The Holocaust

THE COLUMBIA GUIDE TO

The Holocaust

Donald Niewyk and Francis Nicosia

COLUMBIA UNIVERSITY PRESS

NEW YORK

Columbia University Press
Publishers Since 1893
New York   Chichester, West Sussex
Copyright © 2000 Columbia University Press
All rights reserved

Library of Congress Cataloging-in-Publication Data
Niewyk, Donald L., 1940–
The Columbia guide to the Holocaust / Donald Niewyk and Francis Nicosia.
p. cm.
Includes bibliographical references (p.) and index.
ISBN 0-231-11200-9
1. Holocaust, Jewish (1939–1945) 2. Holocaust, Jewish (1939–1945) — Causes. 3.
Holocaust, Jewish (1939–1945) — Psychological aspects. 4. World War,
1939–1945 — Atrocities. 5. Germany — History — 1933–1945. 6. Holocaust, Jewish
(1939–1945) — Sources.   I. Nicosia, Francis R., 1944–   II. Title.

D804.3 .N54 2000
940.53′18 — dc21   00-024979

Casebound editions of Columbia University Press books are printed on permanent and durable
acid-free paper.
Printed in the United States of America
c 10 9 8 7 6 5 4 3 2 1

CONTENTS

Acknowledgments ix

Introduction xi

PART I. HISTORICAL OVERVIEW 1

Historical Overview 3

Excluding the "Racially Inferior," 1933–1939	3
War and the Beginning of Genocide, 1939–1941	9
The Final Solution, 1941–1944	14
The End of the Holocaust, 1944–1945	36
Aftermath and Legacies	37

PART II. PROBLEMS AND INTERPRETATIONS 43

Defining the Holocaust 45

The Gypsies	47
The Mentally and Physically Handicapped	48
Soviet Prisoners of War	48
Polish and Soviet Civilians	49
Political Prisoners, Religious Dissenters, and Homosexuals	50
Conclusion	51

Roots of the Holocaust 53

Trends in Modern European History	53
The History of the Victims	57
The History of Prejudice	63

How the "Final Solution" Came About 71

Intentionalists   72
Functionalists   74
Synthesizers   77

The Perpetrators and Their Motivations 83

Perpetrators   83
Motivations   88

The Victims' Reactions to Persecution 97

Accommodation   97
Armed Resistance   99
Evasion   101
Surviving the Camps   102
The Survivors' Views   103

The Behavior of Bystanders 109

Germany   109
Eastern Europe   112
Western Europe   116

The Question of Rescue 119

The Allied Powers   120
The Neutrals   125

The Lasting Effect of the Holocaust 129

Participants   129
Legal and Religious Institutions   132
Scholars and Students   134

PART III. CHRONOLOGY 139

Chronology 141

PART IV. ENCYCLOPEDIA 171

Encyclopedia 173

People   173
Places   194

Terms   214
Organizations   249

PART V. RESOURCES 267

Resources 269

Printed Reference Works 270

Printed Sources (Primary and Secondary) 273

Filmography 373

Electronic Resources 389

Resource Organizations, Museums, and Memorials 400

Appendix 1. Tables 419
Appendix 2. Maps 425
Index 437

ACKNOWLEDGMENTS

The preparation of this volume required the generous and enthusiastic assistance of others, and we wish to acknowledge their support and express our gratitude.

Henry Friedlander of Brooklyn College and George Kren of Kansas State University, the consultant scholars for this project, provided the necessary constructive criticism of the initial draft. Their expertise in the history of the Holocaust, along with the thoughtfulness and thoroughness of their review of our work, were invaluable throughout the process of writing this book. Much of the credit for any success that this volume may have belongs to them.

We also wish to thank Peter Black, Bret Werb, and Severin Hochberg of the United States Holocaust Memorial Museum in Washington, D.C., for their patience, and their prompt and friendly responses to telephone, e-mail, and fax inquiries on a variety of subjects. We gratefully acknowledge a grant from the William P. Clements Jr. Department of History, Dedman College, Southern Methodist University, that facilitated completion of the manuscript. Thanks too are due the staffs of the Bailey-Howe Library of the University of Vermont, the Durick Library of Saint Michael's College, and the Fondren and Bridwell Libraries of Southern Methodist University.

Finally, we are especially grateful to Kelly McDonald of Saint Michael's College. Her intelligence and her special computer skills enabled us to use the Internet effectively, to collaborate on a regular basis despite the distance between Texas and Vermont, and to bring the different parts of the volume together in one complete and, we hope, coherent manuscript.

INTRODUCTION

◆

This book provides a general introduction for readers coming to the study of the Holocaust for the first time, as well as a guide to specialized studies and controversial issues for those wishing to delve more deeply into the subject. It is divided into five parts.

Part I offers a concise summary of the factual history, placing the Holocaust within the larger context of Nazi Germany and World War II.

Part II is divided into eight chapters devoted to more detailed explorations of issues and problems that interest scholars and laypersons alike. The first chapter ponders how best to define the Holocaust. Were the Jews the sole targets of Nazi genocide, or must other groups, such as Gypsies, handicapped people, Eastern European civilians and prisoners of war, political and religious dissenters, and homosexuals, be included? The second chapter examines the trends in modern European history that made Nazi genocide possible. It also explores the historical developments and social situations of the various victim groups and examines the history of prejudice, giving special attention to conflicting views on the relationship between pre-Nazi racism and antisemitism and the Holocaust. The third chapter delves into debates about why the Nazi leaders abandoned emigration and deportation of the Jews in 1941 in favor of genocide, while the fourth chapter considers the motivations of those who tormented and killed vast numbers of innocent civilians during the Holocaust. The fifth chapter explores the Jews' resistance to Nazi policies and their survival strategies in ghettos and camps and in hiding. The sixth chapter probes the reactions of ordinary Germans, Poles, Hungarians, and other Europeans as the victims were being persecuted and deported. The seventh chapter examines charges that the Allied powers and neutral countries failed to seize opportunities to save the victims. The eighth chapter considers the legacy of genocide for survivors, perpetrators, bystanders, and everyone else. Of special interest here are the legal and religious ramifications of the Holocaust and scholars' efforts to locate Nazi genocide within world history.

Our exploration of these controversial issues seeks to establish the nature of the debates and the strengths and weaknesses of the opposing positions. In most cases no attempt is made to reach conclusions about which interpretations best capture the truth. Readers are encouraged to continue their reading and research in the books mentioned throughout these chapters. Full bibliographical information is provided for these titles in the resource section that concludes this book.

Part III consists of a concise chronology of major events and developments during the Holocaust. It concentrates on the Nazi era, 1933–1945, but it also lists a few key events before and after those years. The chronology may be used in conjunction with and as a supplement to the earlier parts of the guide.

Part IV is an encyclopedia of people, places, terms, and institutions that are central to understanding the Holocaust. These are highlighted in the earlier parts of the guide, enabling the reader to employ the encyclopedia as a source of additional information. Or one may use the encyclopedia for ready reference of highly specific topics or more general concepts, such as "camp system" or "genocide."

Part V presents a guide to print, video, electronic, and institutional resources on the Holocaust. These include books, articles, primary source collections, journals, films, CD-ROMs, Web sites, and resource institutions. Most are annotated to indicate how they might best be put to use. There is a large literature on the Holocaust in other languages, especially German, but we have listed only printed sources in English or English translations of works in other languages. Therefore, some important works on the Holocaust not available in English translation are not included in Part V.

We want to note at the outset that precise statistics of Jewish and Gypsy losses during the Holocaust are not always available. For all their vaunted recordkeeping proclivities, the Germans did not keep accurate count of individuals who were gassed, and records of labor and concentration camps were sometimes lost or destroyed. In this volume the statistics given for losses in various countries and camps represent minimum figures that have been authenticated in existing scholarship. The actual figures may be much higher, and future research may require upward adjustment. In a few cases a range of numbers is given, reflecting the minimum and maximum estimates of losses in cases where documentary evidence is thin.

PART I

Historical Overview

Historical Overview

This brief summary of the Holocaust begins by outlining the stages in which Nazi racial policies evolved. During the 1930s **Adolf Hitler** sought to exclude Jews, Gypsies, and others he considered to be "racially inferior" from the German national community. During the first two years of World War II, the Nazi state turned to **genocide**, starting with the German handicapped, then the Soviet Jews, and finally all European Jews and Gypsies. From late 1941 to late 1944 the concentration, deportation, enslavement, and extermination of Jews and Gypsies were in full swing. At the same time millions of Soviet prisoners of war and Slavic civilians were killed in less organized ways. During the last months of the war the Germans stopped the gassings, but they continued to exploit their victims as slave workers and tried to use them as bargaining chips in ransom negotiations. Following the Nazi defeat victims, perpetrators, and bystanders, at different times and in different ways, came to terms with the immediate legacies of the Holocaust.

In addition to summarizing the evolution of the Holocaust, this overview describes the variety of camps and reactions of victims. It also shows why the Holocaust functioned differently in the various countries controlled by or allied with Nazi Germany. What emerges is a sense of the complexity of these events and the diversity of Holocaust experiences for all the groups involved.

EXCLUDING THE "RACIALLY INFERIOR," 1933–1939

On March 21, 1933, the German Reichstag passed the "Enabling Act" that gave Adolf Hitler dictatorial powers, ending three years of political strife. At the time no one could be sure what he and his Nazi Party would do. Their numerous supporters (just over one-third of German voters; the Nazis never won a free nationwide election) expected bold moves to revive the economy and put the millions of unemployed back to work. Hitler's army of brown-shirted **SA** (Sturmabteilung, or Storm Troopers) had smashed their political opponents in street battles, and many Germans anticipated equally militant action to end the depression. Members of the conservative establishment who had handed power to Hitler in a backstairs political deal hoped to be able to control him and his followers and use them to crush the threatening Communist movement. Hitler's enemies put on a confident front and predicted his early failure. With all eyes fixed on the economic depression and political turmoil that surrounded the destruction of Germany's democratic Weimar Republic, few Germans paid close attention to Hitler's ideas about race.

In fact, race stood at the very heart of Nazi ideology. Hitler called his political philosophy **National Socialism** — the official name of his party was the National Socialist German Workers' Party, or Nazi for short — by which he meant to suggest that he had reconciled the two great competing political ideas of the nineteenth century, nationalism and socialism. What made it possible for him to bring the two together was his belief that racial thinking would lead to national greatness and social justice. During his formative years before World War I in Austria, Hitler had been deeply influenced by Social Darwinism. This now discredited offshoot of biological Darwinism taught that life was eternal struggle between individuals and groups, nature's way of ensuring the survival of the fittest. Hitler saw a lot of struggle in prewar Vienna — between classes, nationalities, political parties, and business firms — and took it as the central law of history. As a confirmed pan-German nationalist, he concluded that only a ruthlessly united and racially purified Germany could survive in the brutal struggle with other races and nations.

These ideas came through clearly in Hitler's book *Mein Kampf*, published in the 1920s. In it he wrote of Germany's need to conquer **Lebensraum** (living space) at the expense of its Slavic neighbors in Eastern Europe and the necessity of racial conflict with Jews and others who stood in the way of German superiority. The future dictator linked the Jews with communism and identified them as Germany's chief internal foe. "If, with the help of his Marxist creed, the Jew is victorious over the other peoples of the world, his crown will be the funeral wreath of humanity. . . . Hence today I believe that I am acting in accordance with the will of the Almighty Creator: *by defending myself against the Jew, I am fighting for the work of the Lord.*"[1] Often ignored or dismissed as pseudo-intellectual posturing at the time, and later obscured by overriding political and economic concerns, the centrality of race in Hitler's thinking became apparent only gradually.

1. Adolf Hitler, *Mein Kampf*, trans. Ralph Manheim (Boston: Houghton Mifflin, 1943), p. 65. Emphasis in the original.

Once firmly in power, Hitler and his followers moved quickly to satisfy Germans' longings for jobs and an end to political conflict. The latter was achieved rapidly and brutally by outlawing all political organizations but the Nazi Party, creating a much feared Gestapo (Secret State **Police**), and sending leading anti-Nazis to newly created **concentration camps** such as **Dachau**, just outside Munich. By the time World War II began in 1939 there would be seven large concentration camps in various parts of Germany and the territories annexed to it, including **Buchenwald** near Weimar; **Ravensbrück**, the women's concentration camp north of Berlin; and **Mauthausen** in Austria. They would also come to hold more than just political opponents of the Nazi Party. Jews, homosexuals, religious dissidents, and common criminals also entered these camps. Run by Hitler's elite **SS**, the concentration camps imposed draconian discipline on the prisoners, many of whom were killed outright or worked to death. But these were not **extermination camps**. Sometimes prisoners were even released, but only after promising never to speak of camp conditions. Their existence, however, was known to all. Although the regime won the support of an increasingly large number of Germans, the terror served to intimidate political opponents.

Fixing the economy took longer, but the Nazis moved to end unemployment with characteristic determination. They bullied private employers to hire workers, spent vast sums on government building projects, and placed young men in a one-year compulsory national service program called the Arbeitsdienst (Labor Service). By the late 1930s, when Germany was rapidly rearming, unemployment disappeared. Naturally, all this cost a fortune, and Hitler had no idea how to pay off Germany's massive debts, except perhaps by conquering and looting most of Europe. But he was not saying so openly, and few asked where the money was coming from. Nothing did more to enhance Hitler's popularity than this spectacular economic recovery.

Hitler's foreign-policy successes likewise impressed Germans. Loudly affirming his peaceful intentions while denouncing the iniquities of the Treaty of Versailles, which had been imposed on Germany at the end of World War I, Hitler set about burying the treaty one clause at a time. The democracies were preoccupied with their own problems and hoped that concessions would calm the dictator. Hence they stood by as Germany rearmed (March 1935), moved its armies into the demilitarized Rhineland (March 1936), seized Austria (March 1938), and annexed the German-speaking Sudetenland from Czechoslovakia (October 1938). Achieving all this without firing a shot, Hitler lifted the pride of a humiliated nation.

These political, economic, and foreign policy victories were the basis of

Hitler's great popularity in the 1930s. They also made the less attractive aspects of Nazism easier for ordinary Germans to swallow. The people might grumble about the obtrusiveness of party hacks in all areas of life and worry about being overheard expressing the "wrong" opinion, but this seemed an acceptable price to pay for national resurgence. As for the sufferings of political dissidents and those deemed racially unworthy, there was nothing one could do. As was true of people in other totalitarian regimes, Germans retreated into their private lives to find shelter from, and avoid offending, the omnipresent Nazi state.

In the case of the Jews, Hitler initially encouraged this attitude of popular indifference by gradually excluding them from the national community and encouraging them to emigrate. He may have been influenced to take this legalistic approach by the results of his first direct attack on the Jews after becoming dictator, the nationwide boycott of Jewish businesses set to begin on April 1, 1933. Hitler placed it under the direction of **Julius Streicher**, one of the early leaders of the Nazi Party, a vicious antisemite and the editor of the scurrilous weekly newspaper *Der Stürmer*. Although Streicher urged Germans not to buy goods in Jewish shops, and Storm Troopers sometimes physically intimidated people from doing so, many patronized them anyway. Foreign reactions were also negative, with Jewish groups and their sympathizers threatening to organize boycotts of German-made goods. The Nazis called off their boycott after the first day and opted instead for less confrontational policies.

These consisted of a series of laws and edicts designed to **Aryanize** German institutions and reverse Jewish emancipation and assimilation. The "Law for the Restoration of the Professional Civil Service" of April 7, 1933, removed anti-Nazis and Jews from government jobs as judges, lawyers, teachers, and officials. Subsequent laws limited Jewish enrollment in schools and universities to 1.5 percent of the student body, barred Jewish dentists and physicians from public insurance programs, revoked the naturalization of Eastern European Jews, and specified that only **Aryans** could edit German newspapers. Simultaneously extralegal pressures on Jewish businessmen to sell their firms, often for only a fraction of their real value, began the gradual process of excluding Jews from the German economy. When local Nazi hotheads revived the practices of boycott and physical attacks aimed at Jews, Hitler firmly returned them to the legal path by promulgating the **Nuremberg Laws** in September 1935.

The Nuremberg Laws enabled the state to limit the rights of Jews as German citizens and banned marriage and sexual relations between Jews and Germans. Legal codicils later defined Jews as persons having more than two Jewish grandparents. Those with two Jewish grandparents were defined as *Mischlinge* (mixed breeds), and they were grouped with the Jews only if they were married to Jews or belonged to Jewish congregations. Persons with one

Jewish grandparent were also considered *Mischlinge* but normally were not grouped with the Jews. Later, in 1938, Hitler decided to create a special category of "privileged mixed marriages" for interracial couples that had married before the Nuremberg Laws went into force. Jewish women married to German men were exempted from anti-Jewish measures. The same was true for Jewish men married to German women if they had children. In making these exceptions Hitler showed that he wanted to minimize the number of Germans who would be hurt by his campaign against the Jews.

Hitler's preference for legal methods of isolating the Jews reflected his sensitivity to public opinion both at home and abroad. As Germany prepared to host the 1936 Olympic Games in Berlin, the Nazis wanted nothing to stain their law-and-order image. This had the unintended result of sending mixed signals to the Jews. Nazi antisemitic policies were designed to demoralize the Jews and induce them to emigrate. In fact, emigration was the original Nazi solution to the "Jewish problem," and it remained in force until 1941. Economically and psychologically devastated, some Jews had left the country already or else planned to go soon. And yet most Jews still hoped that conditions would not get worse and that they could ride out the storm. Moreover, departing was never easy. Quite apart from the mental anguish involved in leaving home, it was hard to find a country willing to accept refugees in a time of world economic depression. Further complicating matters was the German emigration tax, which confiscated a considerable portion of an emigrant's wealth. Hence only about 105,000 of the approximately 600,000 German Jews emigrated in the first four years of the Third Reich.

In 1937, as Hitler entered the fifth year of his dictatorship, he felt increasingly confident of his power and less dependent on conservatives at home or popular opinion abroad. In that year the dictator informed his generals of his plans for a war of conquest in the near future. To prepare for war he wanted to cleanse Germany by speeding the Jews on their way. Pressures to Aryanize Jewish businesses increased, as did random acts of anti-Jewish violence. Such acts were conspicuous accompaniments to Germany's forcible **Anschluss** (union) with Austria in March 1938. Also in 1938 foreign Jews and Gypsies were expelled from the Reich. Radical pressures culminated in the **Crystal Night** pogroms of November 9–10, 1938, in which Nazi Storm Troopers, following orders from Berlin, vandalized Jewish shops and homes and burned 267 synagogues. Twenty thousand Jews were sent to concentration camps, and at least ninety-one were actually murdered. The American consul in Leipzig, David Buffum, described the pogroms as the carefully organized work of Nazi fanatics: "Having demolished dwellings and hurled most of the movable effects onto the streets, the insatiably sadistic perpetrators threw many of the trembling inmates into a small stream that flows through the Zoological Park, commanding horrified spectators to spit at them, defile them with mud and jeer at their plight. . . . The slightest manifestation of sympathy evoked a positive fury on the part of the perpetrators, and the crowd was powerless to do anything but turn horror-stricken eyes from the scene of abuse, or leave the vicinity."[2] Soon thereafter Jews were excluded by law from every conceivable area of German life, including schools, universities, and business activities. The **Aryanization** of Germany's culture and economy was complete.

Although relatively few ordinary Germans joined in the Crystal Night carnage, it was now abundantly clear to the Jews that the Nazi leaders wanted them out. As always, the problem was where to go. Most countries, including the United States and Western European nations such as France and Great Britain, restricted entry to those least likely to swell the welfare rolls — and immigrants, it was widely assumed, were sure to become wards of the state. The British limited Jewish immigration to Palestine in response to protests from the Arab majority there. The **Evian Conference**, held in July 1938 at the suggestion of American president Franklin D. Roosevelt with the goal of finding new homes for German Jewish refugees through intergovernmental cooperation, had been a conspicuous failure. The refugees' plight was dramatized in May 1939 when 930 German Jews left Germany aboard the German luxury liner *St. Louis*, believing they would be admitted to Cuba. Refused permission to debark there, they sailed to the coast of the United States but were again rebuffed and forced to sail back to Europe.

To break through these obstacles, the German leaders in January 1939 established a **Reich Central Office for Jewish Emigration** under the direction of **Reinhard Heydrich**, chief of the Security Police and the Security Service of the SS. This office coordinated and streamlined everything involved in promoting Jewish emigration both legally and illegally. Whenever sufficient visas could not be obtained, the Germans simply chased groups of Jews across unguarded sections of Germany's borders. All of these procedures were modeled on a smaller Central Office for Jewish Emigration established the previous year in Vienna by **Adolf Eichmann**, the SS specialist in Jewish affairs. Throughout this SS takeover of Jewish emigration, Eichmann continued to distinguish himself by his diligence. By 1939 the Jews were leaving at the rate

2. Quoted in J. Noakes and A. G. Pridham, eds., *Nazism: A History in Documents and Eyewitness Accounts, 1919–1945* (Exeter: University of Exeter Press, 1983–1988), p. 1:556.

of nearly 70,000 yearly, and only about 185,000 Jews were left in Germany proper when World War II began on September 1, 1939.

Jews were not the only "racially dangerous" group targeted by the Nazis for exclusion. Germany's 30,000 **Gypsies** were identified as racially alien and subjected to the terms of the Nuremberg Laws; some were placed in special Gypsy camps. Male homosexuals, blamed for undermining the racial community by failing to produce children, were sometimes sent to regular **concentration camps**. As racial Germans they might (theoretically) be rehabilitated and returned to the community, but in fact few of those sent to concentration camps survived. A third group, also consisting of racial Germans, was already partially excluded by being confined to hospitals and nursing homes. These were the mentally and physically handicapped, considered dangerous carriers of hereditary diseases. The Nazis were firm believers in **eugenics**, the selective breeding of humans for the purpose of improving the race by weeding out the weak and inferior. Starting in 1934 they subjected the handicapped to compulsory sterilization, excluding their future progeny from the national community and, indeed, from life itself.

WAR AND THE BEGINNING OF GENOCIDE, 1939–1941

During the first two years of World War II, the Germans radicalized their racial policies with astonishing speed and began subjecting their victims to **genocide**. The first to be exterminated were the German handicapped, who were gassed during the very first year of the war. Simultaneously the Germans brutally ghettoized the Jews and Gypsies in occupied Poland and later extended the exclusionary policies already in force in Germany to occupied Western Europe. In June 1941, when Hitler widened his war by attacking the Soviet Union, the German armed forces were accompanied by special mobile killing squads whose orders were to kill Jews and other "enemies of the Reich" on Soviet territory. By the end of the year preparations were being made to exterminate the Jews and Gypsies in Europe. Evidently Hitler believed that he could camouflage genocide under the cover of war. The truth might eventually leak out, but a swift victory would render knowledge of mass murder moot.

The Euthanasia (T4) Program

The mass murder of mentally and physically handicapped Germans was planned shortly before the outbreak of war, in the spring of 1939. It began with the **euthanasia** of around 5,000 severely handicapped children in German hospitals during the winter of 1939–1940. This turned out to be merely a prelude to a massive expansion of the "mercy killing" of the handicapped at Hitler's order in 1940 and 1941. Whether they had been sterilized or not, these individuals were held to be "useless eaters," an economic drag on society, having "lives not worth living." In a secret program, informally named T4 (after the address of the unit's Berlin headquarters, Tiergartenstrasse 4), German doctors systematically killed at least 70,000 handicapped Germans: the mentally ill, retarded, blind, deaf, mute, senile, epileptic, and physically deformed. This was done chiefly at six killing centers where experiments revealed that the best method was injecting carbon monoxide gas into rooms disguised as showers. Although T4 was to be kept secret, word of it leaked out, and in 1941 courageous leaders of the **Catholic** and **Protestant churches** publicly denounced this murder of the defenseless. Early in August Bishop Galen of Münster delivered a stinging rebuke in a public sermon: "Woe to mankind, woe to our German nation if God's holy commandment, 'Thou shalt not kill' . . . is not only broken, but if this transgression is actually tolerated and permitted to go unpunished."[3] Perhaps even more significant were protests from the German public. Hitler, infuriated at this interference but unwilling to risk dissension during wartime, officially ordered an end to gassings in the killing centers on August 24, 1941. However, the murders of handicapped Germans continued on a decentralized basis throughout the war and took perhaps another 80,000 lives.

T4 was both a logical extension of earlier exclusion policies and a precedent for the coming **Final Solution** of the Jewish problem. The killing centers developed techniques of mass murder that served as models for the **extermination camps**. Additionally, starting in 1941 T4 trained personnel would carry out mass murder on a far larger scale in the east.

Nazi Racial Policies in Occupied Poland

As the German armies swept across western and central Poland in September 1939, some 2,000,000 Polish Jews and smaller numbers of Gypsies and the handicapped were singled out for unusually brutal treatment. At first they were

3. Quoted in J. Noakes and A. G. Pridham, eds., *Nazism: A History in Documents and Eyewitness Accounts, 1919–1945* (Exeter: University of Exeter Press, 1983–1988), p. 2:1038.

the targets of beatings, shootings, lootings, and other random acts of violence. Then the Germans set about conducting more organized atrocities. In the broad band of territory annexed directly to Germany, which constituted about one quarter of prewar Poland, the handicapped were brought under the umbrella of the T4 program and exterminated, whereas the Jews and Gypsies initially were to be rounded up for expulsion to the remaining Polish territory that was under German occupation. This territory, known as the **General Government**, was ruthlessly administered by Governor General **Hans Frank** in **Kraków**. The Germans briefly planned to establish a "Jewish Reservation" at **Nisko**, near **Lublin** in the General Government, and some Jews were actually sent there. However, the reservation was totally unprepared to accept large numbers of deportees, and those who were resettled there died by the thousands. German officials in the General Government as a whole protested that it could not accommodate such large numbers (more than 1,000,000) of Jews and Gypsies in addition to the multitudes of Poles who were also being deported there. Hence Nazi officials in the annexed territories relented and permitted the establishment of a large (with 160,000 inhabitants) ghetto in the industrial city of **Łódź**. This ghetto, intended as a purely temporary expedient, lasted until August 1944, in part because its leadership organized the ghetto inhabitants to produce essential war material for the Germans.

Throughout the annexed territories and the General Government the Germans confiscated the Jews' property and gradually herded them into **ghettos,** where they were expected to perform various forms of **forced labor.** Comparatively small numbers of Gypsies went along with them. In carrying out these measures the Germans were helped by **Volksdeutsche**, ethnic Germans who had lived in Poland and other eastern European countries for generations. They were often the most enthusiastic supporters of ethnic cleansing.

There were a great many ghettos in the General Government, and they varied in size from the one in **Warsaw**, with 445,000 inhabitants, to small-town ghettos of only a few thousand. The largest ghettos and many of the small ones were sealed off from the remaining local populations, but a few of the ghettos were open to traffic back and forth. However, all of the ghettos had three features in common. First, they were governed by **Jewish Councils** that consisted of Jewish leaders appointed by and responsible to the Germans. Second, they were overcrowded and poorly supplied with food and medicines, resulting in many deaths from malnutrition and disease. Third, they were initially conceived of by the Germans as temporary holding pens until some place could be found to which the inhabitants could be permanently expelled.

Some German officials spoke of expelling the Jews to new homes in "the

East," presumably referring to the Soviet Union. Other German documents referred to **Madagascar** as a possible destination. Before the war began the Polish and French governments had discussed creating a home for the unwanted Jews of Europe on that Indian Ocean island off the coast of Africa, then a French colony (today the Malagasy Republic). Hitler had happily endorsed the idea. Once Germany conquered France in 1940, Madagascar was Hitler's to dispose of as he saw fit, but only if he could defeat or sign an armistice with Great Britain and gain access to the sea routes. In the first years of the war Hitler believed that victory was imminent. Hence in this early stage of the struggle the German policy on Jews and Gypsies remained one aimed at expulsion rather than genocide. That changed at some point in 1941.

Germany and Occupied Western Europe

In these regions, too, the Germans prepared the Jews for expulsion to Madagascar or some other remote spot. In Germany itself the Nazi leaders in 1939 established a kind of Jewish Council, the **Reich Association of Jews in Germany**, and made it responsible for all the remaining German Jews. Most of the Jews who had lived in small towns moved to the big German cities where they found shelter with larger Jewish communities. There the Nazi authorities concentrated them in special Jewish apartment blocs, informal ghettos that further isolated the Jews from German society. The able-bodied were forced to work in war factories. In September 1941 Jews were required to display a yellow Star of David with the inscription *Jude* (Jew) sewn on the front of their clothing whenever they appeared in public. In October the SS began systematic deportations of German Jews and Gypsies to ghettos in Eastern Europe, where they were made to share the fate of the victims already there. Later that same month SS leader Heinrich Himmler banned the voluntary emigration of Jews except in special cases that would enrich the Reich (that is, a few very rich Jews could, and did, buy their way out).

Following the German conquest in 1940 of most Western European countries — France, Belgium, Luxembourg, the Netherlands, and Norway — policies there on Jews and Gypsies were brought into line with those in Germany. The Jews were registered, expropriated, denaturalized, isolated, and required to wear the **yellow badge.** The cooperation of local officials in carrying out these measures was made easier because the harshest treatment was always reserved for foreign Jews. In France, which had the largest Jewish population in Western Europe (350,000), officials of the collaborationist **Vichy** regime rounded up 25,000 foreign Jews and placed them in French concentration camps in preparation for future expulsion. In Western Europe deportations to the East did not begin until 1942. The only exception was Denmark, where the small Jewish population was relatively unmolested until 1943.

The Attack on the USSR and the Einsatzgruppen Actions

By early 1941 Hitler's war against England had reached a stalemate. In order to bring the war to a rapid conclusion the dictator decided to attack the Soviet Union in the expectation that rapid victory there would also bring the British to their knees. Additionally, as Hitler saw it, conquest of the Soviet Union would solve the problem of German Lebensraum (living space) and bring about a final reckoning with the most dangerous Jews of all, the Russian Communists. Operation **Barbarossa**, as the attack was called, began on June 22, 1941. At first it was fabulously successful, penetrating all the way to Moscow before winter weather forced a temporary halt to the invasion. Vast sections of the western Soviet Union were placed under the administration of the leading Nazi Party theoretician, **Alfred Rosenberg**, who was named Reich Minister for the Eastern Occupied Territories.

Included in the planning of Operation Barbarossa was the formation of four **Einsatzgruppen,** mobile killing squads made up of Security Police and Security Service personnel. They were instructed to follow the invading German armies and kill primarily Jews but also Communist officials, Gypsies, and the handicapped. The single largest Einsatzgruppen massacre occurred at the end of September 1941 when 33,000 Jews and Gypsies from Kiev were shot and buried at **Babi Yar** just outside the city. Before the war was over these Einsatzgruppen had shot and buried in mass graves more than 1,000,000 defenseless civilians of all ages, often with cooperation from the **German army**. Units of the German Order Police engaged in similar actions. Jews and Gypsies not thus disposed of were herded into ghettos like those in Poland. The largest of these were in **Minsk** (100,000), Kovno (30,000), and **Riga** (30,000). In rounding up these victims the Germans needed the aid of volunteers from among the conquered peoples of the Soviet Union, especially the Ukrainians and Lithuanians. Called **Hiwis,** these volunteers were also trained to help guard **labor** and **extermination camps**.

During the early phase of the war against the USSR, vast numbers of Soviet soldiers were also taken captive. As "subhuman" Slavs they were not treated according to the rules of war but rather were shot or mistreated in prisoner of war camps. More than 3,000,000 Soviet soldiers perished after surrendering to the Germans. The "racially inferior" Polish, Russian, and Ukrainian civilians, too, were starved and exploited. Food and other resources needed to sustain life in Eastern Europe were sent to Germany. Before the war was over millions of Slavic civilians were dead.

The mass murder of Soviet Jews by the Einsatzgruppen may have been part of an existing overall plan to kill every Jew in Europe, although we cannot be certain of this. But three facts are certain. First, the astounding brutality of the war in the Soviet Union nurtured extremist thinking about ways to solve the "Jewish problem." Hitler had told his generals to carry out a "war of extermination" in the USSR, resulting in increasingly desperate resistance by the defending Red Army. Second, the refusal of the Soviet Union to collapse on schedule spoiled German plans to deport the Jews of Poland, Germany, and Western Europe in the near future. Overcrowding and disease in the East European ghettos worried German occupation officials about how much longer they could cope with so many Jews and Gypsies. The fact that Soviet Jews were being murdered seemed to suggest that killing them was an acceptable alternative to having them die slowly in captivity. Third, the Einsatzgruppen were proving imperfect instruments of mass murder. Shooting people one by one took too much time and was too visible. Worse, the men of those killing squads found mass murder so stressful that nervous breakdowns and alcoholism were common. Late in 1941 SS officials began searching for a more efficient and less public method of mass extermination. In September they carried out experimental gassings of Soviet prisoners of war at what was then the small Polish concentration camp at **Auschwitz**. In November construction of what were to become extermination camps began at **Belzec** and **Chelmno**, and in December Jews and Gypsies were being killed in gas vans at Chelmno. Hence many scholars believe that by the end of 1941 what the Germans called the "**Final Solution** to the European Jewish Problem**" had begun.

THE FINAL SOLUTION, 1941–1944

The actual plan for the Final Solution was conveyed to the heads of other German government agencies by **Reinhard Heydrich** at the **Wannsee Conference** in 1942. This plan involved sending Jews from all over German-controlled Europe to ghettos, labor camps, and extermination camps in the East. The impact of these policies varied from country to country, and much depended on where the victims lived. News of the camps filtered out, but it was not always believed, and even when it was believed it was difficult to interpret. Many of the victims found ways to resist their tormentors, but for various reasons armed resistance was not a common response during the Holocaust.

The Wannsee Conference

In July 1941 Reich Marshall **Hermann Göring**, after Hitler the most powerful German leader, had authorized SS security chief **Reinhard Heydrich** to draw up "an overall plan of the organizational, functional, and material measures to be taken in preparing for the implementation of the aspired final solution of the Jewish question."[4] Heydrich headed the Reich Security Main Office, which coordinated all German **police** and security agencies in Germany and the occupied countries. It took him nearly six months to come up with a plan, which suggests that Nazi policies may still have been in flux at that time. Heydrich called a meeting of leading government, party, and SS officials at Wannsee, a suburb of Berlin, on January 20, 1942, to inform them of the project. Hitler, he stated, had authorized the systematic deportation of all 11,000,000 European Jews to camps in Eastern Europe. There they would be forced to work for the Germans until they dropped. Gypsies were not mentioned at the conference, but in practice they would be included in the deportations. Nor was any specific mention made of extermination camps, but it was made clear that those incapable of work would be "dealt with appropriately." (The Nazi leaders always used the euphemisms "Final Solution" and "special treatment" to keep the genocide a secret.) Adolf Eichmann, who took the official notes of the Wannsee Conference, was placed in charge of arresting and deporting the victims to the camps. Once the various agencies represented at the conference had agreed to cooperate, the Final Solution could proceed.

Ghettos

At Wannsee Heydrich spoke of sweeping Europe from west to east. In practice, the Germans found it preferable to deal first with the far larger populations of Jews and Gypsies in Eastern Europe. There most of the Jews were already concentrated in urban **ghettos**, and some of these were emptied during 1942 and their residents sent to labor and extermination camps. But not all the ghettos could be liquidated during the first year of the Final Solution. It took time to complete the forced labor and killing installations, and even then their capacities were limited. Moreover, several of the ghettos were proving useful to the Germans. Ghetto factories and workshops were turning out everything from uniforms for German soldiers to toys for German children. Sometimes these

---

4. Nuremberg Document NG-2586, quoted in Raul Hilberg, ed., *Documents of Destruction* (Chicago: Quadrangle, 1971), p. 89.

enterprises were owned and run by German businessmen, such as **Oskar Schindler** in Kraków. Elsewhere, as in Łódź, the Jews organized and ran the factories themselves. Hence these ghettos were permitted to last into 1943 and, in a few cases, 1944.

The **Jewish Councils** that ran the ghettos for the Germans hoped that such productivity would make the Jews indispensable to the war effort and buy life for at least some of them. Hence the councils sought to maintain strict order and to combat all forms of armed resistance to the Germans, believing that disorder or uprisings would bring down massive retaliation on the whole ghetto. Jewish **police** forces were organized by the councils to keep the ghettos in line and, whenever necessary, to hand troublemakers over to the Germans. Sometimes the police were also expected to supervise the roundups and deportations from the ghetto, as ordered by the Germans; at other times the Germans came in to do the job themselves.

Naturally the Jewish Council members and their families and employees, including the police, were the last to be deported, and they often enjoyed other privileges as well, such as better rations and living quarters. All of this made them controversial in the ghettos, but as they themselves saw it someone had to hold the Germans at bay and keep at least some ghetto inhabitants alive. Some Jewish Council leaders went out of their way to impress the Germans and emulate their authoritarian style, as did **Mordecai Chaim Rumkowski,** "Eldest of the Jews," in **Łódź.** Other Jewish Council leaders played the dangerous game of working with the Jewish underground while giving priority to keeping the Germans satisfied, as did **Jacob Gens,** chief of the **Vilna** Jewish Council. Council leaders who did not do as they were told were replaced, and defiance in the ghettos led to immediate roundups followed by mass shootings or deportations. Some council heads despaired. When **Adam Czerniaków,** chairman of the **Warsaw** Jewish Council, learned in July 1942 that he could do nothing to halt the massive deportations from the ghetto, he committed suicide. More compliant leadership took his place.

For ghetto inhabitants life was a constant struggle to obtain food and avoid deportation. The Germans granted them only the most minimal food supplies — sometimes as little as 500 calories a day per person — and the smuggling of food was essential to survival. The Jewish Councils typically established soup kitchens and rationing to assure that everyone got something to eat. But it was never enough, and disease and malnutrition brought on high death rates. Equally vital to survival was having a job. Without a work card certifying gainful employment, ghetto dwellers were vulnerable to being rounded up and deported at any time. Newly arriving Jews from Germany and Western

Europe, as well as those herded in from nearby towns and villages, had to be accommodated, another task that fell to the Jewish Councils. Jews in the ghettos, sometimes acting independently of the councils, also worked to keep spirits alive by organizing schools, concerts, plays, libraries, literary societies, and open or clandestine religious services. Secret archives, such as the **Oneg Shabbat** organized by **Emmanuel Ringelblum** in Warsaw, documented and preserved the history of life in the ghettos.

Cooperating with the Germans and promoting Jewish survival were the two poles of Jewish Council policies, but ultimately they could not be reconciled. By August 1944 the last of the big ghettos, Łódź, was being liquidated. Only one ghetto survived to the end, and it was a special case. The Germans made **Theresienstadt**, a town in occupied Czechoslovakia, into a "model ghetto" for privileged Jews, especially elderly German and Austrian Jews and Jewish war veterans who had fought for Germany in World War I. Comparatively good conditions there were exploited by the Germans when they took inquisitive **Red Cross** representatives on a tour of the ghetto in June 1944. At the same time German propagandists made a film of the ghetto showing idyllic conditions. In fact, the ghetto was usually overcrowded, and there were frequent deportations to camps in Poland. Especially in the last year of the war food and sanitary conditions deteriorated and deaths from disease rose. Of the nearly 140,000 Jews sent to Theresienstadt, fewer than 17,000 were freed when the ghetto was liberated in May 1945.

Forced Labor

Jews and Gypsies deported from Eastern European ghettos or from their homes or camps elsewhere in Europe were put through "**selections**." These might happen in a ghetto before deportation, at the final destination, or during a temporary stop at a transit camp along the way. Selections separated those who were capable of (and needed for) work from those who were not. The former usually went to labor camps and concentration camps; the latter went to extermination camps.

The **labor camps** were both very numerous and extremely varied. Most of them were in Poland, but others could be found in the Soviet Union and in Germany itself. Some labor camps, such as those located at the armaments plants at Skarzysko-Kamienna and Częstochowa in Poland, were enormous. Others might have only a few hundred workers. Some were placed next to existing factories, but in other cases the workers built both their own camps and the factories in which they worked from scratch. Although some labor camps were owned lock, stock, and barrel by the SS, others were operated by the German army, the Luftwaffe, the Organisation Todt (German construction battalions), and private German firms. But all of them were under the jurisdiction of local SS and police leaders. Assisting the German authorities were guards, often Ukrainian Hiwis, and **prisoner functionaries** consisting of the camp senior and his helpers. In 1943 most of the labor camps were absorbed into the concentration camp system, becoming concentration camps in their own right or else external subcamps of existing concentration camps. The rest were shut down and their prisoners deported or killed.

Other prisoners were sent to forced labor in concentration camps, the numbers of which increased dramatically as they spread from Germany to other parts of Hitler's wartime empire. Most Jews in the prewar German concentration camps were deported to new concentration camps in the East. In all these new camps the existing system of colored triangles distinguished the categories of prisoners: red for political prisoners; green for common criminals; black for "asocials," including Gypsies; and pink for homosexuals. Jews had an inverted yellow triangle sewn over a red one, forming a Star of David. Only at Auschwitz and its satellite camps were the working prisoners tattooed with their serial numbers on the left forearm. Jewish inmates had a triangle added to their tattoos to distinguish them from non-Jews.

In order to run the labor camps as efficiently as possible, the SS carried over an administrative system from the German **concentration camps** that placed important aspects of camp life in the hands of **prisoner functionaries**. These included "capos," who acted as foremen of prisoner work details; "block seniors," who were responsible for the prisoners when they were in their barracks; clerks, who kept camp records and made work assignments; and "runners," usually teenagers who carried messages all over the camps. Their authority was backed up by "enforcers," prisoners armed with whips and truncheons. All of these prisoner functionaries were responsible to a "camp senior," a prisoner who reported directly to the camp commandant, usually an SS officer. At times the SS gave these jobs to the professional criminals among the prisoners, confident that they would demonstrate the requisite lack of pity. At other times, and especially when superior organizing skills were needed, the Germans appointed Jews and other political prisoners to the positions.

The prisoner functionaries had considerable power in the camps, and they were rewarded by being given special privileges, such as private sleeping quarters, more and better food, and exemption from harsh work details. Because these could be withdrawn at any time, members of this camp aristocracy worked hard to satisfy the SS, often treating their fellow prisoners with unbelievable cruelty. As one survivor recalled: "If he [the prisoner functionary] lost his position, he would go down just like the others, and he was ready, rather, to kill a hundred others. The Germans didn't have to bother with the whole camp population at all; just appoint one Jew, and then he would arrange everything in the best order to their satisfaction, and very often, much beyond their demands."[5] But that was not always the case. Some of the prisoner functionaries used their positions to shield their comrades from the very worst treatment by faking beatings, reassigning threatened prisoners to easier work details, and sending the sick to infirmaries where prisoner doctors could look after them.

The Germans spoke of forced labor as "extermination through work." This was an appropriate description, for only the fittest prisoners could survive backbreaking work, long hours, brutal punishments, poor and insufficient food, and inadequate medical care. The SS was not alone in profiting from their misery. Giant German firms such as the chemicals conglomerate I. G. Farben, the aircraft manufacturer Heinkel, and the armaments firm Krupp exploited forced labor. Camp products included raw materials such as food and coal as well as all sorts of industrial products, such as synthetic rubber, textiles, aircraft parts, rifle and artillery shells, and electronic components. Toward the end of the war prisoners in Eastern European camps were also sent out to dig trenches for the retreating German army.

Surviving forced labor required both determination and luck. A prisoner had to be determined to survive and willing to take chances to do it. This might include volunteering for extra work in return for additional rations or risking the wrath of some powerful prisoner to ask for a better work assignment. Or it might mean stealing food from the kitchen or faking an illness and hiding from selections and deportations in the sick ward. A prisoner who lost this determination, who gave up — in camp slang a **Muselmann** — was considered to be as good as dead. Such persons either died in the camp or were identified at the frequent camp selections for shooting or deportation to an extermination camp. But prisoners had only limited opportunities to take risks and thus determine their fate. More often than not luck played a decisive role. Did the Germans happen to need workers on the day of your selection? Did you have a skill they could use? Were you young and healthy? Was the prisoner in charge of work assignments from your hometown or country? Any number of purely fortuitous situations could tip the balance one way or the other.

5. Donald L. Niewyk, ed., *Fresh Wounds: Early Narratives of Holocaust Survival* (Chapel Hill: University of North Carolina Press, 1998), pp. 40–41.

Extermination

Jews and Gypsies who were sent to **extermination camps** were too young, too old, or too sick to work, women with children, or simply not needed for forced labor. Four of the six extermination camps were devoted almost entirely to mass murder: **Chełmno, Bełzec, Sobibór,** and **Treblinka.** No large labor or concentration camps were attached to them, and only a few hundred prisoners were kept alive there to dispose of the bodies (the work of the **Sonderkommando**), sort the victims' belongings, and generally assist the SS in running the camps. The two remaining camps, Majdanek and Auschwitz, were extermination and concentration camps combined. In these camps selections done upon entry determined who lived or died. At the other camps, arrival almost invariably meant death that very day.

Chełmno, just north of Łódź, was the first and smallest of the extermination camps. It was also the only extermination camp in which **gas vans** were used to kill the victims. These were trucks that had been modified to divert engine exhaust into the rear compartments, suffocating those who had been sealed inside. The victims were told to disrobe because they were going to be taken to the showers by truck before continuing on their travels to the East. Most were taken in by the ruse; those who held back were forced to climb aboard. The doors were closed and the engines run until the screams stopped. Then the trucks took the bodies into the nearby forest where Jewish Sonderkommandos burned them or buried them in mass graves. Chełmno operated from December 1941 to March 1943 and reopened for a few months in mid-1944 to finish off some of the remnants of the Łódź ghetto. Altogether it took the lives of at least 152,000 Jews and Gypsies, mainly those from the area of western Poland annexed to Germany.

Bełzec, Sobibór, and Treblinka, the remaining extermination camps devoted solely to gassing, are usually treated together as the **Operation Reinhard** camps, named for Reinhard Heydrich after his May 1942 assassination near Prague by Czech patriots. These camps, established primarily to exterminate Polish Jewry, were under the dynamic command of **Odilo Globocnik**, SS and Police Leader in **Lublin,** Poland. Each camp had a staff of around thirty SS men, most of whom had been engaged in the **euthanasia** program, assisted by Ukrainian guards trained at the SS **Trawniki** training camp. Bełzec, near L'vov in southeastern Poland, operated from March to December 1942. Sobibór, in eastern Poland, started in May 1942 and shut down in October 1943. Treblinka, in northeastern Poland, specialized in gassing the Warsaw Jews between July 1942 and August 1943.

All three of these Operation Reinhard camps employed specially constructed **gas chambers** deceptively identified as shower rooms. These fixed installations had come to be regarded as far more efficient than the gas vans used at Chełmno. The victims were told that they had arrived at a transit camp where they were to be cleaned up before continuing on to places of resettlement. Misleading signs, railroad timetables, and check-ins for clothing and valuables disguised what was really happening. Once the doors were closed, exhaust from a motor salvaged from a tank or truck was piped into the sealed structures. The bodies were buried or burned by the men of the Sonderkommando. Prisoner work details also gathered and sorted the victims' possessions. Bełzec claimed the lives of 600,000 victims, Sobibór 250,000, and Treblinka 870,000.

Majdanek, just outside Lublin in the **General Government,** shared with Auschwitz the distinction of combining extermination and concentration camp facilities. It was established in 1941 as a camp for Soviet prisoners of war, and a year later Jews, Gypsies, and Polish political prisoners were added to the mix of about 50,000 inmates. Majdanek functioned primarily as a giant concentration camp, with emphasis on "extermination through work." A small carbon monoxide gas chamber, later supplemented by another that used **Zyklon B** (hydrogen cyanide) and a **crematorium,** took tens of thousands of lives, but most of the more than 200,000 who died there were shot or fell to hyperexploitation, malnutrition, and disease. About 30 percent of them were Jews. The worst massacre occurred on November 3, 1943, when virtually all 18,000 Jews from Majdanek and its subcamps were machine-gunned by SS men as part of **Operation Harvest Festival,** which was designed to eradicate all remaining Jews in the Lublin district. The camp was evacuated before the Soviet army reached Lublin in July 1944, and the surviving prisoners were sent to Auschwitz and concentration camps in Germany.

Auschwitz, far larger than Majdanek, likewise became an extermination camp when gas chambers and crematoria were added to an existing concentration camp. Located just outside the Polish town of Oświęcem (Auschwitz is its German name), it had been a Polish army camp until 1939 when the Germans made it over into a concentration camp for Poles. In March 1941 **Heinrich Himmler** visited Auschwitz and ordered its expansion into the largest of the German concentration camps. He was probably influenced by its site at the intersection of two main railroad lines about thirty miles southwest of Kraków and close to the large Jewish population of Eastern Upper Silesia. In the course of expanding Auschwitz during the next three years, the Germans also turned it into the largest extermination camp, responsible for at least 1,100,000 dead, more than 90 percent of them Jews.

Auschwitz came to be a vast undertaking, holding 105,000 prisoners and covering eighteen square miles in three distinct sectors, each separated from the others by a few miles of open land or by the town itself. The original camp (Auschwitz I), with its brick barracks and a small gas chamber and crematorium, housed the central administrative offices, housing for 30,000 prisoners, a medical ward, and various workshops. A far larger new section of the camp was built on the site of the tiny hamlet of Birkenau (Auschwitz II). Its Polish residents were cleared out and prisoners from the original camp, mainly Soviet prisoners of war, built a vast collection of barracks and administrative structures. Later four huge gas chamber–crematorium complexes were added. Expansion of Birkenau continued nonstop almost up to the time when plans had to be made to evacuate the camp. The heavy industrial sector of Auschwitz was located at Monowitz (Auschwitz III), often referred to by the name of its principal product, Buna, an artificial rubber. In addition to these three sectors of Auschwitz itself, a network of forty external subcamps, some of them many miles away, supplied the main camp with food, coal, and building materials.

The four large gas chamber–crematorium buildings at Birkenau (Auschwitz II) were designed for murder on a truly industrial scale. The largest of them could gas 2,000 people at one time. Its gas chambers were located underground; the bodies were put on elevators to reach the crematoria directly above. These facilities were not completed until 1943. Until then small gas chambers improvised in old farmhouses at the edge of the camp served the purpose. Hydrogen cyanide gas, an industrial-strength pesticide known by its commercial name **Zyklon B,** was used throughout. In the words of camp commandant **Rudolf Höss,** "It took from 3 to 15 minutes to kill the people in the death chamber depending upon climatic conditions. We knew when the people were dead because their screaming stopped. We usually waited about one-half hour before we opened the doors and removed the bodies."[6]

The gas chambers and crematoria were operated by prisoners of the **Sonderkommando** under direct SS supervision. Their job was to remove the dead from the gas chambers, salvage any valuables hidden in the bodies (including gold dental fillings), and dispose of the remains. Body disposal was always a big problem at Auschwitz. The gas chambers could kill far more people than the crematoria could burn. Hence whenever the gas chambers were running at full capacity, the Sonderkommandos were forced to burn the excess bodies in open pits at the edge of the camp.

6. U.S. Government, *Nazi Conspiracy and Aggression* (Washington, D.C.: U.S. Government Printing Office, 1946), p. 6:788.

A rail spur was built right into the center of Birkenau, and **selections** were made on the ramp by SS doctors. Almost before newly arrived prisoners knew what was happening, they had been separated into two groups. Those selected to die were moved directly to the gas chamber, where the usual methods of deception were used to make the bewildered victims believe they were entering showers. Those selected for work were assigned to a sector of the main camp or sent to one of the Auschwitz satellite camps. The sexes were separated, with just two exceptions. A special Gypsy family camp, numbering 20,000, was housed in Birkenau until it was liquidated in August 1944 and its inmates either gassed or sent to other camps. The second exception, a family camp of 5,000 Czech Jews sent to Birkenau from Theresienstadt in September 1943, lasted as long as the SS thought it might be a useful ruse should the **Red Cross** insist on inspecting the camp. When that likelihood dimmed, this family camp, too, was liquidated in July 1944.

A few of the Auschwitz prisoners who survived the initial selections were used as guinea pigs in ghastly **medical experiments** done by Dr. **Josef Mengele** and other SS physicians. Few of these prisoners survived the ordeal. Perhaps the luckiest prisoners were those assigned to the Birkenau storerooms for property confiscated from the victims. This sector was nicknamed "Canada" by inmates who imagined it a land of endless wealth. There many of them were able to "organize" (prisoner slang meaning "steal") valuables to trade on the black market for extra food and other privileges.

Small gas chambers functioned at six of the "ordinary" concentration camps in Germany: **Sachsenhausen, Neuengamme, Mauthausen, Stutthof, Gross-Rosen**, and **Ravensbrück**. These took the lives of thousands of Jews, Gypsies, German and Polish political prisoners, and religious dissenters.

Netting the Victims

The German plan to sweep all of Europe and net every single Jew and Gypsy could not be completed. Nor could it be carried out with uniform effectiveness everywhere in Nazi-dominated Europe. In fact, whether one lived or died during the Holocaust often depended on where one was born. Gypsies and Jews under direct German rule were usually at greater risk than those living in countries ruled by allied or collaborationist governments. The attitudes of the surrounding population helped determine whether one's neighbors would extend or withhold aid. Geography, too, played a role by establishing whether there were hills and forests in which to hide or nearby neutral countries that might offer refuge. Timing was another factor. Populations of Jews and Gypsies that were swept up in the first months of the Final Solution were less likely to survive than those taken later in the war. A country-by-country survey will demonstrate the diverse impact of the Final Solution on the various parts of Hitler's Europe. We begin with those areas of Eastern Europe that were under direct German control, for nowhere else were Nazi policies so harsh or enforced so brutally from the very start. Then we will turn to Germany and the rest of Europe.

Poland, a country that had been revived at the end of World War I after more than a hundred years of foreign domination, was home to more than 3,250,000 Jews (10 percent of the total population) and 50,000 Gypsies. Many Poles resented the Jews' prominence in the business and financial life of the country, which led to policies in the 1920s and 1930s designed to diminish it. However, nothing that the Poles had done approached the level of persecution by the Germans starting in 1939: confiscation of property, concentration in ghettos, and deportation to labor and extermination camps. These were welcomed by a minority of Poles, whereas another minority of them tried to help the victims hide or pass as Poles. This was always dangerous, for many Jews and Gypsies did not look at all like Slavs or speak good Polish. Poles discovered helping them were shot, along with their families and sometimes their whole villages. Hence most Poles chose not to get involved. They had their own hands full trying to cope with extraordinarily harsh German rule.

Given the length and severity of German rule in Poland, the priority given to the large numbers of victims there, the many German **police** units stationed there, and the unassimilated status of most Polish Jews, few of the targeted victims survived. About 90 percent (2,900,000) of the Polish Jews and at least 16 percent (8,000) of the Polish Gypsies perished.

The Soviet Union had emancipated its nearly 3,000,000 Jews and encouraged their assimilation following World War I. When Hitler attacked in June 1941 Soviet officials managed to evacuate some Jews into the interior, but hundreds of thousands were trapped by the rapid German advance. Harsh German occupation policies were intensified by Hitler's association of Jews with communism. Sweeps by Einsatzgruppen and subsequent deportations to labor and extermination camps decimated the Jewish and Gypsy populations. At least 700,000 Soviet Jews and 30,000 Soviet Gypsies died in the Holocaust.

The Baltic states of Latvia, Lithuania, and Estonia had been absorbed by the Soviet Union in 1940. Extreme nationalists in these small countries believed that the Jews had welcomed Communist rule, and those in Lithuania actually attacked the Jews when the German armies overran the Baltic region in June 1941. These sentiments and actions enhanced the work of the Einsatzgruppen and made ghettoization and deportation easier. In most respects the Final Solution paralleled that in the USSR. About 80 percent of the 245,000 Jews and more than 35 percent of the 7,000 Gypsies in the Baltic states died.

Germany, now enlarged by Austria and lands annexed from Czechoslovakia (the **Protectorate of Bohemia and Moravia**, roughly coterminous with today's Czech Republic) and from Poland, deported virtually all its remaining Jews and Gypsies to Eastern European ghettos and camps in 1942 and 1943. A small number of comparatively fortunate Jews were sent to **Theresienstadt**. By the end of 1942 only a few thousand Jews working in important war industries had been exempted from the transports, and they, too, were taken during the following year. About 5,000 German Jews managed to hide with the help of sympathetic friends and neighbors, although this was risky business for all concerned. Some ordinary citizens expressed delight with the deportations, but many others ignored them out of a sense of being able to do nothing about them or because they had other things on their minds.

Many of the Germans who were actively opposed to Hitler and joined the resistance in order to bring his government down were appalled by the persecutions of the Jews. This group included men of the left, such as Julius Leber, conservative resisters, such as **Claus Schenk von Stauffenberg**, and those opposing Hitler on religious grounds, such as **Dietrich Bonhoeffer**. Students belonging to the **White Rose** resistance group centered at Munich University denounced antisemitism and exposed the extermination of the Jews in their anti-Nazi pamphlets. Another German resister, **Kurt Gerstein**, infiltrated the **SS** in order to get firsthand evidence of Nazi crimes. He informed foreign diplomats about the Final Solution in 1942, but he was not believed. Had efforts by the German resistance to kill Hitler and neutralize the SS succeeded, the Final Solution would have ended.

On the eve of the Final Solution about 150,000 Jews remained in the original German lands, more than 50,000 Jews in Austria, and 92,000 Jews in the annexed Czech lands. Of these groups about 135,000 German Jews, virtually all the Austrian Jews, and 78,000 Czech Jews died. Additional numbers of Jews from these countries who had fled to nearby countries were swept up there. Of the Gypsy populations in those areas, 75 percent of the 20,000 in Germany, 58 percent of the 11,200 in Austria, and 38 percent of the 13,000 in the Czech lands succumbed during the Holocaust.

Yugoslavia was occupied by the Germans in April 1941 and immediately partitioned. Much of it was turned over to the newly created German satellite state of Croatia, but the south, mainly Serbia, was under direct German rule. There the Jews were held responsible for **partisan** attacks on German forces, and thousands of Jews, Gypsies, and communists were shot in reprisals by the **German Army**. The rest were rounded up and dispatched by gas vans. By June 1942 the head of the German military government in Serbia, Harald Turner, could claim that he had solved his Jewish and Gypsy problems. In fact, hundreds of people from both groups had fled to the mountains to find refuge with the partisans. The rest, 24,000 Jews and at least 1,000 Gypsies, were killed in Serbia itself.

Greece was occupied at the same time as Yugoslavia (April 1941), and part of it was handed over to Germany's ally Bulgaria. The rest was divided into German and Italian occupation zones. Most Greek Jews lived in the German zone, and in 1943 they were placed in a ghetto in Salonika and later deported to Poland. The Italians at first refused to hand over the Jews in their zone, but when Italy surrendered and changed sides in the war, the Germans took over their zone and deported the remaining Greek Jews, including those from the Greek islands and the adjacent country of Albania. Evidently most Greek Jews believed German stories about being resettled in Poland. Only a few thousand went into hiding. About 80 percent of the 73,000 Greek Jews and an unknown number of Greek Gypsies fell victim to the Final Solution.

Hungary, a German ally, did not come under direct German control until March 1944. Before that Hungary's right-wing government, directed by **Miklós Horthy,** passed some anti-Jewish laws but refused to participate in the Final Solution. Only Jews who did not have Hungarian nationality, numbering about 20,000, were deported to German-controlled territory. The 725,000 Jews living inside Hungary's border during World War II were safe until early 1944, when Hitler learned that leading Hungarian politicians were holding secret negotiations for a separate peace with the Allies. Furious, the German dictator ordered his army to occupy the country in March 1944, and Horthy was forced to replace the peacemakers with pro-German politicians. **Adolf Eichmann** traveled to Budapest and personally took charge of the Final Solution in Hungary.

Eichmann forced the Hungarian Jews to form a Central Jewish Council and told them that they would be safe as long as they followed orders. In April they were told to form ghettos, and a month later deportations began. Hungarian police supervised the entire process. Eichmann reassured both the deportees and the Hungarians that the destination was **labor camps** in Germany and Poland, a story that was widely accepted. In fact, some Jews and Gypsies were sent to do forced labor in concentration camps, but the majority of them were killed at Auschwitz, which reached its destructive peak in July and August 1944 with the gassing of approximately 400,000 victims. Although Horthy was swayed by foreign protests over the deportations and feared having to answer for them should the Allies win, his attempts to block the transports from July on were only partially successful. Eichmann's deportations were slowed but not stopped. Finally, the Germans ousted Horthy in October 1944, and the deportations resumed. Jews who were not sent away were formed into labor battalions to dig fortifications against the Russians. In the end thousands were slaughtered by the Germans or by the Hungarian fascists, members of the **Arrow Cross** movement. More than 200,000 Hungarian Jews survived because the Germans did not have time to finish the job and because Horthy had slowed them down. Roughly two-thirds of the Hungarian Jews had died, as had at least 1,000 Hungarian Gypsies.

Slovakia, another German ally that was taken over by the Germans in 1944, willingly cooperated with Germany at the beginning of the Holocaust. Slovakia had been part of Czechoslovakia before the war, but the Germans had rewarded it for helping destroy that country in 1939 by making it an "independent" country. In fact it was a German satellite ruled by a Catholic priest, Father **Jozef Tiso**. When the Germans asked for the Slovakian Jews, Tiso's government enthusiastically complied and even paid the Germans five hundred marks per Jew, ostensibly to defray the costs of resettlement. Between March and June 1942 around 56,000 of the 89,000 Slovakian Jews were rounded up by the paramilitary **Hlinka Guard** and sent to Poland. Then the Slovakian leaders changed their minds and stopped the transports. They had heard rumors about the extermination camps, and they were being pressured by the Vatican to stop deporting the Jews.

From June 1942 to August 1944 most of the remaining Slovakian Jews were placed in **labor camps** in Slovakia itself. Compared with the German labor camps, these were humanely run. When Soviet forces approached Slovakia in August 1944, an unsuccessful uprising of anti-Tiso partisans led to a German takeover of the country and a resumption of the deportations. In all at least 60,000 (68 percent) of the Jews who had remained in Slovakia and at least 400 Slovakian Gypsies fell victim to the Final Solution.

Croatia, another German satellite state that was created by the Germans, governed most of northern Yugoslavia during World War II. It was ruled by Ante Pavelić, head of the fascist **Ustasha** movement and every bit as brutal and racist as Hitler. From the start Pavelić pursued a policy of ethnic cleansing aimed at removing Serbs (who were hated for dominating Croatians when both groups lived in Yugoslavia between 1919 and 1941) as well as Jews and Gypsies. Jews and Gypsies were sent to Croatian labor camps in 1941, and the following year they began to be deported at the request of the Germans. Only those in the Italian occupation zone of Croatia were spared, and, as in Greece, that changed when Italy surrendered in September 1943 and the Germans took over the entire area. By then, however, most of the Jews and Gypsies had fled to the partisans that were active in the area. The distinguishing feature of the Holocaust in Croatia was the very large proportion of victims killed in Croatia at the hands of the Croatians themselves, perhaps 75 percent of the total. Estimated total losses were 500,000 Serbs, 25,000 Gypsies, and 32,000 Jews (about 80 percent of the Jewish population).

The remaining Eastern European countries allied with Germany — Bulgaria and Romania — declined to deport their Jews to the extermination camps in Poland, and because they were never occupied by the Germans, they were not forced to do so. And yet, the Holocaust touched them too, in diverse ways.

Bulgaria, with a fairly small Jewish population of 50,000 and no history of strong **antisemitism**, insisted on solving its "Jewish problem" at home, putting off German demands for deportations. Effectively that meant some comparatively mild anti-Jewish legislation, but nothing more. Jews from neighboring countries fled to Bulgaria for refuge, with the result that there were more Jews in the country at the end of the war than at its start. The great exception to this was the fate of the Jews and Gypsies in Macedonia and Thrace, parts of Yugoslavia and Greece given to Bulgaria by Hitler in 1941. There the grateful Bulgarians agreed to round up and deport as many as they could find. More than 11,000 Jews living there were transported to Poland.

Romania, with a far larger Jewish population (441,000 in mid-1941) and a powerful tradition of antisemitism, likewise rebuffed German requests to transport its Jews to Poland. Even more so than in Bulgaria, national pride was an issue. The Romanians disliked the Germans' arrogance and their failures to deliver promised military aid at a time when Romanian and German forces were fighting side by side in the Soviet Union. Hence they chose to intensify existing anti-Jewish laws but did not go through with plans to deport the Jews. The story might have been very different had the highly antisemitic **Iron Guard** managed to seize power in Romania when it rose up in January 1941. In fact the government remained firmly in the hands of Marshal **Ion Antonescu**, a more moderate antisemite, for the remainder of the war.

Greatly complicating the situation in Romania was the prewar occupation of the disputed border provinces of **Bessarabia** and Bukovina by the USSR. Forced to accept this loss in 1940 by Hitler, who was then observing his 1939 Nazi-Soviet Pact with Stalin, Romania regained the provinces when it joined the German assault on the Soviet Union in June 1941. The Romanians claimed that the 300,000 Jews who lived there had welcomed Soviet rule, and in fact some of them had. In retaliation, Romanian troops and members of a German Einsatzgruppe killed thousands of Jews and Gypsies in Bessarabia and Bukovina and herded most of the rest into ghettos across the Dniester River (**Transnistria**) in Romanian-occupied Ukraine. There many more of them were massacred or else left to die from hunger and exposure. Other Jews were killed in Romania proper. Altogether at least 121,000 Jews fell victim, along with a minimum of 19,000 Gypsies.

In Western Europe conditions were crucially different from Eastern Europe, in several ways. Because there were fewer Jews and Gypsies in Western Europe, the Germans went after the more numerous Eastern European victims first. There were also fewer Germans there. With the heaviest fighting going on in the East, their police forces in the West were usually stretched very thin. Jews native to Western Europe were, for the most part, highly assimilated, which made it easier for them to "pass" as Gentiles. Antisemitism was less pronounced in the west and hence less of a barrier to aiding Jews. Finally, several Western European countries shared borders with neutral states that might grant asylum to refugees.

But the Final Solution did not have a uniform impact on the various Western European countries that were under German control. Much depended on the size of a country's Jewish population, the attitudes of local officials and ordinary people, and the availability of hiding places and neutral refuges. These varied greatly from country to country, and they explain why the Holocaust took a far higher toll in some countries than in others.

France, with 350,000 Jews (many of them refugees) and 40,000 Gypsies, had the largest such populations in Western Europe. It also had a pro-German government during the Final Solution. Known as the **Vichy** regime and led by World War I hero Marshal **Henri Pétain**, the government had been formed by right-wing Frenchmen to collaborate with Germany after France's defeat in 1940. Pétain's prime minister, Pierre Laval, was especially keen on demonstrating France's qualifications for junior partnership in German-dominated Europe and willingly brought French laws into line with German antisemitic legislation. Foreign Jews and Gypsies were placed in French concentration camps, and in 1942 they were deported to Poland. French Gypsies were especially hard hit. Almost 40 percent (just over 15,000) of them died, in part because of a long-standing law that required nomads to be registered with the police and prewar requirements that they stay in designated camps. Vichy officials were less willing to send away native French Jews, but in the end they caved in to German pressure. Without the cooperation of Vichy police and other officials, the Germans would have had a much harder time enforcing the Final Solution in France. And yet, only just over 20 percent of the Jews in France (75,000) died in the Holocaust. How can this comparatively low figure be explained?

In contrast to much of Europe, France contained a vast and sparsely populated hinterland in the south and west of the country. A significant number of Jews fled there when the Germans invaded, and many had the good sense to stay there in hiding rather than return home. Other Jews fled to these rural backwaters when deportations threatened. There they received help from sympathetic Frenchmen who either hid them or assisted in their escape to Switzerland or Spain, both neutral countries bordering on France. Others made their way to the small Italian zone of occupation from which Jews were not deported until the Germans took it over in September 1943. The village of Le Chambon-sur-Lignon, where the local Protestant ministers influenced the people to help thousands of Jews, has come to symbolize this aid, although it was an extreme case. Timing, too, has to be taken into account. The first Jews to be deported were the foreign Jews, always less popular than assimilated French Jews. By the time orders came to arrest the latter, Frenchmen were no longer certain that Hitler was going to win his war and were beginning to shake off defeatism. French policemen became increasingly unreliable, and the Germans lacked the manpower to do the job for themselves. Hence geography, Jewish flight, French helpfulness, and declining German fortunes combined to frustrate German and Vichy plans to deport all the French Jews.

The Netherlands' experience of the Holocaust was very different and far more tragic. About 75 percent of the 140,000 Jews who lived there in 1940 did not survive, as was also true of about half of its 500 Gypsies. The Germans regarded the Dutch as fellow **Aryans** who eventually would be incorporated into the Reich. Therefore they imposed a stern civilian (that is, Nazi Party) regime directed by an Austrian Nazi, **Arthur Seyss-Inquart**. The Dutch did not take kindly to direct German rule or to the anti-Jewish measures that came with it. When several hundred Dutch Jews were deported to German concentration camps for defending themselves against attacks by Dutch Nazis, the Dutch unions responded with a general strike in February 1941. This was the only act of its kind in any country during World War II. The Germans only cracked down harder, forcing an end to the strike by threatening even more deportations and ruling the Netherlands with an iron fist. In general the Dutch civil service cooperated in identifying and deporting Jews and Gypsies.

When mass deportations from the Netherlands began in 1942, most Dutch Jews followed directives from the **Jewish Council** to report as ordered. The great majority of them were native-born and well to do, used to trusting their leaders and perhaps incapable of facing up to the dangers that faced them. About 26,000 Jews went into hiding with the help of sympathetic friends and neighbors. But this proved difficult. The Netherlands was small, heavily populated, and lacking any remote rural areas. Hiding had to be done in attics and walled-off rooms, which multiplied the chances of discovery over a three-year period. Discovery and denunciation by the minority of Dutch collaborators and informers was always possible. The fate of **Anne Frank**, whose diary became famous after the war, was similar to that of many in hiding. She and her family were detected when someone reported hearing a toilet flush in a supposedly unused part of a building where they were concealed. Flight, too, was difficult. Neutral countries were far away, and crossing the North Sea to England was all but impossible. The Dutch Jews were trapped.

Belgium in many ways was in a similar position: small, heavily populated, and remote from safe havens. And yet, roughly 60 percent of the 66,000 Jews in Belgium at the start of the war survived the Final Solution. Compared with the Netherlands, German rule in Belgium was less severe. Belgium was not at first slated for annexation to Germany and hence was placed under military administration. Belgian officials were able to exploit the German army's relative indifference to racial policies by refusing to carry out some of the more extreme directives against the Jews. Moreover, the vast majority — more than 80 percent — of the Jews in Belgium were recent immigrants, refugees from Germany and Eastern Europe and hence extremely wary of official policies. Hence many of them evaded registration, went into hiding, sabotaged the work of the Jewish Council, joined underground organizations, and fled to France. In April 1943 an armed Jewish resistance group attacked a deportation train and enabled more than 200 Jews to escape. Still, at least 25,000 Jews from Belgium died in the Holocaust, as did at least 350 Gypsies (60 percent of the total Gypsy population in Belgium).

Denmark is famous for having saved most of its 8,000 Jews by slipping them across to neutral Sweden in small boats in October 1943. That was possible because very unusual conditions prevailed in German-occupied Denmark. Before 1943 the Germans treated the Danes with kid gloves. Danish agricultural products were very important to the German economy, and the Danes made no trouble, in part because the Germans kept the Danish king and government in place. The Germans also refrained from deporting the Danish Jews because they knew that the Danes despised Nazi racism and would react with hostility to antisemitic policies. The story probably would have been very different had the Danish Jewish community not been so small.

Relations between Germans and Danes deteriorated in 1943 as the Germans increased their demands and the Danish underground began to resist. Hitler ordered the German army to take control of the government, and the SS made plans to deport the Jews. But other German officials leaked word of these plans to the Danish underground because they did not want the deportation of Jews to make German-Danish relations even worse. The Danes then organized the flight to Sweden by fishing boats, and fewer than one hundred Danish Jews died in the Holocaust. This was possible because the small Jewish community was concentrated mainly in Copenhagen, neutral Sweden was just a few miles away and willing to take the refugees, and the Germans were divided about how best to deal with the Danes and their Jews.

Italy, alone among the countries of Western Europe, began the war as an ally of the Third Reich. But Italian Fascism was no carbon copy of German Nazism, and **Mussolini**'s views on race differed from Hitler's. The Italian dictator did not especially like Jews, but he was not a radical antisemite, and support for him among the 48,000 Italian Jews was fairly widespread. Racial laws adopted in the late 1930s to cement Italy's new alliance with Germany were only weakly enforced. During the first years of World War II Italian Jews and Gypsies were safe from the Final Solution, and those in Italian occupation zones in France, Greece, and Croatia were shielded from deportations. Several thousand foreign and stateless Jews were placed in Italian concentration camps in 1940, but they, too, were spared worse treatment.

All that changed when Mussolini fell from power following the Allied invasion of Sicily in July 1943. In September Italy surrendered and the German army swiftly seized control of central and northern Italy to prevent the Allies from striking northward. The SS went after the 35,000 Italian Jews who lived there, but they did not find it easy. Italians were not antisemitic, and they despised the Germans. Jews found refuge with friends, neighbors, and various institutions of the **Catholic church.** They were assisted in this by a joint Jewish-Gentile underground group called Delasem, which also helped a considerable number of Jews escape to Switzerland. Only a few Italian policemen were enticed by financial rewards for arresting Jews, and the Germans lacked the manpower to track down many on their own. On the other hand, Mussolini's Fascist militia cheerfully assisted in the deportations. The final death toll, around 8,000 Jews and 1,000 Gypsies, was less than 20 percent of the Italian Jews and about 4 percent of the Italian Gypsies.

Norway, Finland, and Luxembourg, all of which had very small Jewish populations, experienced the Holocaust in diverse ways. Nearly half of Norway's 1,700 Jews crossed the long border with Sweden and were warmly welcomed there. A few others managed to hide from German deportations, but nearly half were arrested by the German and Norwegian police and sent to Auschwitz. Exactly 762 died. Finland, a German ally but independent and remote, firmly declined Himmler's requests to turn over its 2,000 Jews. Just seven out of approximately 300 alien Jews were turned over to the Germans. Luxembourg was effectively annexed to the Third Reich in 1940, and its 3,500 Jews and 200 Gypsies suffered the same fate as those in Germany. Around half the Jews and Gypsies perished.

Evasion and Armed Resistance

The victims responded to Nazi genocide with both evasion and armed resistance. Evasion, nonviolent action aimed at staying alive, took many forms. In Western Europe this might include evading registration, fleeing to neutral countries (or helping others to flee), and hiding from the police. More broadly it involved placing children with Gentile foster parents, jumping from deportation trains, passing as Gentiles, and hiding with Gentile helpers. Evasion in Eastern European **ghettos** involved smuggling food, hiding from deportations, and escaping to nearby forests. The last of these rarely succeeded unless **partisans** could be found to offer protection. A rabbi in eastern Poland who took 350 of his flock into the forests explained their fate: "[The Germans] were raiding the woods constantly. . . . During the whole summertime we were able to hide in the forest because the leaves [hid the underground] bunkers. The moment the snow fell, since we had to go out on the snow occasionally, we left a trail. They tracked them down to each bunker. . . . Out of the 350, no more than 15 remained."[7] Evasion also included efforts to keep victims from losing hope (often called "spiritual resistance"): providing concerts, libraries, plays, education, religious observances, and welfare services. In labor and concentration camps evasion by prisoners took such forms as helping one another at work, sharing food, and even organizing escapes from the smaller, poorly guarded camps.

Most attention, however, has been focused on armed **resistance,** which was much more difficult to pull off. Ordinary Europeans rarely owned firearms, and they were hard to come by during the war. Escape to the forests to join

---

7. Donald L. Niewyk, ed., *Fresh Wounds: Early Narratives of Holocaust Survival* (Chapel Hill: University of North Carolina Press, 1998), p. 229.

anti-German partisans (assuming there were any nearby) succeeded only if one could bring along a gun. Even if one could, partisans might not accept Jews; especially in Poland there were cases of the underground Home Army murdering Jews who asked to join. Yet another obstacle to armed resistance was the German policy of collective responsibility: holding everyone in the community responsible for the actions of individuals and small groups. Armed attacks on Germans were met with mass executions of entire neighborhoods or ghettos. Even those who believed rumors about the extermination camps hoped to evade deportations, whereas collective responsibility assured that armed defiance would bring down immediate and certain retaliation on the whole community. Finally there is the problem of who knew what about the **Final Solution** at the time it was happening, and when they knew it. Jews and Gypsies from Western and Southern Europe, far from the killing fields of Poland, arrived in genuine ignorance of the camps. News of Einsatzgruppen actions and extermination camps did get out to ghettos and labor camps in Eastern Europe, but it was not always believed. "Denial," the mind's inability to assimilate a terrible truth, led many of the potential victims to disbelieve what they heard about mass murder or to believe that it could only happen to some other group that had done something deserving of punishment. Ignorance and denial deprived many Jews and Gypsies of the sense of urgency required for armed resistance.

Armed resistance in Eastern European ghettos occurred only after the Jewish Council strategy of survival through work was discredited by repeated deportations. Such revolts usually were confined to small ghettos where German control was weak and the ghetto underground well developed. They permitted several thousand Jews to take their chances in hiding with peasants or else forming or joining partisan groups. The one large ghetto to rise up in full armed revolt was Warsaw, and it, too, happened only in the last stages of the deportations, in April 1943, at which time only about 60,000 of the original 455,000 Jews remained. As the Germans moved in to deport them, too, the Jewish underground, led by Mordechai Anielewicz, fought back. Very poorly armed and numbering only about 1,500 fighters, they held off larger and far better armed German forces for more than three weeks (April 19–May 15). The SS and Police Leader in Warsaw, General **Jürgen Stroop**, reported, "The resistance offered by the Jews and bandits could be broken only by the energetic day and night commitment of our assault units. . . . [I] decided to embark on the total destruction of the Jewish quarter by burning down every residential block, including the housing blocks belonging to the armament enterprises. One enterprise after another was systematically evacuated and destroyed by fire."[8] Around 56,000 surviving Jews were deported. German losses were negligible, and only a few of the resisters managed to escape through the sewers. A much smaller uprising, in the **Białystok** ghetto at the time of its liquidation in August 1943, was also unsuccessful. Virtually all of the members of the underground who tried to break out of the ghetto at that time died fighting along with their commander, **Mordechai Tennenbaum**. A brief rebellion by the **Vilna** ghetto underground in September 1943 was put down by the Jewish Council under its director, **Jacob Gens**.

Armed resistance in the extermination camps was the work of men belonging to work squads and Sonderkommandos who had learned that they were about to be shot. Truly desperate men, they believed that revolt was the only way to give a few of them a chance to survive. The first such uprising was at Treblinka on August 2, 1943. Having learned that the Germans planned to shut the camp down in a short time and shoot the work crews, the camp underground overpowered some guards, seized arms from the arsenal, and tried to break through the barbed wire and mine fields. About 150 made it to the forest, but only twelve survived the subsequent German manhunt. A short time later, on October 14, 1943, a similar revolt occurred at Sobibór, masterminded by Soviet prisoners among the workers. This time about sixty survived to join Soviet partisans in the nearby forest. At Birkenau (Auschwitz II), 450 members of the Sonderkommando, believing with good reason that their days were numbered, rose up on October 7, 1944. With weapons and explosives smuggled in to them by women arms workers at a nearby camp factory, they were able to kill a capo and three SS men and set fire to one of the crematoria. But most were killed, and not one of them was able to make good his escape.

Jewish armed resistance in underground formations occurred in both Eastern and Western Europe. In Eastern Europe Jews were most in need of the **partisans** in 1942, before very many such units had been formed. From 1943 on perhaps as many as 20,000 Jews fought with the partisans in Poland and the Soviet Union, sabotaging trains, attacking isolated police and army units, and the like. They did so in mixed units, often organized by Soviet officers or Polish communists, as well as in separate Jewish groups. The best known of the latter operated in the Vilna region and was led by the young poet **Abba Kovner**. Jews also fought in partisan units in Slovakia, Serbia, Croatia, and Greece. In Western Europe, where Jews were well assimilated and no ghettos existed, Jewish fighters usually joined mixed underground organizations, in which they were

8. Sybil Milton, ed., *The Stroop Report: The Jewish Quarter of Warsaw Is No More* (New York: Pantheon, 1979), pp. 9–11.

over-represented. There were also specifically Jewish units of young Zionists and Communists, made up chiefly of Eastern European immigrants.

THE END OF THE HOLOCAUST, 1944–1945

In 1944 the increasingly critical need for labor in Germany induced the Germans to transport prisoners from the eastern camps to **concentration camps** in the Reich. With that these camps, which had been depopulated of most Jews in 1942, once again contained large numbers of them, and from that point on their fate paralleled that of all other concentration camp prisoners. The last six months of the Holocaust, stretching from November 1944 to May 1945, corresponded to the invasion from both east and west and increasingly rapid disintegration of the Third Reich. Although the last remaining extermination camp, **Auschwitz**, no longer functioned as a killing center, and the Germans kept Jews and Gypsies alive as slave workers and bargaining tools, deaths from mistreatment, malnutrition, and exhaustion continued. Indeed, many of those liberated by the Allies were already too far gone to recover.

At the end of October 1944 Himmler ordered an end to the gassings at Auschwitz, and a few weeks later he had the crematoria blown up. The German leaders wanted to cover their crimes as much as possible, but these moves may also have been motivated by secret negotiations then going on to exchange Jews for Allied concessions. Already at that time tens of thousands of slave workers were being evacuated from concentration camps all over Eastern Europe to camps in Germany. In January 1945 Auschwitz, too, was abandoned, although about 6,000 sick prisoners were left behind to be liberated by the Soviet army. Almost all these evacuations were done on foot to railheads inside Germany, forced marches appropriately called "**death marches**" by their survivors. In deep snow and freezing temperatures many of the already weakened prisoners dropped in their tracks and were shot by the SS guards. Some daring escapes occurred when prisoners slipped away during snowstorms or blended into crowds of German refugees fleeing the Russians.

Many survivors of these death marches were jammed into **Gross-Rosen**, the easternmost of the German concentration camps and itself the nucleus of a large complex of sub-camps. Others were sent directly to equally overcrowded camps deeper inside Germany. They frequently ended up in new subcamps of the concentration camps, such as those that surrounded **Dora-Mittelbau**, where the V-1 and V-2 rockets were built and which itself had started out as a satellite of Buchenwald. Those still needed as workers were, for the most part, fortunate at this stage, because those left idle were fed little or nothing. The worst camp, **Bergen-Belsen,** had been established in 1943 as a transit camp to accommodate a few thousand prisoners being held for exchange with the enemy. But by the end of the war it was hopelessly overcrowded with 60,000 walking skeletons. When British forces entered the camp on April 15, 1945, they found it littered with corpses; thousands more died after liberation. There were several cases of SS men shooting survivors in the last days of the war, but for the most part they were too busy running away or trying to hide their uniforms to commit further atrocities. The major concentration camps, such as **Buchenwald** and **Mauthausen,** fell without struggle, but there, too, the death rate in the last days was staggering.

AFTERMATH AND LEGACIES

Survivors of the Holocaust numbered more than 2,000,000 Jews and at least 400,000 Gypsies. Whether they had been liberated from German camps, had just come out of hiding, or were still living in countries that had given them refuge, their natural inclination was to return home and look for surviving relatives as soon as health and travel conditions permitted. Most did, but not all stayed. Particularly in Eastern Europe survivors commonly found no other family members alive, and houses and apartments, if they still stood, were occupied by others who did not want to give them up. The roughly 300,000 Jewish survivors from Poland also found themselves caught in the middle of an undeclared civil war between supporters of the country's new communist government, imposed by the Soviet Union, and its enemies within the bitterly anticommunist Polish underground and the general population. The antigovernment forces often identified Jews as procommunist and made their return as difficult as possible. Tensions culminated in an actual **pogrom** in Kielce, Poland, in July 1946. Forty-two Jews were killed and many more injured. In the end less than 10 percent of the Polish survivors decided to stay. Most of those who left slipped illegally into the American zone of Germany where they became **displaced persons** (DPs) living in camps and awaiting resettlement.

Elsewhere in Communist Eastern Europe surviving Jews were labeled as "capitalists" and "cosmopolitan elements" and made unwelcome. This induced large numbers of Jews to leave Romania and Bulgaria after 1945. Hungarian survivors had an easier time going home. Soviet policies there were less harsh and less unpopular at first, although the strong representation of Jews in the leadership of the Hungarian Communist Party stimulated postwar **anti-**

semitism. Ironically, it was communist persecution of religion and private enterprise that induced many Hungarian Jews to leave. About one quarter (55,000) of the Hungarian survivors became DPs in the west. Smaller numbers of refugees filtered out of Czechoslovakia and Yugoslavia. Soviet Jews, and Jews in the Baltic states, now once more under Soviet control, found it far harder to leave.

Elsewhere, and particularly in Western Europe, return was the norm. The approximately 250,000 Holocaust survivors awaiting resettlement in DP camps after the war had almost all been born in Germany and Eastern Europe. It took six years for all of them to be accommodated, and additional years of camp life were hard to take. The Jewish refugees were not alone, however. Initially there were millions of European DPs . Moreover, there were still laws restricting immigration to Palestine and the United States, destinations preferred by most Jewish DPs. Young Holocaust survivors were often militant advocates of **Zionism** who organized illegal immigration to Palestine. Pressure on Great Britain by the United States to help solve the Jewish DP problem contributed to the decision to partition Palestine and create the State of Israel in 1948. Ultimately about 57 percent of the Jewish DPs found new homes in Israel, 29 percent came to the United States, and the remainder entered Canada and a host of other countries.

Gypsy survivors had it even harder. They, too, were often reduced to DP status as a result of the shattering of their clans. Traditionally suspicious of authority and unused to dealing with bureaucracies, they encountered difficulties handling all the red tape. Nor did Gypsies enjoy the benefits of well-heeled foreign allies. Doubtless many wished to emigrate, but few succeeded. The Gypsies were trapped in a Europe that had no more use for them after the war than before.

Perpetrators of genocide were the subjects of various **trials of war criminals,** but for various reasons justice was not always perfectly applied. The major surviving German leaders were tried by the International Military Tribunal at Nuremberg, where judges from the United States, Great Britain, France, and the Soviet Union found all but three of the twenty-two defendants guilty and sentenced twelve to death, including **Göring, Seyss-Inquart, Streicher, Frank, Rosenberg,** and **Ernst Kaltenbrunner,** Heydrich's successor as head of the Reich Security Main Office. Three other defendants were sentenced to life in prison, and the rest to prison terms of varying length. The Nuremberg Trials also provided the first massive documentation of the Final Solution as one of several Nazi "crimes against humanity." Unfortunately several of the major architects of genocide were not present. **Hitler, Himmler,** and **Goebbels** had escaped justice by committing suicide, and **Adolf Eichmann** could not be found. Only later, in 1960, would he be discovered in hiding in Argentina and be brought to trial and executed in Israel. Thousands of lesser perpetrators, mostly pro-Nazi collaborators from Eastern Europe, succeeded in disguising themselves as ordinary DPs and emigrating to the United States and Canada. Years later some were recognized and prosecuted as war criminals. Additional trials in courts set up by the individual military governments in the three Western zones of Germany resulted in more than 5,000 convictions and 794 hangings. In the Soviet zone a great many Nazis were secretly executed and deported, but reliable statistics on them are not available. Trials of war criminals were also held in the four zones of occupation in Austria.

Many war criminals, including labor and extermination camp staff, Einsatzgruppen officers, and local helpers were tried in the states whose citizens were victims of atrocities. These trials occurred in both Eastern and Western Europe. Those in Poland and the Soviet Union were especially numerous and often resulted in the death penalty. Their most famous defendant, Auschwitz commandant **Rudolf Höss**, was convicted by a Polish court and hanged on the gallows at Auschwitz. These trials continued for many years. As late as 1987 Klaus Barbie, who as a Gestapo chief in France had deported hundreds of Jews, was sentenced to life in prison by a French court.

Additional trials of Holocaust perpetrators took place in German courts. The West German government at first extended and then abolished the statute of limitations in cases of murder. In 1958 it established the Central Office for the Investigation of National Socialist Crimes to convict former Nazis suspected of murder. The most sensational of the trials that resulted, the "Auschwitz Trial," ended in 1965 with the conviction of sixteen SS staff members and a capo. Six received life sentences (the death penalty had been abolished in West Germany). Altogether the West German courts tried more than 91,000 defendants for war crimes, and sentenced approximately 6,500 to long prison terms. Of these, fewer than 1,000 convictions came after 1951. As time passed it became increasingly difficult to get convictions. Sometimes those charged with crimes could not be found, or the evidence was not strong enough to convict. West German courts attempted to distinguish between those guilty of excessive cruelty, and hence deserving of harsh sentences, and those guilty of following orders given by superiors and hence mere "accessories." In East Germany, 329 convictions for Nazi crimes were handed down between 1951 and 1964.

Germans as a whole were uncomfortable with these trials, in part because they sensed that a few individuals were being held responsible for crimes in which most Germans were complicit. Among the first to face up to this complicity were the **Catholic** and **Protestant churches**. To be sure, they had not been responsible for genocide, and Hitler and his closest advisors held Christianity in utter contempt. But the German churches had kept silent as Jews and Gypsies were persecuted and deported. Only a few individual clerics, such as the Berlin priest Bernhard Lichtenberg, had taken a stand for the victims. Lichtenberg had prayed openly for the Jews in the Berlin cathedral and, following his arrest, asked to share their fate. He died in the hands of the Gestapo in 1943. That there had been so few like him troubled the postwar German churches, which openly acknowledged their failures and sought to reverse their traditional negative view of Judaism.

West German political leaders also acknowledged Germany's responsibility for the consequences of the **Final Solution** by agreeing to pay **reparations** and restitution to Jewish institutions and individuals. Under the terms of a 1953 Reparations Agreement with Israel, West Germany agreed to deliver goods worth $845,000,000 to defray the costs of absorbing 500,000 Jews who had been victims of Nazi persecution. In the same year West Germany adopted a Restitution Law to indemnify individual Jews for suffering and loss of property. Since then it has paid more than $73,000,000,000 to individual survivors living in many countries, and the payments continue. Little restitution has gone to the Gypsies, however. German courts typically ruled that the Gypsies had been arrested as actual or putative criminals, not for racial reasons, and therefore were not eligible to claim restitution. East Germany denied any responsibility for the crimes of the Third Reich but compensated Holocaust survivors who settled there as "Victims of Nazism."

Generational changes were chiefly responsible for Germans coming to terms with the crimes committed by their leaders during the Nazi years. Young Germans who had grown up since World War II, their curiosity piqued by revelations during the Eichmann and Auschwitz trials in the 1960s, began to ask troubling questions of their elders. Later the American television docudrama *Holocaust*, which captured a huge audience when it was shown in Germany in 1979, had a similar effect. Schools and universities in West Germany responded by teaching the history of the Nazi period in some detail. Top German scholars, such as Karl Dietrich Bracher and Hans Mommsen, and able journalists, such as Heinz Höhne and Joachim Fest, revealed Hitler's crimes in all their particulars, and their books were widely read.

Elsewhere willingness to confront participation in the Holocaust has been less dramatic. Austria, which was part of the Third Reich at the time and contributed disproportionately to the SS murder machinery, has preferred to hide behind the fiction that it was simply and purely the first victim of Nazi aggression. In Eastern Europe the widespread belief that the Jews and Gypsies were treated no worse than the Slavs was reinforced by communist regimes that generalized German crimes and minimized the sufferings of minorities. In Western Europe, too, the cooperation of local officials in persecuting Jews and Gypsies is often forgotten in the rush to blame the Germans for everything.

PART II

Problems and Interpretations

Defining the Holocaust

The Holocaust is commonly defined as the mass murder of more than 5,000,000 Jews by the Germans during World War II. Not everyone finds this a fully satisfactory definition. The Nazis also killed millions of people belonging to other groups: Gypsies, the physically and mentally handicapped, Soviet prisoners of war, Polish and Soviet civilians, political prisoners, religious dissenters, and homosexuals. Can it be said that any of these groups were treated the same way as the Jews and for the same reasons and hence deserve to be included in the history of the Holocaust? A positive answer to this question would require a broader definition of the Holocaust and acknowledging as many as 17,000,000 victims. A more expansive view might also induce us to push the start of the Holocaust back from 1941 to 1939 (if we include the handicapped) or even to 1933 (if we assume that the whole thing was premeditated).

The word *holocaust* itself does not tell us whom to include. It is derived from the Greek translation of the Hebrew word *olah*, meaning "a sacrificial offering burnt whole before the Lord." In English *holocaust* has been used for hundreds of years in a largely secular sense when referring to massive sacrifices and great slaughters or massacres. During World War II it was used to describe the fate of both Jewish and non-Jewish victims of Nazi atrocities. Only later, during the 1960s, was it appropriated (and usually capitalized as "the Holocaust") by scholars and popular writers to denote the genocide of the Jews in particular. That is the way most people still understand it. Efforts to replace *holocaust* with the Hebrew words *sho'ah* (meaning "catastrophe") or *hurban* (*khurbn* in Yiddish, meaning "destruction") have not met with much success.

Proponents of an essentially Judeocentric approach to the Holocaust, such as Steven T. Katz in *The Holocaust in Historical Perspective*, contend that the Jews alone were targeted for **genocide**, or total physical annihilation. That emphasis is obvious in the titles of such standard works as *The Holocaust: A History of the Jews of Europe during the Second World War* by Martin Gilbert and *The War against the Jews, 1933–1945* by Lucy S. Dawidowicz. Scholars who limit the Holocaust to the genocide of the Jews rest their case variously on issues of motive (fear and hatred of the Jews that was not felt on the same level for any other group); intent (total, not selective, destruction); and scale (the annihilation of roughly half of the 11,000,000 European Jews, a higher percentage than that of any other group of victims). They go on to note that only the Jews were mentioned at the **Wannsee Conference**, and the **Final Solution** referred specifically to the "Jewish Problem." The Germans, these scholars argue, persecuted many others in hideous ways but did not plan to eradicate them completely. Such victims ought to figure prominently in general studies of the Third Reich, they conclude, but not in works about the Holocaust. Hence books by such scholars either ignore the other victims altogether or else mention them only briefly. Although rarely saying so openly, at least some of these writers may fear that the special tragedy of the Jews will be forgotten if all victims of Nazi persecution are made part of the Holocaust story.

Those who favor a more expansive definition of the Holocaust acknowledge that the Germans identified the Jews as their chief enemy and therefore persecuted them more ruthlessly than any other group. They point out, however, that Nazi Germany had a broadly racist biological vision that was by no means limited to **antisemitism**. They maintain that the Nazi state was ideologically driven to "purify the body of the nation" from *everything* "alien," "asocial," and "hereditarily ill," and that Nazi racial and social policy must be understood as an indivisible whole. The best statement of this more expansive view is *The Racial State: Germany 1933–1945* by Michael Burleigh and Wolfgang Wippermann. Some advocates of greater inclusivity would add only the Gypsies and/or the handicapped, for whom an argument can be made that they were targeted for genocide in the same way and at about the same time as the Jews. Still other such advocates, less impressed with arguments centering on documented genocidal intentions, would cast the net still wider. They argue that if members of the other groups (such as Poles and Soviet prisoners of war) were not officially, or not yet, intended for total physical annihilation, they clearly were subjected to mass slaughter, to holocaust. The fact that smaller percentages of any of these groups were murdered may only mean that the Germans did not have time to finish the job. After all, they did not have time to kill all the Jews, either. Those who propose a more inclusive definition conclude that the arbitrary appropriation of the word *holocaust* to describe the genocide of the Jews alone must not be allowed to stand. A glance at each of the other groups will help to sort out the arguments for and against inclusion.

THE GYPSIES

Of the nearly 1,000,000 Gypsies (Sinti and Roma) in Nazi-dominated Europe, at least 130,000 died at the hands of the Germans. Traditionally a secretive and largely nonliterate people, only rarely have they told their personal stories or written their own history of persecution under German rule. Only a few non-Gypsy scholars have attempted to fill the gap. Hence we know less about the fate of the Gypsies than about that of any other group of victims. That lack of knowledge has made it easier to relegate the Gypsies to little more than a footnote in most books about the Holocaust.

Yehuda Bauer, a leading Israeli historian of the Holocaust, has advanced specific reasons for excluding the Gypsies from the mainstream of Holocaust history in his article "Gypsies" in *Anatomy of the Auschwitz Death Camp*, edited by Yisrael Gutman and Michael Berenbaum. The Gypsies, he maintains, were persecuted by the Nazis for racial reasons, but they were not condemned to total physical annihilation, as were the Jews, and therefore ought to be placed in an entirely different category. Bauer maintains that in Germany "pure" Gypsies were considered an **Aryan** population and spared. Only the Gypsy **Mischlinge** (mixed breeds) were considered dangerous and hence sent to **concentration** and **extermination camps**. Outside of Germany the Nazis distinguished primarily between Gypsies who had settled in permanent residences, and hence could be tolerated, and those who were rootless nomads and therefore deserved to be annihilated. Bauer concludes that the murder of Gypsies was selective, resulting in a smaller percentage of Gypsy deaths, and cannot be equated with the Nazi plan to kill all the Jews. This is also the conclusion of Guenter Lewy in *The Nazi Persecution of the Gypsies*.

Scholars who think that the Gypsies ought to figure prominently in Holocaust history admit that the Germans treated them differently than they did the Jews but deny that those differences ought to be regarded as decisive. The Gypsies were less numerous, were less wealthy, and were considered to be less dangerous than the Jews. Hence the Nazis at first paid them less attention. Donald Kenrick and Grattan Puxon have assembled suggestive evidence in *The Destiny of Europe's Gypsies* that **Himmler** waited until the summer of 1942 before deciding to kill *all* the Gypsies along with the Jews. Starting about then SS documents about racial policies routinely mention the Gypsies along with the Jews. In "Holocaust: The Gypsies," in S. Totten et al., *Century of Genocide*, Sybil Milton argues that whatever reluctance Himmler may have felt about killing the "pure" and non-nomadic Gypsies probably was overcome by Hitler's personal intervention in December 1942. Just six days after the two German leaders met, Himmler issued an order to deport Gypsies to Birkenau (**Auschwitz** II). Thereafter exemptions for certain classes of Gypsies were no longer honored in practice. Ian Hancock's "Responses to the Parrajmos: The Romani Holocaust," in Alan S. Rosenbaum, ed., *Is the Holocaust Unique?* also concludes that by 1943 the Gypsies were being treated the same way as the Jews; both were being subjected to genocide. That a smaller proportion of Gypsies died in the Holocaust is explained chiefly by the late start of the Gypsy genocide and the higher priority that the Germans continued to give to destroying the Jews.

THE MENTALLY AND PHYSICALLY HANDICAPPED

Handicapped Germans were considered genetically defective by the Nazis and systematically killed in the secret **euthanasia** program starting in 1939. Several of the major studies of the Holocaust briefly acknowledge that the compulsory euthanasia program condemned a whole class of people to death for racial reasons, and that it developed the administrative and technical tools later employed in the Final Solution. And yet, they commonly hold that the murder of the German handicapped merely prefigured the genocide of the Jews. That Hitler officially stopped the gassings in 1941 following public protests may help to explain this marginalization of the 150,000 victims of the T4 program.

Arguing against their exclusion from the Holocaust, Henry Friedlander's *The Origins of Nazi Genocide* portrays the handicapped as biologically selected targets of systematic mass murder, just as the Jews and Gypsies were. Indeed, the secret compulsory euthanasia of the handicapped preceded the killing of the other two groups and hence initiated the Holocaust. Nor did euthanasia end when the gassings ceased, but continued by other means until the end of the war. All three groups would have to disappear because Nazi racial ideology taught that they were inferior, degenerate, and criminal elements. The gene pool of the German nation would have to be cleansed. German bureaucrats involved in each genocidal action readily and consistently cooperated with their counterparts in the others. Friedlander concludes that it is impossible to explain the genocide of any one of these groups without explaining the others as well.

SOVIET PRISONERS OF WAR

Of the 5,700,000 Soviet soldiers who surrendered to the Germans during World War II, more than 3,000,000 were either shot shortly after capture, starved to death in prisoner of war camps, gassed in extermination camps, or worked to death in concentration camps. They are usually ignored in books about the Holocaust because at the time they were not targeted for total extermination. Those who offer explicit or implicit arguments for including them among the victims of the Holocaust, such as Bohdan Wytwycky in *The Other Holocaust* and Christian Streit and Jürgen Förster in *The Policies of Genocide*, point out that the appallingly high losses among Soviet prisoners of war were racially determined. The Germans did not usually mistreat prisoners from other Allied countries, but in the Nazi view Soviet prisoners were Slavic "subhumans" who had no right to live. Moreover, young Slavs of reproductive and fighting age were dangerous obstacles to resettling Eastern Europe with Germans. Hence it is reasonable to conclude that all of them were destined to be killed or else sterilized so that their kind would disappear.

POLISH AND SOVIET CIVILIANS

Slavic civilians, ordinary citizens of Poland and the Soviet Union in particular, were held no higher in Nazi racial ideology. Millions were forced to work for the Germans under frequently murderous conditions. Their natural leaders, such as teachers, professors, lawyers, clergymen, and politicians, were ruthlessly exterminated by the Germans. Others perished in massive German reprisals against various forms of resistance. Three million Poles (10 percent of the population) and 19,000,000 Soviet citizens (11 percent of the population) died at the hands of the Germans. Because these deaths were far more selective than was the case with Jews, Gypsies, and the handicapped, it is possible to place them in a different category. Those who would exclude them from the Holocaust emphasize that the Germans did not plan to kill all the Slavs. On the contrary, Germany considered the Slavs of Slovakia and Croatia as valuable allies, not candidates for extermination. Complicating the issue is the difficulty of distinguishing racially motivated killings of Poles and Soviet citizens from those that resulted directly or indirectly from German military actions. Bohdan Wytwycky has estimated that nearly one-fourth of the Soviet civilian deaths were racially motivated, namely, those of 3,000,000 Ukrainians and 1,500,000 Belarusans.

Those who would include Polish and Soviet civilian losses in the Holocaust include Bohdan Wytwycky in *The Other Holocaust*, Richard C. Lukas in *The Forgotten Holocaust: The Poles Under German Rule, 1939–1944*, and Ihor Kamenetsky in *Secret Nazi Plans for Eastern Europe*. These scholars point out that the deaths were a direct result of Nazi contempt for the "subhuman"

Slavs. They note that the "racially valuable" peoples of Western European countries like France and the Netherlands were not treated anywhere near as badly. Moreover, Nazi plans for the ethnic cleansing and German colonization of Poland and parts of the Soviet Union suggest that a victorious Germany might well have raised the level of genocide against the civilian populations of those areas to even more appalling proportions. Slovakia and Croatia did not figure as victims in Hitler's plans to secure *Lebensraum*, and their Slavic populations could be spared. In *A World At Arms: A Global History of World War II*, Gerhard Weinberg suggests that experiments done on concentration camp inmates to perfect methods of mass sterilization probably were chiefly aimed at keeping Slavs alive to perform slave labor in the short term while assuring their long-term disappearance.

POLITICAL PRISONERS, RELIGIOUS DISSENTERS, AND HOMOSEXUALS

It is difficult to incorporate political prisoners and religious dissenters into the Holocaust. The former consisted of German communists, socialists, and democrats who were joined in the concentration camps during the war by anti-Nazis from all the occupied countries. Most of the religious dissenters were Jehovah's Witnesses. Both of these groups were harshly persecuted, and many of them died alongside Holocaust victims in the concentration camps. However, they were not victims of Nazi racial ideology and were not slated for total annihilation. Rather, they were punished for advocating views that challenged the Nazis' claim to a monopoly on political power. Moreover, they could redeem themselves in some cases by changing their minds, which was not an option for those held to be "racially unfit."

Homosexuals, however, seem to present a special case. They were arrested under laws that long predated Hitler. During the Nazi years these laws were strictly enforced against the roughly 1,500,000 male homosexuals in Germany. It is estimated that between 50,000 and 63,000 gay men were sentenced by Nazi courts. Of these, fewer than one quarter — between 5,000 and 15,000 — were sent to concentration camps after serving their regular prison sentences. There they were treated with particular brutality by both guards and fellow inmates. As many as 60 percent of those sent to concentration camps died, a higher percentage than among the political prisoners and religious dissenters. (The law said nothing about female homosexuality, and the Nazis rarely persecuted lesbians, perhaps because they could always bear children.) The fact that a majority of men convicted for homosexual acts were not sent on to concentration camps from ordinary prisons would seem to justify excluding them from the Holocaust, as do most histories of the subject. Evidently the Nazis thought that at least some homosexuals could be reformed, which was impossible for a Jew, Gypsy, Slav, or handicapped person. Those who would include homosexuals in the Holocaust, such as Richard Plant in *The Pink Triangle: The Nazi War Against Homosexuals* and F. Rector in *The Nazi Extermination of Homosexuals*, maintain that thousands of them died because the Nazis considered them racially degenerate, just as they did the Jews and others. The contrary view, which stresses the complete absence of any Nazi plan for a final solution to the homosexual problem, is developed in essays by Günter Grau and Rödiger Lautmann in Michael Berenbaum and Abraham J. Peck, eds., *The Holocaust and History.*

CONCLUSION

Broadly speaking, it is possible to resolve the problem of defining the Holocaust in one of four ways. First, we may hold to the traditional view that it was the genocide of the Jews alone. Because no sane person will deny that the Germans killed members of other groups, too, one will have to be satisfied that they belong to a different category to be included in general studies of Nazi crimes but not in any substantial way in the history of the Holocaust. Brief attention to the fate of these non-Jewish groups would continue to serve the purpose of underlining the uniqueness of the genocide of the Jews.

A second definition might recognize several parallel Holocausts, one for each of several victim groups (the exact number being debatable), and each displaying special characteristics. This would justify continued separate treatment of the Jewish Holocaust while acknowledging that non-Jews, too, suffered genocide. The result, however, might be further neglect of the other genocides. This approach would also be linguistically awkward, always requiring specification of which Holocaust is meant.

A third definition would broaden the Holocaust to embrace Gypsies and the handicapped along with the Jews. It will appeal to those who believe that all three groups, but only these groups, were equal victims of Nazi racism and **genocide**. In this view members of other groups were killed selectively and can safely be excluded.

A fourth definition would insist on seeing Nazi racism whole and describe the Holocaust as an inseparable complex of policies and events encompassing all racially motivated German crimes and all their victims. This most expansive conceptualization would further complicate an already complex subject and place additional burdens on scholars and their students. Although the trend in recent years has been in the direction of greater inclusiveness, each student of the Holocaust will have to decide whether and how far to embrace it.

The authors of this volume have adopted the third approach to a working definition: The Holocaust — that is, Nazi genocide — was the systematic, state-sponsored murder of entire groups determined by heredity. This applied to Jews, Gypsies, and the handicapped. This section also makes it clear that other definitions are defended by scholars who deserve a respectful hearing.

Roots of the Holocaust

Several historical trends came together in the early twentieth century to make the Holocaust possible: extreme nationalism, industrialism, antisemitism, racism, Social Darwinism, totalitarianism, and the nature of modern war. This section begins with a broad survey of developments in modern Europe up to 1933 with emphasis on the situation in Germany. It then focuses more closely on the history of the Jews, Gypsies, and the handicapped in order to understand what made them targets of prejudice. It concludes with an exploration of the prejudice itself. Throughout this section a central question is whether the Holocaust is better thought of as a culmination of European and German history or as a monstrous aberration.

TRENDS IN MODERN EUROPEAN HISTORY

Nationalism was the single most powerful idea at work in Europe in nineteenth and early twentieth century Europe. From the French Revolution on, liberal political movements broke down the sovereignty of kings and princes and replaced it with popular sovereignty, the rule of the people. Defining "the people" was usually done in ethnic terms, stressing common language, history, customs, and culture. Nationalists wanted political and ethnic boundaries to coincide, which they often did not. Particularly where nationalities were politically divided or subject to foreign rule, nationalism became a passionate force for change. It made it possible for Germany and Italy to become unified countries and for Greece, Belgium, Romania, Bulgaria, and Serbia to achieve independence. Everywhere international tensions and wars engendered patriotic passions, and never more so than during World War I. At the end of that war the principle of national self-determination was incorporated into the peace settlement to revive countries such as Poland and Hungary and create new ones such as Czechoslovakia and Yugoslavia. Long before that time nationalism had become a secular religion for the peoples of Europe.

Nationalism was undoubtedly a liberating idea, but it created as many problems as it solved. For centuries Europe, and especially Eastern Europe, had possessed many national minorities that did not fully share in the language, history, customs, and culture of most of their neighbors. These might be minorities whose cohorts lived in other countries, as, for example, the Polish minority in Germany before World War I or the Hungarian minority in Romania after that war. Or they might be minorities without established homelands, such as the Jews and the Gypsies. Nationalists commonly abused minorities and pressured them to assimilate completely into the dominant culture or else get out. They also used minorities as foils in creating national identities. As nationalist intellectuals sought to define the national characteristics of their own people, they often did so by assigning such positive traits as cleanliness, piety, diligence, and honesty to themselves and the opposites to one or more of the minorities. Hence nationalism spawned hatred and intolerance of outsiders even as it freed oppressed nationalities and organized modern European nation-states.

Science and technology ranked almost as high as nationalism among Europeans. These had enabled Europe to achieve unprecedented heights of wealth and power by the start of the twentieth century. The industrial revolution had greatly expanded its economy, providing jobs for growing populations and generating wealth that penetrated even to the lowest orders of society. Modern medicine and sanitation had improved the length and quality of people's lives. European technological prowess and military might had been projected all over the globe in the form of colonial empires. A few pessimists pondered the prospects of the advanced nations using modern weapons against each other, but no one imagined the industrial mass murder of innocent civilians. More commonly, Europeans looked to science and technology for ever-expanding progress and prosperity.

Poisoning this hopeful prospect was the difficulty many people had in distinguishing between genuine and phony science. Pseudosciences such as racism, Social Darwinism, and **eugenics** undermined traditional moral values and liberal ideas about the value of the individual and the brotherhood of man. It had long been common to call the various cultures of the world "races," but in the nineteenth century biologists and anthropologists began to posit a biological basis for the differences between them. Anthropologists who believed that the various races had originated at different times and evolved in different ways opened the door to theories of their inequality. Starting in the 1850s with the French intellectual Arthur de Gobineau, racists taught that there was a biological basis for the belief that some races were more advanced and hence superior. Unsurprisingly, they placed some or all Europeans in that exalted spot. The powerful nationalisms of the late nineteenth century combined easily with racism. Racist nationalism often strove for racial homogeneity and held minorities in contempt as inferior or corrupting elements and threats to racial purity. Racism likewise underpinned the colonial empires that expanded rapidly between 1870 and 1900.

Social Darwinism, too, claimed the mantle of scientific certainty. Like racism, it drew unwarranted conclusions from biology. From about 1870 on, leading Social Darwinists like Herbert Spencer in England transferred Darwin's theory of natural selection from the evolutionary process over eons to human social relationships in the present. Just as Darwin taught that "survival of the fittest" in nature had determined the evolutionary progress of plants and animals, so the Social Darwinists argued that struggle was the key to human advancement as well. Not all Social Darwinists were racists, but those who were concluded that life was chiefly a struggle between races for land and power. They welcomed it as furthering humanity by securing the victory of the superior race. That, of course, would become Hitler's opinion; it is an open question how many Germans and other Europeans agreed with him.

Eugenics, the third popular pseudoscience, was the last to develop. Initially advanced in the 1880s by the British scientist Francis Galton, it sought to improve "the race," however defined, by selective breeding. Eugenicists hoped to minimize the number of human beings born with undesirable traits and maximize those with desirable traits in the same way plant and animal biologists bred for particular characteristics. They received a powerful boost early in the twentieth century when Gregor Mendel's discoveries about genetics began to catch on. Heredity came to be thought of as determining temperament and behavior as well as physical characteristics. "Positive eugenics" sought to encourage the socially worthy to marry early and have large families. "Negative eugenics" seemed to provide hope of minimizing the numbers of paupers, criminals, and the mentally and physically handicapped by discouraging or blocking their reproduction. This might be achieved through marriage restrictions, sexual segregation in institutions, voluntary or forced sterilization, or even **euthanasia**.

Although eugenics stressed purifying "the race" from within, it also reinforced assumptions about genetic differences between races and embraced notions of the hereditarily biological inferiority of races held to have "undesirable" traits. Joined to Social Darwinism, it could lead to the conclusion that, unless drastic preventive measures were taken, one's own race was in danger of being overwhelmed by prolific but morally and intellectually inferior aliens.

Nineteenth-century nationalism had divided Europe along ethnic lines; racism, Social Darwinism, and eugenics fortified them by introducing notions of biological superiority and racial struggle that anticipated twentieth-century "ethnic cleansing" and **genocide**.

It is possible that no great evil would have come from these trends had it not been for World War I. That great conflict, the first truly modern total war, prepared the way for still greater carnage in the future and set in motion a series of developments that led to the victory of Nazism in Germany. By generating violence on a staggering scale, it brutalized millions of men at the front and convinced some of them of the heroic virtues of war and struggle. Much of the public at large likewise concluded that problems were best solved by organizing savage force. Governments, faced with coordinating their full resources for total war, centralized political power, controlled economies, and molded public opinion with propaganda and censorship. These were considered temporary expedients at the time, but political radicals would later reassemble them on a permanent basis to form totalitarian systems such as Communism and Nazism. Hence total war gave the world its first experience of totalitarianism and predisposed many Europeans to spurn moderation in favor of militant action. This war was also the occasion for what many scholars believe was the first major case of modern **genocide,** that of the Armenian minority in Turkey. More than 1,000,000 Armenians were massacred or starved to death because the government believed they sided with Turkey's traditional enemy, Russia.

World War I also left behind vast social and political problems that undermined liberal democracies and played into the hands of people with "total" solutions. Nowhere was this truer than in defeated and despondent Germany. Its new government, the democratic Weimar Republic, was assailed from the first by extremists of both right and left. The republic inherited an empty treasury and was forced to take responsibility for the harsh Treaty of Versailles with its steep reparation payments. It also fell heir to a political culture established fifty years before by Otto von Bismarck that was lacking in experience with representative government and was authoritarian in nature. And yet the Weimar Republic survived early political and economic crises and developed considerable popular support during the rich years of the late 1920s. The Nazis denigrated it as the "Jew Republic" for its liberal values and the prominence of a few Jews in its economy, culture, and politics. However, as long as prosperity lasted, Hitler's movement remained a marginal force.

All that changed when the world depression reached Germany in 1930. Support for the Weimar Republic plummeted as unemployment went through the roof. The Communists benefited from the crisis, but the Nazis did so even more. They still blamed the Jews for all their country's problems, but now they shifted the main thrust of their attacks to the Republic and its failure to overcome the depression and maintain order. German voters, exasperated at fractious and inept politicians and frightened of the Communists, voted for Hitler in ever greater numbers until by 1932 his was the largest party in Germany. It never won a majority, however, and victory required backstairs political deals between **Hitler** and the conservative politicians who believed, erroneously, that they could control him. On January 30, 1933, President Paul von Hindenburg appointed Hitler chancellor in a coalition government with those conservative allies. A short time later Hitler succeeded in neutralizing his allies and making himself dictator. With Hitler in power all the pieces were brought together in Germany: extreme nationalism, antisemitism, racism, Social Darwinism, eugenics, and totalitarianism. These were supported by a dynamic police and terror system and located within an advanced industrial society fully capable of resorting yet again to total war.

THE HISTORY OF THE VICTIMS

We begin with Hitler's chief victims, the Jews. Fortunately, their history is, for the most part, extremely well documented. The central facts of Jewish history for most of the last two thousand years are the Jews' dispersion from their original homeland in Palestine and their failure to become fully assimilated into the nations in which they settled. Jewish particularism coupled with anti-Jewish prejudice carved out a unique position for the Jews in European society.

Around 1700 B.C. the Jews, originally a nomadic Middle Eastern people who spoke a Semitic language, settled in the Nile delta. Five hundred years later they made their exodus from Egypt to escape slavery and conquered Canaan in what is today Palestine. The new Hebrew state was neither large nor strong, and in the tenth century B.C. it was weakened still further when internal divisions caused it to split into two separate kingdoms, Judah and Israel. Hence from the eighth century B.C. on they were conquered by one more powerful nation after another: Assyria, Babylon, Persia, Greece, and Rome.

What kept the consciousness of a separate Jewish people alive through all of these catastrophes was the Jews' religion. Judaism evolved a set of beliefs that promised the ultimate salvation of God's chosen people, the Jews. It taught that Abraham, the traditional founder of the Jewish people, had entered into a Covenant with God. His people were to obey His commandments, accept that He was the only true god, live upright lives, and lead all nations to worship Him. In return God promised never to forsake His people. One day a Messiah would appear to restore the Jews to Israel and establish world peace.

Armed with this powerful message, Judaism elaborated customs and traditions that preserved the Jews' sense of ethnic distinctiveness for thousands of years. At the same time these customs and traditions made the Jews unruly subjects who frequently rose up against their conquerors. Finally, in A.D. 70, following several Jewish rebellions, the Romans razed Jerusalem and forced the Jews to scatter. This migration away from Palestine, known as the Diaspora, would characterize Jewish existence for the next 1,900 years.

The Jewish farmers and merchants who migrated to Europe during the Diaspora preserved their ethnic identity by centering their lives on their synagogues. While welcoming converts, they generally kept themselves apart from nonbelievers, who responded with suspicion. The early Christian church, which competed with Judaism for souls, taught that the Jews were the enemies of God for having rejected and crucified Jesus. Failing to convert them, it sought to keep them isolated and subservient. On the other hand, medieval Europe possessed secular rulers who considered the Jews' commercial and financial talents useful in promoting the economic development of their realms. Hence, in the sixth century the kings of France placed the Jews under their protection and made that country an important center of Jewish settlement. From there the Jews spread into the German lands and the rest of Europe, wherever they could secure protection and privileges from the kings or other (mainly) secular authorities.

The Jews entered a Europe shattered by the Germanic invasions and the collapse of the Roman Empire. Commercial and financial activities had reached low ebb, and the Jews found opportunities to participate in their recovery. Successful Jewish merchants started lending money, which was not an option for Christians given the church's ban on "usury," the making of loans at interest. But as Christians began to compete with Jews as merchants and to find ways around the ban on usury, opposition to the minority grew and became particularly dangerous in times of religious enthusiasm. During the Crusades fanatics took up the church's teachings that Jews were Christ-killers and deliberate misbelievers and used them to organize **pogroms** (violent attacks on Jews). Stories about Jews desecrating the sacred host and killing Gentile children to use their blood in making Passover matzos (variously known as "ritual murder" or the "blood libel") intensified religious antipathies. Canon law forbade social intercourse between Christians and Jews. In the late Middle Ages the Black Death was explained as the result of Jews' having poisoned the wells. The Protestant Reformation brought the Jews little respite. Martin Luther himself was outspokenly bitter toward them as a result of their refusal to be won over to his new religion.

Increasingly the Jews moved from this unfriendly environment to underdeveloped parts of Eastern Europe, where the rulers of Poland and Lithuania had need of their skills as merchants and bankers and were prepared to grant them privileges and protection. They brought with them a form of the German language, Yiddish, and a thriving Jewish culture strongly devoted to Talmudic studies. They were even granted limited self-government through their own provincial councils. But among the common people Jews were probably no more popular in Eastern Europe than elsewhere. As managers of noble estates they were particularly hated by the peasants. In the small remaining Jewish communities of Western Europe, "Court Jews" often became prominent financial advisors to cash-strapped secular rulers. The Court Jews were loathed at least as much as any tax collectors who have ever lived.

The development of rationalist thought during the eighteenth-century Enlightenment opened new opportunities for the European Jews. Some of Europe's leading thinkers advocated emancipating the Jews from the dozens of restrictions then imposed upon them. That, the advocates of emancipation argued, would improve the Jews and encourage their assimilation and acculturation. Simultaneously, a minority of Jews attempted to modernize their religion and customs and reconcile them with European culture. This culminated in the development of Reform Judaism in Western Europe during the nineteenth century. The Reform movement adopted the vernacular in religious services and stripped Judaism of its nationalist content. Eastern European Jewry held fast to Orthodoxy. But for the increasing numbers of Western European Jews who embraced Reform Judaism, being Jewish applied to religion alone; in every other respect these Jews strove to be good Europeans and loyal citizens of the countries in which they lived.

The growth of capitalist economies in Western and Central Europe also opened doors to the Jews, who had never lost their skills as merchants and financiers. Many left Eastern European villages to seek new business opportunities in Western Europe or in large Eastern European cities like Warsaw and Budapest. There they abandoned Yiddish in favor of the vernacular and adopted the ways of other bourgeois citizens. As a result of these religious and economic developments a great gap opened up between the large mass of rural Eastern European Jews, poor, isolated, and devoutly Orthodox, and the growing Jewish communities in the big cities and in Western Europe that were modern and increasingly assimilated. That gap would persist well into the twentieth century, with the poor Jews of Eastern Europe always constituting the majority even as their numbers declined from emigration to Western Europe and America.

Jews who chose the modern path often did so in ways that reflected their Jewish past. Adept as middlemen and financiers, they succeeded in their traditional roles as small businessmen and bankers. Their offspring might or might not conform to this pattern. Those who branched off commonly chose professional careers as doctors, lawyers, and writers, often preferring to be self-employed and hence free from supervision by possibly antisemitic Gentiles. Significant numbers of Jewish journalists established controversial reputations in mostly liberal and socialist publications. Some Jews became prominent as intellectuals, reflecting traditional Jewish respect for the life of the mind. Hence the Jews became highly visible in a few sectors of the economy. In Germany, for example, they were closely associated with the textile and clothing trades, publishing, and department and chain stores. They were also still identified with banking, even though their prominence in that field was slipping. It was also well known that disproportionately large numbers of German doctors, lawyers, and journalists were Jewish.

Jewish peculiarities were also evident in politics. In Western and Central Europe the Jews stood to the left, which was not surprising in view of liberal sponsorship of Jewish emancipation. As one country after another ended restrictions on the Jews and made them equal citizens — France in 1790–1791, England in 1826, Austria in 1867, and Germany in 1871 — it was the result of liberal pressure. This bound the Jews to liberal political parties and movements, to which they loyally contributed votes, money, and candidates. A few Jewish intellectuals moved further to the left by embracing the cause of the new working-class movements, seeing in socialism a broader liberating cause. Those who did so were no more popular among the solidly middle-class Jewish majority than they were with more conservative Europeans.

Jewish emancipation and assimilation in Western and Central Europe made rapid and impressive strides in the nineteenth century. Intermarriage in particular aroused Jewish concerns about religious and ethnic dissolution and racist fears of biological contamination. And yet, throughout this process of modernization most Jews remained readily recognizable as Jews. The expectations of some liberals that emancipated Jews would leave their old identities behind and become *totally* assimilated into Gentile society were not realized. Most held fast to Judaism and continued to socialize with and marry other Jews. Jewish traditions were too powerful to lose their hold overnight, and even those Jews who abandoned Judaism often reasserted their Jewishness in purely secular terms by interesting themselves in their people's history and culture.

Conditions for the Jews in Eastern Europe were very different. Except for those who lived in a few large urban centers, these Jews turned inward upon their own communities in defense of traditional ways of life. Their economic role as village shopkeepers, cattle traders, and moneylenders kept peasant hostility alive. Especially after World War I, when newly independent states such as Poland, Lithuania, and Hungary adopted anti-Jewish laws designed to promote Gentile competitors, the Jews of this region became increasingly desperate. **Zionism** and Communism vied for the support of young Eastern European Jews with rival versions of salvation. Zionism provided a modern support network for the present and promised refuge and national revival in a Jewish state in the future. Communism could compete well, for in its early years the Soviet Union granted equal rights to Jews and promoted those who renounced their old faith in favor of Marxism.

The more prosperous Jews of Western and Central Europe felt no such desperation. They were well aware that **antisemitism** persisted, but most viewed it as a dying relic of the medieval past. Even those who were impressed by its staying power believed that it could be contained by appeals to justice and reason. Hence they formed self-defense organizations that countered anti-Jewish propaganda, supported liberal candidates for public office, and sued Jew-baiters for libel, boycott, and other illegal acts. Small Zionist minorities instead preferred to emphasize Jewish pride and raise money to help Jews emigrate to Palestine, but even they doubted that people in the advanced nations seriously wished to roll back Jewish emancipation. Imbued with the liberal faith in progress, European Jews were ill equipped to deal with the realities of Nazi rule.

By the eve of the Holocaust the interaction of nearly two thousand years of Jewish particularism and European antisemitism had placed the Jews in precarious economic, political, and social positions. Whether they were village shopkeepers and moneylenders or urban merchants and lawyers, their comparatively high incomes drew negative attention, especially when times were hard. Jewish support for liberals, socialists, and communists outraged the political right. Nationalists who equated national greatness with national homogeneity, looked askance at the Jews' incomplete assimilation and acculturation. Although Jewish peculiarities were slowly declining and might well have disappeared in time, Hitler intervened. For him the facts of Jewish life meant nothing; their place was taken by an abstract image of the Jews as evil incarnate.

The Gypsies, like the Jews, were an unpopular minority, but they occupied a very different place in European society. Poor and nonliterate, they could hardly be charged with excessive power over money and public opinion, and as people of color they were rarely invited to merge with the majority. They originated in northern India; their language, Romani, is based on Hindi but also includes many borrowings from various European languages. *Gypsy* is a name given by Europeans to people who usually refer to themselves as Roma or Sinti. When they entered Europe during the fifteenth and sixteenth centuries, they were erroneously thought to have come from Egypt; *Gypsy* is a corruption of *Egyptian*. Their dark skin, thick black hair, and distinctive clothing made them immediately recognizable.

Some Gypsies settled in permanent residences in Europe, but most lived nomadic lives and tried to earn livings as blacksmiths, metalworkers, horse dealers, and fortunetellers. They usually adopted the dominant religion of the regions through which they wandered, but in Europe they were widely regarded as insincere about their conversion to Christianity and fundamentally irreligious. Banned from competing with the guilds in European cities and towns, the Gypsies sometimes resorted to begging, petty thievery, and sharp practices, which gave local officials excuses to force them on their way again. The distrust of settled people for nomads combined with racial prejudices and doubts about the Gypsies' honesty and religious faith to make them unwelcome everywhere.

To survive, most European Gypsies broke up into smaller groups and carried on their traditional nomadic life in lightly settled areas and border regions. A few formed into bands of robbers. Others attempted to settle down in permanent homes, and some even became merchants and professionals. The isolation of those who resisted assimilation was intensified by a rigid Gypsy purity code that placed taboos on relations with non-Gypsies, who were regarded as unclean. Hence the hopes expressed by a few eighteenth-century rationalists that the Gypsies might be assimilated into European civilization were not fulfilled, although they did promote some degree of toleration for the minority. So, too, did the fascination of some nineteenth-century romantics with Gypsy music, dance, customs, and superstitions. One result of this somewhat more tolerant attitude was a new migration of Gypsies from the Balkans and Hungary to Northern and Western Europe late in the nineteenth century. This led to renewed demands to combat the "Gypsy nuisance" that persisted well into the twentieth century.

The severely handicapped, including the physically impaired, the mentally ill, and the retarded, were neither racially nor religiously alien. Here the issue was how to care for them and at what expense to the community. In ancient times (and among primitive tribes more recently), seriously deformed and crippled children were killed outright or else abandoned in remote spots to die of exposure. This was regarded not so much as cruel as a necessary sacrifice for the good of the group. In more recent centuries Europeans assigned the care of the handicapped to the extended family. Starting in the seventeenth century handicapped people who were indigent, abandoned, or very severely disabled were placed in charitable institutions, conditions in which varied greatly.

In subsequent centuries a number of efforts were made to reform the treatment of handicapped people. Advocates of special education sought to provide the less severely retarded with basic skills that would make them into productive citizens. Psychologists and psychiatrists attempted to cure the mentally ill and return them to society. Rehabilitation programs originally designed to restore the victims of industrial accidents and war wounds were adapted to the needs of those born with physical impairments so that they might gain a measure of independence. But those too severely disabled to benefit from these reforms continued to be warehoused in state and private institutions. They were commonly stereotyped as defective and deviant, and on the rare occasions when people thought of them it was with pity and fear. Incapable of working, they were also regarded as a costly burden on society. Whether institutionalized or not, they came to be thought of as carriers of defective genes who might reproduce their degenerate kind and degrade the race from within.

THE HISTORY OF PREJUDICE

Antisemitism, hostility to Jews, is a modern word for a very old prejudice. The word was first popularized around 1880 by the German antisemite Wilhelm Marr, who wanted a new word to distinguish his secular and racist views from traditional Judeophobia based chiefly on religion. Some scholars believe that *antisemitism* should be used exclusively in that sense in order to dramatize a major shift in thinking about the Jews. And yet, the word almost immediately started to be used to describe all types of opposition to Jews at all times, and that is the way it is used here.

There are many popular misconceptions about the history of antisemitism, and it is best to confront them head on. Antisemitism is not endemic to Christian Western civilization. It may be found elsewhere as well, including in the Arab and Islamic worlds, where it takes on nonracial, political, and religious forms. Nor is antisemitism an unchanging set of ideas. Notwithstanding the persistence of popular stereotypes of Jews over the centuries, antisemitism has experienced significant historical metamorphoses. Just how significant they are is a matter of historical debate. Finally, antisemitism is not a constant feature in European history. Although it has always been present in one form or other, it has tended to erupt at moments of great social stress. At other times it has gone dormant, permitting Jews and Gentiles to live in harmony for long stretches of time. It would be misleading to assume an "eternal antisemitism" that simply grew and grew until it culminated in the Holocaust.

Antisemitism made its appearance in the first centuries A.D. as the Jews of the Diaspora settled in mostly pagan communities throughout the Mediterranean world. The ancient Greeks and Romans were fairly tolerant of religious and ethnic diversity, but they frequently took offense at the Jews' separatism. Rather than associate and intermarry freely with Gentiles, the Jews stood apart. Rather than acknowledge the gods of their neighbors, they held fast to their own monotheistic faith, special dietary laws, and sense of chosenness. The very success of Judaism at winning converts inspired a reaction against the penetration of "oriental religion" into the Hellenistic world. Although there was little actual anti-Jewish violence in the ancient world, the negative stereotype of Jews as hostile to Gentiles was well established even before the triumph of Christianity.

It is generally accepted that antisemitism intensified during the Christian Middle Ages. Christianity, after all, claimed to be the fulfillment of biblical prophecy and the sole recipient of God's covenant, which had shifted from the Jews to all those who believed that Jesus was the Messiah and the son of God. The church taught that the Jews had rejected Jesus' claim to be the Messiah, demanded his crucifixion, and stubbornly refused to see the error of their beliefs. Having cut themselves off from God's true message, it went on, the Jews' religion had curdled into meaningless ritual, and their true god had become Mammon. The rival claims of Jews and Christians to the true interpretation of the same Hebrew scriptures gave medieval antisemitism a sharply religious edge.

Although Christian theologians condemned and ridiculed the Jews, they also taught that God would not entirely abandon His people and would lead them to Jesus in His own good time, thus setting limits to Christian antisemitism. Moreover, the very suffering and isolation of the Jews was often held up as God-willed proof of Christianity's truth. A people that played such an important rule in God's plan might be despised but could not be dispensed with. Hence during the early Middle Ages Christians and Jews lived together peacefully for hundreds of years, their relations limited almost entirely to business transactions.

During the late Middle Ages, however, crusades, social dislocations, and plague (the Black Death) generated religious fanaticism and violence directed against the Jews. **Pogroms**, discriminatory laws, and expulsions became more common. Although economic motives have to be taken into account, these actions were invariably justified in religious terms as Christian self-defense against a people that had become a plaything of Satan. Popes and other Church leaders at times condemned anti-Jewish excesses and the demonization of the Jews, but their own contemptuous attitudes toward Judaism partially undermined their words. The legacy of medieval antisemitism was the image of the Jews as sinister and demonic enemies of Christ and all who believed in Him.

That image persisted for centuries, long after secular rationalism began to make headway during the seventeenth century. Gradually over the next three hundred years the religious basis of antisemitism was partly replaced, and partly supplemented, by one that emphasized worldly objections to the Jews. Progressive thinkers of the eighteenth century Enlightenment sincerely wanted to emancipate the Jews as individuals, but they had no use for Judaism and Jewish communities. These they considered as much sinkholes of superstition and obstacles to human progress as they did the Christian churches. Hence Voltaire could invite the Jews to join the rest of humanity in building a better, freer world while heaping abuse on their religion and historical traditions. This essentially revived ancient pagan accusations that the Jews as a people were enemies of mankind.

Enlightenment ambivalence about the Jews influenced liberals as well as socialists in the nineteenth and twentieth centuries. Liberals enthusiastically and successfully sponsored Jewish emancipation, but they did so in the expectation that the Jews would stop being Jews as a result. Jewish peculiarities, they reasoned, were caused by discrimination. End it and the peculiarities would dissolve, permitting complete Jewish assimilation. When that did not happen on anything like the scale anticipated, the liberals felt betrayed and criticized Jewish aloofness. Socialists demanded Jewish assimilation, too, but into the working-class struggle against capitalism. In their view the Jews, as a persecuted but talented and wealthy minority, had a special obligation to work for the emancipation of the whole human race through socialism. That most Jews clung to their middle-class identities and politics scarcely endeared them to working-class leaders, who perpetuated the stereotype of Jews as greedy capitalists.

Conservatives, who in Europe were committed to maintaining the Christian character of the state, kept traditional religious antisemitism alive in the nineteenth and early twentieth centuries. In keeping with the times they added secular objections. They accused liberal Jewish politicians of systematically undermining traditional institutions by working to limit the powers of churches and kings. Jewish writers, the conservatives maintained, poisoned the minds of readers against those institutions and undermined people's morals with yellow journalism. Jewish businessmen were the targets of conservative reproach for ruthlessly cutting down traditional sectors of the economy, such as farming and handwork, in the soulless pursuit of wealth. With the Jews firmly associated with the political left, virtually all the European conservative parties were, to one extent or another, antisemitic.

An ominous development of the second half of the nineteenth century was the growing belief in scientific racism. European antisemites pounced on this pseudoscience to propound a view of the Jews as an alien race made up of morally and ethically depraved intruders from the Orient. The new word "antisemitism" that came into vogue in the 1880s suggested opposition to Jews as a Semitic "race," not to their religion. Among the best-known racial antisemites was Houston Stewart Chamberlain, a British writer who settled in Germany. His *Foundations of the Nineteenth Century* (1899) pointed to the Jews as a threat to Europe's racial and cultural purity and advanced a program of **eugenics** to improve the race through selective breeding. This paranoid image of the Jews as concocting conspiracies to enslave **"Aryans"** and corrupt them biologically would reappear later in the Nazi movement. Racial antisemitism left the Jews no way out. They might, if they wished, change religion, politics, and jobs, but not their race.

The antisemitism that blossomed in Europe during the hard times following World War I drew upon all the previous strands. In Germany the Jews were accused of betraying the Fatherland during the War and later saddling it with an unwanted liberal democracy. In the new nation states of Eastern Europe they were identified with national oppressors and denounced as alien parasites. Everywhere they were blamed for spreading communism and economic misery. That Jews such as Leon Trotsky in Russia, Béla Kun in Hungary, and Rosa Luxemburg in Germany were prominent Marxist revolutionaries gave rise to the canard "Communism is Jewish." Radical antisemites distributed copies of the *Protocols of the Elders of Zion,* purportedly the Jews' secret plans to subvert Gentile institutions and take over the world. Although research during the 1920s showed that it was a forgery done by the Russian secret police before World War I, Jew-haters continued to believe in its authenticity. Not all postwar antisemites were conscious racists, but in Germany Hitler's National Socialists certainly were.

This brief survey of nearly two thousand years of antisemitism reveals elements of both continuity and change. Negative stereotypes of Jews as exploiters of Gentiles and enemies of their religion and culture have remained fairly constant over the centuries. On the other hand, antisemitism's ideological context and its power to damage the Jews have not been constant at all. We have seen that hostility for Jews underwent considerable change as it adopted pagan, Christian, secular rationalist, and modern racist forms. We have also noted that periods of intense antisemitism have alternated with times of relative peace and harmony. Which phenomena — the steady stereotypes or the changing programs — are more significant? Should the Holocaust be viewed primarily in *continuity* with events that preceded it, or as a *revolutionary rupture* with the past?

A vigorous debate on these questions has emerged from scholars' attempts at tracing the roots of the **Final Solution**. Some argue that those roots penetrate nearly two thousand years of European history, all the way to the earliest encounters between Christians and Jews. Other scholars believe that the roots of genocide are far shallower, perhaps not much deeper than **Adolf Hitler's** mind.

One case for continuity has been made by those who believe that the demonization of the Jews by the early Christian church endured at the core of all subsequent forms of European antisemitism, even those that appeared to be purely secular. Some scholars, such as Hyam Maccoby in *A Pariah People: The Anthropology of Antisemitism*, believe that the view of the Jews as allies of Satan and an accursed people was rooted in Christian doctrine and taught by the church from the very beginning. Others suggest that Christians became passionately antisemitic only during the eleventh and twelfth centuries as a result of intensifying piety or else of agonizing doubts about their own faith. For the latter view one may consult Joshua Trachtenberg, *The Devil and the Jews*, and Gavin I. Langmuir, *Toward a Definition of Antisemitism*.

All of these scholars agree that from at least the twelfth century on the utterly negative stereotypes of Jews became deeply embedded in European culture at an instinctual and mythic level and attained such emotional strength that they easily survived the decline of religion. Reclothed with modern arguments of various kinds, these stereotypes retained their power to turn the excitable masses against the Jews in times of crisis. Proponents of this view, including Uriel Tal in *Christians and Jews in Germany*, often argue that antisemitism was always particularly virulent in Germany and was powerfully reinforced by Martin Luther during the Protestant Reformation. Hence, they conclude, the causes of the Holocaust are not mysterious at all. Hitler and his followers merely built upon many centuries of anti-Jewish vilification, a point of view that is also advanced in Jacob Katz's *From Prejudice to Destruction: Anti-Semitism, 1700–1933,* and Leon Poliakov's *The Aryan Myth: A History of Racist and Nationalist Ideas in Europe.*

Other scholars stress continuity in the history of antisemitism over a much shorter span of time, identifying nineteenth-century European, and especially German, antisemitism as the seedbed of the Holocaust. Economic historians trace modern Judeophobia to vagaries in the development of modern industrial capitalism in Germany. The victims of economic calamities — downwardly mobile groups such as shopkeepers, peasants, and artisans — repeatedly blamed the Jews for their plight, an analysis developed by Paul Massing in *Rehearsal for Destruction: A Study of Political Anti-Semitism in Imperial Germany.* Intellectual historians, impressed by the growing popularity of racism at the time, point out that the essential arguments that Hitler used against the Jews were being made even before he was born. For that view see Peter Pulzer, *The Rise of Political Anti-Semitism in Germany and Austria,* and Fritz Stern, *The Politics of Cultural Despair.* Other scholars stress the frustrations felt by Germans over their country's delayed unification and the identification by German nationalists of Jews with everything that opposed the German national character, as does Paul Lawrence Rose in *German Question/ Jewish Question: Revolutionary Antisemitism from Kant to Wagner.* Hence some of these scholars conclude that antisemitism had become widely accepted in Germany by the 1920s and aided greatly in bringing the masses to Hitler. An example of that approach is John Weiss, *Ideology of Death: Why the Holocaust Happened in Germany.*

The opposing view, which holds that changes in the history of antisemitism are more meaningful than continuities, is based on several arguments. One of these denies that medieval Christian teachings about the Jews should be linked directly to the Holocaust. Christianity, after all, never considered the Jews irredeemable or advocated their extermination; if it had, they would never have survived in Europe for nearly two thousand years, as Salo W. Baron points out in *A Social and Religious History of the Jews.* In fact, Eva G. Reichmann argues in *Hostages of Civilisation,* the very decline of Christian influence in the modern world made genocide possible by removing moral obstacles to mass murder. An influential argument by Hannah Arendt in *The Origins of Totalitarianism* explicitly writes off the religious roots of antisemitism and stresses instead the Jews' economic role in helping to build the modern European nation-states. Closely associated with those regimes, the Jews shared in their unpopularity when hard times brought unemployment and political unrest, especially after World War I.

The belief that antisemitism was unusually long-lived and virulent in Germany has been attacked as overdetermined by events under the Nazis in *The Downfall of the Anti-Semitic Political Parties in Imperial Germany* by Richard S. Levy. For one thing, antisemitism was hardly confined to Germany. For another the most common forms of antisemitism in Germany before World War I had little in common with Hitler's. They were abstract and verbal rather than concrete and action-oriented, as Shulamit Volkov argues in "Antisemitism as a Cultural Code" (in *Leo Baeck Institute Yearbook* 23). Most of them also lacked any murderous intent, looking to the assimilation or segregation of the Jews for solutions. Only the most radical of them called for expelling the Jews, or worse, and these were limited to the lunatic fringe. Those who stress change in the history of antisemitism see a big difference between conditions in Germany before and after World War I and a considerable gap between Hitler and most of his alleged predecessors. In this view, the agony of the German people during the Weimar years and the pathological antisemitism of Adolf Hitler are far more persuasive explanations of the Holocaust than are theories about Christian antisemitism and long-term trends in German history.

The critics of continuity admit that long-held stereotypes of the Jews made it easier for some Germans to vote for the clearly antisemitic Nazi Party, but they doubt that antisemitism was its chief attraction. Had that been the case, it seems likely that the Nazis would have drawn a mass following *before* the depression hit. In fact, the critics note, the growth in votes for the Nazi Party coincided with its shift in emphasis from specific attacks on the Jews toward purely economic and political issues. Hitler himself seems to have realized that his views about the Jews were too radical for most Germans and deliberately downplayed them during his rise to power in the early 1930s. Hence he never spelled out his plans for the Jews, and his followers backed off from attacking them whenever antisemitism failed to arouse a positive response. These points come through in local and regional studies such as William S. Allen's *The Nazi Seizure of Power* and Geoffrey Pridham's *Hitler's Rise to Power: The Nazi Movement in Bavaria, 1923–1933*. It is possible that many Germans who gave their votes to Hitler, if they were conscious of the "Jewish problem" at all, assumed that he represented the comparatively benign prewar form of antisemitism rather than a potentially murderous brand of racism. These critics acknowledge some degree of continuity between prewar and postwar antisemitic ideas, but not between those ideas and the Holocaust.

Nothing comparable to the debate over antisemitism marks the history of the persecutions of Gypsies and the handicapped. Because they were not thought to be anything like as powerful, influential, or religiously offensive as the Jews, simple contempt was more common than fear. And yet both came under increasing pressure in the early decades of the twentieth century, the Gypsies as racially alien, the handicapped as racially unfit.

The Gypsies, regarded as shiftless and criminal elements everywhere in Europe, were forced to register with local authorities and experienced all kinds of harassment designed to get them to move on or else settle down and assimilate. The handicapped, still for the most part warehoused in public and private institutions, became special targets of the eugenicists, who argued that improving the race required sterilizing defective persons. Between the two world wars sterilization laws were enacted in Switzerland, Denmark, Norway, Sweden, and Germany as well as in twenty-seven of the American states. Tens of thousands of mentally and physically disabled persons were sterilized, many without their consent and a few even without their knowledge. The measures taken against Gypsies and the handicapped enjoyed widespread popular approval, but there was no comparable support for more drastic actions, such as euthanizing the disabled. These would require the creation of a ruthless dictatorship dedicated to implementing a radical racist agenda.

How the Final Solution Came About

At first glance the answers to these questions might seem obvious. **Hitler** wanted the ethnic purification of his Reich and began killing handicapped Germans in 1939 and Jews and Gypsies in 1941. But did he plan to do it all along? If so, why did he wait so long and let so many Jews escape by emigrating? And can we be sure that it was always his orders that brought about the victims' deaths?

Scholars are divided on these matters. One group, referred to as "intentionalists," affirms that Hitler intended to kill the Jews from the very beginning of his political career and awaited only the right moment to do so. Hence they commonly treat early Nazi persecution of the Jews as preparation for genocide and think of the Holocaust as spanning the whole history of the Third Reich from 1933 to 1945. "Functionalists," on the other hand, argue that there was no long-standing plan for **genocide**. They doubt that Hitler gave much thought to solving the "Jewish problem" or that he ordered the **Final Solution**. Rather, they place immediate responsibility for it on lower-level Nazi functionaries who believed that they were acting in the spirit of the Führer's wishes. A third group of "synthesizers" attempts in various ways to draw insights from both intentionalists and functionalists in an effort to find middle ground.

The focus of this controversy, obviously, is on the motives behind and timing of the "Final Solution to the Jewish Problem." Until recently the genocide of the handicapped was rarely considered an integral part of the Holocaust, but including it would raise additional questions. Did Hitler consciously regard the **euthanasia** of disabled Germans as preparation for the Final Solution when he began the T4 Program in 1939? Does the attempt to exterminate the handicapped and Gypsies demonstrate that antisemitism and Hitler's hatred for the Jews are insufficient to explain the Holocaust? Was the reassignment of T4 personnel to the genocide of the Jews and Gypsies in 1941 largely fortuitous, or was it part of an existing plan aimed at annihilating all three groups? These questions have yet to be deeply probed by scholars and may not be answerable at all. In examining the debate between intentionalists, functionalists, and synthesizers about the decision to exterminate the Jews, this section reflects the current state of research. Certainly that decision was critical in the history of the Holocaust. Additionally, it offers a chance to plumb Hitler's mind and learn more about how decisions were made and implemented in Nazi Germany.

INTENTIONALISTS

The intentionalists focus on Hitler and his ideology because they believe he had definite ideas about what he intended to do with the Jews of Europe from a fairly early date and systematically moved to implement them once in power. For many years this was the dominant view, and it still appears without critical comment in many general studies of the Holocaust and of Nazi Germany. It also dominates some of the best biographies of Hitler, including Alan Bullock's *Hitler: A Study in Tyranny* and Joachim Fest's *Hitler*. This Hitlercentric explanation of genocide dovetails with traditional notions of "great men" providing the motive force in history. It also accords nicely with the totalitarian model of Nazi Germany as an efficient, well-coordinated dictatorship and with beliefs about the powerful influence of **antisemitism** in Germany that we surveyed in the previous section.

The intentionalists naturally expend considerable energy in trying to pinpoint the origins of Hitler's fixation on the Jews. Writing in his book *Mein Kampf* in the 1920s, the future dictator claimed that he became an antisemite as a youth in prewar Vienna after reading anti-Jewish literature and observing the Jews up close. But books by scholars with a psychological bent raise doubts that he made a purely rational choice. These include Rudolph Binion's *Hitler among the Germans*, Walter C. Langer's *The Mind of Adolf Hitler*, and Robert G. Waite's *The Psychopathic God, Adolf Hitler*. They speculate that Hitler's hatred for the Jews stemmed from some youthful trauma, such as his mother's death while under the care of a Jewish physician, and was intensified by the need to rationalize his rejection for study at the Vienna Art Academy. All of this is possible, but unprovable.

The first hard evidence of Hitler's antisemitism comes from his speeches in postwar Munich, following his experience there of an abortive Communist uprising in which Jewish leaders played prominent roles. From that time forward Hitler made both public and private attacks on the Jews that intentionalists consider proof of unswerving genocidal purpose. Identifying the Jews with everything he thought wrong with Germany — democracy, capitalism, internationalism, communism, pacifism — Hitler employed increasingly radical antisemitic rhetoric. His earliest statements implied the wish to expel the Jews, but after the failed Beer Hall Putsch of 1923 his invective began hinting at murder. In *Mein Kampf* Hitler blamed the Jews for Germany's defeat in 1918 and observed that if "these Hebrew corrupters of the people had been held under poison gas" the story would have ended differently. He called for a "bloody" effort to "dislodge the fist of the implacable world Jew" from Germany's throat.[1] Although Hitler did not use such deadly imagery in his public speeches before 1933, the intentionalists believe it represents his innermost convictions.

On January 30, 1939, six years after coming to power and seven months before the outbreak of World War II, Hitler revived his threat to eliminate the Jews in words that the intentionalists regard as conclusive. If the Jews succeeded in causing another world war, he told the Nazi Reichstag, "then the result will not be the Bolshevization of the earth and with it the victory of Jewry, it will be the annihilation of the Jewish race in Europe."[2] He repeated his threat in three public speeches in 1942, and in two of them he referred to his 1939 statement as a "prophecy." In 1945, shortly before committing suicide as his war ended in defeat, Hitler concluded his political testament by admonishing Germans to carry on "merciless resistance to the poisoners of all peoples, international Jewry." That Hitler would make this his last message to the world proves his fixation on the Jews as the fount of all evil, Gerald Fleming concludes in *Hitler and the Final Solution.*

Hitler's other great long-term obsession, conquering **Lebensraum** (living space) for Germany in Eastern Europe, was closely linked to his hatred of Jews, the intentionalists argue. Identifying Jews with Communism, Hitler planned a war that would simultaneously provide cover for genocide and bring down what he regarded as the most dangerous citadel of Jewish power, the Soviet Union. The intentionalists are unimpressed by resettlement schemes for the Jews, such as the **Nisko and Lublin** and **Madagascar Plans**, that the Nazis bandied about during the first two years of the war. These, they argue, were subterfuges. The concentration of Jews in **ghettos** and **labor camps** at that time was not designed to ready them for resettlement but to place them conveniently for the extermination that began with the invasion of Russia.

Given the intentionalists' belief that genocide was always Hitler's goal, they usually downplay issues of timing but give the impression that his intentions

---

1. Quoted in Eberhard Jäckel, *Hitler's Weltanschauung: A Blueprint for Power* (Middletown, Conn.: Wesleyan University Press, 1972), p. 60.
2. J. Noakes and G. Pridham, eds., *Nazism: A History in Documents and Eyewitness Accounts, 1919–1945* (Exeter: University of Exeter Press, 1983–1988), p. 2:1049.

became fixed at about the time of the German attack on the Soviet Union in June 1941. In this view, advanced by Lucy Dawidowicz in *The War against the Jews* and Gerald Reitlinger in *The Final Solution*, genocide began with the **Einsatzgruppen** sweeps in Russia; **Göring**'s famous mandate to **Heydrich** at the end of July to formulate a "comprehensive solution" to the Jewish problem was undoubtedly the result of an order from the Führer to broaden annihilation to all the Jews of Europe. The order was probably verbal since Hitler wanted to maximize secrecy. He had learned from the T4 Program that a written order over his signature risked revealing his personal responsibility for mass murder. An alternative intentionalist perspective on the implementation of the **Final Solution** is put forward by Eberhard Jäckel in *Hitler in History*. Jäckel perceives a series of increasingly radical Führer orders (again probably verbal) stretching from mid-1940 to late 1941 as Hitler gradually eased his lieutenants into a genocidal mode.

The intentionalist explanation of the Holocaust has the advantages of simplicity, familiarity, and clarity. Hitler deeply hated the Jews, he was absolute master of the Third Reich, and his war against the Soviet Union gave him the opportunity to commit genocide. But this explanation is also vulnerable on several counts. For one thing, there is absolutely no solid evidence that Hitler or his helpers were preparing to kill all the Jews before 1941. During the previous eight years the Third Reich had isolated the German Jews, squeezed them economically, encouraged them to emigrate, and later forcibly deported them. In occupied Poland it had ghettoized the Jews and considered herding them into a "reservation" or shipping them abroad. But nowhere were Jews subjected to mass murder. Nor are Hitler's threats against the Jews absolute proof that he long planned to kill them. He often used the most extreme vocabulary without necessarily meaning it to be taken literally. He may also have intended his threats to intimidate foreign Jews, whose power he always exaggerated. Finally, no one has ever conclusively proved that Hitler gave a written or verbal order to start the Final Solution. All of these considerations have contributed to alternative thinking about the decision to annihilate the Jews.

FUNCTIONALISTS

As the functionalists see it, the intentionalists are wrong on both central issues. There was no premeditated master plan to annihilate the Jews, and Hitler did not give an order to begin the Final Solution. The intentionalists err, these critics hold, because they do not fully comprehend Hitler and the workings of

Nazi Germany. The Third Reich was less a well-coordinated totalitarian regime than a polycratic police state, and Hitler was less a strong leader than a "weak dictator" who left most matters to his cronies and subordinates, the functionalist argument goes. As a result, rival personalities and institutions constantly jockeyed for power and influence, with the Führer only nominally in control. This was particularly true in Jewish affairs as lower-level party and state officials improvised a series of rather haphazard anti-Jewish measures that culminated in genocide, all of them functionally related to one another. (Hence the term *functionalist*. Sometimes the terms *structuralist* and *structural-functionalist* are used instead, referring to these scholars' emphasis on the structures of Nazi Germany rather than on Hitler and his ideology.)

When the functionalists reconstruct pregenocidal Nazi Jewish policy they see a "twisted road" rather than a straight path. They acknowledge that the Nazis cherished a generalized wish to get the Jews to emigrate, but beyond that they perceive more chaos than plan. On one hand were radical Nazis who wanted to attack the Jews as often and as forcefully as possible. Some of them hoped to profit from the "**Aryanization**" of Jewish property. On the other hand were more pragmatic leaders of party and state who feared the consequences of such attacks. At home were millions of conservative Germans who disliked Jews to some degree but also valued law and order and showed little understanding of violence and breaches of property rights. There were also thousands of non-Jewish employees of Jewish businesses who might be thrown out of work just when Hitler's government was trying the curb unemployment. Abroad were governments and private institutions that denounced Germany and boycotted German goods when Jews were openly persecuted. As the functionalists see it, most of the time Hitler either could not or would not make up his mind whom to support, leaving the factions to fight it out. With no one consistently in charge, matters drifted.

The functionalists acknowledge that Hitler did take a position on anti-Jewish policies from time to time, but chiefly to react to radical pressures from below. He ordered the boycott of Jewish businesses on April 1, 1933, in order to satisfy the blood thirst of Nazi Party activists and **SA** men, but he also called it off when the public reaction proved disappointing. In September 1935 the dictator responded to renewed violence against the Jews by party radicals with the **Nuremberg Laws**. Evidently Hitler hoped to quash random attacks by regularizing the status of the Jews by law. The **Crystal Night** pogrom, too, appears to have been improvised. Hitler seems impulsively to have approved **Goebbels**'s idea of using the assassination of a German diplomat in Paris as an excuse for violence. But a few days later, surveying the property damage and the negative foreign response, he called in **Hermann Göring** to return Jewish affairs to an orderly, legal path. Most of the time, however, Hitler ignored the Jews. Functionalists such as Karl Schleunes in *The Twisted Road to Auschwitz* conclude that the dictator had more important things on his mind, particularly foreign and military affairs.

The functionalists also stress that the Nazi regime, far from preparing to annihilate the Jews, consistently sought to remove them from Germany until well after World War II began. It encouraged them to depart for any country that would have them. It even encouraged their emigration to Palestine by signing the Haavara Agreement with the **Jewish Agency** in 1933. This agreement made it possible for 60,000 German Jews to leave for Palestine and transfer some of their wealth there in the form of German exports. German propaganda regularly mocked the democracies for not opening their doors more widely to the minority with whose plight they claimed to sympathize. By 1939 the Germans had established a **Reich Central Office for Jewish Emigration** to coordinate legal departures, and they were also deporting them illegally. None of this, the functionalists contend, made any sense if Hitler had already decided on the Final Solution, for the Jews would only have to be gathered up again.

The functionalists go on to claim that Nazi plans to resettle the Jews in **Madagascar**, Siberia, or the **Nisko and Lublin** reservation were meant in deadly earnest. They interpret Göring's July 31, 1941, order for Heydrich to devise a "comprehensive solution" as referring to an overall plan for Jewish resettlement. They argue that until at least September 1941 the concentration of Jews in **ghettos** and **labor camps** was meant to facilitate relocation, not annihilation. That changed only when the war took unexpected and threatening directions. Hence the functionalists view the genocide of the Jews as a distinct departure from earlier Nazi policies, not their logical culmination.

This departure, the functionalists argue, was not the result of a single order from on high. Rather, genocide began during the second half of 1941 with decisions made by local Nazi officials in Poland who were struggling with purely local conditions. These officials were confronted with the impossible task of finding food and shelter for hundreds of thousands of Jews and Gypsies uprooted from their homes in western Poland and Germany. They also feared that diseases caused by overcrowding and malnutrition in the ghettos would spread to the Polish population and the German occupation forces. These local officials certainly knew of Hitler's threats against the Jews, and many of them were familiar with the T4 Program and the murderous actions of the Einsatzgruppen in the Soviet Union. The functionalists reason that in this environment German officials probably concluded that killing Jews would not be frowned upon. Hence they experimented with increasingly radical ways of eliminating their surplus Jewish population. The larger genocidal enterprise evolved from these small beginnings, but only after it was apparent that stiffening Soviet resistance made resettling the Jews impossible. Once started, the process of annihilation continued almost automatically, requiring minimal high-level involvement. Hitler unquestionably knew what was going on and did not disapprove, but the initiative was not his. A useful summary of this approach may be found in an article by Hans Mommsen, "The Realization of the Unthinkable," in Gerhard Hirschfeld, ed., *The Policies of Genocide*.

These arguments hardly make the functionalists apologists for Hitler. On the contrary, they uniformly reject the opinion advanced by David Irving in *Hitler's War* that Hitler was completely unconcerned about the Jews and knew nothing about the Final Solution until late in the war. They readily acknowledge that his passionate antisemitism established the climate for the continuous radicalization of Nazi Jewish policy. Party and state leaders, motivated chiefly by careerism, competed to come up with more effective ways of pleasing Hitler by hounding the Jews out of Germany. Once an impasse was reached in the war against the Soviet Union and deportation was no longer feasible, they moved to the only remaining alternative, genocide. None of this would have happened without Hitler's example.

The great strength of the functionalist view of Holocaust origins is its consonance with recent research showing that Hitler and Nazi Germany were anything but models of totalitarian efficiency. Behind its imposing facade the Third Reich was an anarchic collection of rival power centers. Hitler evidently preferred it that way, seeing it as a means to encourage initiative and develop leadership qualities. Recognizing this complexity, the functionalists place the Holocaust within the institutional anarchy that characterized Nazi Germany. Their arguments also broaden responsibility for genocide and make it more difficult for Germans to use Hitler as their alibi. But critics believe that the functionalists go too far when they marginalize Hitler's role in decision-making. Given his fanatical antisemitism, they continue, it stretches credulity to argue that he was not centrally involved in making key decisions relating to the Jews, most especially those for their annihilation.

SYNTHESIZERS

Today it is less common to encounter "pure" intentionalists and functionalists than once was the case. Recent scholarship has stressed the interaction of intentions and contingencies and attempted to develop a synthesis of the two approaches. However, full agreement has yet to emerge about how best to do so.

A few broad generalizations may be made about scholars who adopt intermediate positions. First, they incline toward the functionalists in doubting that Hitler consciously planned the Final Solution from a very early date. Rather, again in agreement with the functionalists, they locate the decision to annihilate the Jews in events surrounding the 1941 German attack on the Soviet Union. Second, they incline toward the intentionalists in assigning a greater role to Hitler in the evolution of Nazi anti-Jewish policies before 1941, and they think it probable that Hitler himself ordered (or authorized) the mass murders of Jews to begin. Finally, they differ among themselves on the *degree* of Hitler's personal involvement in formulating anti-Jewish policies and on the *exact timing and motivation* of his decision to shift from resettlement to annihilation.

Hitler always had a plan for the Jews, but it was not always the same plan, argue synthesizers Saul Friedländer in *Nazi Germany and the Jews* and Philippe Burrin in *Hitler and the Jews*. Before 1941 the plan called for emigration and resettlement; thereafter it was for extermination. During the first eight years of the Nazi dictatorship the general direction was always clear: Germany was to be made *judenrein* (literally, Jew-cleansed) by isolating the Jews from other Germans and demoralizing them so that they would depart. When "voluntary" emigration proved too slow, German officials resorted to enforced emigration and deportation. If Hitler really wanted the Jews to die, it seems unlikely that he would have let them go. Even during the first year of the war, when the Polish Jews were being barbarously mistreated, there was no sign of genocide. On the contrary, the synthesizers believe, Hitler and his lieutenants were seriously considering placing some or all of the Jews on a reservation in Poland or shipping them to Madagascar or Siberia. When the Nazi leaders used the term Final Solution between 1939 and 1941, they always referred to resettlement, not annihilation.

Throughout the period 1933–1941, many of these scholars continue, Hitler was very much in control of Nazi anti-Jewish policies. True, he had other things on his mind, such as rebuilding his military forces and supervising German foreign policy. Sometimes these matters distracted him completely, and Jewish affairs momentarily drifted into the hands of other Nazi officials. But far from leaving the status of the German Jews entirely to his underlings, Hitler always returned to shaping their fate. This went well beyond making propaganda statements and setting the general goal of making Germany *judenrein*. Synthesizers see Hitler's guiding hand in shaping even some of the details of antisemitic policies. Hence they note his personal attention to promoting Jewish emigration during the 1930s, defining the status of part-Jews in 1935, regrouping the Polish Jews in 1939, and pushing the **Nisko and Lublin** and **Madagascar** resettlement plans in 1940. Hitler's dominance of the situation was also evident when he reined in Nazi Party radicals who wanted to move faster than he thought prudent.

Just as Hitler dominated the evolution of the original plan for emigration, the synthesizers argue, so too did he determine the switch to genocide by giving verbal orders to his lieutenants. The change in plan, the argument goes, came at some point in 1941, by which time the resettlement schemes were exhausted and the invasion of the Soviet Union was either planned or actually underway. Exactly when and why genocide began is disputed. One opinion is that Hitler gave the order early in the year during the planning stages of Operation Barbarossa, the German attack on the USSR that began on June 22, 1941. Prior to the attack Hitler informed his generals to prepare for a war that would be different from those they had fought so far. It was to be a war of "annihilation" against racially dangerous peoples, and its goals were to smash Bolshevism and clear the way for German settlement of Eastern Europe. In this view the SS Einsatzgruppen that accompanied the attack were given verbal orders to kill *all* the Jews they encountered, not just those in a position to resist German rule. On this one may consult Richard Breitman's *The Architect of Genocide: Himmler and the Final Solution*, and Helmut Krausnick's *Anatomy of the SS State*.

Other synthesizers place Hitler's decision to begin the annihilation of the Jews somewhat later, after Operation **Barbarossa** began. They point out that the Einsatzgruppen did not at first attempt to kill all the Jews who fell into their hands, and that in any case they were initially too small to attempt it. They began to do so only in July and August, when they were augmented by battalions of German Order Police and Eastern European collaborators (Latvians, Lithuanians, Ukrainians, and so on). Orders to strengthen the Einsatzgruppen and kill all the Russian Jews occurred in an atmosphere of elation over breathtaking German triumphs over Soviet forces. They also corresponded with Göring's July 31 order to Heydrich to draw up a plan for a "comprehensive solution" to the Jewish problem in Europe, which in this view was to be, in all likelihood, a feasibility study for the annihilation of the Jews. Then, no later than October 1941, as the seemingly unstoppable Wehrmacht continued to smash its way toward Moscow, a rapturous Hitler took the final step by further broadening his killing orders to encompass all the Jews of Europe. At the same time he authorized the deportation of Jews to the east, banned any further Jewish emigration from German-held territory, and ordered the SS to start building extermination camps at **Chełmno** and **Bełzec.** Hence these scholars conclude that the plan to exterminate the Jews of Europe originated in the euphoria of victory that prevailed between July and October 1941. The most original statement of this view appears in two books by Christopher Browning, *Fateful Months* and *The Path to Genocide.*

Yet a third school of synthesizers places the key decisions even later and holds that Hitler was motivated by despair, not euphoria. In this view, Hitler had expected victory in the east in a matter of weeks. During the summer months, when the Göring order to Heydrich was handed down, the dictator was still expecting imminent victory and planning to resettle the Jews forthwith. But by September his mood had ceased to be anything but euphoric as stiffening resistance by the Red Army slowed the progress of the Wehrmacht. He feared that his Blitzkrieg against Russia had failed and that the United States was about to enter the war, leading to a prolonged and probably unwinnable struggle on two fronts. Frustrated and infuriated, the Führer lashed out at his favorite scapegoats, ordering more comprehensive murders by the Einsatzgruppen in Russia and preparations for the annihilation of all the remaining European Jews. In one influential version of the "rage over impending defeat" argument, the annihilation of the Jews had always been latent in Hitler's thinking but required the specific circumstances of looming military defeat to be translated into action. By the end of October 1941 what had earlier been latent had become fully manifest, and Hitler had delivered the order to begin the **Final Solution,** according to Philippe Burrin in *Hitler and the Jews.* A somewhat different version of this argument attributes less importance to Hitler than to broadly held anticommunist convictions in Nazi Germany. According to Arno J. Mayer in *Why Did the Heavens Not Darken?* the process of venting revenge on the Jews for stiffening Soviet resistance began with the **Babi Yar** massacre at the end of September 1941 and spiraled until it became broadly genocidal during the course of the following year, a byproduct of Germany's increasingly desperate anti-Bolshevik crusade.

Debates between and among intentionalists, functionalists, and synthesizers concerning the immediate origins of the Final Solution can be expected to continue for some time. This is true for two reasons. First, the sources are inadequate and unreliable. Records have been lost, and it seems likely that crucial decisions were made in secret meetings attended for people who were all dead by war's end. Postwar testimony from participants is tainted by an understandable desire to cover one's own responsibility and attribute everything to dead leaders. Hence there is much room to sketch in missing portions of the picture in different ways. Second, scholars will continue to differ in their assessments of Hitler and the decision-making process in Nazi Germany.

And yet, there may be more potential for significant, even dramatic, redirection of this debate than on any other covered in this volume. The newly opened Eastern European archives in particular may yield startling evidence concerning such key issues as Hitler's orders concerning the Jews, the initial instructions given to the Einsatzgruppen in 1941, and local initiatives taken against the Jews by party and state officials. Less dramatic results can be expected from painstaking case studies of the Nazi bureaucracy, especially as it dealt with Holocaust victims. Cumulatively they have the potential to revise our understanding of how Nazi rule operated in practice.

The Perpetrators and Their Motivations

For a long time we have known that Holocaust killers were not limited to Hitler's elite corps, the SS, but also included German physicians, police, and army men. Nor were Germans the only perpetrators. Hundreds of thousands of volunteers in Nazi-occupied territories and officials of collaborationist regimes contributed to genocide.

Perpetrator motivations, on the other hand, are more difficult to establish. Human motives are never easy to understand, made up as they usually are of complex mixtures of hopes, fears, beliefs, and ambitions, not all of them conscious and often varying widely from person to person and group to group. A healthy scholarly debate has grown up about why the killers killed and sometimes willingly went beyond what was expected of them.

PERPETRATORS

Studies of the persecution of Jews, Gypsies, and the handicapped have demonstrated the broad participation of individuals and institutions throughout German society. German civil servants oversaw the removal of Jews from their ranks and defined such terms as *Jew, Gypsy,* and *hereditarily diseased*. Additionally, they regulated such matters as Jewish housing, the "**Aryanization**" of Jewish property, and prohibitions on mixed marriages. Various German businesses sought to acquire Jewish firms; during the Holocaust they supplied poison gas, gas chambers, and **crematoria** in addition to taking advantage of forced labor in camps and ghettos. German lawyers saw to it that German law harmonized with measures that were planned against the victims. German physicians sterilized the "hereditarily diseased," performed race research, and assisted in determining the **Aryan** status of individuals in doubtful cases. Officials of the German Reichsbank and the Justice, Interior, and Economics ministries saw to the disposal of Holocaust victims' property. However, here we are more narrowly interested in perpetrators who took a direct hand in extermination or who participated in organizing arrests and deportations. These include the **SS** and **police**, the **German army**, German physicians, high and mid-level German civil servants, and non-German volunteers and governments.

The SS and Police

No single agency was ever put in charge of the Holocaust, but the one that came closest was the **SS** (Schutzstaffel, or Protective Detachments). Originally founded in 1923 as an elite corps to provide personal security for Hitler and other Nazi leaders, it swiftly grew after 1933 to become the central agency of terror in the Third Reich. Under Reichsführer SS **Heinrich Himmler** the organization made a fetish of unquestioning loyalty to Hitler, who assigned it the task of destroying the regime's opponents. Hence Himmler was also given control over all the **concentration camps** and **police** forces in Germany, including the Security Police (of which the Secret State Police, the Gestapo, was a part). The SS also established its own elite military force, known after 1939 as the **Waffen SS**.

The SS conceived of itself as more than a weapon of terror. It was also intended to be an instrument of racial cleansing, conquering territory for ***Lebensraum***, scouring it of inferior elements, and ultimately resettling it with perfect **Aryan** specimens drawn in part from its own ranks. Although technically racial issues were assigned to the SS **Race and Settlement Main Office,** in fact they permeated the whole SS apparatus. By 1939 the SS had been put in charge of Jewish emigration and deportation from Greater Germany, and during the first two years of the war it carried out both selective and random executions of Jews, Gypsies, Poles, and handicapped people in occupied Poland. With the widening of genocide in 1941 and 1942, the SS organized Einsatzgruppen for mass executions in the Soviet Union as well as **forced labor** and **extermination camps.** Additionally, a team of SS officers headed by Obersturmbannführer **Adolf Eichmann** coordinated Europe-wide deportations of Jews and Gypsies to the Eastern European killing fields.

The merger of the SS and all **police** forces in Germany gave Himmler vast powers to dispose of Jews and Gypsies there. Between 1939 and 1941 the German police concentrated German Jews in special apartment houses and assigned them to forced labor in designated war industries. Thereafter some of the police forces were sent east to provide extra manpower in killing and sweeping operations. Both regular and reserve order police battalions serving in anti-partisan operations behind the German lines often were ordered to round up and kill Jews and Gypsies, too.

The German Army

Although the SS killed most Holocaust victims, the Wehrmacht willingly joined in, especially in the Soviet Union. Criminal orders issued by the generals to **German army** officers and men at the beginning of Operation **Barbarossa** stipulated that communist functionaries, **partisans**, and Jews were to be ruthlessly dealt with. In practice this often meant shooting them or handing them over to the Einsatzgruppen for execution. In carrying out these orders, the German army became deeply involved in genocide. It provided logistic support for the Einsatzgruppen in Russia and itself participated in the killings. Direct killings of Jews, Gypsies, and partisans by army personnel also occurred in Serbia and Greece.

The Wehrmacht contributed to **genocide** in other ways as well. It assisted in forming **ghettos** in the occupied USSR, and throughout Eastern Europe it exploited **forced labor** in armament plants and army offices. It also organized deportations of victims from Western Europe. The German army ran prisoner of war camps in which more than 3,000,000 Soviet soldiers died from starvation and disease. Finally, Wehrmacht policies of economic exploitation and scorched earth resulted in millions of additional civilian casualties in the occupied territories of the Soviet Union. Without the active collaboration of German army generals, junior officers, and rank and file, the Holocaust could not have been carried out on anything like the scale it was.

German Physicians

The role of SS doctors in the Holocaust is well known. They made **selections** that determined whether victims lived or died, supervised the actual gassings at the **extermination camps**, and performed ghastly **medical experiments** on the inmates. Less well known is the participation of physicians in the T4 **euthanasia** program. Not every doctor belonging to this second group was a member of the SS, but all certainly shared the racial and eugenic goals of the Nazi regime.

German Civil Servants

German civil servants responsible for public health matters in the Reich Ministry of the Interior collaborated with the chancellery of the Führer in carrying out the **euthanasia** program. T4 was organized and administered by the chancellery to maintain maximum secrecy. Interior Ministry officials assisted by recruiting physicians for the killings, helping to select the patients to be killed, and sponsoring medical research on the victims. High officials in the Reich Justice Ministry collaborated with T4 by silencing opposition to euthanasia within the judiciary and sweeping aside every legal barrier to the killing operation.

The looting, deportation, and extermination of Jews and Gypsies likewise drew on the services of German civil servants at many levels. These included officials of the finance, interior, justice, armaments, and railroad ministries. As an example one may cite officials of the Jewish desk of the German Foreign Office who were assigned the task of negotiating with allied and collaborationist countries for the deportation of their Jews and Gypsies. By late 1941 Foreign Office officials were aware that the deportations were part of a plan that involved **forced labor** and mass murder. These negotiations succeeded mainly with countries that were heavily dependent on Germany, including Slovakia, Croatia, and **Vichy** France. Elsewhere, as in Bulgaria, Italy, and Denmark, they met with only limited success or outright failure.

Non-German Volunteers

During the Holocaust the Germans were also fighting major military campaigns on which their survival depended. Their manpower was stretched very thin, but they were at first reluctant to recruit large numbers of fighting forces among the "inferior races" of Eastern Europe. They were, however, entirely prepared to make use of volunteers to assist in genocide.

In the Baltic States (Latvia, Lithuania, and Estonia) and the Ukraine, right-wing nationalist groups welcomed the Germans as liberators from "Jewish Bolshevism" and launched pogroms against the Jews either independently or under the benevolent gaze of the Wehrmacht. Organized variously as patriotic militias or "self protection" units, they killed thousands of Jews and so impressed the Germans that the latter formed them into Schutzmannschaften (police) battalions under the command of German officers. These collaborators were encouraged to recruit volunteers from among their countrymen in German prisoner of war camps. The Germans called those who stepped forward **Hilfswillige** (volunteer helpers), Hiwis for short; eventually they came to number in the hundreds of thousands. After receiving training at SS camps such as **Trawniki** in eastern Poland, most of them assisted German order police in various actions against Jews, Gypsies, and partisans. The Germans found that they could usually rely on the Hiwis to perform the least pleasant tasks, such as flushing Jews out of ghetto hiding places and shooting on the spot those too frail to walk to deportation vehicles. Other volunteers became guards at camps and ghettos all over Eastern Europe. More than three quarters of the guards at **Treblinka, Bełzec,** and **Sobibór** were Hiwis. Eventually, in 1943 and 1944, Hitler authorized combat units made up of Eastern European volunteers, including two **Waffen SS** divisions made up of Latvians and one each of Ukrainians and Estonians.

Volunteer auxiliaries in Slovakia, Croatia, and Hungary contributed to the high death tolls in those countries. In Slovakia the Jews were rounded up and turned over to the Germans by the **Hlinka Guard**, the militia of the ruling Slovak People's Party. In Romania the **Iron Guard** and in Croatia the **Ustasha** carried out genocide within the borders of their own countries. In Hungary, following the end of deportations and the removal of Admiral **Horthy** in October 1944, members of the fascist **Arrow Cross** movement shot Jews in Budapest and force-marched Jewish labor battalions into Germany under horrific conditions. In Eastern Europe only Poland and Bulgaria failed to provide significant numbers of native auxiliaries to the killers.

In occupied Western Europe small numbers of volunteers from various ultra right-wing parties assisted in the roundups of Jews. In the Netherlands it was the Dutch Nazis, in Belgium the Rexists, and in **Vichy** France members of the Parti Populaire Français. Vichy France also relied on its volunteer militia to fight resisters and hunt down Jews. Following the German takeover of northern Italy in 1943, fanatical fascists formed militia units to assist the **SS** and the Italian police in arresting Jews.

Non-German Government Officials

As we have seen, the fate of many Holocaust victims depended heavily on the attitudes and policies of governments allied with or dominated by Nazi Germany. Jews and Gypsies living in Croatia and Slovakia, both German satellites, were treated almost as badly as if they had been under direct German rule. The most notable difference was that both countries were more prepared to except wealthy and well-connected Jews from deportations and killings than would have been true of the Germans.

Germany's allies, Bulgaria, Romania, Hungary, and Italy, were primarily interested in conquering territory. Bulgaria chose to shield its Jews from deportation, Romania carried out limited genocide on its own in the eastern provinces, and Hungary and Italy avoided the Holocaust until they we taken over by German forces late in the war. Then, as was also true in the conquered countries of Western Europe, varying degrees of support from native police, militia, and government officials made the deportations possible. Especially in

Vichy France, the Netherlands, and Norway, where German manpower was stretched very thin, local administrative assistance was essential in registering, arresting, and deporting the Jews and Gypsies. Although it cannot be said with certainty that government officials in all these countries knew that the victims were being sent to their deaths, by 1943 no one could any longer suppose that the process of "relocation" was a benign one. Only Finnish and Danish government officials refused to cooperate at all in the Holocaust.

MOTIVATIONS

The willingness of Holocaust perpetrators to follow or exceed orders has been explained in several ways: as arising from ideological convictions, obedience to superior orders, peer pressure, career ambitions, and self-preservation. Although some scholars have advanced one or another of these motivations as the preferred explanation, it is also possible that two or more of them interacted and that the mix varied from person to person and group to group.

Ideology

Ideas and values unquestionably have the power to motivate people, and racist and antisemitic ideas and values were certainly present in Germany and elsewhere in Europe during World War II. Among the simplest explanations of perpetrator motivations is that Hitler's intense racism was shared (or came to be shared) by a very large number of Germans and also by non-Germans who collaborated in the Holocaust. This interpretation can be made to follow logically from studies of German and European **antisemitism** that stress continuities between older and newer forms of the prejudice and that view it as growing stronger in the decades before Hitler.

The argument that German Holocaust perpetrators were motivated by murderous antisemitism has been restated recently in extreme form in Daniel Goldhagen's *Hitler's Willing Executioners*. According to this view, Germans became obsessed with purifying their race and eliminating the Jews in the nineteenth century. Racial antisemitism became deeply embedded in German culture, and the belief that the Jews were deadly enemies penetrated every level of German society, the argument continues. Defeat in World War I and the experience of the Weimar Republic only intensified that fixation. By 1933 Germans were ready to follow Hitler in a crusade against the Jews. When he ordered Jews to be killed, Germans with few exceptions willingly joined in and even exceeded what was expected of them because they shared his lethal racial fantasies. In this interpretation, Hitler did not create exterminationist antisemitism; he had only to unleash it.

This sweeping monocausal explanation of perpetrator motivations has attracted little support from scholars, some of whose reactions may be sampled in Norman Finkelstein's *A Nation on Trial: The Goldhagen Thesis and Historical Truth*. Critics say that it ignores evidence that most forms of antisemitism in pre-Nazi Germany were not eliminationist at all. They point out that during the Third Reich most Germans showed little sympathy with acts of violence and cruelty against Jews. Finally these critics consider an explanation based entirely on suppositions about German society and culture inadequate in view of the widespread participation of non-Germans in the Holocaust.

More pointed and cautious approaches to ideological motivation during the Holocaust seek to identify groups that were most susceptible to racist and eugenic thinking. In Germany members of the Nazi Party and its militant formations (the **SA** and **SS**) always constituted minorities of the population but, not surprisingly, were over-represented among the most willing perpetrators. Of all the professions in Germany, medicine had the highest proportion of party members, as Michael Kater has shown in *Doctors Under Hitler*. Studies of doctors and supervisors in the Nazi **euthanasia** program have shown that most were party men whose ideological reliability was taken for granted. Naturally the SS, with its highly selective membership and intense ideological training, represents the epitome of readiness to engage in genocide, as is clear from studies by Robert Koehl, *The Black Corps: The Structure and Power Struggles of the Nazi SS*, and Charles W. Sydnor, *Soldiers of Destruction*.

Did ideological commitment automatically prepare one to be a perpetrator? A controversial study of SS doctors by Robert Jay Lifton, *The Nazi Doctors: Medical Killing and the Psychology of Genocide*, suggests that it was not always easy for them to become killers in the extermination centers. According to this interpretation, the tension between the doctors' traditional role as healers and the new demands that they act as mass murderers threatened their sanity. They coped by acquiring new, ideologically conditioned identities without being able fully to break with their old selves. In this psychological process called "doubling," they then possessed two autonomous selves. Their "pre-Auschwitz self" permitted them to go on thinking of themselves as healers and decent human beings devoted to traditional morality. It also enabled them in some instances to return to normal lives after the war. The second or "Auschwitz self" made it possible for them to believe that killing subhumans was necessary to the health of the human race. If there is anything to this interpretation, we may conclude that Nazi ideology was essential to these men becoming killers but that it was a recent acquisition that never fully possessed them.

Studies of the **German army** during World War II by Omer Bartov, *Hitler's Army* and *The Eastern Front, 1941–45: German Troops and the Barbarization of Warfare*, argue that acceptance of genocidal ideology may have been more a result of Nazi indoctrination and warfare on the Eastern Front than a preexisting condition. Young German conscripts, already exposed to racist teachings in the schools, received additional propaganda on the subject in the army itself. Alone this may not have been sufficient to prepare them to kill defenseless civilians, this argument continues, but combined with the experience of combat on the Eastern Front it was. War in the Soviet Union reached a horrific scale of human destruction that brutalized men on both sides of the conflict. Increasingly the German soldiers found themselves in a desperate struggle for survival in the most primitive conditions imaginable. The enemy soldiers and civilians they encountered, both Jews and Gentiles, struck them as so savage and backward as to confirm Nazi stereotypes of Slavic subhumans led by Jewish Bolshevik criminals. Hence Wehrmacht troops not only carried out the criminal orders issued to them at the beginning of hostilities but also engaged in a variety of unauthorized atrocities, including shooting prisoners and civilians and plundering and destroying property. The extreme barbarity of war on the Eastern Front made German soldiers more receptive to indoctrination and willing to internalize Nazi ideology and act upon it.

The centrality of racism and antisemitism in Nazi ideology cannot be ignored in any analysis of perpetrator motives, but few scholars are satisfied that it offers a fully satisfactory explanation. The Nazis never openly advocated murdering every single Jew, and it is by no means clear that indoctrinating Germans with anti-Jewish propaganda necessarily prepared them to kill defenseless women and children. Not all of the perpetrators were Nazis, and some of them who were had no strong feelings against the Jews. Hannah Arendt's classic study *Eichmann in Jerusalem* portrays SS official Eichmann not as a militant racist but as a dull bureaucrat who personified the "banality of evil." Nor did all the perpetrators experience intense indoctrination or the brutality of warfare on the Eastern Front. Ideology alone seems insufficient to account for participation in mass murder.

Superior Orders

Germany before 1945 is often thought of as the land of authoritarianism par excellence. The unification of the country under authoritarian Prussian leadership did much to entrench the tradition of obedience to authority. In Hitler's Third Reich that tradition was glorified. Within the Nazi Party the Führer principle demanded unquestioning obedience under the slogan "Führer command, we follow!" The whole German nation was expected to follow suit. **Concentration camps** awaited those who stepped out of line. Naturally the German military required officers and men to follow orders, as did the party's uniformed formations, the **SA** and **SS**. All of these authoritarian trends intensified during wartime.

In postwar **trials of war criminals** the defendants usually claimed that they were "only following orders" and that severe punishment, perhaps even death, awaited them if they refused. These claims are contradicted by the availability of transfers out of killing units and the fact that no case has ever come to light of a Holocaust perpetrator being severely punished by his superiors for refusing to follow orders, as David Kitterman shows in *Refusing Nazi Orders to Kill*. And yet, we cannot completely rule out the possibility that some of them may have *believed* they would be punished if they disobeyed (usually referred to as "putative duress"). Moreover, if transfers to other units meant being sent to the fighting front, they probably were perceived as tantamount to harsh punishment.

Although it is possible that some perpetrators followed orders out of fear, a more interesting possibility is that they did so out of habit and because they viewed authority as legitimate. This is hardly a uniquely German phenomenon. Everyone senses that without deference to respected authority figures, such as political leaders, judges, police, and teachers, society cannot function. This has been ingrained over thousands of years of human evolution, for groups that showed deference to authority were better able to organize for self-defense. As a result people tend to be uncritical of authority and comply automatically with orders from above.

Socially conditioned deference to authority within hierarchical structures was the subject of a classic series of postwar experiments designed to see if individuals would follow orders from authority figures to inflict extreme pain in situations where they themselves did not feel coerced. As described by Stanley Milgram in *Obedience to Authority*, naïve volunteers were instructed by white-robed clinicians to deliver increasingly severe (but faked) electrical shocks to other persons. Most of the volunteers fully complied, but only upon the insistence of the authority figure. The experimenters chillingly concluded that ordinary people (and not just ordinary Germans) could be induced out of deference to authority to kill people whom they neither know nor hate. Although these experiments are often cited in analyses of perpetrator motivation, their results are not entirely conclusive. No experiment can fully replicate the social and political context of Nazi Germany or the experience of actually killing other people.

Peer Pressure

Conformity to the group may be an even more powerful social predisposition than deference to authority. That can be particularly true of uniformed units in time of war operating far from home in hostile environments. Such units become closely knit and develop an intense sense of comradeship, each member sensing that his well-being, and perhaps even survival, depends on the help and support of every other member. This places a premium on group solidarity rather than individualism.

That peer pressure could turn "ordinary men" into mass murderers emerges from an important study by Christopher Browning, *Ordinary Men: Reserve Police Battalion 101 and the Final Solution in Poland.* The men of this unit were average middle-aged German conscripts, not specifically selected to have a majority of Nazi Party or SS members. Nor had they been very heavily indoctrinated with racist ideology or subjected to the brutalizing experience of war on the Eastern Front. Their easygoing commander permitted those who did not want to engage in shooting helpless Jews and Gypsies to perform other jobs, but no more than 20 percent of the nearly five hundred men took advantage of this. The great majority of the men did not want to be seen as shirkers who left the "dirty work" to their companions. They did not want to be ostracized by their comrades for appearing weak, cowardly, or "too good" to follow such orders. Other motivations worked on the men of this police battalion. Nazi racist propaganda made it easier to round up and kill "subhumans." The unit experienced brutalization once the mass shooting became routine. Most of the men grew numbed to the violence, while a few of them came to enjoy it and volunteered for raids at every opportunity. But, in this view, the mainspring that kept the unit going was social psychological pressure for group conformity.

Careerism

The Holocaust was organized bureaucratically and drew on the expertise of many government bureaucrats and professionals in Germany and elsewhere in German-dominated Europe. Several Holocaust scholars have argued that the career aspirations typical of bureaucrats were among the most common reasons for willingness to participate in the Holocaust. This motivation is extremely basic and hence easily understood. Who, after all, does not want to be regarded at the very least as competent at his job? Who does not aspire to the praise, raises, and promotions that come from a job well done?

A broad survey of the Holocaust by Raul Hilberg, *The Destruction of the European Jews,* emphasizes its bureaucratic dimensions and notes that middle-level German civil servants did everything from schedule deportation trains to distribute the property of the victims. In doing so, this argument goes, they showed no strong animus against the victims. Many of them were not even Nazi Party members. Their attitude was very much that of morally neutral, technically competent professional bureaucrats. These individuals valued efficiency and took pride in their ability to surmount obstacles and solve problems. The more ambitious among them sought out opportunities to win the favorable attention of their bosses with creative ideas and enterprising initiatives. In these respects the Holocaust was no different from any other bureaucratic venture.

Two additional features of bureaucratic life made it easier for civil servants to put careerism first, according to this argument. Bureaucrats enjoyed the luxury of working at a distance from the filth and horror that resulted from their diligence. Additionally, each bureaucrat performed only a single, highly specialized segment of the project. Such a person scheduled trains, not gassings, or ordered crematoria, but did not determine their use. Everything outside the area of his immediate responsibility was dismissed as "not my department." Insidiously, the bureaucrats became dehumanized almost as much as their victims, albeit in very different ways.

Careerism's power to motivate perpetrators is confirmed in two specialized studies of the Holocaust bureaucracy. The first, Christopher Browning's *The Final Solution and the German Foreign Office,* examines German diplomats involved in gaining access to Jews and Gypsies in areas that were not under direct German control. These ambitious career civil servants were not forced to become involved. Nor were they particularly antisemitic or devoted to the Nazi Party. Rather, they were so intent upon maintaining unblemished work records that they lost any sense of personal moral responsibility. Hence they welcomed Nazi interest in solving the "Jewish Problem" as a means to promote their careers. The energetic head of the Foreign Office Jewish desk even made suggestions to the SS for better ways to kill Jews.

The second specialized study, Henry Friedlander's *The Origins of Nazi Genocide,* delineates similar patterns that were at work in the T4 **euthanasia** program. Its managers, doctors, and supervisors were young, ideologically committed Nazi Party members who strongly endorsed the value of negative **eugenics**. They were less likely than other bureaucratic killers to enjoy the cushioning effects of distancing and fragmentation of tasks. And yet, they too seem to have been motivated chiefly by career considerations and personal profit. They expected the efficient performance of their duties to bring promotions, influence, and power, and they relished being at the center of a secret, high-priority project. Hence they took the initiative in starting the "euthanasia" of German children even before Hitler gave his personal approval to the program, and thereafter they looked for opportunities to expand it in various ways, even following the official stop order in 1941. Additional evidence that career ambitions motivated some of those who killed at first hand comes from the study of the German reserve order police battalion mentioned above.

Self-Preservation

Doubtless the bureaucratic "desk murderers" preferred their draft exemptions to dangerous front line duty. So, too, must the men attached to **extermination camps** and killing squads have feared the alternative of being transferred to combat units on the Eastern Front. Both groups could rationalize their positions as necessary to the war effort, as Gerhard Weinberg argues in "Crossing the Line in Nazi Genocide: On Becoming and Being a Professional Killer." From what little is known about the Eastern European Hiwis, volunteering to help the Germans may have seemed the only way to avoid almost certain death in a German POW camp. Civil servants and policemen in occupied countries who registered and rounded up Jews had good reason to fear that noncompliance would mean losing their jobs and being sent to Germany as forced laborers.

What emerges from this survey of perpetrator motivations is the impression that they interacted in complex and diverse ways for various groups and individuals, making generalizations hazardous. Human motives are too complicated and enigmatic to be reduced to single, universalized explanations. Certain motivations undoubtedly fit the characteristics of some groups better than others, but few of the groups we have examined were uniform in their composition or behavior. Further complicating matters is the nature of some of the evidence on which we base our judgments. Statements made after the fall of Nazi Germany naturally minimize the motivational power of self-interest and ideology in favor of coercion and psychological pressures. And yet, claims to the latter may be perfectly sincere and truthful. To some degree scholars must intuit motivations, and they can never completely divorce themselves from their own subjective feelings about people and events when they do so. Because no one has yet found a way to see into human hearts and minds with absolute clarity, perpetrator motives are likely to remain among the most difficult and contentious issues in Holocaust history.

The Victims' Reactions to Persecution

Holocaust victims attempted to survive the Nazi onslaught in ways that ranged from accommodation to various forms of active resistance and evasion. Apart from self-preservation, their motives included wanting to help family members, take revenge, and tell the world what had happened. In this section we examine the variety of victim responses, giving special attention to opportunities for, and obstacles to, resistance. We begin with the most common reaction, accommodation, and ponder charges that it should have been recognized as the least appropriate response. We then turn to forms of armed resistance by groups in ghettos, forests, and camps. After that we consider the efficacy of nonviolent survival strategies and the opinion that survival, in and of itself, constituted a form of resistance. We conclude by testing the scholars' views against what Holocaust survivors have to say about their experiences.

ACCOMMODATION

Throughout Nazi-dominated Europe most of the victims of racial persecution complied with German demands. Small, unarmed minorities, they felt powerless to do otherwise. The Germans often exploited their psychological vulnerability by tightening the screws on them only gradually and keeping **genocide** a secret as long as possible. Handicapped people in German hospitals were in no position to resist instructions given by T4 physicians. During the 1930s the German Jews, hoping that things would not get worse and might get better, took advantage of opportunities to foster their own cultural, educational, and self-help programs. For them armed resistance was obviously not an option, although individual Jews participated in Communist and Social Democratic underground organizations, including the **Baum Group**. In many parts of Europe **Gypsies** were already under police surveillance, and in Germany they were confined to special "Gypsy camps" before the war began. The Jews who came under German control before 1941 were mistreated but promised resettlement if they cooperated. Then, once genocide began, it took time for reality to sink in.

Jewish leaders and organizations usually accommodated the Germans in order to buy time and minimize losses. They also saw little alternative. The slightest **resistance** brought down draconian reprisals from the Germans, whose policy of "collective responsibility" held large numbers or whole communities of Jews responsible for the acts of individuals or small groups. Arms were hard to come by. The Germans had confiscated all the firearms they could find, and the non-Jewish underground was reluctant to share the few arms it had. Escape from the **ghettos** and camps was possible, albeit risky, but finding hiding places was difficult in places where forest cover was absent. In much of Eastern Europe the farmland is flat and open; in eastern Poland and parts of the Soviet Union, where forests abound, the chief problems were securing food and shelter during the winter. Peasants might or might not aid fugitives. Partisans were not numerous until 1943, and even then Jewish **partisan** units were hard to find. Non-Jewish partisans normally accepted new recruits only when they brought their own guns with them, and a few such units were actively antisemitic, killing Jews who approached them for help.

To these practical obstacles to resistance must be added a powerful psychological block. For one to fight back under these conditions required an overwhelming sense that one's life was in danger and that resistance was the only way to save it, but that was missing for many European Jews. Many, and perhaps most, of them either did not know or could not bring themselves to believe that death awaited them. In *The Terrible Secret: Suppression of the Truth about Hitler's Final Solution*, Walter Laqueur shows that reports about mass exterminations trickled out of Nazi occupied Europe during 1942. Allied and neutral radio broadcasts immediately relayed this information all over Europe, but it was not always believed. In much of Europe these reports were commonly dismissed as war propaganda. Jews and Gypsies in Eastern Europe, having experienced German rule at first hand, might have been expected to believe the worst, and some did. But many more did not, preferring to deny that their lives were in danger. In *The Holocaust and the Crisis of Human Behavior* George Kren and Leon Rappoport trace this denial to what they call the "fallacy of innocence," the psychologically comforting belief that only people who had done something wrong could possibly be in danger. Those who were killed, the victims reasoned, must have engaged in sabotage or failed to follow German orders — all the more reason to avoid such behavior. Psychic innocence blocked them from clear awareness of the reality of their situation and assured conscientious accommodation to the Germans.

Such accommodation drew a sharply critical analysis from Raul Hilberg in *The Destruction of the European Jews*. Hilberg, who is anything but lacking in sympathy with the victims, nonetheless sees the practical and psychological obstacles of resistance as less significant than the Jews' own intellectual and imaginative failures. In his opinion the Jews were the prisoners of deeply ingrained thinking and habits. For two thousand years they had survived persecution by appeasing their tormentors and appealing for help to established authority. During the Holocaust the authorities themselves were trying to kill them, but they could not break out of the habits of submission. Even in cases when death seemed unavoidable, Hilberg continues, the Jews complied with their killers to avoid unnecessary pain. By concluding that Jewish accommodation made it possible for comparatively small numbers of Germans and Hiwis to kill millions of victims, Hilberg implies that a different response might have saved an incalculable number of lives.

An even stronger attack on Jewish accommodation during the Holocaust appeared in Hannah Arendt's *Eichmann in Jerusalem*. She reserved special condemnation for Jewish leaders during the Holocaust, and particularly the members of the **Jewish Councils** and their **police** forces. By controlling and reassuring their own people and then handing them over to the Germans, she avers, these leaders implicated themselves in the mass murders. Arendt concludes that the Jews would have been better off leaderless. That would have produced chaos and thereby increased the chances of survival. These books by Hilberg and Arendt received shocked responses when they appeared in the early 1960s. Before then readers had been used to thinking of Holocaust victims as martyrs; now they were being told that the Jews missed opportunities to save the lives of their own people.

ARMED RESISTANCE

Scholars were not slow to respond to this charge by arguing that Hilberg and Arendt underestimated both the extent of Jewish **resistance** and the obstacles that stood in its path. In many ways the most important of these responses was Isaiah Trunk's *Judenrat: The Jewish Councils in Eastern Europe under Nazi Occupation*. This massively documented study of ghetto leaders appointed by the Germans argued that they adopted not one but many patterns of behavior. Some of the **Jewish Councils** secretly aided the Jewish underground or themselves resisted the Germans by collecting arms and organizing mass escapes. In a few cases such resistance succeeded, but far more often the Germans simply shot these leaders and replaced them with more compliant ones. What emerges from Trunk's book is the impression that German policies were so brutal that there were few opportunities for resistance. The council leaders had good reason to believe that putting ghetto Jews to work producing goods useful to the Germans offered the best chance for survival, but that resistance meant almost certain death. Hence Trunk concludes that most Jewish Council members were honorable men doing their best to save some of their co-religionists, and that they were in no position to alter the final outcome in any substantial way. The highly coercive environment in which the Jewish Councils acted also comes through in a short book by Leonard Tushnet, *The Pavement of Hell,* which examines three major ghetto leaders: **Mordechai Rumkowski** in **Łodź, Jacob Gens** in **Vilna,** and **Adam Czerniaków** in **Warsaw.**

Another response to charges of Jewish passivity during the Holocaust may be found in specialized studies of armed **resistance** by Jews in ghettos, in **partisan** groups in the forests, and in **labor** and **extermination camps.** Yisrael Gutman's *The Jews of Warsaw, 1939–1943: Ghetto, Underground, Revolt* details the development of the ghetto underground and the 1943 revolt by about 1,500 poorly armed Jews. Yitzhak Arad's *Ghetto in Flames: The Struggle and Destruction of the Jews in Vilna in the Holocaust* acknowledges the failure of the **Vilna** ghetto underground to arouse the majority of Jews to revolt, but it also describes the harrowing escape of a hundred resisters and their battles with the Germans in the forests of Lithuania. Other books, such as Shmuel Krakowski's *War of the Doomed: Jewish Armed Resistance in Poland, 1942–1944,* Reuben Ainsztein's *Jewish Resistance in Nazi-Occupied Eastern Europe,* and Nechama Tec's *Defiance: The Bielski Partisans* chronicle the operations of Jewish **partisans** to save Jews and attack German forces in Eastern Europe. They show that it took time to recover from the initial shocks inflicted by the Germans, and in this the Jews were no different from non-Jews. Neither group mustered much organized opposition before the start of 1943, and by then most Holocaust victims were already dead. Reliable numbers are hard to come by, but there may have been as many as 30,000 Jewish fighters in mixed and specifically Jewish partisan units in Poland, Belarus, the Ukraine, and the Baltic states.

Studies such as those by Krakowski, Ainsztein, and Tec also give a powerful sense of the hurdles Jewish resisters had to overcome and the atrocious casualties they sustained. Under the circumstances, such studies imply, the fact that there was any Jewish armed resistance at all in Eastern Europe is more impressive than its modest dimensions. In Western Europe Jewish fighters usually joined mixed resistance groups, although in France young Zionists founded a "Jewish Army" to fight the Germans on their own, as Annie Latour points out in *The Jewish Resistance in France*. In Yugoslavia both Jews and Gypsies joined either Tito's Communist underground or the rival Chetniks.

Armed resistance in the camps was even rarer. Constantly watched by German and Hiwi guards as well as by **prisoner functionaries**, prisoners did not often get chances to escape or arm themselves. Small wonder, then, that the few cases of armed resistance were acts of extreme desperation and doomed to almost total failure.

EVASION

In view of the many obstacles to armed **resistance**, it will surprise no one that many more victims responded to German policies by trying to evade them. This included smuggling food into ghettos, building "bunkers" (hiding places in basements, attics, and closets), and placing Jewish children with Gentiles or else spiriting them to some safe haven abroad. It also involved carrying on clandestine religious, cultural, and educational programs, which is sometimes called "spiritual resistance." Isaiah Trunk credits most of the **Jewish Councils** with trying to evade deportations and preserve at least a remnant of their communities. Some Jews were saved because the Jewish Councils made them work for the Germans while providing them with a cultural life and welfare services such as soup kitchens and orphans' homes. This argument is sustained by recent studies such as Charles G. Roland's *Courage under Siege*, which documents the **Warsaw** Jewish Council's heroic efforts to combat filth, hunger, and disease in the ghetto. Yehuda Bauer, in *The Jewish Emergence from Powerlessness*, goes further with the controversial argument that "resistance" ought to be defined more broadly so as to include all of these acts of unarmed opposition to German policies. In his view, any group action that thwarted German plans and kept the intended victims alive ought to count as resistance.

Survival required individual initiative when group solidarity could not be brought into play. This might involve making a break for refuge in a neutral country or hiding with the aid of non-Jewish friends or acquaintances. Or it might take the form of jumping from a deportation train or trying to "pass" as a Gentile. All were extremely hazardous. Jumpers who were not shot by train guards were often severely hurt in the fall. Unassimilated Eastern European Jews had trouble "passing" or hiding, as Nechama Tec has shown in *When Light Pierced the Darkness: Christian Rescue of Jews in Nazi-Occupied Poland*. Jews who looked too "Jewish" or lacked fluency in the Gentile vernacular were likely to be picked up, and those without Gentile contacts or money had trouble securing aid in hiding. In *Perpetrators Victims Bystanders* Raul Hilberg refers to victims who took risks in order to survive as "the unadjusted," reaffirming his belief that the great majority of victims adjusted themselves step-by-step to German control. Hilberg identifies the characteristics of the nonconformists as realism, the ability to make split-second decisions, and a tenacious holding on to life.

Handicapped people were in no position to help themselves, but suspicious German relatives sometimes complained so forcefully as to get family members released from the clutches of T4 personnel. Eventually such complaints helped to bring about the official order "stopping" euthanasia in August 1941. Except where the small number of mixed marriages was concerned, Jews and Gypsies could expect no intervention from relatives. Gypsies often survived by fleeing to remote and thinly populated regions, as they always had done. In Yugoslavia, for instance, they sought refuge in the mountains. Others fled to safety in the Italian occupation zones or in Italy itself.

SURVIVING THE CAMPS

Survival in the camps is the subject of a controversy that revolves around the victims' ability to influence their own fate. Bruno Bettelheim, a survivor of a prewar German **concentration camp** and later a leading American psychologist, offered a much discussed interpretation of camp survival in *Survival and Other Essays*. Camp conditions so crushed the human mind and spirit, he argued, that most prisoners became completely depersonalized and dehumanized. Their entire existence revolved around self-preservation; only rarely could they afford the luxury of looking out for others. Hence, the argument continued, they tended to regress to childlike behavior and to identify with the SS guards. Bettelheim, it should be noted, was not attacking the victims but rather indicting the Germans for systematically crippling the victims' personalities. If he is correct in his view that they usually succeeded in this, the prisoners could do little to save themselves; survival depended mostly on luck.

George Kren and Leon Rappoport take a similar position. The "fallacy of innocence" among camp inmates contributed to psychic collapse and the loss of the will to live. Only those with a fanatical determination to stay alive and a lot of luck had a chance. A Polish sociologist who survived **Auschwitz** supports this interpretation. In *Values and Violence in Auschwitz*, Anna Pawel-czynska recalls that Jews and Gypsies were less well prepared to survive the camp than were Polish political prisoners precisely because, unlike the latter, they had done nothing to deserve incarceration. It did not take long for the camp to destroy their psychic world, following which they lost the will to live. Only a lucky few survived.

Challenging this image of powerless victims is the influential view advanced by Terrence Des Pres in *The Survivor* that the captives helped one another survive. Acts of mutual kindness and aid in the camps took many forms: propping up and supporting sick compatriots during roll calls and marches, sharing rations with those in greater need, helping the weak complete their work, and hiding threatened prisoners in sick wards. Des Pres concludes that the survivors' experiences exemplify the human need to help others. Prisoner survival depended less on luck than the maintenance of a moral and social order in the face of massive cruelty. Whether women prisoners were better prepared than men to maintain that moral and social order is debated in Dalia Ofer and Lenore Weitzman, eds., *Women in the Holocaust*.

THE SURVIVORS' VIEWS

Memoirs and interviews of Holocaust survivors permit us to glimpse events at first hand. They are extremely important for many reasons, not least because they convey the sheer psychological terror experienced by the victims that is so often lost in scholarly tomes. There are now thousands of primary accounts of Holocaust survival, each one offering a small piece of a very complex puzzle. Together they can help us sort out questions related to accommodation, evasion, resistance, and survival in the Holocaust, but they do not lead to simple answers. What emerges from the survivor accounts is a sense of the diversity of Holocaust experiences and of the inadequacy of any one perspective to take the whole event into account. A glance at a few of the most important published memoirs suggests why this is true.

It was natural for Holocaust survivors to recall accommodation of the Germans by Jewish leaders with contempt. The unpopularity of Jewish Council exactions is unmistakable in Bertha Ferderber-Salz's *And the Sun Kept Shining* and Michael Diment's *The Lone Survivor*. The Jewish ghetto police usually come across as monsters, as they do in *Out of the Ashes* by Leon Thorne. And yet the memoir of one of these policemen suggests that they, too, could be victims. Calel Perechodnik's *Am I a Murderer?* tells of his decision to join the Otwock ghetto police in order to save himself, his wife, and their small daughter. His story, written shortly before his death in Warsaw in 1944, reminds us that the Germans succeeded in turning the victims against one another by granting (or appearing to grant) privileges to a few. It also anticipates the more understanding attitudes toward accommodation that have made way in Holocaust studies in recent decades.

The obstacles to breaking with accommodation come out clearly in many eyewitness accounts. Charles Gelman describes the mutually reinforcing effects of hope and repression in a small Polish ghetto in his memoir *Do Not Go Gentle*. Initially most of his neighbors believed that the Germans would limit the killings to Communists, Gypsies, and Polish resisters, and even when word came of massacres of Jews in nearby towns they refused to believe that the Germans would harm peaceable workers like themselves. An escape plan by Gelman and a small group of like-minded Jews was vigorously opposed by the majority, which feared it would endanger the whole community. Gelman escaped, but more typical was the decision of Yitzhak Arad to stay in his Lithuanian ghetto lest the Germans take reprisals against his family and neighbors, as he explains in *The Partisan*. The belief that the Germans would impose collective responsibility also kept Jews in **labor camps** and **concentration camps** from exploiting opportunities to flee and hide. For a case in point read Thomas Geve's memoir of Auschwitz, *Guns and Barbed Wire*.

The accounts by Gelman and Arad also highlight the limits and the achievements of Jewish armed struggle behind the German lines. Both ended up in communist partisan units, in which antisemitism was less of a barrier to acceptance than was true of units made up of Lithuanian or Polish nationalists. In *Fighting Back* Harold Werner describes the hunger that drove his band of Jewish partisans in Eastern Poland to steal food from the peasants and winters so severe that some of them returned to their ghetto rather than go on fighting. Filip Müller's *Eyewitness Auschwitz*, the memoir of one of the few surviving members of Birkenau's Sonderkommando, relates a few individual acts of violent resistance as well as the circumstances surrounding the doomed revolt of October 1944. Significantly, the camp underground refused to support the uprising, not wanting to risk annihilation when the war appeared about to end.

As we have seen, survival in the camps is variously attributed to good luck and self-help. Survivors' accounts provide evidence for both sides in the debate. The case for luck gets indirect support from one of the most famous survivor memoirs, *Survival in Auschwitz* by **Primo Levi.** Levi describes the victims being plunged into a primitive struggle for existence in which demoralization and exhaustion were inevitable. Hence many a prisoner became a **Muselmann** to one degree or another, incapable of individual or group resistance. Levi's own luck was in arriving late (1944) and having a knowledge of chemistry that the Germans needed in one of the camp laboratories.

Indeed, having work skills that were useful in the camps was probably the most important single factor in determining whether one lived or died. George Topas, in *The Iron Furnace*, explains that he survived **Majdanek** because of training as a mechanic he had received earlier in a labor camp attached to a Luftwaffe base. That doctors and dentists were needed, too, and were in positions to help other prisoners comes through in Gisella Perl, *I Was A Doctor in Auschwitz*, and Benjamin Jacobs, *The Dentist of Auschwitz*.

Luck rolled the dice even in the extermination camps. As Richard Glazer explained to Gita Sereny in *Into That Darkness*, he happened to arrive at **Treblinka** at exactly the moment when the guards needed another slave worker to sort the victims' clothing. Had he stepped off the train a moment sooner or later he would have been gassed along with everyone else who arrived that day.

Is there any evidence of prisoners identifying with and emulating their oppressors, as Bettelheim contends? This phenomenon seems to have been limited to some of the capos and other **prisoner functionaries** who ran the camps for the Germans in return for more food and other concessions. Contrary to common opinion, not all of them were drawn from the criminal elements, although it is certainly true that this group made up the worst of the lot. Some of these functionaries were political prisoners, and some were Jews. No single description fits all these groups. Kind and sadistic capos could be found among all of them, as a comparison of several memoirs attests. Eva Schloss *(Eva's Story)* and Trudi Birger *(A Daughter's Gift of Love)* encountered brutish capos, whereas Louis J. Micheels *(Doctor 117641)* survived in part because his capo protected him from antisemitic Poles at **Auschwitz**. Thomas Geve dedicated *Guns and Barbed Wire* to his block senior, a German political prisoner at Auschwitz who taught Geve to be a bricklayer and thereby saved his life. Fania Fenelon's *(Playing for Time)* friend Clara went mad with power when made a capo at **Bergen-Belsen**, whereas Isabella Leitner *(Fragments of Isabella)* was removed as a capo at a camp in Germany because she refused to beat her charges. Primo Levi, in *The Drowned and the Saved*, argues that the prisoner functionaries occupied a "gray zone" precisely because they were at once victims and persecutors. That makes it difficult to peg them as a group in any absolute dichotomy of good and evil.

There is abundant evidence that the victims sometimes helped each other survive the camps. At times prisoner solidarity appears to have been spontaneous, as described by Jenö Schwarz in *A Promise Redeemed*. When a **Maut-**

hausen block senior stole his shoes and his feet became infected, the men in his work crew saved him by keeping him going at work and getting medical aid. Moshe Garbarz relates a unique form of help in *A Survivor*. As he was about to commit suicide by throwing himself on Auschwitz's electrified fence, a fellow prisoner knocked him out with a blow to the head. More often than not, however, such acts of mutual aid occurred between victims who were tied to each other by family relationships, professional bonds, or long-standing friendships. Alexander Donat's survival at **Majdanek**, related in *The Holocaust Kingdom*, was possible because two fellow prisoners, an old friend and a fellow journalist, found him indoor work. Eva Schloss might have died in the **Auschwitz** infirmary had the head nurse not turned out to be a relative who saw to it that she received special care and extra food. Strong Jewish family ties come through again and again in the survivors' accounts. Typical was Trudi Birger's determination to stand by her mother through almost unbelievable privations in the Kovno ghetto and **Stutthof** concentration camp.

The view that Holocaust victims were thrown back on their own inner resources is advanced in Viktor Frankl's extremely influential memoir *Man's Search for Meaning*. Frankl believes that he and many other prisoners survived the camps because they were able to give meaning to their lives, often simply by helping others through the day. Those who lost faith in the future and the need to help their comrades ultimately lost the will to live.

One of the most balanced portrayals of camp survival, Hermann Langbein's *Against All Hope*, is based in part on his experiences of **Dachau, Auschwitz,** and several other camps. Langbein, an Austrian political prisoner, shows that the **SS** deliberately undermined prisoner solidarity by pitting Jews against Gentiles, Communists against Social Democrats, and political prisoners against the professional criminals. That worked well enough to limit resistance, but it was never entirely successful. The prisoners found ways of getting food to the starving, corrupting guards and prisoner functionaries, and saving comrades slated for execution by giving them the identities of inmates who had already died. Additionally, they kept up morale in the camps with musical, literary, and educational activities. Langbein's analysis works better for the camps with diverse prisoner populations than for the mainly Jewish camps in Eastern Europe. For a useful anthology of Jewish camp experiences read Donald L. Niewyk's *Fresh Wounds: Early Narratives of Holocaust Survival*.

Survivors' memoirs acquaint us with the great diversity of Holocaust experiences and ought to make us thoughtful about how far to push any generalization about victim responses. They also have their limits. They tell us much about what happened, but we can never know what *might* have happened had the victims behaved differently. We will never be sure, for example, how the Germans and their helpers would have reacted had the victims fought back in greater numbers. On this and similar issues more than the usual caution and humility are in order.

The Behavior of Bystanders

Bystanders, Europeans who witnessed the persecution of Jews, Gypsies, and the handicapped, found themselves willy-nilly before a choice: they could act by helping to **rescue** the victims or by joining in persecuting them, or they could do nothing. Reactions were not uniform, but in general only minorities of varying sizes acted one way or the other. The majorities remained disengaged. Who came to the aid of the victims, and why did they do it? Did the majorities passively approve of discrimination, care nothing about the victims one way or the other, or fear the consequences of becoming involved? Once again most of our comments will be about bystander reactions to the fate of the Jews, reflecting the current state of research.

Some answers to these questions have been advanced on the basis of broad surveys of Europe as a whole during the Holocaust. An analysis of rescuers of Jews in several countries by Samuel and Pearl Oliner, *The Altruistic Personality: Rescuers of Jews in Nazi Europe*, portrays them as socially connected and committed individuals who cared about the helpless because they came from backgrounds that emphasized justice and nonviolent discipline. Helen Fein's *Accounting for Genocide: National Responses and Jewish Victimization during the Holocaust* argues that, in most cases, the degree of popular cooperation with the Germans was determined mainly by the degree of prewar anti-semitism and the extent of SS control. However, conditions varied greatly from country to country, making broad generalizations questionable. We will divide our analysis of bystander reactions into three parts: Germany, Eastern Europe, and Western Europe.

GERMANY

In the years immediately following World War II it was commonly assumed that Germans under Hitler had been uncritically supportive of all Nazi racial policies, including **genocide**. More recently that general view has been qualified in significant ways. Research on German public opinion during the Nazi years has been based on internal Nazi Party and secret police reports as well as in reports by the Social Democratic underground, and it reveals that most Germans refused to become as racist as Hitler wanted them to be. The minority of Nazi Party activists always excepted, they shied away from actual attacks on the Jews, such as the one on **Crystal Night** in 1938. This and the public outcry against the genocide of the handicapped helps to explain why the mass murder of Jews and Gypsies was done in secret outside of Germany. On the other hand, research also shows that, with a few notable exceptions, there was little opposition to the persecution of Jews and Gypsies in Germany during the 1930s and to their deportation during the war, even when rumors about annihilation began to circulate. Why was this so?

One approach to that question stresses the German people's indifference and apathy toward the victims, arising from the increasingly difficult wartime situation, the repressive nature of Nazi rule, and the invisibility of the sufferers. This is forcefully argued in Marlis Steinert's *Hitler's War and the Germans* and Ian Kershaw's *Popular Opinion and Political Dissent in the Third Reich.* As these scholars see it, Germans were progressively overwhelmed by such wartime concerns as finding food, worrying about relatives at the front, and dodging bombs. Even if they had a bit of time and energy to spare, the harshness of the Nazi police state made any statement or action on behalf of the victims extremely perilous. Preoccupation and fear combined to cause Germans to seek refuge in purely private spheres such as the family and circles of close friends. Popular passivity permitted the aggressive minority, backed by the full power of the Nazi Party and state, to set the agenda. Moreover, the Jews had been almost totally isolated from the general population, and the Gypsies were even less likely to be noticed since they, unlike the Jews, rarely were even partially assimilated. Neither group had been exactly popular in Germany before the war; now both were literally out of sight and out of mind.

Apathy and indifference, the argument continues, were reinforced by the unreliability of information available to Germans. Rumors about mass murders, based on information brought back from Eastern Europe by German soldiers and civilians, circulated widely in Germany, but hard evidence of actual genocide was impossible to come by. It was easier to assume that the rumors were based on isolated excesses of the kind that are bound to happen in wartime. Because ordinary Germans had no way of seeing the big picture, most of them dismissed Allied radio reports of genocide as atrocity propaganda of the kind used against Germany in World War I and later shown to be false. If they thought about the deportations at all, they assumed that the Jews were being resettled; if any were being shot, they probably had done something to deserve it.

A rather different characterization of Germans during the Holocaust emerges from David Bankier's *The Germans and the Final Solution* and Marion A. Kaplan's *Between Dignity and Despair: Jewish Life in Nazi Germany*. Whereas Steinert and Kershaw downplay the influence of radical **antisemitism** on German public opinion, Bankier and Kaplan view ordinary Germans as profoundly racist and eager to get the Jews out of Germany once and for all. Hence they were anything but apathetic and indifferent, in this view, and they took an active role in persecuting and ostracizing the Jews before the war began. They wanted the Jews to leave, not die; Bankier and Kaplan do not accept Daniel Goldhagen's characterization of them as "willing executioners." But during the war Germans correctly sensed the direction of events and concluded from public statements made by the Nazi leaders and stories told by soldiers on the Eastern Front that the Jews were being killed. Most chose to distance themselves from genocide and salve their conscience by repressing the truth, but it came out when they uttered fears of "Jewish revenge" should Germany lose the war. Bankier and Kaplan are in agreement that the Germans' zeal to solve the Jewish problem led them into deep complicity in genocide.

There is less disagreement about the heroism of the few Germans who helped Jews in various ways during the war. Hiding Jews from arrests and deportations was undoubtedly the most difficult form of aid, and yet between 3,000 and 5,000 Jews survived the Holocaust in Germany that way, becoming "U boats," as they called themselves, submerging with the assistance of bystanders who were often, though not always, relatives. Several of their stories are gathered into a fascinating anthology edited by Erich Boehm, *We Survived: Fourteen Histories of the Hidden and Hunted of Nazi Germany*. A controversial study of Gentile aid to Jews in Düsseldorf, *Hitler, Germans, and the Jewish Question* by Sarah Gordon, found that arrests of Germans for helping Jews actually increased during the war even as anti-Jewish propaganda increased. However, Gordon found that her mostly older and middle-class helpers were unusual people; most Düsseldorf citizens were indifferent and apathetic concerning racial persecution, and their knowledge of the Holocaust was scanty.

Studies of the German **resistance** to Hitler have shown that opposition to racial persecution was a major force in turning some of its leading figures into active anti-Nazis. Doubtless the most unusual of these resisters was a conscience-stricken SS officer whose story is told by Saul Friedländer in *Kurt Gerstein: The Ambiguity of Good*. **Gerstein**, who had turned against the Nazis when a relative had been killed in the **euthanasia** program, delivered firsthand knowledge of the Holocaust to German church leaders, a Swedish diplomat, and members of the German and Dutch undergrounds. His message appears to have had an important impact on the conservative resistance in Germany, although Theodore Hamerow points out in *On the Road to the Wolf's Lair: German Resistance to Hitler* that many of these anti-Nazis had to overcome traditional anti-Jewish prejudices in order to act. Only **Dietrich Bonhoeffer** came out unequivocally against antisemitism from the start. More typical was the leading civilian resister, Carl Goerdeler, who saw no possibility of Germans and Jews living together in the long run and advocated removing the Jews to Palestine. Goerdeler and most other resisters, however, drew the line at violent persecution, and news of genocide that reached them in 1942 clinched the revulsion against Hitler that they had begun to feel four years before on Crystal Night. As Peter Hoffmann has shown in his biography of the German army officer who set the bomb that came close to killing Hitler in July 1944, *Stauffenberg: A Family History, 1905–1944*, information about the mass killings of Jews in the East convinced Count **Claus Schenk von Stauffenberg** to turn against the Nazi regime. Had the resistance succeeded in killing Hitler and overturning his government, the Holocaust would have ended.

The failure of the **Catholic** and **Protestant churches** to take organized stands against racial persecution in the Third Reich is widely held to be among the saddest chapters in German history. Such books as John Conway's *The Nazi Persecution of the Churches* and Richard Gutteridge's *The German Evangelical Church and the Jews* show that the churches as institutions were too preoccupied with defending themselves against the anti-Christian Nazi state to stand up for the victims of racial persecution. And yet they also show that individual church leaders took courageous stands. Count Clemens August von Galen, the Catholic bishop of Münster, publicly protested the euthanasia of the handicapped in August 1941, shortly before Hitler issued his "stop" order. Bernhard Lichtenberg, the Catholic provost of St. Hedwig's cathedral in Berlin, led his congregation in prayers for the persecuted Jews. In Berlin also the Protestant pastor Heinrich Grüber established an office to provide Jews with medical and social services. Both clerics paid dearly for these acts. The Protestant bishop of Württemberg, Theophil Wurm, wrote letters protesting the treatment of the Jews to Hitler, Himmler, Goebbels, and other German leaders in 1943. But for the most part the churches confined themselves to trying to protect Jewish converts to Christianity, and that to little avail.

EASTERN EUROPE

Throughout Eastern Europe powerful traditional **antisemitism** was strengthened by the stereotype of Jews as supporters of communism against local nationalism. Nowhere was that stereotype stronger than in regions that had been under Soviet control before the Holocaust: the Baltic states, **Bessarabia**, eastern Poland, and the USSR itself. In these areas it was widely believed that Jews had welcomed Soviet rule and served the Communist regime as political commissars and police officers. On the other hand, most of those regions plus western Poland came under direct, and exceedingly harsh, German rule in which growing hatred for the occupiers might have been expected to translate into sympathy for their most conspicuous victims, the Jews, But the evidence suggests that only minorities of Eastern Europeans deliberately harmed or helped the Jews. As was true in Germany, the majority remained uninvolved.

A lively debate has developed about the behavior of Poles during the Holocaust. A position sharply critical of the Poles was advanced during the Holocaust itself by Jewish historian **Emmanuel Ringelblum**, *Polish-Jewish Relations during the Second World War.* Completed while he was in hiding in Warsaw in 1943 after the unsuccessful ghetto revolt, this book was begun as part of the ghetto's underground research project code-named **Oneg Shabbat** (Sabbath Delight). Ringelblum drew attention to the special situation that prevailed in Poland and the rest of Eastern Europe and cautioned against hasty comparisons with the very different conditions in Western Europe. He also praised Poles who took enormous risks to aid the Jews in various ways. But his overall conclusion was bleak in the extreme: so infected was the majority of the Polish people by antisemitism and fascism that few Jews could be saved.

This negative assessment is buttressed by Yisrael Gutman and Shmuel Krakowski in *Unequal Victims*, a searing indictment of Poles for turning away from Jews during the Holocaust. The scene the authors describe is grim in the extreme. Gangs of Poles blackmailed Jews trying to pass as Gentiles. Others informed on Jewish fugitives and their Polish helpers, with the result that both were shot. In rural areas Polish peasants joined the Germans in raiding and killing Jews who had escaped from ghettos and in some cases carried out such raids on their own. So difficult was it for Jews to get help from the Poles that escapees sometimes gave up and returned to their ghettos or turned themselves in to the German police. Jewish **resistance** groups, such as the ZOB in Warsaw, could rarely get arms from the official Polish underground, the Armia Krajowa (Home Army), and when they could they were expected to pay for them. Indeed, some Polish underground and **partisan** units were explicitly antisemitic. Gutman and Krakowski honor the Poles who assisted the Jews, but they conclude that bystander crimes against the victims were far more common than acts of aid.

The reluctance of the Polish government in exile in London to support the

Polish Jews is a theme in two books by David Engel, *In the Shadow of Auschwitz* and *Facing a Holocaust*. Engel shows that the Polish leaders in London were slow to publicize information that reached them about the Holocaust and to instruct Poles at home to aid Jews threatened with annihilation. Traditional religious antisemitism was only one motive, however. The London Poles, convinced that most Jews were pro-Soviet, saw them as obstacles to restoring Poland to its prewar borders after the war. The Polish leadership also feared that it would lose credibility among Poles if it spoke too loudly on behalf of the Jews.

A study of Poles who rescued Jews during the Holocaust, Nechama Tec's *When Light Pierced the Darkness*, stresses the extraordinary risks they took. Their motives, as Tec sees it, had less to do with politics, class, or religion than with altruism and autonomy. (She limits her study to helpers who acted without thought of personal gain.) These Polish rescuers, she believes, were socially marginal individualists who came from backgrounds that put a premium on standing up for those in need. This contrasts with the Oliners' analysis of rescuers from many countries, which emphasizes their social engagement. Tec also makes it clear that the Polish rescuers were truly exceptional people in a society in which antisemitism was prevalent.

A far more favorable assessment of Polish society during the Holocaust appears in *The Forgotten Holocaust: The Poles under German Occupation, 1939–1944* by Richard Lukas. Lukas stresses the oppressive nature of Nazi rule in Poland. Holding that Hitler's policies toward the Poles were also genocidal, he notes that Poland was the only occupied country in which the death penalty was automatically imposed for helping Jews. He finds it amazing under the circumstances that tens of thousands of Poles risked their lives in order to aid the victims. Hiding Jews was both risky and difficult given wartime food shortages and frequent German searches. Lukas also notes that Poland was unique among the occupied countries in forming an underground organization specifically to aid the Jews, **Zegota** (an acronym for Council for Aid to Jews). It helped the victims find shelter, food, and medical assistance, and it furnished them with forged documents that enabled some Jews to pass as Gentiles.

Lukas admits that there was considerable antisemitism in wartime Poland, but he insists that it was different from that of the Germans in that it was economic rather than racial in character. He concedes that Polish antisemitism did increase during the war, but he attributes it to German propaganda, the belief that Jews supported the Soviets in eastern Poland from 1939 to 1941, and craven behavior on the part of the Jews toward the Germans throughout the period. No wonder, Lukas continues, that the Polish Home Army rarely supplied the Jewish underground with arms, especially in view of their limited numbers and the need to hoard them for the moment when a general uprising might succeed. But the high death toll among Polish Jews had little to do with local antisemitism and everything to do with German brutality and the limited opportunities for Poles to help the victims. Lukas concludes that a more balanced judgment of the Holocaust in Poland would recognize that the Poles were fellow victims, not perpetrators or collaborators.

Lukas and others have pointed out that the Polish underground took great pains to get word of the Holocaust to the outside world during the first months of the genocide. **Jan Karski** in particular is recognized as an authentic hero. Karski personally witnessed conditions in the **Warsaw** ghetto and then smuggled himself inside a transit camp for Jews and Gypsies on their way to **Bełzec** disguised as a Ukrainian militiaman. He escaped across Germany and France in November 1942 and brought news of all he had heard and seen to the Polish government in exile and British and American leaders. His story is related in *Karski: How One Man Tried to Stop the Holocaust* by E. Thomas Wood and Stanislaw Jankowski.

Much less is known about bystander reactions in parts of the USSR occupied by the Germans between 1941 and 1944. On the basis of what we have learned so far, the picture resembles that in Poland: small minorities who helped the victims or helped persecute them, and a larger majority that was preoccupied with staying alive and mostly indifferent to the fate of minorities. Here, too, there is an interpretive divide between scholars who emphasize popular antisemitism and acts of cruelty against Jews and Gypsies, and writers who stress lifesaving aid from Slavs who themselves lived under conditions of almost indescribable fear and oppression. This division is reflected in a collection of articles edited by Zvi Gitelman, *Bitter Legacy: Confronting the Holocaust in the USSR*.

The very different conditions that prevailed in Hungary are described in Randolph Braham's massive *The Politics of Genocide: The Holocaust in Hungary*. The Germans treated the Hungarians as allies, even after occupying the country and staging a coup against Admiral **Horthy** in 1944. That may help to explain why a significant minority of Hungarians openly and actively collaborated with the Germans and their **Arrow Cross** confederates by denouncing Jews who tried to avoid deportations and Christians who tried to help them. The Germans declared themselves well pleased with the level of assistance they received from the population. And yet it required German initiative to get the transports moving. As Braham notes, most Hungarians were passive, taken aback by the swiftness of the deportations, ignorant of the ultimate fate of the victims, and fearful of being caught aiding the Jews. Moreover, a small minority of individuals aided them anyway, including both Protestant and Catholic churchmen. As Soviet forces approached Hungary, government officials became more willing to place Jews in labor service battalions or grant them exemption certificates.

WESTERN EUROPE

The situation in Western Europe was radically different. There was less **antisemitism,** the Jews were better assimilated, the killing fields were far away, and the Germans were fewer and their policies less oppressive. Here it was easier to aid the victims, but at the same time they seemed to be in less imminent danger. Deportations of Jews and Gypsies from Western Europe did not seem all that unusual at first when civilian workers were being sent to Germany nearly every day. It was usual for local civil servants and police in Western Europe to cooperate in registering and deporting the victims, and once started the policy was hard to reverse. It took time for the special status of the Jews to sink in. When it did, help was forthcoming. Opinion is divided about how decisive it was in determining the outcome.

An important study of France during the Holocaust, *Vichy France and the Jews*, by Michael Marrus and Robert Paxton, argues that more victims died than would otherwise have been the case because of widespread public indifference to their fate and outright antisemitism. That the death toll among French Jews was not higher still they attribute primarily to factors other than popular aid: the availability of rural havens, the proximity of neutral countries, and the effectiveness of Jewish rescue networks. Other studies emphasize the fact that most French Jews survived the Holocaust and give much of the credit to French bystanders. John Sweets's *Choices in Vichy France* finds less inclination among ordinary Frenchman to support **Vichy** policies and greater determination to help Jews avoid deportation than do Marrus and Paxton. That is also the thrust of Susan Zuccotti's *The Holocaust, the French, and the Jews*, which underlines growing sympathy for the victims in 1942 as their suffering became unavoidably apparent. She credits Catholic leaders with issuing public protests, the French underground with furnishing false identity cards and escape routes to Switzerland and Spain, and ordinary citizens with hiding the hunted. The most dramatic case of French aid, the **rescue** of thousands of Jews by the inhabitants of the isolated Protestant town, Le Chambon-sur-Lignon, is set forth in Philip Hallie's *Lest Innocent Blood Be Shed*.

A similar difference of opinion exists about the role of bystanders in saving Jews in Denmark and Italy. Leni Yahil, in *The Rescue of Danish Jewry*, lauds Denmark's liberal and democratic traditions and the moral influence of the Danish Lutheran Church for motivating Danes to save virtually all 8,000 Danish Jews. Susan Zuccotti attributes the survival of 84 percent of the Italian Jews to help from their friends and neighbors in *The Italians and the Holocaust*. The Italian people, she argues, lacked any substantial tradition of antisemitism and expressed their disgust with the war and the Fascists by helping the Jews avoid arrest. But here, too, Marrus and Paxton warn against placing too much emphasis on bystander reactions. In a comparative overview, "The Nazis and the Jews in Occupied Western Europe, 1940–1944," they point out that conditions in Denmark and Italy were special. Neither country had large numbers of Jews, neutral countries (Sweden, Switzerland) were close, and the Germans waited until 1943 to go after the Jews, by which time it looked like Hitler might lose the war and anti-German resistance forces were beginning to act.

At the opposite extreme, the Netherlands enjoyed no such advantages. Louis de Jong has noted in *The Netherlands and Nazi Germany* that the Dutch people's rejection of antisemitism and contempt for German racial policies could not prevent around 75 percent of the Dutch Jews from being deported and gassed. The conditions that led to that fate — subjection to direct German rule for the entire period and the absence of nearby rural havens and neutral countries — comes through in Bob Moore's *Victims and Survivors: The Nazi Persecution of the Jews in the Netherlands 1940–1945*. Although 16,000 Dutch Jews survived by hiding with their neighbors, many more were discovered and arrested, sometimes as a result of denunciation by Dutch collaborators. Under such conditions bystanders could help only in limited ways.

Comparing Denmark and Italy on one hand and the Netherlands on the other hand illustrates the pitfalls of generalizing about bystanders during the Holocaust. Conditions varied widely from country to country, and the nature of German rule was the most decisive factor of all. Local officials and populations might speed or slow the deportations, but in the last analysis they ended only with Germany's military defeat.

The Question of Rescue

This chapter is chiefly about people outside the lands controlled by Nazi Germany and its allies during World War II. It should be noted at the outset that these outsiders showed little interest in helping the victims of racial persecution *before* the Holocaust began. Although governments and private groups lodged protests against the most conspicuous acts of persecution, legal barriers to immigration were being raised at a time when the Germans were still trying to coerce the Jews to leave. This was true of the democracies, the USSR, and most neutral countries. Books such as *The Unwanted: European Refugees in the Twentieth Century* by Michael R. Marrus and *No Haven for the Oppressed: United States Policy towards Refugees* by Saul S. Friedman show that these restrictions had less to do with **antisemitism** than with a general bias against immigration at a time of high unemployment during the world depression of the 1930s. In the special case of Palestine, the British mandatory government limited Jewish immigration in response to protests by the Arab majority against the influx of Jews. In evaluating this unwillingness to receive Jewish refugees, bear in mind that no one could predict the Holocaust, that many German Jews waited until after **Crystal Night** to try to leave, and that opening the doors to refugees would have seemed to reward Germany for its anti-Jewish policies and might have encouraged others to emulate them.

Outsiders started hearing about the Holocaust during 1942, within months of the start of massacres of Jews and Gypsies. At the time no one outside the Nazi leadership could know the dimensions or systematic nature of the **genocide**. As Martin Gilbert has shown in *Auschwitz and the Allies*, the extermination center that today is emblematic of the Holocaust was virtually unknown to the outside world until four Jewish prisoners escaped in mid-1944. And yet, the general direction of events might have been grasped had there been the will to understand. Some scholars believe that the powers arrayed against Hitler and the neutral countries bordering his empire missed opportunities to thwart the murder machinery and lower the death toll. Others are not so sure.

In addressing the question of whether different policies by Allied and neutral powers might have saved lives we venture into speculative territory. No one can be certain how the perpetrators, victims, and bystanders would have reacted to different outsider policies. There is also a strong element of "wisdom after the fact" in this speculation that goes well beyond trying to understand why things happened as they did. This critical examination of charges that more could have been done to aid the victims of genocide begins with those that touch on the Grand Alliance against Germany and then turns to the neutral governments, including the Vatican.

THE ALLIED POWERS

A number of scholars have been severely critical of the United States government for failing to **rescue** the victims of genocide during World War II. Henry Feingold has charged the American President Franklin D. Roosevelt with indifference to the Jews in *The Politics of Rescue: The Roosevelt Administration and the Holocaust*. In his view Roosevelt lacked the courage to take political risks entailed in diverting resources from military programs to civilian rescue. As a result issues related to rescuing Holocaust victims were left to the State Department, where they found little sympathy. An even sharper indictment of Roosevelt appears in David Wyman's *The Abandonment of the Jews: America and the Holocaust, 1941–1945*, which lists no fewer than twelve programs that in Wymans's opinion might have saved hundreds of thousands of lives. The programs were not put into effect, the argument continues, because the American president feared that appearing too friendly to the Jews would hurt him and the Democrats in the 1944 elections. In *The Jews Were Expendable*, Monty Penkower advances similar arguments but partially exculpates Roosevelt and his advisors with a psychological explanation: the reports of mass murder they were hearing were so outrageous that no one could fully absorb them at the time. Bernard Wasserstein has argued that indifference also marked British policy in *Britain and the Jews of Europe, 1939–1945*. He goes on to point out that Britain was reluctant to embark on policies that might result in Jewish refugees demanding entrance into Palestine, where the British mandatory administration was caught between an aroused Arab majority and militant Jewish advocates of **Zionism**.

Until recently few scholars were willing to respond in a systematic way to this literature, perhaps because so much of it is based on unprovable assumptions about the efficacy of alternative action. Now, however, we have William D. Rubinstein's rather combative *The Myth of Rescue: Why the Democracies*

Could Not Have Saved More Jews from the Nazis. Because the only way that outsiders could have rescued Holocaust victims was to defeat Germany as swiftly as possible, he argues, the Allies' single-minded emphasis on military priorities was entirely appropriate. More favorable assessments of Roosevelt's role are also found in Verne W. Newton, ed., *FDR and the Holocaust.* Let us examine the debate point by point.

One of the charges made by critics of the Allies is that they failed to bomb **Auschwitz** and the rail lines leading to it. Starting in 1944, the **extermination camp** was within range of American heavy bombers based in Italy, and the huge industrial complex at Monowitz (Auschwitz III), which produced vital military products, was successfully bombed on several occasions. Those bombers, or possibly the British Mosquito precision bomber, it is argued, could have destroyed the **gas chambers** and **crematoria** at Birkenau (Auschwitz II) during the summer of 1944 when they were consuming hundreds of thousands of Hungarian Jews along with other victims.

Scholars who doubt the efficacy of bombing Auschwitz point out that American heavy bombers dropped their loads from high altitudes to saturate their targets and everything nearby. Because the gas chambers and crematoria at Birkenau were very close to the prisoners' barracks, many of them would surely have been hit. The all-wood Mosquito would have been extremely vulnerable flying over such long range, and the Royal Air Force would have had to risk a substantial number of these scarce and valuable planes for a nonmilitary mission at a time when such aircraft were needed to prepare for and support the Allied invasion at Normandy. Even the Mosquito could not be relied on for absolute accuracy. The likelihood that hitting Auschwitz would cause casualties among the prisoners prevented many Jewish leaders from endorsing proposals to bomb the camp. As for bombing the rail lines from Hungary to Auschwitz, the doubters point out that there were seven of them, not just one, and the Germans were adept at speedy repairs. Such bombing would have had to be constant to do any good. Finally, even if Auschwitz could have been shut down by bombing raids, the Germans still had other methods of mass murder at their disposal, including shootings and starvation.

A second charge made against the leaders of the democracies is that they did not take advantage of opportunities to negotiate with the Germans to ransom Jews. In *Jews for Sale? Nazi-Jewish Negotiations, 1933–1945,* Yehuda Bauer demonstrates that the Nazis never totally abandoned a willingness to let at least some Jews emigrate, even after the mass annihilations began, as long as it enriched the Reich or benefited it in some other tangible way. Some scholars believe that many lives could have been saved had the Allies responded favorably to German offers. The most famous of these was delivered to the Western powers in June 1944 by **Joel Brand**, a Jew who had been released from Hungary to strike a deal between them and Nazi Germany. The Germans offered to release 1,000,000 Jews in return for the delivery of 10,000 trucks or other wartime supplies (sometimes called the "blood for trucks" offer). The story of Brand's ill-fated venture is told in *Desperate Mission: Joel Brand's Story* by Alex Weissberg. Later **SS** leader **Heinrich Himmler** made similar offers to Jewish leaders in an apparent attempt to curry favor with the western Allies and perhaps secure a separate peace. He even released small numbers of Jews to neutral Switzerland in 1945 in a gesture of good faith.

The case against the view that negotiations could have saved lives is based on doubts that **Hitler** would ever have let substantial numbers of Jews go. When he heard about Himmler's transport of Jews to Switzerland, he angrily forbade any more. Martin Gilbert and Rudolph Braham believe that the "blood for trucks" offer was a sham designed to lull the Hungarian Jews into a false sense of security. Peter R. Black, the author of *Ernst Kaltenbrunner: Ideological Soldier of the Third Reich*, argues that the Nazis might have been willing to let some Jews go, but only if that had brought about the collapse of the Grand Alliance and the preservation of the Nazi system in some form. That was too high a price to pay.

A third point made by the critics of Allied leaders is that they failed to pressure Germany and its satellites to release Jews, neutral countries to accept them, and the International **Red Cross** and the Vatican to act on behalf of the victims still in German hands. Pressure on the satellites, such as Romania, Hungary, and Bulgaria, would have been efficacious from 1943 on, this argument goes, because by then they knew Hitler could not win and hence were eager to curry favor with the democracies by freeing their Jews. David Wyman goes so far as to suggest that the Allies failed to pressure the satellites out of reluctance to deal with problems of feeding and relocating large numbers of Jewish refugees. Putting pressure on the International Red Cross might have encouraged it to press more forcefully for the right to inspect the camps and supply them with food and medicine. The Vatican might have been convinced to take a public stand condemning Nazi extermination policy and requiring Catholics to help the victims.

The counterargument is that Hitler was committed to **genocide** and would not have been moved by any attempts to pressure him. William D. Rubinstein notes that when Admiral **Horthy** stopped the deportations from Hungary in the summer of 1944 the Germans ousted him, placed their **Arrow Cross** puppets in charge, and would certainly have resumed the mass expulsions had the military situation permitted. As for Romania and Bulgaria, the Germans were not in direct control, the Jews were not being sent to extermination centers anyway, and they were essentially out of danger by the time the war turned against Hitler in 1943. The Romanian leader, **Ion Antonescu**, was a virulent antisemite, but he protected the Jews from the retreating German army because he did not want to answer for their extermination before a postwar tribunal. The Red Cross and the Vatican had no power to demand anything of the Germans and would only have endangered their neutral status had they tried.

A fourth accusation leveled at the Western leaders is that they failed to publicize what was known about the Holocaust with sufficient force and frequency. Had those leaders done so, their critics aver, the Germans would have concluded that saving the Jews was a top priority for the Allies and slowed or ended the killings earlier than they did. The victims would have been alerted to the threat of annihilation by such publicity and hence would have been more likely to hide, flee, or resist.

Unimpressed by these arguments, the critics of rescue theories point out that the Allies did publicize what they knew about the genocide. The problem was getting victims and bystanders to internalize and act on it. The Nazi leaders did not have to be convinced that the Jews were important to the Western leaders. In fact, they always greatly exaggerated the influence of what they called "world Jewry" on the Allied governments, which partially explains the ransom offers that came in serious form only after it was clear that Germany could no longer win the war.

A final charge, aimed squarely at Roosevelt, is that he waited too long to establish the **War Refugee Board** (WRB), America's official rescue and relief office, and then funded it inadequately. Had it been created in 1942 instead of January 1944 and properly supported, many more victims could have been saved from genocide, the accusation continues. As it was, the WRB produced an admirable record of financing Jewish underground operations and escape systems and supplying food and medical aid to the victims. David Wyman asserts that in its short span of activity it saved around 220,000 lives, most notably the Jews in Budapest and those of eastern Romania. Delaying the WRB for fourteen crucial months denied such assistance to tens of thousands of victims who might otherwise have been saved.

Nonsense, replies William D. Rubinstein. At most the WRB saved 20,000 lives, and the figure would not have been higher had it been established earlier because the Board had no access to the victims in 1942 and 1943. Nor did the WRB have any substantial impact on sparing the Jews of Budapest and

Eastern Romania in 1944–1945, Rubinstein continues. They survived for reasons determined almost entirely by local conditions. The Romanians wanted to avoid the consequences of their alliance with Hitler and eventually changed sides in the war in August 1944. The Jews of Budapest were spared because Admiral Horthy learned about the genocide of Hungarian Jews who had been deported earlier and delayed further mass deportations until resuming them was no longer possible.

The Jewish communities of the free world have not escaped criticism for their responses to the Holocaust. The report of a historical commission that investigated Jewish responses in the United States, *American Jewry during the Holocaust*, described them as timid and ineffectual and the Jewish community itself as divided, squabbling, and unwilling to put much pressure on the Roosevelt administration to take an active role in rescue. A far less critical assessment is made by Yehuda Bauer in *American Jewry and the Holocaust*. This study of the **American Jewish Joint Distribution Committee**, a charitable organization that helped European Jews during the Nazi era, leaves the impression that American Jewish leaders did everything in their power to influence the course of events. Their failures were determined principally by the indifference of the public and the politicians and by the impotence of the small Jewish minority. In *The Terrible Secret* Walter Laqueur usefully reminds us that Jews in America and elsewhere in the free world found it no easier than anyone else to absorb the full significance of reports about mass murder that filtered out of Europe. For them, too, shock and bewilderment limited the capacity to respond quickly and effectively.

The Jewish community in Palestine, often referred to as the **Yishuv**, has been the subject of similar controversy. Tom Segev characterizes the Palestinian Jews as apathetic, complacent, and irresolute during the genocide of their European brethren in *The Seventh Million: The Israelis and the Holocaust*. An article by Bela Vago, "Some Aspects of the Yishuv Leadership's Activities During the Holocaust," in *Jewish Leadership in the Nazi Era* sums up the view that Yishuv leaders were slow to grasp what was happening in Europe, preoccupied with their own problems, and unwilling to mobilize resources to help European Jews. An opposing interpretation is advanced by Dina Porat in *The Blue and Yellow Stars of David: The Zionist Leadership in Palestine and the Holocaust*. This study argues that Yishuv leaders sensibly concentrated on the one area in which they might do some good for the European Jews, namely pressuring Great Britain to open Palestine to immigration by Jews who managed to escape the killers. Beyond that there was little that the Jewish minority there could do, although rescue and illegal immigration projects had some impact.

As Dalia Ofer has shown in *Escaping the Holocaust: Illegal Immigration to the Land of Israel*, these projects brought thousands of Jews from the periphery of Hitler's empire to Palestine during World War II.

And what of the USSR? It, too, has been faulted by some scholars for abandoning the victims of the Holocaust. More than half of the 5,000,000 Jews under Soviet control were threatened by the Germans, and not all of them were evacuated in time. An earlier generation of scholars, perhaps influenced by Cold War tensions or by Stalin's postwar antisemitism, alleged that between 1939 and 1941 (the period of the Nazi-Soviet Pact) the Soviets failed to warn the Jews of what awaited them should the Germans attack because they were fixated on maintaining Hitler's friendship. Once the invasion began, the criticism continues, too little was done to move them out of harm's way. An example of this view may be found in Solomon Schwarz, *The Jews in the Soviet Union*. Recently a more nuanced assessment has been advanced by Mordechai Altschuler, "Escape and Evacuation of Soviet Jews at the Time of the Nazi Invasion," in Lucjan Dobroszycki and Jeffrey S. Gurock, eds., *The Holocaust in the Soviet Union*. As Altschuler sees it, the Soviet Jews were reasonably well informed about Nazi antisemitism from pre-1939 news reports, rumors, and Soviet reports of German atrocities from the start of the invasion on. Altschuler also takes into account the panic and confusion that reigned during the rapid German advance into the USSR. There was no deliberate or central Soviet policy favoring the evacuation of Jews, but local authorities frequently gave the Jews preference once it became clear that they faced greater danger than did other Soviet citizens. Hence Jews made up a larger proportion of refugees and evacuees than they did of the population as a whole, and hundreds of thousands of them owed their lives to Soviet rescue measures.

THE NEUTRALS

Switzerland, Sweden, Spain, Portugal, and Turkey were close to German-held territory and might grant or deny refuge to those targets of genocide who could make it to their borders. A sixth neutral, the Vatican, was important chiefly for the influence it wielded over millions of Catholics on both sides of hostilities. Proximity to the Germans also made all six of these weak neutral states extremely sensitive to Nazi retribution, especially before 1943 when it looked like Hitler would win his war. Although their policies tended to become more liberal during the last year of the struggle, all have been criticized for doing less than they might have for the victims of genocide.

Switzerland, traditionally neutral and democratic, was mostly hostile to Nazism but also completely surrounded by Axis territory during the war. Hence its leaders felt that it had no choice but cooperate with Germany on several levels, including the economic and the financial. Even before 1939 the Swiss had grown apprehensive about an influx of political refugees that might strain relations with Nazi Germany and overtax the small country's capacity to aid and absorb them. Hence in 1938 the Swiss government persuaded the Germans to stamp the passports of German Jews with a **J** so that they could not enter Switzerland posing as tourists and not return. Following the fall of France in 1940 anxiety about a possible German invasion and a new wave of refugees led the Swiss to maintain their restrictive policies, which included the identification of Jews as "racial" rather than "political" refugees and hence ineligible for admission. Exceptions were made for children, pregnant women, and the elderly, and a few thousand Jewish refugees slipped into the country illegally and managed to avoid discovery.

Sadly, many others were turned back at the border or expelled after being arrested for illegal entry, and it is known that at least some of them perished as a result. Not until July 1944 did the Swiss stop distinguishing between racial and political refugees and begin accepting Jews without question. Altogether about 300,000 persons, around 22,000 of them Jews, were given sanctuary in Switzerland during the war. It should be added that Swiss diplomats in Budapest handed out 7,800 protective passports to local Jews in 1944, more than those supplied by any other neutral country. Postwar soul-searching by the Swiss concerning their country's restrictive wartime refugee policies is reflected in Alfred A. Häsler's *The Lifeboat Is Full: Switzerland and the Refugees, 1933–1945*, which argues that many more of the hunted could have been given refuge and laments that the country succumbed to "panic" over being inundated with refugees.

Sweden was also traditionally neutral and democratic and also surrounded by the Germans. Hence it, too, cooperated with the Germans. On the other hand, it accepted without question approximately 11,000 Jews who reached its borders, including about half of Norway's Jews and virtually all the Danish Jews. Its geographical position limited the numbers who could get there. In *The Stones Cry Out: Sweden's Response to the Persecution of the Jews 1933–1945*, Steven Koblik points out that Sweden's strictly neutral conduct during the war prevented it from publicizing what it knew about the genocide but also enabled it to rescue an additional 20,000 inmates from German concentration camps during the last months of the war. Neutrality also made it possible for **Raoul Wallenberg** to enter Budapest in 1944 for the purpose of distributing protective passports and providing food, medicine and shelter for Jews in "safe houses." A generous account of Wallenberg's mission is found in John Bierman's *Righteous Gentile: The Story of Raoul Wallenberg, Missing Hero of the Holocaust.*

Spain's neutrality during World War II derived principally from exhaustion following its civil war (1936–1939). General Francisco Franco had won that struggle over the democratic Spanish Republic with help from Hitler and Mussolini, so he naturally inclined toward the Axis. But he had the practical sense to keep Spain nonbelligerent. Neither Franco nor contemporary Spanish society was particularly antisemitic, and throughout the war Spanish officials did not discriminate between Jewish and non-Jewish refugees. People fleeing the Nazis were allowed to cross Spanish territory from France on transit visas, but stateless refugees were at first turned back at the border. Pressure from the Allies induced Franco to reverse that policy in November 1942, following which about 2,000 refugees were allowed to stay at any one time. Altogether Spain saved about 11,000 Jews. According to Haim Avni in *Spain, the Jews, and Franco*, the number might have been higher had the democracies acted sooner and placed more pressure on the Spanish government. Portugal, which had no border with the Axis powers, permitted refugees reaching it through Spain to depart through the port of Lisbon.

Turkey, fearful that the Germans would try to link their forces in the USSR with a victorious Afrika Korps in North Africa, was likewise extremely cautious on refugee issues. Although Stanford J. Shaw, in *Turkey and the Holocaust*, emphasizes Turkey's willingness informally to permit Jews to use the country as a bridge to Palestine, it is equally clear that it was not prepared to take any of them in. Hence the tragedy of the SS *Struma*, an unseaworthy ship that had stopped at Istanbul carrying 769 Romanian Jews on their way to Palestine. Denied permission to land in Palestine by the British, the ship was ordered out of Turkish waters and towed into the Black Sea in February 1942. There it was torpedoed, probably by mistake by a Soviet submarine, and all but two of the refugees perished.

Vatican neutrality was consistent with the Roman **Catholic church's** practice of ministering to the spiritual needs of believers on both sides of conflicts and playing the role of peacemaker whenever possible. Pope Pius XII held firmly to that tradition and famously remained silent during the Holocaust. Although he was well informed about Nazi genocide from an early date, he issued no public condemnation of the murderers. Nor did he instruct Catholics at large to help the victims. Individual church leaders did try to help in various ways, as when they used their influence to stop deportations from Slovakia in

1942 and Hungary in 1944. Pius XII, however, gave no central coordination to this aid. John F. Morley roundly condemns the pope for his silence and the Vatican for its feeble diplomatic response in *Vatican Diplomacy and the Jews during the Holocaust, 1939–1943*. In his opinion lack of empathy for the Jews and preoccupation with defending church interests led the Vatican to betray its own ideals of charity and justice. If anything Saul Friedländer paints an even darker picture in *Pius XII and the Third Reich*, in which he argues that the Pope's strongly anticommunist views led him to sympathize with Nazi Germany in its war with the Soviet Union.

A more favorable assessment of the Pope is advanced by John Conway's "The Silence of Pope Pius XII" in *The Papacy and Totalitarianism between the Two World Wars*. In this view the pontiff was under no illusions about the evils of Nazism but could not extricate himself from the horns of a terrible moral and political dilemma. A forceful protest against genocide might do more harm than good. It might bring on serious reprisals against German Catholics and especially Jewish converts to Catholicism. It would also end any hope that the Vatican might mediate a peaceful settlement of the war. Guenter Lewy in *The Catholic Church and Nazi Germany* agrees with Conway that there was no chance that a papal protest would have changed Hitler's mind.

Writing of the neutral powers during the Holocaust in *The Holocaust in History*, Michael R. Marrus points out that from our vantage point it is extremely tempting to condemn one or another of them for not doing more to help the victims of genocide. We, after all, know that Hitler was going to lose and go down fighting. But things looked different in places like Bern, Stockholm, and the Vatican during most of the war. The Allies made their policy decisions on the basis of their own wartime priorities rather than fears of German retaliation. And yet they, too, were constrained by military considerations and the Germans' alternately intransigent and manipulative attitudes. Are these sufficient to explain the alleged Allied "failures" to save the victims? Assessing the chances for successful rescue during the Holocaust requires that we grasp how conditions were understood at the time and take all the limiting factors into account.

The Lasting Effect of the Holocaust

In this chapter we consider some of the wider historical and philosophical issues raised by the Holocaust. We begin by examining its impact on those who
were personally touched by genocide, both surviving victims and perpetrators.
We then turn to the ways in which legal and religious institutions have been
influenced by Nazi genocide. The section concludes by surveying attempts by
scholars and their students to place the Holocaust in historical context.

PARTICIPANTS

The destruction of two-thirds of European Jewry in the Holocaust removed
the center of Jewish life in the world from Europe to Israel and the United
States. The virtual eradication of Jewish life and culture in most of Eastern Europe was particularly dramatic. Little remained of what had once been thriving Jewish communities in Poland, the Ukraine, and White Russia. Survivors
from these areas either did not try to revive the communities or quickly despaired of success. Hence hundreds of thousands of them settled for long de-
lays and incarceration in **Displaced Persons** (DP) camps and waited for the
chance to emigrate. Yehuda Bauer sets this scene and lauds the work of the
American Jewish Joint Distribution Committee in assisting the DPs in *Out
of the Ashes: The Impact of American Jews on Post-Holocaust European Jewry*.
The departure of large numbers of survivors from Europe, followed by assimilation, intermarriage, and low birth rates among the remaining Jews, has
caused Bernard Wasserstein to predict the coming extinction of European
Jewry in *Vanishing Diaspora: The Jews in Europe since 1945*. The contribution
of Holocaust survivors to creating the state of Israel is exalted in Abram L.
Sachar's *The Redemption of the Unwanted*. On the other hand, John Quigley
points out that this involved the displacement of most Palestinian Arabs and
the creation of a Palestinian diaspora in the Middle East, Europe, and North
America in *Palestine and Israel: A Challenge to Justice*.

Jews and Gypsies who had survived the Holocaust in ghettos and camps or else in hiding were certain to carry emotional scars for a long time afterward. Would their wounds ever heal, or would they prove disabling? Postwar studies by psychologists implied that significant numbers of survivors were beyond hope of recovery. The American psychologists William G. Niederland and Henry Krystal interviewed hundreds of Holocaust survivors who had made restitution claims on the West German government and concluded that they suffered what Niederland called the "survivor syndrome." Its symptoms include: (1) anxiety in the form of fear of renewed persecution, repeated nightmares, and apprehension about being alone; (2) memory loss and confusion of the past with the present; (3) chronic depression; (4) self-isolation; (5) psychosomatic ailments, such as ulcers, headaches, respiratory problems, and heart conditions; (6) severe feelings of guilt over having survived when so many others had not; and (7) blocked maturational development that in severe cases took the forms of complete inertia, delusions, and paranoia. It was further argued that these symptoms frequently affected the development of the survivors' children, causing them, too, to suffer chronic depression and obsessional traits. Niederland and Krystal summarized their findings in Henry Krystal's *Massive Psychic Trauma*. They concluded that many survivors were so deeply troubled that psychotherapy could do little to help them live normal lives.

Other scholars have denied that large numbers of Holocaust survivors are psychologically impaired and have challenged the evidence for a "survivor syndrome." Studies on which this evidence is based, the critics contend, used relatively small samplings made up of severely impaired, unrepresentative survivors. Their findings are influenced by now dated Freudian theories of traumatic neurosis, the argument continues. Finally, the critics imply, the need to document mental health impairment to West German restitution panels colored the earlier studies. Broader studies show far less evidence of widespread psychological difficulties. These arguments are well summarized in an article by Paul Marcus and Alan Rosenberg, "A Philosophical Critique of the 'Survivor Syndrome' and Some Implications for Treatment," in Randolph Braham, ed., *The Psychological Perspective of the Holocaust and Its Aftermath*. Suggestive evidence favoring this view is advanced by William B. Helmreich, *Against All Odds: Holocaust Survivors and the Successful Lives They Made in America*. Here survivors are pictured as typically normal and thriving, with stable families, solid work patterns, and wide circles of friends. The distinct identity that their experiences had forged for them in no way impaired their effectiveness as human beings.

A middle position has been taken by the Norwegian psychiatrist Leo

Eitinger, whose study of *Concentration Camp Survivors in Norway and Israel* compares the postwar adjustments of Jewish survivors living in Norway and Israel and of Norwegian Gentiles who had spent time in German **concentration camps**. Eitinger found clear evidence of the "survivor syndrome" among the Jewish survivors but not among the Norwegian Gentiles; he attributed this to the extreme dangers endured by Jews in the camps as well as survivor guilt. Paradoxically, he also found that most of the Jewish survivors led active and productive lives and that many of them held responsible jobs and prominent social positions, proving the human potential for regeneration. Eitinger found that it was easier for Jewish survivors to start over again in Israel, possibly because of the proximity of larger numbers of other Holocaust survivors. Additional evidence that survivors displayed both the effects of trauma and amazing resilience is presented in Aaron Hass's *The Aftermath: Living with the Holocaust.* Various psychotherapeutic approaches to helping survivors recover from trauma are summarized in Paul Marcus and Alan Rosenberg, eds., *Healing Their Wounds.*

Gypsy survivors, too, must have experienced long-term psychological aftereffects, although we know of no studies of them. *The Destiny of Europe's Gypsies* by Donald Kenrick and Grattan Puxon points out that not a single Gypsy was called on to give testimony at the **trials of war criminals** held at Nuremberg. For many years the West German courts denied restitution to Gypsies, asserting erroneously that Gypsies had been persecuted for alleged criminal activities rather than racial reasons. Only recently have Gypsies won compensation from the German government. With no homeland or chorus of foreign supporters, they have remained a largely despised and neglected minority.

And what of the perpetrators? The complexities of trying and convicting the surviving Nazi leaders, most of whom were connected in one way or another with the Holocaust, is told in Telford Taylor's *The Anatomy of the Nuremberg Trials.* Taylor, one of the American prosecutors at Nuremberg, defends the Nuremberg precedent while conceding the uneven quality of justice meted out by the International Military Tribunal. Subsequent trials of around 70,000 Nazi war criminals, many of them Holocaust perpetrators, by the victorious Allies and German courts are documented in Adalbert Rückerl's *The Investigation of Nazi Crimes, 1945–1978.* Rückerl also points out that many individuals sought for various crimes were either dead or could not be found, and that the destruction of records and the fading of memory over time sometimes made it impossible to secure convictions. A view sharply critical of postwar German courts for allegedly being seriously deficient in punishing Nazi war criminals is presented by Ingo Müller in *Hitler's Justice.*

Little is known about the fate of the numerous **Hilfswillige** who were forcibly repatriated to the Soviet Union after 1945, although it may safely be assumed that they were treated savagely by Stalin's officials. A few managed to avoid repatriation and enter the United States and other countries as refugees. Efforts by the **Office of Special Investigations** to expose Nazi war criminals living in the United States are the subject of Allan A. Ryan's *Quiet Neighbors: Prosecuting Nazi War Criminals in America*. Perhaps inevitably there have been errors, as happened in the case of John Demjanjuk, wrongly accused of being a sadistic camp guard at **Treblinka** known as "Ivan the Terrible" and stripped of his American citizenship. The story of his trial and acquittal in Israel is told in Yoram Sheftel's *The Demjanjuk Affair*.

LEGAL AND RELIGIOUS INSTITUTIONS

The Holocaust gave the world the idea of **genocide**. The word *genocide* itself was coined by the Polish Jewish jurist Raphael Lemkin in his 1944 book *Axis Rule in Occupied Europe*. Lemkin defined genocide as the planned annihilation of a national, religious, or racial group. The term was included in the Nuremberg indictments of the Nazi leaders for crimes against humanity. At the time it was noted that there was no precedent for punishing what seemed an unprecedented crime. Moreover, prosecuting Nazi war criminals for genocide was possible only because of Germany's military defeat. In 1948 the United Nations adopted the Genocide Convention, outlawing all acts committed with the intent to destroy all or part of a national, racial, or religious group. But as Leo Kuper shows in *Genocide: Its Political Use in the Twentieth Century*, the convention is difficult to enforce and has not prevented subsequent genocides. The proposed creation of a world criminal court may yet make it possible to put teeth in the Genocide Convention.

The impact of Nazi genocide on Jewish religious thought has been profound. Judaism teaches that God's covenant with His chosen people, the Jews, assures them a special place in the working out of the divine plan. But where was the merciful, loving, and omnipotent God during the Holocaust? A survivor's loss of faith as a consequence of Nazi genocide is dramatized in **Elie Wiesel's** semiautobiographical novel, *Night*.

The shattering of belief entered Jewish theological discourse with Richard L. Rubenstein's 1966 book *After Auschwitz: Radical Theology and Contemporary Judaism*. It boldly stated that after Auschwitz belief in a covenanted God of history was no longer possible. To believe in such a God was to accept that

Hitler did His will and that the Jews were punished for their sins. Rubenstein concluded that the post-Holocaust era was the time of the death of God, by which he meant that the thread connecting God and man had been broken.

Less radical Jewish theologians have attempted to reassert belief in God's presence in history in light of the Holocaust. In *The Face of God after Auschwitz*, Ignaz Maybaum reaffirmed the traditional God of covenant and election by locating the Holocaust within a long history of God-ordained communal disasters. Emil Fackenheim took issue with Maybaum in *To Mend the World*. For him the Holocaust was not divine punishment, but it had shattered the covenant, which needed to be mended and restored. For Jews to abandon Judaism would have the effect of granting Hitler a posthumous victory. Fackenheim went on to argue in *The Jewish Return into History* that the Holocaust had made the creation of the modern state of Israel possible by goading Jews into fighting for their future. Yet another view was advanced by Eliezer Berkovits in *Faith after the Holocaust*, which argued that God limits His own power in order to make history possible. The Holocaust was man's responsibility, not His. These and other post-Holocaust theological debates are analyzed in *(God) after Auschwitz* by Zachary Braiterman.

For Christian thinkers the Holocaust called for a reevaluation of traditional church teachings about Judaism. Both Protestant and Catholic theologians correctly sensed that Christian triumphalism and contempt for the Jews had contributed to the climate of opinion that made genocide possible. Among the first to say so was the French scholar Jules Isaac in *The Teaching of Contempt*. From this point of view Christian **antisemitism** is a medieval intrusion into the faith and essentially foreign to authentic Christianity. Popular beliefs that Christianity had superseded Judaism and that Jewish misery demonstrated God's displeasure with those who rejected Jesus are historical accretions that must be swept away. Returning to biblical Christianity would place Jewish-Christian relations on a solid footing. It was in this spirit that the postwar German churches ultimately came to confront their failure to stand up for the victims of racial persecution under Hitler. This viewpoint also corresponded with the Catholic confrontation with Christian Judeophobia during the reforming pontificate of John XXIII. One of the central documents that emerged from the Second Vatican Council in 1965, *Nostra Aetate*, recognized the common patrimony of Christianity and Judaism and denounced all forms of antisemitism.

Radical Christian theologians consider this approach to be well-meaning but inadequate and conceptually flawed. In their opinion antisemitism is no mere corruption of Christianity but lies at its very heart. Rosemary Ruether subjects the churches to a rigorous ideological critique in *Faith and Fratricide*, in which she locates anti-Judaism at the center of the early Christian move-ment's self-understanding as the "true Israel." Although Jesus himself did not share this anti-Judaism, the argument goes, Christian scripture and doctrine were deeply infected with it from the start. Hence, Ruether concludes, there must be a radical reinterpretation of the gospel to rid Christianity of its pro-found anti-Jewish bias. A similar conclusion is to be found in Franklin H. Lit-tell's *The Crucifixion of the Jews,* which argues that Christian antisemitism is firmly rooted in the myth that Christianity displaced Judaism as the one true religion.

SCHOLARS AND STUDENTS

The earliest scholarly studies of the Holocaust concentrated on detailing events and demonstrating responsibility. More recently historians and scholars in related fields have turned their attention to establishing the place of the Holocaust in the wider sweep of modern history and determining its meaning for the present and the future. Was the Holocaust "unique" and hence an "in-comparable crime," or should it be compared to other instances of **genocide** before and since? Was the Holocaust an expression of the modern world's ca-pacity for rationally planned mass murder, or was it a regression to barbarism?

The first of these questions is posed by Steven T. Katz in the first volume of a proposed three-volume set, *The Holocaust in Historical Perspective.* Katz's an-swer is unequivocal: the Holocaust, which he limits to the Jewish victims, was the only instance of true genocide in world history and hence unique. Defin-ing genocide as the deliberate, systematic and total physical annihilation of a specific people, Katz argues that the Germans set out to eliminate the biolog-ical stock of the Jews alone. Their other racial targets were subjected to only unsystematic and partial annihilation. The same was true of all other cases of mass murder. Katz argues that the Holocaust of the Jews was the only case of one group of people intentionally setting out to kill all members of some other group. The critical issue is not the absolute numbers of victims or the propor-tion of the victim group that was killed — Katz admits that other historical atrocities rival the Holocaust in those categories. What makes the Holocaust unique is that the Jews alone were targeted for the extermination of every man, woman, and child. That was not true of the mass murders of Native Ameri-cans, Armenians, Gypsies, Ukrainians, Poles, Cambodians, or any other group, Katz maintains.

Other scholars reject this view. To say that something is "unique" denotes that it is one of a kind. But who can say that there will never again be a deliberate attempt to eradicate every single member of some ethnic group? "Unprecedented" might be a better word, inasmuch as it is easier to argue that the Holocaust was the first planned attempt to murder all members of a condemned group. But not everyone is prepared to go even that far. Some scholars believe that such groups as the Native Americans and Armenians were also intentionally subjected to mass murder. And, as we have seen, there are those who would include Gypsies and the handicapped along with the Jews as targets for extermination in the Holocaust. Moreover, these criticisms continue, there is no incontrovertible evidence that the Germans wanted to kill every single Jew. After all, they were often willing to let some Jews get away if it would profit them, most dramatically in their offer to spare 1,000,000 Jews in the "blood for trucks" offer of 1944. The critics are obviously uncomfortable with what they view as attempts to privilege the Holocaust above other cases of modern genocide. A generous sampling of their views appears in a collection edited by Alan S. Rosenbaum, *Is the Holocaust Unique? Perspectives on Comparative Genocide.*

German scholars have debated the uniqueness or comparability of the Holocaust in especially acrimonious tones. In what is known as the *Historikerstreit* (historians' dispute), they divided over whether the Holocaust has a claim to special horror among all the atrocities of the twentieth century. Beginning in the 1970s a few conservative German historians, including Ernst Nolte, Andreas Hillgruber, and Michael Stürmer, began to argue that entirely too much attention was being paid to the Holocaust to the exclusion of other genocidal acts, resulting in one-sided condemnation of German crimes. Nolte and others maintained that Stalin taught Hitler about mass murder when he annihilated millions of peasants and political dissenters during the 1930s. Hillgruber compared the Soviet orgy of revenge against German civilians at the end of the war directly to the Final Solution, and thereby joined Nolte in relativizing the Nazi policy of genocide toward the Jews. Placing the Holocaust in a larger, comparative context, these historians argued, did not excuse Nazi genocide but rather demonstrated that it was only one of many monstrous acts of mass murder. The dispute broke into the open spectacularly in 1986 when the German philosopher Jürgen Habermas, supported by liberal historians, accused the conservative scholars of advancing an apologetic revisionism designed to revive German nationalism. Denying the uniquely barbaric nature of the Holocaust, they feared, would encourage Germans to distance themselves from historical responsibility. The outlines of the *Historikerstreit* are judiciously laid out by Charles S. Maier in *The Unmasterable Past: History,*

Holocaust, and German National Identity. The dispute continues in abated form to this day.

The question about whether the Holocaust is best viewed as an aspect of or a revolt against modernism has set off fewer fireworks, but it is equally crucial in setting the Holocaust in a larger context. If, as is frequently argued, Nazi genocide represents regression to barbarism and hence should be regarded as an irrational revolt against modern science and ethics, one may doubt its recurrence short of a catastrophic takeover by a Nazi-style radical right-wing movement. On the other hand, if the Holocaust was no aberration but belongs to the very mainstream of modernity, genocide on a massive scale may have a more promising future.

The former view that links antisemitism and the Holocaust to a revolt against liberal, bourgeois modernity is advanced in two classic books: George Mosse's *The Crisis of German Ideology* and Ernst Nolte's *Three Faces of Fascism.* Both view Nazi ideology as a radical rejection of the basic values and moral foundations of Western civilization. The Jews had to die because they were symbols of the liberalism and rootless modernity that Hitler and his followers considered fundamental causes of Germany's social and political agony.

Richard L. Rubenstein was among the first to express the contrary opinion. In *The Cunning of History* he argued that the Holocaust expressed some of the most significant tendencies of twentieth-century Western civilization. These include the nature of modern warfare, the expansion of state power, and the organizational methods of modern corporate enterprises. Genocide, Rubenstein concluded, is well within the capacity of any modern state and will become ever more a temptation as expanding populations push against limited resources. A similar view was advanced by Zygmunt Bauman in *Modernity and the Holocaust.* The Holocaust was not an exceptional historical event representing regression to barbarism, he maintains. It was a central event in modern history that was made possible by modern science and the rational bureaucratic organization of industrial society. These not only provided the means and justification to commit genocide, but they also offered a modern substitute morality that valued organizational discipline more highly than ethical responsibility. George Mosse came to embrace at least some of these arguments in *Nationalism and Sexuality.* There he portrays Nazism as an expression of modern middle-class morality corrupted by extreme nationalism and hence intolerant of outsiders such as Jews, Gypsies, and "cripples."

The most controversial version of the "Holocaust as modernism" argument is advanced by the German scholars Götz Aly and Susanne Heim. Their study of Third Reich economic planners involved in the **Final Solution** portrays them as motivated by cold economic logic rather than irrational racism. Excluding Jews from the German economy gave jobs to Germans. Exploiting **forced labor** saved vast sums for the Reich, and killing the "surplus" population saved it even more. Hence, Aly and Heim conclude, the Holocaust was a vast program of capitalist socioeconomic modernization. In comparing it to the massive loss of life that accompanied Stalin's modernizing Five Year Plans in the Soviet Union, they align themselves with those who downplay the "unique" characteristics of the Final Solution. Aly and Heim summarize many of their conclusions in English in "The Economics of the Final Solution: A Case Study from the General Government," in *Simon Wiesenthal Center Annual* (1988).

The arguments of Rubenstein, Bauman, Aly, and Heim have stimulated much discussion. Critics such as Michael Burleigh and Wolfgang Wippermann in *The Racial State* accuse them of ignoring Nazi ideology and the domination of political leadership over economic planners in the Third Reich. The critics also note that premodern societies, such as Turkey before World War I and more recently Cambodia and Rwanda, have been the scenes of genocide. Finally, they note that modernization theories of the Holocaust fail to account for the choice of victims; why did the Germans not set out to kill all the Poles rather than the Jews and Gypsies?

Scholarly interest in the Holocaust has been matched or exceeded by public fascination with the subject. This is indicated by the proliferation of books, high school and college courses, and museums, research institutes, and memorials dedicated to the Holocaust. Apart from the natural curiosity that people feel when contemplating monstrous human evil, this popular interest may betray unease over racial and ethnic tensions that continue to cause strife in many parts of the world and a realization that what could happen once could happen again. Many people also sense that some of the distinctive (and perhaps indispensable) features of our modern world — bureaucracy, technology, nationalism, and secularism — are revealed by the Holocaust as latent threats to the future of our civilization. The potential for abusing public interest in the Holocaust through oversimplification, vulgarization, or downright misrepresentation is explored in Judith Miller's *One, by One, by One: Facing the Holocaust.*

Debates such as the ones summarized in this section and those preceding it are signs of deepening interest in the Holocaust and healthy indications of determination to learn more. Given the complexity of Nazism and the Holocaust and the many approaches that scholars take to them, there is good reason to believe that such debates will continue indefinitely. To learn from them requires an open mind and a willingness to read and think deeply about the Holocaust. The resources guide that concludes this volume is designed to assist in that quest.

PART III

Chronology

Chronology

1918

November 11   The armistice ending World War I is signed.

1919

January 9   The German Workers' Party (Deutsche Arbeiterpartei or DAP) is founded in Munich.

June 28   German representatives sign the Treaty of Versailles.

July 31   The constitution of the Weimar Republic is adopted.

September 12   Adolf Hitler attends his first meeting of the German Workers' Party.

November 13   Adolf Hitler becomes the chief speaker and propagandist for the German Workers' Party.

1920

February 24   The German Workers' Party (DAP) announces its 25 Point Program. Soon after, the party changes its name to the National Socialist German Workers' Party (Nationalsozialistische Deutsche Arbeiterpartei or NSDAP).

December 17   The NSDAP acquires the newspaper *Völkischer Beobachter*.

1921

July 29   Adolf Hitler becomes chairman of the Nazi Party with dictatorial powers.

August 3   The formation of the SA (Sturmabteilungen) is announced in the *Völkischer Beobachter*.

1923

March   The SS (Schutzstaffel) is created as Hitler's personal bodyguard.

November 9   In their famous "Beer Hall" Putsch, the Nazis fail to seize

control of the Bavarian government. The Nazi Party is
banned in Bavaria.

1924

February 26	Hitler stands trial for the Beer Hall Putsch.
April 1	Hitler is convicted of high treason and sentenced to five years' detention and a fine of two hundred gold marks.
April 9	The Dawes Plan provides for American loans and German economic reforms to revive the German economy and resume German reparation payments.
December 20	Hitler's sentence is commuted and he is released from the Landsberg fortress.

1925

February 26	The Nazi Party is reinstated in Bavaria.
April 26	Field Marshal von Hindenburg becomes president of the Weimar Republic.
July 18	The first volume of *Mein Kampf* is published in Munich.
October 5–16	At the Locarno Conference, Germany, France, Belgium, Great Britain and Italy guarantee the German-French and the German-Belgian borders.

1926

September 8	Germany enters the League of Nations as a permanent member of the League Council.
December 10	The second volume of *Mein Kampf* is published in Munich.

1928

May 28	In Reichstag elections, the Nazis receive 2.8 percent of the vote and twelve seats in the German parliament.

1929

January 6	Heinrich Himmler is appointed Reich Leader of the SS (Reichsführer-SS).
June 7	The Young Plan is signed, reorganizing German reparations payments.

October 3   Gustav Stresemann, Germany's foreign minister and former chancellor, dies.

1930

January 23   Wilhelm Frick, appointed minister for domestic affairs and popular education in Thuringia, becomes the first Nazi minister in a state government.

April 27   Joseph Goebbels is appointed Nazi propaganda chief.

September 14   The Nazis receive 18 percent of the votes in Reichstag elections and 107 seats, making the NSDAP the second-largest party in the German parliament.

December 31   The SS creates the Race and Settlement Main Office (Rasse- und Siedlungshauptamt or RuSHA).

1931

January 5   Ernst Röhm is appointed chief of staff of the Stürmabteilungen (SA).

September 18   Japanese forces invade Manchuria.

October 11   The Harzburg front, a right-wing coalition including the conservative German Nationalists and the Nazis, is established in opposition to the Weimar Republic.

1932

January 27   In a speech to the Industrie-Club in Düsseldorf, Hitler blames the economic crisis in Germany on Weimar democracy and cites Germany's need for greater "living space" (*Lebensraum*) in Europe as the only solution to its economic problems.

February 25   Hitler obtains German citizenship.

March 13   Hitler receives 30.2 percent of the popular vote to Hindenburg's 49.5 percent in the first ballot of the presidential elections.

April 10   In the second ballot of the presidential elections Hitler receives 36.6 percent of the vote to 52.9 percent for Hindenburg, who wins a second term.

July 31   The Nazis receive almost 38 percent of the vote in Reichstag elections and 230 seats, making the NSDAP the largest party in the German parliament.

November 6   In new Reichstag elections, the Nazis receive 33 percent of the vote. Their seats decline from 230 to 196, but the Nazis remain the largest party.

1933

January 30   President von Hindenburg appoints Adolf Hitler Reich Chancellor. Hitler and the Nazis enter into a coalition government with the conservative German National Peoples' Party (DNVP).

February 22   As Interior Minister in Prussia, Hermann Göring authorizes the use of SA and SS men as auxiliary police.

February 27   The Reichstag in Berlin is set on fire. The Nazis arrest a Dutch communist and claim a communist revolution is imminent.

February 28   President von Hindenburg grants Hitler emergency powers with the "Decree for the Protection of the People and the State." Civil rights in Germany are suspended.

March 5   In Reichstag elections the Nazis win 44 percent of the vote and 288 seats in parliament.

March 13   Joseph Goebbels becomes a member of the cabinet as Reich Minister for Public Enlightenment and Propaganda (Reichsminister für Volksaufklärung und Propaganda).

March 20   The first major concentration camp is opened at Dachau near Munich.

March 24   The Reichstag passes the "Law for Removing the Distress of the People and the Reich," also known as the Enabling Law, by an overwhelming majority, allowing Hitler to rule by decree for four years.

March 28   The Fulda Conference of (Catholic) Bishops gives tentative approval for German Catholics to support Hitler's government.

April 1   The Nazi regime orchestrates a one-day boycott of Jewish businesses throughout Germany.

April 7   The "Law for the Reestablishment of the Professional Civil Service" begins the process of removing Jews from the civil service in Germany. War veterans are exempted.
The "Law Concerning Admission to the Legal Profession" places restrictions on Jewish lawyers and judges in Germany. War veterans are exempted.

April 22	The "Decree Regarding Physicians' Services with the National Health Service" bars payment of medical bills by national health insurance for Aryans who consult Jewish doctors. War veterans are exempted.
April 25	The "Law against the Overcrowding of German Schools" places quotas on the number of Jewish students in institutions of higher education.
April 26	The Secret State Police (Geheimstaatspolizei or Gestapo) is consolidated in Berlin.
May 10–11	Books written by Jews and others deemed objectionable by the Nazis are burned publicly throughout Germany.
May 11	The Ministry of Economics issues the "Decree for the Protection of Retail Trade" stipulating that the anti-Jewish clauses of legislation passed in April do not apply to commercial activities.
June 22	The Social Democratic Party (SPD) is banned in Germany.
June 27	The Conservative Party (DNVP), Hitler's coalition partner, dissolves itself.
July 5	The Catholic Center Party dissolves itself.
July 14	The "Denaturalization Law" allows the Reich government to revoke the citizenship of anyone who settled in Germany after November 9, 1918. Beginning on July 26, it is used against some of the more than 100,000 East European Jews living in Germany, and against Gypsies.

The "Law against the Establishment of Parties" declares the Nazi Party to be the only legal political party in Germany.

The "Law for the Prevention of Progeny of Sufferers from Hereditary Diseases" introduces compulsory sterilization of some categories of the mentally and physically handicapped and Gypsies in Germany. |
July 20	Nazi Germany and the Vatican sign a Concordat guaranteeing the rights of the Catholic Church in Germany.
August 25	German officials and Zionist representatives from Germany and Palestine sign the "Haavara Transfer Agreement." Jews emigrating from Germany to Palestine are permitted to take with them a small portion of their assets in the form of German goods.
September 17	German Jewish leaders establish the Reich Representation of German Jews (Reichsvertretung der deutschen Juden), uniting major Jewish organizations to deal with Nazi policies and

their impact on Jews in Germany. Its name is changed to the Reich Representation of Jews in Germany (Reichsvertretung der Juden in Deutschland) in 1935 in compliance with the Nuremberg Racial Laws.

September 22   The "Law Creating a Reich Chamber of Culture" effectively removes Jews from German cultural life and the media.

October 14   Germany withdraws from the Disarmament Conference and the League of Nations.

November 12   In Reichstag elections in which the NSDAP is the only legal political party, the Nazis win 92 percent of the vote. In a simultaneous referendum, 95 percent of those participating express their approval of the regime.

1934

January 26   Nazi Germany signs a nonaggression treaty with Poland.

January 30   The "Law for the Reorganization of the Reich" transforms Germany from a federal to a unitary state.

June 30   In the "Night of the Long Knives," Hitler orders the murder of Ernst Röhm and other SA leaders, along with other political rivals. The SS carries out the operation with the support of the German army. As a political force, the SA is neutralized.

July 20   The SS becomes independent of the SA within the framework of the NSDAP.

July 25   Austrian Nazis assassinate Chancellor Engelbert Dollfuss in an unsuccessful attempt to seize power.

August 2   President von Hindenburg dies, and Hitler combines the offices of president and chancellor into the new office of "Führer and Reich Chancellor."

August 19   In a plebiscite on Hitler's new powers, 89.9 percent of those voting approve.

August 20   Public officials and members of the armed forces are required to swear an oath of loyalty to Adolf Hitler.

1935

January 13   The Saarland is returned to Germany.

March 16   Hitler repudiates the military clauses of the Versailles Treaty by reintroducing conscription and announcing the expansion of the German army to thirty-six divisions.

April 11	Britain, France, and Italy announce in Stresa their determination to protect the independence of Austria.
May 2	France concludes a mutual assistance pact with the Soviet Union.
May 21	The "Military Service Law" excludes Jews from serving in the German army.
June 18	Germany and England sign the Anglo-German Naval Pact, allowing the Germans to rebuild a navy up to 35 percent of the British navy in strength, and a submarine force equal to that of the British.
June 25	The "Sterilization Law" of July 14, 1933, is amended to permit abortions on the "eugenically unfit."
September 15	The Nuremberg Racial Laws are announced at the Party Rally in Nuremberg. The "Law for the Protection of German Blood and Honor" outlaws marriage and sexual intercourse between Jews and non-Jews in Germany, while the "Reich Citizenship Law" places German Jews in a lower citizenship category. The laws are also applied to Gypsies and blacks after November 26, 1935.
October 3	Italy invades Ethiopia.
November 14	The first supplementary decree to the "Reich Citizenship Law" of September 15, 1935, defines a Jew as someone with at least three full Jewish grandparents, or someone with two Jewish grandparents and married to a Jew or an adherent of Judaism. Jewish veterans exempted from earlier anti-Jewish laws lose their exemptions.
December 31	Jews remaining in the German civil service are dismissed.

1936

March 7	Hitler repudiates the Versailles and Locarno Treaties as German troops occupy the demilitarized Rhineland.
June 5	The Central Office to Combat the Gypsy Menace (Zentralstelle zur Bekämpfung des Zigeunerwesens) is established in Munich.
June 17	Hitler consolidates all police agencies in Germany under the SS and appoints Heinrich Himmler Reich Leader of the SS and Chief of the German Police (Reichsführer-SS und Chef der deutschen Polizei).

July 16	Police arrest 600 Gypsies in Berlin before the Olympic Games and incarcerate them in a Gypsy camp in the Berlin suburb of Marzahn.
July 18	Civil War breaks out in Spain as right-wing officers under General Francisco Franco rebel against the Spanish republic.
August 1–16	The Olympic Games take place in Berlin.
September 9	At the Nuremberg Party rally, Hitler announces a Four-Year Plan for the German economy to make the German economy and armed forces ready for war within four years. All Jews are made liable for any damage by individual Jews to the German economy.
October 25	Germany and Italy establish the Rome-Berlin Axis.
November 25	Germany and Japan sign the Anti-Comintern Pact.

1937

March 21	Pope Pius XI issues the papal encyclical *Mit brennender Sorge* (*With Deep Anxiety*), which condemns racism and Nazi persecution of the Catholic Church.
July 7	Japanese forces invade northern China.
July 16	The concentration camp at Buchenwald is opened.
November 5	In a meeting in the Reich Chancellery, Hitler announces to military and civilian leaders his intention to annex Austria, destroy Czechoslovakia, and conquer "living space" (*Lebensraum*) for Germany in Europe.
November 6	Italy joins Germany and Japan in the Anti-Comintern Pact.
December 11	Italy withdraws from the League of Nations.
December 14	Himmler decrees that persons deemed "asocial" but not guilty of criminal acts can be arrested. The decree is applied to Gypsies.

1938

February 4	Hitler assumes direct command of the German Armed Forces.
March 12	The German army marches into Austria and the formal union (Anschluss) of Austria with Germany takes place.
March 28	The Nazi regime revokes the official status of all Jewish communities in Germany.

April 10   A plebiscite is held in Austria. 99.75 percent vote in favor of union with Germany.

April 26   The "Decree Regarding Registration of Jewish Property" requires all Jews in Germany to register their assets, domestic and foreign, in excess of 5,000 Reichsmarks. A directive is issued for the expropriation of Jewish property in Austria.

May 16   Prisoners begin working in the quarries at Mauthausen.

May 20   Hitler sends the German army the draft of a plan for an attack on Czechoslovakia.

June 13–18   "Gypsy Clean-up Week" is declared in Germany. One thousand Gypsies are arrested and sent to concentration camps at Dachau, Buchenwald, Sachsenhausen, and Lichtenburg.

July 6   Racially mixed marriages can be legally annulled in Germany.

July 6–15   Thirty-two nations attend an international conference on refugees at Evian-les-Bains. They fail to agree on action to solve the Jewish refugee crisis.

July 8   The Great Synagogue in Munich is torn down.

August 17   In Germany, Jewish men are required to add "Israel" to their names, and Jewish women "Sarah" to theirs.

August 26   Adolf Eichmann of the Security Service [SD] of the SS opens the Central Office for Jewish Emigration (Zentralstelle für jüdische Auswanderung) in Vienna.

September 2–3   Italy announces that foreign Jews can no longer establish residence in Italy or its possessions. Those living in Italy must leave within six months. Jews nationalized after January 1, 1919, lose their Italian citizenship.

September 15   Neville Chamberlain meets Hitler at Berchtesgaden in Bavaria to discuss the crisis over the Sudetenland.

September 22   Neville Chamberlain meets again with Hitler at Bad Godesberg in the Rhineland to discuss changes in Hitler's demands in the Sudeten crisis.

September 27   Jews are prohibited from practicing law in Germany.

September 29–30   Germany, Great Britain, France, and Italy sign the Munich Agreement approving Germany's peaceful annexation of the Sudetenland.

September 30   The Nazi regime revokes the licenses of Jewish physicians in Germany.

October 5	German Jews are required to have their passports marked with the letter **J** *(Jude)*.
October 6	Germany officially annexes the Sudetenland. Slovakia becomes autonomous.
October 8	The Hlinka Guard, a right-wing, antisemitic, nationalist militia, is created in autonomous Slovakia.
October 28	Almost 17,000 stateless (mostly Polish) Jews are expelled from Germany to Poland.
November 6	Herschel Grynszpan, a Jewish student in Paris whose parents are among the Jews deported from Germany on October 28, fatally shoots the Third Secretary of the German Embassy in Paris, Ernst vom Rath.
November 9–10	The Crystal Night (Kristallnacht) pogrom takes place throughout Germany and Austria following Herschel Grynszpan's assassination of Ernst vom Rath. Some 30,000 Jews in Germany are interned in concentration camps, and 91 are killed. Hundreds of Jewish stores, homes, and synagogues are damaged or destroyed.
November 12	Following Crystal Night, the German government imposes a fine of 1 billion Reichsmarks on the Jews of Greater Germany.
November 15	Any Jewish pupils remaining in German schools are expelled.
November 17	Italy announces racial laws prohibiting intermarriage between Italians and Jews, restricting Jewish economic activity, and defining who is a Jew.
November 18	Jews are excluded from all public assistance in Germany, effective January 1, 1939.
December 8	Himmler issues a decree "Fighting the Gypsy Plague" in which he defines the Gypsy problem as a racial one.

1939

January 1	The "Law Excluding Jews from Commercial Enterprises" takes effect, forcing Jewish businesses to close.
January 24	The Reich Central Office for Jewish Emigration (Reichszentrale für jüdische Auswanderung) is opened in Berlin, centralizing all authority over Jewish emigration from Greater Germany in the hands of the SS.
January 30	Hitler speaks to the Reichstag, threatening the annihilation of the Jews in Europe in the event of a war.

March 1 Gypsies are classified as either racially "pure" or "mixed" (*Mischlinge*).

March 2 Cardinal Eugenio Pacelli becomes Pope Pius XII.

March 14 Slovakia declares independence.

March 15 German forces occupy Bohemia and Moravia and immediately arrest Jews, German émigrés, and Czech intellectuals.

March 16 Hitler signs a decree establishing the Protectorate of Bohemia and Moravia in the former Czech lands of Czechoslovakia.

March 22 Germany annexes the Lithuanian territory of Memel (Klaipeda).

March 31 Great Britain and France guarantee the sovereignty and territorial integrity of Poland.

April 3 Hitler orders German armed forces to prepare for an attack on Poland to begin some time after September 1.

April 7 Italy invades Albania.

May 15 A concentration camp for women is opened at Ravensbrück, north of Berlin.

May 17 The British White Paper on Palestine establishes a limit of 75,000 Jewish immigrants over the next five years, subject to the wishes of the (Arab) majority.

May 22 Nazi Germany and Fascist Italy forge a military alliance known as the Pact of Steel.

July 4 The Reich Association of Jews in Germany (Reichsvereinigung der Juden in Deutschland) is officially established, replacing the Reich Representation of Jews in Germany (Reichsvertretung der Juden in Deutschland).

August 18 The Reich Interior Ministry requires midwives and physicians to report newborns, infants, and children under three with physical and mental handicaps.

August 23 German Foreign Minister Joachim von Ribbentrop and Soviet Foreign Minister Viacheslav Molotov sign the Nazi-Soviet Pact in Moscow, which includes economic cooperation, a nonaggression pact, and the division of eastern Europe into German and Soviet spheres.

September 1 Germany invades Poland and World War II in Europe begins. A curfew is imposed on Jews in Germany.

The Nazi program to exterminate the physically and mentally handicapped in Germany formally begins as physicians are empowered to determine which of the incurably sick are to be killed.

September 3 Great Britain and France declare war on Germany.

September 6–8 German forces occupy Kraków, Łódź, Radom, and Tarnów.

September 17 In conjunction with the terms of the Nazi-Soviet Pact, Soviet forces enter eastern Poland.

September 21 Reinhard Heydrich orders the expulsion of Poles, Jews, and Gypsies from the Polish territories to be incorporated into the Reich (Danzig, West Prussia, Posen, and eastern Upper Silesia). In the rest of German-occupied Poland, Jews from the countryside are ordered concentrated in ghettos in the major cities. Smaller Jewish communities (under 500 inhabitants) are to be dissolved and absorbed by Jewish communities in the nearest large cities. The Reich Interior Ministry requires all asylums and clinics in Germany that treat the handicapped to register with the state.

September 23 Jews in Germany are forbidden to own radios.

September 27 Heinrich Himmler orders the amalgamation of the State Security Police (Gestapo and criminal police) and the Security Service (SD) of the SS to form the Reich Security Main Office (Reichssicherheitshauptamt or RSHA) under Reinhard Heydrich.

September 28 In a revision of the Nazi-Soviet Pact, Germany receives the district of Lublin and the eastern part of the Warsaw district in Eastern Poland, and turns over Lithuania to the Soviet Union. Reinhard Heydrich orders the expulsion of Gypsies from Polish territories to be incorporated into the Reich into what will soon become the General Government of Poland.

October 8 Nazi authorities establish the first ghetto in Poland, in Piotrków Trybunalski.

October 12 Hitler decrees the creation of a civilian administration in Polish territories not incorporated into the Reich, known as the General Government (Generalgouvernement). Hans Frank is appointed Governor General.

October 16 The Germans designate Kraków as capital of the General Government in Poland.

October 17 Gypsies and part-Gypsies not already interned in camps are forbidden to change their registered domiciles.

October 18	The first trainloads of Jews from Austria and the Protectorate of Bohemia and Moravia arrive in Nisko in the Lublin district of Poland as part of the short-lived plan to concentrate Jews from the Reich on a Jewish Reservation (Judenreservat) in the Lublin area.
October 26	Governor General Hans Frank issues a decree imposing compulsory labor on the Jewish population of the General Government in Poland.
November 12	German authorities begin the deportation of the Jews from Łódź, recently annexed to the Reich and renamed Litzmannstadt, to other parts of Poland.
November 15	The Germans begin the destruction of synagogues in Łódź.
November 23	Jews above the age of ten living in the General Government in Poland are required to wear a Star of David on a white armband.
November 28	German authorities enact laws governing the establishment of Jewish Councils (Judenräte) in the General Government in Poland.
November 30	Soviet forces invade Finland.
December 1	The Jewish Agency for Palestine proposes to the British government that Palestinian Jews form a separate Jewish fighting force under British command.
December 11	Jews are forbidden to change their domicile without permission.

1940

January 4	The first gassing of disabled patients takes place at the Brandenburg asylum.
January 30	The decision is made that all Gypsies are to be expelled from Germany to occupied Poland.
February 8	German authorities order the establishment of a ghetto in Łódź.
March 11	Jews are excluded from special allocations of foodstuffs, but receive the same normal rations as other Germans. Ration cards for Jews are stamped with a **J**.
March 24	Göring issues a directive temporarily halting the deportation of Jews from German-annexed Polish territories to the General Government.

April 9	Germany invades Denmark and Norway.
April 27	Himmler orders the establishment of a concentration camp at Auschwitz.
April 30	The Germans seal off the Łódź ghetto.
	Rudolf Höss begins work as commandant of Auschwitz.
May 10	Germany launches its western offensive against the Low Countries and France.
	Neville Chamberlain resigns as British prime minister and is replaced by Winston Churchill.
May 18	2,800 Gypsies are deported from Germany to Lublin in the General Government in Poland.
May 26	The evacuation of British and Allied troops at Dunkirk begins.
June 10	Italy enters the war as Germany's ally.
June 14	German troops enter Paris.
	The first prisoners, more than 700 Poles, arrive at Auschwitz.
June 15–16	Soviet forces occupy the Baltic states.
June 22	France surrenders and signs an armistice with Germany.
June 24	France and Italy sign an armistice.
July 3	The German Foreign Ministry recommends a territorial solution to the Jewish question in which all Jews would leave Europe as part of a peace settlement. Madagascar is suggested as a destination.
July 9	The German bombing campaign against England begins.
July 19	The Nazi regime confiscates all telephones from Jews in Germany.
July 31	In a meeting with military and naval chiefs at Berchtesgaden, Hitler orders preliminary plans for an invasion of the Soviet Union.
August 3	Hungary annexes northern Transylvania.
August 15	Adolf Eichmann produces a plan to settle 4,000,000 European Jews on the island of Madagascar.
September 14	Hitler postpones the invasion of England.
September 27	Germany, Italy, and Japan sign the Tripartite Pact.
October 3	The Vichy government in France enacts the first "Jewish Law" (Statut des Juifs).
October 12	The Warsaw ghetto is established.
October 22–23	The Jews of southwestern Germany are expelled to the Gurs transit camp in France.

November 15 The Warsaw ghetto is sealed.

December 18 Hitler issues a military directive for Operation Barbarossa, the invasion of the Soviet Union, to commence on May 15, 1941.

1941

March 1 Bulgaria officially joins Germany, Italy, and Japan in the Tripartite Pact.

Himmler inspects Auschwitz and orders the expansion of the camp.

March 3 German authorities order the creation of a ghetto in Kraków.

March 13 The SS is assigned special tasks, independent of Wehrmacht authority, regarding the civilian population in the invasion of Russia.

March 29 A General Commissariat for Jewish Affairs (Commissariat General aux Questions Juives) is established by the Vichy government in France with German support.

March 30 Hitler orders his generals to conduct a war of destruction (Vernichtungskrieg) in Russia, including the extermination of communist civilian and military leaders.

April 6 The German army simultaneously invades Yugoslavia and Greece.

April 7 The Jews of Radom are moved into two ghettos.

April 9 German forces occupy Salonika.

April 10 Germany and Italy create an independent Croatia.

April 24 German authorities seal the Lublin ghetto.

May 11 Rudolf Hess, Hitler's deputy, flies to Scotland in what he terms a "peace mission."

May 20 The Germans stop all Jewish emigration from Belgium and France.

June 2 Vichy France enacts a second Jewish Law.

June 17 Einsatzgruppen commanders receive orders to exterminate Jews during the invasion of the USSR.

June 22 Operation Barbarossa, the Axis invasion of the Soviet Union, begins.

June 23 SS Einsatzgruppen units begin exterminating Jews and Gypsies in the Soviet Union.

June 26 The German army enters Białystok. Part of the Jewish quarter is burned down immediately and hundreds of Jews die when they are locked in a burning synagogue.

June 27	Hungary joins the Axis and enters the war.
June 28	German forces occupy Minsk.
June 30–July 1	German forces take Riga and L'vov.
July 6	In reaction to the program to exterminate the handicapped, a pastoral letter from the Fulda Conference of Catholic Bishops condemning the killing of innocent human beings is read from the pulpits of Catholic churches throughout Germany.
July 11	A ghetto is established for the Jews in Kovno, Lithuania.
July 20	German authorities establish a Jewish ghetto in Minsk.
July 21	Romanian forces occupy Bessarabia and join SS Einsatzgruppe D and German army units in the mass murder of more than 150,000 Jews by the end of August.
July 24	A Jewish ghetto is established in Kishinev in Bessarabia.
July 25–27	In two days of violence known as the Petliura days, Ukrainians in L'vov stage a pogrom and kill about 2,000 Jews.
July 31	In a letter hand-delivered to Reinhard Heydrich, Hermann Göring conveys Hitler's instructions to the SS to devise a comprehensive plan for the total solution (*Gesamtlösung*) to the Jewish question in Europe. The term *Endlösung* (Final Solution) derives from this instruction.
August 1	Eastern Galicia, with its capital L'vov, is separated from the rest of the Ukraine and becomes the fifth district in the General Government in Poland. Nazi authorities establish a Jewish ghetto in Białystok.
August 3	Cardinal August Count von Galen, the Roman Catholic Bishop of Münster, condemns Nazi extermination of the handicapped.
August 5–7	Thousands of Jews are murdered in Pinsk.
August 14	Roosevelt and Churchill sign the Atlantic Charter.
August 23	Himmler issues a directive ordering a halt to all Jewish emigration.
August 24	Hitler calls a halt to the killing of handicapped persons in Germany.
August 31–September 3	Some 8,000 Jews are murdered in Vilna.
September 1	The Jews in Greater Germany are ordered to wear the yellow badge as of September 19.
September 3	About 900 people, mostly Russian prisoners of war, are gassed with Zyklon B at Auschwitz.
September 6	The Germans establish two Jewish ghettos in Vilna. More than 40,000 Jews in Vilna are killed by the end of 1941.

September 15   In Holland, German authorities confiscate most Jewish assets, and Jews are banned from appearing in public places.
Germany and Romania begin transporting some 150,000 Jews from Bessarabia and Bukovina to Transnistria, where about 90,000 are killed.

September 18   Himmler informs officials in the Warthegau that Hitler has decided to deport all remaining Jews from Greater Germany to the east by the end of the year.

September 29–30   SS Einsatzkommando 4A murders more than 33,000 Kiev Jews at Babi Yar.

October 1   The beginning of an "action" (*Aktion*) in which more than 33,000 Vilna Jews and an unknown number of Gypsies are killed by the end of December.

October 8   The Germans liquidate the ghetto at Vitebsk near Smolensk and kill more than 16,000 Jews.

October 10   In Serbia the German army adopts a policy of holding Communists, suspected Communists, and Jews as hostages. One hundred hostages are to be shot for each German soldier killed, and fifty for each German soldier wounded, resulting in the extermination of all male Jews and many Gypsies in Serbia in the fall of 1941.

October 12   The German army reaches the outskirts of Moscow.

October 15   The death penalty is introduced in the General Government for any Jews leaving the ghetto or those assisting them.

October 16   The first trainload of Jews from Greater Germany arrives at the Łódź ghetto. Some 5,000 Gypsies are included in the transports throughout October. German forces take Odessa.

October 23   All Jewish emigration from Germany is prohibited.
In Odessa 19,000 Jews are killed.

October 25   Orders are given for the deportation of Jews from Germany to the ghettos in Riga and Minsk.

November 1   Construction of the Bełzec extermination camp begins.

November 4   Jewish workers in Germany no longer receive sick pay, accident insurance, paid vacations, or pensions, and they can be fired without notice.

November 5–9   5,000 Gypsies deported from Austria arrive in the Łódź ghetto. They are gassed at Chełmno in December 1941 and January 1942.

November 6–7   More than 33,000 Jews are murdered outside Rovno in the Ukraine and near Minsk. Another 20,000 Jews from Minsk are killed two weeks later.

November 8   The second phase of deportations of Jews from Germany to the East begins.

November 20   More than 30,000 Jews are slaughtered for two weeks in the Rombuli forest outside Riga.

November 24   The first Jews from the Protectorate of Bohemia and Moravia arrive in Theresienstadt to establish a concentration camp, reclassified later as a ghetto.

November 25   A supplemental decree to the Reich Citizenship Law authorizes the Reich government to confiscate the property of Jews deported to the East by claiming they lose their German nationality when they move abroad.

November 25, 29   Five trainloads of German Jews are massacred in Kovno, Lithuania, soon after their arrival.

November 29–30   14,000 Jews from Riga and 1,000 Jews from Berlin are shot in the Rombuli forest outside Riga.

December 7   Japanese forces attack the American naval base at Pearl Harbor, bringing the United States into World War II.

December 7–8   The SS opens the first extermination camp at Chełmno near Łódź in the Warthegau, the territory in western Poland incorporated into the Reich.

December 8   Another 13,000 Jews are massacred outside Riga.

December 11   Germany and Italy declare war on the United States.

December 16   Himmler orders the deportation and extermination of all remaining Gypsies in Europe.

1942

January 1   Twenty-six nations sign the United Nations Declaration.

January 13   The St. James Palace declaration on war crimes is announced by representatives of nine governments in exile in London.

January 16   The first Jews and Gypsies are deported from the Lodz ghetto to the extermination camp at Chełmno.

January 20   At a conference in the Wannsee section of Berlin, Reinhard Heydrich and fourteen representatives of the SS, government, and party agencies meet to discuss the implementation of the Final Solution, the plan to exterminate the Jews of Europe.

February 23	The refugee ship *Struma* sinks off the Turkish coast after being refused entry into Palestine. 768 refugees drown.
March 1	Construction begins on the Sobibór extermination camp.
March 2	Some 5,000 Jews are killed in Minsk.
March 10	The Bełzec extermination camp begins killing Jews deported from L'vov.
March 13	Mass gassings of Jews from Upper Silesia begin at Auschwitz-Birkenau.
March 17	Jews from Lublin begin arriving at Bełzec for extermination.
March 26	The deportation of more than 57,000 Jews from Slovakia to extermination camps in Poland begins. Almost 1,000 women from Ravensbrück and another 1,000 Jews from Slovakia arrive in Auschwitz.
March 27	The first Jews are deported from France to Auschwitz.
April 17–18	In the middle of the night the Nazis murder about fifty people in the Warsaw ghetto, including members of the ghetto underground.
April 29	In Holland, Jews are ordered to wear the yellow badge.
April 30	A Jewish ghetto is established in Pinsk.
May 6–11	At the Biltmore conference in New York City, the Zionist movement condemns Nazi atrocities against the Jews of Europe and the British White Paper on Palestine of 1939. The Zionists demand the creation of a Jewish state in Palestine after the war.
May 8	The Dutch embassy in Switzerland reports that Dutch Jews have been killed in Germany in experiments using poison gas.
May 10	About 1,500 Jews are deported from Sosnowiec to Auschwitz.
May 20	The Jewish Agency for Palestine office in Geneva begins reporting that the Germans are pursuing a policy of exterminating the Jews of Europe.
May 27	Czech partisans fatally wound Reinhard Heydrich, Chief of the RSHA and Reich Protector of Bohemia and Moravia, near Prague. Belgian Jews are ordered to wear the yellow badge.
May 28	German authorities begin the deportation of some 6,000 Jews from Kraków to the Bełzec extermination camp.
May 29	Jews in occupied France are required to wear the yellow badge.

June 10	German forces murder all the men and some women in the village of Lidice, Czechoslovakia, in retaliation for the assassination of Reinhard Heydrich.
June 11	Adolf Eichmann informs the German Foreign Ministry that beginning in mid-July Jews from France, Holland, and Belgium are to be transported daily to the East. The Vichy government in France agrees to the deportation of foreign Jews only.
June 15	The deportation of more than 10,000 Jews from Tarnów to Bełzec begins.
June 20	The transport of Jews from Vienna to Theresienstadt begins.
June 22	The first transport from the Drancy transit camp in France leaves for Auschwitz.
July 8	About 7,000 Jews from L'vov are interned at the Janówska labor camp.
July 15	The deportation of Jews from Holland to Auschwitz begins.
July 16–17	More than 42,000 Jews are rounded up throughout France and sent to the Drancy transit camp.
July 17–18	Heinrich Himmler visits Auschwitz. He orders the enlargement of the Birkenau camp (Auschwitz II) and the extermination of Jews and Gypsies unfit for work.
July 19	Himmler orders Operation Reinhard, the liquidation of all ghettos and the extermination of all Jews in the General Government in Poland by the end of the year.
July 22	The Treblinka extermination camp is completed. The first deportations from the Warsaw ghetto to Treblinka begin.
July 23	The mass murder of Jews at Treblinka begins.
July 28	The Jewish Fighting Organization (Zydowska Organizacja Bojowa or ZOB) is created by the Jewish underground in Warsaw.
July 28–30	The majority of German and Austrian Jews in Minsk, about 30,000, are killed.
August 2	The deportation of Jews from Belgium to Auschwitz begins. The first to be deported are stateless Jews.
August 5	The Germans liquidate the smaller ghetto in Radom and send about 6,000 Jews to Treblinka.
August 10–23	German authorities deport some 50,000 Jews from L'vov to Bełzec.

August 13–20   Most Jews in Croatia are deported to Auschwitz.

August 16   The SS liquidates the large ghetto in Radom. Most of the inhabitants are deported to Auschwitz, and about 1,500 who resist deportation are shot.

August 19   The battle of Stalingrad begins.

August 20–24   About 18,000 Jews from Kielce are deported to Treblinka.

August 27   The deportation of about 3,000 Jews from Ternopol to Bełzec begins.

September 7–8   Thousands of Jews are deported from ghettos in Kolomyia and Tarnów to Belzec for extermination.

September 14   The German Sixth Army reaches the suburbs of Stalingrad.

September 26   200 Gypsies are transferred from Buchenwald to Auschwitz to build a Gypsy camp (*Zigeunerlager*) at Birkenau.

October 13   Himmler orders that "pure" Gypsies and some "mixed" Gypsies are exempt from deportation but must remain under supervision.

October 23   The battle of El Alamein in Egypt begins. The British Eighth Army routs Axis forces within two weeks.

October 27   The Germans begin deporting some 7,000 Jews from Kraków to Bełzec.

October 29–November 1   Nazi forces murder most of the Jews in Pinsk.

October 30   Some 800 Jewish prisoners at Auschwitz are transferred to the newly established Buna-Monowitz subcamp to work for I. G. Farben.

November 7–8   Operation Torch, the invasion of North Africa, begins as Allied troops land in Morocco and Algeria.

November 10   A Jewish ghetto is established in L'vov in eastern Galicia.

November 11   German and Italian forces occupy Vichy France in response to the Allied invasion of North Africa.

November 17   Jews in Norway are required to register with the police.

November 20   The first Jews are deported from Norway to Auschwitz. The main deportation from Norway takes place on November 26.

December 4   The Council for Aid to the Jews, code-named Zegota, is founded by Polish and Jewish underground organizations.

December 16   German authorities order the establishment of a Jewish ghetto in Khar'kov in the Ukraine.
Himmler orders the deportation of most Gypsies in Greater Germany to Auschwitz.

December 17   An Allied statement condemns Nazi extermination policies.

December 28   Dr. Carl Clauberg begins sterilization experiments in the medical blocks of the Birkenau women's camp. Dr. Horst Schumann begins the sterilization of men.

1943

January 13   German authorities deport 1,500 Jews from Radom to Auschwitz.

January 14–24   Roosevelt and Churchill meet at Casablanca to discuss the unconditional surrender of Germany.

January 18   Nazi forces try to liquidate the remnants of the Warsaw ghetto but meet with armed resistance. Some 5,000 Jews are killed.

January 25   53 Polish prisoners, mostly officers and intellectuals, are shot in Auschwitz.

February 2   The German Sixth Army at Stalingrad surrenders to Soviet forces.

February 5   In Białystok more than 2,000 Jews are killed and some 10,000 are deported to the Treblinka extermination camp.

February 18   In Munich the police destroy the White Rose student resistance movement and arrest its leaders, including Hans and Sophie Scholl.

February 24   The Jews of Salonika are forced to move into a ghetto.

February 26   The first large transport of Gypsies from Germany arrives at the Gypsy Camp at Auschwitz.

March 14   In Kraków more than 2,000 Jews are deported to Auschwitz and 700 are shot.

March 15   The deportation of Jews from Salonika to Auschwitz begins.

March 17   In L'vov, 1,500 Jews are murdered and some 800 are sent to Auschwitz.

April 13   German propagandists announce the discovery of mass graves at Katyn near Smolensk containing the bodies of thousands of Polish officers massacred by the Soviet Union during the early years of the war.

April 19–30   British and American officials meet on Bermuda to discuss refugee problems and the rescue of European Jews.

April 19–May 16   The Warsaw Ghetto Uprising takes place. German troops destroy the ghetto, and most of the more than 56,000 survivors are sent to Treblinka.

April 30   The Bergen-Belsen concentration camp is opened for Jews holding certain foreign passports to be exchanged for German nationals in Allied hands.

May 5
: The transport of the remaining Jews from Croatia to Auschwitz begins.

May 19
: The German government declares Berlin to be *judenfrei*, free of Jews.

May 23
: Tunis, the last remaining Axis position in North Africa, falls to the Allies.

May 25
: Josef Mengele orders the gassing of more than 1,000 Gypsies suspected of carrying typhus.

June 1
: The SS begins the liquidation of the L'vov ghetto.

June 10
: The Reich Association of Jews in Germany (Reichsvereinigung der Juden in Deutschland) is dissolved.

June 20
: The SS liquidates the ghetto at Ternopol and kills most of the Jews in the city — more than 3,000. Some resist.

July 4–22
: The Battle of Kursk takes place in which the last major German offensive against the Soviet Union fails.

July 9
: Allied forces begin the invasion of Sicily.

July 21
: Heinrich Himmler orders the liquidation of all ghettos in the Reich Commissariat for the East (Reichskommissariat Ostland).

July 25
: Mussolini is dismissed as head of government in Italy and arrested. The Fascist regime is replaced with a military dictatorship under Marshal Badoglio.

August 1
: The SS liquidates the Będzin and Sosnowiec ghettos. Most of their inhabitants are sent to Auschwitz.

August 2
: A prisoner revolt breaks out in the Treblinka extermination camp.

August 16
: The ghetto in Białystok is liquidated despite resistance from the Jewish underground. The deportation of the remaining Białystok Jews occurs through August 21.

September 2
: The ghetto at Tarnów is liquidated and most of its inhabitants are deported to Auschwitz or the Płaszów labor camp.

September 3
: The Allies land in southern Italy. The last Jews of Belgium are deported to the East.

September 6
: The first transport of Jews leaves Theresienstadt for Auschwitz.

September 8
: The government of Marshal Badoglio in Italy surrenders to the Allies.

September 9
: The German army begins the occupation of Italy and the dis-

armament of Italian forces following Italy's surrender to the Allies.

September 11–14   The SS liquidates the ghetto in Minsk and murders most of its inhabitants.

September 23-24   The SS liquidates the ghetto in Vilna.

September 29   The last Jews leave Amsterdam for the Westerbork transit camp.

October 1   German authorities begin arresting Jews in Denmark for deportation. More than 7,000 Danish Jews are smuggled to safety in Sweden.

October 14   Jewish workers at the Sobibór extermination camp stage an uprising.

October 18   The first Jews from Rome are deported to Auschwitz.

November 1   Churchill, Roosevelt, and Stalin issue the Moscow Declaration condemning Nazi atrocities in Europe and promising to prosecute Nazi perpetrators after the war.

November 3   Nazi authorities launch Operation Harvest Festival (Aktion Erntefest), the liquidation of the Jews in the Lublin district at the Poniatowa and Trawniki labor camps and the Majdanek extermination camp. By the end of November the three extermination camps used in Operation Reinhard, Sobibór, Treblinka, and Bełzec, are closed.

November 6   Soviet forces liberate Kiev.

November 9   The United Nations Relief and Rehabilitation Agency (UNRRA) is established to aid refugees in countries liberated from the Axis powers.

November 19   Prisoners at the Janówska labor camp in L'vov revolt, and more than 1,000 are killed.

November 28–December 1   Churchill, Roosevelt and Stalin meet at Teheran.

November 30   German authorities order the concentration of Italian Jews in camps.

1944

January 22   President Roosevelt creates the War Refugee Board.

March 19   With Soviet forces approaching the Hungarian border German forces occupy Hungary.

March 27   Nazi forces murder some 1,800 Jews in Kovno.

March 31   The Hungarian government requires Jews to wear the yellow badge as of April 5.

April 16	Jews in Hungary are forced into ghettos.
April 27	German authorities begin the deportation of Jews from Hungary to Auschwitz.
May 19	Joel Brand, a Hungarian Zionist, arrives in Istanbul from Vienna with an offer from the SS to exchange 1,000,000 Jews for large quantities of food, 10,000 trucks, and German prisoners of war.
June 5	Allied troops enter Rome.
June 6	D-Day. The western Allies land in Normandy in France.
June 17	The Jews in Budapest are confined to specially marked buildings.
July 3	Soviet forces recapture Minsk.
July 8	The Kovno ghetto is liquidated.
July 9	The Hungarian leader Miklós Horthy orders a halt to the deportation of Jews from Hungary to Auschwitz.
July 13	Soviet troops liberate Vilna.
July 15	Britain rejects the German exchange offer made through Joel Brand.
July 20	An assassination attempt against Hitler at his headquarters in East Prussia fails. The conspiracy to overthrow the Nazi regime and end the war is brutally suppressed. Most of the Jews on the Greek island of Corfu are sent to Auschwitz.
July 23	A delegation from the International Red Cross visits the Theresienstadt ghetto.
July 24	The Jews on the Greek island of Rhodes are deported to Auschwitz.
July 25	Soviet forces liberate Lublin and the Majdanek extermination camp.
August 1	The Polish rebellion against the Germans begins in Warsaw.
August 2	The Gypsy camp at Auschwitz is liquidated. Almost 4,000 Gypsies are gassed.
August 15	American forces land in southern France.
August 24	Paris is liberated.
August 25	The regime of Ion Antonescu is overthrown and Romania declares war on Germany.
August 29	The last transport of Jews leaves the Łódź ghetto for Auschwitz.
September 1	Britain rejects the suggestion of the Jewish Agency for Pales-

	tine to bomb the extermination camp at Auschwitz-Birkenau and the rail lines leading to it.
September 3	The last transport of Jews from Holland leaves the Westerbork transit camp for Auschwitz.
October 2	German troops crush the Warsaw Polish uprising.
October 6	The Sonderkommando at the Auschwitz-Birkenau extermination camp revolts.
October 13	Russian troops liberate Riga.
October 15	The government of Miklós Horthy in Hungary announces a truce with the Allies. The Horthy government is overthrown by the fascist Arrow Cross Party with German support.
November 2	The gassings at Auschwitz are stopped.
November 3	The last recorded transport of Jewish prisoners arrives at Auschwitz.
November 5	With the rail connection to Auschwitz cut, Adolf Eichmann begins deporting Jews from Budapest by foot in so-called death marches to Austria.
November 13	The Nazis establish a ghetto in Budapest for Jews without international protection.
November 25	The destruction of the crematoria at Auschwitz to conceal Nazi mass murder from the advancing Russians begins.
December 16	The Battle of the Bulge begins as the German army launches an offensive in the Ardennes forest.

1945

January 8	The German army is forced to withdraw in the Battle of the Bulge.
January 14	Soviet forces enter East Prussia.
January 17	The last roll call takes place at Auschwitz, where 67,012 prisoners are still incarcerated.
	Soviet authorities in Hungary arrest Raoul Wallenberg.
	Russian troops liberate Warsaw.
January 18	The SS begins the hasty evacuation of Auschwitz, with most of the surviving prisoners sent on the infamous death marches to camps in the West.
January 19	Soviet forces liberate Łódź.
January 27	Soviet troops liberate the Auschwitz camp complex, where they find some 7,000 prisoners still alive.
February 7–11	Churchill, Roosevelt, and Stalin meet at Yalta in the Crimea.

	They discuss postwar plans for Germany, Soviet entry into the war against Japan, and the United Nations.
February 7	The International Red Cross has 1,200 Jews moved from the Protectorate of Bohemia and Moravia to Switzerland.
March 7	American forces cross the Rhine at Remagen.
March 12	Himmler's personal physician, Felix Kersten, reports in Stockholm that Himmler has blocked Hitler's order to have concentration camps destroyed and their prisoners killed and has ordered the camps be turned over to the Allies intact.
April 11	American forces liberate the Buchenwald concentration camp.
April 12	President Franklin D. Roosevelt dies in Warm Springs, Georgia.
April 13	Soviet forces enter Vienna.
April 15	British forces liberate the Bergen-Belsen concentration camp.
April 20–21	Heinrich Himmler meets in Berlin with a Jewish representative from Sweden and the Swedish mediator Folke Bernadotte and agrees to release some 15,000 Jewish and non-Jewish women from Ravensbrück concentration camp.
April 22	Soviet troops enter Berlin.
April 25	The United Nations meets in San Francisco. American and Soviet troops link up at Torgau on the Elbe River.
April 28	Italian partisans execute Benito Mussolini.
April 29	Soviet troops liberate Ravensbrück concentration camp. American troops liberate Dachau concentration camp.
April 30	Adolf Hitler commits suicide in his bunker beneath the Reich Chancellery in Berlin.
May 2	German forces in Berlin capitulate. German armies in Italy surrender. President Truman appoints Robert Jackson chief American prosecutor of Nazi war criminals.
May 3	German authorities turn over Theresienstadt to the Red Cross.
May 5	German armies in northern Germany, Denmark, and Holland surrender.
May 7	Soviet troops enter the Theresienstadt ghetto. Nazi Germany surrenders to the Allies at Rheims.
May 8	The war in Europe officially ends.
May 9	In Berlin, Nazi Germany formally surrenders to the Soviet Union.

June 26   Fifty nations sign the United Nations Charter in San Francisco.

July 17–August 2   Churchill, Truman, and Stalin meet at Potsdam in Germany to discuss the postwar settlement for Germany. Clement Atlee replaces Churchill after July 28.

August 8   The London Agreement is signed by Great Britain, France, the United States, and the Soviet Union authorizing the trial of Nazi war criminals in Germany.

August 14   Japan accepts Allied terms for surrender.

September 2   Japan signs Allied surrender terms aboard the USS *Missouri* in Tokyo harbor.

September 20   The Jewish Agency for Palestine makes its first formal claim for German reparations to Jewish victims of the Third Reich.

October 6   The four Allied chief prosecutors bring indictments against twenty-four major Nazis and six Nazi organizations.

November 20   The International Military Tribunal (IMT) opens in Nuremberg.

December 20   The military governors of the four occupation zones in Germany adopt "Control Council Law No. 10," which authorizes the individual zones to establish courts to try Nazi war criminals.

1946

January 10   The first session of the United Nations General Assembly meets in London.

January 17   The first session of the United Nations Security Council meets in London.

August 31   The defendants at the Nuremberg Trials make their final statements before the International Military Tribunal.

October 1   The IMT at Nuremberg issues its verdicts and imposes sentences on the defendants.

October 16   Those condemned to death by the IMT are executed.

1948

May 14   The state of Israel is established in part of the former British Mandate of Palestine.

1949

May 23   The "Basic Law" (*Grundgesetz*), the constitution of the Federal Republic of Germany (West), is promulgated.

1951

January 16   Israel asks the occupation powers in Germany to facilitate German restitution of Jewish property in Germany and indemnification of survivors.

March 12   The Israeli government presents to the Allied powers an estimate of German reparation obligations to the Jewish people living inside and outside of Israel.

September 27   In a speech to the Bundestag, the West German parliament, Chancellor Konrad Adenauer formally accepts German responsibility for Nazi crimes against the Jews and the obligation to pay restitution to the Jewish people.

1952

March 21   Reparations negotiations between the Federal Republic of Germany, Israel, and the Conference of Jewish Material Claims against Germany (the combined representatives of twenty-three Jewish organizations) begin in the Netherlands.

September 10   West German Chancellor Konrad Adenauer and Israeli Foreign Minister Moshe Sharett sign a "Reparations Agreement" between West Germany and Israel. Adenauer also signs an agreement with Nahum Goldmann representing the Conference of Jewish Material Claims against Germany.

1953

August 28   The Israeli parliament, the Knesset, establishes Yad Vashem in Jerusalem.

1961

December 2   Adolf Eichmann is sentenced to death in Jerusalem.

1963

December 20   The trials of former SS commanders at Auschwitz begin in Frankfurt and last until August 20, 1965.

1993

April 22   The United States Holocaust Memorial Museum is dedicated in Washington, D.C.

PART IV

Encyclopedia

Encyclopedia

PEOPLE

Antonescu, Ion (1882–1946) General and dictator of Romania during World War II, Antonescu united with the right-wing and antisemitic **Iron Guard** in 1940 to form a new Romanian government, ending a period of political unrest. When the Iron Guard revolted against him in January 1941, Antonescu suppressed it and made himself dictator. He allied his country with Nazi Germany, hoping to regain Romania's eastern territories, **Bessarabia** and Northern Bukovina, recently lost to the Soviet Union.

Marshal Antonescu's **antisemitism** was not as intense as that of the Iron Guard, but like many Romanians the dictator blamed the Jews for pro-Soviet sympathies and subjected them to legal discrimination. When German and Romanian forces retook Bessarabia and Northern Bukovina in June 1941, Antonescu ordered the expulsion of most of the 126,000 Jews of those provinces across the Dniester River (**Transnistria**) where the majority perished. Romanian soldiers fighting alongside the Germans in those areas joined German **Einsatzgruppen** (action squads) in mass shootings of Jews. The Romanian dictator also ordered his soldiers to carry out massive reprisals against the Jews in Odessa for an explosion that destroyed the Romanian army headquarters in that occupied Ukrainian city. In 1942 Antonescu authorized negotiations with German representatives for the deportation of the remaining 315,000 Romanian Jews to camps in Poland. But as the war turned against Germany and its allies, the negotiations were put on hold and, in fact, never occurred. The dictator was overthrown in August 1944, and two years later he was tried and executed. Among his crimes was the murder of more than 121,000 Romanian and Ukrainian Jews.

Baeck, Leo (1873–1956) The Chief Rabbi of Berlin and president of the **Reich Association of Jews in Germany** (Reichsvereinigung der Juden in Deutschland), Baeck was the most important leader of German Jewry in the Nazi era. Throughout the Weimar years he strove with mixed success to overcome divisions between assimilationists and Zionists, and his commitment to

Jewish unity made him the natural leader of the German Jews from 1933 until his deportation to **Theresienstadt** in January 1943. Although harassed by the Gestapo, Baeck declined invitations from abroad to immigrate during the 1930s. He wanted, he said, to stay as long as there were Jews in Berlin. In Theresienstadt he became a member of the **Jewish Council** (Judenrat) and endeavored to raise the spirits of the ghetto inhabitants; to that end he declined to pass on information he had received about **Auschwitz**. After liberation Baeck moved to London, where he continued to teach and write.

Ben-Gurion, David (1886–1973) Chairman of the Zionist Executive and head of the Jewish Agency, Ben-Gurion was the leading figure of the **Yishuv** (Jewish community in Palestine) during World War II. His single-minded pursuit of opening Palestine to large-scale Jewish immigration was stymied in the late 1930s by British quotas in response to Palestinian Arab unrest. Ben-Gurion's call for Jews to resist the British was only partially tempered by the outbreak of war in Europe and news of the Holocaust. Deeply moved by the fate of European Jewry, he believed that small-scale rescue operations and continued illegal Jewish immigration to Palestine were the only significant contributions that the Yishuv could make under the circumstances. Ben-Gurion went on to become the first prime minister of Israel from 1948 to 1963.

Bonhoeffer, Dietrich (1906–1945) A German Protestant theologian active in the anti-Nazi resistance, Bonhoeffer was among the first to recognize the antisemitic implications of traditional Christian teachings about the Jews. As a member of the "Confessing Church" (Bekennende Kirche) he both opposed all intrusions of Nazi ideology into the German Evangelical Church and helped persecuted German Jews find hiding places in Germany and escape to Switzerland. His revulsion at the treatment of the handicapped and the Jews contributed to his decision to become an active participant in the anti-Hitler **resistance**. Bonhoeffer was arrested in April 1943 and executed in the last days of the war. His writings, most of them published posthumously, have influenced Christianity's post-Holocaust reassessment of its relationship with Judaism.

Brack, Viktor (1904–1948) An official of the Chancellery of the Führer, Brack implemented the T4 **euthanasia** program. He joined the **Nazi Party** and the **SS** soon after completing study at the University of Munich in 1928. When the Nazis came to power he was named head of the office of party and state affairs in Hitler's personal chancellery. In 1939 Brack was instructed to organize the euthanasia of handicapped Germans and create front organizations to disguise the fact that the order came from Hitler's office. Brack helped recruit T4 personnel and create its administrative structure. Later he ordered the transfer of

T4 personnel to **Lublin**. In August 1942 he left for the front as a **Waffen SS** officer. After the war an American military court sentenced him to death.

Brand, Joel (1907–1964) A Budapest businessman and active Zionist, Brand was selected by Adolf Eichmann to convey the "blood for trucks" offer to the Allies in May, 1944. Brand had long been active in refugee affairs and belonged to the Va'da, an organization that aided Jews from Poland and Slovakia who had fled to Hungary. He took the German offer to release 1,000,000 Jews in return for 10,000 trucks very seriously, and he was shattered when the Allies turned it down and refused to negotiate with the Germans at all. Only late in his life, after settling in Israel, did he acknowledge that the German offer was a cynical attempt to split the Allies and save the Third Reich.

Czerniaków, Adam (1880–1942) Until his suicide on July 23, 1942, Czerniaków headed the Warsaw **Jewish Council** (Judenrat) that presided over the **Warsaw** ghetto. For many years before World War II he taught at a Warsaw Jewish vocational school and served on the Jewish community council. Shortly after conquering Warsaw in October 1939 the Germans appointed Czerniaków to head a new Jewish Council and ordered him to name its other members. He refused to take advantage of opportunities to leave Poland in the early months of the occupation, and he held Jewish leaders who did so in contempt as traitors to their people.

Under Czerniaków's leadership the Jewish Council vastly expanded its work force and activities, taking responsibility for all areas of Jewish life from health and nutrition to work and housing. Czerniaków had no choice but to follow German orders for the creation of the Warsaw Ghetto in November 1940. Although badly treated by the German authorities, he long believed that most of the Jews of the ghetto would be spared as long as they provided a steady work force for the German factories located in the city.

Czerniaków's sense of duty held fast when the Germans began to deport ghetto residents in 1942. At first he accepted German assurances that the Jews were being resettled in order to alleviate overcrowding in the ghetto. But in July, finding that the Germans had lied to him about the extent of the deportations, and suspecting that rumors about **Treblinka** were true, Czerniaków swallowed poison. His diary survived the war and provides invaluable information about the functioning of the ghetto.

Eichmann, Adolf (1906–1962) The SS officer whose belated trial and conviction in 1961 reminded the world of the Holocaust, Eichmann was responsible for deporting Jews to ghettos and extermination and forced labor camps. He was born in Solingen, Germany, but his family moved to Linz, Austria, when he was eight. During the 1920s he joined the Austrian branch of the Nazi Party and the SS, and in 1933 he moved back to Germany where he was assigned to the Jewish section of the intelligence section at SS headquarters in Berlin. Dedicated and ambitious, Eichmann learned a smattering of Hebrew and Yiddish to enhance his job skills.

Eichmann's big chance came following Germany's **Anschluss** (union) with Austria in March 1938. Sent to Vienna to organize the emigration of Austrian Jews, he established the first Central Office for Jewish Emigration (Zentralstelle für jüdische Auswanderung), which engaged the cooperation of Jewish officials in forcing the Jews to leave. Thereafter he distinguished himself in organizing expulsions of Jews from Germany and western Poland to the **General Government**. In 1941 Eichmann was rewarded by being made head of the Jewish Section of the Reich Security Main Office (Reichssicherheitshauptamt). He participated in the **Wannsee Conference** and was assigned the task of coordinating the transport of all the European Jews to camps in Poland. Members of his staff operated virtually everywhere in German-dominated regions, and Eichmann himself supervised the deportations from Hungary in 1944.

After Germany's defeat Eichmann managed to slip away to Argentina with the help of sympathetic Vatican officials. He was discovered and kidnapped by Israeli agents in 1960. His trial in Jerusalem created a sensation and introduced the Holocaust to members of the postwar generation. Eichmann's defense that he was merely following orders carried no weight with the court, and he was executed in 1962.

Frank, Anne (1929–1945) *The Diary of Anne Frank* has made Anne Frank the best-known victim of the Holocaust. She was born in Frankfurt am Main, Germany, although Anne's father, Otto Frank, took his family to live in Amsterdam when Hitler came to power in 1933. When the Germans began to deport the Dutch Jews in 1942, the Franks were hidden with the help of Dutch friends in an unused office room. The Germans arrested them all following an anonymous telephone tip in August 1944. The Franks were sent to **Auschwitz**, while two of their friends were sent to Dutch concentration camps. Anne and her older sister Margot were brought from Auschwitz to **Bergen-Belsen** in October 1944. There they died of typhus in March 1945 and were buried in a mass grave. After the war Otto Frank returned from Auschwitz, and in 1947 he published the diary Anne had written while in hiding in the original Dutch. Since then it has been translated into more than fifty languages, has sold more than 20,000,000 copies, and has been made into a play and a film. The Amsterdam hiding place is today a museum visited by hundreds of thousands every year.

Frank, Hans (1900–1946) Nazi Germany's leading lawyer, Frank became infamous for his harsh rule as governor of German-occupied Poland during World War II. Frank was fresh out of law school when he joined the Nazi Party during the 1920s and made a name by defending party militants accused of various violent crimes. When Hitler took over, Frank became the President of the Academy of German Law but enjoyed little real power.

Following the German conquest of Poland in October 1939, Frank was appointed governor of the **General Government** and quickly found himself at odds with other Nazi officials who wanted to use his lands as a dumping ground for Poles and Jews from the annexed regions of Poland and from Germany itself. Above all he wanted to defend his turf from intrusions by **Himmler** and the **SS**. In 1942 Hitler overruled Frank and punished him by stripping him of his party offices and transferring racial matters in Poland to the SS. Frank tried to resign his governorship, but Hitler insisted that he stay at his post. He was convicted as a major war criminal at Nuremberg and hanged.

Gens, Jacob (1905–1943) As head of the **Vilna** ghetto **Jewish Council** (Judenrat), Gens attempted unsuccessfully to save his community by placating the Germans. While still a teenager he fought against the Poles and the Bolsheviks for Lithuania's independence, and for a time served as an officer in the new country's army. When the USSR occupied Lithuania in July 1940, Gens feared arrest and fled to Vilna, where few people knew him. There he became director of the Jewish hospital, and following the creation of the Vilna ghetto he was named head of the Jewish **police**. Gens's military background enabled him to build an efficient and disciplined ghetto police force that participated in the roundups of Jews in the ghetto in the last months of 1941. The Germans came to view him as the ablest ghetto leader, and in July 1942 they appointed him chairman of the Vilna Jewish Council and also put him in charge of several smaller ghettos in the area.

Gens ruled with an iron hand in order to keep the Vilna ghetto working and hence productive for the Germans. He could not avoid delivering Jews for deportations, but whenever possible he sent the old and sick rather than young women and children, hoping to preserve the biological stock. Gens was in constant contact with the ghetto underground, always urging it to avoid a premature revolt. His strategy of buying time worked for about a year, but as the Germans began to empty the Vilna ghetto in the summer of 1943 his friends urged him to flee and join his Lithuanian wife and child outside the ghetto. Gens, fearing immediate reprisals against the ghetto if he left, stayed at his post. He was shot on September 14, 1943, only days before the ghetto was liquidated.

Gerstein, Kurt (1905–1945) An anti-Nazi SS officer, Gerstein tried to alert the world to the mass murder of Jews. He joined the Nazi Party in 1933, but he was also a member of the "Confessing Church" (Bekennende Kirche), which fought off attempts by the party to meddle in **Protestant Church** affairs. This got Gerstein expelled from the party and sent to a concentration camp. After his release in 1938 he became a medical student, but the death of his sister-in-law in the T4 program induced him to infiltrate the Nazi system by volunteering for the **Waffen SS** in 1941. His medical background caused him to be appointed head of the Technical Disinfection Department, and as the chief SS hygiene officer he delivered **Zyklon B** to the camps and witnessed the gassings at first hand. He informed Swiss and Swedish diplomats, German and Vatican churchmen, and the Dutch underground, but the recipients either could not or would not act on the information. After the war Gerstein was charged as a war criminal by the French and found hanged in his cell, either a suicide or the victim of murder at the hands of other SS prisoners incarcerated with him.

Globocnik, Odilo (1904–1945) Odilo Globocnik was the high SS officer who directed **Operation Reinhard**. Born in Trieste, he was a construction engineer in Austria when he joined the Nazi Party and the SS in the early 1930s. He spent time in prison during the years when the party was illegal in Austria, but following **Anschluss** (Union) with Germany he became the Gauleiter (Nazi Party district leader) of Vienna. Ousted from that post for corruption in 1939, he was given a second chance by **Himmler,** who then appointed him SS and Police Leader in Lublin in eastern Poland. In that capacity he was responsible for building and running **Majdanek** and the three Operation Reinhard extermination camps. Globocnik also directed the clearing of the Zamość area of eastern Poland for resettlement by **ethnic Germans**, sending the Jews to labor and extermination camps and the Poles to **forced labor** in Germany or elsewhere in Poland. Conflicts with rival SS officers resulted in his transfer to Trieste in August 1943. Globocnik committed suicide in May 1945.

Goebbels, Joseph (1897–1945) The Nazi propaganda minister, Goebbels established a climate of opinion in Germany that made racial persecution and genocide possible. Born in the Rhineland, he earned a doctorate in German literature in 1921 and aspired to a career as a writer, but he came into his own only after joining the Nazi Party in 1924 and editing its Rhineland newspaper. **Hitler** recognized Goebbels's talents as a propagandist by making him Gauleiter (Nazi Party district leader) of Berlin (1926), Nazi Party propaganda chief (1930), and German Minister of Public Enlightenment and Propaganda (1933).

As propaganda minister Goebbels organized the banishment of Jews from German culture and disinformation campaigns to prepare public opinion for **euthanasia** and anti-Jewish actions. It was his idea to conduct the **Crystal Night** (Kristallnacht) pogroms in 1938, although Göring and Himmler blocked his goal of winning control over Jewish affairs. During the war Goebbels pushed for the rapid expulsion of Jews from Berlin so that he could declare the Reich capital "Jew-free." In July 1944 Hitler placed him in charge of the total mobilization of the German people for war. As the Third Reich crumbled Goebbels attempted to stiffen morale by raising the specter of victorious Jews wreaking terrible revenge on Germany. Goebbels and his wife, Magda, committed suicide in the Führerbunker after killing their six children on May 1, 1945.

Göring, Hermann (1893–1946) The second most powerful figure in Nazi Germany and Hitler's appointed political heir, Bavarian-born Göring joined the Nazi Party in 1922 and a year later was seriously wounded in the abortive Nazi seizure of power known as the Beer Hall Putsch. Later he became head of the Nazi delegation in the German Reichstag and, when the Nazis became the largest party, president of that body. Outgoing and urbane, Göring lent the Nazis an aura of social respectability.

During the Third Reich Göring held many top posts, including head of the Luftwaffe and chief of the Four Year Plan, which in 1936 began to ready the German economy for war. His economic powers extended to "**Aryanizing**" Jewish property in Germany and, after Crystal Night, forcing the Jews out of the economy altogether. Göring confined his activities to confiscating Jewish wealth, relegating other anti-Jewish measures to the SS. Hence when he authorized the creation of a **Reich Central Office for Jewish Emigration** (Reichszentrale für jüdische Auswanderung) in 1939, he turned it over to **Reinhard Heydrich** and the SS. Similarly, his July 1941 order to Heydrich to formulate a "comprehensive solution to the Jewish problem" was composed by Heydrich himself and merely signed by Göring.

Göring lost much of his influence over Hitler during World War II as a result of the Luftwaffe's failure to stop the bombing of Germany. He was tried by the Allies at Nuremberg, where he refused to renounce Hitler or National Socialism. Claiming that he only wanted the Jews to emigrate, he insisted he knew nothing of genocide. Göring was sentenced to death but took his own life by swallowing poison a short time before he was to be hanged.

Grynszpan, Hershel. See Crystal Night

Heydrich, Reinhard (1904–1942) After Himmler the most powerful SS leader in Germany, Heydrich was responsible for planning and executing genocide. He was born in Halle and embarked upon a career as a naval intelligence officer during the 1920s. In 1931 **Himmler** recruited him to set up an SS intelligence office within the Nazi Party called the Sicherheitsdienst (Security Service, or SD). As Himmler's faithful servant Heydrich assisted in bringing all the police forces in Germany under SS control, and by 1936 he occupied powerful positions in both party (SD) and state (police) offices. When Göring turned most anti-Jewish policies over to the SS in late 1938 and 1939, Heydrich took these, too, in hand, including direction of the **Reich Central Office for Jewish Emigration** (Reichszentrale für jüdische Auswanderung) in January 1939.

The creation of the **Reich Security Main Office** (Reichssicherheitshauptamt) under Heydrich's direction in 1939 institutionalized his power within the police and SS. Two years later his **Einsatzgruppen** (action squads) ghettoized and expelled the "racially undesirable" during the first year and a half of World War II and murdered them thereafter. Although the origins of the decision to begin the systematic mass murder of all the Jews are unclear, it is certain that Heydrich drew up plans to implement the **Final Solution** that were unveiled to other party and state officials at the **Wannsee Conference** in January 1942. Six months before Heydrich himself had cleared the way by having Hermann Göring, who was nominally in charge of Jewish affairs, authorize him to move ahead with a "comprehensive solution to the Jewish problem." Heydrich was also named deputy Reich Protector of the **Protectorate of Bohemia and Moravia** in 1941. Following his assassination by Czech agents in May 1942, he was succeeded in all his posts save that in the protectorate by **Ernst Kaltenbrunner.**

Himmler, Heinrich (1900–1945) As head of the SS, Himmler was responsible for clearing Europe of "racially undesirable" elements during World War II. He was born in Bavaria, studied agriculture in Munich in the early 1920s, and was attracted to the Nazi Party by its blood-and-soil mysticism. He worked his way up through the Nazi Party bureaucracy, evincing diligence, dedication, and absolute loyalty to Hitler, who in 1929 made him chief of the SS. Following the Nazi victory in 1933 Himmler became head of the political police in Bavaria and began a three-year struggle to assemble all the **police** forces in Germany under his own personal control. He took a giant step forward in 1934 when Hitler ordered him to purge the **SA** (the Nazi Storm Troopers), which freed the SS from SA control and made it the chief agency of terror in the Third Reich.

By 1936 Himmler ran both the SS and the police, combining in his person both party and state offices with the power of life and death over everyone in Germany. This included control of the growing network of German **concentration camps.** During the war his powers increased further with the creation of the **Waffen SS,** which rivaled the army as Germany's chief military force, and with his appointment as Reich Commissar for the Strengthening of German Nationality, which gave him authority to cleanse Eastern Europe of Slavs and Jews. Hence Himmler had overall responsibility for carrying out the Final Solution, including the actions of the **Einsatzgruppen** (action squads) and the operation of the **labor** and **extermination camps**.

During the last ten months of the war Himmler attempted to ingratiate himself with the Western Allies, offering to ransom the Hungarian Jews and ending the gassings at **Auschwitz** at the end of October 1944. But when he tried to convince **Hitler** to surrender in the west, Hitler stripped him of all his offices. Captured by the British shortly after the war ended, Himmler committed suicide.

Hitler, Adolf (1889–1945) Born in Braunau am Inn, Austria, Hitler was the son of middle class parents who disapproved of his youthful interest in art and architecture. Following his father's death in 1903, Hitler dropped out of high school and moved to Vienna in an unsuccessful attempt to get admitted to the Vienna Art Academy. He stayed in Vienna and interested himself in right-wing and pan-German politics. In 1913 Hitler moved to Munich, Germany, and a year later volunteered to fight for Germany in World War I. Wounded and highly decorated, Hitler came to view war as a heroic adventure.

Hitler returned to Munich after the war and became leader of the Nazi Party in 1921. He dedicated himself wholeheartedly to smashing the liberal and democratic Weimar Republic, and after failing to overturn it by force in 1923 he worked to build his party and come to power legally. His chance came during the depression years of the early 1930s. In 1933 he was appointed German Chancellor, after which Germany's demoralized parliament, the Reichstag, granted him dictatorial powers that he retained to the end of what he called Germany's "Third Reich."

As dictator of Germany Hitler embarked upon racial policies aimed at removing "racially undesirable" groups such as handicapped people and Jews and preparing Germany for war to conquer **Lebensraum** (living space) for an expanding German population. He committed suicide as the Russians closed in on Berlin at the end of April 1945. Hitler's legacy to humankind is the costliest war and the bloodiest **genocide** in history.

Horthy, Miklós (1868–1957) The Hungarian strongman during World War II, Horthy at first accepted and then tried to stop the German policy of deporting Jews from Hungary in 1944. A former admiral in the Austro-Hungarian navy during World War I, he was elected Regent of Hungary and remained head of state until 1944. He agreed to various anti-Jewish laws that were adopted during the 1930s, but he was not a virulent antisemite.

When the Germans occupied Hungary in March 1944 and began sending the Hungarian Jews to **Auschwitz,** Horthy initially accepted German assurances that they were going to **labor camps**. But by July he was beginning to have doubts and was also under pressure from the Vatican, the **Red Cross**, and the Western Allies to stop the deportations, which he did on July 6. Horthy then offered to let the Jews emigrate, but the Germans would not allow them to leave without some quid pro quo. And yet, Horthy's actions put the Hungarian government on record as opposing further persecutions of the remaining Hungarian Jews and made it easier for Swiss, Swedish, and other neutral diplomats to help them.

The Germans ousted and imprisoned Horthy in October 1944 and replaced his government with one run by the fascist and antisemitic **Arrow Cross**. After the war the Allies determined that Horthy was not a war criminal and allowed him to move to Portugal, where he spent his last years.

Höss, Rudolf (1900–1947)   The first commandant of **Auschwitz** was also its architect and builder. A veteran of World War I, Höss joined the Nazi Party in 1922 and after Hitler came to power joined the **SS** and learned the skills of **concentration camp** administration at **Dachau** and **Sachsenhausen**. In May 1940 he was promoted and sent east to establish a concentration camp at Auschwitz. A year later Höss introduced **Zyklon B** gassing techniques and began a vast expansion of the camp and its facilities that made it into the largest concentration and extermination camp.

Höss was relieved of his duties in November 1943 after an internal SS investigation established that there was widespread corruption among the Auschwitz staff. He was put to work in the SS Inspectorate for Concentration Camps at Oranienburg, but he arranged to return to Auschwitz in March 1944 to supervise the gassing of large numbers of Hungarian Jews. At the end of the war Höss was arrested and sent to Poland to be tried. Before being hanged on the gallows at Auschwitz, Höss wrote his memoirs, in which he portrayed himself as an officer who was duty bound to follow orders and hence another victim of Hitler's racial mania.

Kaltenbrunner, Ernst (1903–1946)   Kaltenbrunner succeeded **Reinhard Heydrich** as SS coordinator of the **Final Solution** in 1942. He joined the Nazi Party and the SS as a young Austrian lawyer in 1932, and following **Anschluss** (union) with Germany he was placed in charge of the Gestapo in Austria. When Heydrich was assassinated in May 1942, Himmler named Kaltenbrunner to replace him as head of the **Reich Security Main Office** (Reichssicherheitshauptamt), which included both the SS police and intelligence branches. In these capacities he faithfully carried through the genocidal program already underway. Brought before the International Military Tribunal at Nuremberg in 1946, Kaltenbrunner unsuccessfully argued that he knew nothing about SS crimes and blamed the dead SS leader, **Heinrich Himmler**, for them. He was convicted and hanged.

Karski, Jan (1914–) A Polish civil servant before World War II, Karski joined the anti-German underground during World War II and acted as one of its couriers to the Polish government in exile in London. Karski is a cover name that he adopted at the time; his real name is Kozielewski. In 1942 he made the hazardous clandestine trip from Poland to England to inform the London Poles of conditions under German rule. Before leaving, Karski took great risks in order to familiarize himself with the **Final Solution**, twice sneaking into the **Warsaw** ghetto and later disguising himself as a Ukrainian **Hiwi** to inspect Jews being readied for extermination at **Bełzec**.

Karski made it to London in November 1942 and spoke with Winston Churchill and other English and Polish leaders. As a result the Allies and the London Poles publicly demanded an end to genocide. Later Karski met with President Roosevelt, staying in the United States and informing the public about the plight of civilians under German rule in Poland.

Kasztner, Rezsö (1906–1957) Hero to some, villain to others, Kasztner negotiated with the Germans in an effort to **rescue** Hungarian Jews from deportations and death marches. As an active Zionist and leader of Va'da, which operated an underground railroad for Jews fleeing the Nazis, he was among those Budapest Jews approached by **Eichmann** with the "blood for trucks" offer that was conveyed to the Western Allies in July 1944 by **Joel Brand**. Kasztner, exploiting SS hopes for a separate peace with the Western powers, convinced the Germans to release 1,684 Hungarian Jews to Switzerland as a good faith gesture. Among them were his family members and friends. Evidently he hoped that this would be the first of many such releases, but **Hitler** banned them when he learned of it.

After the war Kasztner settled in Israel, where in 1954 he engaged in a court battle over charges that he had sold out his fellow Jews in Budapest for personal advantage. The court found against him, and he appealed to the Israeli Supreme Court. Eventually it exonerated Kasztner of all charges, but before it could rule he was assassinated by a rabid nationalist. To this day some still revile Kasztner as a traitor who failed to warn his fellow Jews about the nature of the Nazi threat in order to save himself and those close to him. More commonly, he is venerated for discerning that negotiation was the most promising way to delay deportations from Budapest and save the remaining Hungarian Jews in 1944–1945.

Korczak, Janusz (1878–1942) A physician and educator, Korczak directed the

Warsaw ghetto orphanage. Long before that he had established an international reputation as an educational reformer and child psychologist. Korczak put his theories to work in running Jewish and Polish orphanages before World War II. When the ghetto was formed, Korczak stayed with his Jewish orphans and worked tirelessly to provide them with their basic needs. He declined offers to escape to the Polish side and seems to have believed that the 1942 deportations meant resettlement. On August 5, 1942, the German order came, and Korczak himself led his orphans to the rail siding. He perished with them at **Treblinka.**

Kovner, Abba (1918–1988) After the Holocaust a prominent Israeli writer, Kovner was the most important Jewish underground and partisan leader in the **Vilna** area during the war. Intuiting Nazi plans, he refused to believe that the massacres of Jews and others in the early days of German rule were exceptional or temporary. On the last day of 1941 he called upon the Jews of the Vilna ghetto to come together for armed **resistance** under left-wing Zionist leadership. In January 1942 young Jews from several groups heeded his call by forming the United Partisans Organization, and when its first leader, Yitzhak Wittenberg, was arrested and executed in July 1943, Kovner took his place. He led the breakout of a hundred Jews from the ghetto at the time of its liquidation in September 1943, and thereafter he commanded a Jewish partisan force in the nearby forests. After the liberation Kovner helped organize Jewish **displaced persons** for emigration to Palestine. Until his death he was one of Israel's leading poets.

Levi, Primo (1919–1987) An **Auschwitz** survivor, Levi became one of the best-known memoirists of the Holocaust experience. He was born in Turin, Italy, and earned a doctorate in chemistry in 1943, only a short time before Italy changed sides in the war and Germany occupied the northern part of the country. Levi fled to the mountains to join the Italian resistance, but he was taken by **Mussolini**'s fascist militia and turned over to the Germans. They sent him to Auschwitz with 650 other Italian Jews, only twenty of whom survived.

Levi survived because his knowledge of chemistry made him useful in the Buna laboratories at Monowitz. He avoided evacuation from Auschwitz on one of the **death marches** because he had fallen ill and was one of the few thousand prisoners left behind to be liberated by the Soviet army. Throughout his ordeal Levi was sustained by determination to live to tell his story. His most influential books, *Survival at Auschwitz* and *The Drowned and the Saved*, are characterized by acute psychological insight and great emotional restraint. Levi committed suicide in 1987.

Mayer, Saly (1882–1950) A Swiss Jewish leader, Mayer tried to buy time for the surviving European Jews by negotiating with the SS in the last year of World

War II. From 1936 to 1942 Mayer headed the Federation of Swiss Jewish Communities, and from 1940 on he represented the **American Joint Distribution Committee** (JDC), which aided Jewish refugees in Europe. In 1943 Mayer used some of the money at his disposal to bribe the **SS** into not resuming deportations of Jews from Slovakia, although it is not clear whether the bribe was decisive in making German policy at that time.

Late in the war Mayer entered into ransom negotiations with the SS to prevent further Jewish deportations, especially those from Budapest. In order to keep the Germans interested, he delivered tractors to Germany and arranged a meeting between SS and American **War Refugee Board** officials. It may be that these negotiations helped to keep most of the Budapest Jews alive during the last months of the Holocaust, although this cannot be proved. Nor can it be said with certainty that providing still more bribes to the Germans would have saved additional lives, as some have alleged. After the war Mayer supervised the distribution of JDC aid to Jewish Holocaust survivors in Germany and Eastern Europe.

Mengele, Josef (1911–1979) Dr. Mengele, perhaps the best known **SS** physician at **Auschwitz,** was responsible along with other SS doctors for selections and **medical experiments** that used prisoners as guinea pigs. Born in Günzburg, Germany, he joined the Nazi Party and the SS in the late 1930s. In 1940 the young physician volunteered for the medical corps of the **Waffen SS** and was assigned to its Viking Division. He was wounded in May 1943 and transferred to the relative comfort of Auschwitz.

Mengele's medical experiments at Auschwitz reflected the SS preoccupation with race. He deliberately infected prisoners with contagious diseases such as tuberculosis and typhus to compare the reactions of various races to disease. His research on Gypsy and Jewish twins sought means of increasing multiple births among Germans to increase the **Aryan** population. When finished with his human guinea pigs, many of them children, he usually gave them fatal injections. Mengele sent the results of his research, together with blood samples and body organs of the victims, to his former professor Otmar Verschuer, who by then was director of the Kaiser Wilhelm Institute for Anthropology in Berlin.

In 1945 Mengele managed to disguise himself and slip away to Argentina. The West German government issued a warrant for his arrest and asked Argentina to extradite him in 1960, but Mengele escaped to Brazil and Paraguay and always managed to elude his pursuers. In 1985 it was learned that he died in a swimming accident in Brazil in 1979.

Merin, Moshe (1906–1943) Merin was chairman of the Central **Jewish Council** (Judenrat) in Eastern Upper Silesia from 1940 to 1943. Active in Zionist and

Jewish community affairs in his hometown of Sosnowiec, Poland, before the war, he was appointed to head the regional Jewish Council by the Germans in January 1940. This placed Merin in charge of 100,000 Jews in more than forty communities of various sizes scattered throughout Eastern Upper Silesia, a large area of Western Poland annexed to the Third Reich in 1939.

From his headquarters in Sosnowiec Merin pursued a classic "rescue through work" strategy, recruiting Jewish volunteers for **forced labor** and co-operating with the deportations in the belief that sacrificing part of the population would save the rest. In this he was supported by most of the rabbis. Whenever possible he turned over the young Zionists and Communists of the Jewish underground to the Gestapo, believing that their strategy of defiance doomed every single Jew. On June 21, 1943, Merin and the other Jewish Council members were sent to **Auschwitz**, and during the next two months the Jewish communities and ghettos of Eastern Upper Silesia were liquidated.

Mussolini, Benito (1883–1945) The Italian Fascist dictator from 1922 to 1945 ended his career as a German puppet and deeply implicated in the Holocaust in Italy. Mussolini began his political career as a Socialist but went over to the extreme right as an advocate of Italian entry into World War I against Germany and Austria-Hungary. After the war he founded the Fascist party, which came to power in 1922 with the connivance of the monarchy and the conservative political establishment. Mussolini was not a racial antisemite, and his party had the support of many Italian Jews. However, Mussolini was frequently critical of Jews who were Zionists or Communists, and these criticisms formed the basis of an anti-Jewish campaign that accompanied Italy's growing closeness to Nazi Germany starting in 1936. Two years later Mussolini cemented his alliance with Hitler by passing racial laws that were loosely based on the German **Nuremberg Laws**. But until 1943 Italian Jews were never as badly treated as the German Jews had been in the 1930s, and Mussolini would not allow the Italian Jews to be deported to Poland.

All that changed in 1943 when Mussolini was overthrown and the new Italian government surrendered and then brought Italy back into the war on the side of the Allies. In a daring commando raid the Germans freed Mussolini from captivity and installed him as head of the "Italian Social Republic" in German-occupied northern Italy. His Fascist militia aided in rounding up thousands of Jews for deportation to **Auschwitz.** In the last days of the war Mussolini was captured by Italian partisans and, together with his mistress, publicly hanged.

Pétain, Henri Philippe (1856–1951) A World War I French war hero, Pétain surrendered to the Germans in June 1940 and became head of the new French government at **Vichy**. He transformed France into a Fascist state and ally of Germany, and supported the persecution of Jews in France, including the deportation of foreign Jews to the East. Pétain was convicted of treason by a French court in 1945, but Charles de Gaulle commuted his death sentence to life imprisonment. He died at the age of ninety-six.

Pius XII (Eugenio Pacelli, 1876–1958). See Catholic Church

Pohl, Oswald (1892–1951)   An SS overseer of the economics of the Final Solution, Pohl joined the **Nazi Party** in 1926 and the SS in 1929. In 1935 he became chief of administration in the SS Main Office (Hauptamt). During the war Pohl helped to develop SS economic enterprises. In 1940 he became chief of Budget and Construction and of Administration and Economy, two offices consolidated in 1942 under him as the **Economic Administration Main Office** (Wirtschaftsverwaltungshauptamt). In this capacity, he supervised slave labor, camp industrial projects, and the shipment of the personal possessions of victims back to Germany until 1945. He made available hundreds of thousands of **concentration camp** prisoners to SS and other German industries. In 1947 the **American Military Tribunal** in Nuremberg condemned Pohl to death for war crimes and crimes against humanity, for which he was executed in 1951.

Ringelblum, Emanuel (1900–1944)   Jewish historian and chronicler of Jewish life in German-occupied Poland, Ringelblum was born in Buczacz, Eastern Galicia. He received a doctorate from the University of Warsaw in 1927, taught Jewish history in high schools, and wrote about Jewish history in Warsaw. He worked with the **American Jewish Joint Distribution Committee** in Poland helping Jews expelled from Germany in 1938, and with Jewish self-help organizations during the war. Ringelblum is best known for his accounts of Jewish life under German occupation, especially in **Warsaw**. He established and administered the clandestine **Oneg Shabbat** Archive, which included reports and testimonies of Jews entering Warsaw from the provinces. This material, passed on to the Polish underground and sent to London, provides an extensive archival source on Jewish life under German rule. Ringelblum's own wartime writings are also an important source. He was connected to the **Jewish Fighting Organization** (Zydowska Organizacja Bojowa or ZOB), the Jewish resistance organization, and survived the Warsaw ghetto uprising in 1943. He escaped from the **Trawniki** labor camp in July, was recaptured in March 1944, and was executed with his family.

Rosenberg, Alfred (1893–1946)   Rosenberg was the unofficial racial theorist of the **Nazi Party** during its early years. He was born in Estonia and fled to Munich after the Russian Revolution in 1917. In 1919 he joined the fledgling Nazi Party, and four years later became editor of its newspaper, *Völkischer Beobachter*. An early Hitler adviser and the NSDAP's racial theorist, Rosenberg wrote several books on the alleged Jewish world conspiracy and its agents, Bolshevism and Zionism. His influence on Hitler declined dramatically after 1933. In July 1941 Hitler appointed him Minister for the Occupied Eastern Territories, the territories conquered in the Soviet Union, giving him an indirect role after the SS in the extermination of Jews and **Gypsies** in the USSR and in the germanization of Baltic peoples. Rosenberg was convicted at **Nuremberg** and hanged in October 1946.

Rumkowski, Mordechai Chaim (1877–1944)   Born in Ilino, Russia, Rumkowski was chairman of the **Jewish Council** (Judenrat) in the **Łódź ghetto** from 1939 to 1944. Between 1939 and 1944 he helped establish more than one hundred factories employing Jews for the German administration in Lodz. In late 1941 the Germans forced Rumkowski to begin organizing deportations to the **Chełmno** extermination camp. He was unable to have the deportations reduced, but believed that working for the Germans and maintaining peace within the ghetto was the best way to save Jewish lives. He managed to extend the life of the **Łódź** ghetto longer than other ghettos in Poland, resulting in a relatively large number of survivors. With the advance of the Soviets, the Germans liquidated the ghetto, closed the factories and dissolved the **Jewish Council** in August 1944. Rumkowski and his family were deported to **Auschwitz**, where they were killed.

Sauckel, Fritz (1894–1946)   The wartime overseer of **forced labor** in the Third Reich, Sauckel was born in Hassfurt am Main. He joined the **Nazi Party** in 1923 and became Gauleiter (Nazi Party district leader) in Thuringia in 1925. Sauckel was responsible for mobilizing labor for Germany's war machine. In 1942 he was appointed Plenipotentiary-General for Labor Mobilization, ruthlessly deporting more than 5,000,000 people from occupied countries to Germany as slave labor for Germany's war economy. Some were Jews and **Gypsies** who were worked to death. He was convicted of war crimes and crimes against humanity at **Nuremberg**, and was hanged in October 1946.

Schindler, Oskar (1908–1974)   A German industrialist and **Nazi Party** member who saved more than 1,000 Jews during the war, Schindler was born in Zwittau in the Sudetenland. He came to German-occupied **Kraków** in late 1939 and purchased a former Jewish factory that produced enamel kitchenware. His firm, employing Jewish workers from the Kraków ghetto, produced pots and pans for the German army. When the ghetto was liquidated in early 1943, those not murdered were sent to nearby Plaszów **labor camp**. Schindler's Jewish workers continued to work for him. He protected them from the brutality at Plaszow and deportation to **Auschwitz**. In October, with the Russian army approaching Kraków, Schindler moved his 1,100 Jewish workers to the Sudetenland to another factory he planned to operate. His good connections with and payoffs to high **SS** officials enabled him to do this. Most of Schindler's Jewish workers survived the Holocaust, and Schindler was declared a "**Righteous Gentile**" after the war by Yad Vashem.

Seyss-Inquart, Arthur (1892–1946) The leading Austrian Nazi, Seyss-Inquart was born in Stannern, Moravia. He was Hitler's point man in Austria in the campaign for the **Anschluss** (union) of Germany and Austria. In February 1938, after considerable pressure from **Hitler** on Austria's government, Seyss-Inquart was appointed Austrian Minister of the Interior with control over the police and internal security. When Austrian Chancellor Kurt Schuschnigg was forced to resign on March 2, Hitler demanded that Seyss-Inquart succeed him. German troops entered Austria, the union was accomplished, and Hitler appointed him Governor of the Ostmark (Austria). In October 1939 he was appointed deputy to **Hans Frank**, the governor of the **General Government** in Poland. In May 1940 he became Reich Commissioner for the Netherlands, a post he held until the end of the war. Seyss-Inquart supervised the recruitment of Dutchmen for forced labor in Germany and the deportation of Dutch Jews and **Gypsies** to Poland. He was arrested by Allied troops in May 1945, tried at **Nuremberg,** found guilty of crimes against humanity, and executed in October 1946.

Speer, Albert (1905–1981) Architect and wartime Minister of Armaments and Munitions, Speer was born in Mannheim. He joined the **Nazi Party** in early 1931, developing a personal relationship with **Adolf Hitler,** who promoted his career as an architect. In 1933 Speer was put in charge of designing the large Nazi Party rallies, and Hitler soon entrusted him with significant architectural projects. These included the new Reich Chancellery in Berlin, and the eventual rebuilding of Berlin and other German cities according to Hitler's grandiose visions for future. Speer became Minister of Armaments and War Production in 1942, and his control over war production made him responsible for the exploitation of **slave labor**. He kept the German military machine going in spite of shortages and Allied bombing. In 1945 he became disillusioned and resisted Hitler's orders to destroy German industry in the face of advancing Allied armies. At his trial in Nuremberg in 1946, Speer admitted to serving the Nazi state and using slave labor. He was found guilty of crimes against humanity and sentenced to twenty years in prison. For his efforts to end the war sooner and his cooperative manner, his life was spared. While in prison he wrote his best-selling memoir of his role in the Third Reich, published in English in 1970 as *Inside the Third Reich.*

Stangl, Franz (1908–1971) Born in Altmünster, Austria, Stangl was Commandant of the **Sobibór** and **Treblinka extermination camps** in 1942 and 1943. He joined the Austrian police in 1931, and became a member of the **Nazi Party** in Austria in 1936. In 1938, he joined the **SS** and served with the **Gestapo** in Linz before being assigned to the **euthanasia** killing center in Hartheim, near Linz, where handicapped people and political prisoners from concentration camps were murdered. In the spring of 1942 he became commandant of the Sobibór extermination camp, where he oversaw the murder of some 100,000 Jews before being transferred to Treblinka in September. In less than a year, he supervised the murder of approximately 800,000 Jews at Treblinka. He was transferred to Trieste with **Odilo Globocnik** and Lublin T4 (euthanasia) personnel in August 1943 to participate in the campaign against Yugoslav partisans. Stangl was captured by American forces in 1945 and handed over to Austrian authorities for prosecution. His record at Sobibór and Treblinka was unknown at the time. He escaped to Rome in 1948 and made his way to Syria. In 1951 he and his family moved to Brazil, where he lived and worked for sixteen years before he was extradited to West Germany in 1967. He was convicted of murder for his actions at Treblinka, received a life sentence, and died in prison in 1971.

Stauffenberg, Claus Schenk Graf von (1907–1944) Born in Greifenstein Castle in Upper Franconia, Stauffenberg was a key figure in the conspiracy to assassinate **Adolf Hitler** on July 20, 1944. He joined the **German army** as an officer cadet in 1926. A devout Roman Catholic, he believed in Germany's rebirth and was initially positive toward aspects of the Nazi program. After witnessing the extermination of Jews in the Soviet Union, Stauffenberg joined the **resistance**. He declared himself ready to kill Hitler, and in June 1944, as chief of staff to General Fromm of the Reserve Army and therefore having access to Hitler, Stauffenberg was selected to carry out the assassination. On July 20 he carried two concealed bombs to a meeting at Hitler's headquarters in East Prussia, but he was able to arm only one of the bombs and to leave the compound just before it exploded. He returned to Berlin to lead the coup d'état, believing the bomb had killed Hitler. Hitler survived, the Home Army refused to join the coup, and the conspiracy collapsed. Stauffenberg was arrested and shot that same day.

Streicher, Julius (1885–1946) Born in Fleinhausen, Bavaria, Streicher was a rabid antisemite, Nazi Germany's leading Jew-baiter, and publisher of the **antisemitic** newspaper *Der Stürmer*. He joined the **Nazi Party** in 1921, was Gauleiter (Nazi Party district leader) of Franconia from 1925 until 1940, and Hitler's close friend. He gained notoriety in Nazi circles through *Der Stürmer*, which he founded in 1923 and edited until 1945. It was devoted to sensationalist and obscene Jew-baiting with repellent illustrations of Jews and continuous

allegations of ritual murder, sexual perversion and other crimes. He organized
the April 1, 1933, anti-Jewish boycott, and, according to some, helped to write
the **Nuremberg Laws** of 1935. He was captured in May 1945, convicted at
Nuremberg, and hanged on October 16, 1946.

Stroop, Jürgen (1895–1951) The SS officer in charge of liquidating the **Warsaw Ghetto** in 1943, Stroop was born in Detmold. In 1932 he joined the Nazi
Party and the SS, becoming an SS-Oberführer and **police** commander by 1939.
After liquidating the Warsaw Ghetto in April 1943 and crushing the ghetto uprising, Stroop continued to serve as SS and police commander in the Warsaw
district. He was arrested after the war, tried by an American military court in
Dachau, convicted, and sentenced to death. He was extradited to Poland,
where he was convicted by a Warsaw court in July 1951 and hanged.

Tenenbaum, Mordechai (1916–?) Born in **Warsaw**, Tenenbaum was a leader
in the Jewish underground in **Vilna**, Warsaw, and **Białystok**. He fled Warsaw to
Vilna in 1939 to avoid the Germans. When the Germans entered Vilna in June
1941 he worked in the underground providing forged papers. He traveled
around occupied Poland on forged papers helping Jews to escape. He was a
founder of the Blok Antyfaszystowski (Anti-Fascist Bloc), a union of Jewish underground organizations whose activities included the publication of underground newspapers and other forms of resistance. He was also a founding member of the **Zydowska Organizacja Bojowa (Jewish Fighting Organization** or
ZOB), a Jewish underground resistance organization. In late 1942 he arrived in
the Białystok ghetto, where he organized an underground movement and
archive containing documents describing Jewish life in the ghetto. Throughout
1943 he organized, trained, and armed the ghetto resistance in Białystok. In August, anticipating the ghetto's liquidation, Tenenbaum gave the order for the
uprising to begin. Some escaped to the forests, but most did not. Tenenbaum
was never seen again.

Tiso, Jozef (1887–1947) A Slovak nationalist, Roman **Catholic** priest, and proGerman collaborator, Tiso ruled Slovakia from 1939 to 1945. He opposed the
union of Czechs and Slovaks after World War I. After the Munich conference
of September 1938, Slovakia became an autonomous state with Tiso as its
leader. In March 1939, after Hitler's takeover of **Bohemia and Moravia**, Tiso
declared Slovakia an independent state, allied to Germany. As Hitler's loyal
ally, Tiso agreed to the deportation of Slovakian Jews to Nazi camps in Poland
in 1942. But a few months later, alarmed by reports of mass exterminations and
pressured by the Vatican, he suspended the deportations. At the end of the war
he was tried in Czechoslovakia, sentenced to death, and executed.

Wallenberg, Raoul (1912–?) A Swedish businessman, Wallenberg was sent to

Budapest in July 1944 by the Swedish Foreign Ministry to help protect the 200,000 Jews who remained in the city after more than 400,000 had been deported from Hungary to **Auschwitz**. The Hungarian government had temporarily stopped the deportations in response to international pressure, but the intensely antisemitic **Arrow Cross Party** seized power in October, threatening to cooperate with the Germans and resume the deportations. Wallenberg issued Swedish passports to Jews and set up protective hostels, saving many from deportation to Auschwitz and **Eichmann's** "death marches" to the Austrian border. When the Soviets liberated Budapest in January 1945 they accused Wallenberg of spying for the Germans. He disappeared and was never seen again. After claiming no knowledge of Wallenberg's whereabouts after the war, Moscow announced in 1956 that he had died in a Soviet prison in 1947. Wallenberg has been memorialized throughout the world for his rescue efforts. Yad Vashem declared him a "**Righteous Gentile**," and the U.S. Congress bestowed on him honorary American citizenship.

Weissmandel, Rabbi Michael Dov (1903–1956) A leader in the Jewish underground in Slovakia, Weissmandel worked to save Slovakian Jews from deportation to **Lublin, Majdanek,** and **Auschwitz** in 1942. He sought help from Jewish and non-Jewish sources in Slovakia and abroad, and he criticized the outside world for not helping the Jews. He advocated ransom payments to the Nazi authorities in Slovakia, believing they would stop the deportations in return for money. He passed on information to Jewish organizations abroad about the extermination of Jews, and he demanded that the Allies bomb Auschwitz and the rail lines to it. He and his family were deported to Auschwitz in 1944, but he managed to escape and to make his way to Switzerland and to the United States.

Weizmann, Chaim (1874–1952) Scientist, statesman, and first president of Israel, Weizmann was born in Motol, Russia. He studied in Germany and Switzerland and eventually settled in England in 1904, where he taught biochemistry at the University of Manchester. He became active in the English Zionist Federation and the **World Zionist Organization** before World War I, becoming the principal **Zionist** leader in England in the negotiations with the British government for the Balfour Declaration in 1917. Weizmann was president of the World Zionist Organization from 1920 to 1931, and again from 1935 to 1946. He worked to bring German and other persecuted Jews to Palestine, both to save them and to build up the Jewish National Home. Weizmann published his autobiography, *Trial and Error*, in 1949.

Wiesel, Elie (1928–) Born in Sighet, Transylvania, Wiesel has been one of the most prominent Holocaust survivors for more than forty years. His first book,

Night, published in English in 1958, is a semiautobiographical novel about his experiences as an adolescent during the Holocaust. His other novels also deal with the anguished memories of his ordeal during World War II. Wiesel was chairman of the U.S. Holocaust Memorial Council from 1980 to 1986, and in 1986 he received the Nobel Peace Prize. Currently a professor at Boston University, he has helped to bring the Holocaust to the forefront of the American conscience.

Wiesenthal, Simon (1908–) Known best for his efforts since 1945 to find Nazi perpetrators and bring them to justice, Wiesenthal was born near **L'vov** in eastern Poland. He was educated as an architect and was working in L'vov when it was occupied by the Soviet Union in September 1939. After the Germans invaded the Soviet Union and occupied Lvov in 1941, Wiesenthal was sent to several camps and barely survived. After the war he assisted the U.S. Army in identifying Nazi **war criminals** and bringing them to trial. He has continued the search for Nazi war criminals as director the Jewish Documentation Center in Vienna. His several books about his life and work include *The Murderers Among Us*.

Wirth, Christian (1885–1944) Wirth was an administrator at the T4 **euthanasia** killing center in Hartheim, Austria, and roving inspector for all the T4 centers in Germany in 1940 and 1941. Born in Württemberg in 1885, he joined the **Nazi Party** in 1931, the **SA** in 1933, and in 1939 he transferred to the **SS**. He became commandant of the **Belzec extermination camp** in 1942, and acted as inspector for the **Operation Reinhard** extermination camps (Belzec, **Sobibór**, and **Treblinka**) in 1942 and 1943. His administration of the camps was brutal, earning him the nickname "Christian the Terrible." After his transfer to Trieste in 1943, Wirth was killed by Yugoslav partisans in 1944.

Wise, Rabbi Stephen Samuel (1874–1949) An American Jewish leader and reform rabbi, Wise was a founder of the **Zionist** movement in the United States. He was among the founders of the American Jewish Congress in 1920 and the **World Jewish Congress** in 1936. In response to German persecution of Jews in the 1930's, he was active in promoting the boycott of German products in the United States. Wise tried to mediate conflicts between Jewish groups and the Roosevelt administration regarding the American response to persecution of the Jews.

Zuckerman, Yitzhak (1915–1981) Active in the **Jewish resistance** in Poland during the war, Zuckerman was born in **Vilna**. When Germany invaded Poland, he left for Soviet-occupied eastern Poland. In April 1940 he entered German-occupied territory to promote underground activity, and he became one of the leading Jewish underground figures in Poland throughout the war.

In early 1942, with the start of the **Final Solution**, Zuckerman helped to organize armed Jewish resistance. He was a founder of the **Zydowska Organizacja Bojowa (Jewish Fighting Force or ZOB)** in 1942, helped prepare the **Warsaw ghetto** uprising in 1943, and acted as a liaison between the ZOB and the Polish underground in an effort to supply the ghetto fighters with arms. In the summer of 1944 he and remnants of the ZOB supported the Warsaw Polish uprising. He was liberated by the Soviet army in January 1945 and emigrated to Palestine in 1947, where he helped found the Ghetto Fighters' Kibbutz in western Galilee and sponsored the Ghetto Fighters Museum.

Zygelbojm, Samuel Artur (1895–1943)   Active in the wartime Jewish underground in Poland, Zygelbojm was born in Borowice, near **Lublin**. He was a leader of the Polish Bund, a Jewish socialist organization in Poland between the wars. At the beginning of the German occupation, Zygelbojm and others organized the Bund underground, and he was responsible for its relations with the **Jewish Council** (Judenrat) in the **Warsaw ghetto**. In December 1939 he fled to Belgium, where he told of the German persecution of Polish Jews. He went to France and then to the United States in 1940, and was sent to London in 1942 as a member of the National Council of the Polish Government in Exile. There he argued for a free, egalitarian, and pluralistic Poland. Beginning in May 1942, he received reports from **Warsaw** via the Polish underground on the extermination of the Jews, and alerted the Allies. In May 1943, when he received word of the final deportations of Jews from Warsaw, among them his wife and son, he committed suicide. Zygelbojm was critical of humanity, and of Allied governments in particular, for not doing enough to save the Jews of Europe.

PLACES

Auschwitz   The largest **concentration camp** and **extermination camp** in Nazi-ruled Europe, Auschwitz started out in 1940 as a modest "ordinary" concentration camp for Polish political prisoners. It was located near a main rail line in Lower Silesia, a part of Western Poland that had been annexed to Germany in 1939. Between 1941 and 1943 it was vastly expanded under the direction of its first commandant, **Rudolf Höss**. During that period two new camps were built near the original camp. Birkenau (Auschwitz II) was constructed by Soviet prisoners of war, for whom the extension was at first designed; later it was the site of four modern **gas chambers** and **crematoria**. Monowitz (Auschwitz III) exploited prisoner labor in industrial plants run by the German firms I. G. Farben, Krupp, and Siemens. Around forty remote subcamps also were brought into the Auschwitz network.

Auschwitz employed **Zyklon B** exclusively in its gas chambers. Unlike the other big extermination camps, which concentrated chiefly on murdering Eastern European Jews, Auschwitz received deportation trains from all over Nazi-ruled Europe. Approximately 405,000 prisoners, including Jews, Gypsies, Poles, and others, were actually registered to live and work at Auschwitz at one time or other, about half of whom died of overwork and disease. Additionally at least 900,000 were sent directly to the gas chambers without being registered at the camp. Recent research has shown that the total number of deaths at Auschwitz was between 1,100,000 and 1,500,000. Earlier, far higher estimates are no longer considered reliable.

Late in 1944, as the Soviet army neared Auschwitz, **Heinrich Himmler** ordered an end to the gassings, the destruction of the gas chambers and crematoria, and the removal of prisoners to concentration camps inside Germany. On January 18, 1945, the SS began to evacuate 58,000 of the remaining prisoners on foot, leaving behind more than 6,000 of the sick and dying to be liberated by the Russians. The evacuation was too hasty to permit extensive destruction of the camp, and today Auschwitz I and II are part of a museum and research center that receives thousands of visitors every year.

Babi Yar This partially wooded ravine on the outskirts of the Ukrainian capital of Kiev was the scene of systematic mass murders following the German conquest of the city in September 1941. The first occurred on September 29 and 30, when the Germans retaliated for the bombing of their headquarters in the city by shooting around 34,000 Jews and burying them in the ravine. Subsequent massacres at Babi Yar of Jews, Gypsies, and Soviet prisoners of war brought the total number of victims to as many as 100,000. In 1943, as the Red Army counterattacked in the Ukraine, the Germans forced concentration camp prisoners to exhume and burn the bodies. In 1961 the Soviet poet Yevgeni Yevtushenko commemorated Babi Yar with a poem that Dmitri Shostakovich later set to music in his Thirteenth Symphony. In 1974 a monument to the victims was erected on the site.

Bełzec The prototype of the three **extermination camps** of **Operation Reinhard**, Bełzec was located in southeastern Poland on the main railroad line between Lublin and L'vov. In November 1941 Poles and Jews from the area began constructing three carbon monoxide **gas chambers**, which were tested the following February and put into regular operation on March 17, 1942. When the original gas chambers proved too small to handle the influx of victims, they were replaced in June 1942 with six interconnected gas chambers having a total capacity of 1,200 people. The usual subterfuge about the arriving prisoners' taking showers before continuing their journey was effective because everything happened so fast; when the camp functioned smoothly the victims were dead an hour after their arrival.

Belzec was run by about two dozen operatives drawn from the T4 **euthanasia** program, assisted by around one hundred Ukrainian **Hiwis**. Much of the work of the camp was done by more than seven hundred "work Jews" who were kept alive as long as they were needed to clean the railroad cars, sort prisoners' clothing and valuables, empty the gas chambers, and bury the bodies in mass graves. Only one of these prisoners succeeded in escaping.

By the end of 1942 Belzec had completed its task of exterminating most of the Jews and Gypsies of southern Poland and the transports ceased. At least 600,000 had died at Belzec, most of them Jews. Early in 1943 the work Jews were ordered to open the graves and cremate the remains, after which they were sent to **Sobibór** to be gassed. The camp was then dismantled and all traces of it were obliterated. Today a monument to the victims marks the spot.

Bergen-Belsen   Located in northern Germany near the city of Hanover, Bergen-Belsen was established in April 1943 as a "detention camp" within the SS **concentration camp** system. It was built by prisoners brought in from other concentration camps and was designed to house prisoners, mostly Jews, who were to be exchanged for German nationals held by the Allies. The number of such exchanges fell far short of German expectations. In 1944 the camp began to fill up with thousands of prisoners who were too sick to work, most of whom were left to die. As the camp grew it increasingly took on the features of a standard concentration camp, and in December 1944 it became one officially.

During the last months of the war Bergen-Belsen was overwhelmed with tens of thousands of prisoners brought in on **death marches** from camps farther east. Hence a camp originally designed for a few thousand prisoners came to contain more than 60,000. As the Third Reich collapsed, the camp food supply and sanitation systems completely broke down and typhus took a fearful toll on the prisoners. Of the 61,000 prisoners who were liberated on April 15, 1945, at least 11,000 were too sick and weak to live more than a few more days. Before liberation at least 35,000 had died at Bergen-Belsen. A British military court tried forty-eight camp staff members in November 1945 and sentenced eleven of them to death and twenty-three to prison terms.

Bermuda Conference   On April 19, 1943, representatives of Great Britain and the United States convened a conference on the Atlantic island of Bermuda to discuss ways of aiding wartime refugees. By that time some sense of widespread Nazi atrocities against civilian populations was becoming known, and public opinion in both countries demanded action to help the victims. The conference ended with a pious statement of intent to do just that, but the only practical result was the establishment of a small camp for refugees in North Africa in March 1944. Although the Bermuda Conference was chiefly a public relations exercise to placate public opinion, there were few Holocaust refugees to help because the Germans would not let them go on terms acceptable to the Allies.

Bessarabia The region between the Prut and Dniester rivers in what is today Moldova and Ukraine, Bessarabia had a population of 3,000,000 before World War II, made up of Romanians (55%), Jews (10%), and Slavs (35%). The region was taken from Russia and made part of Romania in 1918, but in 1940 Hitler let the USSR take it back as part of his understanding with Stalin while the Nazi-Soviet pact was in force. When the Romanians sided with Germany and conquered Bessarabia in June 1941, they accused the local Jews of pro-Soviet sympathies and staged **pogroms** that left thousands dead. The Romanian strong man, **Ion Antonescu**, then ordered the remaining Bessarabian Jews and Jews from neighboring Bukovina removed across the Dniester River into **Transnistria**, where many of them died in concentration camps and shootings. Jews who had fled from Bessarabia with the retreating Soviet forces frequently were overtaken and killed by German and Romanian units. At least 104,000 of the 300,000 Jews of Bessarabia and Bukovina did not survive.

Białystok Ghetto An industrial town in northeastern Poland, Białystok had a prewar population of 100,000, about half Jewish. The surrounding Białystok district was home to an additional 350,000 Jews. In August 1941 around 50,000 Jews from the city and some of the nearby villages were crowded into a closed ghetto and forced to work in German-run factories. A **Jewish Council** (Judenrat) directed by Efraim Barasz was appointed to keep order and provide basic services in the ghetto.

The Jewish Council retained the confidence of virtually everyone in the Białystok ghetto until large-scale deportations began in February 1943. The ghetto underground, heretofore hopelessly divided along ideological lines, came together under the leadership of **Mordechai Tenenbaum**, who had been sent from the Warsaw ghetto to organize resistance in Białystok. When the Germans began to liquidate the ghetto on August 16, 1943, the poorly armed Jewish underground fought back but was easily crushed. In the next few weeks the remaining Jews were sent to **Treblinka** and **Majdanek**. A few dozen Jews survived by hiding in the city, and about 150 escaped to join the **partisans** in the forests.

Buchenwald One of the largest **concentration camps** in prewar Germany, Buchenwald was established near Weimar in July 1937. Its first inmates were German political prisoners as well as **Gypsies** and others designated as "asocial elements," and for a short time after **Crystal Night** (Kristallnacht) they were joined by thousands of German Jews. During the war additional German and other political prisoners and Polish and Soviet prisoners of war swelled the camp, and the inmates were put to work at armament factories just outside the gates. Some 20,000 Jewish prisoners were sent to Buchenwald from the east during the last year of the war. By 1945 the main camp held more than 80,000 prisoners, and additional numbers were held in Buchenwald's eighty-five sub-camps, the most famous of which was **Dora-Mittelbau**.

A corruption scandal involving **SS** men and German convicts serving as **prisoner functionaries** caused the camp commander to turn camp functions over to the political prisoners in 1938. This gave the camp underground some influence over camp life and made Buchenwald less hellish than other concentration camps. When the SS guards abandoned the main camp in April 1945, the prisoners liberated themselves shortly before the arrival of the American army. Prisoners at some of the subcamps were not so lucky. Those at Ohrdruf, for example, were massacred by the SS. Of the approximately 239,000 prisoners who passed through Buchenwald and its subcamps, it is estimated that more than 56,000 perished.

Chełmno Sometimes referred to by its German name, Kulmhof, this small village in western Poland was the site of the first German camp to begin regular mass killings and the only one of the **extermination camps** to employ mobile **gas vans**. It began to operate on December 8, 1941, having been given the assignment of eliminating the Jewish and Gypsy populations of Western Poland and the **Łódź** ghetto. The victims were brought by rail to a nearby station and then loaded into trucks for the trip to the village. There they were forced into gas vans, which eventually drove their bodies a few miles out of town for burial in the forest. The digging of mass graves and disposing of the bodies was the work of Jewish workers, one of whom escaped early in 1942 and told his story in the **Warsaw** ghetto.

Chełmno was shut down in March 1943 but reopened in April 1944 to receive some of the remaining Jews from Łódź. The Germans abandoned it in September after forcing Jewish workers to exhume and burn the corpses. Estimates of the Chełmno dead range from 152,000 to 320,000. After the war the Poles tried and executed two of the Germans who ran the camp, and in 1962 West German courts began trials of twelve members of Chełmno's staff, four of whom received long prison sentences.

Dachau The first of the major German **concentration camps**, Dachau was established in March 1933 on the outskirts of the village that gave it its name, a suburb of Munich. It was created by **Heinrich Himmler**'s Bavarian state police, which soon turned it over to the SS. In June 1933 Theodor Eicke became camp commandant and made it the model for subsequent concentration camps and a training center for the SS Death's Head units, which guarded the camps. To the political prisoners who made up the camp's first inmates the Nazis later added Gypsies, common criminals, homosexuals, and Jehovah's Witnesses. In 1937–1938 Dachau was greatly expanded to accommodate the growing numbers of prisoners.

During the last year of the war the SS intensified Dachau's role in war production and increased the number of its subcamps to more than thirty. Thousands of Jews and Gypsies were brought in from the East to perform **forced labor**. By April 1945 malnourishment and overcrowding at the main camp and several of the subcamps brought about a typhus epidemic. It is estimated that of the 206,000 prisoners registered at Dachau at one time or other, at least 31,000 died. A crematorium disposed of the bodies on site. A gas chamber was built but never used. When Dachau was liberated by the Americans on April 19, 1945, about 60,000 survivors remained, one-third of them Jews. Others were liberated at the subcamps and from **death marches**. Later that year an American military court tried forty Dachau SS guards and sentenced thirty-six of them to death.

Dora-Mittelbau As Germany came under increasing air bombardment during the last years of World War II, the SS employed concentration camp prisoners to build and man secret underground armaments factories. The most important of these, code named Dora-Mittelbau, was located in the southern Harz Mountains near the town of Nordhausen. It began in 1943 as a subcamp of **Buchenwald**, whose prisoners constructed it under appalling conditions. In August 1944 it became a **concentration camp** in its own right with thirty-two subcamps and fifteen underground installations. Its most important products were the V-1 and V-2 rockets. Slave workers from Eastern Europe, including many Jews, augmented the work force, which ultimately numbered 35,000. Of the 60,000 prisoners sent to Dora-Mittelbau, some 20,000 died. A **death march** from Dora-Mittelbau to **Bergen-Belsen** during the first days of April 1945 alone resulted in thousands of deaths.

Drancy In this police internment and transit camp located in the Paris suburb of Drancy, French Jews were assembled for deportation to **labor** and **extermination camps** in Poland. It was established by **Vichy** French officials at the order of the Germans in August 1941 and modeled on the German concentration camps. Located in a former police barracks, Drancy was run by the French police under fairly tolerable conditions until July 1943. Later, under German control, conditions deteriorated. Of the roughly 70,000 Jews taken to Drancy, about 65,000 were sent east in sixty-four transports between June 1942 and July 1944. The majority were Jews from other countries who lived in France. Few of them survived. The camp was liberated in August 1944.

Evian Conference Convened at Evian-les-Bain, France, in July 1938, this conference attempted to assist European Jewish refugees but came too late to do much good. By 1938 intensifying persecution of the German Jews and Hitler's recent seizure of Austria had generated thousands of racial and political refugees in need of safe havens. American president Franklin D. Roosevelt proposed an international conference to find ways of helping them and announced that the United States would drop all barriers to filling its German and Austrian immigration quotas, opening the door to tens of thousands of additional refugees. In all, thirty-two countries, not including Germany or its allies, responded to the call and met at Evian on July 6–15 to explore ways of facilitating emigration and creating an international committee to carry the task forward.

The results were disappointing. Most countries took the stand that they already had accepted as many refugees as they could accommodate in a time of economic depression. The conference also established the Intergovernmental Committee on Refugees and charged it with promoting the emigration of refugees and finding additional places for them to go. With few funds and little authority, it had achieved nothing by the time war broke out in 1939 and thereafter became inactive.

Flossenbürg This **concentration camp** was built in 1938 near Weiden, a town between Nuremberg and the German-Czech border. At first it held 1,600 criminal and political prisoners who worked at a nearby quarry. During the war the camp was expanded to accommodate Eastern European prisoners of war and Western European resisters, and production was shifted to arms manufacture. In 1944 large numbers of Jews and other slave workers were sent to Flossenbürg and its extensive system of subcamps. As the war neared its end, all of these camps were flooded with survivors evacuated from camps in the East. A **death march** by 14,000 prisoners left the camp on April 20, 1945. Several thousand died before the Americans overtook it a few days later. Around 1,500 prisoners who had been left behind were liberated in the camp itself on April 23. Of more than 96,000 prisoners registered at Flossenbürg, just over 28,000 died.

General Government Officially called the General Government of the Occupied Polish Territories, this area initially comprised all of Poland occupied by Germany in 1939 except for the regions in the west that were incorporated directly into the Reich. To the original four districts of Kraków, Lublin, Radom, and Warsaw, a fifth, Galicia, was added in 1941. Its population of 12,000,000

(1,800,000 of them Jews) included large numbers of Polish and Jewish refugees expelled to the General Government from western Poland. Nazi governor **Hans Frank**, ruling from his capitol in **Kraków**, was expected to exploit the area's human, agricultural, and industrial resources to the benefit of the Reich. For the Poles this exploitation involved **forced labor** at home or in Germany, near starvation resulting from German confiscation of agricultural products, and destruction of their cultural and educational institutions. The Jews of the General Government were exploited in the same ways, but they were also ghettoized starting in 1940 and sent to extermination camps two years later. **Operation Reinhard** was set into motion specifically to annihilate the Jews of the General Government. When it ended in November 1943, only the Jews in **labor camps** or in hiding were still alive.

Draconian German policies in the General Government generated increasingly desperate underground resistance. Poles joined either the right-wing nationalist Armia Krajowa (Home Army) or the Communist Armia Ludowa (National Army) for small-scale raids on the Germans. In August 1944 the former staged a major uprising in Warsaw in hopes of liberating the city before the arrival of the Russians, but the Russians refused support and it was savagely crushed after two months of fighting. With the exception of the **Warsaw ghetto** uprising in 1943, armed resistance by Jews in ghettos and labor camps was negligible in the General Government. Without weapons or places to hide, there was little they could do.

The Russians liberated the General Government during the last five months of 1944. Hard fighting and more than four years of German exploitation left it a wasteland. Few surviving Jews chose to return.

Gross-Rosen Originally established in 1940 as a subcamp of **Sachsenhausen**, Gross-Rosen became a **concentration camp** in its own right in 1941. It was located in Lower Silesia near the Polish border. Its prisoners worked at an adjacent quarry producing building material for the **SS**. The camp expanded between 1942 and 1944, first by absorbing the Organization Schmelt Jewish **labor camps** and then establishing subcamps of its own using Jewish workers from the East. Hence Gross-Rosen was unusual among the concentration camps in Germany in having a majority of Jewish prisoners. The total population of the main camp and subcamps in 1944 was 78,000 (52,000 men and 26,000 women), about three-quarters of whom were Jewish.

Gross-Rosen and its subcamps became seriously overcrowded late in 1944 as the SS dumped prisoners evacuated from camps farther east. Gross-Rosen's turn for evacuation came in February 1945. Its prisoners were taken to other camps, most notably **Bergen-Belsen**, by foot and rail. It is estimated that by war's end 40,000 of the 120,000 prisoners registered at Gross-Rosen had perished.

Kraków The ancient capital of Poland, Kraków became seat of the Nazi-occupied **General Government** in 1939. In 1940 the Germans set about ridding this city of 250,000 of its 60,000 Jews. By the time the Germans established a ghetto in March 1941, only 18,000 Jews were left in Kraków. The ghetto Jews worked in German-owned factories, including the one taken over by Oskar Schindler. The Kraków **Jewish Council** (Judenrat) refused to cooperate with the Germans in rounding up the ghetto inhabitants, resulting in many of them being shot as the Germans moved in to do the job themselves. The chairman of the Jewish Council, Artur Rosenzweig, was executed as a reprisal. The ghetto underground succeeded in helping a few Jews escape, and it also carried out several hit-and-run attacks on German targets outside the ghetto walls. On March 13, 1943, the ghetto was liquidated and its residents sent to Płaszów labor camp (later made a concentration camp) on the outskirts of the city. Around 4,000 Kraków Jews survived in **labor camps**.

Łódź Ghetto Łódź, a large industrial city in western Poland with a population of 665,000, one-third of it Jewish, was home to the second largest **ghetto** in Poland during the Holocaust. Shortly after taking the city and annexing the district in September 1939, the Germans renamed it Litzmannstadt (after a World War I general), established a **Jewish Council** (Judenrat) under **Chaim Rumkowski**, and made plans to expel the Jews to the **General Government**. When the expulsion plans proved impractical, the Jews who had not fled were pushed into a ghetto between February and April 1940, and their numbers were swelled with Jews from nearby areas and Germany. Many of the 205,000 Jews were put to work in a variety of factories, especially textile mills, run by the Jewish Council. A separate enclave adjacent to the ghetto held around 5,000 **Gypsies**. Between December 1941 and September 1942 the Jewish Council believed that it had no choice but to cooperate when the Germans deported 80,000 Jews and all the Gypsies to the extermination camp at **Chełmno**.

For nineteen months after September 1942 there were no deportations from the Łódź ghetto, but disease and malnutrition took a toll of more than 43,000 ghetto residents. The Jewish Council induced the Germans to keep the ghetto going for longer than originally planned by making it productive to their war effort. Additionally it rationed scarce food supplies, promoted ghetto cultural and welfare activities, and recorded a clandestine history of the ghetto known as the *Łódź Ghetto Chronicles*. That lasted until Russian victories in Poland led the Germans to empty the ghetto from June to August 1944. Most of the 77,000 Jews went to Chełmno and **Auschwitz**, although others were sent to **concentration** camps in Germany. The Jewish Council's success in keeping the ghetto going longer than any other large ghetto enabled a relatively high percentage of Łódź ghetto residents to survive.

Lublin This city of 120,000 in Eastern Poland was also the capital of Poland's Lublin District. Jews made up one-third of its population. After the city fell to the Germans in September 1939, it became headquarters for **Odilo Globocnik**, the SS officer in charge of the **Final Solution** in the **General Government**. In the Fall of 1939 Lublin became an assembly center for Jews destined for a "Jewish reservation" under the **Nisko and Lublin Plan**. Following the collapse of that plan the **Jewish Council** (Judenrat) cooperated in providing Jews for **forced labor** along the nearby border with the Soviet occupation zone and in Lublin itself. Also in Lublin was a prisoner of war camp for Jewish soldiers from the Polish Army.

Early in 1941 the Germans began to deport Lublin Jews to other towns in Poland, and in April they established a **ghetto** that lasted exactly one year. In April 1942 more than 30,000 ghetto residents were sent to the newly opened **Bełzec** extermination camp. The few thousand Jews left in Lublin, for the moment considered "essential workers," were transferred to a "small ghetto" on the edge of town, but they, too, were gradually sent away, most to **Majdanek**. **Operation Harvest Festival** (Erntefest) in November 1943 did away with the remnants of the community, including the men in the POW camp. Only a handful of Lublin Jews survived in the camps or in hiding.

L'vov The capital of the Polish province of Galicia (now part of Ukraine) before World War II, L'vov was a city of just over 300,000 inhabitants divided almost equally between Poles, Ukrainians, and Jews. From 1939 to 1941 the city was occupied by the USSR and crowded with 40,000 Jewish refugees who had come in from the German occupation zone. Only about 10,000 Jews were able to escape the city when the Germans attacked in June 1941. Ukrainian nationalists welcomed the Wehrmacht and, encouraged by the Germans, went on a rampage that resulted in 6,000 Jews being killed. The Germans established several forced **labor camps** in L'vov, the largest of which, Janówska (or Janow Street), was also a place of execution where thousands of Jews were shot.

In December 1941 more than 100,000 Jews were herded into the L'vov **ghetto,** the third largest in Poland. During its one year of existence it was gradually depleted by deportations to labor camps and to **Bełzec.** The **Jewish Council** chairman, Henryk Landsberg, demanded compliance with the Germans, even though he knew the fate of the deportees, because he believed the Germans would do the job far more brutally if forced to act alone. By the end of 1942 just 10,000 Jews were left, and the ghetto was redesignated a labor camp.

In June 1943 it was liquidated altogether. The Jewish underground in L'vov was poorly organized. Its efforts to smuggle Jews out of the ghetto were hampered by Ukrainian hostility and the lack of nearby forests in which to hide. However, in the end the underground fought back and forced the Germans to burn and blow up the ghetto in order to liquidate it. About 3,000 Jews died in the process, and the remaining 7,000 were taken to the Janówska camp, which was liquidated five months later.

Majdanek Both a **concentration camp** and an **extermination camp**, Majdanek was established on the southern outskirts of Lublin, Poland, in October 1941 to hold Soviet prisoners of war. It soon came to hold other categories of prisoners, including Polish political offenders and Jews. Although Majdanek had several small **gas chambers** that employed both carbon monoxide and **Zyklon B**, most who died there were shot or succumbed to camp conditions. In 1943 a large **crematorium** was built to dispose of the bodies. Majdanek also operated six large subcamps in southern Poland.

Majdanek was evacuated in July 1944, but virtually all the Jews in the camp were shot in November 1943 as part of **Operation Harvest Festival** (Erntefest). Estimates of total casualties range from 200,000 to 360,000. Majdanek was the only extermination center where Jews made up a minority of the victims. The camp was hastily evacuated and only partially destroyed; today it stands as a museum and research center. Polish and West German trials of 116 members of Majdanek's **SS** staff resulted in death for fifteen and long prison sentences for ninety-seven others.

Mauthausen The Mauthausen **concentration camp** was built next to a stone quarry near Linz, Austria, by prisoners from **Dachau** and opened in August 1938, just five months after **Anschluss** (union) with Germany. Its first inmates were mostly political prisoners from Germany and Austria, presided over by brutal professional criminals who were chosen by the SS to be **prisoner functionaries**. Starting in 1940 Mauthausen held an increasingly varied international population in which Poles came to be the largest single group. Ultimately 198,000 prisoners were enrolled in the camp. As it expanded it added a large subcamp at Gusen, also located at a quarry. The **SS** designated Mauthausen and Gusen to receive the prisoners it considered the most dangerous and hardened. They were treated with exceptional cruelty, and the mortality rate was high. Adjacent to Mauthausen was Hartheim, one of the killing centers of **Operation 14f13**, where sick and dying prisoners were gassed.

Large numbers of Jews were sent to Mauthausen from the east in 1944 as the camp expanded its war production and built more than thirty additional subcamps all over northern Austria. During the last months of the Reich Mauthausen and its subcamps became seriously overcrowded with additional prisoners. As the American army approached, the SS marched the surviving 17,000 Jews to a new subcamp, Gunskirchen, near Wels, Austria, where conditions were so bad that only 5,400 of them were still alive when the Americans arrived on May 5, 1945. Altogether Jews made up about 38,000 of the more than 102,000 prisoners who died at Mauthausen.

Minsk Ghetto Today the capital of Belarus, Minsk was the site of the largest **ghetto** on German-occupied Soviet territory. About one-third of the city's 250,000 inhabitants were Jews, and in June 1941 they were unable to flee because of the rapid advance of the German army. Shootings of Jews by **Einsatzgruppen** (action squads) took more than 20,000 lives during the first months of German rule. In July 1941 the Germans established a ghetto for 100,000 Jews from Minsk and the surrounding region. A separate ghetto held 35,000 Jews sent there from Germany. Noncooperation and resistance by **Jewish Council** leaders and the proximity of Soviet partisans and heavily forested land to Minsk enabled several thousand Jews to escape the ghetto and form seven Jewish partisan groups in the area. But the vast majority of the Jews in the ghetto died. The last group of 4,000 Jews was taken from Minsk in October 1943 and dispatched by shooting or **gas vans.**

Neuengamme Neuengamme **concentration camp** opened near Hamburg in December 1938. Initially a subcamp of **Sachsenhausen** concentration camp, it became autonomous in June 1940. A center for **SS** and other German industries, Neuengamme opened subcamps throughout northwestern Germany to serve the shipbuilding, armaments, and other industries. Prisoners, including Soviet prisoners of war and **Gypsies**, were used as slave labor after the fall of 1941. By 1945, Neuengamme had some seventy annexes with a combined prisoner population of almost 40,000. In 1944 Jewish prisoners arrived from the east, about 13,000 in 1944 and 1945. Approximately 106,000 prisoners were sent to Neuengamme and its subcamps, and about half of them perished. The camp was evacuated in April 1945.

Protectorate of Bohemia and Moravia This was the area of western Czechoslovakia incorporated into the Reich in March 1939. The Munich Agreement of September 29–30, 1938, ceding the Sudetenland to Germany, left the Czech lands of Bohemia and Moravia in a reduced Czechoslovakia. On March 15, 1939, Hitler violated the Munich Agreement by occupying Bohemia and Moravia and incorporating them into the Reich as a protectorate. After ceding some of its lands to Hungary, Slovakia became independent and allied to Germany.

There were about 118,000 Jews and 13,000 Gypsies in Bohemia and Moravia in 1939. Violence against Jews, arrests, and the burning of synagogues by the Germans and Czech collaborators began almost immediately. In June 1939 **Adolf Eichmann** established the **Central Office for Jewish Emigration** (Zentralstelle für jüdische Auswanderung) in Prague to promote large-scale Jewish emigration. Modeled on his Vienna operation, Eichmann's office forced Jews out quickly, often without valid immigration visas to other countries.

When the war began, German authorities unleashed a reign of terror against the Jews in the Protectorate, including arrests, dismissals from schools and jobs, loss of freedom of movement and use of public utilities, and forced labor. By October 1941, when Jewish emigration from the Reich ceased, about 30,000 Jews had left the Protectorate and some 80,000 remained. About half the **Gypsies** had left as well.

Initially, several transports of Jews were sent to ghettos in **Łódź, Minsk,** and **Riga**. Most sent to Łódź eventually died in **Chełmno** and later **Auschwitz**. Most sent to Minsk and Riga died there, in **Stutthof** concentration camp, or on "death marches" to the Reich. Gypsies were initially sent to small camps in the Protectorate, and later to the Gypsy camp at Auschwitz. From November 1941 to March 1945 most Jews in the Protectorate (some 74,000) were sent to the **Theresienstadt** (Terezin) ghetto. About 60,000 of these were sent to Auschwitz and other extermination camps. When Bohemia and Moravia were liberated in May 1945 only about 2,800 Jews remained. About 78,000 Jews from the provinces had perished, along with about 5,000 Gypsies.

Radom About one hundred kilometers (sixty miles) south of **Warsaw**, Radom was settled by Jews in the early nineteenth century. About 30,000 Jews (33% of the city's population) were living in Radom when the German army entered the city on September 8, 1939. Radom became one of four district capitals in the **General Government** in Poland, the Polish territories not annexed by Germany. Many Jews and **Gypsies** from western Polish provinces annexed by Germany were deported to Radom.

In December 1939 the Germans appointed a **Jewish Council** (Judenrat) with Josef Diament as chairman. In March 1941, they established two **ghettos**. Several operations (**Aktionen**) in the ghettos early in 1942 resulted in the execution of some Jewish leaders and deportation of others to **Auschwitz**. In August 1942 the two ghettos were liquidated. Many were shot immediately, some were chosen for forced labor, and thousands were sent to the **Treblinka** extermination camp. Several hundred from the ghetto underground escaped and fought in partisan units. Only a few hundred Radom Jews survived.

Ravensbrück A **concentration camp** for women ninety kilometers (fifty-six miles) north of Berlin, Ravensbrück opened in May 1939 for about 1,000 female prisoners transferred from Lichtenburg concentration camp. A camp for men and another for children were joined to Ravensbrück in 1941 and 1942. By the end of 1942, the prisoner population was almost 11,000, and by 1944 Ravensbrück and its thirty-four subcamps had a prisoner population of more than 80,000. It employed 150 female supervisors (SS-Aufseherinnen) and became a training base for some 3,500 female SS personnel who served there and at other camps. Tens of thousands were murdered or died of starvation, disease, or from medical experiments that began in 1942. Prisoners were killed using a variety of methods, including shootings, deportation to **euthanasia** facilities or to **Auschwitz**, and phenol injections. A **crematorium** was installed in 1943, and gas chambers were constructed late in 1944 in which almost 6,000 prisoners were killed. Some 132,000 women, 20,000 men, and 1,000 youths passed through Ravensbrück, including Poles, Germans, Russians, Ukrainians, and more than 15,000 Jews and 6,000 **Gypsies**. In late March 1945 most prisoners were evacuated, and on April 30 the Soviets liberated the 3,000 who remained.

Riga Ghettos The capital of Latvia, Jews first arrived in Riga in the early part of the seventeenth century. In 1939, about 83,000 Jews lived in Latvia, about half of them in Riga. Although several thousand left the city with retreating Soviet troops, some 40,000 Jews remained when the Germans arrived on July 1, 1941. Latvian volunteers launched **pogroms** against the Jews, killing almost 3,000 by mid-July. The Germans issued the usual decrees restricting Jewish life and confiscating Jewish property.

A "Big **Ghetto**" was set up in August with some 30,000 inhabitants, a Council of Elders (Ältestenrat), and a Jewish ghetto **police** force (Jüdischer Ordnungsdienst). Many worked for the Germans inside and outside the ghetto. On November 19 those who worked were separated from those who did not and moved to another location known as the "Little Ghetto." Those who remained in the "Big Ghetto" were massacred on the night of November 29–30, with estimates of the number killed ranging between 10,000 and 15,000. A second massacre on December 8 resulted in another 12,000 murdered, leaving only about 4,500 Jews in the "Little Ghetto" and perhaps 9,000 Jews in Latvia by the end of 1941.

The liquidation of the "Big Ghetto" might have been meant to make room for Jews deported from Greater Germany in the fall of 1941, some 15,000 of whom arrived in the "Big Ghetto" by December. Others never reached the ghetto, and were murdered in the forests surrounding the city. About 20,000 Jews from the Reich perished in and around Riga between December 1941 and the spring of 1942. More Jews arrived from **Kovno** in 1942, and the two ghettos were consolidated in early November. A Jewish underground movement oper-

ated with little success. In November 1943 several operations (Aktionen) liquidated the ghetto, and the approach of the Soviet army led to more killing sprees
throughout 1944. When the Soviets liberated Riga in October, only about 150
Jews remained in the city.

Sachsenhausen A concentration camp in Oranienburg, north of Berlin, Sachsenhausen opened in the summer of 1936. A smaller camp operating in
Oranienburg since March 1933 closed before Sachsenhausen opened. Following the **Crystal Night** (Kristallnacht) pogrom in November 1938 some 1,800
Jews were sent there, and about 450 were shot. Initially, prisoners worked
mainly in a new brickyard, but in 1943 they began working in armaments plants
near Berlin. About 200,000 persons were imprisoned there between 1936 and
1945, including Soviet prisoners of war, Poles, Jews, **Gypsies**, and others. Mass
executions by shooting began in 1941, and a **gas chamber** was installed, probably in 1943. It is not known how many prisoners perished at Sachsenhausen. Soviet troops liberated Sachsenhausen on April 27, 1945.

Sobibór Sobibór **extermination camp,** located in eastern Poland, functioned
from May 1942 until October 1943. Along with the extermination camps at
Bełzec and **Treblinka,** Sobibór was part of **Operation Reinhard** (Aktion Reinhard), the Nazi plan in 1942 to exterminate the Jews of the General Government. SS-Obersturmführer **Franz Stangl** was commandant until his transfer to
Treblinka in August of 1942. About thirty **SS** men and several hundred Ukrainians and **ethnic Germans** (Volksdeutsche) ran the camp. Some 250,000 Jews
from Poland, the Soviet Union and elsewhere were killed at Sobibór, mostly in
the camp's **gas chambers,** which used carbon monoxide gas.

A prisoner revolt broke out in Sobibór on October 14, 1943. Many prisoners
were killed, but about three hundred managed to escape into the nearby forest.
Most were eventually caught by the Germans or killed by local Poles, while
some found friendly partisan units. About fifty managed to survive the war.
Those who had not joined the escape and had stayed in the camp were killed.
Shortly after the uprising, the camp was liquidated.

Stutthof Established in September 1939, Stutthof **concentration camp** was located near Danzig (Gdansk). The staff included **SS** men and Ukrainian auxiliary police. Before 1943 mostly non-Jewish prisoners from German-occupied
countries were imprisoned there. Jews from **Warsaw** and **Białystok** began arriving in 1943, and by mid-1944 mostly Jewish women entered the camp. By
1944, Stutthof had a **gas chamber** and a **crematorium.** Jews were also killed by
shooting and lethal injection. By the time of its liquidation in late January 1945,
some 110,000 persons had been imprisoned there, of whom 70 percent were
Jews. About 65,000 perished there and on the **death march** to the west after the
camp's liquidation. Stutthof was not liberated until May 9, 1945.

Theresienstadt (Terezin) This fortress town in northwestern Czechoslovakia became a **ghetto** for some 140,000 Jews from central and western Europe, and an unknown number of **Gypsies** during World War II. The Germans established the ghetto in November 1941 for the Jews of the **Protectorate of Bohemia and Moravia**, for German-Jewish World War I veterans, and prominent Jews from Germany and western Europe. It served to camouflage the nature and purpose of Jewish "resettlement," described by the Nazis as a "retirement" town for elderly and prominent Jews. Beginning in 1942, Jews from Theresienstadt were deported to the ghettos of **Białystok, Łódź, Minsk, Riga,** and **Warsaw,** where most died or were sent to **extermination camps.** Many were sent directly to **Auschwitz, Majdanek,** and **Treblinka.** Others died in Theresienstadt, mostly from starvation or disease. The Germans turned over Theresienstadt to the **Red Cross** on May 3, 1945, and the Soviet army liberated it on May 8.

Transnistria A region in the western Ukraine, Transnistria was conquered by Axis forces in the summer of 1941 and turned over to Romania. Of the approximately 300,000 mostly Ukrainian Jews who lived in this region before World War II, Romanians and Germans murdered some 150,000. Beginning in the fall of 1941, the Romanian dictator **Ion Antonescu** deported more than 120,000 Jews who had survived killings in other territories annexed by Romania (**Bessarabia,** Bukovina, and Moldavia), along with thousands of **Gypsies,** to Transnistria. Thousands perished during the deportations, and those who survived were confined to camps and **ghettos** where they endured hunger, disease, **forced labor** and brutality. At least 54,000 deported Romanian Jews died in Transnistria. By November 1942, Romania stopped all deportations to Transnistria.

Transylvania An area of mixed Romanian and Hungarian population and part of the Austro-Hungarian Empire until 1918, Transylvania was ceded to Romania after World War I. About 200,000 Jews lived there in 1939, most of them of Hungarian descent living in northern Transylvania, which Romania ceded to Hungary in August 1940. They were subjected to the same anti-Jewish laws as Hungarian Jews, with restrictions on their professional and economic activities and livelihood and loss of basic rights. About 40,000 Jews lived in southern Transylvania, which remained part of Romania.

When the Germans occupied Hungary in March 1944, the Jews of northern Transylvania, like Jews elsewhere in Hungary, were forced into **ghettos** and faced deportation to **Auschwitz.** In May and June 1944 almost 132,000 Jews were deported from northern Transylvania, part of the total of more than 400,000 Jews deported from Greater Hungary to Auschwitz.

Although persecuted by Romanian authorities in 1940 and 1941, the Jews of southern Transylvania were spared deportation. Jewish leaders, some Christian supporters, and the Romanian government foiled German plans to deport them. The Jews of northern Transylvania under Hungarian and German control were virtually wiped out, while most of the Jews under Romanian control in the south survived. Transylvania was liberated in the fall of 1944.

Trawniki A **labor camp** opened in the fall of 1941 near **Lublin**, Trawniki initially housed Soviet prisoners of war and Polish Jews. In the spring of 1942 Jews from Greater Germany, including Austria and the **Protectorate of Bohemia and Moravia**, were sent to Trawniki, where they died of starvation or were murdered in the nearby forest or at the **Bełzec** extermination camp. Factories were established in the camp, employing thousands of slave laborers. As part of **Operation Harvest Festival** (Erntefest), the plan to exterminate the Jews in the Lublin district, 10,000 Jews in Trawniki were killed on November 5, including members of the camp underground. In the spring of 1944, the remaining prisoners were transferred to a camp further west, near **Radom**. There was also a separate training site in Trawniki for Hiwis (**Hilfswillige**), civilians in the German-occupied areas of the Soviet Union who volunteered to work for the Germans.

Treblinka Treblinka was opened in July 1942 as part of **Operation Reinhard** (Aktion Reinhard), the Nazi plan to exterminate the Jews of the **General Government** in Poland. Like **Bełzec** and **Sobibór**, Treblinka was established for the purpose of killing Jews and **Gypsies** in this operation. Situated about 130 kilometers (80 miles) northeast of Warsaw, it was the killing center primarily for Jews from the ghettos of central Poland, especially Warsaw. The camp's **gas chambers** used carbon monoxide gas. SS-Obersturmführer **Franz Stangl** was camp commandant from September 1942 until August 1943, with a staff of about thirty **SS** men and more than a hundred Ukrainian guards. By the time Treblinka was shut down in the fall of 1943, more than 800,000 Jews and several thousand Gypsies had been murdered there.

An underground **resistance** movement planned an uprising and break out in August 1943, but the plot was uncovered by the SS and the revolt put down. Hundreds tried to escape, but only seventy survived. German authorities used those left behind to demolish the camp and then murdered them.

Vichy A spa town in south central France, Vichy became the capital of a new French state following Germany's victory over France in June 1940. Although the Germans occupied northern and western France, including Paris, and the central and southern region remained unoccupied, the Vichy government was responsible for the civilian administration of all of France. Under Marshal **Henri Philippe Pétain,** the Vichy regime was an authoritarian state that collaborated with Nazi Germany. The Allied invasion of North Africa in November 1942 brought Vichy France under full Axis occupation, which became a purely German occupation in the fall of 1943 after Italy's surrender to the Allies.

Vichy cooperated with German authorities in persecuting the Jews of France. In June 1940 there were about 350,000 Jews in France. About half were foreign Jews, some of whom had arrived from Germany during the 1930s or from neighboring Western European countries following the German onslaught in 1940. Most were Eastern European Jews who had immigrated to France much earlier. The "Jewish Law" (**Statut des Juifs**) of October 1940 and a follow-up law in June 1941 defined a Jew and drastically reduced the presence of Jews in French society. An **Aryanization** program in the summer of 1941 led to the confiscation of Jewish assets. Foreign Jews were particularly vulnerable and thousands were forced into **labor camps** where they lived under terrible conditions. Beginning in the summer of 1942, Vichy cooperated in implementing the **Final Solution** by helping to round up and deport Jews from France to the East. The first to go were foreign Jews, but French Jews soon followed.

Vichy collaboration in the deportations heightened opposition to the regime and split the French **Catholic Church,** which hitherto had supported the regime. The deportations continued until the summer of 1944, when France was liberated. About 77,000 Jews from France perished in the Holocaust, most at **Auschwitz.** About two-thirds were foreign Jews.

Vilna Ghettos Under Polish rule between the wars, Jews had lived in Vilna (Vilnius in Lithuanian, Wilno in Polish), since the beginning of the sixteenth century. By 1939, there were more than 55,000 Jews in Vilna, about one third of the city's population. Vilna reverted to Lithuania, which reverted in turn to Soviet control under the Nazi-Soviet agreement of September 17, 1939. The city's Jewish population swelled to about 70,000 from 1939 to 1941 as Jewish refugees from German-occupied Poland arrived. When the Germans arrived in June 1941 there were still almost 60,000 Jews in the city.

Two **ghettos** were created in September 1941, each with a **Jewish Council** (Judenrat). At the same time, **Einsatzgruppen** killings began, and by the end of the year some 40,000 Jews had been killed. The more than 15,000 surviving Jews in the one remaining ghetto continued working for the Germans in relative peace through 1942 and early 1943.

Jacob Gens, chairman of the Jewish Council since July 1942, pursued a policy of working for the Germans and making the Jews indispensable to German needs. The Jewish Council established schools and cultural and welfare institutions that helped to keep the mortality rate relatively low. But in the summer of 1943 German authorities began to liquidate the labor camps and murder Jewish workers in the Vilna ghetto. In August and September, the ghetto was liquidated. Some 2,500 remained to work in Vilna, but most were sent to other camps, or to **Sobibór** or elsewhere to be killed. Some went into hiding, but most were caught. Vilna was liberated on July 13, 1944. Between 2,000 and 3,000 Vilna Jews survived.

Wannsee Conference At a meeting in the Wannsee district of Berlin on January 20, 1942, Nazi leaders discussed the implementation of the **Final Solution** (Endlösung), the plan to exterminate the Jews of Europe. **Reinhard Heydrich**, head of the **Reich Security Main Office** (Reichssicherheitshauptamt or RSHA), called this meeting of fourteen top Nazi officials from the **police**, government, and party agencies to secure their cooperation.

The decision to exterminate the Jews of Europe had already been made in late 1941, and the mass murder of Jews in the Soviet Union had been under way since July. Thus, the meeting was not intended to debate extermination, but rather to implement it throughout Europe. Most in attendance knew that Jews were being systematically murdered in the Soviet Union, and some were **SS** and police officers who had participated in the killing operations.

Heydrich asserted his authority and that of the SS in the Final Solution. He outlined the plan to evacuate millions of Jews from all over Europe to the East, where they would be used for labor and exterminated. There was broad agreement and enthusiasm for the plan among the conference participants.

Warsaw Ghetto The population of Warsaw, the capital of Poland, was more than 1,300,000 when the city surrendered to the Germans on September 28, 1939. In October, it became one of four district centers in the **General Government** (Generalgouvernement), Polish territories not annexed by Germany or occupied by the USSR.

German occupation was characterized by terror, with frequent arrests, public and secret executions, deportations, and forced labor in Germany. German authorities restricted the economic, educational, and cultural life of the city and the rest of occupied Poland. Polish **resistance** movements, centered in Warsaw, engaged in military resistance. In early August 1944, with Soviet troops approaching from the east, the Polish resistance staged a full-scale rebellion against the Germans in Warsaw. The uprising was crushed and German authorities ordered the destruction of much of the city. When Soviet and Polish forces liberated Warsaw in January 1945, about 80 percent of the city had been destroyed. Almost 700,000 Warsaw residents, including almost the entire prewar Jewish population of about 370,000 Jews, had perished.

Jews had lived in Warsaw since the fifteenth century. When the war began in September 1939, more than 3,000,000 Jews lived in Poland, and Warsaw's population was almost 30 percent Jewish. The Warsaw Jewish community, the largest in Europe and second largest in the world after New York City, was the center of Jewish life in Poland. Jews were attacked on the streets and Jewish shops were plundered. Many were arrested and put into **forced labor**, most lost their jobs and livelihoods, and the economic restrictions of November 1939 severely curtailed Jewish economic activity and excluded Jews from public assistance. Jewish schools and other institutions were closed and Jewish property was confiscated. German authorities created a **Jewish Council** (Judenrat) under **Adam Czerniaków**, and a ghetto, established in October 1940, was sealed off from the rest of the city a month later. Jews were crammed into about 2.5 percent of the area of Warsaw.

German firms set up factories in the ghetto to exploit Jewish labor. Jews from towns outside of Warsaw, from Germany, and from other occupied areas, as well as several thousand **Gypsies,** were forced into the Warsaw ghetto in 1941 and 1942. Up to 400,000 people lived in the ghetto at any one time, and the mortality rate averaged between 4,000 and 5,000 per month. Between July and October 1942, about 300,000 Jews (83% of the entire ghetto population) were deported to extermination camps, most to **Treblinka**. By early October, when the mass deportations ended, about 55,000 people remained in the ghetto.

Underground Jewish political organizations and youth groups operated from the beginning of the German occupation. There was an underground press and a secret archive established by **Emanuel Ringelblum**, code-named **Oneg Shabbat** (Sabbath Delight), which collected thousands of documents chronicling the fate of the Jews in Poland. During the mass deportations of the summer and fall of 1942, underground leaders formed two armed self-defense organizations, the **Jewish Fighting Organization** (Zydowska Organizacja Bojowa or ZOB), and the Revisionist-Zionist Jewish Military Union (Zydowski Zwiazek Wojskowy). The renewal of deportations from the Warsaw ghetto in April 1943 was the signal for an armed uprising. From mid-April to mid-May, the Warsaw ghetto uprising was the most significant armed Jewish resistance against the Germans. About seven hundred Jewish fighters engaged in street battles with several thousand **SS** troops commanded by SS-Oberführer **Jürgen Stroop,** who destroyed the ghetto and flushed Jewish fighters out into the open. About 13,000 Jews were killed in the uprising, and most of the rest were sent to their deaths at Treblinka and **Majdanek** extermination camps. Probably a few hundred survived the uprising.

Westerbork   Situated in northeastern Holland, Westerbork was a **transit camp** (Durchgangslager) for Jews deported from the Netherlands to the East between 1942 and 1944. The German **Security Police** took over the camp in the summer of 1942 and used Dutch police as guards. Almost 100,000 Jews were deported from the Netherlands via Westerbork to **Auschwitz, Sobibór, Theresienstadt,** and **Bergen-Belsen**. A small, more or less permanent population consisting of Jewish police and workers was employed in workshops, health services, metal-working, education and welfare, and other jobs. When Westerbork was liberated in April 1945 about 900 prisoners, mostly Dutch Jews, remained in the camp.

TERMS

Anschluss (Union) In the Nazi era the term *Anschluss* invariably referred to the union of Austria and Germany into "Greater Germany." The idea long predated the Nazis. Pan-German nationalists had advocated the union of all Germans since the time of the wars against Napoleon in the early nineteenth century. It was thwarted by Prussian-Austrian rivalry and banned by the peace treaties that ended World War I.

When **Adolf Hitler** came to power in Germany in 1933, Anschluss looked less inviting to Austria's political leaders, who established a dictatorship and banned the Austrian Nazi Party in 1933. Hitler, however, made Anschluss one of his chief foreign policy objectives, and his opportunity came when Italy became a German ally in the late 1930s and dropped its objections to the union. In March 1938 Hitler sent the German army into Austria, which did not resist. The German dictator then returned to the land of his birth to great acclaim and announced that Austria was a province of the Third Reich.

The joy with which most Austrians greeted Anschluss was not shared by the 185,000 Austrian Jews, who immediately were made targets of violence and intimidation by Austrian Nazis. This so impressed the **SS** that it used Vienna for an experiment in forcing the Jews to leave, Adolf Eichmann's Central Office for Jewish Emigration (Zentralstelle für jüdische Auswanderung). Its success led to programs of forced emigration from the Reich as a whole in 1939. In general, Austrian Jews, Gypsies, and handicapped people were treated exactly like their counterparts in the rest of Germany during the Holocaust. Austrians such as **Adolf Eichmann, Odilo Globocnik, Franz Stangl,** and **Ernst Kaltenbrunner** played prominent roles in Nazi genocide. After World War II Austrians consistently promoted their own identity in order to mask their initial support for Anschluss.

Antisemitism *Antisemitism*, a term first used widely in Germany in the 1870s to distinguish modern from traditional antipathy toward the Jews, has come to mean hostility to Jews in all its forms throughout history. Among the oldest forms is religious antisemitism, notably Christianity's traditional contempt for Judaism as the religion of deicides and deliberate misbelievers. Equally old is cultural antisemitism, which objects to the Jews' aloofness from the larger societies within which they live. Economic antisemitism draws attention to "excessive" Jewish wealth and power growing out of the Jews' success in commerce, banking, and the professions. Political antisemitism opposes the Jews' associations with liberal and socialist political parties and movements. Racial antisemitism combines easily with any or all of the above resentments but views Jewish characteristics as biologically determined and hence immutable.

Antisemitism has existed for at least two thousand years, and yet most of the time Jews and Gentiles have lived together peacefully. Strong antagonism and even violence against Jews have broken out mainly in times of great social, political, and economic stress. Those who have shown the greatest susceptibility to antisemitism have often been losers in the process of historical change, such as farmers who lost their farms or small shopkeepers who could not compete against department stores. During the nineteenth century antisemites of all kinds referred to the "Jewish problem," by which they meant the issue of whether the Jews were qualified to enjoy equal rights with Gentiles. At the time virtually all of them opposed introducing Jewish emancipation or wanted to roll it back.

It required a strikingly venomous form of antisemitism to lead to **genocide**, and such was the case with Hitler and his closest followers. For them the Jews were not merely objectionable but the racially irredeemable masterminds of an insidious world conspiracy from which only Germany could save **Aryan** civilization. Just how widespread this extreme view was among ordinary Germans is a matter of debate.

Aryan   Derived from the Sanskrit word for "noble," the term *Aryan* originally referred to groups of people speaking Indo-European languages that included the various Germanic, Romance, and Slavic tongues as well as Romany, the language of the **Gypsies**. During the nineteenth century European writers began to use the word in a racial sense, assuming that language was an expression of ethnic and cultural traits. Racists in Europe and North America understood Aryans to be the "superior" peoples descended from Northern Europeans. Nazi anthropologists argued that Aryans were mixtures of various Northern European races having high admixtures of the blond-haired, blue-eyed Nordic race and found most commonly among the Germans, Dutch, and Scandinavians. Other Western European peoples, including the British, French, and Italians, had smaller percentages of Nordic blood and, while Aryan, were of lesser racial worth. Eastern Europeans, such as Poles, Latvians, Lithuanians, and Estonians, might have some Aryan blood, but not enough to belong to the "master race."

Nazi anthropologists supposed that proof of Aryan status could be drawn from physical characteristics, such as skull shape and hair and eye color, but family genealogies showing Aryan ancestry were required in order to obtain the "Aryan certificate" that was required for many official transactions in Nazi Germany. In practice an Aryan was defined as anyone who had no "alien" ancestors. The "Aryan paragraph" was imposed upon all German institutions during the 1930s in order to exclude Jews, leading to the **Aryanization** of Germany's economy and culture. Hitler's entire racial agenda was inspired by a determination to purify the Aryan population of Germany and keep it pure by eliminating imperfect Germans and all alien genes and influences.

Informally, "Aryan" came to mean anyone who was not Jewish or Gypsy during the Holocaust. Eastern European Jews referred to the area outside a ghetto as the "Aryan side."

Aryanization The removal of non-**Aryans** from Germany's economy and culture, Aryanization began immediately upon Hitler's coming to power in 1933 and intensified in spurts during the years that followed. It was intended to segregate the Jews from other Germans and impoverish and demoralize them so that they would emigrate.

Economic Aryanization began in 1933 with boycotts of Jewish businesses. The nationwide boycott of April 1, 1933, failed for lack of popular support, but local boycotts continued and in some localities brought Jewish businesses down. Extortion by greedy Nazi Party members also led to the sale of Jewish enterprises at bargain basement prices. This process of forcing Jews out of business and transferring their property to Aryans accelerated in 1936 following Hitler's great propaganda victory in the Olympic games. It reached its peak two years later when a series of laws banned Jews from one business or profession after another. After **Crystal Night** (Kristallnacht) the Jews were ordered to sell all their enterprises, land, jewels, works of art, and the like by the end of 1938. German Jews who did not have savings to fall back on became paupers.

Cultural Aryanization developed much more rapidly. The Nazis had long railed about the pernicious role played by Jews in "corrupting" the culture of the Weimar Republic. Under Hitler all German cultural institutions were placed under the control of the Reich Chamber of Culture, which was part of **Goebbels's** Propaganda Ministry. By November 1935 the last Jews had been ousted from the chamber, effectively excluding them from all levels of German art, music, theater, press, radio, cinema, and literature. Jews were, however, permitted to participate in strictly Jewish cultural institutions. Shortly after Crystal Night the expulsion of Jewish children still remaining in German schools put the final touch on cultural Aryanization. Hence well before the last Jews were deported from Germany in 1943, Aryanization had separated them almost entirely from contact with Germans.

Barbarossa, Operation The German assault on the Soviet Union that began on June 22, 1941, Operation Barbarossa was intended to bring World War II to a victorious conclusion by delivering a knockout blow in the East. Two years earlier **Hitler** had signed a nonaggression pact with Stalin in order to have a free hand in Poland and Western Europe. But by 1941 Britain's refusal to be defeated had produced stalemate, which Hitler hoped to break by rapid and spectacular victory over Russia. The initial victories were spectacular indeed, but they could not be sustained. By December 1941 German forces made it to the suburbs of Moscow but were then bogged down by the harsh Russian winter. In 1943 the battles of Stalingrad and Kursk decisively turned the tide on the Eastern Front against Germany.

Operation Barbarossa quickly brought several million additional Jews, Gypsies, and handicapped people under German control in eastern Poland, the Baltic states, and the USSR. Additionally, it unleashed the **Einsatzgruppen** for massacres behind the German lines. Some scholars believe that the Germans' early victories during the summer of 1941 energized them to begin the **Final Solution**. Other scholars argue that it derived from doubts about final victory inspired by stiffening Soviet resistance during the fall. Certainly the progressive barbarization of warfare on the Eastern Front, including massacres of prisoners of war and starvation of civilians, established a climate conducive to **genocide**.

Block Seniors. *See* Prisoner functionaries

Camp Seniors. *See* Prisoner functionaries

Camp System Between 1933 and 1945 the Germans elaborated a system of camps designed to isolate enemies of the Nazi regime, exploit their labor, and exterminate the racially undesirable. The first to be created were the **concentration camps**, which were extended into the conquered territories during World War II. Also during the war the Germans established a vast number of **labor camps** and six **extermination camps**. The victims were assembled for transport at transit camps. Additionally, six killing centers of the **euthanasia** program (Operation T4) gassed the handicapped between 1939 and 1941.

Capos. *See* Prisoner functionaries

Concentration Camps First developed for military purposes by the Spanish in Cuba during the 1890s, concentration camps came to be the favored instruments of modern dictators to isolate and punish nonconformists and terrorize whole populations. They were established in Germany during the very first days of Nazi rule as the first component of the **camp system**. They held **Hitler's** political opponents, mainly Communists, Social Democrats, and labor union leaders. By July 1933 there were 27,000 prisoners. The concentration camps were turned over to the SS in 1934, at which time **Himmler** appointed **Dachau** commandant Theodor Eicke inspector of the camps with orders to reorganize and expand them. Eicke shut down all but Dachau and in 1936 began to build new camps, including **Sachsenhausen, Buchenwald, Neuengamme, Flossenbürg, Mauthausen, Ravensbrück,** and **Gross-Rosen.** New categories of prisoners were added to the political prisoners already in the camps: **Gypsies,** habitual criminals, religious dissenters (especially Jehovah's Witnesses), homosexuals, vagrants, prostitutes, and others defined by German authorities as "asocial elements." Following the **Crystal Night** pogrom of November 1938, thousands of Jews were sent to concentration camps for a short time to extort promises of early emigration. The total prisoner population, which had sunk to 6,000 in 1936, rose temporarily to around 60,000 in 1938 and then declined to 21,400 in 1939. The inmates were forced to work in SS industries that helped prepare Germany for war.

During World War II the concentration camp empire expanded greatly, so that by January 1945 it held more than 700,000 prisoners. Concentration camps were established all over German-controlled Europe, especially in the East where they sometimes evolved out of **labor camps. Auschwitz** and **Majdanek** combined concentration camp and extermination camp facilities. (The pure **extermination camps** were not linked organizationally to the concentration camp system.) The concentration camps now held captured resistance fighters, Spanish Republicans, and Soviet and Polish prisoners of war in addition to the previous categories if prisoners. In Germany itself additional concentration camps were established, most notably **Bergen-Belsen** and **Dora-Mittelbau,** and large numbers of subcamps of the concentration camps were set up all over the country. During the last months of the war survivors of camps in the East were brought in to keep arms production going. Overcrowding of the camps and the consequent malnutrition and disease in the last phase of the war took many lives, as did **death marches** from the camps that sought to keep the prisoners from being liberated.

Crematoria The disposal of bodies at the German camps presented great problems that ultimately were solved by incinerating corpses in crematoria. **Concentration camp** prisoners who died from mistreatment or natural causes were at first taken to municipal crematoria, but as the numbers of such victims increased, crematoria were built at the camps themselves. At the **extermination camps** bodies were at first buried in mass graves, but this proved impractical because the ground heaved and noxious gases from the graves filled the air during hot weather. Hence the bodies were exhumed and burned; new victims were likewise incinerated and the ashes used for fertilizer.

At large, well-established camps such as **Auschwitz, Majdanek**, and the concentration camps in Germany, cremation was done in brick furnaces built especially for the purpose. At Auschwitz the new facilities at Birkenau combined both **gas chambers** and cremation furnaces in the same buildings, which everyone referred to simply as "crematoria." Elsewhere bodies were burned in cremation pits, holes dug in the ground in which fires were fueled with wood, alcohol, and various petroleum products. Cremation pits also disposed of excess bodies at Auschwitz whenever very large numbers of victims were being gassed and the furnaces were overtaxed.

Crystal Night (Kristallnacht) The only large-scale **pogrom** in Nazi Germany, Crystal Night occurred on the night of November 9–10, 1938, and is sometimes referred to as the "November pogrom." Some of the Nazi leaders were looking for an excuse to unleash violence against the Jews in order to speed up their emigration from Germany. The opportunity arose when a Jewish teenager living in Paris, Herschel Grynszpan, assassinated a German diplomat there. Grynszpan was taking revenge on Germany for mistreating his parents, part of a large group of Polish Jews who had just been expelled from Germany under appalling conditions. At that moment the Nazis were celebrating the fifteenth anniversary of the Beer Hall Putsch, and **Goebbels** convinced **Hitler** to exploit the assassination by instructing party activists to attack Jews and their property. The Nazi leaders hoped that popular indignation over the crime committed in Paris would induce ordinary Germans to join in.

Few ordinary Germans did join in, and many were outraged at the violence, but the Storm Troopers and other Nazi fanatics were sufficiently numerous and well-organized to do a great deal of damage all by themselves because the police and firefighters had been instructed not to interfere. The rioters looted and destroyed thousands of Jewish businesses, littering the streets with broken glass — whence the name "Crystal Night." Jewish homes and apartments were attacked, ninety-one Jews were murdered, and 267 synagogues were destroyed, many by being set afire. Around 20,000 Jews were arrested and taken to **concentration camps** where they were kept until they promised to emigrate in the near future.

Goebbels had hoped that Crystal Night would enhance his position in Hitler's inner circle, but the true beneficiary of the pogrom was **Hermann Göring**, who as boss of the German economy fined the Jews 1 billion marks in order to pay for the damages. Göring also moved swiftly to complete the

Aryanization of the German economy by ending all Jewish business activity by the end of the year. These and other anti-Jewish measures in the immediate aftermath of Crystal Night spelled the end of hope for Jews who had expected to tough it out in Nazi Germany. At the time no one could know just how little time was left for them to leave.

Death Marches   Coined by prisoners who survived them, this apt phrase refers to evacuations, usually on foot (but sometimes by rail or ship) and under horrific conditions, of German camps in danger of being liberated by the Allies. Forced marches had been inflicted on Jews, Soviet POWs, and others before 1944, but the truly massive movements of prisoners occurred during the last nine months of World War II. The prisoners, already weakened by long stretches of heavy labor, malnutrition, and disease, often could not make it, particularly when the marches occurred in the dead of winter. Those who fell were shot on the spot. Others died in their sleep from exposure. Allied planes sometimes bombed trains and ships crowded with prisoners. In some cases the death marches from camps in Eastern Europe proceeded directly to railheads in Germany where the prisoners boarded trains destined for **concentration camps** deeper in the Third Reich. But not always. With the rail net disrupted and the enemy close at hand, the **SS** guards sometimes directed their exhausted charges in one direction after another, scarcely knowing where to go. Additional death marches of Jews and Gypsies from Hungary and Yugoslavia into Germany were likewise costly in lives.

Something similar happened in the last days of the war as enemy forces reached the German concentration camps into which the remaining prisoners had been crowded. Many of these were wholly or partially evacuated and their inmates marched out of liberation's way. Again thousands of severely weakened prisoners could not keep up and were shot, although the confusion reigning in Germany at that time afforded some opportunities for prisoners to escape. At the last moment the SS guards either abandoned their charges or massacred them before running away. Altogether as many as 250,000 prisoners may have died in these death marches.

The death marches are sometimes portrayed as a final frenzy of gratuitous torture and killing by the SS. However, they are better viewed as the product of chaos as Nazi Germany experienced its death throes. The SS guards, knowing only that their orders were to keep able-bodied slave laborers out of Allied hands, and preferring guard duty to actual fighting, kept them marching to the end.

Displaced Persons (DPs)   Of the 14,000,000 European refugees uprooted by World War II, many refused to return home, becoming Displaced Persons.

These included large numbers of anti-Soviet Eastern Europeans and smaller numbers of Holocaust survivors. Jewish survivors who had attempted to return to homes in Eastern Europe sometimes found conditions so difficult and **anti-semitism** so strong that they left again. That was particularly true in Poland. An underground railroad of Zionist activists channeled the flight of Polish Jews through Czechoslovakia to Displaced Persons camps in Western Europe. Hence the numbers of Jewish DPs increased as refugees from other categories declined. By 1947 Jews made up around one-third of the 700,000 DPs remaining in Western Europe.

Jewish DPs sought out camps in the American occupation zones where they were not required to live with non-Jewish DPs from Eastern Europe, whom they suspected of pro-German sympathies. These camps were housed at former German military installations and converted concentration camps. Other Jewish DPs lived in homes that were scattered throughout Western Europe and supported by Jewish charities. All were the responsibility of the newly founded United Nations Relief and Rehabilitation Administration. The Jewish DPs, many of whom had already spent years in camps, were particularly impatient to get back to something like normal life. Their fate became a contentious issue as Zionists pressed for open admission to Palestine and the British government attempted to honor its pledge to the Arab majority there to limit Jewish immigration. Many of the DPs would have welcomed the opportunity to enter the United States, but American immigration quotas slowed the way. Illegal Jewish migration to Palestine became a serious problem for the British administration in Palestine.

In 1948 the British departure from Palestine and the establishment of the state of Israel opened the door to Jewish DPs. At about the same time the United States Congress adopted special legislation admitting additional numbers of DPs of all nationalities. Altogether about 250,000 Jewish DPs found new homes, more than half of them in Israel, and most of the rest in the United States and Canada.

Einsatzgruppen Variously translated as "operational groups," "special strike forces," or "action groups," the Einsatzgruppen operated as mobile killing units of the SS from 1941 to 1945. Before that small Einsatzgruppen had supervised the expulsions of Poles and Jews from territories annexed to the Reich to the **General Government** and the formation of **ghettos** there and in Łódź. However, four new Einsatzgruppen were formed to accompany the **German army** as it swept into eastern Poland and the USSR in June 1941. Their task was to round up and annihilate Jews, Gypsies, handicapped people, Soviet prisoners of war, and Communists. Consisting of a total of 3,000 men drawn principally from the **Security Service of the SS** and the German **Security Police**, the Einsatzgruppen were assisted by Eastern European **Hiwis**, German **Order Police**, and the **Waffen SS**. Whenever possible they also incited local antisemites to **pogroms**.

Each Einsatzgruppe was responsible for a particular sector of the Eastern Front: Einsatzgruppe A for the Baltic states and the northern USSR; Einsatzgruppe B for the north central sector around Minsk; Einsatzgruppe C for most of the Ukraine; and Einsatzgruppe D for the southern region, including Eastern Romania and the Crimea. Their usual method was to herd the victims into existing trenches and shoot them, although they also employed **gas vans** on a small scale. The total number of victims exceeds 1,000,000, the majority of them Jews. Although **extermination camps** were set up to do the job more efficiently and less publicly, the Einsatzgruppen continued to operate until the end of the war.

Ethnic Germans. See Volksdeutsche

Eugenics The "science" of improving the human race (or a race of humans) by selective breeding, eugenics was influential among anthropologists, biologists, and the general public during the early decades of the twentieth century. Its proponents believed that encouraging the "best" people to breed while discouraging (or preventing) the "unfit" from having children would better the gene pool and spur progress. An international movement, eugenics advocated government action to sterilize those deemed genetically flawed (negative eugenics) and provide tax and other incentives to encourage the best specimens to have large families (positive eugenics). Various combinations of these approaches were adopted in many countries, including the United States and the Scandinavian states, in the early decades of the twentieth century.

No country embraced eugenics more ardently than Nazi Germany. **Hitler's** preoccupation with race improvement was expressed in programs of positive eugenics that provided government subventions and lower taxes to Germans with large families. Laws banned abortions for German women, whereas illegitimate pregnancies were tolerated as long as the babies were of "good blood." Negative eugenics sought to cleanse the gene pool by forbidding Germans to marry Jews and Gypsies, inducing people with "alien blood" to emigrate, and sterilizing the physically and mentally impaired. Nazi eugenics measures won the applause of eugenicists around the world, including the United States.

The Holocaust was the radicalization of this eugenic imperative. The emigration of Jews and sterilization of the handicapped moved too slowly for Hitler. **Genocide** — first of the handicapped and then of the Jews and Gypsies — was both swifter and more final, and World War II provided the necessary cover.

Euthanasia A word meaning "merciful death," euthanasia is usually understood to be the mercy killing of the incurably ill who want to die. That was not its meaning in Nazi Germany, where the interests of the race superseded those of the individual. As convinced advocates of **eugenics**, the Nazis sought to weed out "genetically tainted" Germans and end "life unworthy of life," first by sterilizing the physically and mentally handicapped beginning in 1934 and then, starting in 1939, by gassing them. These victims did not want to die, and their relatives and friends could hardly be expected to approve of their summary elimination. Hence Hitler ordered that euthanasia be carried out as a secret program, named Operation T4, under the direction of an official from his personal chancellery, **Viktor Brack.**

The T4 euthanasia program employed carefully selected doctors to screen the medical records of handicapped and disabled patients in hospitals and asylums and identify those to be killed. Additional victims were found by combing the **concentration camps** for prisoners unfit for work or whom the SS wanted out of the way. All of these were sent to one of six regional T4 killing centers: Grafeneck, Brandenburg, Hartheim, Sonnenstein, Bernburg, and Hadamar. There they were gassed with carbon monoxide in **gas chambers** disguised as shower rooms. The victims' relatives were informed that death was the result of natural causes. But word leaked out about what was really happening to the victims, and public opinion against euthanasia, heightened by public protests from church leaders, induced Hitler to end the gassings in August 1941. In two years it had taken the lives of around 70,000 victims.

But that was not the end of Nazi euthanasia. T4 merely decentralized its operations in August 1941. Nazi doctors continued informally to kill "incurable' patients by withholding medication or by giving drug overdoses. There were more than 80,000 additional victims in Germany alone. Moreover, physicians in **Operation 14f13** gassed sick and disabled prisoners in the German concentration camps. The gassing methods used in the Holocaust were perfected in the euthanasia program, and almost a hundred of the T4 personnel went on to use their expertise against Jews, **Gypsies,** and others in the Eastern European **extermination camps.**

Extermination Camps These camps, the final components of the German camp system, were devoted entirely or in large measure to the immediate mass annihilation of prisoners. They took between 2,700,000 and 3,500,000 lives between 1941 and 1944. All six were located on Polish soil. The first, **Chełmno,** began operating in December 1941. It was followed in 1942 by **Auschwitz, Majdanek,** and the three **Operation Reinhard** camps: **Bełzec, Sobibór,** and **Treblinka.** The last three, exclusively extermination centers using carbon monoxide gas, were run by the SS and Police Leader of Lublin, **Odilo Globocnik.** Auschwitz and Majdanek, where **Zyklon B** gas was employed, were **concentration camps** as well as extermination camps and hence were administered by the SS Economic-Administrative Main Office (Wirtschaftsverwaltungshauptamt). Chełmno killed its victims with **gas vans** and was under the jurisdiction of the Higher SS and Police Leader of the Warthegau, former Polish territory that had been annexed to the Third Reich.

The six extermination camps are sometimes called "death camps," but that term should be avoided since death was commonplace at all German camps. The extermination camps were distinguished by their facilities for industrial mass murder and hence should be compared with the killing centers of the **euthanasia** program (Operation T4). The concentration camps were primarily designed to hold political prisoners, and labor camps were primarily devoted to supplying prisoner labor to factories, often as an alternative to extermination.

Final Solution (Endlösung) The Nazi "Final Solution to the Jewish Problem" is commonly understood to be **genocide** as practiced by Germany from 1941 to 1944. But that was not always its meaning. In the early years of the Third Reich the German leaders did everything possible to encourage Jewish emigration, chiefly through **Aryanization** policies. When that proved too slow, they advanced to deporting German Jews and planning the deportation of all the European Jews. During the first months of World War II Final Solution meant a "territorial solution" to the European Jewish problem. Possible destinations included **Madagascar,** Siberia, and the **Nisko and Lublin** "Jewish reservation." Hitler himself spoke of the Madagascar Plan as a "territorial final solution." But at some point in 1941 the Final Solution was redefined as the genocide of all the Jews in Europe.

Forced Labor With millions of men and women serving in their armed forces during World War II, the Germans exploited the forced labor of both Jews and non-Jews in Germany and the occupied countries. By 1944 non-Jewish foreign workers doing forced labor for the Reich numbered more than 5,000,000, the majority of them from Poland and the Soviet Union, the remainder from Western Europe. Although often poorly treated, these non-Jewish civilian workers were not always subjected to concentration camp-like conditions, as were the Jews and Gypsies.

Jewish forced labor began in the early days of World War II. German Jews were assigned to jobs in war factories, and some of the more skilled Jewish workers were not deported until 1943. Jews in the occupied nations of Western Europe were subjected to similar treatment starting in 1940. Polish Jews were formed into work groups to clean up and repair war damage as well as dig trenches along the new border with the Soviet occupation zone. In 1940 the **Jewish Councils** (Judenräte) were ordered to organize work crews for forced labor in **ghetto** workshops or in factories and work sites outside the ghetto boundaries. The Councils were also compelled to deliver able-bodied Jewish workers for deportation to special **labor camps**, some for Jews only, and others with mixed populations. Forced labor was likewise imposed on Jews who arrived in the East from Germany and Western Europe and then, in 1941, on those in the Baltic states, the Soviet Union, the Balkans, and even North Africa. Workers who weakened were sent to **extermination camps** and replaced. Forced labor was also imposed on all types of prisoners in **concentration camps**.

Tensions between Germans who wanted to exploit cheap Jewish labor as much as possible and those who wanted to get on with **genocide** were partially resolved in 1943 with the liquidation of most of the **ghettos**. But the following year acute labor shortages in Germany and the advance of the Soviet army into Poland induced a change of plan. For the first time large numbers of Jews — as many as 100,000 — were brought into Germany and set to forced labor in the concentration camps and their burgeoning satellite systems. Forced labor was also imposed on Jews by countries allied with Nazi Germany, including Slovakia, Croatia, Romania, Bulgaria, and Hungary.

Forced labor under conditions of sadistic treatment and inadequate nourishment and health care took the lives of hundreds of thousands of Holocaust victims. On the other hand, for the young, the tough, and the determined it could offer an escape from extermination. Hence Jews frequently vied for work permits and bribed Jewish Council members and German policemen for assignments to labor camps, believing that they increased one's chances of living.

Genocide A word invented by Raphael Lemkin in 1944 to describe the deliberate and systematic destruction of an ethnic or national group, *genocide* referred directly to Nazi racial policies then being carried out. It appeared in some of the indictments of German officers in postwar **trials of war criminals**. In 1948 the United Nations adopted the "Genocide Convention," which made genocide a crime in international law. It explicitly bans killing, causing grievous bodily or spiritual harm, preventing births, or transferring children from a targeted group to some other group with genocidal intent. Hence the meaning of the word is somewhat fluid. It is sometimes used to refer to the actual physical annihilation of all members of an ethnic or national group. At other times it is employed to mean the killing of large numbers of such group members or to "spiritual" or "cultural" destruction.

Gas Chambers Fixed installations to asphyxiate prisoners with poisonous gas,

gas chambers were first used to execute convicted criminals in the United States during the 1920s. They were used for genocidal purposes for the first time during the Nazi **euthanasia** program, in which experiments perfected the use of chambers disguised as shower rooms to kill many victims at once with carbon monoxide. In 1942 similar gas chambers were erected at **Majdanek** and the three **Operation Reinhard** camps, the only difference being that carbon monoxide was generated on the spot by internal combustion engines rather than coming from canisters. Euthanasia (Operation T4) personnel carried their experience with mass gassing to the new extermination centers in the East. The gas chambers proved superior to the **gas vans** and mass shootings employed by the **Einsatzgruppen** (action squads). Not only were they more efficient and secret, but they also minimized the stress on **SS** personnel by employing prisoner **Sonderkommandos** to perform the unpleasant tasks of body removal and disposal.

The largest of the gas chambers were built at Birkenau (Auschwitz II) in 1943. They were housed together with cremation furnaces, and the prisoners referred to the combined installations simply as **crematoria**. Before they came into use the **Auschwitz** commandant, **Rudolf Höss**, had experimented with **Zyklon B** in a small gas chamber improvised at Auschwitz I and found that it worked much quicker than carbon monoxide. While the big crematoria were being built, Höss used Zyklon B in gas chambers housed in small peasant cottages at Birkenau. Zyklon B was also used at gas chambers at Majdanek and several of the regular **concentration camps** inside Germany.

Gas Vans Trucks whose exhaust pipes had been diverted into hermetically sealed rear compartments, gas vans were in effect mobile gas chambers. Trucks were first used in conjunction with carbon monoxide canisters in 1940 during the **euthanasia** program; the victims were hundreds of German and Polish mental patients in the newly conquered eastern territories. In November 1941 the **Einsatzgruppen** (action squads) began to use the modified trucks to kill civilians and Soviet POWs; eventually more than twenty gas vans were placed at their disposal and continued to function until the end of the war. Gas vans were the only method of gassing used at the **Chełmno** extermination camp, where they killed at least 152,000 Jews and Gypsies. They were also employed in killing Jews and Gypsies in Yugoslavia.

Gas vans had the advantage of mobility, but otherwise they were found to be much inferior to the fixed **gas chambers** in the **extermination camps**. They could gas only sixty or seventy prisoners at a time. The hermetic seals often failed when poor Eastern European roads damaged the trucks' frames. Moreover, slave workers were not always readily available to unload the corpses, and

SS men displayed symptoms of mental stress when they had to do it themselves. And yet, gas vans took hundreds of thousands of lives during the Holocaust.

Ghettos In the Middle Ages Jews in the towns of Christian Europe and Islamic Asia and Africa were sometimes confined to specific residential areas called ghettos. Some were walled in, but most were not. At the time Jews did not find them objectionable since they, too, wanted to minimize contacts with their neighbors. By the nineteenth century ghettos had disappeared from Europe.

The Nazis revived ghettos in very different form starting in western Poland in 1939. They were intended to be temporary centers to collect Jews in preparation for mass deportations to the **General Government** in occupied Poland or, perhaps, abroad. At the time the Germans justified them in the name of fighting disease and "Jewish profiteering." The first large ghetto, **Łódź**, was closed in April 1940, and ghettos were then established throughout the General Government and later in Russia and the Baltic states. Eventually there were more than 350 ghettos in German-occupied Eastern Europe. These were usually located in slums and overcrowded with Jews from nearby villages and, sometimes, Germany and Western Europe. Ghettos also appeared in **Transnistria,** Greece, and Hungary. There were no true ghettos in Germany or Western Europe, with the exception of **Theresienstadt** in the **Protectorate of Bohemia and Moravia.**

Ghetto formation did not follow a master plan, with the result that ghettos took diverse forms. However, virtually all the ghettos were administered by **Jewish Councils** (Judenräte) that were granted a degree of autonomy as long as they followed German orders. Poorly supplied with food and medicine, the ghettos experienced high death rates; the Germans found this acceptable, but it does not appear to have been part of any premeditated plan for extermination. The ghettos lasted longer than originally intended because the Germans could not deport or exterminate all the Jews at once and because the ghettos provided valuable **forced labor**. But in 1943 the advocates of extermination won out over the promoters of ghetto forced labor, and the Germans liquidated most of the ghettos and confined the best slave workers to **concentration camps**. The last ghetto, Łódź, was liquidated in August 1944.

Gypsies The Gypsies, or Roma and Sinti, were predominately nomadic people of color who originated in Northern India. The Nazis designated the Gypsies as racially undesirable and, grouping them with other "asocial elements," sent many of them to **concentration camps** in the 1930s. Other Gypsies were confined in Gypsy camps that were located in the suburbs of the largest German cities. The biggest of these, Marzahn, was established adjacent to a sewage dump near Berlin just before the 1936 Olympic Games. German public health and police officials cooperated in segregating entire Gypsy families in these camps and setting them to **forced labor**. When the Gypsies were deported to the East starting in 1939, Gypsy family camps existed for a short time adjacent to the Łódź ghetto and, later, in Birkenau (Auschwitz II). Both were ultimately liquidated. Many scholars believe that, like the Jews, the Gypsies were targeted for total annihilation by the Germans. It is estimated that at least 130,000 of the 950,000 European Gypsies died in the Holocaust.

Hiwis/Hilfswillige In order to alleviate manpower shortages on the Eastern Front, the Germans recruited Soviet POWs and civilians to serve as Hilfswillige (volunteer helpers), during World War II. Hiwis were given special training at camps such as **Trawniki,** put in German uniforms, and ordered to duties behind the front lines as auxiliaries of the **German army** and the **SS**. Sometimes this involved service as drivers, mechanics, and cooks, but Hiwis were also employed as camp guards and in **Einsatzgruppen** (action squads) and police battalion actions against Jews, Gypsies, and **partisans**. As many as 1,000,000 men served in these capacities. Eventually the Hiwis were absorbed into special "Eastern Battalions" of the German army, which were used mainly for military support services in Western Europe and the Balkans.

What motivated Eastern Europeans to collaborate with the Germans as Hiwis? Some doubtless hated Communism and Jews and hoped to strike a blow for Ukrainian, Lithuanian, or some other nationalism. Others may have wanted simply to escape lethal conditions in the German POW camps. The Soviets routinely executed Hiwis who fell into their hands and insisted on their repatriation to the USSR after the war. A few eluded this fate and started new lives in countries around the world.

International Military Tribunal. See Trials of War Criminals/International Military Tribunal

Labor Camps These camps, wartime components of the German **camp system**, exploited prisoner **forced labor** under conditions similar to those in **concentration camps**. The first German labor camps were established in 1940 in Western Poland, which had been annexed to the Third Reich. The SS Organization Schmelt, named for its commander, Albrecht Schmelt, administered them. By 1942 there were at least 160 Organization Schmelt camps with more than 50,000 Jewish slave workers from Poland. These included separate labor camps for women. The prisoners themselves usually built the camps near existing factories, although in some cases they were required to build the factories, too. Camps on this model were established throughout German-dominated Eastern Europe to provide forced labor in SS enterprises and also concerns run by private German companies producing for the German war effort. The German armed forces and Organisation Todt, the German construction battalions, ran other labor camps.

Conditions in the labor camps varied considerably. Hence, when the camps were folded into the concentration camp system in 1943, prisoner environments improved in some cases but deteriorated in others. Labor camps for Jews were also run by several of Germany's allies, including Slovakia, Hungary, and Romania.

Lebensraum The German word meaning "living space," *Lebensraum* refers to the theory that nations "naturally" compete for territory and resources to satisfy the basic needs of their people. The theory was popularized by scholars of geopolitics in many nations before World War I and reflected the vogue of Social Darwinist "survival of the fittest" thinking. In Germany Lebensraum was taught during the 1920s by Munich University professor Karl Haushofer, who may have influenced **Adolf Hitler** and Rudolf Hess. It was also popularized by the German writer Hans Grimm, whose 1926 novel *Volk ohne Raum (People Without Space)* was widely read.

Hitler made his ideas about *Lebensraum* clear in the mid-1920s in his book *Mein Kampf.* Germany, he argued, was overpopulated and needed more territory. Colonies were out of the question for Germany because they would draw **Aryans** away from their homeland and alienate Great Britain. Germans had a "moral right," as the "superior race," to conquer and settle Eastern Europe, specifically Poland and parts of the USSR. Unstated, but implied, was the ethnic purification of these lands. Hence *Lebensraum* theory, together with racism, was the intellectual foundation for World War II and the Holocaust. The "lesser" races of Eastern Europe would have to be displaced or enslaved in order to make way for Germans.

Madagascar Plan The German Foreign Ministry proposed to deport European Jews to the French-controlled island of Madagascar in June 1940. Poland had attempted to win French approval to settle Polish Jews in Madagascar in 1937. In 1938, Nazi officials, and possibly **Hitler** himself, expressed support for a Madagascar option. The victory over France in June 1940, the expected collapse of England, and the difficulty of resettling Jews from Polish territories incorporated into the Reich revived the Madagascar idea in Germany. The SS supported the idea, and Hitler gave his approval in principle in May 1940. However, Germany's inability to defeat England rendered the Madagascar option unfeasible. The Madagascar Plan of 1940 was a serious but short-lived approach to eliminating the Jews from Europe.

Medical Experiments Nazi racial ideology, which called for the creation of a pure and "genetically improved" German master race, was quickly incorporated into the practice of medicine in Germany. SS physicians, working closely with German universities and research institutes, conducted medical research in **concentration** and **extermination camps** between 1939 and 1945. They performed painful, crippling, and often fatal experiments on prisoners, using them as guinea pigs to serve both Nazi racial ideology and the German war effort.

Some experiments had military applications, testing human endurance under harsh conditions. Prisoners at **Dachau** were subjected to high altitude and freezing temperatures and to drinking salt water instead of fresh water. At the women's concentration camp at **Ravensbrück,** prisoners were deliberately wounded and their wounds infected to test new medical treatments. Other experiments involved breaking bones of healthy women, and transplanting bones, muscle, nerves, and even whole limbs. At **Auschwitz** and **Buchenwald,** doctors burned inmates while conducting experiments to develop new burn treatments, while at Dachau they inoculated prisoners with chemical agents meant to assist coagulation of the blood. At **Neuengamme** and **Sachsenhausen,** the treatment of chemical-warfare victims was studied by exposing prisoners to poisonous chemicals. At Sachsenhausen and Dachau, physicians infected prisoners with hepatitis, malaria, and typhus to test new treatments. In these experiments, victims were deliberately injured, and subjected to treatments that were often just as lethal. Thousands died in these experiments.

SS physicians like **Josef Mengele,** Carl Clauberg, and Horst Schumann also conducted racial-ideological experiments on Jews and **Gypsies** designed to improve the "genetic health" of Germans and eliminate "racial enemies." Mengele's experiments on dwarves and twins at Auschwitz involved injecting victims with chemicals, infectious diseases, and other lethal substances to document racial differences and find ways of improving the **Aryan** genetic health. A project on Jewish skeletons involved murdering 115 Jews and using their skeletons to demonstrate Jewish inferiority. Sterilization remained a part of Nazi policy during the war. Experiments on men, women, and children for mass sterilization using X-rays on men and the injection of chemical substances into the wombs of women were carried out at Auschwitz and Ravensbrück. Mass sterilization, it was believed, would make Jews, Gypsies, and others useful as slave laborers, while insuring their ultimate elimination.

Physicians and others in the German medical establishment were tried at **Nuremberg** after the war. Charged with crimes against humanity and other crimes, some were sentenced to death and others received prison terms. The court ruled that the medical experiments violated universal medical ethics, served only the ideological and military objectives of Nazi Germany, but had little scientific value.

Mischlinge (Mixed Breeds) *Mischlinge* were persons of mixed German and

Jewish or German and **Gypsy** descent who were legally classified as such. Regarding the Jews, the "First Supplementary Decree to the Reich Citizenship Law" of November 14, 1935, defined two categories of Mischlinge. Reliable numbers for each category are difficult to ascertain. Mischlinge of the first degree (half Jews) numbered about 75,000 in 1935 and included people who had two Jewish grandparents, did not practice Judaism, were not married to a Jew as of September 15, 1935, and were not the offspring of "illegitimate" unions between Jews and **Aryans**. They retained most of the rights of other German citizens, but were restricted to marrying Jews or other Mischlinge of the first degree. They were excluded from military service in 1940 and from high schools in 1942. Individuals with two Jewish grandparents and at least one of the above conditions were considered Jews. Mischlinge of the second degree (quarter Jews), those with one Jewish grandparent, are more difficult to quantify, but might have numbered as many as 125,000. They were generally treated as Aryans. Because the intent was to absorb them into the German people, they could marry only full Germans. Those with just one Jewish grandparent but an affiliation with a Jewish religious community were defined as Jews. In late 1941 there were proposals to sterilize Mischlinge of the first degree, repeated at the **Wannsee Conference** in January 1942, along with proposals to treat them as full Jews and include them in the **Final Solution**.

About 90 percent of the Gypsies in Germany were also classified as Mischlinge. The **SS** classified them as follows: pure Gypsies (Z, or Zigeuner); mixed-race Gypsies of predominantly Gypsy blood (ZM+, or Zigeuner-Mischlinge +); mixed-race Gypsies of predominantly Aryan blood (ZM -, or Zigeuner-Mischlinge -); and mixed-race Gypsies with half Gypsy and half Aryan blood (ZM, or Zigeuner-Mischlinge). The Nazi regime kept Gypsies and Germans, as well as pure and Mischlinge Gypsies, apart.

The place of Mischlinge in the implementation of the Final Solution was never resolved. Confusion and lack of uniformity seem to have characterized Nazi treatment of Mischlinge, Jewish and Gypsy.

Muselmann Prisoners in camps applied this term to fellow prisoners close to dying from starvation, exhaustion, and despair. Their bodies were reduced to skeletons covered with tight yellow skin, their eyes devoid of expression, and they could barely stand up. Other prisoners avoided contact with them, while camp authorities tormented them because they could not work. Those who reached this stage did not survive. The term appears to have been used to compare the dying victims to Muslims, possibly pointing to the similarity between the image of the dying Muselmann wrapped in a blanket and that of a Muslim prostrating himself in prayer.

National Socialism (Nazism) National Socialism was an ideology that developed in post–World War I Germany under **Adolf Hitler**. It was intensely nationalistic and xenophobic, racist and antisemitic, militaristic, bitterly antidemocratic, and fiercely hostile to Marxism (social democracy and communism). It was distrustful of capitalism and big business and condemned labor unions. It championed German farmers, shopkeepers, small businesses, and workers who rejected all forms of Marxism.

The National Socialist German Workers' Party (Nationalsozialistische Deutsche Arbeiterpartei or NSDAP), also known as the Nazi Party, grew out of the German Workers' Party (Deutsche Arbeiterpartei or DAP) founded in Munich in 1919. Hitler took over as Leader (Führer) of the party in 1921. Its initial political agenda in Germany in the 1920s included opposition to the democracy and culture of the Weimar Republic, the establishment of a Nazi dictatorship under Hitler, and an end to the Treaty of Versailles. The Nazis demanded the reversal of Jewish emancipation and assimilation in Germany, as well as Jewish emigration. During World War II Hitler's regime pursued the German conquest of Europe and its racial reorganization. The Germanic peoples would secure a vast living space (**Lebensraum**) in Europe; the Jews, **Gypsies**, and the disabled would be exterminated; and the Slavs would be reduced to slave labor and eventually eliminated.

Nisko and Lublin Plan This was an SS plan in September 1939 to expel Jews and **Gypsies** from Greater Germany and German-annexed Polish territory to a Jewish reservation (Judenreservat) near **Lublin**. The war significantly reduced the possibilities for Jewish emigration, and **Hitler** approved plans to deport Jews to Polish territory not earmarked for annexation and Germanization. The German-Soviet agreement of September 28, 1939, placed the **Lublin** region under German control in return for Soviet control of Lithuania.

In October, Jews from Mährisch-Ostrau, Vienna, and Kattowitz arrived at Nisko near Lublin, where a transit camp had been built to receive and disperse them. The plan proved unfeasible because of the enormous numbers from western Poland who would have to be accommodated there. Only 4,760 Jews were deported to the Lublin area, all in October 1939. The camp at Nisko remained in existence until the entire plan was scrapped in April 1940. Most of its inhabitants were dispersed throughout the Lublin district, and about five hundred were returned to Austria and the Protectorate. German interest in a territorial solution to the Jewish Question turned briefly in 1940 to a plan to resettle European Jews on the island of **Madagascar**.

Nuremberg Laws Announced on September 15, 1935, at the annual **Nazi Party** rally in Nuremberg, the Nuremberg Laws consisted of two laws that furthered the legal exclusion of Jews from German life. The "Law for the Protection of

German Blood and Honor" (Gesetz zum Schutze des deutschen Blutes und der deutschen Ehre), prohibited marriages and sexual intercourse between Germans and Jews, and the employment of German maids under the age of forty-five by Jewish households. Jews were also forbidden to raise flags with the traditional German colors. Exemptions for Jewish World War I veterans and state officials in earlier anti-Jewish legislation were rescinded. Sexual relations between Jews and Germans henceforth constituted the crime of Rassen-schande (racial defilement). The "Reich Citizenship Law" (Reichsbürgerge-setz) did not alter the status of Jews as citizens (Staatsangehörige), but stigma-tized them as citizens of lesser worth by elevating Aryans to the status of "Reich Citizens" (Reichsangehörige), a status reserved for those with German or re-lated blood.

The application of the laws to **Mischlinge**, persons of mixed German and Jewish background, was not settled at Nuremberg. The definition of a Jew only came in the "First Supplementary Decree to the Reich Citizenship Law" of November 14, 1935. Full Jews and three-quarter Jews (three Jewish grandpar-ents) were declared legally Jews. Half Jews (two Jewish grandparents) were con-sidered Jews if they practiced Judaism, were married to Jews, or were the off-spring of "illegitimate" unions between Jews and **Aryans**. Half Jews to whom none of these conditions applied were classified Jewish Mischlinge. Even someone with only one Jewish grandparent was still legally Jewish if he or she practiced Judaism. Although not mentioned in the Nuremberg Laws, **Gypsies** were included in their implementation.

Operation 14f13   Operation 14f13 was the code name for the extension of the **euthanasia** program to **concentration camp** prisoners. The victims were sick and disabled prisoners and those who had repeatedly violated camp regula-tions. In the spring of 1941, Operation T4 doctors selected those to be gassed based on information supplied by camp officials. The victims were gassed at three T4 killing centers: Bernburg, Hartheim, and Sonnenstein. Although Op-eration 14f13 was ended in April 1943, prisoners continued to be gassed at Hartheim until late 1944. The total number of victims was between 10,000 and 20,000. Collaboration between T4 personnel and the **SS** in gassing concentra-tion camp prisoners formed an important link between euthanasia and the **Final Solution**.

Operation Harvest Festival (Aktion Erntefest)   This was the SS operation to exterminate the Jews in the **Lublin** district of the **General Government** of Poland in 1943. Throughout 1943 **Jewish resistance** in **ghettos** and camps in-creased. After uprisings in the **Warsaw** and **Białystok** ghettos, as well as in the **Treblinka** and **Sobibór** extermination camps throughout 1943, the Germans decided to eliminate the Jews around Lublin. SS-Gruppenführer Jakob Sporrenberg, **Odilo Globocnik's** successor as SS and Police Leader in the Lublin district, planned and directed Aktion Erntefest. The killings took place in the **Majdanek**, Poniatowa, and **Trawniki** camps, and a total of about 40,000 Jews were murdered in the operation.

Operation Reinhard (Aktion Reinhard) Operation Reinhard was the plan to exterminate the approximately 2,200,000 Jews in the Nazi-administered **General Government** in Poland in 1942 and 1943. It was named after **Reinhard Heydrich**, head of the **Reich Security Main Office** (Reichssicherheitshauptamt or RSHA), the man in charge of the **Final Solution** who had been assassinated near Prague by Czech resistance fighters in May of that year. **Heinrich Himmler** placed SS and Police Leader (SS- und Polizeiführer) **Odilo Globocnik** in charge of the operation. Three extermination camps, **Bełzec, Sobibór** and **Treblinka**, were built as part of the operation. A team of about 450 Germans, some participants in the earlier euthanasia killings in Germany, along with several hundred Ukrainian auxiliaries recruited from captured Soviet prisoners of war, were involved.

The operation included deportations, construction and operation of the **extermination camps**, and confiscation and processing of the victims' possessions. It was extended in late 1942 and 1943 to **Białystok**, from which the entire Jewish population of some 200,000 was sent to the extermination camps. Operation Reinhard claimed the lives of more than 2,000,000 Jews from the General Government and Białystok by November 1943.

Operation T₄. See Euthanasia

Partisans, Jewish Jewish partisan activity varied throughout occupied Europe, with problems unlike those of non-Jewish partisan groups. The Germans specifically identified the Jews and **Gypsies** as a whole and made them targets. This reality, and the reluctance of many Jews to leave families and loved ones for fear of never seeing them again, made flight into the forests and armed partisan activity problematic. Individual Jewish partisans and Jewish partisan groups could not rely on the support of non-Jewish partisans or the general population, especially in Eastern Europe. Jews in non-Jewish partisan units often concealed their Jewish identities, while Jewish partisan units in Eastern Europe were often shunned or betrayed by hostile populations and non-Jewish partisan units.

Beginning in 1942, Jewish partisan groups existed in the densely forested areas of the Soviet Union and Baltic states, with some 30,000 Jews fighting in mixed and Jewish partisan units. Many escaped from **ghettos** and camps, or emerged from hiding. Between 12,000 and 15,000 Jewish partisans were active in Belarus alone. Jewish partisans were also active in Lithuania and the Ukraine beginning with the German invasion of the USSR in June 1941. In occupied Poland, Jewish underground movements in ghettos and camps were extensive, but armed partisan activity was not nearly as widespread. Polish partisan groups tended to be more **antisemitic** than those in the Soviet Union, and Poland lacked the vast, densely forested terrain of Belarus, Lithuania, and the Ukraine. Moreover, Jews in Poland bore the main brunt of the **Final Solution**. Between 1942 and 1944 only about 2,000 Polish Jews fought as partisans, mostly in Polish communist units or other Polish units in which they often concealed their Jewish identities, or in some twenty-seven small Jewish units.

In Western Europe and the Balkans, Jews were generally accepted into the ranks of partisan units as equals, and there were few separate Jewish units. An exception was the **Jewish Army** (Armée Juive), formed by Jewish underground groups in France in 1942 and active in military operations against German targets.

Pogroms From the Russian term for "devastation," pogroms are violent attacks against Jews or others, often inspired by government officials. Pogroms against Jews occurred from time to time in Christian Europe before the French Revolution. Christians were incited by their governments and churches to attack Jews, their homes, shops and synagogues, usually in times of political and social upheaval and economic uncertainty. The term is most commonly used when referring to outbreaks of popular violence against Jews in Tsarist Russia between the 1880s and World War I, resulting in the emigration of millions of Jewish refugees from Eastern Europe to Western Europe, North and South America, and elsewhere. Immediately following World War I, there were pogroms against Jews in some of the new states of Eastern Europe. In Germany, some Nazi leaders did not favor pogroms. However the infamous **Crystal Night** (Kristallnacht) pogrom in Germany on November 9–10, 1938, a pogrom in Kielce in occupied Poland in September 1939, and one in **L'vov** (Ukraine, later part of the **General Government**) in July 1942 were exceptions.

Prisoner Functionaries Everyday life in German **concentration** and **labor camps** was determined largely by prisoners directed by the **SS** to perform various administrative functions. Prisoner functionaries included the camp senior, who was appointed by and directly responsible to the SS commandant or camp leader for the overall operation of the camp; block seniors (sometimes translated "block chiefs" or "barracks seniors"), usually chosen by the camp senior to supervise the barracks where prisoners ate and slept; room seniors, who assisted the block seniors in keeping the prisoners under surveillance; capos (or kapos), who supervised work crews, assisted by work foremen when the crews were very large; and clerks, the camp bureaucrats who kept office records, prepared reports, and allocated supplies. Prisoner self-administration of the camps permitted the Germans to minimize the number of guards and run the installations more efficiently.

In camps with mixed prisoner populations the SS often appointed hardened German criminals to positions as prisoner functionaries. They were usually willing tools who showed the desired levels of violence and cruelty. But too much of that could undermine the prisoners' capacity for work. Hence the SS sometimes chose political prisoners with some education and skills, including Jews, to help run the camps. Occasionally prisoners turned down such tasks, usually without reprisal, but more commonly they welcomed the chance to enjoy the special privileges — better food, clothing, and quarters, and easier work assignments — and perhaps assist their fellow prisoners in some manner.

Prisoner functionaries stood between the SS and the prisoner population, and where they felt a sense of solidarity with the rank and file they could often help in small ways. These included assigning the weak to easier work, pretending to inflict harsh punishments for infractions of the rules, and undermining the positions of corrupt and brutal prisoner functionaries. However, their ability to help was limited by their ultimate dependence on the SS. As accomplices of the SS, prisoner functionaries had to make the camps run smoothly. Functionaries displayed a broad range of behavior, from the best to the worst, and this was true of criminal and political prisoners, Jews and non-Jews alike.

Privileged Mixed Marriages Jews living in mixed marriages in Germany generally did not suffer the same plight as other Jews. Marriages in which the husband was **Aryan** and the wife Jewish were classified as privileged mixed marriages (priviligierte Mischehen). After the **Crystal Night** pogrom, Jewish spouses in mixed marriages were afforded a reprieve from some of the worst anti-Jewish measures that followed, including the decision to **Aryanize** Jewish apartments and property, the wearing of the **yellow star**, and deportations to the **ghettos** and **extermination camps** in the East. In December 1938 Hitler ruled that in privileged mixed marriages the families could remain in their apartments and the wife's assets could be transferred to her husband. If the husband was Jewish and there were children, families could remain where they were at least temporarily. Jewish wives received some privileges if their Aryan husbands were in the army, although Jewish spouses of Aryans were required to wear the yellow star when it became obligatory for Jews in September 1941. Jews in mixed marriages had to abide by the restrictions imposed on all Jews and to look on helplessly as their Jewish relatives suffered. In February 1945 Jewish wives and husbands in mixed marriages were deported to **Theresienstadt,** but most survived.

Reparations, West German   Between 1953 and 1965, the Federal Republic of Germany indemnified individual Jewish victims of **National Socialism** and the Jewish people as a whole. During World War II Jewish leaders made plans to seek restitution from Germany for the property it had stolen from Jews in Germany and throughout Europe.

The **Jewish Agency for Palestine** made the first official postwar claim to Allied governments for German reparations to the Jewish people. Recovered Jewish property was to be returned to the original owners if they had survived, to their heirs if they had not, or to Jewish organizations and institutions for distribution to other Jewish victims. The Jewish Agency proposal also suggested that a percentage of total German reparations be turned over to the Jewish Agency for Palestine for rehabilitation and resettlement of survivors in Palestine. Occupation authorities in Germany endeavored to restore Jewish property to its rightful owners between 1945 and 1947.

In 1951 Israel pressed for the restoration of Jewish property and compensation for victims living outside of Germany, citing the enormous cost to Israel of absorbing some 500,000 Jewish victims since the war. Israel estimated the value of stolen Jewish assets at $6 billion, and the absorption of Jewish victims at $1.5 billion ($1 billion from West Germany and $500 million from East Germany). The major West German political parties agreed to assume responsibility for German crimes against the Jewish people and to pay reparations.

Some Israelis and other Jews opposed direct negotiations with Germany over reparations, preferring instead to work through the Allied powers. The Israeli government and majorities in major Jewish organizations were willing to deal directly with the Germans, and negotiations opened in the Netherlands in March 1952. On September 10, 1952, West German Chancellor Konrad Adenauer and Israeli Foreign Minister Moshe Sharett signed the Reparations Agreement. The Federal Republic of Germany agreed to pay Israel DM3.45 billion ($845 million) over twelve to fourteen years, mostly in the form of goods. From that amount, Israel would turn over DM450 million ($110 million) to Jewish survivors abroad.

The scope of restitution to Jewish victims has expanded considerably since then, and it is estimated that a total of DM85 billion will have been paid out to the victims of the Third Reich by the year 2000. During its existence, the German Democratic Republic (East Germany) refused to assume responsibility for the crimes of the Third Reich, but did pay pensions to survivors who remained in the East.

Rescue   The rescue of Jews between 1933 and 1945 was multifaceted but enormously problematic and dangerous. Jews needed and sometimes received help from a variety of sources. These included neutral, foreign, and even Axis governments; Jewish and non-Jewish relief and rescue organizations inside and outside occupied Europe; Jewish underground and **partisan** movements in the **ghettos,** camps, and forests; and courageous non-Jews, German and non-German, acting as individuals or in groups to save Jews.

During the 1930s, when Germany was coercing Jews to emigrate, most European and overseas countries were reluctant to open their doors to refugees. During the war, the Jewish refugee crisis only worsened as hundreds of thousands of Jews in Eastern and Western Europe attempted to escape German control. Some found refuge in a reluctant Switzerland, a generous Sweden, the Soviet Union, or temporarily in countries allied to Nazi Germany such as Italy and Hungary; others managed to escape overseas through Spain and Turkey. With few exceptions, most were trapped and there was little commitment if any among the nations of the world to actively rescue Jews.

Jewish and non-Jewish relief organizations outside occupied Europe sent food and other supplies to Jews in ghettos and camps. Jewish **resistance** and partisan movements in the ghettos, camps, and in the countryside, as well as non-Jews in churches, government bureaucracies, diplomatic representations, or simply on their own, hid Jews or smuggled them out of ghettos and camps into hiding or across borders to safety. The **Jewish Agency for Palestine** tried to ransom Jews from the Nazis, to have the Allies bomb **Auschwitz** and the railway lines leading to it, and to parachute Jewish commandos into Eastern Europe to rescue Jews.

Resistance, Jewish Jewish resistance has been a sensitive and emotional question in the post-Holocaust era. Notions of Jews as docile, passive victims have given way in recent years to evidence that Jewish resistance was widespread. Given the single-minded nature of Nazi persecution and the vulnerability of the Jews, most forms of individual or group noncompliance or opposition by Jews can be characterized as "resistance." Armed resistance, particularly before 1942, was virtually unthinkable. Thus, Jewish resistance took different forms between 1933 and 1945.

In Germany during the 1930s, acts of disobedience, "spiritual resistance," and legal challenges to anti-Jewish legislation and policies were the main forms of resistance in which German Jews and their organizations engaged. Some were involved in underground socialist and communist resistance movements. The **Baum Group** (Baum Gruppe), a clandestine organization of young communist and **Zionist** Jews in Berlin, published illegal brochures and organized educational, cultural, and political events and meetings. Between 1937 and 1942, most of its members were caught and executed or deported to **Auschwitz**.

In German-occupied Eastern Europe, Jewish resistance was varied and included organized, armed Jewish resistance against the Germans and their collaborators after 1942. Underground movements sprang up in the **ghettos** in Poland in 1939 and 1940. Smuggling food and other necessities of life; "spiritual resistance" and the establishment of schools, archives, and cultural groups; the publishing of clandestine newspapers and pamphlets; and the refusal of individual Jews to comply with German directives were common. As the situation became more desperate with the beginning of the extermination process in 1942, Jewish underground movements produced armed resistance fighters who tried to hinder the deportations from the ghettos. A major armed Jewish resistance organization in Poland was the **Jewish Fighting Organization** (Zydowska Organizacja Bojowa or ZOB), established in August 1942 by young Zionists in **Warsaw**. Almost every ghetto had its lightly armed fighters and several major ghettos, most notably the Warsaw ghetto in the spring of 1943, staged open rebellions against the Germans. Of course, virtually every attempt by Jewish fighters to combat Nazi troops was crushed, and most of the fighters killed. There were also underground movements, armed groups, and uprisings in the extermination camps, most notably in **Sobibór** and **Treblinka** in 1943 and Auschwitz-Birkenau in 1944. Most perished in these uprisings.

Escape was a major aspect of resistance activity, and some fighters managed to escape from the ghettos and camps during the uprisings. Jewish partisan activity, both individual Jews in largely non-Jewish partisan units and units that were wholly Jewish, was a manifestation of Jewish resistance in occupied Europe. Jewish partisans engaged in military activities and attempts to rescue Jews from ghettos, transports and camps.

"Righteous Among the Nations" This honor has been bestowed by Israel on thousands of non-Jews who risked their lives to save Jews during the Holocaust. In 1953, the Israeli parliament (Knesset) passed the "Martyrs' and Heroes' Remembrance Law" which charged Yad Vashem, Israel's national memorial institution for Holocaust commemoration, to establish a memorial for "Righteous Gentiles."

Since 1963, a committee of the Yad Vashem Remembrance Authority in Jerusalem has designated some 16,000 men and women as "Righteous Among the Nations." Ordinary Germans and other Europeans, including bureaucrats, businessmen, clergymen, and foreign diplomats in countries occupied by or allied to Nazi Germany, risked their lives to save Jews. Among them were the German industrialist **Oskar Schindler**, the Swedish businessman **Raoul Wallenberg**, the Swiss diplomat Charles Lutz, the Japanese diplomat Sempo Sugihara, the Portuguese diplomat Aristides de Sousa Mendes, the Italian diplomat

Giorgio Perlasea, the French pastor André Trocme, the Polish underground group **Zegota**, and all 117 inhabitants of the Dutch village of Nieuwlande. It is not known how many Jews were saved by "Righteous Gentiles," nor is it possible to know the identity of every non-Jew who risked his or her life to save them.

Selections (Selektionen) Selection was the process of separating those prisoners in the camps who could work from those who could not. The latter were usually sent on to "**special treatment**" (Sonderbehandlung), that is, death in the gas chambers at one of the extermination camps. At **Auschwitz**, for example, a concentration and **extermination camp**, the selection process usually took place immediately on the platform as the deportation trains arrived with their human cargo from all over Europe. SS physicians quickly inspected the prisoners assembled on the platform and "selected" those deemed fit to work (healthy-looking young and middle-aged men and women without children). The rest, usually the elderly and small children and their mothers, were sent directly to the gas chambers. The SS also undertook periodic selections of sick and exhausted prisoners in labor and **concentration camps** and either killed them immediately or sent them to the extermination camps.

Sho'ah This is the Hebrew word used by some instead of "Holocaust" when referring to the destruction of some 6,000,000 Jews in Europe during World War II. The word *sho'ah* was first used in the booklet *The Destruction of the Jews of Poland*, published in Hebrew (*Sho'at Yehudei Polin*) in Jerusalem in 1940. But the term was rarely used thereafter, and by the 1950s the term *Holocaust* (from the Greek *holokauston*, meaning a totally burnt offering or sacrifice) had become the accepted term used around the world. However, as **Zionists** responded to the destruction of the Jews in Europe after the war, the Hebrew term *sho'ah* came into use among many Jews, particularly in Israel.

Shtetl *Shtetl* is a Yiddish word meaning "small town," commonly referring to a small Jewish village or town in Eastern Europe before World War II. Thousands of shtetls dotted the rural landscape of the Jewish Pale of Settlement in Eastern Poland, Lithuania, Belarus, and the Western Ukraine before World War II. Most shtetls were destroyed and their mostly poor Jewish inhabitants killed during the Holocaust.

Sonderkommando (Special Commandos) Different kinds of "Special Commandos" were involved in the killing operations of the **Final Solution**. About ten were made up of German **SS** troops who assisted the **Einsatzgruppen** in the occupied territories of the Soviet Union, or worked at **extermination camps**. Others were special units, German and non-German, charged with digging up burial pits, burning corpses, and eliminating all traces of mass murder. There were Jewish Sonderkommandos, Jewish prisoners at extermination camps whose task it was to remove bodies from gas chambers, burn them in crematoria, and dispose of the remains. In the **Łódź ghetto** a Jewish Special Commando functioned as part of the **Jewish ghetto police.**

Special Treatment (Sonderbehandlung) *Sonderbehandlung* was a term of concealment used by the Nazi bureaucracy when referring to the murder of Jews and other victims during World War II. Nazi officials used the term routinely in conversations, documents, and in the "Books of the Dead" kept in the camps to camouflage clerically the murder of countless victims and thereby conceal the **genocide** from those not directly involved in its implementation.

Statut des Juifs (Jewish Law) In October 1940 and June 1941 the **Vichy** government in France passed comprehensive anti-Jewish laws for occupied and unoccupied France. The October 3, 1940, law defined a Jew as a person with at least three Jewish grandparents or someone with two Jewish grandparents but married to a Jew. It reduced or eliminated the role of French Jews in the civil service, the military and most professions. The second "Jewish Law" of June 2, 1941, eliminated Jews from the professions, commerce, and industry, with exemptions for only a few well-established French Jews. The anti-Jewish laws in France mirrored the legalistic approach of the Nazis in Germany during the 1930s and the deep-rooted **antisemitism** in both countries.

Trials of War Criminals/American Military Tribunal Law No. 10 of the Allied Control Council in Berlin, promulgated on December 20, 1945, empowered Allied authorities to conduct further war-crimes trials in their respective occupation zones. All four Allied powers did so.

American military courts conducted twelve trials in **Nuremberg**, the so-called Nuremberg Successor Trials, between December 1946 and April 1949. The first to be tried were twenty-three Nazi physicians and members of the German medical establishment for **T4** (**euthanasia**) killings and **medical experiments** in the camps. Field Marshal Erhard Milch of the Main Planning Office was tried for state-sponsored **slave labor.** In the Justice Case, sixteen judges were tried for crimes that included enforcing the **Nuremberg Racial Laws** of 1935. **Oswald Pohl** and seventeen members of the **SS Economic and Administrative Main Office** (Wirtschaftsverwaltungshauptamt or WVHA) were tried for their role in the administration of **concentration camps** and the policy of killing people through work. In the Flick Case, Friedrich Flick, a coal and steel producer, and five associates were tried for the program of **Aryanization** of Jewish businesses and for the exploitation of slave labor. In the I. G. Farben trial, twenty-four representatives of the company were tried for the sale of **Zyklon B** to the **SS** and the construction of industrial facilities at **Auschwitz.** In a case against twelve army generals, the defendants were tried for abductions and mass shootings of Jews as hostages in Serbia and deportations of Jews from Greece. Fourteen officials of the **Race and Settlement Main Office** (Rasse- und Sied-lungshauptamt or RuSHA) were tried for their role in deporting Jews from Western Europe to the East. In the **Einsatzgruppen** case, twenty-four members of the Mobile Killing Units were tried for the extermination campaign in the Soviet Union. Alfred Krupp and eleven directors of his company were tried for the enslavement of Jews through **forced labor** under **concentration camp** conditions. The Ministries Case put members of various government ministries on trial for certain activities: Wilhelm Stuckart of the Interior Ministry was tried for his involvement in the preparation of the **Nuremberg Racial Laws** and forced labor; former Minister of Agriculture Walther Darre for the **Aryanization** of agricultural property; German Foreign Office personnel (among them Ernst von Weizsäcker) for waging an aggressive war; former chief of the Reich Press Corps Otto Dietrich for antisemitic indoctrination of the population; former Minister of Finance Lutz Schwerin von Krosigk for the illegal confiscation of Jewish property; and Reichsbank vice-chairman Emil Johann Puhl for hoarding dental gold in the Reichsbank from Auschwitz victims. Finally, in the High Command (Oberkommando der Wehrmacht or OKW) Case, fourteen German officers were tried for providing logistical support for the Einsatzgruppen in the Soviet Union and for murdering Soviet prisoners of war.

A total of 185 persons were indicted, of whom 177 stood trial. Twenty-four were condemned to death, twenty received life in prison, ninety-eight prison terms between eighteen months and twenty-five years, and thirty-five were acquitted. Only twelve death sentences were carried out, with eleven commuted to life in prison. A pardon by U.S. High Commissioner in Germany in January 1951 further reduced many sentences. In addition to these trials in Nuremberg, American authorities conducted trials in Ludwigshafen, Wiesbaden (the Hadamar Trial), **Dachau, Mauthausen,** and elsewhere in 1945 and 1946.

Trials of War Criminals/British Military Tribunal Between September 1945 and December 1949, Great Britain conducted 357 trials in its occupation zone of German, Austrian, and Italian nationals, civilian and military, for war crimes. From September to November 1945 a British military tribunal at Lüneburg tried the commandant and forty-seven male and female staff of the **Bergen-Belsen** concentration camp for crimes against humanity committed against Jews and others at **Auschwitz** and Bergen-Belsen. Eleven were sentenced to death. In March 1946 a British military tribunal at Hamburg tried three owners of Tesch & Stabenow Co., a firm that manufactured **Zyklon B** gas used to kill prisoners at Auschwitz-Birkenau. Two were sentenced to death and one was acquitted. The British prosecuted individuals for crimes against Allied civilians and military personnel, including concentration camp internees and Allied POWs. Those indicted included commandants, guards and other staff of **concentration** and **extermination camps,** as well as high-ranking officers in the German army such as Albert Kesselring (in Venice), Nikolaus von Falkenhorst, Erich von Manstein, Eberhard von Mackensen, and Karl von Rundstedt.

Trials of War Criminals/Federal Republic of Germany In late 1945 the four Allied occupation powers in Germany decided to allow rehabilitated German courts to try Germans for Nazi crimes against German citizens or stateless persons. During the postwar years few Germans wished to confront the Nazi past, and the politics of the Cold War distracted attention from prosecuting Nazi war criminals. Nevertheless, in the late 1940s and 1950s German courts tried Germans for denunciation, coercion, and more serious crimes committed in **concentration camps**, the murder of innocents in the **euthanasia** program, and the murder of German soldiers and civilians toward the end of the war.

By the late 1950s it was clear that apart from Allied military tribunals in the immediate postwar years, many of the worst Nazi crimes had escaped prosecution. In 1958 West Germany established the Central Office of the Judicial Administrations of the States for the Investigation of Nazi Crimes in Ludwigsburg to investigate Nazi crimes. The work of the Ludwigsburg office led to prosecutions involving **Einsatzkommando** mass murders, the murderous activity of the various **police** units and units of ethnic Germans (**Volksdeutsche**), and mass murder in the **extermination camps** in Poland. The Frankfurt Trial, also known as the **Auschwitz** Trial, took place between December 1963 and August 1965, at which **SS** officers who worked at Auschwitz were tried. Governments in Eastern Europe, especially Poland, cooperated with the Ludwigsburg office and German prosecutors by providing relevant documents for these investigations.

After repeated extensions, the West German parliament (Bundestag) abolished the statute of limitations for murder by former Nazis. By the late 1980s West German courts had indicted almost 91,000 persons for Nazi crimes. The German Democratic Republic (East Germany) claimed that it had convicted almost 13,000 persons of "fascist" crimes by the end of 1976.

Trials of War Criminals/International Military Tribunal (IMT) In 1942, when news of German atrocities against civilian populations in occupied Europe reached the outside world, Allied leaders promised that the perpetrators would be brought to justice after the war. In the Moscow Declaration of November 1, 1943, Britain, the Soviet Union, and the United States announced their support for trials of suspected German perpetrators in countries where their crimes were committed. They eventually decided on a trial to be held in **Nuremberg** under the auspices of an International Military Tribunal composed of judges from the four principal allied powers: Great Britain, France, the United States, and the Soviet Union. Nuremberg was chosen as the trial site for its symbolic significance as a major Nazi town, and because it had one of the few courthouses still standing in Germany.

For about a year, between October 1945 and October 1946, the IMT tried twenty-two of Nazi Germany's most important leaders and six organizations including the **Nazi Party** leadership, the **Gestapo** and **SD**, the **SS**, the **SA**, the Reich Cabinet, and the Army General Staff. The Tribunal identified crimes that fell under its jurisdiction, and charged the defendants with some or all of them. "Crimes against peace" involved the planning, preparing and waging a war of aggression or in violation of international treaties. "War crimes" were violations of the laws and customs of war, such as the ill treatment, deportation for **forced labor**, or murder of civilian populations and prisoners of war. "Crimes against humanity" included the enslavement, murder, extermination, or general religious, racial and political persecution of civilian populations throughout Europe. The judgments dealing with crimes against humanity were in large measure a response to the extermination of the Jews during World War II.

Martin Bormann, head of the Party Chancellery and **Hitler's** secretary, was tried in absentia and sentenced to death. Karl Dönitz, Grand Admiral of the German Navy and German head of state after Hitler's suicide, was sentenced to ten years in prison. **Hans Frank**, governor of the **General Government** in Poland, was sentenced to death and hanged. Wilhelm Frick, Minister of the Interior from 1933 to 1943 and later Reich Protector of Bohemia and Moravia, was sentenced to death and hanged. Hans Fritsche, director of radio broadcasting in the Propaganda Ministry, was acquitted. Walther Funk, Minister of Economics from 1937 to 1945, was sentenced to life in prison, but released in 1957. **Hermann Göring**, Reich Marshal, Commander of the German Air Force, Plenipotentiary of the Four Year Plan, and Hitler's one-time designated successor, was sentenced to death. He committed suicide before his execution. Rudolf Hess, deputy Führer of the Nazi Party, was sentenced to life in prison. He committed suicide in Spandau prison in Berlin in 1987. Alfred Jodl, an army general, was sentenced to death and hanged. **Ernst Kaltenbrunner**, successor to **Reinhard Heydrich** as chief of the **Reich Security Main Office** in the SS, was sentenced to death and hanged. Wilhelm Keitel, General Field Marshal and Chief of Staff of the Armed Forces High Command, was sentenced to death and hanged. Constantin von Neurath, German Foreign Minister from 1933 to 1938 and later Reich Protector of Bohemia and Moravia, was sentenced to fifteen years in prison but was released in 1954. Franz von Papen, Hitler's deputy Chancellor in 1933 and 1934 and German ambassador to Turkey from 1939 to

1945, was acquitted. Erich Raeder, Grand Admiral of the German Navy from 1935 to 1943, was sentenced to life in prison but released in 1955. Joachim von Ribbentrop, German Foreign Minister from 1938 to 1945, was sentenced to death and hanged. **Alfred Rosenberg**, Nazi racial theorist and administrator of the occupied territories in the Soviet Union, was sentenced to death and hanged. **Fritz Sauckel**, director of labor mobilization (**forced labor**), was sentenced to death and hanged. Hjalmar Schacht, president of the Reichsbank and Minister of Economics from 1933 to 1937, was acquitted. Baldur von Schirach, leader of the Hitler Youth and later governor of Vienna, was sentenced to twenty years in prison. **Arthur Seyss-Inquart**, the Austrian Nazi leader in the 1930s, deputy to **Hans Frank** in the **General Government** in Poland, and later Reich Commissioner in the occupied Netherlands, was sentenced to death and hanged. **Albert Speer**, Hitler's architect and Minister for Armaments and War Production from 1942 to 1945, was sentenced to twenty years in prison. **Julius Streicher**, Nazi leader in Franconia and editor of the rabidly antisemitic newspaper *Der Stürmer*, was sentenced to death and hanged. One other Nazi official, Robert Ley, the leader of the German Labor Front, had been indicted but committed suicide in his cell before the trials began.

The court held that the defendants were individually responsible for their actions, not the agencies or organizations for which they worked, and that carrying out the orders of their superiors did not relieve them of responsibility for the crimes of which they were accused. The court also ruled that there would be no statute of limitations on these crimes. Judgments reached at Nuremberg were applied subsequently to international conventions on war, **genocide,** and human rights.

Trials of War Criminals/Occupied Europe Countries allied to or occupied by Germany also prosecuted war criminals, both Germans and non-German collaborators. Important German perpetrators were tried and convicted outside of Germany. **Rudolf Höss**, commandant of **Auschwitz; Jürgen Stroop**, the SS commander who crushed the **Warsaw ghetto** uprising; and Amon Göth, commandant at the Plaszow labor camp, were executed in Poland. Werner Best, SS officer and German plenipotentiary in occupied Denmark, was initially sentenced to death in Denmark. His sentence was commuted to twelve years in prison, but he was released in 1951. In Czechoslovakia Kurt Daluege, head of the **Order Police** (ORPO) and Reichsprotektor of Bohemia and Moravia after the assassination of **Reinhard Heydrich**, along with SS officers Dieter Wisliceny and Hermann Höfle, were executed for their roles in the deportations from Slovakia. The USSR executed Friedrich Jeckeln, SS and Police Leader in the **Reichskommissariat Ostland** (Reich Commissariat for the East). Belgium tried military commander Alexander von Falkenhausen and sentenced him to twelve years in prison. In Italy, SS and Police Leader for Rome Herbert Kappler was sentenced to life in prison. Yugoslavia executed Siegfried Kasche, German Minister to Croatia, and Alexander Löhr of the Army Group E Southeast. Holland sentenced to death Willy Lages, SD officer in Amsterdam, and Hans Albin Rauter, SS Police Leader. Lages's sentence was reduced to life, and Rauter was executed. In France, SS officer Karl Oberg was sentenced to death (later commuted to life), and Otto Abetz, German ambassador to France, was sentenced to twenty years (he was released in 1954).

Collaborators were also brought to justice throughout Europe. In Hungary, former Prime Minister Laszlo Bardossy and former Interior Minister Laszlo Endre were executed. Romania executed its former dictator **Ion Antonescu**, and Czechoslovakia did the same to **Jozef Tiso**, former president of Slovakia. Bulgaria executed former Prime Minister Bogdan Filov, and Yugoslavia executed the Croat Defense Minister Slavko Kvaternik. France executed Pierre Laval, former Premier of **Vichy France**.

Uprisings, Jewish. See Resistance, Jewish, and entries for various camps and cities/ghettos

Volksdeutsche (Ethnic Germans)   Ethnic Germans who lived as minorities in other countries, mostly in Eastern Europe, the Volksdeutsche were a significant factor in Nazi plans to reorganize Central and Eastern Europe racially during World War II. The term *Volksdeutsche* distinguished ethnic Germans living outside the Reich from Reichsdeutsche (Reich Germans) who were German citizens. In 1931 the Nazi Party established the Foreign Organization of the NSDAP (Auslandsorganisation der NSDAP) to disseminate Nazi propaganda among the Volksdeutsche. In 1936 the SS set up the Ethnic Germans' Welfare Office (Volksdeutsche Mittelstelle) to cultivate relations with Nazi elements among Volksdeutsche, who soon included many non-ethnic Germans (mainly Czechs, Poles, and Slovenes) who could prove some family ties to ethnic Germans. For instance, some 1,800,000 Poles became eligible for classification as *Volksdeutsche*. Between 1939 and 1941 about 350,000 ethnic Germans from the Baltic states and Russia settled in the western regions of Poland annexed by Germany, and an additional 100,000 lived in the **General Government**. The SS permitted Volksdeutsche to seize the property of Poles and Jews deported from annexed and occupied territories. Many joined the **German army**, the SS and **police** units operating against Jews, **Gypsies,** and partisans in the East.

Yellow Badge   During World War II Jews in Germany and occupied Europe were compelled to wear a distinguishing sign on their clothes to facilitate their identification as Jews and their physical and psychological separation from the non-Jewish population. They wore such markings on their clothing in occupied Poland beginning in 1939. In the **General Government** and **Białystok**, Jews wore white armbands with a blue Star of David, later changed to yellow badges in the shape of the Star of David. In the Warthegau and the occupied Soviet Union, Jews had to wear yellow six-pointed stars on the left side of their breasts and on their backs. Inside Greater Germany, including Austria and the **Protectorate of Bohemia and Moravia**, and in some of Germany's client states Jews were first ordered to wear the yellow star with the inscription Jude (Jew) in September 1941. In some occupied countries in Western Europe the yellow badge with the inscription Jood, Juif, and so on was imposed in the spring and summer of 1942. Hungary resisted imposing the badge on its Jews until the Germans occupied the country in March 1944, while Denmark was able to resist its imposition on the Danish Jewish community entirely.

Yishuv (Jewish Community of Palestine) In 1914 there were about 75,000 Jews in Palestine, mostly **Zionist** settlers of European origin, out of a total population of 650,000. Britain's Balfour Declaration of November 1917 promised the Zionists a "Jewish National Home" in a British-administered Palestine. The declaration and the National Home were incorporated into Britain's postwar Mandate in Palestine, and Jewish immigration from Europe into Palestine increased dramatically during the interwar years as a result of economic and political turmoil in Europe. On the eve of World War II there were about 470,000 Jews in a total population of almost 1,300,000.

Yishuv attitudes toward the Jews in the Diaspora had always been complex and uneasy. Zionist pioneers in Palestine considered themselves a radical departure from Jewish life in the Diaspora, with a new Jewish identity, culture, and existence based on strength, self-defense, and independence. However, the catastrophe that befell European Jews during World War II induced the Yishuv to act on behalf of Jews in Europe.

Putting aside differences with the British over Jewish immigration to Palestine and the 1939 White Paper, some 30,000 Palestinian Jews enlisted in the British army during the war. In January 1943 the Jewish Agency for Palestine created the "Joint Rescue Committee" to facilitate the rescue of Jews and their immigration to Palestine. The Jewish Agency established offices in Geneva and Istanbul to make contact with Jews in occupied Europe and assist Jews in the **ghettos** and camps. It earmarked more and more of its budget for rescue efforts in cooperation with Jewish organizations in the Diaspora. It tried to pay ransom for Jews in captivity, secure more immigration certificates for Jews to enter Palestine, have the Allies bomb **Auschwitz**, allow Jewish commandos to be parachuted into German-occupied Europe to **rescue** Jews, and continue the illegal immigration of Jewish refugees into Palestine. But there was little the Yishuv could do to save large numbers of Jews; the Allies were not interested, the Germans murdered millions of Jews with speed and efficiency, and the Yishuv itself lacked the means, military, political and financial, to effect large-scale rescue.

Zionism A modern Jewish nationalist movement, Zionism was a secular Jewish response to the dilemmas of Jewish emancipation and assimilation, and the growing virulence of racial **antisemitism** in the second half of the nineteenth century. Early proponents of Zionism were the German Moses Hess in the 1860s, the Russian Leo Pinsker in the 1880s, and, with the publication of his famous book *The Jewish State* (*Der Judenstaat*) in 1896, the Austrian journalist Theodor Herzl. They argued that emancipation and assimilation would not eliminate antisemitism and solve the Jewish question. Jew-hatred would always exist, regardless of its religious or racial content or rationale. They concluded that Jews must seek emancipation as a people through the revival of a Jewish national identity and culture, and emigration to their own state in Palestine.

The first international Zionist congress in Basel, Switzerland, in 1897 signaled the beginning of a movement that culminated in the establishment of Israel in 1948. Young Zionist pioneers, mostly from Russia, established agricultural settlements in Palestine before World War I. With the "Jewish National Home" under the British Mandate in Palestine after the war, Jewish immigration to Palestine grew steadily, particularly in the 1930's with the depression and the rise of Fascism in Europe. In Germany, the Nazi regime encouraged Zionism among German Jews and Jewish emigration to Palestine, and generally facilitated Zionist work that coincided with the regime's determination to reverse Jewish assimilation and push Jews out of Germany and Europe. The **Final Solution** and the consequent end to Jewish emigration in the fall of 1941 ended Zionism's utility for Nazi Jewish policy.

Most emancipated and assimilated Jews of Central and Western Europe were indifferent to or actively opposed Zionism before the Holocaust. Most immigrants to Palestine before 1933 were poor, unassimilated Eastern European Jews. Persecution of Jews in Germany after 1933 led more and more Western Jews to immigrate to Palestine. The murder of some 6,000,000 Jews during World War II changed Jewish attitudes toward Zionism after 1945, as the success of Zionist efforts in Palestine and the survival of Israel after 1948 became essential to the vast majority of the world's Jews.

Zyklon B The commercial name for hydrogen cyanide, Zyklon B was a pesticide used to exterminate Jews and **Gypsies** at **Auschwitz**-Birkenau and **Majdanek**. Carbon monoxide poisoning, used in **vans** and smaller **gas chambers** at the

Sobibór, Bełzec, and **Treblinka extermination camps**, was not used at Auschwitz. The SS conducted experiments using Zyklon B on Russian prisoners of war at Auschwitz-Birkenau in September 1941. The gas was delivered in the form of pellets in sealed canisters and dropped into large chambers. When exposed to the air, the pellets turned into a lethal gas that asphyxiated its victims within minutes. The tests proved successful, and Zyklon B became the preferred instrument of extermination at Auschwitz. It was produced primarily by the German Vermin-Combating Corporation (Deutsche Gesellschaft für Schädlingsbekämpfung mbH or DEGESCH), partly owned by the chemical giant I. G. Farben but controlled by the German Gold and Silver Metallurgical Institute (Deutsche Gold und Silber Scheide-Anstalt or DEGUSSA).

ORGANIZATIONS

American Jewish Joint Distribution Committee   This American charitable organization, usually abbreviated JDC, extended valuable assistance to countless European Jews before, during, and after the Holocaust. It was formed in 1914 with the support of all the important factions among American Jews to relieve needy and threatened Jewish populations abroad. During the 1930s it sent funds to support German Jews who were being impoverished by Nazi **Aryanization** policies. As an American organization the JDC was permitted to function inside German-occupied Europe during the first two years of the war, distributing food, medicine, clothing, and funds for schools, hospitals, and other important Jewish institutions in Poland and Western Europe.

After the entrance of the United States into the war in December 1941, the JDC was no longer able to transfer large sums to Europe or operate openly in German-controlled territory. Only in 1943 did the Swiss government renew United States currency exchanges. This enabled the JDC to send aid to the remnants of the Jews in **Transnistria** and to supply funds to **Raoul Wallenberg** and other neutral diplomats assisting Jews in Budapest. JDC funds also supported illegal emigration of Jews from Europe to Palestine throughout the war.

Truly massive JDC aid came after World War II when Jewish **Displaced Persons** were in dire need of assistance. Virtually all of the 250,000 Jewish DPs benefited in one way or another from various rehabilitation programs funded by the JDC. These included vocational programs designed to prepare Holocaust survivors for new lives and assistance in emigrating abroad. The JDC also received and distributed **reparations** funds from the West German government to Holocaust survivors.

Army, German The Holocaust was directed by the SS, but from time to time the German army was called on to assist. For the most part it complied. From the very beginning of the Third Reich most of the generals made their support for Hitler and National Socialism unmistakable, and they willingly cooperated in excluding Jews from the German armed forces. Later they endorsed Hitler's racial policies in occupied Poland and his criminal plans for a war of extermination against the USSR. Hence army units dutifully assisted the **Einsatzgruppen** (action squads) in rounding up Jews, Gypsies, and handicapped people during **Operation Barbarossa** and in some cases joined in the shootings.

The German army also carried out savage reprisals against Jews during actions against **partisan** forces, exploited the products of **forced labor**, and presided over the deaths of more than 3,000,000 Soviet POWs. A small number of German officers were revolted by these and other Nazi atrocities and participated in the German **resistance**. Most, however, stayed with Hitler to the end.

Arrow Cross The main Hungarian fascist political party, the Arrow Cross was founded in 1937 with the merger of four right-wing parties under the leadership of Ferenc Szálasi. Two years later it won 25 percent of the votes in elections to the Hungarian parliament with appeals based on social justice combined with extreme nationalism, antisemitism, and anticommunism. Although the Arrow Cross stood little chance of coming to power on its own, its growth reinforced the Hungarian government's readiness to adopt anti-Jewish legislation in order to steal the issue from the radical right.

The Arrow Cross was put in power by the Germans in October 1944 after they ousted Admiral **Horthy** and his government for trying to make a separate peace with the Allies. During its short time in power the Arrow Cross obediently supplied the Third Reich with **forced labor**. Tens of thousands of Jews were marched to Germany under Hungarian guards. The remaining Hungarian Jews, most of them in Budapest, were confined to a **ghetto** and subjected to looting and random violence at the hands of Arrow Cross fanatics. Thousands of Jews were shot and their bodies dumped into the Danube River before the Soviets liberated the city in February 1945. A year later Szálasi and most of the other Arrow Cross leaders were tried and executed in Hungary.

Baum Group The largest Jewish **resistance** group in Nazi Germany, the Group was named for Herbert and Marianne Baum, Berlin Communists who were also active in Jewish youth organizations. Starting in 1936 they were ordered to infiltrate legal Jewish youth groups in order to influence them ideologically. Additionally the Baum Group secretly printed and distributed anti-Nazi leaflets and scrawled anti-Hitler slogans on walls in Berlin. Altogether about 150 individuals were involved in these resistance cells; the militant core of the Baum Group was much smaller.

In May 1942 the group attempted to set fire to the Nazi exhibition "The Soviet Paradise" and managed to do it minor damage. Most members of the group were arrested, and in reprisal the Nazis seized five hundred Berlin Jews, including some of the leaders of the **Reich Association of Jews in Germany** (Reichsvereinigung der Juden in Deutschland). Of these, half were shot and the rest sent to **Sachsenhausen** and, later, to **Auschwitz**. Among those executed were Herbert and Marianne Baum. The Baum Group illustrates both the courage of a few young, ideologically committed Jews and the futility of overt Jewish resistance in the Third Reich.

Catholic Church Germany's Catholic leaders opposed the rise of Nazism, but in July 1933, shortly after **Hitler** made himself dictator, the Vatican signed a Concordat with his government. This treaty, Catholics hoped, would guarantee the rights of the church, but the fundamentally anti-Christian attitude of the Nazi state kept Catholicism on the defensive. Preoccupied with defending its own interests, the Catholic Church did not protest increasingly severe measures against the Jews, although in March 1937 Pope Pius XI denounced Nazi racism in his encyclical *Mit brennender Sorge* (*With Burning Anxiety*). Individual German Catholics assisted some victims of racial persecution, especially baptized Jews, and protests by high Catholic churchmen against the **euthanasia** program were among the reasons Hitler decided to end the Operation T4 gassings in 1941.

During World War II the new pope, Pius XII, studiously pursued a policy of neutrality in the hope of mediating between the warring powers. Hence, although he learned of the **Final Solution** early in 1942, he made no public statements specifically condemning German atrocities or calling upon Catholics to help the victims of genocide. Rather, he employed traditional diplomacy, instructing papal representatives to intervene on behalf of the Jews. Vatican diplomacy met with only limited success, chiefly in halting deportations of Jews from Slovakia in 1942 and Hungary in 1944. The Nazi state, however, was impervious to such diplomatic pressure. The Vatican also quietly encouraged individual **rescue** attempts. Pius XII's great reserve in all of this is variously attributed to the desire to preserve the influence and independence of the church, the fear of losing the allegiance of Catholics in Germany, and the commitment to maintaining a conservative social order against encroachments by liberalism and Bolshevism.

In the absence of a forthright condemnation of German policies backed by the moral authority of the papacy, traditional Catholic **antisemitism** sometimes neutralized or even overshadowed sympathy for the victims. Hence in France and elsewhere in Western Europe the deportations of foreign-born Jews inspired little criticism from leading Catholic spokesmen. In Poland some Catholic priests actively assisted Jews and urged their parishioners to do the same, but others commended the Germans for solving Poland's Jewish problem. Most European Catholics, like most Protestants, however, appear to have remained indifferent to the fate of the Jews. After 1945 this led to a rethinking of traditional Catholic teachings.

Central Office for Jewish Emigration (Reichszentrale für jüdische Auswanderung). See Reich Central Office for Jewish Emigration

Confessing Church. See Protestant Churches

Council of Elders (Ältestenrat). See Jewish Councils

Criminal Police (Kriminalpolizei or KRIPO). See Police, German

Economic and Administrative Main Office (Wirtschaftsverwaltungshauptamt or WVHA). See SS

German Christians. See Protestant Churches

Gestapo (Secret State Police). See Police, German

Hlinka Guard A fascist paramilitary organization, the Hlinka Guard functioned as the rough equivalent of the SS in Slovakia from 1939 to 1945. It was named for Andrej Hlinka, a priest and founder of the Slovakian People's Party, which worked to achieve greater autonomy for Slovakia within Czechoslovakia between the two world wars. The Hlinka Guard was formed in 1938 from the party's most militant and antisemitic elements. Hitler's destruction of Czechoslovakia and creation of an "independent" Slovakia in 1939 produced a clericofascist state under Father **Jozef Tiso** in which the Hlinka Guard was made responsible for internal security. Its commander, Alexander Mach, was also Slovakia's Interior Minister and director of the secret police.

At first the Hlinka Guard engaged in random attacks on Jews, and with the onset of the **Final Solution** it participated in roundups of 58,000 Jews and smaller numbers of Gypsies for deportation to camps in Poland between March and October 1942. Following the Slovak National Uprising of August 1944, the Guard joined the German SS in sweeps against **partisans** and Jews and renewed deportations to **Auschwitz.**

Iron Guard One of the largest and most successful fascist parties in the Balkans, Romania's Iron Guard was founded in 1927 by Corneliu Zelea Codreanu. Its official name was "All for the Fatherland," but it was commonly known by the name of its paramilitary organization, the Iron Guard. This intensely antisemitic party employed both parliamentary and terrorist methods. In 1938 the Romanian monarch, King Carol II, outlawed the party and had Codreanu shot.

The Iron Guard revived its fortunes in 1940 when it joined General **Antonescu** in overthrowing the King's dictatorship and establishing a new, unabashedly pro-German government. Codreanu's successor as Iron Guard leader, Horia Sima, became Antonescu's vice premier. The Iron Guard unsuccessfully attempted to overturn Antonescu and seize power in January 1941, but before the fighting was over its members had killed hundreds of Jews. Party leaders fled to Germany but failed to get Hitler's backing since he believed he could work with Antonescu. Had the Iron Guard coup succeeded, it seems likely that the death toll among Romanian Jews would have been far higher than it was.

Jewish Agency for Palestine. See Yishuv

Jewish Army. See Partisans, Jewish

Jewish Councils (Judenräte) Throughout Nazi-dominated Europe the Germans ordered the Jewish communities to establish such councils to act as intermediaries between the Jews and officials of the Third Reich. A Jewish Council (sometimes called a Council of Jewish Elders [Judenältestenrat]) might govern a single ghetto or cluster of **ghettos**, as was the case in most of Eastern Europe. Or it might be held responsible for the Jews of entire countries, as was true in Germany, France, Belgium, the Netherlands, and Slovakia. Whether elected by the Jewish communities or appointed by the Germans, council members usually were prominent figures in prewar Jewish political and religious affairs and hence enjoyed popular confidence, at least initially.

With the Jews cut off from public services and often confined to ghettos, the Jewish Councils were obliged to provide for a far broader range of basic needs than had been true for the prewar Jewish community councils. These included food rationing, health programs, orphanages, schools, and aid to Jewish refugees. German expectations of absolute order and obedience in the ghettos were met by Jewish **police** forces, often corrupt and brutal and likewise under Jewish Council direction. In return for limited autonomy the Jewish Councils were expected to keep track of the Jews for the Germans and move them to ghettos or prepare them for deportations when so ordered. Additionally they were called on to collect Jewish valuables for delivery to Nazi officials and supply Jews for **forced labor**, at home at first, and later in distant **labor camps**. Compliance, the council members hoped, would save at least some Jews from death. Hence they usually opposed all forms of armed Jewish **resistance** or else urged the resisters to strike only if the whole community was threatened by liquidation. Councils or individual council members who refused to implement German policies were removed (and sometimes shot), which yielded increasingly compliant council actions. Inevitably under such circumstances corruption crept in as council members, their employees, and members of their families sometimes enjoyed special privileges in ghettos and (temporary) exemptions from deportations.

Once almost universally reviled for "collaborating" with the Germans and undermining the Jews' will to resist, today the Jewish Councils are the subjects of more nuanced analysis. It is now clear that the councils were not uniform in their compliance with German orders, their susceptibility to corruption, and their interactions with the Jewish underground. Today there is also a deeper appreciation of the councils' greatly limited range of options and of their efforts to maximize survival under the most difficult circumstances imaginable.

Jewish Fighting Organization (Zydowska Organizacja Bojowa or ZOB). See Resistance, Jewish

Nazi Party. See National Socialism

Office of Special Investigations (OSI) The OSI was established in the Criminal Division of the U.S. Department of Justice in 1979 to prosecute Nazi **war criminals** living in the United States. Many war criminals, mostly Eastern Europeans who participated in the murder of Jews and **Gypsies**, emigrated to the United States after World War II. The OSI has investigated some 1,500 persons and prosecuted 103 for violating U.S. immigration and naturalization laws prohibiting perpetrators from entering the United States and acquiring U.S. citizenship. Its success over the years has influenced other governments, including Great Britain, Australia and Canada, to investigate and prosecute war criminals living in their countries.

Oneg Shabbat (Sabbath Delight) The code name for a secret archive administered by the **Warsaw ghetto** underground, Oneg Shabbat is an important source for the history of Polish Jewry during the Holocaust. "Sabbath Delight" normally refers to physical pleasures after the Sabbath, but probably reflects here Isaiah's use of the term to convey his vision of a socially just world.

In October 1939 **Emanuel Ringelblum** began collecting information on Jewish life in German-occupied Poland. Initially, he recorded what he saw in a diary that became a chronicle of Jewish life under German occupation. He collected materials documenting the suffering of the Jews in Poland. The archive soon became an organized underground operation employing writers and history students who collected underground newspapers, minutes of meetings, letters, information from Jewish welfare organizations in the ghetto, the testimony of Jews who had been in other ghettos, in camps, and in hiding, and personal diaries. It sponsored papers and reports on all aspects of Jewish life under occupation, collected German documents, particularly those relating to deportation and extermination policies, recorded the testimonies of Jews who escaped from **extermination camps** at Chełmno and **Treblinka**, and alerted the world via the Polish underground about the extermination of the Jews. Oneg Shabbat also collected information on the Warsaw ghetto underground. The archive was hidden and most of it survived the war and the ghetto's destruction.

Order Police (Ordnungspolizei or ORPO). See Police, German

Palestine Office (Palästinaamt) Part of the **Jewish Agency for Palestine**, Palestine Offices were attached to **Zionist** organizations in the Diaspora to organize Jewish emigration to Palestine. In Germany the Palästinaamt was located in the headquarters of the Zionist Association for Germany (Zionistische Vereinigung für Deutschland) in Berlin. It was responsible for Jewish emigration from Germany to Palestine, and functioned until it was closed in April 1941.

Police, German In June 1936 the German police system was reorganized and placed under the authority of the **SS**. **Heinrich Himmler** became the Reich Leader of the SS and Chief of the German Police (Reichsführer-SS und Chef der Deutschen Polizei). Its two main divisions were the **Security Police** (Sicherheitspolizei or **SIPO**) and the **Order Police** (Ordnungspolizei or **ORPO**). SIPO consisted of the **Criminal Police** (Kriminalpolizei or **KRIPO**) and the Secret State Police (Geheime Staatspolizei or **Gestapo**), and operated under the command of SS General **Reinhard Heydrich**. Heydrich already controlled the **Security Service** (Sicherheitsdienst or SD) of the SS, and this personal union of state and party security agencies under Heydrich became the chief instrument of Nazi terror and mass murder during the Third Reich. ORPO, commanded by Kurt Daluege, included the uniformed municipal police (Schutzpolizei), the rural police (Gendarmerie), and the police in small towns (Gemeindepolizei).

Under the authority of the individual German states before 1936, the criminal police handled nonpolitical criminal activity. KRIPO officers wore civilian clothes in Germany and SS uniforms when on duty in German-occupied countries. They often assisted the Gestapo in its actions against the regime's racial and political enemies. Responsible for the suppression of political opponents of the Nazi regime, the Gestapo established regional and district offices directed from Berlin in 1933. The emergency regulations of February 28, 1933, and the Enabling Law of March 24, 1933, gave it unlimited authority to deal with political opponents and enforce Nazi racial laws without regard to the civil rights of German citizens. In 1934 the Gestapo was placed under the SS, which already controlled the developing concentration system in Germany.

The Gestapo grew rapidly after 1936. It targeted political opponents such as communists, social democrats, outlawed trade unions, monarchists, and conservatives, as well as Jews, **Gypsies**, religious groups, and Freemasons. In 1938, it joined in enforcing Jewish emigration policy and other anti-Jewish measures of the regime.

In September 1939, the Gestapo joined with the Security Service (SD) of the SS to form the **Reich Security Main Office** (Reichssicherheitshauptamt or RSHA) under SIPO and SD chief Reinhard Heydrich, operating along separate but parallel lines. The SD had been the intelligence and security agency in the Nazi Party prior to 1939. Its Jewish Section had carried out close surveillance of Jewish organizations in Germany, but SD functions overlapped with those of the Gestapo, leading to their closer relationship in 1939. The new RSHA constituted a powerful police empire dominated by SS officers, devoted to the ruthless implementation of Nazi racial policy, including deportation, confinement to ghettos, organization of **forced labor,** and the extermination of Jews, Gypsies, and others, and to the eradication of all anti-Nazi **resistance** in Germany and occupied Europe.

With the threat of war in 1938 and 1939, ORPO expanded rapidly, reaching 131,000 by September 1, 1939. Order Police units were soon made available to the army as occupation troops and military police, while the rest were exempt from military service. By mid-1940 ORPO had expanded to 244,500 men, with more than 15,000 in the **General Government** in Poland participating in the murder of Jews and Gypsies by late 1942. Some were assigned to three of the four Einsatzgruppen engaged in killing Jews in the Soviet Union beginning in 1941. Others worked as guards on trains transporting Jews to the East. Order Police units were active in **Operation Reinhard**, the campaign to kill all the Jews in the General Government of Poland beginning in 1942, and **Operation Harvest Festival** late in 1943.

After the war, the **International Military Tribunal** at **Nuremberg** declared the SS, including the SD and the Gestapo, to be criminal organizations. Postwar investigations in Germany of Order Police members led to few indictments and even fewer convictions.

Police, Jewish German authorities established Jewish police units to enforce German policies in the **ghettos.** The motives of Jews willing to serve the Germans in this way ranged from a will to survive (they often received better rations and living conditions), to a belief that they could help other Jews survive.

When the Germans established ghettos in Eastern Europe, they ordered the **Jewish Councils** (Judenräte) to create Jewish ghetto police forces, referred to in German as Jüdischer Ordnungsdienst (Jewish Order Service). Technically subordinate to the Jewish Councils, the Jewish police were controlled by German authorities. They varied in size and structure, depending on the ghetto. They assisted in selections for deportation, rounded up Jews for **forced labor** and those hiding to avoid deportation, guarded ghetto walls and gates, and escorted Jewish workers who worked outside the ghettos. The Jewish police also helped improve sanitation, and distribute food rations and aid to the needy. Smuggling food and supplies into the ghetto would have been impossible without the help of the Jewish police. Their relationship to the Jewish underground was usually one of cross purposes, but the police often cooperated with the underground or looked the other way. Thus, the ghetto population both detested the police for helping their Nazi tormentors, and appreciated them for trying to alleviate suffering. After the war, the conduct of the Jewish ghetto police was investigated in Germany and in Israel. Some members were convicted of improper conduct, but most were acquitted due to the circumstances under which they operated.

Protestant Churches Hitler's efforts to subordinate the Christian churches to **National Socialism** produced a split among Protestants (mostly Lutherans) in Germany. Those who wished to reconcile Christian doctrine with the racism and the political philosophy of Nazism formed the radical wing of German Lutheranism, the German Christian movement. "**German Christians**" enthusiastically supported Hitler and his racial policies and attempted to remove all traces of Judaism from Christian liturgy and practice, including the Old Testament. The orthodox members of the Lutheran church, known as the **Confessing Church** (Bekennende Kirche), opposed these efforts, condemned them as heresy, and repudiated all attempts to control church teachings. The Confessing Church wished to retain church autonomy and defend Jewish converts to Lutheranism, maintaining its traditional antipathy toward the Jews on theological and social, rather than racial or biological, grounds. Its Barmen Declaration of May 1934 condemned the idea of dictatorship, but said nothing about **antisemitism** and the Jews. Most Lutherans generally did not object to anti-Jewish laws that restored restrictions on Jews that had existed before emancipation. Only a few, such as the theologian **Dietrich Bonhoeffer** or the bishop of Württemberg, Theophil Wurm, condemned the persecution and murder of the Jews and others, and actively resisted the regime for this reason.

Outside Germany, Protestant churches more actively opposed the Nazis. For them the Germans were foreign conquerors, occupiers, and wartime enemies, and resistance was patriotic, not treasonous. Reformed or Calvinist churches in Western Europe were more sympathetic to the Jews on theological grounds. At times Protestants protested Nazi persecution of Jews, resisted Nazi occupation, **rescued** Jews and other victims, or mounted relief efforts for Jews in the ghettos and camps of Eastern Europe; but most did very little.

In general, the Protestant churches responded slowly to Nazi crimes. In Germany, traditional antipathy toward Jews, Gypsies, and the handicapped, and the appeal of Nazi racial theories, nationalism and patriotism, precluded significant opposition to the persecution and mass murder of the victims.

Race and Settlement Main Office (Rasse- und Siedlungshauptamt or RuSHA) Established in 1931 as the **SS** authority on racial matters, it was elevated to the status of a "Main Office" (Hauptamt) in January 1935. The RuSHA was charged with maintaining the racial purity of the SS. It was active in conquered territories in dispossessing Jews, Czechs, Poles and others, and settling ethnic Germans from Eastern Europe on their lands. The RuSHA conducted the germanization of Poles deemed to possess the necessary racial attributes, and investigated the racial background of ethnic Germans from Eastern Europe who settled in territories annexed by Germany. It also ran the Lebensborn program that supervised the kidnapping and transfer to Germany of Polish children considered suitable for germanization. The role of the RuSHA declined during the war due to jurisdictional overlap and friction among the multiplicity of agencies dealing with racial matters.

Red Cross, International   The International Committee of the Red Cross was founded in 1863 in Switzerland to maintain links between national Red Cross societies around the world. It acted as a neutral intermediary between belligerents in wartime, and monitored the application of humanitarian laws to protect soldiers and prisoners of war.

The IRC undertook humanitarian initiatives on behalf of political prisoners during the 1930s, including visits to prisons and camps in Nazi Germany. However, there was no international law designed to protect civilian populations in wartime in 1939. Although the IRC could help civilians held in enemy countries, it was unable to protect civilians in their own countries occupied by Germany. It did little to confront the deportation, **forced labor,** confinement to ghettos, and mass murder of Jews and Gypsies, the mass killing of Polish and Soviet civilian officials and prisoners of war, the murder of tens of thousands of hostages, and the brutal suppression of anti-Nazi **resistance** and **partisan** movements.

It is difficult to assess how much the IRC knew of Nazi atrocities. With the exception of two visits to **Buchenwald** in 1940 and 1941, and a carefully staged visit to **Theresienstadt** in 1944, IRC officials could not enter Nazi camps until the war was almost over. Attempts by the IRC to discover the fate of Jews deported to the East from France and Belgium in 1942 and to provide humanitarian assistance were rebuffed by German authorities. Moreover, IRC officials in Geneva declined to make a public appeal to the German government in the summer of 1942 out of fear of German reprisals against neutral Switzerland. However, it intervened with the governments of German satellite states (Croatia, Slovakia, Romania, Bulgaria, and Hungary) on behalf of their Jewish populations, and sent material assistance (food, clothing, medicine, and other necessities) to prisoners in **ghettos** and camps. These efforts met with limited success. Relief assistance was beset with bureaucratic problems, Allied and

German, and intervention with pro-German governments in 1944 saved relatively few Jews from deportation. Negotiations with the SS to suspend deportations and spare the remaining Jews and other prisoners in German camps in 1944 and 1945 also had mixed results.

Reich Association of Jews in Germany (Reichsvereinigung der Juden in Deutschland) Following the dissolution of Jewish organizations in Germany in 1938, their representative body, the Reich Representation of Jews in Germany (Reichsvertretung der Juden in Deutschland), was eventually replaced with the Reich Association of Jews in Germany in July 1939. Unlike its predecessor, which was a voluntary umbrella organization representing major Jewish organizations in Germany, the Reichsvereinigung was a compulsory body representing Jews as a whole. Its responsibilities were similar to the defunct Reichsvertretung, namely retraining and education, social welfare, and emigration. Cut off from public welfare, Jews had to rely on the Reichsvereinigung for assistance. It was closed in June 1943.

Reich Central Office for Jewish Emigration (Reichszentrale für jüdische Auswanderung) The Reichszentrale was opened in Berlin in January 1939 to function as the central office responsible for all Jewish emigration from Greater Germany. On November 12, 1938, **Hermann Göring** authorized the **SD** to administer all Jewish emigration from Greater Germany according to the procedures it had established in Austria earlier that year. Beforehand Jewish emigration in Germany was controlled by various government agencies, principally the ministries of the interior and economics. In Austria, **Adolf Eichmann's Central Office for Jewish Emigration** (Zentralstelle für jüdische Auswanderung) in Vienna had exercised exclusive control over Jewish emigration from Austria since August 1938, following emigration procedures different from those used in the rest of Germany. Eichmann's methods were harsh and arbitrary. Austrian Jews were concentrated in Vienna, stripped of their assets, and expelled from the country, often without valid immigration visas for other countries. These methods resulted in faster emigration from Austria than from Germany prior to 1938. On January 30, 1939, **Reinhard Heydrich**, chief of the **Security Service** (Sicherheitsdienst or SD) in the SS, placed Heinrich Müller of the **Gestapo** in charge of the Reichszentrale in Berlin. Eichmann's Vienna office and a similar office in Prague became its branches.

Reich Commissariat for the Eastern Territories (Reichskommissariat Ostland) One of two German civilian administrative districts in Alfred Rosenberg's Ministry for the Occupied Eastern Territories (Reichsministerium für die Besetzten Ostgebiete), the occupied territories in the Soviet Union, the Reichskommissariat Ostland was run by Reich Commissar Heinrich Lohse, and included Estonia, Latvia, and Lithuania, and the western half of Belarus. Each of the four became a subdistrict under the authority of a German General Commissar. A few hundred German bureaucrats supported by local pro-Nazi collaborators administered the Reich Commissariat. German plans called for German settlement of the Baltic states and their incorporation into the Reich. **Einsatzgruppen** A and B, and other **police** units killed almost all of the Jews and **Gypsies** remaining in the three Baltic states between July and December 1941, and in western Belarus in the first half of 1942. The major ghettos included **Kovno, Vilna,** and **Minsk**. Soviet forces liberated most of the Reichskommissariat Ostland by the summer of 1944.

Reich Commissariat for the Ukraine (Reichskommissariat Ukraine)

One of two German civilian administrative districts in Alfred Rosenberg's Ministry for the Occupied Eastern Territories (Reichsministerium für die Besetzten Ostgebiete), the occupied territories in the Soviet Union, the Reichskommissariat Ukraine was under the authority of Reich Commissar Erich Koch, who was also governor of the **Białystok** district. The Reich Commissariat expanded in the summer and fall of 1941 as German armies advanced into the USSR, but it never included all of the Ukraine. Eastern Galicia, including the city of **L'vov**, was transferred to the **General Government** of Poland, while southern areas such as the Crimea and eastern territories remained under German military occupation. As of early 1943, the Reich Commissariat included the districts of Volhynia-Podolia, Zhitomir, Kiev, Nikolayev, Dnepropetrovsk, and Tauria. Several hundred German bureaucrats, supported by local collaborators, administered the Reich Commissariat. The major **ghettos** in the Reich Commissariat included Rovno, Khar'kov, Tuchin, and Zhitomir. **Einsatzgruppen** C and D operated in the Ukraine and, along with other **police** units, murdered hundreds of thousands of Jews and **Gypsies**.

Reich Representation of Jews in Germany (Reichsvertretung der Juden in Deutschland)

Initially created by German Jews as the Reich Representation of German Jews (Reichsvertretung der deutschen Juden) in September 1933, it was forced to change its name to the Reich Representation of Jews in Germany in accordance with the **Nuremberg Laws** in 1935. The Reichsvertretung was established in order to give the Jewish community in Germany a representative body vis-à-vis the state. It united the major Jewish organizations in Germany in the common task of dealing with the traumatic changes in Jewish life in Germany after 1933. It assisted Jews in education, vocational training, social welfare and economic assistance, and emigration. As best it could, the Reichsvertretung represented and defended the Jewish community in the face of intensifying persecution during the 1930s. It was replaced by the **Reich As-**

sociation of Jews in Germany (Reichsvereinigung der Juden in Deutschland) in July 1939.

Reich Security Main Office (Reichssicherheitshauptamt or RSHA). *See* **Police, German**

Relief Organization of German Jews (Hilfsverein der deutschen Juden) Established by German Jews in 1901, the Hilfsverein promoted the social welfare and educational needs of poorer Jews in Eastern Europe and the Middle East. After the Nazi assumption of power, circumstances forced it to focus its energies and resources on assisting Jews in Germany with all aspects of emigration, including information on destination countries, vocational counseling, technical and bureaucratic matters, and financial advice. The Hilfsverein reached an understanding with the **Jewish Agency for Palestine**, whereby the latter's **Palestine Office** (Palästinaamt) dealt with Jews emigrating to Palestine, while the Hilfsverein worked with Jews emigrating elsewhere. It also assisted Jews in migration and resettlement within Germany. The Hilfsverein functioned independently until it was absorbed by the **Reich Association of Jews in Germany** (Reichsvereinigung der Juden in Deutschland) in 1939. When the Nazi regime prohibited all emigration in September 1941, the Hilfsverein was dissolved.

SA (Storm Troopers) (Sturmabteilung) The military arm of the **Nazi Party** during the Weimar and early Nazi years, the SA was formed in August 1921. It received some military training from army (Reichswehr) units in the Munich area. Initially, the SA was under the command of **Hermann Göring**, but the failure of Hitler's Beer Hall Putsch in November 1923 resulted in its dissolution. When it was reinstated in 1924 along with the rest of the Nazi Party, Hitler restricted SA activities to intimidation of his political opponents rather than the overthrow of the state. The SA leadership objected to this role and never fully accepted the principle of total obedience to Hitler. Moreover, it envisioned itself as the nucleus of a new, revolutionary Nazi army that would replace the traditional German army led by the conservative, aristocratic elite.

Ernst Röhm, a former army captain who emerged as a leader in the SA in the wake of the Beer Hall Putsch, opposed Hitler's policy but accepted his invitation to command the SA in 1931. SA membership grew from 260,000 in 1931 to more than 4,000,000 in June 1934. But its penchant for independent action and its desire to replace the regular army as Germany's main armed force, conflicted with Hitler's drive for total power and his plans for conquest in Europe. As a result, Hitler moved against the SA leadership on the night of June30-July 1, 1934. In the so-called Night of the Long Knives, SS units with logistical support from the **German army** murdered Röhm and some fifty SA leaders. The

SA was disarmed and neutralized, and its membership fell to about 1,000,000 by 1938.

Although the SA's function became largely ceremonial, its members retained a presence in the police on the local level. During the war it participated in the military training of army conscripts and often constituted auxiliary units attached to the army and the SS, at times helping to run **ghettos** and **labor camps**. The decline of the SA after 1934 was accompanied by the rise of the SS as the main instrument of coercion in Nazi Germany.

Security Police (Sicherheitspolizei or SIPO). *See* **Police, German**

Security Service of the SS (Sicherheitsdienst or SD). *See* **Police, German; SS**

SS (Schutzstaffel) (Protective Detachment) Initially recruited from the SA as Hitler's elite personal bodyguard in 1923, the SS became the embodiment of Nazi racial ideology and the backbone of the Nazi police state. It was a vast police, military, and economic empire dedicated to the destruction of Hitler's political and racial enemies and the creation of a new order in Europe.

Unlike the SA, the mass, semi-independent military arm of the **Nazi Party**, the SS was an exclusive, "racially elite" organization loyal to Hitler alone. In the late 1920s SS activities expanded beyond guarding Hitler to gathering information on political opponents, Jews and Freemasons. After 1929, when **Heinrich Himmler** was appointed Reich Leader of the SS (Reichsführer-SS), the SS assumed responsibility for security in the Nazi Party. It created its own secret intelligence office, the **Security Service** (Sicherheitsdienst or SD), under **Reinhard Heydrich**, and a **Race and Settlement Main Office** (Rasse- und Siedlungshauptamt) to oversee the racial education and purity of SS members and the future settlement of Germans in the East. The SS institutionalized Nazi racial ideology and mythology, requiring its officers and their spouses to have **Aryan** appearances and pure Aryan ancestry.

Under Himmler, SS membership expanded rapidly to about 52,000 by early 1933. In 1934, the SS was rewarded for its role in the neutralization of the **SA** on June 30–July 1, when Himmler assumed authority over the **Gestapo** and the **concentration camp** system. In July, the SS was freed from SA control and became autonomous. In 1936 Heinrich Himmler assumed control of all police functions, including the **Criminal Police** and the **Order Police**, when he became Reich Leader of the SS and Chief of the German Police (Reichsführer-SS und Chef der Deutschen Polizei). In late 1938, after the **Crystal Night pogrom**, the SS took control over Jewish emigration from Germany.

The size and mission of the SS expanded dramatically during the war. Its police functions were manifested in its responsibility for destroying Hitler's political opponents, promoting Nazi racial ideology and enforcing its policies. The latter included the murder of the Jews and **Gypsies, medical experiments** on Jews and other victims in the pursuit of a "genetically perfect" Aryan race, and the expulsion of millions of Slavs from lands in the East that were to be resettled by Germans.

The SS took on an expanding role in economic and industrial activities. Its Economic Administrative Main Office (Wirtschaftsverwaltungshauptamt or WVHA) was formed in 1942 out of two previous SS offices, Budget and Construction (Haushalt und Bauten), and Administration and Economy (Verwaltung und Wirtschaft). Under the direction of **Oswald Pohl**, the WVHA absorbed the Inspectorate of the Concentration Camps, and used the camps and ghettos, and the **forced labor** they provided, to serve its industrial enterprises, which numbered more than forty with some 150 factories and plants.

In the fall of 1939, the SS also established an elite military force, the **Waffen SS**, from the old SS-Verfügungstruppen (Special Purpose Troops) and Death's Head (Totenkopf) units. The Waffen SS became the military arm of the SS, an elite armed force indoctrinated in Nazi ideology and obedient to Hitler alone. By the end of the war, the Waffen SS consisted of thirty-nine divisions, all but one created after 1939. Almost 1,000,000 men of fifteen nationalities served in the Waffen SS during the war, reflecting Himmler's wish to make it an international armed force of Germanic peoples in the ruthless pursuit of Nazi political and racial goals in Europe. Standards for entry into the Waffen SS reflected Nazi racial ideology in general, and SS policy in particular. Its elite units were considered to be of high quality, comparable to the best units in the regular army. At the Nuremberg trials the Waffen SS was one of the organizations indicted as a criminal organization for its role in atrocities against Jews and other victims.

Storm Troopers. See SA (Sturmabteilung)

***Stürmer, Der.* See Streicher, Julius**

T₄. See Euthanasia

Ustasha An extreme right-wing Croatian nationalist movement, the Ustasha was created in 1930 amid ethnic tensions and conflict between Serbs and Croats in Yugoslavia. Led by Ante Pávelic, the Ustasha engaged in terrorism against the Yugoslav government in the 1930s, seeking an independent Croatia. Ideologically, the Ustasha was a mix of reactionary Catholicism, Italian Fascism, agricultural populism, and hatred of Serbs, Muslims, Jews, and **Gypsies. Mussolini** gave the Ustasha considerable support, as did Hitler when, in April 1941, the Germans established an independent Croatia allied to the Third Reich. Between 1941 and 1945 the Ustasha killed more than 500,000 Serbs, 32,000 Jews, and about 25,000 Gypsies in Croatia. When the war ended most of its leaders escaped to Spain and South America.

Waffen SS. *See* **SS**

War Refugee Board Established in January 1944 by President Franklin Roosevelt, the WRB was charged with rescuing the victims of Nazism facing imminent death. It received little assistance, financial or otherwise, from other agencies of the U.S. government. Jewish organizations provided most of the WRB's funding, including close to $17 million from the **American Jewish Joint Distribution Committee**. Its work included rescuing people from Axis territory, finding places to which they could emigrate, using both diplomacy and threats of criminal prosecution to prevent deportation to **extermination camps**, and sending relief supplies to prisoners in Nazi camps. There is disagreement about the effectiveness of the WRB. Estimates of the number of Jews it was able to save range from 20,000 to 200,000, largely through evacuation from Axis territory, protection within Axis territory, or psychological pressure on German allies to cease deportations.

White Rose A small group of anti-Nazi university students in wartime Germany, the White Rose began printing and distributing leaflets in Munich in the summer of 1942 urging an end to the war and the overthrow of **Hitler.** The leaflets told of the mass murders perpetrated by Germany in the East, and urged passive **resistance** to Germany's war effort. White Rose groups were established in other German cities as well. The **Gestapo** infiltrated the group and arrested most of its members, including brother and sister Hans and Sophie Scholl, Christoph Probst, Willi Graf, Alexander Schmorell, and other students and young soldiers, as well as University of Munich philosophy professor Kurt Huber. They and others were tried and executed in 1943 and 1944.

World Jewish Congress (WJC) An international Jewish organization founded in 1932 to defend Jews against the threat of Nazism and **antisemitism,** the World Jewish Congress and its American affiliate, the American Jewish Congress, undertook initiatives to combat Nazi persecution of Jews beginning in 1933. It organized rallies and an international boycott of German goods to protest Nazi Jewish policy. It sought to influence governments, particularly the U.S. government, to relax immigration restrictions to accommodate the growing number of Jewish refugees. Its reports of German atrocities in Eastern Europe in the summer of 1942 provided some of the earliest indications of Nazi extermination policy. The WJC led Jewish relief and **rescue** efforts, lobbying the U.S. and other governments to provide relief aid to Jews in the **ghettos** and camps in occupied Europe, and to save the remnants of European Jewry by whatever means possible.

World Zionist Organization. See Jewish Agency for Palestine

Zegota The code name for the Council for Aid to the Jews (Rada Pomocy Zydom), Zegota was an underground group of Poles and Jews working to assist Jews in German-occupied Poland between 1942 and 1945. It provided Jews with hiding places, forged documents, foster homes for Jewish children, medical attention, and money, and appealed to the Polish government in exile to persuade Poles to help Jews. By the end of 1944 Zegota was providing financial assistance to about 4,000 Jews, and supporting some 2,500 Jewish children in foster homes. In October 1963 Zegota as an organization was declared **Righteous Among the Nations** by Yad Vashem.

PART V

Resources

Resources

Part V is divided into five sections, which are further divided into subsections. The first section contains printed reference works, including encyclopedias, dictionaries, bibliographies, atlases, and photographic collections. The second is the most comprehensive, with printed primary and secondary sources, books, articles, memoirs and diaries, collections of documents, and journals. Its subsections include the history of the Holocaust and the prosecution of war criminals; racism and antisemitism in Germany and Europe before World War II; perpetrators, victims, bystanders and rescuers; and the legacy of the Holocaust since 1945. There are specifically Holocaust journals and journals that cover the Holocaust and Holocaust-related topics. Although the printed sources deal overwhelmingly with the Jewish Holocaust, we have included literature on non-Jewish victims, including the disabled, Gypsies, homosexuals, and members of religious and political groups. We have not included foreign-language publications that are not available in English translation.

The third section, a filmography, lists documentaries, dramas, and docudramas on the Holocaust and the history of Nazi Germany. Most of the documentaries are survivor accounts of ghettos and camps; others deal with antisemitism, world reaction to the Holocaust, rescue, Hitler, war crimes trials, Nazi propaganda, liberation, and displaced persons after the war. The fourth section directs readers to available electronic resources. These include H-Net discussion networks that offer useful information and connections to others involved in Holocaust studies. This section also lists available CD-ROMs on the Holocaust and Nazi Germany and a selection of Web sites not housed at Holocaust institutions, memorials, museums, and the like. The last section provides a list of Holocaust resource institutions, memorials, and museums in North America, Europe, and Israel, including addresses, telephone and fax numbers, and E-mail and Web site addresses, if available.

All the printed resources, the films, and most of the electronic resources are annotated. We have not annotated the Web sites in the fourth section or those Web sites located in the Holocaust institutions listed in the last section. The organization and the content of Web sites frequently change, and any descriptions given here would probably not remain accurate for long. Readers can easily connect to these sites and quickly determine their usefulness.

PRINTED REFERENCE WORKS

Encyclopedias, Bibliographies, Guides

Bloomberg, Marty, ed. *The Jewish Holocaust: An Annotated Guide to Books in English*. San Bernardino, Calif.: Borgo Press, 1991.

This volume includes references to revisionist views of the Holocaust, the search for missing Nazi war criminals, starvation in the ghettos and camps, and a useful list of core title recommendations for college libraries.

Cargas, Harry. *The Holocaust: An Annotated Bibliography*. Chicago: American Library Association, 1985.

This annotated bibliography of the Holocaust includes sections on antisemitism and the rise of Nazism, ghettos, camps, Jewish resistance, world indifference, and survivors and the second generation. There is also a brief list of Holocaust resource centers in the United States.

Edelheit, Abraham, and Hershel Edelheit, eds. *Bibliography on Holocaust Literature*. 2 vols. Boulder, Colo.: Westview, 1993.

Each section begins with an introductory essay, followed by references to books, document collections, periodical literature, and eyewitness accounts. Sections include Jewish life before World War II, world reaction to the Holocaust, and Holocaust literature.

Eitinger, Leo, and Robert Krell, eds. *The Psychological and Medical Effects of Concentration Camps and Related Persecutions on Survivors of the Holocaust*. Vancouver: University of British Columbia Press, 1985.

Epstein, Eric, and Philip Rosen. *Dictionary of the Holocaust: Biography, Geography, and Terminology*. Westport, Conn.: Greenwood, 1997.

This volume contains 2,000 short entries useful in identifying people, places, organizations, and specialized terminology. Entries are cross-referenced, and many end with suggestions for further reading.

Gutman, Israel, ed. *Encyclopedia of the Holocaust*. 4 vols. New York: Macmillan, 1990.

This is the most comprehensive encyclopedia of the Holocaust, covering its background, history, and impact. The entries are by leading scholars from many countries. There is a detailed chronology, a glossary, and useful tables, charts, and maps.

Snyder, Louis. *The Third Reich, 1933–1945: A Bibliographical Guide to German National Socialism.* New York: Garland, 1987.

This annotated bibliography with some 850 titles is divided into thirteen categories, including antisemitism and the Holocaust. The editor provides a short introductory essay that analyzes the various interpretations of the decision to exterminate the Jews.

Szonyi, David. *The Holocaust: An Annotated Bibliography and Resource Guide.* New York: Ktav, 1985.

This volume lists works on Jewish resistance, ghetto life, war crimes trials, survivors and their children, and Holocaust literature. It also lists audiovisual materials, research institutes and archives, oral history projects, traveling exhibits, and educational information.

Tong, Diane, ed. *Gypsies: A Multidisciplinary Annotated Bibliography.* New York: Garland, 1995.

This annotated bibliography on Gypsies concentrates on English-language books and articles on the Roma and their history. It also contains some non-English sources.

Tyrnauer, Gabrielle, ed. *Gypsies and the Holocaust: A Bibliography and Introductory Essay.* Montreal: Inter-University Center for European Studies and Montreal Institute for Genocide Studies, 1991.

Beginning with a brief historical overview of the Holocaust, this bibliography contains almost 600 entries describing books and articles on the fate of the Gypsies during the Holocaust.

Zentner, Christian, and Friedemann Bedürftig, eds. *Encyclopedia of the Third Reich.* 2 vols. New York: Macmillan, 1991.

These two volumes contain more than 3,000 entries and longer articles on the personalities, events, organizations, and historical and ideological terms associated with the Third Reich, the Versailles Treaty, the Weimar Republic, Hitler's early life, and the early history of the Nazi movement. Post–World War II topics such as denazification, the Nuremberg Trials, and neo-Nazism are also covered.

Atlases

Gilbert, Martin. *Atlas of the Holocaust.* New York: Macmillan, 1993.

316 maps present a cartographic history of the Holocaust from the antisemitic violence of prewar Germany to the liberation of the camps in 1945. They chronicle the random killings, mass expulsions and ghettoization, deportations, extermination

camps, death marches, Jewish resistance, and escape and rescue. Numerous photographs supplement the maps.

———. *The Atlas of Jewish History*. New York: Routledge, 1995.

This is a comprehensive map history of the migrations, achievements, and tragedies of the Jewish people from ancient Mesopotamia to the present day, including the Holocaust. Sidebars with useful information accompany 123 maps in chronological order.

United States Holocaust Memorial Museum. *Historical Atlas of the Holocaust*. New York: Simon & Schuster, 1996.

More than 230 full-color maps with accompanying text detail events and places such as ghettos and camps. They depict the deportations, Eastern European cities with Jewish ghettos, and Nazi concentration and extermination camps.

Photographic Collections

Arad, Yitzhak, ed. *The Pictorial History of the Holocaust*. Jerusalem and New York: Yad Vashem and Macmillan, 1990.

More than 400 photographs, with maps and narrative, make up this pictorial history of the Holocaust. They cover rise of Nazism, European Jews under German occupation, ghettos, deportation, the camps, and emigration of survivors to Israel.

Dobroszycki, Lucjan, ed. *Image before My Eyes: A Photographic History of Jewish Life in Poland before the Holocaust*. New York: Schocken, 1994.

Almost 200 black-and-white photographs document Jewish life in Poland from 1864 to 1939. They depict social change, wars, pogroms, modernization, and political turmoil that shaped Jewish life in Poland before World War II, and developments such as Hasidism, Jewish life in Warsaw, education, Zionism, and the cinema.

Grossman, Mendel. *With a Camera in the Ghetto*. New York: Schocken, 1977.

Grossman took thousands of photographs in the Łódź ghetto with a camera he kept hidden under his coat. He hid the negatives in the ghetto before he died, and they were discovered after the war. Fewer than a hundred are presented here.

Hellman, Peter. *Auschwitz Album: A Book Based upon an Album Discovered by a Concentration Camp Survivor, Lili Meier*. New York: Random House, 1981.

This collection contains 185 photographs of Jews in Auschwitz-Birkenau. The collection presents a visual record of tragedy, explained and connected by the author's text.

Keller, Ulrich. *The Warsaw Ghetto in Photographs: 206 Views Made in 1941.* New York: Dover, 1984.

More than 200 photographs, all taken in 1941, document Jewish life in the Warsaw and Łódź ghettos. Subjects include the ghetto administration, Jewish labor, religious practice, children, amusements, and the scourge of hunger and disease.

Milton, Sybil, and Roland Klemig, eds. *Bildarchiv Preussischer Kulturbesitz, Berlin. Vol. I–1, 1933–1939, Vol. I–2, 1939–1945. Archives of the Holocaust: An International Collection of Selected Documents.* Edited by Henry Friedlander and Sybil Milton. Vol. I. New York: Garland, 1990.

These photographs from 1933 to 1945 are from the "Photo Archive of the Prussian Cultural Trust" in Berlin, from its collection of photographs about Jewish life in Europe and the Holocaust. Each volume contains a list of the photographs with dates and descriptions.

Scharf, Rafael, ed. *In the Warsaw Ghetto Summer 1941: Photographs by Willy Georg with Passages from Warsaw Ghetto Diaries.* New York: Aperture, 1993.

These photographs of the Warsaw ghetto were taken on a single day in 1941 by Willy Georg, a German soldier and photographer. They are accompanied by passages from several Warsaw ghetto diaries, the Polish underground press, and Himmler's final liquidation decree.

Swiebocka, Teresa, ed. *Auschwitz: A History in Photographs.* Bloomington: Indiana University Press, 1993.

This is a photographic history of the Auschwitz camp system. It contains almost 300 photographs, along with maps, documents, and artwork, from the archives of the Auschwitz-Birkenau State Museum in Poland.

Vishniac, Roman. *A Vanished World.* New York: Noonday, 1997.

This is a collection of photographs by the author of Jews living their everyday lives in Eastern Europe in the 1930s. There are 180 black and white pictures of porters, peddlers, rabbis, students, children, and others.

PRINTED SOURCES (PRIMARY AND SECONDARY)

History of the Holocaust

GENERAL HISTORIES, ANTHOLOGIES

Bauer, Yehuda. *A History of the Holocaust.* New York: Franklin Watts, 1982.

This survey places the Holocaust into the larger context of the history of the Jews and their relationship with the non-Jewish world since the beginning of Christianity. It also considers the impact of the Holocaust on the postwar world.

Benz, Wolfgang. *The Holocaust: A German Historian Examines the Genocide*. New York: Columbia University Press, 1999.

This work of synthesis outlines the mounting persecution of the Jews in Germany, culminating in mass murder during World War II. Its focus is on German Jews, the deportation of Europe's Jews to the East, and the bureaucratic structures of the Final Solution.

Berenbaum, Michael. *The World Must Know: The History of the Holocaust as Told in the United States Holocaust Memorial Museum*. New York: Little Brown, 1993.

This is a well-documented history of the Holocaust with hundreds of photographs and images of artifacts housed in the United States Holocaust Memorial Museum in Washington, D.C, and eyewitness accounts of survivors.

Berenbaum, Michael, and Abraham Peck, eds. *The Holocaust and History: The Known, the Unknown, the Disputed, and the Reexamined*. Bloomington: Indiana University Press, 1998.

This collection of essays by prominent scholars on the many dimensions of the Holocaust range from antisemitism to the Final Solution, from resistance and rescue to liberation and post-Holocaust recovery.

Botwinick, Rita. *A History of the Holocaust: From Ideology to Annihilation*. Englewood Cliffs, N.J.: Prentice Hall, 1996.

This basic text poses questions about whether the Holocaust was inevitable, whether Jews passively submitted to their own deaths, when the world knew about the mass murders, and whether the world could have done anything to stop it. Designed for high school and college students, it contains a brief glossary, some maps, and a bibliography.

Dawidowicz, Lucy. *The War against the Jews, 1933–1945*. Philadelphia: Jewish Publication Society, 1975.

Hitler's early racial views and German antisemitism are linked to the mass murder of the Jews during World War II. There is an appendix with detailed information on the fate of the Jews in each country under Nazi control.

Gilbert, Martin. *The Holocaust: A History of the Jews of Europe during the Second World War*. New York: Henry Holt, 1987.

The author sees the evolution from persecution to mass murder as a consequence of historic hatreds, and the cooperation or acquiescence of many groups. These included industry, science and medicine, the bureaucracy, the media, foreign collaborators, and the general indifference of non-Jews.

Hilberg, Raul. *The Destruction of the European Jews.* 3 vols. New York: Holmes & Meier, 1985.

The first major history of the Holocaust based on the documentary evidence, this is the standard work that a generation later spawned countless histories and studies of the destruction of European Jewry during World War II. A comprehensive account of the Final Solution, it focuses on the administrative and bureaucratic process of the genocide. A one-volume student edition is available.

———. *Perpetrators Victims Bystanders: The Jewish Catastrophe, 1933–1945.* New York: HarperCollins, 1992.

The author considers the multiplicity of perpetrators, victims, and bystanders in the Holocaust. Perpetrators include Hitler, physicians and lawyers, non-German governments, and others. The victims are Jewish leaders, children, Christian Jews, mixed marriages, and others. Other European nations, the Allies, and the churches are bystanders.

Mayer, Arno. *Why Did the Heavens Not Darken? The "Final Solution" in History.* New York: Pantheon, 1990.

Although antisemitism was always virulent, it did not reach genocidal proportions until well into World War II when Hitler's campaign against the Soviet Union began to falter. The Holocaust is placed within the context of the larger European upheaval of the first half of the twentieth century.

Marrus, Michael, ed. *The Nazi Holocaust: Historical Articles on the Destruction of European Jews.* 9 vols. Westport, Conn.: Meckler, 1989.

These nine volumes contain important, previously published articles and chapters by noted scholars of the Holocaust. Reproduced in facsimile form, they deal with all aspects of the Holocaust.

Niewyk, Donald, ed. *The Holocaust: Problems and Perspectives of Interpretation.* Boston: Houghton Mifflin, 1997.

This anthology compares selected interpretations of key Holocaust issues: the origins of the Final Solution; the victims' reactions to persecution; the problem of Jewish resistance; the motivations of the perpetrators; Gentiles during the Holocaust; and the possibilities of rescue.

Weinberg, Gerhard. *A World at Arms: A Global History of World War II.* New York: Cambridge University Press, 1994.

A synthesis of the military, diplomatic, and human dimensions of World War II, this volume places the Holocaust within the context of that larger struggle.

Yahil, Leni. *The Holocaust: The Fate of European Jewry*. New York: Oxford University Press, 1990.

This comprehensive study rejects arguments that Hitler had no plan for the extermination of the Jews and that the Jews went passively to their deaths. Nazi policies were often inconsistent and contradictory, but Hitler envisioned a final reckoning with the Jews.

THE FINAL SOLUTION

Aly, Goetz. *Final Solution: Nazi Population Policy and the Murder of the European Jews*. New York: Oxford University Press, 1999.

This study places the decision to exterminate the Jews into the context of Hitler's racial reorganization of Europe and the resettlement of ethnic Germans in the East. The author examines the role of lesser officials in the ghettos and camps of Eastern Europe as they struggled to deal with the enormity of this task.

Aly, Goetz, and Susanne Heim. "The Economics of the Final Solution: A Case Study from the General Government." *Simon Wiesenthal Center Annual* 5 (1988): 3–48.

This essay views the planning and implementation of the Final Solution as a process engineered by pragmatic men driven more by considerations of political economy than by Nazi racial ideology.

Bartov, Omer. *Murder in Our Midst: The Holocaust, Industrial Killing, and Representation*. New York: Oxford University Press, 1996.

These essays by the author consider the industrialization and impersonalization of warfare in the nineteenth and early twentieth centuries, linking modern warfare after 1914 to the industrial and impersonalized slaughter of World War II and the Holocaust.

Breitman, Richard. *Official Secrets: What the Nazis Planned, What the British and Americans Knew*. New York: Hill & Wang, 1998.

Beginning in June 1941, British intelligence intercepted, decoded, and analyzed secret radio messages of the SS and German police regarding the extermination of Jews in Russia. These messages reveal British knowledge of German atrocities as early as the summer of 1941.

Browning, Christopher. *Fateful Months: Essays on the Emergence of the Final Solution*. New York: Holmes & Meier, 1985.

The Final Solution did not result from a single decision by Hitler to implement long-standing plans, or implementation by a monolithic structure blindly obeying orders. Political repression, "euthanasia," bloody occupation policies in Poland, and atrocities in the Soviet Union were preliminary steps in an evolutionary process resulting in mass murder.

——. *The Path to Genocide: Essays on Launching the Final Solution.* New York: Cambridge University Press, 1992.

The evolution of Nazi Jewish policy from 1939 to 1941 included massive resettlement of Jews to ghettos in the East, to a reservation in Eastern Poland (Lublin), and to Madagascar. Ordinary people were quickly and easily brought into the process of mass murder.

——. "Nazi Ghettoization Policy in Poland, 1939–1941." *Central European History* 19/4 (1986): 343–368.

The movement of hundreds of thousands of Polish Jews into ghettos between 1939 and 1941 was not part of a conscious plan and the Final Solution. Largely local Nazi officials implemented it at different times, in different ways, and for different reasons.

Burrin, Philippe. *Hitler and the Jews: The Genesis of the Holocaust.* London: Edward Arnold, 1994.

A synthesis between the intentionalist and functionalist interpretations of the Final Solution, the author argues that Hitler held mass murder as an option that depended on circumstances. The Final Solution was the result of genocide against Jews in the Soviet Union, and stiffening Soviet resistance in 1941.

Fleming, Gerald. *Hitler and the Final Solution.* Berkeley: University of California Press, 1984.

Rejecting the view that Hitler knew nothing of the Final Solution until 1943, the author documents Hitler's involvement in the Final Solution from the beginning and lends support to the intentionalist interpretation of the Final Solution.

Gerlach, Christian. "The Wannsee Conference, the Fate of German Jews, and Hitler's Decision in Principle to Exterminate All European Jews." *The Journal of Modern History.* 70 (1998): 759–812.

This essay sheds new light on the significance of the Wannsee Conference of January 20, 1942, in the decision-making process of the Final Solution. It was a precondition for the Final Solution, the result of Hitler's decision in early December to proceed with the extermination of the Jews.

Goldhagen, Daniel. *Hitler's Willing Executioners: Ordinary Germans and the Holocaust.* New York: Alfred A. Knopf, 1996.

This book claims that German antisemitism was unique, arguing that the enthusiastic killers in the police and SS were merely a reflection of the German people as a whole, who enthusiastically supported the extermination of the Jews.

Headland, Ronald. *Messages of Murder: A Study of the Reports of the Einsatzgruppen of the Security Police and the Security Service, 1941–1943*. Rutherford, N.J.: Fairleigh Dickinson University Press, 1992.

This study of the Einsatzgruppen reports of atrocities against the Jews and other citizens in the USSR between 1941 and 1943 examines the role of the German military and the peoples of Eastern Europe as support for the Einsatzgruppen.

Mommsen, Hans. "The Realization of the Unthinkable." In Gerhard Hirschfeld, ed., *The Policies of Genocide: Jews and Soviet Prisoners of War in Nazi Germany*, pp. 93–144. London: Allen Unwin, 1986.

This essay argues that it is unlikely that mass murder was set in motion by a direct order from Hitler, and concludes that lower-level officials devised increasingly radical measures that received Hitler's approval.

Poliakov, Leon. *Harvest of Hate: The Nazi Program for the Destruction of the Jews of Europe*. New York: Holocaust Library, 1979.

This study of the Nazi extermination of the Jews includes the systematic destruction of other "racial enemies" of the Third Reich, particularly the Gypsies and the Slavs. The author focuses on the official and bureaucratic character of German brutality.

Reitlinger, Gerald. *The Final Solution: The Attempt to Exterminate the Jews of Europe, 1939–1945*. New York: A. S. Barnes, 1961.

Published in 1953, this was the first formal history of the Final Solution. Based on documents from the Nuremberg Trials, the author reconstructs the events, the administrative machinery, and the lives and characters of the individuals who were responsible for implementing mass murder.

THE HOLOCAUST IN OCCUPIED EUROPE

Adler, Jacques. *The Jews of Paris and the Final Solution: Communal Response and International Conflicts, 1940–1944*. New York: Oxford University Press, 1989.

This is a personal memoir of the Jews of Paris under German occupation by a member of the Jewish resistance in France. Anti-immigrant sentiments of the Vichy regime and little support from French Jews left foreign Jews as the primary targets of the Germans and their Vichy collaborators.

Braham, Randolph. *The Politics of Genocide: The Holocaust in Hungary*. 2 vols. New York: Columbia University Press, 1993.

The extermination of the Jews of Hungary did not begin until 1944, relatively late in World War II. The extermination process had become routine, and the annihilation of Hungary's Jews proceeded quite rapidly, with the eager collaboration of many Hungarians.

——, ed. *The Nazis' Last Victims: The Holocaust in Hungary*. Detroit: Wayne State University Press, 1998.

These essays consider the rapid deportation and murder of more than 400,000 Hungarian Jews in the summer of 1944. The authors address questions such as bombing Auschwitz, appeals of the Vatican and neutral leaders to stop the deportations, and possible ransom payments to the Germans.

Chary, Frederick. *The Bulgarian Jews and the Final Solution, 1940–1944*. Pittsburgh: University of Pittsburgh Press, 1972.

The Jews in Bulgaria were relatively safe due to the government's reluctance to deport them to the extermination camps. Jews in areas occupied by Bulgaria, in Greece and Yugoslavia, were turned over for deportation. Pressure from the Allies rather than Bulgarian sympathy saved Bulgarian Jews.

Cohen, Richard. *The Burden of Conscience: French Jewish Leadership during the Holocaust*. Bloomington: Indiana University Press, 1987.

Focusing on the Jewish leadership in France during the Vichy period, the author examines the struggles of Jewish leaders against nativist antisemitism directed against foreign Jews in France.

Dobroszycki, Lucjan, and Jeffrey Gurock, eds. *The Holocaust in the Soviet Union*. Armonk, N.Y.: M. E. Sharpe, 1993.

This anthology examines Soviet reactions to the Holocaust and sources for the study of the Holocaust in the Soviet Union. It also contains local and regional case studies, including examinations of events in Transnistria, Riga, and Lithuania.

Ezergailis, Andrew. *The Holocaust in Latvia, 1941–1944: The Missing Center*. Washington, D.C.: United States Holocaust Memorial Museum, 1996.

The author examines German policies in Latvia, the mass killings of Jews, and the role of Latvian auxiliaries in the killings. He argues that Latvian antisemitism and complicity in Nazi mass murder were minimal.

Lemkin, Raphael. *Axis Rule in Occupied Europe*. Washington: Carnegie Endowment, 1944.

The author, a Polish Jewish émigré scholar who coined the term *genocide*, here defines it and applies it to German policies.

Marrus, Michael, and Robert Paxton. *Vichy France and the Jews*. New York: Basic Books, 1981.

This volume documents the active role of the Vichy government in the persecution of the Jews in France. Vichy officials followed German orders to persecute Jews, often taking the initiative themselves.

——. "The Nazis and the Jews in Occupied Western Europe." *Journal of Modern History* 54 (1982): 687–714.

In 1940 Hitler anticipated a postwar mass resettlement of Jews outside Europe. Failure to achieve quick victory by the fall of 1941 prompted the Final Solution, leading to roundups and deportations from Western Europe to extermination in the East after 1942.

Michaelis, Meir. *Mussolini and the Jews: German-Italian Relations and the Jewish Question in Italy, 1922–1945*. Oxford: Clarendon Press, 1978.

This book examines German-Italian relations and Italian policy toward the Jews. Italian antisemitism was more a consequence of Mussolini's alliance with Hitler than a logical development of Italian Fascism.

Moore, Bob. *Victims and Survivors: The Nazi Persecution of the Jews in the Netherlands, 1940–1945*. London and New York: Arnold, 1997.

Despite its traditions of liberalism and tolerance, a large proportion of Holland's Jewish citizens were killed in the Holocaust. The author considers the civilian German administration in Holland, the compliant nature of the Dutch bureaucracy and police, and the deference to authority of the Jewish Council and the Dutch population.

Poliakov, Leon, and Jacques Sabille. *Jews under the Italian Occupation*. New York: Howard Fertig, 1983.

This volume examines German and Vichy pressures on Italy to implement anti-Jewish measures in Italian occupation zones. The Italians acted to thwart German and French efforts against the Jews.

Presser, Jacob. *The Destruction of the Dutch Jews*. New York: Dutton, 1969.

This is an abridgement of the original Dutch edition, written by a Holocaust survivor. It covers the history of the Jews in Holland from the German occupation in May 1940 to the end of the war, focusing on Dutch collaboration in Nazi persecution of the Jews in Holland.

Schneider, Gertrude. *Exile and Destruction: The Fate of the Austrian Jews, 1938–1945*. Westport, Conn.: Praeger, 1995.

This book describes the expulsion of Austrian Jews in 1938 and 1939, deportations to and experiences in ghettos and camps, and the homecoming of survivors after World War II. There is a glossary of names, a family tree, and a complete list of camp survivors with statistics on the victims from each camp.

Schwartz, Solomon. *The Jews in the Soviet Union*. Syracuse, N.Y.: Syracuse University Press, 1951.

This is a traditional, highly negative view of the treatment of Soviet Jewry by Stalin's regime during World War II.

Sweets, John. *Choices in Vichy France: The French under Nazi Occupation*. New York: Oxford University Press, 1986.

This is a generally positive assessment of French reactions to German rule during World War II, including aid given to Holocaust victims.

Weisberg, Richard. *Vichy Law and the Holocaust in France*. New York: New York University Press, 1996.

This study examines the role of the French legal system in the German persecution of Jews in France. Vichy laws reflected Catholic hostility toward the Jews and illustrate the relative ease with which democratic legal systems can be subverted.

Zuccotti, Susan. *The Italians and the Holocaust: Persecution, Rescue and Survival*. New York: Basic Books, 1987.

This book examines the fate of the Jews of Italy during the Holocaust and what it took for 85 percent of them to survive, including courageous decisions of individual Italian Jews in the face of persecution, and the high degree of public and private support from Italians.

——. *The Holocaust, the French, and the Jews*. New York: Basic Books, 1993.

French bureaucrats and police cooperated with the Nazis in the persecution of the Jews. The attitude of the French public ranged from indifference to sympathy for the victims, to satisfaction over their plight.

PROSECUTION OF WAR CRIMINALS

Freiwald, Aaron. *The Last Nazi: Josef Schwammberger and the Nazi Past*. New York: W. W. Norton, 1994.

This is the story of the former SS officer in charge of three slave labor camps in southeastern Poland during World War II. The author examines Schwammberger's life and career, his escape after the war to South America, his years in hiding, his capture, and his trial in Germany in 1992.

Friedlander, Henry. "The Judiciary and Nazi Crimes in Postwar Germany." *Simon Wiesenthal Center Annual* 1 (1984): 27–44.

This essay considers the German legal system after World War II and its record in confronting the Nazi past. West German courts compiled a record of prosecuting Nazi criminality unmatched by anyone, but failed to bring many Nazi criminals to justice, or adequately punish those convicted.

Harel, Isser. *The House on Garibaldi Street: The First Full Account of the Capture of Adolf Eichmann, Told by the Former Head of Israel's Secret Service.* New York: Viking Press, 1975.

The author directed the Israeli search, capture, and abduction of Adolf Eichmann from Argentina to Israel in 1960. He describes the first tentative identification of Eichmann and the suspense of his abduction from Argentina to Israel.

Hausner, Gideon. *Justice in Jerusalem.* New York: Herzl Press, 1978.

The author was the attorney general of Israel and the prosecuting attorney at the trial of Adolf Eichmann. From the documentary evidence used at the trial, he reaffirms Eichmann's guilt.

Kuper, Leo. *Genocide: Its Political Use in the Twentieth Century.* New Haven: Yale University Press, 1982.

This study examines the nature of genocide and presents examples from antiquity to the present. Modern technology and great-power politics have facilitated genocide. The author highlights the inability of the United Nations to prevent or punish its perpetrators.

Rosenbaum, Alan. *Prosecuting Nazi War Criminals.* Boulder, Colo.: Westview Press, 1993.

The author makes a moral, legal, and political case in support of the process of prosecuting Nazi war criminals since World War II. Not doing so would have been an assault on the basic values of civilization and democracy.

Rückerl, Adalbert, ed. *The Investigation of Nazi Crimes, 1945–1978: A Documentation.* Hamden, Conn.: Archon, 1980.

This brief study examines the International Military Tribunal at Nuremberg, the trials by the four Allied Powers in their occupation zones, and those in Germany, Austria, and other European countries after World War II.

Ryan, Allan. *Quiet Neighbors: Prosecuting Nazi War Criminals in America.* New York: Harcourt Brace Jovanovich, 1984.

The author, former head of the Office for Special Investigations in the U.S. Department of Justice, examines public opinion and official attitudes toward Nazi war criminals in the United States and their prosecution after World War II.

Sheftel, Yoram. *The Demjanjuk Affair: The Rise and Fall of a Show Trial*. London: Gollanz, 1994.

John Demjanjuk was wrongly accused of being the sadistic Treblinka camp guard known as "Ivan the Terrible." This is the story of his trial and acquittal in Israel.

Smith, Bradley. *Reaching Judgment at Nuremberg*. New York: Basic Books, 1977.

This book examines pretrial decisions about where the trials would be held, selection of the defendants to be tried, and the makeup of the prosecution team. The author considers the charges and the verdicts, the defendants, the judges, and the law.

———. *The Road to Nuremberg*. New York: Basic Books, 1981.

This book describes how the U. S. government developed its policy for postwar trials of Nazi leaders. It formulated the concepts of charging political organizations with criminal conspiracy and with conspiracy to wage aggressive war.

Taylor, Telford. *Anatomy of the Nuremberg Trials: A Personal Memoir*. New York: Alfred A. Knopf, 1992.

The author, chief counsel and a key member of the American prosecution staff during the Nuremberg trials, considers conflicts within the U.S. government and among the Allies over the nature and purpose of the trials.

Wiesenthal, Simon. *Justice Not Vengeance*. New York: Grove Weidenfeld, 1989.

The author recounts the stories of some of the many war criminals he tracked down after World War II. He includes successful and failed cases, as well as famous and not so famous ones.

DOCUMENT COLLECTIONS

Arad, Yitzhak, Yisrael Gutman, and Abraham Margoliot, eds. *Documents on the Holocaust: Selected Sources on the Destruction of the Jews of Germany and Austria, Poland, and the Soviet Union*. Lincoln: University of Nebraska Press, 1999.

A reprint of an important volume of primary sources on the mass murder of the Jews in Europe, it includes extracts from Hitler's speeches and Goebbels's diaries, the text of anti-Jewish legislation, SS orders liquidating ghettos, eyewitness accounts of atrocities, and other sources.

Arad, Yitzhak, Shmuel Krakowski, and Shmuel Spector, eds. *The Einsatzgruppen Reports: Selections from the Dispatches of the Nazi Death Squads' Campaign against the Jews, July 1941–January 1943*. New York: Holocaust Library, 1989.

This collection contains more than 100 operational reports in English translation of Nazi action squads (Einsatzgruppen), mostly in the Soviet Union from 1941 to 1943. They document the daily activities of the squads; statistics on executions of Jews, partisans, and other victims; and information on local populations and auxiliary police units.

Berenbaum, Michael. *Witness to the Holocaust: An Illustrated Documentary History of the Holocaust in the Words of Its Victims, Perpetrators and Bystanders.* New York: HarperCollins, 1997.

These legal documents, government memoranda, diplomatic cables, army orders, and operations reports conceal the brutality of the Holocaust in bland, bureaucratic language. They cover the anti-Jewish boycott of 1933, the Nuremberg Laws, the Crystal Night pogrom, ghettoization, Jewish resistance, the Einsatzgruppen, and the camps.

Botwinick, Rita, ed. *A Holocaust Reader: From Ideology to Annihilation.* Englewood Cliffs, N.J.: Prentice Hall, 1998.

This is a collection of primary source material on the Holocaust, including documents and memoirs, designed to supplement any text on the Holocaust. The sources, mostly excerpts, are organized into chapters with introductory comments.

Braham, Randolph, ed. *The Destruction of Hungarian Jewry: A Documentary Account.* 2 vols. New York: Pro Arte Federation of Hungarian Jews, 1963.

This collection of original German documents in facsimile form details the German occupation of Hungary and the deportation and extermination of Hungarian Jews in 1944. Most of the documents are in German, but there are descriptions in English of the contents of each document, and an informative introduction.

Central Commission for Investigation of German Crimes in Poland. *German Crimes in Poland.* New York: Howard Fertig, 1982.

This documentary evidence on German war crimes was put together by the Polish provisional government after World War II. It consists of German documents, eyewitness testimony, and photographs on the destruction of Polish Jewry, the extermination camps in Poland, the liquidation of the Warsaw ghetto, and German medical experiments.

Dawidowicz, Lucy, ed. *A Holocaust Reader.* New York: Behrman House, 1976.

The first section contains perpetrator documents such as anti-Jewish legislation in Germany, liquidation orders for the Warsaw ghetto, and eyewitness reports on Auschwitz. The second contains accounts by victims on life, resistance, and death in the ghettos and camps.

Ehrenburg, Ilya, and Vasily Grossman, eds. *The Black Book of Soviet Jewry.* New York: Schocken, 1981.

Jews and non-Jews collaborated during and after World War II to collect the material for this volume on the massacre of Soviet Jews by the Germans. Stalin suppressed it after the war, and the manuscript was not published until it was smuggled to Israel.

Friedlander, Henry, and Sybil Milton, eds. *Archives of the Holocaust: An International Collection of Selected Documents.* 22 vols. New York: Garland, 1990–1995.

This series of documents and photographs is drawn from a representative group of archives in five countries. The volumes are arranged by archival provenance, and the records of each institution are presented in one or more volumes. The collection includes official documents from German and Allied governments and documents from private persons and charitable organizations. They appear in facsimile form, with many in English. Each volume has an introduction, a table of contents listing each document with a brief description of its contents and its archival citation, and a glossary.

Hilberg, Raul, ed. *Documents of Destruction: Germany and Jewry, 1933–1945.* Chicago: Quadrangle, 1971.

This small collection of documents includes papers written by German perpetrators and Jewish victims. The former constitutes mostly official documents, while the latter are personal, autobiographical accounts.

International Military Tribunal. *Trial of the Major War Criminals before the International Military Tribunal, Nuremberg, 14 November 1945 to 1 October 1946.* 42 vols. Nuremberg: International Military Tribunal, 1947–1949.

The volumes in this collection contain the trial proceedings (in English) and the documents in evidence (in the original German) used by the prosecution at the International Military Tribunal in Nuremberg in 1945 and 1946.

Kintner, Earl, ed. *The Hadamar Trial: Trial of Alfons Klein, Adolf Wahlmann, Heinrich Ruoff, Karl Willig, Adolf Merkle, Irmgard Huber, and Philipp Blum.* London: William Hodge, 1949.

This is a collection of photographs, selected motions, opening and closing arguments by the prosecution and the defense, testimony, and the court decision in the 1945 trial of perpetrators of the murder of the handicapped at Hadamar in wartime Germany.

Kogon, E., H. Langbein, and A. Rückerl, eds. *Nazi Mass Murder: A Documentary History of the Use of Poison Gas.* New Haven: Yale University Press, 1993.

This volume documents the use of poison gas by Nazi Germany to exterminate Jews and others during World War II. It contains extracts from wartime German documents, postwar trial testimonies of perpetrators, and eyewitness accounts of the victims.

Lang, Jochen von, ed. *Eichmann Interrogated: Transcripts from the Archives of the Israeli Police*. New York: Farrar, Straus & Giroux, 1983.

This is the transcript of the interrogation of Adolf Eichmann by Avner Less, a captain in the Israeli police, in preparation for Eichmann's trial in Jerusalem. The transcript provides insight into Eichmann's character, and how the times and circumstances conditioned his actions.

Marrus, Michael, ed. *The Nuremberg War Crimes Trial, 1945–1946: A Documentary History*. Boston: Bedford Books, 1997.

This small volume contains excerpts from Nuremberg Trials documents, with commentary and analysis by the editor. They are organized into chapters on historical precedent and background, the important personalities, the charges, and the closing statements of some of the defendants.

Mendelsohn, John, and Donald Detweiler, eds. *The Holocaust: Selected Documents in Eighteen Volumes*. 18 vols. New York: Garland, 1982.

These volumes offer documents in facsimile form from the U.S. Archives in Washington, D.C. They deal with Nazi planning and preparations, the mass murder of the Jews, attempts to rescue the Jews, and postwar trials. Each volume has an introduction and a table of contents listing each document with its content and source. More than two-thirds of the documents are in English.

Noakes, J., and G. Pridham, eds. *Nazism: A History in Documents and Eyewitness Accounts, 1919–1945*. 3 vols. Exeter: University of Exeter Press, 1983–1988.

This is a collection of more than 1,500 documents, excerpted and translated into English. Volume I covers the history of the Nazi Party from 1919 to 1934; volume II covers the domestic policies of the regime during the 1930s; and volume III covers German foreign and racial policies from 1933 to 1945.

State of Israel. *The Trial of Adolf Eichmann. Record of Proceedings in the District Court of Jerusalem*. 9 vols. Jerusalem: State of Israel Ministry of Justice, 1992–1995.

This is the first publication in English of the proceedings of the trial of Adolf Eichmann in Jerusalem in 1960. It includes the trial proceedings, a list of exhibits, Eichmann's statements, documents submitted in evidence, the judgment of the court, and Eichmann's appeal to the Israeli Supreme Court.

State Museum of Auschwitz-Birkenau. *Death Books from Auschwitz*. 3 vols. Munich: K. G. Saur, 1995.

These volumes contain death records of victims murdered at Auschwitz, based on the partially preserved original death books compiled by German authorities at the camp. There are essays by ex-prisoners; statistical information and charts on prisoners and transports; a chronology; short biographies of SS personnel at Auschwitz; and photographs, documents in facsimile form, and maps. Two volumes contain the names of 68,864 prisoners killed at Auschwitz.

Smith, Bradley (ed.). *The American Road to Nuremberg: The Documentary Record, 1944–1945*. Stanford: Hoover Institution Press, 1982.

This is a documentary record of the development of the Nuremberg trial system, formulated in 1944 and 1945 almost entirely by American officials. Their aim was to devise a plan to punish Nazi war criminals, eliminate the threat of a Nazi revival, and avoid the economic destruction of Germany.

United States. *Nazi Conspiracy and Aggression*. 11 vols. Washington, D.C.: U.S. Government Printing Office, 1946–1948.

These volumes contain the documentary evidence (in English) and the guide materials prepared by the American and British prosecuting staffs for the prosecution of the Nazis under indictment by the International Military Tribunal in Nuremberg in 1945 and 1946.

——. *Trials of War Criminals before the Nürnberg Military Tribunals under Control Council Law No. 10*. 15 vols. Washington, D.C.: U.S. Government Printing Office, 1949.

These volumes contain indictments, judgments, and portions of the trial records (in English) of prominent figures in the Third Reich, tried by the U.S. Military Court in the American zone of occupation from 1946 to 1949. The defendants were diplomats, politicians, military officers, SS leaders, industrialists, and professionals.

Racism and Antisemitism before World War II

HISTORIES OF RACISM AND ANTISEMITISM
Almog, Shmuel, ed. *Antisemitism through the Ages*. Oxford: Pergamon, 1988.

Addressing the continuity of Jew-hatred from classical antiquity to the present, these essays examine the forms and manifestations of antisemitism in history and the diverse interpretations of contemporary historians.

Arendt, Hannah. *The Origins of Totalitarianism*. Part I: *Antisemitism*. New York: Harcourt Brace Jovanovich, 1973.

This study begins with the author's controversial account of the rise of antisemitism in Europe in the nineteenth century. It concludes with an analysis of the institutions, organization, and operation of totalitarian movements and governments, with a focus on Nazi Germany and Stalinist Russia.

Barkan, Elazar. *The Retreat of Scientific Racism: Changing Concepts of Race in Britain and the United States between the World Wars.* Cambridge: Cambridge University Press, 1992.

This study examines the rejection of the scientific foundations of racism in Great Britain and the United States between the wars. Racial differences were no longer attributed to biological factors, but to cultural factors instead.

Cohn, Norman. *Warrant for Genocide: The Myth of the Jewish World Conspiracy and the "Protocols of the Elders of Zion."* New York: Harper & Row, 1966.

The Nazi drive to exterminate the Jews developed out of demonological superstitions inherited from the Middle Ages. The author examines the continuity of the antisemitic myth of a world Jewish conspiracy, manifested in the so-called *Protocols of the Elders of Zion,* an early twentieth-century forgery purporting to prove the conspiracy.

Efron, John. *Defenders of the Race: Jewish Doctors and Race Science in Fin de Siècle Europe.* New Haven: Yale University Press, 1994.

This study demonstrates the ways in which scientific racism shaped the discourse of Jewish doctors and anthropologists in their effort to combat antisemitism.

Field, Geoffrey. *Evangelist of Race: The Germanic Vision of Houston Stewart Chamberlain.* New York: Columbia University Press, 1981.

This account of the racial ideology of Houston Stewart Chamberlain concludes that while parliamentary antisemitism declined before World War I, antisemitic attitudes spread rapidly through German society.

Fischer, Klaus. *The History of an Obsession: German Judeophobia and the Holocaust.* New York: Continuum, 1998.

This history of German-Jewish relations concludes that although Hitler was the major villain, the German people provided unconditional support. It argues that the ideology behind the Holocaust can be found in "human delusion" and the fear, paranoia, projection, and scapegoating it inspires.

Hertzberg, Arthur. *The French Enlightenment and the Jews: The Origins of Modern Antisemitism.* New York: Columbia University Press, 1990.

This study locates the roots of Jewish emancipation and modern antisemitism in eighteenth-century France and the Enlightenment. Both the hopeful and the tragic elements of modern Jewish history have their genesis in the way the Jewish question was defined in France before the revolution.

Isaac, Jules. *The Teaching of Contempt: Christian Roots of Antisemitism*. New York: McGraw Hill, 1965.

This work of a French-Jewish historian and survivor seeks to provide a better understanding of the Christian roots of antisemitism. He exposes the Christian teaching of contempt for the Jews as the major obstacle to teaching respect for Jews and other non-Christians.

Katz, Jacob. *From Prejudice to Destruction: Antisemitism, 1700–1933*. Cambridge, Mass.: Harvard University Press, 1980.

The author looks at the paradox of modern antisemitism in Europe, considering the rapid growth of anti-Jewish feeling in Europe in an age of Enlightenment, rationality, and Jewish emancipation.

——. *The Darker Side of Genius: Richard Wagner's Anti-Semitism*. Hanover, N.H.: University Press of New England, 1986.

The author argues that Wagner's Judeophobia resulted from conflict with his Jewish mentors and competitors. He maintains that Wagner's music is untainted by his antisemitism.

Katz, Steven. *The Holocaust in Historical Context*. Vol. I: *The Holocaust and Mass Death before the Modern Age*. New York: Oxford University Press, 1994.

This volume compares the Holocaust with mass slaughters in ancient, premodern, and modern times, arguing that the Holocaust is unprecedented because it is the only instance when an entire people was slated for extinction.

Kühl, Stefan. *The Nazi Connection: Eugenics, American Racism, and German National Socialism*. New York: Oxford University Press, 1994.

This book examines contacts between American and German eugenicists during the 1930s. American eugenicists were enthusiastic about forced sterilization and other practices in Germany, and American eugenic policies and forced sterilization practices were admired by Hitler and the Nazis.

Langmuir, Gavin. *Toward a Definition of Antisemitism*. Berkeley: University of California Press, 1990.

The author examines the development of Judeophobia in the Middle Ages, when a concrete, definable antisemitism first appeared. Jews became the target of a hostility in northern Europe in the twelfth and thirteenth centuries identical to Nazi antisemitism.

Levine, Hillel. *Economic Origins of Antisemitism: Poland and Its Jews in the Early Modern Period*. New Haven: Yale University Press, 1991.

This is a study of Poland and its Jewish community from the sixteenth to the eighteenth centuries. It considers the changing circumstances and disastrous consequences for Poland's Jews as the forces of modernization swept into Poland from the West at the end of the eighteenth century.

Levy, Richard. *The Downfall of the Anti-Semitic Political Parties in Imperial Germany*. New Haven: Yale University Press, 1975.

This study rejects the idea that the origins of Nazism are to be found in Germany's earlier antisemitic political parties. By 1914 these parties had failed to marshal public support or pass antisemitic legislation in the Reichstag. The search for prototypes of the Third Reich distorts nineteenth-century German history.

Lindemann, Albert. *Esau's Tears: Modern Anti-Semitism and the Rise of the Jews*. Cambridge: Cambridge University Press, 1997.

This volume explores the variety of modern antisemitism in Europe and the United States from the 1870s to the 1930s. Antisemitism was more ambiguous and less central in the lives of Jews and non-Jews. It did not necessarily point to an inevitable Holocaust.

Massing, Paul. *Rehearsal for Destruction: A Study of Political Antisemitism in Imperial Germany*. New York: Harper, 1949.

In this first post-Holocaust study of modern antisemitism in Imperial Germany, the author affirms the continuity of German antisemitism from nineteenth century racist and antisemitic writers to the Nazis.

Mosse, George. *Toward the Final Solution: A History of European Racism*. New York: Harper & Row, 1978.

This history of modern racism considers how 6,000,000 Jews could be murdered by a modern European state in an efficient and impersonal manner. Racism inculcated every important idea and movement in nineteenth- and twentieth-century Europe, and accepted myths became reality for all racists.

——. *The Crisis of German Ideology: Intellectual Origins of the Third Reich*. New York: Schocken, 1981.

The ideological sources of Nazism can be found in a complex collection of antidemocratic ideas deeply embedded in nineteenth- and twentieth-century German history. A peculiarly Germanic ideology was institutionalized in the schools, youth movements, veterans' organizations, and political parties, and was transformed into a Nazi revolution and anti-Jewish crusade.

——. *Nationalism and Sexuality: Respectability and Abnormal Sexuality in Modern Europe.* New York: H. Fertig, 1985.

This history of European manners and morals argues that bourgeois values excluded Jews, Gypsies, and the handicapped from respectability and thus paved the way for their genocide.

Nicosia, Francis. "Zionism and Palestine in Antisemitic Thought in Imperial Germany." *Studies in Zionism* 13/2 (1992): 115–131.

Zionism was popular among prominent nineteenth-century antisemitic writers as a means of promoting Jewish emigration from Germany. Some considered Zionism a positive phenomenon, while others saw it as a dangerous but useful means of eliminating Jews.

Niewyk, Donald. "Solving the 'Jewish Problem': Continuity and Change in German Antisemitism, 1871–1945." *Leo Baeck Institute Yearbook* 35 (1990): 335–370.

There was little similarity between most pre-1918 antisemitism and the Nazi variety. The former stressed integrating the Jews fully into German society or advocated their segregation. The few advocates of exclusion or extermination were marginal figures, and there is no evidence of large numbers of Germans wishing to annihilate the Jews.

Pauley, Bruce. *From Prejudice to Persecution: A History of Austrian Antisemitism.* Chapel Hill: University of North Carolina Press, 1992.

A general history of Austrian antisemitism from the Middle Ages to the present, this volume focuses on the period from 1914 to Austria's union with Germany in 1938. Antisemitism was stronger in Austria than elsewhere in Central and Western Europe, and Austrian Jews were more vulnerable.

Poliakov, Leon. *The Aryan Myth: A History of Racist and Nationalist Ideas in Europe.* New York: Basic Books, 1971.

This study sees the myth of Aryan origins as the result of a confusion about the nature of humanity (races) and their culture (languages). This confusion persisted until it achieved general acceptance in the late nineteenth century.

——. *A History of Anti-Semitism.* 4 vols. New York: Vanguard Press, 1965–1986.

These four volumes constitute a sweeping history of the Jews and their relations with non-Jews in the Diaspora from classical antiquity to the eve of Hitler's assumption of power in Germany in 1933.

Pulzer, Peter. *The Rise of Political Antisemitism in Germany and Austria.* Cambridge, Mass.: Harvard University Press, 1988.

This study locates the beginnings of the road to Auschwitz by tracing the rise of modern antisemitism in Germany and Austria from the late nineteenth century through World War I. Modern antisemitism was generated by late nineteenth-century cultural despair and social conflict. The Nazis merely exploited something that already existed.

Reichmann, Eva. *Hostages of Civilization: The Social Sources of National Socialist Antisemitism*. Westport, Conn.: Greenwood, 1971.

The author examines the nature of German antisemitism, its interaction with other historical factors in Germany, and the role it played in bringing about the mass murder of the Jews. The Jews and the Jewish Question played a small part in German antisemitism. Nazi persecution was rooted in German society's "spirit of collective aggressiveness," which targeted the Jews.

Rose, Paul Lawrence. *German Question — Jewish Question: Revolutionary Antisemitism from Kant to Wagner*. Princeton, N.J.: Princeton University Press, 1992.

A new edition of the author's earlier *Revolutionary Antisemitism in Germany: From Kant to Wagner*, this study blurs the traditional distinction between pre-modern Christian Judeophobia, and modern, secular, racial antisemitism. The author sees a continuous antisemitism through the centuries based on a continuing mythology about Jews, recast in the Enlightenment, and then again in the nineteenth century. Finally, it appears at the core of biological racism.

Ruether, Rosemary. *Faith and Fratricide: The Theological Roots of Antisemitism*. Eugene, Ore.: WIPF & Stock, 1997.

The author, a Roman Catholic theologian, sees the roots of Christian antisemitism in the Christian New Testament. She ascribes the long tradition of almost unrelenting Christian hatred of the Jews, the prologue to the Holocaust, to a symbolic self-hatred.

Stern, Fritz. *The Politics of Cultural Despair: A Study of the Rise of Germanic Ideology*. Berkeley: University of California Press, 1961.

This study considers the writings of Paul de Lagarde, Julius Langbein, and Moeller van den Bruck to convey the mood of despair that pervaded German culture at the turn of the century. It was a mood that rejected the modern world, idealized a non-existent past, and generated a vision that would become the Third Reich.

Trachtenberg, Joshua. *The Devil and the Jews: The Medieval Conception of the Jew and Its Relation to Modern Antisemitism*. Philadelphia: Jewish Publication Society, 1983.

The author focuses on the demonological character of a unique strand of anti-Jewish prejudice that had its origins in the late Middle Ages. The concept of the Jew as the devil was the product of historical and cultural factors peculiar to Christian Europe in the late Middle Ages.

Volkov, Shulamit. "Antisemitism as a Cultural Code — Reflections on the History and Historiography of Antisemitism in Imperial Germany." *Leo Baeck Institute Yearbook* 23 (1978): 25–46.

Rejecting earlier notions of continuity in German antisemitism from the nineteenth century to Hitler, the author sees a difference between the political cultures of Wilhelminian Germany and Hitler's Third Reich. The Nazis infused antisemitism with new meaning and transformed it with extermination.

Weiss, John. *Ideology of Death: Why the Holocaust Happened in Germany*. Chicago: Ivan R. Dee, 1996.

The Holocaust happened in Germany because of the racist form of antisemitism prevalent in Germany and Austria by the twentieth century. Racist ideas were ingrained in German culture, leading to the development of an extreme form of antisemitism from Martin Luther through the nineteenth century to Nazism.

Weiss, Sheila. "The Race Hygiene Movement in Germany." *Osiris* 3 (1987): 193–236.

German eugenicists possessed diverse political and racial views. Not all believed in notions of "Aryan" supremacy, nor were all of them Nazis. They were indirectly complicit in Nazi crimes because their support for Hitler generally rested on the regime's support for their work.

Zimmermann, Moshe. *Wilhelm Marr: The Patriarch of Antisemitism*. New York: Oxford University Press, 1986.

The author examines Wilhelm Marr's Jew-hatred and his influence on the political, literary, and artistic circles of his time. He demonstrates the ways in which modern racial antisemitism came to permeate German thought and culture before World War I.

RACIST AND ANTISEMITIC TEXTS

Chamberlain, Houston Stewart. *Foundations of the Nineteenth Century*. 2 vols. New York: Howard Fertig, 1968.

An important antisemitic text of the late nineteenth century, Chamberlain's history of European civilization interprets world history as a struggle between the "racially inferior and evil Jews" and the "racially and morally superior Aryans."

Gobineau, Arthur de. *The Inequality of the Races*. Los Angeles: Noontide Press, 1966.

This mid-nineteenth century work attempts to explain the rise and fall of civilizations as the product of racial conflict. It is a synthesis of ideas that generated modern racist thought in Europe and the United States. Drawing on anthropology, linguistics, and history, the author uses race to explain human history.

Levy, Richard, ed. *Antisemitism in the Modern World: An Anthology of Texts*. Lexington, Mass.: D.C. Heath, 1991.

This is a collection of excerpts from important antisemitic texts in the modern era, from the eighteenth century to Nazi Germany and the Holocaust. The editor introduces each section with a brief description of the documents and their meaning. There are suggested readings at the end of each section.

Pois, Robert, ed. *Race and Race History and Other Essays by Alfred Rosenberg*. New York: Harper & Row, 1974.

This volume contains extracts from Alfred Rosenberg's major works on race, principally from his book *The Myth of the Twentieth Century*. Rosenberg was the chief racial theorist of the Nazi Party in the early years of the movement. The extracts are linked by the editor's comments.

Rosenberg, Alfred. *The Myth of the Twentieth Century: An Evaluation of the Spiritual-Intellectual Confrontations of Our Age*. Newport Beach, Calif.: Noontide Press, 1993.

The author's role as the Nazis' chief racial theorist was enhanced by the publication of this book in 1930. It incorporates the theories of nineteenth-century racial philosophers and argues that race is the decisive factor in history. Rosenberg represents the Teutons as the master race and condemns Judaism and Christianity and their ideals of compassion and charity.

THE WEIMAR REPUBLIC AND THE RISE OF HITLER

Allen, William Sheridan. *The Nazi Seizure of Power: The Experience of a Single German Town, 1922–1945*. New York: Franklin Watts, 1984.

Antisemitism, although present in Germany, was not a major cause of the rise of Nazism in the town of Northeim in central Germany. The Nazis did not succeed in making the townspeople into strong antisemites once in power.

Broszat, Martin. *Hitler and the Collapse of Weimar Germany*. London: Berg Publishers, 1987.

This is a systematic analysis of the role of Hitler and the Nazis in the collapse of the Weimar Republic. The author presents the broad structural and ideological preconditions that brought the conservative elite and the Nazis together to destroy the democratic system and constitution.

Brustein, William. *The Logic of Evil: The Social Origins of the Nazi Party, 1925–1933.* New Haven: Yale University Press, 1996.

This book argues that the working class provided considerable support for the Nazis between 1925 and 1933. Workers accounted for 40 percent of the membership in the NSDAP before 1933 and were motivated by material rather than emotional considerations.

Childers, Thomas. *The Nazi Voter.* Chapel Hill: University of North Carolina Press, 1984.

This is the first study based on a large national sample of rural and urban districts in national elections during the Weimar Republic. The sources of support for the Nazis were more diverse than merely the lower middle class. The NSDAP became a broad-based party that crossed traditional social, religious, and regional lines.

Feuchtwanger, Edgar. *From Weimar to Hitler: Germany, 1918–1933.* New York: St. Martin's, 1995.

This book argues that the political failure of the Weimar Republic was not inevitable. The author contends that there were ways out of the political crisis right up to Hitler's assumption of power.

Hamilton, Richard. *Who Voted For Hitler?* Princeton, N.J.: Princeton University Press, 1982.

Using voting records and other election data from fourteen large German cities, the author rejects the view that the Nazis drew most of their support from the lower middle class. Support for the Nazis was conditioned by class in each district. The wealthiest districts generally gave the NSDAP the strongest support.

Mommsen, Hans. *The Rise and Fall of Weimar Democracy.* Chapel Hill: University of North Carolina Press, 1996.

The author argues that the rise of Nazism in Germany was not inevitable, but was the result of particular domestic and international pressures, including foreign recognition of the Nazis, the Weimar parliamentary system, and the depression.

Pridham, Geoffrey. *Hitler's Rise to Power: The Nazi Movement in Bavaria, 1923–1933.* New York: Harper & Row, 1973.

The Nazis' home turf, Bavaria, was not easy for them to win over. The author shows how they did it, and demonstrates that racism was not always a strong attraction.

JEWS IN GERMANY BEFORE 1933

Ascheim, Steven. *Brothers and Strangers: The East European Jews and the German Jewish Consciousness 1800–1923.* Madison: University of Wisconsin Press, 1982.

This study reveals the stereotypical presentations by German Jews of East European Jews, from the largely negative image of half-Asian aliens in the 1880s to the more positive image of Jewish cultural heroes and symbols of Jewish revival.

Brenner, Michael. *The Renaissance of Jewish Culture in Weimar Germany*. New Haven: Yale University Press, 1996.

This study rejects the view that German Jews pursued a linear retreat from Jewish traditions toward full assimilation during emancipation. The indigenous culture of German Jews was neither the total abandonment of Jewish identity, tradition, and community, nor incompatible with the majority's view of belonging to German culture.

Kauders, Anthony. *German Politics and the Jews: Düsseldorf and Nuremberg, 1910–1933*. Oxford: Clarendon Press, 1996.

This book attempts to define the nature of German antisemitism before the Third Reich by examining the history of political antisemitism in two important German cities from 1910 to 1933. Attitudes toward Jews began to change for the worse during the Weimar years, before Hitler's assumption of power in 1933.

Lamberti, Marjorie. *Jewish Activism in Imperial Germany: The Struggle for Civil Equality*. New Haven: Yale University Press, 1978.

This study looks at Jewish lawyers and political organizations that struggled for civic equality for German Jews before World War I. They received some sympathy from non-Jewish liberals and progressives, but little active support. The author argues that German Jewish activism was self-conscious, articulate, and effective.

Low, Alfred. *Jews in the Eyes of the Germans: From the Enlightenment to Imperial Germany*. Philadelphia: Institute for the Study of Human Issues, 1979.

Germans in the eighteenth and nineteenth centuries generally did not preach the removal or elimination of the Jews from Germany. The author argues that nineteenth-century Germans stood apart from the ideology and aims of twentieth-century Nazism.

Lowenstein, Steven. *The Berlin Jewish Community: Enlightenment, Family and Crisis, 1770–1830*. New York: Oxford University Press, 1994.

This social history of the Jews in late eighteenth- and early nineteenth-century Berlin examines the early modernization stimulated by the Jewish economic elite following the Seven Years War. It considers the strains in Jewish life as preliminary signs of emancipation conflicted with Jewish traditions.

Mosse, Werner. *The German-Jewish Economic Elite, 1820–1935: A Socio-Cultural Profile*. Oxford: Clarendon Press, 1989.

The author considers the German-Jewish entrepreneurial elite in the nineteenth and early twentieth centuries. He takes a case-study approach to draw conclusions about the Jewish elite. Most retained their Jewish identity, resisted total assimilation, and only partially integrated into German society.

Niewyk, Donald. *The Jews in Weimar Germany*. New Brunswick, N.J.: Transaction, 2000.

This study of German Jews during the Weimar years explores their role in Germany's economic, political, and cultural life, their self-definitions, and their responses to antisemitism. It rejects the notion of a false sense of assimilation and security, and demonstrates that German Jews were anything but monolithic. Deeply contentious on religious, ideological, and regional issues, they failed to achieve organizational unity.

Poppel, Stephen. *Zionism in Germany, 1897–1933: The Shaping of a Jewish Identity*. Philadelphia: Jewish Publication Society, 1977.

This is a brief survey history of the German Zionist movement from its beginnings to 1933. It focuses on the effects of Zionist ideology on German Zionists who remained in Germany rather than on the activities and contributions of German Zionists in Palestine.

Pulzer, Peter. *Jews and the German State: The Political History of a Minority, 1848–1933*. Oxford: Basil Blackwell, 1992.

The author argues that Jews in Germany never achieved full civic equality in the nineteenth century and remained a distinct ethnic group conditioned only in part by membership in a Jewish religious community. Unlike the Jews of other Western European states, German Jews largely failed to achieve political integration.

Reinharz, Jehuda. *Fatherland or Promised Land? The Dilemma of the German Jew, 1893–1914*. Ann Arbor: University of Michigan Press, 1975.

This is a study of the two major competing views of Jewish identity in Germany before World War I, the "assimilationists" and the Zionists. The former believed that the Jews were German by nationality and Jewish only by confession, while the latter argued that the Jews in Germany and elsewhere were Jewish by nationality and deserved their own state in Palestine.

Schorsch, Ismar. *Jewish Reactions to German Antisemitism, 1870–1914*. New York: Columbia University Press, 1972.

This book traces the resurgence of antisemitism in Germany after unification in 1871 and the consequent reappraisal by German Jews of their status in Germany. Defense strategy shifted from traditional reliance on silence, Christian defenders, and Jewish courtiers, to the establishment of self-defense institutions designed to defend Jewish rights.

Sorkin, David. *The Transformation of German Jewry, 1780–1840.* New York: Oxford University Press, 1987.

The emancipation of German Jews was marked by the dramatic transformation from feudal status to absorption of the most extreme manifestations of Western society. The author examines their encounter with modern culture, and their consequent cultural productivity.

Tal, Uriel. *Christians and Jews in Germany: Religion, Politics, and Ideology in the Second Reich, 1870–1914.* Ithaca, N.Y.: Cornell University Press, 1975.

This book examines Jewish-Christian relations in Germany between unification and World War I. Far from being the object of events and changing conditions, the Jews played an active and influential role in Germany's development.

Wertheimer, Jack. *Unwelcome Strangers: East European Jews in Imperial Germany.* New York: Oxford University Press, 1987.

This book examines the attitudes of German Jews toward East European Jewish immigrants in late nineteenth-century Germany. The author challenges the view that German Jews responded with arrogance, condescension, and even hatred, concluding that German Jews generally acted responsibly and charitably toward East European Jewish refugees.

NAZI POLICY AND GERMAN JEWS, 1933–1939

Adam, Uwe. "An Overall Plan For Anti-Jewish Legislation in the Third Reich." *Yad Vashem Studies* 11 (1976): 33–55.

Although there is no evidence for the existence of a long-term Nazi plan to exterminate the Jews, early plans for anti-Jewish legislation to regulate Jewish life in Germany under National Socialism did exist.

Angress, Werner. *Between Fear and Hope: Jewish Youth in the Third Reich.* New York: Columbia University Press, 1988.

The author offers a memoir of growing up Jewish in Nazi Germany. He reveals that until the Crystal Night pogrom of November 1938 it was possible to lead a "relatively normal life," despite the deteriorating situation.

Baker, Leonard. *Days of Sorrow and Pain: Leo Baeck and the Berlin Jews.* New York: Macmillan, 1978.

This book explores the life and philosophy of Rabbi Leo Baeck, Jewish theologian and spiritual leader of German Jewry during the Third Reich, against the backdrop of Nazi persecution. Baeck teaches that a human being can suffer any tragedy and survive as a moral person.

Barkai, Avraham. *From Boycott to Annihilation: The Economic Struggle of German Jews 1933–1943.* Hanover, N.H.: University Press of New England, 1989.

This is an account of Hitler's efforts to destroy the Jews of Germany economically from very early on. The regime undermined Jewish economic life before 1938 through a combination of boycotts, discrimination, exclusions, and repressive legislation, generally with the support of non-Jewish businesses.

Dippel, John. *Bound upon a Wheel of Fire: Why So Many German Jews Made the Tragic Decision to Remain in Nazi Germany.* New York: Basic Books, 1996.

Case studies of six prominent members of the German Jewish community attempt to ascertain why so many Jews stayed in Germany between 1933 and 1938. They consider arguments critical of German Jews for hanging on for so long, and understanding of the circumstances in which they had to make decisions.

Friedländer, Saul. *Nazi Germany and the Jews: The Years of Persecution, 1933–1939.* New York: HarperCollins, 1997.

The first of what is to be a comprehensive two-volume history of the Holocaust, this book examines the steadily increasing persecution of Jews in Germany from 1933 to 1939. The author considers the interplay between the ideological objectives and tactical policy decisions of the Nazi leadership, the mentalities of the bystanders, and the attitudes and reactions of the victims.

Kaplan, Marion. *Between Dignity and Despair: Jewish Life in Nazi Germany.* New York: Oxford University Press, 1998.

Written from a gender perspective, the author examines the thoughts and feelings of Jewish men, women, and children as they coped with persecution in Nazi Germany. She focuses on the everyday lives of ordinary Jews and their struggle to survive, rather than on Nazi perpetrators and the responses of Jewish organizations.

Nicosia, Francis R. *The Third Reich and the Palestine Question.* New Brunswick, N.J.: Transaction, 2000.

This book includes a detailed account of the role of Zionism in Nazi Jewish policy before World War II. Hitler's regime used Zionism to eliminate Jewish life in Germany before the war while actively opposing the Zionist goal of an independent Jewish state in Palestine.

——. "The End of Emancipation and the Illusion of Preferential Treatment: German Zionism, 1933–1938." *Leo Baeck Institute Yearbook* 36 (1991): 243–265.

Despite the regime's encouragement of Jewish emigration from Germany to Palestine, Zionists were rarely exempt from the persecution inflicted on all German Jews.

This made Zionist work more difficult and, from the perspective of Nazi efforts to promote Jewish emigration, counterproductive.

Paucker, Arnold, ed. *Die Juden im Nationalsozialistischen Deutschland / The Jews in Nazi Germany, 1933–1943*. Tübingen: J. C. B. Mohr Paul Siebeck, 1986.

This is a collection of essays dealing with Jewish life in the Third Reich. They illustrate the deep sense of belonging in Germany even after 1933, Jewish social and cultural achievements in the face of intensifying persecution, and the persistence of political rivalries between Zionists and assimilationists.

Schleunes, Karl. *The Twisted Road to Auschwitz: Nazi Policy toward German Jews, 1933–1939*. Urbana: University of Illinois Press, 1970.

This study argues that the Final Solution was not the product of some grand design or blueprint. The Nazis came to power with no specific plans for an overall solution to the Jewish question in Europe, and the path to the Final Solution was not a deliberate or intended one.

Strauss, Herbert. "Jewish Emigration from Germany — Nazi Policies and Jewish Responses (I)." *Leo Baeck Institute Yearbook* 25 (1980): 313–361.
——. "Jewish Emigration from Germany — Nazi Policies and Jewish Responses (II)." *Leo Baeck Institute Yearbook* 26 (1981): 343–409.

These two essays provide the most detailed account and analysis of German Jewish emigration during the Third Reich. Charts, tables, and other statistical data illuminate the demographics of the German Jewish community and emigration between 1933 and 1945.

Thalmann, Rita, and Emmanuel Feinermann. *Crystal Night, 9–10 November 1938*. New York: Holocaust Library, 1974.

An account of the infamous pogrom in Nazi Germany. The authors use excerpts from the diaries of Jews who witnessed and experienced the violence and destruction. The book also considers the bystanders and the indifference with which other nations responded to the tragedy.

JEWS IN EUROPE BEFORE WORLD WAR II

Baron, Salo. *A Social and Religious History of the Jews*. 18 vols. New York: Columbia University Press, 1952.

This study of Jewish history and civilization surveys developments from ancient times to the early modern period, ending around 1650. The volumes are particularly informative about Jewish-Gentile relations in the European Middle Ages.

Eliach, Yaffa. *There Once Was a World: A Nine-Hundred-Year Chronicle of the Shtetl of Eishyshok*. Boston: Little Brown, 1998.

This is the history of the author's hometown in Lithuania before most of its 5,000 Jewish inhabitants were murdered during the Holocaust. Eishyshok was a typical *shtetl*, one of the oldest Jewish settlements in Eastern Europe. The author brings the community back to life with the aid of Lithuanian archival records, oral histories, diaries, letters, and birth and marriage certificates.

Heller, Celia. *On the Edge of Destruction: Jews of Poland between the Two World Wars*. New York: Schocken, 1980.

An analysis of the political, economic, and social condition of Poland's Jewish population before World War II. The author portrays the more than 3,000,000 Jews in Poland as a complex community ill prepared for the Nazi onslaught in 1939.

Levin, Nora. *The Jews in the Soviet Union since 1917*. 2 vols. New York: New York University Press, 1988.

This is a definitive history of the Jews in the Soviet Union. Volume I covers the period from the overthrow of the Tsarist regime by the Bolsheviks to the immediate Cold War years. It includes chapters that deal with antisemitism in the USSR, World War II, and the Holocaust.

Mendelsohn, Ezra. *The Jews of East Central Europe between the Two World Wars*. Bloomington: Indiana University Press, 1983.

This comparative history of Jews in seven Eastern European countries between the world wars focuses on Jewish-Gentile relations, and Jewish efforts to solve the "Jewish question." Neither the increasing acculturation of Jews in these countries nor their economic role had much impact on the degree of antisemitism.

Vital, David. *A People Apart: The Jews in Europe, 1789–1939*. Oxford: Oxford University Press, 1999.

This is primarily a political history of the Jewish minority in Europe from the French Revolution to the outbreak of World War II, within the context of the dramatic transformation of European society and politics in the modern age.

Weinberg, David. *A Community on Trial: The Jews of Paris during the 1930s*. Chicago: University of Chicago Press, 1977.

This study examines the complex relationship between native French Jews and the large immigrant Jewish community. Their divisions generated a complex response to the growing threat of Nazi Germany and a failure to create a unified or commonly accepted understanding of the crisis they faced.

MEMOIRS, DIARIES, DOCUMENTS

Gay, Peter. *My German Question: Growing Up in Nazi Berlin*. New Haven: Yale University Press, 1998.

The author tells of his youth as an assimilated, secular Jew in Nazi Germany during the 1930s. He describes his family and the life they led under Nazism, why they did not emigrate sooner, and his own ambivalent feelings toward Germany and Germans to this day.

Klemperer, Victor. *I Will Bear Witness: A Diary of the Nazi Years, 1934–1941*. New York: Random House, 1998.

This is the diary of a German Jew, married to a non-Jew, who lived in Dresden and survived the Nazi years. A professor of French literature, he recorded the daily events of life in the Third Reich as they touched him and those around him, and his reactions to and observations on those events. They highlight his isolation and both the meanness and the kindness shown to him by neighbors.

Mendes-Flohr, Paul, and Jehuda Reinharz, eds. *The Jew in the Modern World: A Documentary History*. New York: Oxford University Press, 1980.

This is a rich collection of excerpts from a wide variety of primary sources on all aspects of modern Jewish history. They include Jewish emancipation and shifting patterns in Judaism among European Jews, modern political and racial antisemitism, Jewish experiences in Russia and America, Zionism, and the Holocaust.

Richarz, Monika. *Jewish Life in Germany: Memoirs from Three Centuries*. Bloomington: Indiana University Press, 1991.

This is a social history of German Jewry from 1780 to 1945 using fifty-one autobiographical sketches of ordinary German Jews. The authors describe their childhoods, families, schools, professional and daily lives, as well as their communities, religious practices, culture and politics.

Perpetrators

NATIONAL SOCIALISM AND THE THIRD REICH

Bracher, Karl-Dietrich. *The German Dictatorship: The Origins, Structure and Effects of National Socialism*. New York: Praeger, 1970.

This is a study of authoritarianism in Germany from the years before World War I to the Federal Republic of Germany. The author contends that the German tendency for authoritarian rule, culminating in the Third Reich's unprecedented seductive and destructive power, reflected organizational and structural problems in all modern states in the transition to democracy. These problems were particularly acute in Germany.

Broszat, Martin. *The Hitler State: The Foundations and Development of the Internal Structure of the Third Reich*. New York: Longman, 1981.

This book examines the relationship between the totalitarian nature of National Socialism and the traditional structures of political authority in Germany. These tensions characterized the Nazi state. The author rejects the notion that the Third Reich was a well-oiled, totalitarian super state.

Burleigh, Michael, and Wolfgang Wippermann. *The Racial State: Germany, 1933–1945.* New York: Cambridge University Press, 1991.

Aimed at a popular rather than a scholarly audience, this volume reviews the main historiographical controversies surrounding Nazi Germany and its place in German history. It examines the growth of racism and racial ideology in Germany after the eighteenth century and the institutionalization of these ideas in the Nazi Party and the Third Reich.

Dülffer, Jost. *Nazi Germany, 1933–1945: Faith and Annihilation.* New York: Oxford University Press, 1995.

This survey history of the Third Reich, based largely on recent scholarship, focuses on World War II, German occupation policies, and the persecution and extermination of the Jews and other victims. It considers the question of continuity beyond 1945 in an attempt to place Nazi crimes into a larger historical context.

Fischer, Klaus. *Nazi Germany: A New History.* New York: Continuum, 1995.

A history of Nazism from its nineteenth-century roots through World War II, this volume ponders the question of collective German guilt in the postwar period. The author reaffirms that guilt but argues that it must be allowed to subside while keeping the memory of the war and the Holocaust alive.

Frei, Norbert. *National Socialist Rule in Germany: The Führer State, 1933–1945.* Oxford: Blackwell, 1993.

This interpretation of the Third Reich argues that the path to catastrophe in Germany was not inevitable. The author concludes that there were turning points and alternatives, and that its history was no more predetermined that any other. A collection of documents is included.

Nolte, Ernst. *Three Faces of Fascism.* New York: New American Library, 1969.

This comparative study deals with the origins and development of Fascism in France, Germany, and Italy. The author focuses on the intellectual roots of these related but distinct movements and examines the social and political conditions as well as the personalities that gave each its own character.

Orlow, Dietrich. *The History of the Nazi Party.* 2 vols. Pittsburgh: University of Pittsburgh Press, 1969–1973.

This is the most comprehensive history of the Nazi Party available in English. Volume I considers the organization, administrative history, and rise to power of the NSDAP, while Volume II looks at the implementation of Nazi policies in Germany and the occupied territories during World War II.

Pauley, Bruce. *Hitler and the Forgotten Nazis: A History of Austrian National Socialism.* Chapel Hill: University of North Carolina Press, 1981.

This is the first history of National Socialism in Austria before its union with Germany in 1938. It examines the social composition, structure, and organizations of the Austrian Nazi Party. Austrian Nazis were not easily manipulated by Hitler, nor were they able to produce a local leader able to command the loyalty and support of the movement.

Spielvogel, Jackson. *Hitler and Nazi Germany: A History.* Englewood Cliffs, N.J.: Prentice Hall, 1996.

This is a brief survey of the history of the Third Reich, based on current research and designed for undergraduate students and general readers. It outlines the political, economic, and social forces that made the establishment of Nazism in Germany possible, and surveys Nazi Germany's cultural, social, and institutional life.

HITLER: BIOGRAPHIES, MONOGRAPHS, PRIMARY SOURCES

Binion, Rudolph. *Hitler among the Germans.* De Kalb: Northern Illinois University Press, 1984.

This psychohistory of Hitler traces his antisemitism to his traumatization by poison gas as a soldier in World War I. The author links that trauma to Hitler's repressed memories of his mother, who was treated by a Jewish doctor for cancer. These memories form a psychological basis for Hitler's actions against the Jews and others during World War II.

Bullock, Alan. *Hitler: A Study in Tyranny.* New York: Harper & Row, 1962.

The first major biography of Adolf Hitler and the standard for almost forty years, this study is noted as much for its penetrating insight into Hitler's psychology as it is for its brilliant literary style.

Domarus, Max, ed. *Hitler: Speeches and Proclamations, 1932–1945.* 4 vols. Wauconda, Ill.: Bolchazy-Carducci, 1990–1998.

This is an English translation of the definitive collection of Hitler's speeches, collected by the editor since 1932. The collection is arranged chronologically by calendar year, and each year includes a summary of events. The documents are annotated and accompanied by commentaries.

Fest, Joachim. *Hitler*. New York: Harcourt Brace Jovanovich, 1974.

One of the standard biographies of Adolf Hitler for many years, Fest's book examines Hitler's life and career from his youth to his suicide in 1945. The author devotes relatively little attention to Hitler's racial views, antisemitism, and the persecution of the Jews.

Hamann, Brigitte. *Hitler's Vienna: A Dictator's Apprenticeship*. New York: Oxford University Press, 1998.

In this biographical study, the author examines the events of Adolf Hitler's Vienna years (1906–1913) and their contribution to the development of his antisemitism. She dismisses earlier claims that Hitler harbored a hatred for Jews because a Jewish master had blocked his entry into the city's art academy, and suggests that he arrived in Vienna with an antisemitic worldview already well developed.

Hitler, Adolf. *Mein Kampf*. New York: Reynal & Hitchcock, 1941.

Although Hitler intended this as an autobiography and political testament, he also meant to assert his supreme leadership over the Nazi Party. While he does present his views on political, economic, social, racial, and international issues, they were secondary to the purpose of asserting his absolute authority over the party.

——. *Hitler's Secret Book*. New York: Bramhall House, 1986.

This is Hitler's second book, written in 1928 and published as *Hitlers zweites Buch*. It reflects his concern about his party's modest popular appeal in the midst of economic prosperity and political stability. His focus here is on foreign policy, war and peace, and the German military.

Jäckel, Eberhard. *Hitler's World View: A Blueprint for Power*. Cambridge, Mass.: Harvard University Press, 1981.

Originally published as *Hitler's Weltanschauung: A Blueprint for Power* in 1976, this study examines Hitler's view of the world that was the driving force of his career. The author sees a coherent and rational outlook, centered on his belief in the struggle of races for living space that inevitably culminated in a war of annihilation.

——. *Hitler in History*. Hanover, N.H.: University Press of New England, 1984.

This book argues that Hitler had formulated his major objectives well before coming to power, and that he was the sole instigator of the Final Solution. The author maintains that he gave no single order for genocide, but rather a series of orders in an evolutionary process.

Kershaw, Ian. *The "Hitler Myth": Image and Reality in the Third Reich*. London: Oxford University Press, 1987.

This book traces the creation, growth and decline of the "Hitler Myth." The author describes how a manufactured *Führer*-cult became an important integrating force in the Third Reich, and how the Nazis used it to exploit and build on the beliefs, fears and prejudices of the times in order to attain their aims in Germany and Europe.

——. *Hitler 1889–1936: Hubris*. New York: Norton, 1999.

This, the first of a planned two-volume biography, covers Hitler's life and surrounding events from his early years to the early period of the Third Reich. The author demonstrates the centrality of Hitler's role and the extent to which he and the Nazis transformed all areas of German society between 1933 and 1936.

Langer, Walter. *The Mind of Adolf Hitler: The Secret Wartime Report*. New York: New American Library, 1985.

This is the author's psychological study of Adolf Hitler, prepared in 1943 for the OSS. He examined documents and other writings available at the time, and interviewed people who had known Hitler before the war. He looked into Hitler's family background, his sexual life, fears of death, Messiah complex, vegetarianism, and other personal characteristics, and predicted his suicide.

Maser, Werner. *Hitler: Legend, Myth and Reality*. New York: Harper, 1973.

This was the first biography of Hitler to make use of a variety of new sources. These include accounts by childhood, school, and army friends, relatives, and comrades from the early days of the Nazi movement, as well as a large number of letters and notes in Hitler's own hand, and medical statements and reports of Hitler's doctors.

——, ed. *Hitler's Letters and Notes*. New York: Harper & Row, 1974.

This is a selection of Hitler's letters and notes used in the editor's biography of Hitler. These documents demonstrate that Hitler's political philosophy was not fully formed before World War I, as many had claimed at the time. His views were still similar to other right-wing radicals in Germany as late as 1921.

Stierlin, Helm. *Adolf Hitler: A Family Perspective*. New York: Psychohistory Press, 1976.

This is a German psychologist's examination of Hitler's childhood and youth. He concludes that formative family experiences brought forth a self-destructive personality. Germans as a whole experienced similar formative influences that rendered them vulnerable to Hitler and Nazism.

Trevor-Roper, Hugh, ed. *Hitler's Secret Conversations, 1941–1944*. New York: Octagon, 1981.

This is the complete record of Hitler's table talk, or secret conversations, taken from the collection originally preserved by Hitler's secretary, Martin Bormann. Hitler talks freely about Nazi ideology, the Jews, and his domestic and foreign policies.

Waite, Robert. *The Psychopathic God: Adolf Hitler*. New York: Da Capo, 1993.

This psychohistory contends that Hitler's life raises questions that neither psychology nor history can answer alone. It focuses on Hitler's pathological personality within the context of the events that unfolded around him. Hitler was at the same time a consummately skillful political leader of high intelligence.

SS, POLICE, AND *WEHRMACHT*

Arendt, Hannah. *Eichmann in Jerusalem: A Report on the Banality of Evil*. New York: Penguin, 1994.

This is the author's controversial account of the trial of Adolf Eichmann in Jerusalem in 1960. Contrary to the prosecution picture of Eichmann as the personification of evil, Arendt maintains that he was an average man, a petty bureaucrat interested only in promoting his career. She demonstrates that normal, ordinary people are capable of perpetrating horrible crimes.

Bartov, Omer. *Hitler's Army: Soldiers, Nazis and War in the Third Reich*. New York: Oxford University Press, 1991.

This book challenges the view that the German army was an apolitical, purely professional fighting force during World War II within the context of the struggle between Nazi Germany and the Soviet Union. He demonstrates how the savagery of the war reshaped the *Wehrmacht*, which had become permeated with Nazi ideology.

——. *The Eastern Front, 1941–1945: German Troops and the Barbarization of Warfare*. New York: St. Martin's, 1986.

This study of ordinary German soldiers and junior officers considers their attitudes, education, and conduct on the Eastern Front during World War II. The author concludes that the barbarism that characterized German soldiers was significantly different from the brutal behavior of armies in other wars.

Black, Peter. *Ernst Kaltenbrunner: Ideological Soldier of the Third Reich*. Princeton, N.J.: Princeton University Press, 1984.

This is the only comprehensive biography of the man who succeeded Reinhard Heydrich as head of the Reich Security Main Office in 1942. An unremarkable man who became a major war criminal, Kaltenbrunner, like other top Nazis, was neither demonic nor banal. He sought refuge from the complexities of modern society in the simplistic racism and pan-German ideology of National Socialism.

Breitman, Richard. *The Architect of Genocide: Himmler and the Final Solution*. New York: Alfred Knopf, 1991.

This biography of the leader of the SS focuses on Himmler's relationship with Hitler. Although Hitler was ultimately responsible for the Holocaust, it was Himmler who was responsible for devising the Final Solution in 1941.

Browder, George. *Foundations of the Nazi Police State: The Formation of Sipo and SD*. Lexington: University of Kentucky Press, 1990.

Examining the emergence of the Nazi police state, the author agues that it was not the product of some rational design or plan, but rather "an awkward assemblage of pragmatic compromises made by bitter rivals on the basis of common, but by no means identical, ideological goals."

——. *Hitler's Enforcers: The Gestapo and the SS Security Service in the Nazi Revolution*. New York: Oxford University Press, 1996.

This book examines the rank-and-file members of the Security Police and the Security Service of the SS. The author poses the question: how did so many of these people become mass murderers despite the fact that many were ordinary police detectives hired during the Weimar period with no particular enthusiasm for the Nazis before 1933?

Browning, Christopher. *Ordinary Men: Reserve Police Battalion 101 and the Final Solution in Poland*. New York: HarperCollins, 1992.

A detailed study of one reserve police battalion from Hamburg and its role in the extermination of Jews in Poland. The author reconstructs the battalion's murderous record, paying particular attention to the social background and the actions of its individual members. It demonstrates the capacity for inhumanity of ordinary people.

Deschner, Günther. *Reinhard Heydrich: A Biography*. New York: Stein & Day, 1981.

This work sees Heydrich's single-minded personal ambition as his most significant characteristic. His central role in the mass murder of the Jews derived not so much from hatred of the Jews as from a determination to show his organizational and administrative skills.

Förster, Jürgen. "The German Army and the Ideological War against the Soviet Union." In Gerhard Hirschfeld, ed., *The Policies of Genocide: Jews and Soviet Prisoners of War in Nazi Germany*, pp. 15–29. London: Allen & Unwin, 1986.

This essay links the German army to the mass murder of Soviet prisoners of war and Jews in the East. Genocide occurred in the Soviet Union because of the ideological link between Jews and Bolshevism made by Hitler, the SS, and the German army.

Gellately, Robert. *The Gestapo and German Society: Enforcing Racial Policy, 1933–1945*. Oxford: Oxford University Press, 1990.

This study looks at the day-to-day operations of the Gestapo in Nazi Germany, revealing its methods of detecting noncompliance and opposition. The police were able to enforce Nazi policy with relative ease, particularly with regard to the Jews and foreign workers in Germany, because ordinary German citizens were willing to provide information to the authorities.

Höhne, Heinz. *The Order of the Death's Head: The Story of Hitler's SS*. New York: Coward, 1970.

This is the first organizational history of the SS. The author rejects the view that the SS was an organization driven by demonic, systematic planning. Rather, he depicts it as a group of idealists, romantics, and criminals driven by ambition and opportunism.

Koehl, Robert. *The Black Korps: The Structure and Power Struggles of the Nazi SS*. Madison: University of Wisconsin Press, 1983.

This structural history of the SS illustrates the phases of its development from Hitler's personal protection squad before 1924 to a dominant police, economic and military empire within the Third Reich. The author reveals an organization motivated more by greed than racial ideology, interested in dispossessing and killing the Jews.

Krausnik, Helmut, and Martin Broszat. *Anatomy of the SS State*. London: Paladin, 1973.

This volume contains two of the four depositions prepared for the trial of twenty-two former Auschwitz staff members in Frankfurt beginning in December 1963. They are expert historical statements on the history of antisemitism and Nazi persecution of the Jews, and the organization and function of the SS and its camp system.

Milgram, Stanley. *Obedience to Authority: An Experimental View*. New York: Harper & Row, 1974.

The author describes his controversial experiments at Yale University to measure people's willingness to obey orders to administer increasingly severe electric shocks to innocent subjects. His conclusions that people are socialized to obey authority and can be led to kill with little difficulty are controversial.

Posner, Gerald, and John Ware. *Mengele: The Complete Story*. New York: McGraw Hill, 1986.

This is a biography of Josef Mengele, with a focus on his postwar fugitive years. It is based on thousands of pages of Mengele's notes, letters, and diaries from 1960 until his death. Although Mengele was never punished for his crimes, he suffered in hiding, consumed with self-pity, loneliness, and bitterness.

Reitlinger, Gerald. *The SS: Alibi of a Nation, 1922–1945.* New York: Viking, 1957.

This first scholarly history of the SS examines the complexity of its organization and the multitude of its component parts. The author demonstrates that the SS was part of every facet of Hitler's state, and the German nation as a whole was responsible for the crimes of the Third Reich.

Segev, Tom. *Soldiers of Evil: The Commandants of the Nazi Concentration Camps.* New York: McGraw Hill, 1987.

This study of the fifty commandants of Nazi camps reveals who they were, why they became Nazis, and how they could do the work they did. The author interviewed some of them, and members of their families, and concludes they were mediocre men without imagination, courage, or initiative, who relayed orders from their superiors to their subordinates.

Sereny, Gita. *Into That Darkness: From Mercy Killing to Mass Murder.* London: Deutsch, 1991.

This study is based on more than seventy hours of interviews with Franz Stangl, the commandant of the Treblinka extermination camp. The author reveals a man who always found ways to rationalize his role in the mass extermination of human beings.

Sofsky, Wolfgang. *The Order of Terror: The Concentration Camps.* Princeton, N.J.: Princeton University Press, 1997.

This work examines Nazi concentration camps from the inside. The author places the camps into the context of the political ideology and institutions of the Nazi state. The camps are described as laboratories of cruelty, built on violence, starvation, "terror labor," and the production-line extermination of human beings.

Streit, Christian. "The German Army and the Policies of Genocide." In Gerhard Hirschfeld, ed., *The Policies of Genocide: Jews and Soviet Prisoners of War in Nazi Germany,* pp. 1–14. London: Allen & Unwin, 1986.

This essay links the German army to the mass murder of Jews and Soviet prisoners of war in the USSR. It reveals a changing attitude in the German military toward cooperating with the Einsatzgruppen of the SS in their extermination operations against Soviet prisoners and Jews.

Sydnor, Charles. *Soldiers of Destruction: The SS Death's Head Division, 1933–1945.* Princeton, N.J.: Princeton University Press, 1977.

This is a history of the notorious Waffen-SS Totenkopf division. The division's military operations took place mostly in the East, with a dual role of fighting along side the German army and involvement in the mass murder system of the SS. It rejects the view that the Waffen-SS soldiers were no different from soldiers in the regular army.

Wegner, Bernd. *The Waffen-SS: Organization, Ideology and Function.* Oxford: Basil Blackwell, 1990.

This book provides insights into the political, military, and societal functions of the Waffen-SS and its leadership. It does so within the framework of SS ideology, its training and education, the social structure of its leadership, and its expansion during World War II.

Ziegler, Herbert. *Nazi Germany's New Aristocracy: The SS Leadership, 1925–1939.* Princeton, N.J.: Princeton University Press, 1989.

This quantitative study of the social backgrounds of the SS elite considers age, region, class, religion, education, and occupational background in an attempt to understand the nature of the SS officer corps. The leadership of the SS was not necessarily a racial elite. Like the rest of the Nazi Party, it tended to be young, ambitious, and from all regions and classes in Germany.

OTHER NAZI LEADERS AND ORGANIZATIONS

Browning, Christopher. *The Final Solution and the German Foreign Office.* New York: Holmes & Meier, 1978.

A study of the role of civil service personnel in the evolution of the policy to exterminate the Jews of Europe. The author examines the efforts to nazify the German Foreign Ministry after Ribbentrop's appointment as foreign minister in 1938. These "banal bureaucrats" were motivated neither by ideological fanaticism nor by blind obedience, but by career ambition.

Cecil, Robert. *The Myth of the Master Race: Alfred Rosenberg and Nazi Ideology.* London: B. T. Batsford, 1972.

The first biography of Alfred Rosenberg, the chief racial theorist of the Nazi Party during the 1920s and 1930s. Rosenberg appears as a man who easily contemplated brutal persecution and mass murder, and yet shrank from directly participating in the implementation of his own ideas. He is seen not as a monster but as a misguided human being.

Fest, Joachim. *The Face of the Third Reich.* New York: Pantheon, 1977.

These brief portraits of the leading Nazis provide insight into their personalities and roles in the Third Reich. The author explores their relationships with each other, with Hitler, the party, and the government bureaucracy around them. They were men of mediocre intellect and high ambition, caught up in petty rivalries and infighting.

Heiber, Helmut. *Goebbels*. New York: Da Capo, 1983.

This biography of Goebbels portrays him primarily as an opportunist. The author also argues that Goebbels was convinced by his own propaganda about Hitler and about the righteousness and invincibility of the Nazi cause in Germany and Europe.

Kater, Michael. *The Nazi Party: A Social Profile of Members and Leaders, 1919–1945*. Cambridge, Mass.: Harvard University Press, 1983.

This study examines the structure of the Nazi Party and provides a social profile of its supporters in general, and its leadership in particular. The Nazi Party was not primarily a phenomenon of the lower middle class. The author points to support from the working class, big business, and the aristocracy.

Lang, Jochen von, and Claus Sibyll. *The Secretary, Martin Bormann: The Man Who Manipulated Hitler*. New York: Random House, 1979.

This is a study of Martin Bormann, Hitler's private secretary and the man Hitler called "the most loyal Party comrade." The author portrays him as a "manager" who worked the levers of power, in conformity with Hitler's wishes, but with a surprising degree of independence that he alone enjoyed in Hitler's Germany.

Miller, Richard. *Nazi Justice: Law of the Holocaust*. Westport, Conn.: Praeger, 1995.

This book considers the legal foundations of Nazi persecution of the Jews. It documents how the law can be used to commit crimes any time, anywhere, by using the example of the persecution and mass murder of the Jews of Europe.

Müller, Ingo. *Hitler's Justice: The Courts of the Third Reich*. Cambridge, Mass.: Harvard University Press, 1991.

This is a survey history of the legal system in Nazi Germany. The author ponders how much resistance a legal system can mount against rampant misrule and criminality by the state. He also looks at the way in which the German system was reconstructed after World War II and the role of American and British lawyers in the process.

Overy, Richard. *Goering: The "Iron Man."* London: Routledge & Kegan Paul, 1984.

Goering was a politician whose decisions were based on expedience and a Nazi ideologue seeking Nazi solutions for Germany's problems. His assortment of jobs and titles was a product of more than simple vanity and lust for power. The author contends that Goering was a true Nazi, not a moderate who sympathized with the conservative elites in Germany.

Rempel, Gerhard. *Hitler's Children: The Hitler Youth and the SS*. Chapel Hill: University of North Carolina Press, 1989.

The activities of the Hitler Youth included roles as police informants, and eventually fighting and dying as soldiers for Adolf Hitler. As informants the boys were used to detect "sexual misconduct" in the Nazi drive against homosexuality. The author concludes that the most important alliance in the Nazi system was between the Hitler Youth and the SS.

Reuth, Ralf Georg. *Goebbels*. New York: Harcourt Brace, 1990.

This biography of Joseph Goebbels chronicles his life from his birth in Rheydt in 1897 to his suicide in the ruins of Berlin in 1945. Goebbels was a true believer in Hitler and Nazism, not a Machiavellian.

Sereny, Gita. *Albert Speer: His Battle with Truth*. New York: Alfred Knopf, 1995.

After eight years of personal interviews with Albert Speer, his family, close friends, and professional colleagues, and research into his personal papers, the author seeks neither to blame nor to exculpate Speer. She reveals a schemer and opportunist who lost his moral compass and made himself part of Hitler's crimes. After the war and twenty years in prison, he struggled to accept the truth of his complicity.

Smelser, Ronald, and Rainer Zitelmann, eds. *The Nazi Elite*. New York: New York University Press, 1993.

These twenty-two short biographical sketches of the most important Nazi leaders provide answers to the following questions: Who were the leaders of the Third Reich? What led them to embrace Nazism? What roles did they play in the Third Reich? What were the motives, personalities, and philosophical orientations that determined their actions?

Stachura, Peter. *Nazi Youth in the Weimar Republic*. Santa Barbara, Calif.: Clio, 1975.

This book examines the early Hitler Youth movement within the context of the general youth culture of those years. The author reveals the internal dynamics of the movement and the Nazi Party itself, including the quasi-socialist goals of the Nazis and their youth movement in the early years.

Weitz, John. *Hitler's Diplomat: The Life and Times of Joachim von Ribbentrop*. New York: Ticknor & Fields, 1992.

This is the first complete biography in English of Joachim von Ribbentrop, Hitler's Foreign Minister from 1938 to 1945. Within the context of the men and women of culture and means who surrounded Hitler and supported his quest for European domination, Ribbentrop is depicted as a social climber who married into money and cast his lot with Hitler to the bitter end.

THE PROFESSIONS, NAZISM, AND THE HOLOCAUST

Beyerchen, Alan. *Scientists under Hitler: Politics and the Physics Community in the Third Reich.* New Haven: Yale University Press, 1977.

This book contends that the majority of scientists in the Third Reich were neither pro-Nazi nor anti-Nazi. They were committed to the independence of their profession, even after about 25 percent of all German academic physicists lost their positions in Hitler's Reich.

Borkin, Joseph. *The Crime and Punishment of I. G. Farben: The Unholy Alliance of Adolf Hitler and Germany's Great Chemical Combine.* New York: Free Press, 1978.

This volume considers the role of the German chemical giant I. G. Farben in Nazi Germany's war effort. Despite its role in the building of the slave labor and extermination complex at Auschwitz, the officers at I. G. Farben were not necessarily antisemitic. But they knew that their efforts caused the deaths of thousands of innocent people.

Deichmann, Ute. *Biologists under Hitler.* Cambridge, Mass.: Harvard University Press, 1996.

The author, a biologist, examines the impact of National Socialism on the lives and work of a generation of German biologists forced to emigrate from Germany, and those who stayed and worked under the Nazis. She considers the removal of Jewish biologists, German biologists and eugenic research, their proximity to Nazi crimes, and scientific research by the SS.

Ferencz, Benjamin. *Less Than Slaves: Jewish Forced Labor and the Quest For Compensation.* Cambridge, Mass.: Harvard University Press, 1979.

This is a book about slave laborers, mostly Jews, in the Third Reich. The author establishes the responsibility of German industrialists who paid the SS for the laborers in a system that cared for the machinery in factories but not those who worked them.

Gallagher, Hugh. *By Trust Betrayed: Patients, Physicians, and the License to Kill in the Third Reich.* New York: Henry Holt, 1990.

The author examines the popular hostility in Germany toward the disabled and argues that German physicians "acted out" these feelings by murdering them. He further argues that these exist everywhere, not just in Germany, and that the German experience holds important lessons for the struggle of the disabled today for equal rights.

Gregor, Neil. *Daimler Benz in the Third Reich*. New Haven: Yale University Press, 1998.

An examination of the role of big business in Nazi Germany, this study traces the history of Daimler-Benz during the Third Reich and its ability exploit the German war economy. The firm acquiesced in the use of forced labor, protected its interests during the war, and managed its transition to peacetime despite complicity in the crimes of the Third Reich.

Hayes, Peter. *Industry and Ideology: IG Farben in the Nazi Era*. Cambridge: Cambridge University Press, 1987.

This is an examination of the relationship of the German chemical giant I. G. Farben with Hitler's regime. Thousands of slave laborers, many of them prisoners from Auschwitz, died in Farben's factory and mines near the camp. It was also involved in the production of the gas used to exterminate millions at Auschwitz. The author demonstrates how good men were able to participate in the process of genocide.

Kater, Michael. *Doctors under Hitler*. Chapel Hill: University of North Carolina Press, 1989.

This study examines the German medical profession during the Third Reich. The author considers the institutional framework of the medical profession to demonstrate how physicians participated in euthanasia and mass sterilization of the handicapped, and cruel and often fatal medical experiments on Jews, Gypsies, and others.

——. *The Twisted Muse: Musicians and Their Music in the Third Reich*. New York: Oxford University Press, 1997.

The first history of music and musicians in the Third Reich, this book considers the complex motivations behind the relationship of German musicians to Hitler's regime. They included careerism, professionalism, opportunism, and ideological identification. The author looks at the problematic efforts of German musicologists to distinguish between German and Jewish music and the struggles of Jewish musicians inside Germany and in exile.

Lifton, Robert. *The Nazi Doctors: Medical Killing and the Psychology of Genocide*. New York: Basic Books, 1986.

This study explains how German physicians were transformed from healers to systematic murderers, and the crucial role they played in Nazi genocide. The author focuses on some of the leading medical figures in Nazi Germany, using eyewitness testimony from victims.

Macrakis, Kristie. *Surviving the Swastika: Scientific Research in Nazi Germany*. New York: Oxford University Press, 1993.

This is a history of the Kaiser Wilhelm Gesellschaft (later the Max Planck Gesellschaft) from its beginnings before World War I through the Third Reich. High-quality scientific research survived under Hitler, making important advances despite the complicity of many German scientists in Nazi crimes.

Müller-Hill, Benno. *Murderous Science: Elimination by Scientific Selection of Jews, Gypsies and Others, Germany 1933–1945*. New York: Oxford University Press, 1988.

This volume examines the support of the scientific and medical establishment in Germany for Nazi racial policies toward the Jews, Gypsies, and the disabled. Scientists and physicians justified their participation in Nazi racial programs as scientifically necessary, and they benefited from their complicity with more professional positions, and more funds for their work.

Proctor, Robert. *The Nazi War on Cancer*. Princeton, N.J.: Princeton University Press, 1999.

Although German doctors participated in countless atrocities against Jews and other victims, they also made strides in promoting better health, including the discovery of the link between smoking and lung cancer. Nazi Germany's positive health activism ultimately came from the same twisted roots as its medical crimes against humanity.

——. *Racial Hygiene: Medicine under the Nazis*. Cambridge, Mass.: Harvard University Press, 1988.

This book examines the role of German scientists in the formulation of Nazi racial policy. Nazi racial views and policies appealed to significant numbers of German scientists, including biologists, geneticists, physicians, psychiatrists, and anthropologists. Their collaboration was based on conviction rather than mere careerism or opportunism.

Steinweis, Alan. *Art, Ideology and Economics in Nazi Germany: The Reich Chambers of Music, Theater and the Visual Arts*. Chapel Hill: University of North Carolina Press, 1996.

This volume considers the politics and economics of culture in the Third Reich, revealing how the regime governed the arts, and its consequences. Goebbels easily convinced most German artists that their status and living standards would rise if they supported regime.

Weinreich, Max. *Hitler's Professors: The Part of Scholarship in Germany's Crimes against the Jewish People*. New Haven: Yale University Press, 1999.

Originally published in 1946, this book argues that responsibility for the mass murder of the Jews rests with Germany's ruling class during the Third Reich. The author contends that German scholarship provided the ideas, techniques, and justification for Nazi Germany's crimes against humanity.

COLLABORATORS

Fenyo, Mario. *Hitler, Horthy and Hungary: German-Hungarian Relations, 1941–1944*. New Haven: Yale University Press, 1972.

This book considers Hungary's relations with Germany during World War II. Germany's ally in the war against the Soviet Union, Hungary was the object of economic and racial pressures by the Nazis, including the anti-Jewish campaigns and Jewish deportations to Auschwitz in 1944. Hungary was both antisemitic and sympathetic to the German cause.

Hirschfeld, Gerhard. *Nazi Rule and Dutch Collaboration: The Netherlands under German Occupation, 1940–1945*. Oxford: Berg, 1988.

Dutch collaboration with the Germans was based on a false sense of hope in its benefits. As the requirements of the war placed greater burdens on the people of Holland, cooperation with the Germans created disillusionment, self-deception, and gradual conformity to German demands for labor, production of war materials, and the treatment of the Jews.

Ioanid, Radu. *The Holocaust in Romania*. Chicago: Dee, 2000.

This study of the opportunistic policies of the Antonescu regime toward Jews and Gypsies documents the atrocities of the Iron Guard and the massacres in Transnistria.

Jelinek, Yeshayahu. *The Parish Republic: Hlinka's Slovak People's Party, 1939–1945*. New York: Columbia University Press, 1976.

The author argues that while Hlinka's party cannot be blamed for seeking Slovak autonomy or independence from the Czechs prior to 1938, it was guilty of supporting German policies and following Nazi examples. The extremists in the party undertook initiatives in the extermination of Slovak Jews, harassment of other minorities, and support for Hitler's war effort.

Steinberg, Jonathan. *All or Nothing: The Axis and the Holocaust, 1941–1943*. London: Routledge, 1990.

This book examines the differences in behavior between Fascist Italy and Nazi Germany toward the Jews. The Italians operated with the primary virtues of humanity and compassion and the secondary vices of corruption, incompetence, disobedience, and sloth. The Germans, on the other hand, practiced those vices primarily, and displayed the secondary virtues of punctuality, obedience, efficiency, and impersonality.

Webster, Paul. *Pétain's Crime: The Complete Story of French Collaboration in the Holocaust.* Chicago: Ivan R. Dee, 1991.

This work describes the systematic persecution of the Jews by Vichy France. The author details the central role of French police in the roundup and deportation of Jews to the East, and Pétain's contribution to the extermination of the Jews of Europe.

DIARIES, MEMOIRS, AUTOBIOGRAPHIES

Goebbels, Joseph. *The Goebbels Diaries, 1939–1941.* New York: Putnam, 1983.

These diaries provide insights into the leaders and institutions of the Third Reich, but most importantly into Goebbels's personality and the role he himself played. One sees the ruthless bureaucrat, the warmonger, the devoted family man, and sensitive admirer of many of the works of art he banned.

——. *The Goebbels Diaries, 1942–1943.* New York: Award Books, 1971.

These were the first Goebbels diaries published after World War II. The entries reveal a man who heaped abuse on everyone who disagreed with him. They also reveal his virulent antisemitism and his support for the extermination of the Jews.

——. *Final Entries 1945: The Diaries of Joseph Goebbels.* New York: Putnam, 1978.

These diaries contain Goebbels's personal account of the last weeks of the Third Reich. He alternates between despair and hope, attacking others for treachery and cowardice, and blaming them for Germany's imminent defeat. He is particularly scornful of Hermann Göring whom he blames for leaving Germany defenseless.

Höss, Rudolf. *Death Dealer: The Memoirs of the SS Kommandant at Auschwitz.* Buffalo: Prometheus Books, 1992.

This volume contains Rudolf Höss's autobiography, his own profiles of SS members, and final letters to his family before he was executed. Höss, commandant of the Auschwitz-Birkenau extermination camp from the summer of 1941 until the end of 1943, wrote these documents while in Polish prison from October 1946 until he was hanged on April 16, 1947. He describes how Jews, Gypsies, Poles, and Russians were murdered under his command.

Kersten, Felix. *The Kersten Memoirs, 1940–1945.* New York: Howard Fertig, 1995.

This is based on the author's notes of his conversations with some of the leading men in the Third Reich, particularly with the head of the SS, Heinrich Himmler.

He was Himmler's personal physician and confidant during World War II, and learned much about German and SS thinking and policy on the persecution and extermination of the Jews.

Milton, Sybil, ed. *The Stroop Report: The Jewish Quarter of Warsaw Is No More*. New York: Pantheon, 1979.

This volume contains the daily reports of the German commander in Warsaw, Jürgen Stroop, in which he gives details of the uprising and destruction of the Warsaw ghetto. He provides figures on the number of Jews and German troops killed each day, and shows pride in his efforts to crush the uprising and destroy the ghetto.

Speer, Albert. *Inside the Third Reich*. New York: Macmillan, 1970.

This is the memoir of Albert Speer, Hitler's chief architect and minister for armaments, and one of the highest-ranking Nazi leaders tried at Nuremberg after World War II. Although the book offers a relatively objective account of the Third Reich as seen from the inside, Speer was less than candid about his knowledge of the mass murder of the Jews as it was going on.

——. *Spandau: The Secret Diaries*. New York: Macmillan, 1976.

These diaries provide an account of Albert Speer's daily life at the Nuremberg trials and in the Spandau prison in Berlin. They span twenty years, from 1946 until his release in 1966. More than a chronicle of his life in prison, they provide information about and analysis of Hitler, other Nazi leaders, and the Third Reich.

Victims

GHETTOS AND CAMPS

Arad, Yitzhak. *Ghetto in Flames: The Struggle and Destruction of the Jews in Vilna in the Holocaust*. New York: Holocaust Library, 1982.

This is a study of the systematic destruction of the Jewish community of Vilna. Various documentary sources provide a comprehensive account of the expropriation, ghettoization and extermination of the Jews of Vilna.

——. *Bełzec, Sobibór, Treblinka: The Operation Reinhard Death Camps*. Bloomington: Indiana University Press, 1987.

This study of the three "Operation Reinhard" extermination camps in Poland, built for the extermination of the Jews of the General Government of Poland, examines the physical layouts of the camps, transports to the camps, and the process of extermination.

Beinfeld, Solon. "The Cultural Life of the Vilna Ghetto." *Simon Wiesenthal Center Annual* 1 (1984): 5–25.

This is an overview of the cultural life of the Vilna ghetto. Vilna was an important center of Jewish culture before World War II. Its cultural heritage provided a sense of self-worth in the ghetto that made resistance possible.

Berkley, George. *Hitler's Gift: The Story of Theresienstadt*. Boston: Branden, 1993.

This book chronicles life in Theresienstadt during World War II. It focuses on Jewish and German perceptions of Theresienstadt, including the assumption that Theresienstadt was a better destination than others in the East. There are photographs and drawings of the ghetto and its inhabitants.

Czech, Danuta. *Auschwitz Chronicle, 1939–1945*. New York: Henry Holt, 1990.

This detailed history of Auschwitz from 1940 to 1945 is based on German documents, documents of the camp underground, autobiographies of SS men, and the recollections of camp survivors. It contains photographs and plans of the three camps that made up the Auschwitz complex, and biographical sketches of perpetrators who worked at Auschwitz.

Des Pres, Terrence. *The Survivor: An Anatomy of Life in the Death Camps*. New York: Oxford University Press, 1976.

This study examines life in the extermination camps and how the people who suffered in them endured and returned to bear witness. The author sees survival as an experience with a definite structure, and the book makes that structure visible to the reader.

Dwork, Deborah, and Robert Jan Van Pelt. *Auschwitz: 1270 to the Present*. New York: Norton, 1996.

The authors analyze the links between the 700-year history of the town of Auschwitz and the five-year development of concentration, labor, and extermination camps on the town's outskirts. They use photographs, architectural plans, survivor testimonies, memoirs, diaries, and depositions to demonstrate how Auschwitz evolved to become the focus for the Final Solution.

Friedländer, Albert. *Leo Baeck: Teacher of Theresienstadt*. Woodstock, N.Y.: Overlook Press, 1991.

This book considers the impact of Leo Baeck's teachings on those around him, in Berlin and in Theresienstadt. Baeck relies on religious faith to sustain him throughout the Holocaust.

Friedrich, Otto. *The Kingdom of Auschwitz*. New York: HarperCollins, 1994.

This essay describes everyday life in Auschwitz and the human capacity for survival. It addresses the controversies surrounding the camp since the end of World War II, including efforts to preserve the structures that remain, and its significance for Christians.

Gutman, Yisrael, and Michael Berenbaum, eds. *Anatomy of the Auschwitz Death Camp*. Bloomington: Indiana University Press, 1994.

This collection of essays presents a comprehensive portrait of Auschwitz. Essays consider the history of the camp, its physical dimensions, the perpetrators, the victims, resistance, and the outside world's reaction.

Gutman, Yisrael, and Saf Avital, eds. *The Nazi Concentration Camps: Structure and Aims, the Image of the Prisoner, the Jews in the Camps*. Proceedings of the Fourth Yad Vashem International Conference. Jerusalem: Yad Vashem, 1984.

28 scholarly papers address different aspects of the German concentration camps. Besides examining the structure and aims of the camps, and the social and psychological aspects of prisoner life, the volume looks at the camps and the Holocaust in literature.

Hackett, David, ed. *The Buchenwald Report*. Boulder, Colo.: Westview Press, 1995.

This is a report of the U.S. Psychological Warfare Division in April–May 1945 on the operation of the Buchenwald concentration camp, put together by a team of German-speaking American intelligence personnel. It tells of SS corruption, the use of criminals in running the camp, and widespread resistance against the Nazis.

Hoffman, Eva. *Shtetl: The Life and Death of a Small Town and the World of the Polish Jews*. Boston: Houghton Mifflin, 1997.

The author reconstructs the lost world of Polish Jewry. She probes the ambivalent relations between Poles and Jews from the sixteenth to the twentieth centuries, and the decisions of Christian Poles to hide or betray their Jewish neighbors during the Holocaust.

Kogon, Eugen. *The Theory and Practice of Hell: The German Concentration Camps and the System behind Them*. New York: Berkeley, 1998.

The author was a Catholic opponent of the Nazis incarcerated in Buchenwald in 1939. He survived and went on to become a sociologist and publisher, but not before he published this first analysis of the concentration camp system in 1946.

Lederer, Zdenek. *Ghetto Theresienstadt*. New York: Howard Fertig, 1983.

In this history of the Theresienstadt ghetto, the author, a survivor, describes the setting and organization of the ghetto, ghetto life, and the deportation process to Poland.

Marshall, Robert. *In the Sewers of L'vov: A Heroic Story of Survival from the Holocaust*. New York: Scribner, 1991.

Based on notes and interviews with survivors, this is the story of the survival of a group of Jews in the L'vov ghetto who hid in the city's sewer system and avoided massacre by Germans and their Ukrainian auxiliaries.

Pawelczynska, Anna. *Values and Violence in Auschwitz: A Sociological Analysis.* Berkeley: University of California Press, 1980.

The author rejects the theory that those who identified with their tormentors were best able to survive the camps. She argues that maintaining a love for one's neighbors, adjustment to and acceptance of the brutal conditions of camp life, were the best way to survive.

Roland, Charles. *Courage under Siege: Starvation, Disease, and Death in the Warsaw Ghetto.* New York: Oxford University Press, 1992.

This book examines the practice of medicine by Jewish doctors in the Warsaw ghetto from November 1940 to May 1943. Much of the work of the Jewish Council and other Jewish organizations in the ghetto dealt with problems essentially medical in nature, namely starvation and disease.

Trunk, Isaiah. *Judenrat: The Jewish Councils in Eastern Europe under Nazi Occupation.* New York: Macmillan, 1972.

This is the first comprehensive history of the Jewish Councils in the ghettos of Eastern Europe. The author considers whether the members of the Councils, appointed by Nazi authorities to carry out their directives, supply forced labor, and cooperate in the deportations, unwittingly assisted the murderers.

——. *Jewish Responses to Nazi Persecution: Collective and Individual Behavior in Extremis.* New York: Scarborough Books, 1982.

This book deals with the attitudes of sixty-two survivors toward Jewish emancipation, patriotism and loyalty to their respective governments, and Hitler once he took power. It examines Jewish resistance and Gentile responses to the Jewish plight.

JEWISH RESISTANCE

Ainsztein, Reuben. *Jewish Resistance in Nazi-Occupied Eastern Europe.* New York: Barnes & Noble, 1974.

The author argues that Jews everywhere actively resisted Hitler's war against the Jews in a variety of ways. He is critical of the Soviets and the Poles for not helping the Jews.

Bauer, Yehuda. *The Jewish Emergence from Powerlessness.* Toronto: University of Toronto Press, 1979.

Jewish resistance during World War II constitutes a bridge between lost opportunities to save Jews in Europe and events leading to the establishment of Israel in 1948. The role of Holocaust survivors and former resistance fighters is emphasized in this break with the historical condition of Jewish powerlessness.

Cohen, Asher. *The Halutz Resistance in Hungary, 1942–1944.* New York: Columbia University Press, 1986.

> The resistance of Zionist youth in Hungary during World War II began with the influx of Slovakian Jews in 1942 and ended with the organization of illegal immigration to Palestine after the war. Zionist youth in Hungary rescued Jews rather than battle with the Germans.

Eschwege, Helmut. "Resistance of German Jews against the Nazi Regime." *Leo Baeck Institute Yearbook* 15 (1970): 143–180.

> An account of the role of German Jews in resistance to Hitler's regime in Germany from 1933 to 1943, this essay focuses on the Jews in the communist resistance. Jews were active in other resistance activities and groups, and were neither oblivious nor passive to the Nazi threat.

Gutman, Israel. *Resistance: The Warsaw Ghetto Uprising.* Boston: Houghton Mifflin, 1994.

> This is the story of a small group of lightly armed Jewish youths in the Warsaw ghetto who confronted the German army and police in 1943. The author is a historian of the Holocaust and a survivor of the uprising.

——. *The Jews of Warsaw, 1939–1943: Ghetto, Underground, Revolt.* Bloomington: Indiana University Press, 1983.

> Most of this volume is devoted to the Jewish underground and the Warsaw ghetto uprising of 1943. The author, a survivor of the uprising, presents a broad social and cultural history of the Jews of Warsaw during World War II.

Krakowski, Shmuel. *The War of the Doomed: Jewish Armed Resistance in Poland, 1942–1944.* New York: Holmes & Meier, 1984.

> The author, a survivor of the Lodz ghetto and the communist underground in Poland, surveys the history of Jewish resistance in wartime Poland, in the ghettos of the General Government, in partisan units, and in the camps. Jewish resistance groups were isolated due to the general hostility of the Polish population and underground.

Latour, Annie. *The Jewish Resistance in France, 1940–1944.* New York: Holocaust Library, 1981.

> The author, a veteran of Jewish resistance in German-occupied France, tells the story of rescue as a form of resistance to Nazi Germany. She interviewed hundreds of persons, Jews and Christians, who worked in the underground helping Jews.

Lazare, Lucien. *Rescue as Resistance: How Jewish Organizations Fought the Holocaust in France.* New York: Columbia University Press, 1996.

Jewish resistance in France began with aid to immigrating foreign Jews escaping persecution in Germany and Eastern Europe. During the war its work involved smuggling Jews out of France; hiding them; helping them to pass as Aryans; providing food, shelter, and false papers; and eliminating informers.

Levin, Dov. *Fighting Back: Lithuanian Jewry's Armed Resistance to the Nazis, 1941–1945*. New York: Holmes & Meier, 1985.

This history of Jewish resistance in Lithuania during World War II presents a familiar story of Jewish isolation in a hostile land. Jews played a major role in the Lithuanian division of the Red Army, and resisted the Germans in the ghettos, labor camps, and in the forests.

Rashke, Richard. *Escape from Sobibór*. Boston: Houghton Mifflin, 1982.

This is an account of the famous escape attempt of some 600 Jews from the Sobibór extermination camp in October 1943. About half made it out, and only fifty survived the war, eighteen of whom provided testimony for this book.

Rohrlich, Ruby, ed. *Resisting the Holocaust*. Oxford: Berg Publishers, 1998.

This collection of essays examines Jewish resistance in its many forms. It considers the active and passive resistance of individuals and groups, and covers topics such as the Warsaw ghetto, Jewish partisans, Jewish women in the French resistance, and Primo Levi and survival at Auschwitz.

Steinberg, Lucien. *Not as a Lamb: The Jews against Hitler*. London: Gordon and Cremonesi, 1978.

This study differentiates Jewish resistance from other resistance movements throughout Europe. Others resisted the Germans and Nazism in order to regain their independence and freedom; the Jews resisted in order to live.

Suhl, Yuri, ed. *They Fought Back: The Story of Jewish Resistance in Nazi Europe*. New York: Schocken, 1975.

This volume rejects the notion that Jews were passive victims. Thirty-four essays deal with the various forms of Jewish resistance, particularly armed resistance, that occurred in nearly every ghetto and camp in the East.

Tec, Nechama. *Defiance: The Bielski Partisans*. New York: Oxford University Press, 1993.

This is the history of one of the largest and most successful Jewish partisan organizations during World War II. The Bielski partisans, led by the charismatic Tuvia Bielski, practiced the dual roles of anti-German fighters and rescuers of other Jews.

Tushnet, Leonard. *The Pavement of Hell*. New York: St. Martin's Press, 1973.

This volume examines the leaders of the Jewish communities in the Warsaw, Vilna, and Lodz ghettos, and the dilemmas they faced carrying out German orders while trying to protect as many Jews as possible.

Women and Children

Baumel, Judith. *Double Jeopardy: Gender and the Holocaust*. Portland: Valentine Mitchell, 1998.

These essays examine the Holocaust from the perspective of gender. They consider women's experiences during the Holocaust and demonstrate how gender issues transcend the historical framework of the Holocaust to become part of its cultural heritage for later generations.

——. *Unfulfilled Promise: Rescue and Resettlement of Jewish Refugee Children in the USA, 1934–1945*. Juneau: Denali Press. 1990.

This volume examines the immigration of 1,000 unaccompanied Jewish children to the United States between 1934 and 1945. It considers the role of the United States government, volunteer agencies, public opinion, Jewish organizations, and the machinery of rescue and resettlement.

Buchignani, Walter. *Tell No One Who You Are: The Hidden Childhood of Regine Miller*. Montreal: Tundra Books, 1994.

This is the true story of a young Jewish girl in Belgium, the daughter of Jewish immigrants from Poland, who was sent into hiding after the Germans invaded. She lived with four different Belgian families and learned after the war that her parents had perished.

Dwork, Deborah. *Children with a Star: Jewish Youth in Nazi Europe*. New Haven: Yale University Press, 1991.

This is the story of the everyday lives of Jewish children during the Holocaust. The author examines their education, companions, and ways in which they acquired food, clothing, and shelter, within the context of life at home, in hiding, in the ghettos and camps.

Gilbert, Martin. *The Boys: The Untold Story of 732 Young Concentration Camp Survivors*. New York: Henry Holt, 1996.

This volume looks at the child survivors of the Holocaust, boys and girls, who were brought to England under the auspices of the Central British Fund in 1945. It is a group memoir that offers a coherent, personal recollection of the prewar years, the ghettos, the camps, liberation, and postwar rehabilitation.

Greenfeld, Howard. *The Hidden Children*. New York: Ticknor and Fields, 1993.

Based on the author's interviews with twenty-five child survivors who emigrated to the United States, this book illuminates the stories of thousands of children hidden by Gentiles in homes, convents, and elsewhere during World War II.

Lagnado, Lucette, and Sheila Cohn Dekel. *Children of the Flames: Dr. Josef Mengele and the Untold Story of the Twins of Auschwitz.* New York: William Morrow, 1991.

This is a collection of stories of surviving twins who were victims of Josef Mengele's medical experiments. Based on survivor testimony, the volume offers insights into Mengele, his personality, and his methods.

Lukas, Richard. *Did the Children Cry: Hitler's War against Jewish and Polish Children, 1939–1945.* New York: Hippocrene, 1994.

This study examines Nazi policies toward Jewish and Polish children during the Holocaust. Jewish children were usually the first victims selected for immediate death or medical experiments at the extermination camps. Polish children were often starved, killed, or abducted by SS officials and taken to Germany for "Germanization."

Marks, Jane. *The Hidden Children: The Secret Survivors of the Holocaust.* New York: Fawcett, 1993.

This is a collection of accounts of Jewish child survivors hidden by non-Jews during World War II. The author describes how dependence on the goodness of others affected their lives after World War II.

Milton, Sybil. "Non-Jewish Children in the Camps." *Simon Wiesenthal Center Annual* 5 (1988): 49–60.

This essay examines the fate of non-Jewish children in German-occupied Europe. The author considers the Germanization of Polish children, the abandoned children of partisans in Latvia and White Russia, and the children of Gypsies, Jehovah's Witnesses, and Spanish republican refugees.

Ofer, Dalia, and Lenore Weitzman, eds. *Women in the Holocaust.* New Haven: Yale University Press, 1998.

These essays explore the special trials women faced during the Holocaust and their ways of coping with them. Testimonies of Holocaust survivors, and essays by historians, sociologists, and literary scholars offer insights into women's lives in the ghettos, camps, and in Jewish resistance.

Rittner, Carol, and John Roth, eds. *Different Voices: Women and the Holocaust.* New York: Paragon House, 1993.

This volume contains memoirs, letters, poems, plays, eyewitness accounts, and excerpts from longer works that offer a history of Jewish women during the Holocaust.

Ritvo, Roger, and Diane Plotkin. *Sisters in Sorrow: Voices of Care in the Holocaust.* College Station: Texas A&M University Press, 1998.

This book, a collection of memoirs and the authors' historical narrative, examines the work of women prisoners who cared for the sick in the camps. Women prisoners exhibited techniques for adapting different from those developed by men. Women's survival skills were often the result of their backgrounds as homemakers, nurturers, and caregivers.

NON-JEWISH VICTIMS

Bauer, Yehuda. "Gypsies." In Yisrael Gutman and Michael Berenbaum, eds., *Anatomy of the Auschwitz Death Camp*, pp. 441–455. Bloomington: Indiana University Press, 1994.

The author argues that the fate of the Gypsies in German-occupied Europe paralleled that of the Jews, but was not the same. Gypsies were not viewed as racial enemies as were the Jews, and not targeted for total extermination.

Berenbaum, Michael, ed. *Mosaic of Victims: Non-Jews Persecuted and Murdered by the Nazis.* New York: New York University Press, 1990.

These essays on the persecution of Gypsies, Russian prisoners of war, homosexuals, Jehovah's Witnesses, Catholic activists, pacifists, and others are organized in sections that deal with the politics of extermination, forced labor, non-Jewish children, the position of German Catholics, and sterilization and "euthanasia."

Burleigh, Michael. *Death and Deliverance: "Euthanasia" in Germany, 1900–1945.* Cambridge: Cambridge University Press, 1994.

This volume links the mass murder of the handicapped, the Jews, and the Gypsies. It reveals the redeployment of "euthanasia" personnel to the mobile killing units and the extermination camps in the East. Most "euthanasia" personnel were able to escape justice after the war.

Friedlander, Henry. *The Origins of Nazi Genocide: From Euthanasia to the Final Solution.* Chapel Hill: University of North Carolina Press, 1995.

This is the most comprehensive treatment of the program to exterminate the handicapped in Germany. The author traces the rise of racist and eugenic ideas in Germany and elsewhere in the early twentieth century, and their implementation in Hitler's euthanasia program in 1939, which provided the model and key personnel for the Final Solution after 1941.

Friedman, Ina, ed. *The Other Victims: First-Person Stories of Non-Jews Persecuted by the Nazis.* Boston: Houghton Mifflin, 1990.

This book deals with non-Jewish victims of Nazi persecution. Eleven personal narratives of Gypsies, homosexuals, deaf persons, blacks, and Christians underscore the reality that other groups besides the Jews were persecuted.

Grau, Günter. "Final Solution of the Homosexual Problem? The Antihomosexual Policies of the Nazis and the Social Consequences for Homosexual Men." In Michael Berenbaum and Abraham Peck, eds., *The Holocaust and History: The Known, the Unknown, the Disputed, and the Reexamined*, pp. 338–344. Bloomington: Indiana University Press, 1998.

The daily lives of German homosexuals were deeply affected by the repressive policies of the Nazi state. Unlike political enemies and the Jews, homosexuals could not establish a coherent subculture inside or outside the camps. Those who did not die in the camps had to conform to accepted societal behavior.

Gutman, Yisrael, and Shmuel Krakowski, eds. *Unequal Victims: Poles and Jews during World War II*. New York: Holocaust Library, 1986.

This volume examines Polish-Jewish relations during the Holocaust. It refutes Polish arguments that there was little Polish antisemitism or collaboration with the Germans, and Jewish arguments that there were no Poles who helped the Jews.

Hancock, Ian. "Responses to the Parraimos: The Romani Holocaust." In Alan Rosenbaum, ed., *Is the Holocaust Unique? Perspectives on Comparative Genocide*, pp. 39–64. Boulder, Colo.: Westview Press, 1996.

This essay considers the views of prominent Holocaust scholars on the fate of the Gypsies in Nazi Germany and Europe. The author argues that Hitler considered Gypsies and Jews racial threats and attempted to exterminate both accordingly.

Heger, Heinz. *The Men with the Pink Triangle: The True Life and Death Story of Homosexuals in the Nazi Death Camps*. Boston: Alyson Publications, 1994.

This is the story of an Austrian homosexual who describes his nightmarish years and experience in concentration camps. Remaining anonymous, his story is told by the author, who explains that gay Holocaust survivors did not come forward to tell their stories after World War II because of continuing prejudice against homosexuals.

Hirschfeld, Gerhard, ed. *The Policies of Genocide: Jews and Soviet Prisoners of War in Nazi Germany*. London: Allen & Unwin, 1986.

This volume contains five essays that deal with aspects of Nazi genocide, including the mass murder of Soviet prisoners of war. The German army is connected to the mass murder of Soviet prisoners of war and the Jews.

Kamenetsky, Ihor. *Secret Nazi Plans for Eastern Europe: A Study of Lebensraum Policies*. New York: Bookman Associates, 1961.

This study documents German plans to colonize Eastern Europe with Germans at the expense of other nationalities. It is particularly useful in understanding the different treatment accorded the various groups of Slavs in Eastern Europe during World War II.

Kenrick, Donald, and Grattan Puxon. *The Destiny of Europe's Gypsies*. New York: Basic Books, 1972.

Following a brief examination of Gypsy history and the roots of anti-Gypsy prejudice in Europe, this book surveys the impact of Nazi genocide on these "non-Aryan Aryans." It concludes with a consideration of Gypsy recovery from the Holocaust.

King, Christine. "Jehova's Witnesses under Nazism". In Michael Berenbaum, ed., *A Mosaic of Victims: Non-Jews Persecuted and Murdered by the Nazis*. New York: New York University Press, 1990.

This very brief essay outlines the refusal of the Jehovah's Witnesses to conform to the dictates of the Nazi regime in Germany, and the persecution they endured as a result.

Lautmann, Rüdiger. "The Pink Triangle: Homosexuals as 'Enemies of the State'." In Michael Berenbaum and Abraham Peck, eds., *The Holocaust and History: The Known, the Unknown, the Disputed, and the Reexamined*, pp. 345–357. Bloomington: Indiana University Press, 1998.

Contrasting the persecution of homosexuals with that of the Jews, the author concludes that the former involved preventing sexual relations among men, and not attacking them as human beings. Same-sex relations precluded biological reproduction and were antithetical to the goals of the state.

——. "Gay Prisoners in Concentration Camps as Compared with Jehova's Witnesses and Political Prisoners." In Michael Berenbaum, ed., *A Mosaic of Victims: Non-Jews Persecuted and Murdered by the Nazis*. New York: New York University Press, 1990.

Comparing the plight of homosexuals to that of the Jehovah's Witnesses and political prisoners in the concentration camps, the author argues that Nazi racial ideology and public attitudes placed gay men with the Jews at the bottom of the camp hierarchy.

Lewy, Guenter. *The Nazi Persecution of the Gypsies*. New York: Oxford University Press, 2000.

Drawing on hitherto unused sources for this comprehensive account of the fate of the Gypsies under German rule, the author argues that Nazi policy toward the Gypsies was confused and changeable. He concludes that there was no general program to exterminate the Gypsies analogous to the Final Solution for the Jews.

Lukas, Richard. *Forgotten Holocaust: The Poles under German Occupation, 1939–1945*. New York: Hippocrene, 1997.

The author argues that Poles were also victims. Many resisted as partisans and by helping Jews to hide or escape.

Milton, Sybil. "Nazi Policies Toward Roma and Sinti, 1933–1945." *Journal of the Gypsy Lore Society* 2/1 (1992): 1–18.

This essay examines measures against the Gypsies during the Third Reich, including the decision to exterminate them. The author places the mass murder of the Gypsies into the larger context of Nazi racial ideology and policies that targeted Jews, Gypsies, and the handicapped.

——. "Holocaust: The Gypsies." In Samuel Totten et al., eds., *Century of Genocide: Eyewitness Accounts and Critical Views*, pp. 171–207. New York: Garland, 1997.

This detailed essay argues that although the Jewish question loomed much larger in Nazi ideology that the Gypsy question, there is a striking parallel between the ideology and process of extermination for Jews and Gypsies

Plant, Richard. *The Pink Triangle: The Nazi War against Homosexuals*. New York: Henry Holt, 1988.

Beginning with a survey of German attitudes toward homosexuality at the turn of the century, the author focuses on the campaign against homosexuals after 1933. He examines Nazi homophobia and the evolution of a Nazi policy that included degradation, imprisonment, enslavement, and extermination.

Ramati, Alexander. *And the Violins Stopped Playing: The Story of the Gypsy Holocaust*. New York: Franklin Watts, 1986.

This story focuses on the experience of a Gypsy family of musicians who fled the Germans, were captured, and survived in the Gypsy Camp at Auschwitz. Based on eyewitness testimony, the book also provides a glimpse into Gypsy life and culture.

Rector, Frank. *The Nazi Extermination of Homosexuals*. New York: Stein & Day, 1981.

This volume examines the attempt to eliminate homosexuals and transvestites in Nazi Germany. The author relates how homosexuals were cruelly used in medical experiments designed to help the German war effort.

Wytwycky, Bohdan. *"The Other Holocaust."* Washington, D. C.: Novak, 1980.

This brief survey of Eastern Europe under German rule argues that at least nine million Slavs shared the fate of the Jews and Gypsies.

ART AND MUSIC

Blatter, Janet, and Sybil Milton. *Art of the Holocaust*. New York: Routledge & Kegan Paul, 1981.

This collection of some 350 works of art from ghettos and camps includes portraits and self-portraits, realistic and expressionistic depictions of torture, suffering, and death. The authors describe the difficulty the artists had obtaining supplies and concealing their works.

Bak, Samuel. *Landscapes of Jewish Experience: Paintings by Samuel Bak*. Hanover, N.H.: University Press of New England, 1996.

With an essay and commentary by Lawrence Langer, this is a collection of paintings by Holocaust survivor and artist Samuel Bak. The artist and the writer present a visual and written testimony to the Holocaust.

Bor, Josef. *The Terezin Requiem*. New York: Alfred Knopf, 1963.

Verdi's *Requiem* was played in the Theresienstadt (Terezin) ghetto by prisoners for the German officers who ordered conductor Raphael Schachter to put together an orchestra from the many Jewish musicians in the ghetto. Despite disease, death and deportation, the orchestra played until it was deported as a group to Auschwitz.

Constanza, Mary. *The Living Witness: Art in the Concentration Camps and Ghettos*. New York: Free Press, 1982.

Many works of Holocaust art are reproduced in this volume. It includes interviews with seven of the artists who were inmates of ghettos and camps, providing a pictorial and narrative history of human suffering.

Czarnecki, Joseph. *Last Traces: The Lost Art of Auschwitz*. New York: Atheneum, 1989.

This is a collection of black and white photographs of paintings, drawings, and writings carved on walls at Auschwitz. They depict life in the camp and the state of mind of many of the inmates. There is an introduction by Chaim Potok.

Feinstein, Stephen, ed. *Witness and Legacy: Contemporary Art About the Holocaust*. Minneapolis: Lerner, 1995.

This is a small collection of works of art about the Holocaust by contemporary American artists, some of them survivors, who are working to bring the Holocaust into the cultural dialogue.

Flam, Gila. *Singing for Survival: Songs of the Łódź Ghetto, 1940–1945*. Urbana: University of Illinois Press, 1992.

The author attempts to understand the music culture of the Łódź ghetto, and the effects of singing in times of duress. The music and lyrics of many of the songs embody the history of the ghetto, the lives of its inhabitants, and the forces that drew them together.

Green, Gerald. *The Artists of Terezin: Illustrations by the Inmates of Terezin.* New York: Hawthorne, 1978.

The author traces the experiences of individuals who worked at drawing and painting while prisoners in Theresienstadt (Terezin). There are four main characters who smuggled some of their art out of the ghetto as evidence of the persecution and suffering.

Kalisch, Shoshana, and Barbara Meister. *Yes, We Sang: Songs of the Ghettos and Concentration Camps.* New York: Harper & Row, 1985.

A Jewish child survivor from a town in southern Czechoslovakia brings together songs that she and others sang in Auschwitz. Each song, with music and lyrics in original languages and English translation, is accompanied by a brief description of the song and the composer if known.

Karas, Joza. *Music in Terezin, 1941–1945.* New York: Beaufort, 1985.

This is a history of the musicians and the music they composed and performed at the Theresienstadt (Terezin) ghetto during World War II. It provides insight into life, especially the cultural life, at Terezin. The volume contains biographies of the musicians, and a list of the music they composed while imprisoned at Terezin.

Novitch, Miriam, Lucy Dawidowicz, and Tom Freudenheim. *Spiritual Resistance: Art from the Concentration Camps, 1940–1945.* Philadelphia: Jewish Publication Society, 1981.

The works of forty-eight prisoner-artists are presented in color reproductions, although some of the originals were done in black and white. They capture the suffering of Jewish victims.

HOLOCAUST LITERATURE
Appelfeld, Aharon. *Badenheim 1939.* Boston: David Godine, 1980.

Set in an Austrian resort frequented by middle-class Jews in the spring of 1939, this novel depicts the prelude to the catastrophe as Badenheim is transformed from a vacation retreat to a ghetto.

Borowski, Tadeusz. *This Way for the Gas, Ladies and Gentlemen.* New York: Penguin, 1959.

The author, a survivor of Auschwitz, shows how cruelty and atrocities became an ordinary part of life and how the line between normal and abnormal, sane and insane, virtually disappeared.

Brown, Jean, Elaine Stephens, and Janet Rubin, eds. *Images from the Holocaust: A Literature Anthology.* Lincolnwood, Ill.: NTC, 1996.

This anthology of Holocaust literature contains fiction, nonfiction, poetry, and drama that reveal the experiences of the victims and survivors of the Holocaust. The selections tell of the day-to-day terror and the painful memories and adjustments of the survivors and their descendants.

Hochhuth, Rolf. *The Deputy.* New York: Grove, 1964.

This controversial five-act play deals with the role of Pope Pius XII and the Vatican during the Holocaust. The hero is a Catholic priest who fights the Vatican's refusal to help the Jews. It is an indictment of the Pope for not helping the Jews.

Keneally, Thomas. *Schindler's List.* New York: Simon and Schuster, 1982.

This best-selling novel is based on the true story of German industrialist, Oskar Schindler, who saved some 1,100 Jews who worked as slave laborers for him in Poland and Czechoslovakia during World War II. Steven Spielberg's Academy Award-winning film is based on this novel.

Kosinski, Jerzy. *The Painted Bird.* Boston: Houghton Mifflin, 1965.

This is the story of a young boy, a Jew or a Gypsy, who is left with Christians by his parents during the Holocaust. He is cast adrift in the hostile world of German-occupied Eastern Europe, moving from village to village, alone and brutalized by the local populations.

Langer, Lawrence, ed. *Art from the Ashes: A Holocaust Anthology.* New York: Oxford University Press, 1995.

This anthology is the largest collection of literature and art on the Holocaust in a single volume. It presents the works of artists and writers, men and women, Jews and non-Jews, famous and unknown people, those who experienced the Holocaust and those who did not.

Levi, Primo. *Moments of Reprieve.* New York: Summit Books, 1985.

This is a collection of stories written at different times, centered on characters that represent individuals the author encountered during his experience in Auschwitz. The characters are men who retain their humanity, even if their means of survival do not conform to common morality.

——. *If Not Now, When?* New York: Summit Books, 1985.

This is a novel about Jewish partisans in Russia during World War II. The author confronts the dilemma that a Jew must kill Germans to persuade them that he is a man, but in doing so he violates the commandment against killing.

Rosenfeld, Alvin. *A Double Dying: Reflections on Holocaust Literature.* Bloomington: Indiana University Press, 1980.

The author presents a case for a special status for Holocaust literature among other literatures of the world. Other types of literature express our lives in their variety, while Holocaust literature "is needed to express our deaths, the characteristically violent, dehumanized deaths of the twentieth century."

Siegal, Aranka. *Upon the Head of a Goat: A Childhood in Hungary, 1939–1944*. Madison: Turtleback Books, 1997.

A young Jewish girl and her family in Hungary are deported to Auschwitz in 1944, but she survives. It is based on the author's childhood experience.

Steiner, Jean. *Treblinka*. New York: Simon & Schuster, 1967.

This novel deals with Nazi brutality and Jewish resistance at Treblinka. The author focuses on the blurred line between heroism and villainy in camp life, and creates a prisoner uprising where escapees are hunted by the Germans with the help of local Poles.

Styron, William. *Sophie's Choice*. New York: Bantam, 1980.

Sophie is a Polish Catholic woman who was imprisoned at Auschwitz. She survives and immigrates to America, where she is haunted by the deaths of her two children

Thomas, Gordon, and Max Witts. *Voyage of the Damned: Voyage of the St. Louis*. New York: Stein & Day, 1974.

This novel is based on the story of the tragic voyage of the *St. Louis*, with its 937 Jewish refugees from Nazi Germany. The story is presented as a diary relating the passengers' elation over leaving Europe to fear and despair upon their return.

Wallant, Edward. *The Pawnbroker*. New York: Manor, 1962.

This novel uses a fictional survivor to relive the human suffering of the Holocaust. Sol Nazerman is a Jewish pawnbroker in New York City, a survivor who emerges from Nazi captivity numb and hardened. He is unable to feel, to mourn the family he lost in Europe, or to come to terms with his pain and suffering.

Weiss, Peter. *The Investigation*. New York: Atheneum, 1966.

This play is a dramatic re-creation of the trials of twenty-one Nazi war criminals in Germany between 1963 and 1965. The dialogue is taken from the actual testimony of witnesses and accused alike, without identifying witnesses by name. It addresses the nature of the victims' suffering and the perpetrators' accountability for their actions.

Wiesel, Elie. *The Night Trilogy: Night, Dawn, The Accident*. New York: Hill & Wang, 1987.

Wiesel's trilogy includes *Night*, his autobiographical account of survival during the Holocaust, and two first-person novels containing his thoughts on violence, suicide, and the duty to affirm life. *Dawn* is about a young survivor who joins a terrorist group in Palestine, and struggles with his transition from victim to executioner. *The Accident*, about a man confined to a hospital bed after a car accident he could have avoided, deals with being entrapped in the past.

DIARIES, MEMOIRS, SURVIVOR ACCOUNTS

Adelson, Alan, ed. *The Diary of David Sierakowiak: Five Notebooks from the Łódź Ghetto*. New York: Oxford University Press. 1996.

The notebooks of a teenage boy who perished in the Łódź ghetto are contained in this volume. It provides a detailed account, from June 1939 to April 1943, of life in the longest surviving concentration of Jews in German-occupied Europe.

Adelson, Alan, and Robert Lapides, eds. *Łódź Ghetto: Inside a Community under Siege*. New York: Viking Penguin, 1989.

These diaries, notebooks, poems, photographs, and sketches chronicle life in one of the largest Jewish ghettos in German-occupied Poland. Most of the 200,000 Łódź Jews, and the approximately 20,000 Jews from Greater Germany and Luxembourg who passed through the Łódź ghetto, died from starvation, exhaustion, or were murdered in extermination camps.

Adler, Stanislaw. *In The Warsaw Ghetto, 1940–1943: An Account of a Witness*. Jerusalem: Yad Vashem, 1982.

The author was a Jewish police officer in the Warsaw ghetto. He explains how educated Jews with army training were attracted to the ghetto police, and how conflicts arose between the ghetto inhabitants and police.

Amery, Jean. *At the Mind's Limits: Contemplations by a Survivor on Auschwitz and Its Realities*. New York: Schocken, 1986.

Five autobiographical essays illuminate themes such as the intellectual reaction to the realities of Auschwitz, the victim's confrontation with torture, exile, homelessness, and resentment, and the dilemma of "the catastrophe Jew."

Arad, Yitzhak. *The Partisan: From the Valley of Death to Mt. Zion*. New York: Holocaust Library, 1979.

After a last minute escape from his hometown ghetto in Lithuania, Arad joined a communist partisan group that attacked German units and assisted Jews hiding in the forests. His memoir sheds light on the complicated relations between Jews, Soviet partisans, and the Polish Home Army.

Bartoszewski, Wladyslaw. *The Warsaw Ghetto: A Christian's Testimony*. Boston: Beacon, 1987.

The author was a Polish Catholic, a founder of the "Council for Aid to the Jews" (*Zegota*). He describes how Poles risked their lives to help Jews.

Birger, Trudi. *A Daughter's Gift of Love: A Holocaust Memoir.* Philadelphia: Jewish Publication Society, 1992.

Birger and her mother were German Jews confined to the Kovno ghetto, where Trudi kept them alive by working in a German military hospital. She saved her mother's life at Stutthof concentration camp and outlasted her tormentors by never losing confidence in a better future.

Delbo, Charlotte. *Auschwitz and After.* New Haven: Yale University Press, 1995.

This is a memoir of the author's experiences in Auschwitz and Ravensbrück and her readjustment to society after the war. She tells of her transition from feelings of despair to a determination to survive, and a resolve after her liberation to understand, remember and explain what happened in the camps.

Diment, Michael. *The Lone Survivor: A Diary of the Lukacze Ghetto and Suyniukhy.* New York: Holocaust Library, 1992.

Diment, a native of Ukraine, survived by escaping the Lukacze ghetto at the time of its liquidation in 1942. He describes hiding until the Soviet army arrived eighteen months later. He also examines the attitudes among ordinary Ukrainians toward the Jews and the Germans.

Dobroszycki, Lucjan, ed. *The Chronicle of the Łódź Ghetto, 1941–1944.* New Haven: Yale University Press, 1984.

This chronicle contains the contributions of several authors who were trapped in the Łódź ghetto. It covers 1,296 days and contains information on births, deaths, suicides, the weather, rumors, arrests, and other kinds of information that convey a complete picture of life in the ghetto.

Donat, A. *The Death Camp Treblinka: A Documentary.* New York: Holocaust Library, 1979.

This is a collection of documents, statistics, biographical data, profiles of victims and perpetrators, photographs and maps, and a list of survivors of the Treblinka extermination camp. The author is a survivor of the Warsaw ghetto who narrowly escaped deportation to Treblinka.

——. *Holocaust Kingdom: A Memoir.* New York: Holocaust Library, 1978.

The author experienced the Warsaw ghetto uprising and forced labor at Majdanek and in Germany. He reflects on issues such as resistance and non-resistance, the perpetrators, and the examples of Janusz Korczak and Adam Czerniaków.

Eichengreen, Lucille. *From Ashes to Life: My Memories of the Holocaust.* San Francisco: Mercury House, 1994.

A survivor of Auschwitz and Bergen-Belsen, the author describes the realities of liberation and the revival of feelings that had been numbed for a long time.

Eliach, Yaffa. *Hasidic Tales from the Holocaust*. New York: Oxford University Press, 1982.

This is the only major collection of Hasidic tales and anecdotes compiled from experiences in the Holocaust. Interviews and oral histories conducted by the author with Hasidic survivors offer a glimpse into the spiritual struggle for survival during the Holocaust.

Fenelon, Fania. *Playing for Time*. New York: Atheneum, 1977.

Fania Fenelon was a member of the women's orchestra at Auschwitz-Birkenau. She and the members of the orchestra played over an eleven-month period for the camp administration and visiting officials. Fenelon was evacuated to Bergen-Belsen, where she was eventually liberated.

Ferderber-Salz, Bertha. *And the Sun Kept Shining*. New York: Holocaust Library, 1980.

A native of Kraków, the author sought refuge in the city's ghetto. She and her husband were sent to Plasow concentration camp, and later to Auschwitz and Bergen-Belsen. She emphasizes the role of relatives in survival.

Frank, Otto, and Mirjam Pressler. *Anne Frank, The Diary of a Young Girl: The Definitive Edition*. New York: Doubleday, 1995.

This new edition of the famous diary is a more complete version of Anne Frank's original account of her life in hiding, her capture, and her death. The original edition, edited by Anne Frank's father, omitted details about her emerging sexuality and her relationship with her mother.

Freeman, Joseph. *The Road to Hell: Recollections of the Nazi Death March*. St. Paul, Minn.: Paragon House, 1998.

This brief memoir of a survivor describes the agony he witnessed during a six-week march from the German camp at Spraichingen from mid-March to the end of April 1945. He was liberated by American troops.

Friedländer, Saul. *When Memory Comes*. New York: Farrar, Straus & Giroux, 1979.

This is the Holocaust historian's memoir of survival as a young boy during the Holocaust. After fleeing his native Czechoslovakia with his family and settling in France before World War II, his parents hid him in a Catholic seminary during the war. Baptized and studying for the priesthood when the war ended, he discovered his true identity, and immigrated to Israel.

Garbarz, Moshe. *A Survivor*. Detroit: Wayne State University Press, 1992.

As a young man Garbarz moved from Poland to Paris, where he became a boxer and joined the Communist party. He was sent to Auschwitz and assigned to the clothing commando. His memoir tells of the role of camp prisoner functionaries, some of whom were Jews.

Gelman, Charles. *Do Not Go Gentle: A Memoir of Jewish Resistance in Poland, 1941–1945*. Hamden, Conn.: Archon, 1989.

Gelman was one of sixteen Jews who escaped from the ghetto at Kurenets in eastern Poland. After making his way to Soviet territory, he joined a partisan group that engaged in hit-and-run attacks on the Germans.

Geve, Thomas. *Guns and Barbed Wire: A Child Survives the Holocaust*. Chicago: Academy, 1987.

Geve, born in Germany in 1929, was sent to Auschwitz fourteen years later. Friends and a sympathetic block senior helped him survive. Turning down an opportunity to escape because he feared reprisals against his fellow prisoners, Geve was liberated at Buchenwald in 1945.

Grossman, Chaika. *The Underground Army: Fighters of the Białystok Ghetto*. New York: Holocaust Library, 1987.

The author was a member of the underground Zionist youth movement in Poland, first under Soviet and then German occupation. Using false identity papers, she acted as a contact between Jewish ghettos in Poland and Lithuania, acquired arms for the Białystok ghetto revolt, and maintained contact with outside resistance forces.

Heppner, Ernest. *Shanghai Refuge: A Memoir of the World War II Jewish Ghetto*. Lincoln: University of Nebraska Press, 1995.

The author discusses his life in Nazi Germany before emigration to Shanghai, where he and his mother fled in 1939. Life there was characterized by hunger and terrible heat in the summer and the restrictions imposed on the Jewish ghetto by the Japanese.

Hilberg, Raul, S. Sharon, and J. Kermisz, eds. *The Warsaw Diary of Adam Czerniaków: Prelude to Doom*. New York: Stein & Day, 1979.

Czerniaków was the controversial chairman of the Warsaw Jewish Council for almost three years. The Germans forced him to select those Jews who would be deported to the extermination camps. The diary reveals that he tried to save as many Jewish lives as possible.

Hillesum, Etty. *Letters from Westerbork*. New York: Pantheon, 1986.

A young Dutch Jewish woman wrote these letters from the Westerbork transit camp in Holland before her final deportation to Auschwitz where she was killed. They capture the atmosphere of the transit camp, the reunions with friends and family, and the fear surrounding the deportations.

——. *An Interrupted Life*. New York: Pantheon, 1984.

This is the diary of a Dutch Jewish woman deported to Auschwitz, where she was killed. Most entries are about living under German occupation before her deportation. Like Anne Frank, she is young, writes about her dreams for the future, and says she cannot hate anyone.

Holliday, Laurel, ed. *Children in the Holocaust and World War II: Their Secret Diaries*. New York: Pocket Books, 1995.

This is an anthology of diaries written by children, nine boys and thirteen girls aged 10 to 18, from ghettos, concentration camps, a prison, and bombed-out streets. They document events such as police roundups, mass executions, and their struggle to survive.

Jacobs, Benjamin. *The Dentist of Auschwitz: A Memoir*. Lexington: University Press of Kentucky, 1995.

A dental student in Warsaw when the war began, Jacobs spent several years in labor camps before being sent to the Auschwitz subcamp of Fürstengrube in 1943. There he treated prisoners and SS men. Evacuated to Buchenwald in 1945, he survived.

Kalib, Goldie. *The Last Selection: A Child's Journey through the Holocaust*. Amherst: University of Massachusetts Press, 1991.

The author, a child survivor of Auschwitz and a death march, describes her prewar life in Poland, her lost childhood, and the way in which she and her family were hidden by Christian Poles for money. The book examines the complexities of Polish responses to the mass murder of the Jews.

Katsh, Abraham, ed. *Scroll of Agony: The Warsaw Diary of Chaim Kaplan*. New York: Macmillan, 1973.

Chaim Kaplan, the principal of a Hebrew school in Warsaw and inhabitant of the Warsaw ghetto, perished in late 1942 or early 1943. His diary was not discovered until twenty years after the destruction of the ghetto. The entries describe the German occupation of Warsaw and the destruction of the Warsaw Jewish community.

Kermish, Joseph, ed. *To Live with Honor and Die with Honor! Selected Documents from the Warsaw Ghetto Underground Archives "Oneg Shabbat."* Jerusalem: Yad Vashem, 1986.

These documents, taken from the secret archive Oneg Shabbat kept by the Jewish underground in the Warsaw ghetto, include diaries, notes, and short monographs. They deal with topics such as Jews in the Polish army, forced labor, Jewish Council policies, self-help organizations, children, religious life, resistance, schools, smuggling and the ghetto economy, and German persecution.

Korczak, Janusz. *Ghetto Diary*. New York: Holocaust Library, 1978.

Janusz Korczak compiled this diary in the Warsaw ghetto between 1939 and 1942. It chronicles the author's efforts to care for some two hundred Jewish children and adolescents until he, some teachers, and the children were deported to Treblinka on August 5, 1942, where they were killed.

Krall, Hannah. *Shielding the Flame: An Intimate Conversation with Dr. Marek Edelman, the Last Surviving Leader of the Warsaw Ghetto Uprising*. New York: Henry Holt, 1986.

This book is based on interviews in the 1970s with Marek Edelman, a survivor and leader of the Warsaw ghetto uprising and the only one to remain in Poland after the Holocaust. It describes Polish-Jewish relations before and during World War II, life in the ghetto, and the uprising.

Langbein, Hermann. *Against All Hope: Resistance in the Nazi Concentration Camps, 1938–1945*. New York: Continuum, 1996.

Written by an Austrian Jew who survived French internment camps, Dachau, and Auschwitz, the author considers a wide range of resistance activities, including overt rebellion and sabotage, getting news of genocide to the outside world, and helping to liberate the camps.

Levi, Primo. *Survival in Auschwitz*. New York: Touchstone, 1996.

Originally published in 1947, this well-known Holocaust memoir first appeared in English in 1958 as *If This Is a Man*. It is a profoundly important sociological and psychological study of life in an extermination camp. The author survived Auschwitz because his skills were useful to the Germans. Perpetrator and victim alike were reduced to a level where their humanity was questionable.

Lewin, Abraham. *A Cup of Tears: A Diary of the Warsaw Ghetto*. Oxford: Basil Blackwell, 1988.

This is a memoir from the Warsaw ghetto, part of the ghetto underground archive *Oneg Shabbat*. The author, a schoolteacher in his late forties, did not survive the ghetto, but his memoir provides a glimpse into ghetto life.

Micheels, Louis. *Doctor 117641: A Holocaust Memoir*. New Haven: Yale University Press, 1989.

A Jew newly qualified as a physician in 1942, the author unsuccessfully tried to escape from the Netherlands to Switzerland. He was captured and sent to work in the infirmary at Auschwitz III. The need for friendship and to help one's compatriots is the theme of this memoir.

Müller, Filip. *Eyewitness Auschwitz: Three Years in the Gas Chambers*. New York: Stein & Day, 1981.

This is the memoir of a Slovakian Jew, a survivor whose job it was to burn the corpses of Nazi victims. Providing a first hand account of the gassing process, the author relates how he took pride in the efficiency with which he carried out his tasks.

Nieuwsma, Milton, ed. *Kinderlager: An Oral History of Young Holocaust Survivors*. New York: Holiday House, 1998.

Three Jewish women from the same town in Poland tell of their experiences in the children's section at Auschwitz-Birkenau. They survived roundups, transports, selections, and massacres, and saw the child victims of Mengele's medical experiments.

Niewyk, Donald, ed. *Fresh Wounds: Early Narratives of Holocaust Survival*. Chapel Hill: University of North Carolina Press, 1998.

This collection of thirty-six survivor accounts is drawn from interviews recorded immediately after the war by the Russian-American psychologist David Boder. Their importance lies in the proximity to the events they relate. The survivors range in age from their early teens to their seventies. An introduction provides background and context to the narratives.

Perechodnik, Calel. *Am I a Murderer? Testament of a Jewish Ghetto Policeman*. Boulder, Colo.: Westview, 1996.

This is the memoir of a former Jewish policeman in the ghetto of Otwock near Warsaw, written before his death in 1944. He examines his role in the ghetto police and the ethical compromises he had to make.

Perel, Solomon. *Europa, Europa*. New York: John Wiley & Sons, 1997.

This is the story of a German Jew who as an adolescent survived the Third Reich by passing as an "Aryan." Not certain how to judge his own survival, the author suppressed his story for many years.

Perl, Gisella. *I Was a Doctor in Auschwitz*. Salem, N.H.: Ayer, 1992.

This Hungarian Jew saved lives as a physician in the Auschwitz infirmary before being evacuated to a labor camp near Hamburg and then to Bergen-Belsen. She describes abortion, infanticide, and sex in the camps.

Ringelblum, Emmanuel. *Notes from the Warsaw Ghetto: The Journal of Emmanuel Ringelblum*. New York: Schocken, 1978.

The author, a historian and leader of the Warsaw ghetto underground, buried his notes before he was murdered by the Germans in 1944. Discovered after World War II, the notes chronicle daily life in the Warsaw ghetto.

Rosenberg, Maxine, ed. *Hiding to Survive: Stories of Jewish Children Rescued from the Holocaust*. New York: Clarion, 1994.

Fourteen men and women describe being hidden as children by non-Jews in convents, secret attics, closets, farm buildings, and sewer tunnels. Each story is accompanied by information about the relationship today between the survivors and their rescuers.

Rotem, Simha. *Memoirs of a Warsaw Ghetto Fighter: The Past within Me*. New Haven: Yale University Press, 1994.

This memoir describes the preparations for the defense of the Warsaw ghetto, the battle with German troops, the rescue of Jews who survived the uprising, and the subsequent support of surviving Jews in Warsaw.

Rothchild, Sylvia, ed. *Voices from the Holocaust*. New York: New American Library, 1981.

This book contains transcripts from taped interviews of Holocaust survivors taken by the Oral History Library of the American Jewish Committee. The survivors describe the horrors and heroics they witnessed and the impact on their lives after the war.

Schloss, Eva. *Eva's Story: A Survivor's Tale by the Step-Sister of Anne Frank*. New York: St. Martin's, 1988.

Born in Austria, Schloss fled with her family to the Netherlands in 1938. After hiding, she and her mother were arrested and sent to Auschwitz in 1944, and then liberated by the Soviets. Her mother later married Anne Frank's father, making Eva Schloss Anne's posthumous stepsister.

Schwarz, Jenö. *A Promise Redeemed*. Frome, England: Butler and Tanner, 1964.

A young rabbinical student in Hungary in 1944, Schwarz was sent to Auschwitz and Mauthausen where he survived with help from his fellow prisoners and a few helpful Germans. His memoir suggests the importance of religious faith in overcoming despair.

Senesh, Hannah. *Hannah Senesh: Her Life and Diary*. New York: Schocken, 1972.

Hannah Senesh, a Hungarian Jew who emigrated to Palestine before World War II, joined a group of Palestinian Jewish paratroopers dropped into Hungary and Yugoslavia to warn Jews of Nazi extermination plans. She was captured and executed in 1944.

Sliwowska, Wiktoria, ed. *The Last Eyewitnesses: Children of the Holocaust Speak.* Evanston, Ill.: Northwestern University Press, 1998.

Sixty-five Jewish child survivors of the Holocaust in Poland describe the heroism of some gentile rescuers, and the complicity of others in Nazi cruelty and atrocities.

Tec, Nechama. *Dry Tears: The Story of a Lost Childhood.* New York: Oxford University Press, 1982.

The author and her family survival with the help of Polish Christians who hid them for money. Although the Poles shared the antisemitic views of much of the population of Poland, the two families developed a sympathetic and mutually dependent relationship.

Thorne, Leon. *Out of the Ashes: The Story of a Survivor.* New York: Block Publishing, 1976.

The author escaped the Germans on several occasions, often because he could buy his way to safety. He went into hiding with the help of former Polish employees who were promised rewards after the war.

Toll, Nelly. *Behind the Secret Window: A Memoir of a Hidden Childhood during World War II.* New York: Dial, 1993.

The author, a child survivor from L'vov, kept notes from the time the Germans entered her city in 1941 through the Soviet liberation in July 1944. Christians hid her and her mother. Photographs of her watercolor paintings record her life in hiding during the Holocaust.

Topas, George. *The Iron Furnace: A Holocaust Survivor's Story.* Lexington: University Press of Kentucky, 1990.

A Jew from Warsaw, Topas placed his skills as an aircraft mechanic at the disposal of the German air force. He survived forced labor at several camps, including Majdanek, Płasów, and Flossenbürg.

Tory, Avraham. *Surviving the Holocaust: The Kovno Ghetto Diary.* Cambridge, Mass.: Harvard University Press, 1990.

The author, a survivor of the Kovno ghetto, first revealed the diary's existence in 1982. It is a detailed, often day-to-day account of the fate of the approximately 30,000 Jews of Kovno from June 1941 to January 1944.

Troller, Norbert. *Theresienstadt: Hitler's Gift to the Jews*. Chapel Hill: University of North Carolina Press, 1991.

A memoir of life and survival in Theresienstadt, this book is accompanied by drawings of people, activities, and buildings that together provide a visual and written record of life in Theresienstadt.

Wechsberg, Joseph, ed. *The Murderers among Us: The Simon Wiesenthal Memoirs*. New York: McGraw Hill, 1967.

In four chapters, the editor profiles the life and work of Simon Wiesenthal, Holocaust survivor and Nazi hunter after World War II. The remaining chapters contain Wiesenthal's own narrative account of his life and work.

Werber, Jack. *Saving Children: Diary of a Buchenwald Survivor and Rescuer*. New Brunswick, N.J.: Transaction, 1996.

The author, one of the few Jewish members of the Buchenwald camp underground, survived five and a half years in the camp, and helped to save the lives of hundreds of Jewish children who arrived at Buchenwald late in 1944 by hiding them and getting them false working papers.

Werner, Harold. *Fighting Back: A Memoir of Jewish Resistance in World War II*. New York: Columbia University Press, 1992.

This is the author's memoir of Jewish resistance in the Wlodawa region of Poland, about 150 miles southeast of Warsaw. He and a small group of friends escaped to the woods where they joined escaped Soviet prisoners of war in attacks against the Germans.

Zuckerman, Yitzhak. *A Surplus of Memory: Chronicle of the Warsaw Ghetto Uprising*. Berkeley: University of California Press, 1993.

Zuckerman, a survivor and a leader of the Warsaw ghetto uprising, connects the ghetto resistance to prewar Zionist and Socialist Jewish youth movements in Poland. They were gradually forged into the first major armed Jewish resistance movement in Europe, the "Jewish Fighting Organization," which led the Warsaw ghetto uprising in 1943.

Acquiescence, Resistance, and Rescue

THE CHRISTIAN CHURCHES, NAZISM, AND THE HOLOCAUST

Bergen, Doris. *Twisted Cross: The German Christian Movement in the Third Reich*. Chapel Hill: University of North Carolina Press, 1996.

The approximately 600,000 self-described "German Christians" were Protestants who sought to expunge all Jewish elements from Christianity, including the Old

Testament and the Jewish ancestry of Jesus. They occupied key positions within the Protestant church.

Conway, John. *The Nazi Persecution of the Churches, 1933–1945.* New York: Basic Books, 1968.

This study traces Hitler's efforts to undermine the autonomy of the churches in Germany. Church property was confiscated, clergy were accused of crimes they did not commit, Christian trade organizations and youth movements were abolished, and the religious press was restricted.

Cornwell, John. *Hitler's Pope: The Secret History of Pius XII.* New York: Viking Penguin, 1999.

This study of Pius XII, his career and his pontificate, is based in part on new materials from the Vatican archives. The author sees him as pro-German and as consciously unwilling to denounce Nazi crimes publicly.

Delzell, Charles, ed. *The Papacy and Totalitarianism between the Two World Wars.* New York: John Wiley, 1974.

Seven essays consider the Vatican's relationship with Fascist dictatorships and its role in the Jewish question during World War II. The texts of relevant papal documents are included.

Dietrich, Donald. *Catholic Citizens in the Third Reich: Psycho-Social Principles and Moral Reasoning.* New Brunswick, N.J.: Transaction, 1988.

This volume examines the response of German Catholics to political and moral issues in the Weimar and Nazi periods. The author reveals both Catholic accommodation and resistance to the totalitarianism and anti-Jewish policies of Hitler's regime.

Ericksen, Robert. *Theologians under Hitler.* New Haven: Yale University Press, 1985.

This study examines the adherence to National Socialism of three prominent Protestant theologians, social and political conservatives who despised the Versailles Treaty, Weimar democracy, and Jewish influence in German life. All three became ardent Nazis.

Gutteridge, Richard. *The German Evangelical Church and the Jews, 1879–1950.* New York: Barnes & Noble, 1976.

This history of anti-Jewish sentiment in the modern German Lutheran Church focuses on the Nazi period. The lack of a spontaneous, widespread, public, visible expression of righteous indignation by ordinary Christians was the most serious failure of Christianity.

Helmreich, Ernst. *The German Churches under Hitler: Background, Struggle and Epilogue*. Detroit: Wayne State University Press, 1979.

This volume focuses on the movements and conflicts within the Christian churches in Germany, and their impact on church-state relations during the Third Reich. Two final chapters consider the consequences in postwar Germany.

Lewy, Guenter. *The Catholic Church and Nazi Germany*. New York: McGraw Hill, 1964.

The author argues that the failure of Pope Pius XII to speak out against Nazi crimes against the Jews was consistent with the Catholic church's attitudes toward the Jews over many centuries. German bishops, like the Vatican, knew what was happening to the Jews.

Littell, Franklin, and Hubert Locke, eds. *The German Church Struggle and the Holocaust*. Detroit: Wayne State University Press, 1974.

This is an anthology of conference papers on the behavior of the churches in Nazi Germany. The authors, Jews and Christians, represent a broad range of thought and opinion on the subject.

Passelecq, Georges, and Bernard Suchecky. *The Hidden Encyclical of Pius XI*. New York: Harcourt Brace, 1997.

This is the story of Pope Pius XI's secret encyclical condemning racism and anti-semitism. Called *Humani Generis Unitas*, it was locked away in a secret archive after the pope's death in 1939 until discovered in the late 1960s. The Vatican opposed publication for thirty years.

Scholder, Klaus. *The Churches and the Third Reich*. 2 vols. Philadelphia: Fortress, 1987–1988.

This is a comprehensive history of the Protestant and Catholic churches in Nazi Germany. In a clear indictment of the churches during the Third Reich, the author characterizes their behavior as blind, dishonest, arrogant, stupid, and opportunistic.

WORLD REACTION, RESCUE

Abella, Irving, and Harold Troper. *None Is Too Many: Canada and the Jews of Europe, 1933–1948*. Toronto: Lester & Orpen Denys, 1983.

This book criticizes Canada's response to the persecution and mass murder of the Jews of Europe during World War II. The Canadian government wanted to keep Jews out, and only about 5,000 managed to enter Canada between 1933 and 1945.

Avni, Haim. *Spain, the Jews and Franco*. Philadelphia: Jewish Publication Society, 1982.

Spanish policy toward the Jews during the Holocaust is placed within the context of the troubled history of Spanish-Jewish relations since the Inquisition. Although responsible for rescuing some Jews, Spain refrained from taking full advantage of the opportunities to rescue more.

Bauer, Yehuda. *Jews for Sale? Nazi-Jewish Negotiations, 1933–1945.* New Haven: Yale University Press, 1994.

Jewish organizations negotiated with the Nazis for the safety of Jews before and during World War II. The vulnerability of Europe's Jews, the powerlessness of Jews outside of Europe, and the unwillingness of the Allies to help are considered.

——. *American Jewry and the Holocaust: The American Jewish Joint Distribution Committee, 1939–1945.* Detroit: Wayne State University Press, 1981.

This is the story of Jewish self-help and the organization that controlled most outside aid to Europe's Jews during World War II, the American Jewish Joint Distribution Committee. It concentrates on efforts to get aid to the Jews and to support self-help initiatives within Germany and occupied Europe.

Berman, Aaron. *Nazism, the Jews and American Zionism, 1933–1948.* Detroit: Wayne State University Press, 1990.

The obsession of American Zionists during World War II to secure a Jewish state in Palestine weakened efforts to rescue Jews from Nazi-occupied Europe. Demands for a Jewish state politicized the rescue issue, making it impossible to appeal for American help on humanitarian grounds alone.

Bierman, John. *Righteous Gentile: The Story of Raoul Wallenberg, Missing Hero of the Holocaust.* New York: Viking, 1981.

This is a biography of Raoul Wallenberg, the Swedish businessman turned diplomat who helped rescue thousands of Jews in Hungary in 1944. The author devotes a good portion of the book to Wallenberg's fate in Soviet prison camps after 1945.

Bower, Tom. *Nazi Gold: Switzerland, the Nazis, and Their Plunder of the Innocents.* New York: HarperCollins, 1997.

This is an indictment of Swiss bankers and the Swiss government for allegedly exploiting the misfortune of European Jews during World War II by holding the money the Nazis looted from their Jewish victims.

Breitman, Richard, and Alan Kraut. *American Refugee Policy and European Jewry, 1933–1945.* Bloomington: Indiana University Press, 1987.

American rescue and relief policy rested on restrictive immigration laws, State Department policies, popular opposition to immigration, and Roosevelt's reluctance to help foreign Jews.

Cohen, Michael. *Churchill and the Jews*. London: Frank Cass, 1985.

Why was Churchill regarded as a friend of the Jews when his record during the Holocaust was so poor? The author argues that Churchill was not impeded by a pro-Arab Foreign Office, and that he was not an active gentile Zionist.

Engel, David. *In the Shadow of Auschwitz: The Polish Government-in-Exile and the Jews, 1939–1942*. Chapel Hill: University of North Carolina Press, 1987.
——. *Facing a Holocaust: The Polish Government-in-Exile and the Jews, 1943–1945*. Chapel Hill: University of North Carolina Press, 1993.

These two volumes examine the policies of the Polish government in exile toward the Jews during World War II. They identify the factors that conditioned the responses of Polish policymakers in London to the plight of Polish Jews in German-occupied Poland.

Feingold, Henry. *Bearing Witness: How America and Its Jews Responded to the Holocaust*. Syracuse, N.Y.: Syracuse University Press, 1995.

The author examines the ineffectiveness of the U.S. government and Jewish leaders to halt Nazi genocide against the Jews. America's reaction was the natural result of tensions in American society at the time, making it impossible for American Jews and the government to act differently.

——. *The Politics of Rescue: The Roosevelt Administration and the Holocaust, 1938–1945*. New York: Holocaust Library, 1980.

This volume is a critique of the Roosevelt administration's alleged failure to respond to the disaster that befell the Jews of Europe during World War II. Those in government thought only in terms of winning the war, citing the exigencies of war as a rationale for not helping the Jews.

Finger, Seymour. *American Jewry during the Holocaust*. New York: Holmes & Meier, 1984.

This is a report of a private investigatory committee of scholars headed by Arthur J. Goldberg that examines how much American Jews knew about the Holocaust and their actions in response to it. It is critical of American Jewish leaders for lacking unity and aggressiveness.

Gilbert, Martin. *Auschwitz and the Allies*. New York: Holt, Rinehart and Winston, 1981.

This study examines the failure of the Allies to acknowledge what was happening in Auschwitz. Evidence in Allied hands was ignored. The author cites bureaucratic incompetence and deliberate indifference on the part of Allied governments.

Häsler, Alfred. *The Lifeboat Is Full: Switzerland and the Refugees, 1933–1944.* New York: Funk & Wagnalls, 1969.

This is an account of Switzerland's complex and contradictory refugee policies before and during World War II. Some Swiss officials were antisemitic and tried to keep Jews out, while others fought antisemitism and worked to rescue them.

Koblik, Steven. *The Stones Cry Out: Sweden's Response to the Persecution of the Jews, 1933–1945.* New York: Holocaust Library, 1988.

Thousands of Jews from Scandinavia and the Baltic states found refuge in Sweden. More than 20,000 Holocaust survivors were released from German camps and brought to Sweden in March and April 1945.

Laqueur, Walter. *The Terrible Secret: Suppression of the Truth about Hitler's Final Solution.* Boston: Little Brown, 1980.

The Allied powers learned of German atrocities against the Jews in Eastern Europe in 1941 and 1942 in several ways. The Germans made it relatively easy for outside world to find out, and the Polish underground was an important source of information. The West received the news with disbelief and tried to suppress it.

Laqueur, Walter, and Richard Breitman. *Breaking the Silence: The German Who Exposed the Final Solution.* New York: Simon & Schuster, 1986.

This is the story of German industrialist Edward Schulte who in July 1942 revealed to Allied intelligence Hitler's plans to exterminate the Jews. It illustrates Allied reluctance to act on information coming out of Europe regarding the mass murder of the Jews.

Lester, Elenore. *Wallenberg: The Man in the Iron Web.* Englewood Cliffs, N.J.: Prentice Hall, 1982.

With a foreword by Simon Wiesenthal, this book chronicles Wallenberg's work in Budapest in 1944 and his disappearance after being arrested by the Russians in 1945. It provides insights into Wallenberg's character.

Linnea, Sharon. *Raoul Wallenberg: The Man Who Stopped Death.* Philadelphia: Jewish Publication Society, 1993.

This brief biography of Raoul Wallenberg is based on archival materials and interviews with Wallenberg's family, colleagues, and the Jews he saved.

Lipschitz, C. U. *Franco, Spain, the Jews and the Holocaust.* New York: Ktav, 1984.

The Franco government in Spain helped to protect Jews during World War II. This study, based on archival sources and an interview with Franco himself, credits his government with saving about 45,000 Jews.

Lipstadt, Deborah. *Beyond Belief: The American Press and the Coming of the Holocaust, 1933–1945.* New York: Free Press, 1986.

Despite so much information to the contrary, most Americans refused to believe the Jews were being mass murdered during World War II. Public doubt about the authenticity of the reports resulted from the failure of the American press to treat the stories as urgent or even significant.

Marrus, Michael. *The Unwanted: European Refugees in the Twentieth Century.* New York: Oxford University Press, 1985.

This volume examines refugee crises such as the Armenians, the émigrés from the Spanish civil war, and Cold War refugees from Soviet-controlled states. The author devotes most of his attention to refugees from Nazi and Fascist tyranny from 1918 through 1945.

Morly, John. *Vatican Diplomacy and the Jews during the Holocaust, 1939–1943.* New York: Ktav, 1980.

This study of the Vatican's response to the mass murder of the Jews, written by a Catholic priest, presents a largely negative picture of the church's role. Generally indifferent to the plight of the Jews, the church interceded only for baptized Jews.

Morse, Arthur. *While Six Million Died: A Chronicle of American Apathy.* New York: Random House, 1968.

American reaction to the stories of atrocities against the Jews during World War II was a combination of political expediency, diplomatic evasion, isolationism, indifference, and bigotry. Roosevelt and the State Department come in for particular criticism.

Newton, Verne, ed. *FDR and the Holocaust.* New York: St. Martin's, 1996.

This anthology takes a more positive view of the Roosevelt administration's reaction to the plight of the Jews. The essays consider FDR's attitudes toward Jewish refugees, his knowledge of the atrocities against the Jews, and the question of bombing Auschwitz.

Ofer, Dalia. *Escaping the Holocaust: Illegal Immigration to the Land of Israel, 1939–1944.* New York: Oxford University Press, 1990.

This book assesses the response of Palestinian Jews (the *Yishuv*) to the Jewish catastrophe in Europe. Concepts of rescue changed during the war in response to shifting German policies in Europe, and British and Zionist policies in Palestine.

Packard, Jerrold. *Neither Friend nor Foe: The European Neutrals in World War II.* New York: Scribner, 1992.

This is an account of the five neutrals, Ireland, Switzerland, Sweden, Spain, and Portugal, during World War II, and how they remained neutral against considerable odds. The author considers their policies toward Jewish refugees fleeing from Nazi persecution.

Penkower, Monty. *The Jews Were Expendable: Free World Diplomacy and the Holocaust*. Detroit: Wayne State University Press, 1988.

Saving the Jews during World War II was not a priority for the Allies because it would not contribute directly to a military victory over the Axis. The author discusses the silence of the International Red Cross and the failure of the Allies to help the Jews of Hungary in 1944.

Porat, Dina. *The Blue and the Yellow Stars of David: The Zionist Leadership in Palestine and the Holocaust, 1939–1945*. Cambridge, Mass.: Harvard University Press, 1990.

This book examines the impact of the Holocaust on Zionism and Zionist policy. There was no conflict of interests between Palestinian Jewry and the rescue of European Jews, between Zionism and the Diaspora. The *Yishuv* did what it could to save Jews in Europe.

Rubinstein, William. *The Myth of Rescue: Why the Democracies Could Not Have Saved More Jews from the Nazis*. London: Routledge, 1997.

The author argues that the Allies could not have saved the Jews who perished in the Holocaust. Nothing the Allies could have done, given what they knew and what had actually been proposed at the time, could have saved the lives lost in the Holocaust.

Rautkallio, Hannu. *Finland and the Holocaust: The Rescue of Finland's Jews*. New York: Holocaust Library, 1987.

Finland was Germany's ally from 1941 to 1944, and Finnish Jews fought in the Finnish army. The SS left Finnish Jews alone, never requested that they be deported, and Finland never would have complied had the Germans asked.

Shaw, Stanford. *Turkey and the Holocaust: Turkey's Role in Rescuing Turkish and European Jewry from Nazi Persecution, 1933–1945*. New York: New York University Press, 1993.

This study reveals Turkish efforts to save Turkish and other Jews from deportation and death. The author regrets the unwillingness of Ashkenazi Jews and non-Jewish groups to recognize Turkey's role in saving Jews.

Teveth, Shabtai. *Ben Gurion and the Holocaust*. New York: Harcourt Brace, 1996.

This volume argues that David Ben Gurion and the Palestinian Jewish leadership did everything possible to rescue Jews, in large part because of the realization that the Jews of Europe were needed to build the Jewish state.

Vago, Bela. "Some Aspect of the Yishuv Leadership's Activities during the Holocaust." In Randolph Braham, ed., *Jewish Leadership during the Nazi Era: Patterns of Behavior in the Free World*, pp. 45–65. New York: Institute for Holocaust Studies for the City University of New York, 1985.

A harsh critique of the leaders of the *Yishuv* (the Jews in Palestine), this essay faults them for self-absorption and inadequate responses to the plight of the Jews in German-controlled Europe.

Wahrhaftig, Zorach. *Refugee and Survivor: Rescue Efforts during the Holocaust.* Jerusalem: Yad Vashem, 1988.

The author describes the rescue of Polish Jews in Lithuania during World War II. He was involved in the rescue operation that brought Jews briefly to Japan and Shanghai with the support of Japanese and Soviet officials.

Wasserstein, Bernard. *Britain and the Jews of Europe, 1939–1945.* Oxford: Oxford University Press, 1988.

This study considers Britain's restrictive immigration policy in Palestine, its failure to aid Jewish resistance in Europe, and its rejection of suggestions for Allied bombing of Auschwitz. Britain's policy was characterized by bureaucratic complacency, inhumanity, and indifference.

Weissberg, Alex. *Desperate Mission: Joel Brand's Story.* New York: Criterion, 1958.

This is the author's account of Joel Brand, Zionist and member of the Jewish underground in German-occupied Budapest, and his role in the controversial SS offer to trade 1,000,000 Jews for money, trucks, and other commodities in the summer of 1944. The offer was rejected.

Wood, E. Thomas, and Stanislaw Jankowski. *Karski: How One Man Tried to Stop the Holocaust.* New York: John Wiley, 1994.

Jan Karski, a Polish Catholic, was a courier for the Polish underground who escaped from Poland in 1942. He brought to Allied leaders in London his eyewitness account of the extermination of the Jews.

Wyman, David. *The Abandonment of the Jews: America and the Holocaust, 1941–1945.* New York: Pantheon, 1984.

The response of American society, including the Christian churches and the Jewish community, to the Jewish catastrophe in Europe was inadequate. The author documents the struggle of some Jews and non-Jews in the United States to overcome an obstructive State Department, an indifferent president and public, and inadequate press coverage.

——. *Paper Walls: America and the Refugee Crisis, 1938–1941*. New York: Pantheon, 1985.

This study examines America's reluctance to allow more Jewish refugees to enter the country between 1938 and 1941. Unemployment, nativism, antisemitism, and indifference meant that only about 150,000 visas were granted to Jews seeking refuge from Nazi persecution.

——, ed. *The World Reacts to the Holocaust*. Baltimore: Johns Hopkins University Press, 1996.

This collection of essays on the reactions of twenty-two countries and the United Nations to the Holocaust reveals the existence of antisemitism in each country, with remarkably similar characteristics and varied consequences.

Yahil, Leni. *The Rescue of Danish Jewry*. Philadelphia: Jewish Publication Society, 1969.

This book recounts the unique position of Jews in Denmark, and the rescue operation that successfully evacuated almost all of Denmark's Jews to Sweden.

ORDINARY PEOPLE

Bankier, David. *The Germans and the Final Solution: Public Opinion under Nazism*. Oxford: Basil Blackwell, 1992.

This study of public opinion in Nazi Germany rejects the view that the public blindly supported the dictatorship and antisemitism. But the German public was indifferent to the fate of the Jews.

Block, Gay, and Malka Drucker. *Rescuers: Portraits of Moral Courage in the Holocaust*. New York: Holmes & Meier, 1992.

Forty-nine Gentile rescuers describe their lives before, during, and after World War II as they wrestle with the question of why they acted as they did, and whether they would do it again.

Fein, Helen. *Accounting for Genocide: National Responses and Jewish Victimization during the Holocaust*. Chicago: University of Chicago Press, 1984.

This is an analysis of the forces that facilitated the Holocaust. The causes, especially the history of Christian antisemitism, are examined in detail against the backdrop of the social history of the Jews in Europe.

Fogelman, Eva. *Conscience and Courage: Rescuers of Jews during the Holocaust.* New York: Anchor, 1994.

This volume considers the few who risked everything to help Jews. The author examines the circumstances and motivations that led some to become rescuers while so many others did nothing.

Fritzsche, Peter. *Germans into Nazis.* Cambridge, Mass.: Harvard University Press, 1998.

The author rejects the view that Germans supported the Nazis because they hated Jews, had been humiliated in World War I, or ruined by the Depression. Nazism was part of a larger process of democratization and political populism that began with the outbreak of war in 1914.

Goldberger, Leo, ed. *The Rescue of the Danish Jews: Moral Courage under Stress.* New York: New York University Press, 1987.

These essays and personal narratives examine the rescue of the Jews of Denmark in 1943, a natural and spontaneous phenomenon with virtually the entire Danish nation helping to smuggle Jews to safety in Sweden.

Gordon, Sarah. *Hitler, Germans and the "Jewish Question."* Princeton, N.J.: Princeton University Press, 1984.

This book examines the role of antisemitism in Hitler's rise to power, Hitler's message about the Jews, and what the German people might have understood that message to be. It argues that antisemitism was not the major reason for Nazi electoral success.

Hallie, Philip. *Lest Innocent Blood Be Shed: The Story of the Village of Le Chambon and How Goodness Happened There.* New York: Harper Perennial, 1994.

This is the story of the citizens and clergy of the town of Le Chambon-sur-Lignon in southern France and their efforts to save thousands of Jews. In full view of the Vichy government, they established a network that hid Jews and moved them to safety in neutral countries.

Jong, Louis de. *The Netherlands and Nazi Germany.* Cambridge, Mass.: Harvard University Press, 1990.

Three lectures by the author on Holland during World War II contend that most Dutch citizens resisted Nazi persecution of the Jews. German failure to nazify Holland and prevent a strong anti-German resistance, and Queen Wilhelmina, effectively rallied the Dutch to resist.

Kershaw, Ian. *Popular Opinion and Political Dissent in the Third Reich: Bavaria, 1933–1945.* Oxford: Clarendon Press, 1984.

This study examines the political mentality of ordinary Germans in Bavaria. The author considers the socioeconomic discontent and popular reaction to Hitler's anticlerical and anti-Jewish policies, and he reveals dissent in popular opinion in the Third Reich.

Meltzer, Milton. *Rescue: The Story of How Gentiles Saved Jews in the Holocaust.* New York: Harper Trophy, 1991.

Eyewitness accounts, diaries, letters, memoirs, and interviews, demonstrate how Gentiles risked their lives to save Jews. Stories of personal courage indicate that not all were passive in the face of evil.

Oliner, Samuel, and Pearl Oliner. *The Altruistic Personality: Rescuers of Jews in Nazi Germany.* New York: Free Press, 1988.

The authors, one a Holocaust survivor, seek answers to why some risked their lives to save Jews while so many others stood by and did nothing. Rescuers had certain characteristics in common, including a sense of community responsibility and a belief that their actions could make a difference.

Paldiel, Mordecai. *The Path of Righteousness: Gentile Rescuers of Jews during the Holocaust.* Hoboken, N.J.: Ktav Publishing, 1993.

This volume presents the stories of Gentile rescuers of Jews in German-occupied Europe during World War II. Each chapter is devoted to a different country. The author and his family were hidden by a French priest and smuggled into Switzerland.

Peukert, Detlev. *Inside Nazi Germany: Conformity, Opposition and Racism in Everyday Life.* New Haven: Yale University Press, 1987.

This book describes popular opposition to and enthusiastic support for Hitler's regime, and the impact of Nazism on existing long-term social structures and trends. Everyday life was not characterized by conformity. Germans made choices that involved consent, accommodation, or nonconformity.

Ramati, Alexander. *The Assisi Underground: The Priests Who Rescued Jews.* New York: Stein & Day, 1978.

This is the story of an Italian priest who saved some 300 Jews in Assisi. He dressed some in the clothing of monks and nuns, found jobs for others, made false identity cards, and created an entire underground movement to help Jewish refugees.

Silver, Eric. *The Book of the Just: The Unsung Heroes Who Rescued Jews from Hitler.* New York: Grove Press, 1992.

This book contains the stories of Gentiles who saved Jews during the Holocaust. It demonstrates that there were people who cared, who were not indifferent or intimidated, who risked everything to save Jews.

Steinert, Marlis. *Hitler's War and the Germans: Public Mood and Attitude during the Second World War*. Athens: Ohio University Press, 1977.

The author finds that public opinion in Nazi Germany was not conditioned solely by official propaganda, and that Hitler's regime was responsive to public criticism when it did occur.

Tec, Nechama. *When Light Pierced the Darkness: Christian Rescue of Jews in Nazi-Occupied Poland*. New York: Oxford University Press, 1986.

This study considers Polish Jews who passed as Christians to evade capture by the Nazis. It is also about the people who helped them and the risks they took. Jews who tried to pass as Christians in Nazi-occupied Poland lived with the antisemitism of the Poles who helped them.

GERMAN RESISTANCE

Fest, Joachim. *Plotting Hitler's Death: The Story of the German Resistance*. New York: Henry Holt, 1996.

This history of the German resistance focuses on the events leading to the ill-fated attempt to assassinate Hitler on July 20, 1944. It portrays the human side of the resisters, their convictions, motives, and courage, as well as their indecisiveness.

Friedländer, Saul. *Kurt Gerstein: The Ambiguity of Good*. New York: Alfred Knopf, 1983.

This is the story of Kurt Gerstein, a devout Christian and anti-Nazi, who joined the SS and attempted to resist from within by alerting the churches in Germany, the Vatican, and the Allies to the mass murder of the Jews. The author deals with Gerstein's role as both resister and member of the murderous SS.

Hamerow, Theodore. *On the Road to the Wolf's Lair: German Resistance to Hitler*. Cambridge, Mass.: Harvard University Press, 1997.

This volume focuses on the resisters' views on democracy and the "Jewish Question." Many were as opposed to democracy as they were to Nazi totalitarianism. Most were not motivated by opposition to antisemitism, even if they rejected its implementation.

Hoffmann, Peter. *Stauffenberg: A Family History, 1905–1944*. Cambridge: Cambridge University Press, 1995.

This is a family biography centered on the three Stauffenberg brothers: Berthold, Alexander, and Claus. The brothers are portrayed as men motivated to act primarily by the mass murder of the Jews. Their religious background, noble birth, and intellectual inclinations drove them to action as atonement for Germany's crimes.

——. *The History of the German Resistance, 1933–1945*. Cambridge, Mass.: MIT Press, 1977.

This is the English translation of the first comprehensive history of the German resistance. Each of the attempts to overthrow the regime is presented with meticulous detail, as are the lives and personalities of the individual resisters who are portrayed neither as heroes nor as villains.

Klemperer, Klemens von. *German Resistance against Hitler: The Search for Allies Abroad, 1938–1945*. New York: Oxford University Press, 1992.

This study focuses on the failure of the German resistance to secure the support of the Allies. It examines mainly the conservative opponents of Hitler's regime, and reveals the ways in which some managed to alienate Allied governments.

Scholl, Inge. *The White Rose*. Hanover, N.H.: University Press of New England, 1983.

The White Rose, the resistance group of young German university students, was infiltrated and destroyed by the Gestapo in 1943 and 1944. The organization grew out of the students' conviction that they could not remain silent in the face of German atrocities. The volume includes photographs, leaflets, personal letters, and German documents.

Stoltzfus, Nathan. *Resistance of the Heart: Intermarriage and the Rosenstrasse Protest in Nazi Germany*. New York: W. W. Norton, 1996.

This volume examines the Rosenstrasse protest of 1943, when some 150 non-Jewish Germans in mixed marriages protested the arrest and planned deportation of their Jewish spouses. The larger context of the history of mixed marriages in the Third Reich is considered.

DOCUMENTS, MEMOIRS, LETTERS

Boehm, Erich, ed. *We Survived: Fourteen Histories of the Hidden and Hunted of Nazi Germany*. Santa Barbara, Calif.: ABC-Clio, 1985.

Fourteen people, Jews and non-Jewish resisters, describe their experiences hiding and surviving in Nazi Germany. They describe those who followed Hitler enthusiastically and those who were simply apathetic.

Fittko, Lisa. *Escape through the Pyrenees*. Evanston, Ill.: Northwestern University Press, 1991.

This memoir documents the fate of German émigrés, Jews, antifascists, and social-ists before and immediately after the German conquest of France in 1940. The au-thor is a Jew who fled Germany to France with her non-Jewish husband.

Friedländer, Saul, ed. *Pius XII and the Third Reich: A Documentation.* New York: Oc-tagon, 1980.

This volume supports the argument that Pope Pius XII was sympathetic to Nazi Germany because of his fears of communism in Europe. It contains a selection of documents from German, British, American, and Israeli archives.

Gies, Miep. *Anne Frank Remembered: The Story of the Woman Who Helped to Hide the Frank Family.* New York: Simon & Schuster, 1987.

This is a memoir of the woman who helped to hide Anne Frank and her family from German authorities in Amsterdam during World War II. It describes her life in Aus-tria, immigration to Holland, her relationship with the Frank family, and life in Ger-man-occupied Amsterdam.

Jens, Inge, ed. *At the Heart of the White Rose: Letters and Diaries of Hans and Sophie Scholl.* New York: Harper & Row, 1987.

These are letters and diary entries of Hans and Sophie Scholl, brother and sister in the White Rose student resistance movement in Germany during World War II. The entries run from May 1937 to February 17, 1943, the day before they were ar-rested and five days before they were executed.

Opdyke, Irene. *Into the Flames: The Story of a Righteous Gentile.* San Bernardino, Calif.: Borgo Press, 1992.

The author is a Polish Catholic woman who risked her life to protect her Jewish friends during the Holocaust. She hid twelve Jews in the basement of the villa of a Gestapo officer for whom she worked.

Ringelblum, Emanuel. *Polish-Jewish Relations during the Second World War.* Eds. Joseph Kermish and Shmuel Krakowski. Evanston, Ill.: Northwestern University Press, 1992.

This examination of Polish-Jewish relations during the German occupation is based on the records of the secret archives of the Warsaw ghetto underground, Oneg Shabbat. The author created the archive, and he argues that many Poles helped the Jews, many betrayed them, and most were indifferent.

Ten Boom, Corrie. *The Hiding Place.* New York: Bantam, 1974.

This is the autobiography of a Christian who hid Jews in Holland during World War II. Arrested and imprisoned by the Nazis, she and her family were tortured, and most died. The author survived and stresses the power of love and the rejection of hate.

Wallenberg, Raoul. *Letters and Dispatches, 1924–1944.* New York: Arcade, 1995.

Raoul Wallenberg's letters and dispatches are drawn from his correspondence with his paternal grandfather; his dispatches from Budapest between July 18 and December 12, 1944, describing the deportation of the Jews to Auschwitz; and several letters Wallenberg wrote from Budapest to his mother.

Wollenberg, Jörg, ed. *The German Public and the Persecution of the Jews, 1933–1945.* Atlantic Highlands, N.J.: Humanities Press, 1996.

This volume contains eyewitness testimony of Jews, half-Jews, and non-Jews, and analysis of contemporary writers that address the extent to which the German public was aware of Nazi persecution of the Jews.

Legacies of the Holocaust

MEMORY AND HISTORY

Baldwin, Peter, ed. *Reworking the Past: Hitler, the Holocaust, and the Historians' Debate.* Boston: Beacon, 1990.

This is a collection of essays about the historians' debate in the 1980s on the meaning of the Third Reich and the Holocaust in German history. The debates reflect political divisions between left and right in Germany, and the emotion of German-Jewish relations since 1945.

Dawidowicz, Lucy. *The Holocaust and the Historians.* Cambridge, Mass.: Harvard University Press, 1981.

The author explores Holocaust literature to determine how the Holocaust has been treated in different countries, and argues that Jewish historians face particular emotional problems when dealing with the topic.

Evans, Richard. *In Hitler's Shadow: West German Historians and the Attempt to Escape from the Nazi Past.* New York: Pantheon, 1989.

This is an analysis of the debate among German historians over the meaning of the Third Reich and the Holocaust in German history. Germans and Austrians born since World War II must bear responsibility for the past, but not guilt, and the survival of German democracy requires open and honest confrontation with the past.

Finkelstein, Norman, and Bettina Birn. *A Nation on Trial: The Goldhagen Thesis and Historical Truth.* New York: Henry Holt, 1998.

The authors dispute Daniel Goldhagen's controversial argument that the Holocaust must be explained solely in terms of an antisemitism unique to Germany, one that embodied a national will to exterminate the Jews.

Friedländer, Saul. *Memory, History and the Extermination of the Jews of Europe.* Bloomington: Indiana University Press, 1993.

These seven essays reveal the author's concern over the impact of contemporary events on the memory of the Holocaust. They consider the natural tension between memory and history, and reveal the author's fears of a diminished memory of the Holocaust.

Gilbert, Martin. *Holocaust Journey: Traveling in Search of the Past.* New York: Columbia University Press, 1997.

This narrative describes a two-week trip to the important Holocaust sites in Poland by the author and his students. The author brings together the day-to-day experiences of the group, his knowledge of Jewish history, and personal memories of Holocaust survivors and victims.

Gitelman, Zvi, ed. *Bitter Legacy: Confronting the Holocaust in the USSR.* Bloomington: Indiana University Press, 1997.

These essays deal with the Holocaust inside the Soviet Union, its consequences on post–World War II Soviet society, and on post-Soviet societies. They rely on recently released documentation that reveals details of German crimes on Soviet soil, and the collaboration of Soviet citizens.

Hartman, Geoffrey, ed. *Holocaust Remembrance: The Shapes of Memory.* Oxford: Blackwell, 1994.

Scholars, artists and writers ponder the ways in which the Holocaust is remembered. They consider the enormous volume and variety of records available to current and future generations, and cite benefits and dangers posed by the overwhelming amount of information.

Herf, Jeffrey. *Divided Memory: The Nazi Past in the Two Germanys.* Cambridge, Mass.: Harvard University Press, 1997.

Politicians in both Germanys manipulated and distorted the Nazi past to serve new purposes. The author contrasts the ways in which the two German states recalled the Third Reich, and sees these differences as an impediment to coming to terms with the past in a reunited Germany.

Hilberg, Raul. *The Politics of Memory: The Journey of a Holocaust Historian.* Chicago: Ivan R. Dee, 1996.

This brief memoir recounts the author's decision to study the Holocaust as his life's work, and the obstacles he faced some forty years ago in finding a publisher for his path-breaking book *The Destruction of the European Jews.*

Hirsch, Herbert. *Genocide and the Politics of Memory: Studying Death to Preserve Life*. Chapel Hill: University of North Carolina Press, 1995.

This book attempts to understand the meaning of the Holocaust for the post-Holocaust world. An analysis of the prerequisites for genocide, the author considers how people come to participate in genocidal activity.

Kaplan, Harold. *Conscience and Memory: Meditations in a Museum of the Holocaust.* Chicago: University of Chicago Press, 1994.

The author seeks to find an "ethical testimony" from the confusion of what he calls the apocalyptic event known as the Holocaust. He explores the basis of the terror and despair of the Holocaust, much as visitors might wish to do in the United States Holocaust Memorial Museum in Washington, D.C., and Yad Vashem in Jerusalem.

LaCapra, Dominick. *History and Memory after Auschwitz*. Ithaca, N.Y.: Cornell University Press, 1998.

The author deals with the interaction of history, memory, ethical, and political concerns as they emerged after the Holocaust. He analyzes literature, film, the recent historians' debate, and the role of psychoanalysis in an effort to understand how we understand and remember the Holocaust.

Langer, Lawrence. *Holocaust Testimonies: The Ruins of Memory*. New Haven: Yale University Press, 1991.

The author uses the Fortunoff Video Archives of Yale University to demonstrate how oral testimonies complement historical scholarship on the Holocaust by confronting the human dimensions of the genocide.

Linenthal, Edward. *Preserving Memory: The Struggle to Create America's Holocaust Museum*. New York: Viking, 1995.

This book examines the process of defining the boundaries of Holocaust memory that are incorporated into the United States Holocaust Memorial Museum in Washington, D.C.

Maier, Charles. *The Unmasterable Past: History, Holocaust, and German National Identity*. Cambridge, Mass.: Harvard University Press, 1988.

This is an account of the acrimonious debate in the mid-1980s among German historians over Germany's Nazi past. Were Nazi crimes unique and uniquely German, or were they comparable to other national atrocities? The controversy gave Germans a chance to air the issues just before reunification.

Marrus, Michael. *The Holocaust in History*. Hanover, N.H.: University Press of New England, 1987.

This is a discussion of historical literature on the Holocaust, an overview of the competing interpretations or schools of thought. The book serves as a guide to the literature and major questions of the Holocaust.

Milton, Sybil. *In Fitting Memory: The Art and Politics of Holocaust Memorials*. Detroit: Wayne State University Press, 1991.

This is a collection of photographs of concentration and extermination camp remains, and of memorials and monuments erected to the victims of mass murder throughout Europe. Each photograph is accompanied by a caption with information relevant to the site.

Novick, Peter. *The Holocaust in American Life*. Boston: Houghton Mifflin, 1999.

Examining the sweeping transformation of the Holocaust from a phenomenon long ignored by Americans to one that has moved to the center of American life, the author argues that American Jews have made the Holocaust emblematic of the Jewish experience to the exclusion of all else.

Rousso, Henry. *The Vichy Syndrome: History and Memory in France since 1944*. Cambridge, Mass.: Harvard University Press, 1991.

This is a study of how post–World War II generations in France have come to grips with the troubling legacy of occupation and collaboration. The collective representation of France's wartime past has been marked by myth, polemics, and escapism, and has become obsessive over the past fifteen years.

Steinlauf, Michael. *Bondage to the Dead: Poland and the Memory of the Holocaust*. Syracuse, N.Y.: Syracuse University Press, 1997.

This examination of the mutual perceptions of Poles and Jews after World War II reveals a complex historical relationship. Poles in the postwar Communist period denied the reality of the Holocaust, until the positive changes ushered in by the Solidarity movement of the 1980s.

Young, James. *The Texture of Memory: Holocaust Memorials and Meaning*. New Haven: Yale University Press, 1993.

This is a study of Holocaust memorials in Germany, Poland, Israel, and the United States, the countries where the mass murder of the Jews was formulated, where much of it was implemented, and where the great majority of survivors settled after the war. More than 120 photographs complement the author's text.

SURVIVORS AND POST-WAR JEWISH COMMUNITIES

Bauer, Yehuda. *Out of the Ashes: The Impact of American Jews on Post-Holocaust European Jewry*. Oxford: Pergamon, 1989.

This book examines the work of American Jewish organizations to aid Jewish survivors after the Holocaust, including American Jewish Joint Distribution Committee, the Hebrew Sheltering and Immigrant Aid Society, and the Organization for Rehabilitation and Training.

Bodemann, Y. Michael, ed. *Jews, Germans, Memory: Reconstructions of Jewish Life in Germany*. Ann Arbor: University of Michigan Press, 1996.

These essays describe how the foundations were laid for a new Jewish community in post–World War II Germany. They consider the conflicting interests and aims of Jewish leaders and German politicians, as well as issues of politics, social movements, history, literature, the media, and ethnicity.

Brenner, Michael. *After the Holocaust: Rebuilding Jewish Lives in Postwar Germany*. Princeton, N.J.: Princeton University Press, 1997.

This book examines the streams that make up today's German Jewish community. Eastern European Jewish survivors of the Holocaust, German Jews who escaped before the war and returned, and more recent immigrants from Israel and the former Soviet Union today lack a strong cultural and religious identity.

Eitinger, Leo. *Concentration Camp Survivors in Norway and Israel*. The Hague: M. Nijhoff, 1972.

This study of former concentration camp inmates living in Norway and Israel considers whether the psychic and physical stress of the camps has had any lasting psychological effects on the survivors.

Hass, Aaron. *The Aftermath: Living with the Holocaust*. Cambridge: Cambridge University Press, 1995.

This is a study of the postwar psychological adjustments of survivors of the Holocaust. It examines how people who have lived for years with memories of horror have been able to avoid paralysis and move on with their lives.

Helmreich, William. *Against All Odds: Holocaust Survivors and the Successful Lives They Made in America*. New Brunswick, N.J.: Transaction, 1996.

This is an examination of the approximately 140,000 Holocaust survivors who came to America and the lives they have made. The author finds a surprisingly normal community of people who have built happy lives.

Krystal, Henry, ed. *Massive Psychic Trauma*. New York: International Universities Press, 1968.

The contents of this volume are taken from the proceedings of a conference on massive psychic trauma among survivors of German concentration camps and the atomic bomb attack on Hiroshima. Thirty-five participants, mostly psychiatrists, discuss their examinations of survivors.

Marcus, Paul, and Alan Rosenberg. *Healing Their Wounds: Psychotherapy with Holocaust Survivors and Their Families*. New York: Praeger, 1989.

In this anthology, sixteen scholars discuss a wide range of approaches to helping survivors recover and lead relatively normal lives. These include traditional psychotherapy, self-psychology, group and family approaches, and pastoral counseling.

Rapaport, Lynn. *Jews in Germany after the Holocaust: Memory, Identity, and Jewish-German Relations*. Cambridge: Cambridge University Press, 1997.

This book examines how the memory of the Holocaust has shaped the lives of Jews who were born and grew up in Germany after World War II. It considers the evolution of the views that Jews have of other Germans and of themselves in German society.

Sachar, Abram. *The Redemption of the Unwanted: From the Liberation of the Death Camps to the Founding of Israel*. New York: St. Martin's, 1983.

The author, founding president of Brandeis University, examines the fate of Holocaust survivors in the years immediately following World War II. He focuses on the DP camps, finding new homes for the survivors, and Zionist efforts to bring them to Palestine.

Segev, Tom. *The Seventh Million: The Israelis and the Holocaust*. New York: Hill & Wang, 1993.

This book considers how the Jewish community of Palestine (Yishuv) reacted to Nazi Germany and the Holocaust, and how Israeli society has dealt with the consequences since 1948. It is critical of the Zionist response, and interprets the new Jewish state's reception of survivors as less than enthusiastic.

Wasserstein, Bernard. *Vanishing Diaspora: The Jews in Europe since 1945*. Cambridge, Mass.: Harvard University Press, 1997.

This is a history of the Jews in Europe since the end of World War II, against the backdrop of postwar reconstruction, Soviet occupation and the Cold War, the collapse of communism, the memory of Nazi genocide, the persistence of antisemitism and the creation of Israel.

CHILDREN OF SURVIVORS

Epstein, Helen. *Children of the Holocaust: Conversations with Sons and Daughters of Survivors*. New York: G. P. Putnam, 1979.

The author, a daughter of Holocaust survivors, deals with the children of Holocaust survivors who grew up after the war in freedom and security, possessed by the legacy and tragedy of a history they had never lived.

Hass, Aaron. *In the Shadow of the Holocaust: The Second Generation*. New York: Cambridge University Press, 1996.

This book examines the experiences of the children of Holocaust survivors. These mostly middle-aged men and women describe their relationships with their parents and the impact of the Holocaust on their own lives.

Wardi, Dina. *Memorial Candles: Children of the Holocaust*. New York: Routledge, 1993.

The author is an Israeli psychotherapist who used group therapy to treat the children of Holocaust survivors. The children of Holocaust survivors in Israel and elsewhere had experiences, emotional burdens, and methods of expression that were unique and common to this group.

RELIGIOUS, PSYCHOLOGICAL, AND PHILOSOPHICAL IMPLICATIONS

Bauman, Zygmunt. *Modernity and the Holocaust*. Ithaca, N.Y.: Cornell University Press, 1992.

The author argues that modernity, with its emphasis on technology, efficiency, and bureaucracy, must be viewed as a major cause of the Holocaust.

Berkovits, Eliezer. *Faith after the Holocaust*. New York: Ktav, 1973.

The author seeks to define a future for Jews in the post-Holocaust world. He looks to the "faith history" of the Jewish people, and believes that Jews can be optimistic because their "faith history" is the guarantee of their future.

Bettelheim, Bruno. *Surviving and Other Essays*. New York: Alfred A. Knopf, 1979.

This anthology of essays on psychic trauma includes Bettelheim's classic statement on coping mechanisms in German concentration camps, based in part on his own experiences.

Braham, Randolph, ed. *The Psychological Perspective of the Holocaust and Its Aftermath*. New York: Columbia University Press, 1988.

These ten essays provide various psychological perspectives on the Holocaust and its aftermath. They deal with topics such as "survivor syndrome" and therapeutic alternatives for the treatment of the psychological and psychiatric problems of Holocaust survivors and their descendants.

Braiterman, Zachary. (*God*) *After Auschwitz: Tradition and Change in Post-Holocaust Jewish Thought*. Princeton, N.J.: Princeton University Press, 1998.

This book brings postmodern philosophical and literary approaches together with post-Holocaust Jewish thought. The author draws on the ideas of contemporary Jewish thinkers to recreate religious thought for the post-Auschwitz age.

Burleigh, Michael. *Ethics and Extermination: Reflections on Nazi Genocide*. Cambridge: Cambridge University Press, 1997.

These nine essays by the author are divided into three sections that deal with different aspects of the "euthanasia" program, German behavior in the Soviet Union, and the Final Solution.

Cargas, Harry. *Reflections of a Post-Auschwitz Christian*. Detroit: Wayne State University Press, 1989.

The author, a Catholic scholar, traces the origins of Nazi Jew-hatred to its Christian roots. For Christianity to survive, it must eliminate hate from its teachings, and rediscover love in the teachings of Jesus.

——. *Shadows of Auschwitz: A Christian Response to the Holocaust*. New York: Crossroad, 1992.

It is impossible to detach the Holocaust from its Christian context. Hitler and Himmler were never excommunicated from the Catholic church, Pius XII never condemned Nazi mass murder, the killers came from Christian families and had a Christian education, and many Christian dignitaries supported Hitler.

——. *Voices from the Holocaust*. Lexington: University Press of Kentucky, 1993.

This is a collection of the author's interviews with prominent witnesses to the Holocaust. Those interviewed include Jewish survivors, and Gentiles who saved Jews during World War II.

Cohen, Arthur. *The Tremendum: A Theological Interpretation of the Holocaust*. New York: Continuum, 1993.

Rejecting liberal theologies of the Enlightenment, emancipation, and neo-orthodoxy among Jews, the author seeks a new theological language in response to the Holocaust. He suggests retrieving classic Jewish responses to earlier catastrophes as a place to start.

Davies, Alan. *Antisemitism and the Christian Mind: The Crisis of Conscience after Auschwitz*. New York: Herder & Herder, 1969.

This critique of post-Holocaust Protestant and Catholic theology as it relates to Judaism highlights the divisions within both regarding the Jews, and concludes that the attitude of Christian theologians remains ambivalent.

Dietrich, Donald. *God and Humanity in Auschwitz: Jewish-Christian Relations and Sanctioned Murder*. New Brunswick, N.J.: Transaction, 1994.

This study examines the dramatic impact of the Holocaust on post-Holocaust Christians. It focuses on institutional attitudes, and the biblical and theological scholarship of post-Holocaust Christians that has changed the attitudes of the Christian churches toward Jews and the past.

Fackenheim, Emil. *The Jewish Return into History: Reflections in the Age of Auschwitz and a New Jerusalem*. New York: Schocken, 1978.

The author, a leading Jewish philosopher and theologian, sees the Holocaust and the establishment of Israel as major historical events of our age. Jews must confront the Holocaust honestly and recognize the centrality of Israel in Jewish life.

——. *To Mend the World: Foundations of Future Jewish Thought*. New York: Schocken, 1982.

The author examines the rupture in Jewish thought caused by modernity and its heightened tension as a result of the Holocaust. He points the way toward a renewal of Judaism in an age when our ideas about God and humanity have been shaken.

Frankl, Viktor. *Man's Search for Meaning: An Introduction to Logotherapy*. New York: Pocket Books, 1984.

The author, a survivor, is the founder of a major school of psychology in Vienna. He rejects the view that survival required the victims to be more like the perpetrators. They had to depend on an ability "to retreat from their terrible surroundings to a life of inner riches and spiritual freedom."

Haas, Peter. *Morality after the Holocaust: The Radical Challenge of the Nazi Ethic*. Philadelphia: Fortress Press, 1988.

This book considers the Holocaust as a problem in ethical theory. How was it that a society could participate in an ethic of persecution and mass murder for more than a decade, with virtually no significant opposition from Germany's religious, political, legal, and medical leaders?

Hayes, Peter, ed. *Lessons and Legacies: The Meaning of the Holocaust in a Changing World*. Evanston, Ill.: Northwestern University Press, 1991.

The unifying theme of these essays is the gradual shift of responsibility for understanding and memory of the Holocaust from survivors to historians. They examine the relationship between the dwindling number of eyewitnesses and contemporary historians.

Kren, George, and Leon Rappoport. *The Holocaust and the Crisis of Human Behavior*. New York: Holmes & Meier, 1980.

The authors criticize existing scholarship for failing to confront the implications of the Holocaust for post-Holocaust society. Interpretations of the Holocaust have been unable to integrate it into analyses of the human condition.

Lang, Berel, ed. *Writing and the Holocaust*. New York: Holmes & Meier, 1988.

In this collection of essays, historians, philosophers, and novelists ponder significant questions raised by the Holocaust. Was it unique in human history, or does it fit into a larger context? Is Holocaust fiction justifiable, and is humor appropriate in Holocaust literature?

Langer, Lawrence. *Admitting the Holocaust: Collected Essays*. New York: Oxford University Press, 1995.

These essays interpret the Holocaust as a rupture in human values. They examine memory, Jewish resistance, Holocaust literature, the use and abuse of the Holocaust by contemporary culture, and other questions.

——. *Preempting the Holocaust*. New Haven: Yale University Press, 1998.

Through his analysis of prominent Holocaust writers and artists, the author focuses attention on controversial issues such as the appropriation of the Holocaust for private moral or political agendas, the ordeal of women in the camps, the tendency to conflate the Holocaust with other atrocities and genocides, and other issues.

Levi, Primo. *The Drowned and the Saved*. New York: Vintage International, 1989.

Written shortly before the author committed suicide in 1987, this book reflects his pessimism that the lessons of the Holocaust had not been learned. He argues for the uniqueness of the Holocaust, and fears that it was simply taking its place among the routine atrocities in history.

Littell, Franklin. *The Crucifixion of the Jews*. Macon, Ga.: Mercer University Press, 1987.

A brief history of Christian Jew-hatred begins this treatment of the German churches and the Jewish question in Nazi Germany. It considers the meaning of the Holocaust and the founding of the state of Israel for Christians.

Maybaum, Ignaz. *The Face of God after Auschwitz*. Amsterdam: Polak & Van Gennep, 1965.

The author, a Jewish theologian and refugee from Nazi Germany in 1939, sees the salvation of humanity not in the political universalism of one world government or church, but in the universal application of the commandment "Love thy neighbor as thyself."

Miller, Judith. *One, by One, by One: Facing the Holocaust*. New York: Touchstone, 1991.

This is a book about how people remember the Holocaust in Germany, Austria, the Netherlands, France, the Soviet Union, and the United States. Although the vehicles of remembrance differ from society to society, the mechanisms of self-deception and suppression are very similar.

Quigley, John. *Palestine and Israel: A Challenge to Justice*. Durham: Duke University Press, 1990.

This survey of the conflict between Arabs and Israelis assesses the impact of the creation of the state of Israel on both peoples.

Rosenbaum, Alan, ed. *Is the Holocaust Unique? Perspectives on Comparative Genocide*. Boulder, Colo.: Westview, 1996.

This collection of scholarly essays compares the Jewish Holocaust with the Gypsy Holocaust, the Atlantic slave trade, the Armenian genocide, and the Stalinist terror, raising the question whether all mass murders constitute genocide.

Rosenberg, Alan, and Gerald Myers, eds. *Echoes from the Holocaust: Philosophical Reflections of a Dark Time*. Philadelphia: Temple University Press, 1988.

These twenty-three essays reflect on the extermination of the Jews during World War II. It is a source for philosophical reflection about ethics and the human capacity for evil.

Rosenfeld, Alvin, ed. *Thinking about the Holocaust: After Half a Century*. Bloomington: Indiana University Press, 1997.

Thirteen scholars assess the impact of the Holocaust and of contemporary scholarship on our understanding of it. They examine historical writing, testimonial literature, monuments and memorials, theological reflections, poetry, prose, film, and drama.

Roth, John, and Michael Berenbaum, eds. *Holocaust: Religious and Philosophical Implications*. New York: Paragon House, 1989.

This is an introduction to some of the major religious and philosophical issues raised by the Holocaust. The editors bring together the well-known works of Holocaust survivors and writers, including Hannah Arendt, Primo Levi, and Elie Wiesel.

Rubenstein, Richard. *The Cunning of History: The Holocaust and the American Future*. New York: Harper & Row, 1978.

The Holocaust is part of a larger continuum of slavery that has been at the foundation of Western civilization for centuries. The extermination camps were made possible by Western culture's emphasis on rationality that leads inevitably to the depersonalizing bureaucracies of the modern state.

Rubenstein, Richard, and John Roth. *Approaches to Auschwitz: The Holocaust and Its Legacy*. Atlanta: John Knox, 1987.

This volume deals with the meaning and significance of the Holocaust, particularly for non-Jews. It contains a historical overview of the roots of Jew-hatred from antiquity to the eighteenth century, and the rise of Nazism, its establishment in Germany, and the Holocaust.

Wiesenthal, Simon. *The Sunflower: On the Possibilities and Limits of Forgiveness*. New York: Schocken, 1998.

This is a moral allegory about a dying Nazi who asks the forgiveness of a young Jew who refuses and walks silently away from the man's hospital room. The book poses the question of what the boy's moral obligations were under the circumstances.

ANTISEMITISM, NEO-NAZISM, HOLOCAUST DENIAL

Bergmann, Werner, and Rainer Erb. *Anti-Semitism in Germany: The Post-Nazi Epoch from 1945 to 1995*. New Brunswick, N.J.: Transaction, 1996.

This book provides a quantitative analysis of persistent antisemitic attitudes in contemporary Germany, and concludes that the images that Germans have of Jews have changed little since 1960.

Kurthen, Hermann, Werner Bergmann, and Rainer Erb, eds. *Antisemitism and Xenophobia in Germany after Unification*. New York: Oxford University Press, 1997.

This book offers some of the most recent research by a team of American and German scholars on the reawakening of xenophobia and antisemitism since German unification a decade ago.

Lipstadt, Deborah. *Denying the Holocaust: The Growing Assault on Truth and Memory*. New York: Free Press, 1993.

This study exposes the claims of those who deny the Holocaust and claim it is a myth. It argues that those who make such claims are not harmless cranks on the fringes of society. Despite the evidence and thousands of living witnesses, Holocaust denial has gained adherents.

Stern, Frank. *The Whitewashing of the Yellow Badge: Antisemitism and Philosemitism in Postwar Germany.* New York: Oxford University Press, 1992.

This volume considers the evolution of German public opinion regarding the Jews during the Allied occupation and the first four years of the Federal Republic. A new philosemitism in postwar Germany was not indicative of a national repentance for Nazi crimes, nor was the reemergence of antisemitism necessarily a reversion to Nazi racism.

Stern, Kenneth. *Holocaust Denial.* New York: American Jewish Committee, 1993.

This survey of Holocaust denial in the United States, Europe, and around the world defines Holocaust denial and identifies who is behind it. It refutes the arguments of the deniers, and offers a framework for combating it.

Journals

HOLOCAUST JOURNALS
Dimensions: A Journal of Holocaust Studies

This journal is published twice a year by the Anti-Defamation League's Braun Center for Holocaust Studies, with articles on all aspects of the Holocaust from a variety of disciplines, as well as book reviews.

Holocaust and Genocide Studies

The official journal of the United States Holocaust Memorial Museum in Washington, D.C., it is published three times a year by Oxford University Press. It is multidisciplinary with articles that reflect the latest scholarship on the Holocaust.

Journal of Holocaust Education (formerly *British Journal of Holocaust Education*)

Devoted to interdisciplinary Holocaust education and research, this journal publishes articles, conference and workshop reports, book, video and film reviews, and information on forthcoming events. It is published three times a year by Frank Cass Publishers, the Institute of Contemporary History, and the Wiener Library.

Simon Wiesenthal Center Annual

The *Annual* was published between 1984 and 1990 by Rossel Books, and then Kraus International Publications, and the Simon Wiesenthal Center in Los Angeles. It contains scholarly essays from different disciplines on all aspects of the Holocaust. It is no longer published.

Yad Vashem Studies

This is an annual published by the Yad Vashem Martyrs' and Heroes' Remembrance Authority in Jerusalem. It contains scholarly articles, research papers, reminiscences, and reports on the history and historiography of the Holocaust.

JOURNALS WITH SOME HOLOCAUST CONTENT
Central European History

This quarterly publishes scholarly articles, review articles, book reviews, and conference reports on the history of German-speaking Central Europe. It is published by the Humanities Press International for the Conference Group for Central European History.

German History

Published twice a year by Oxford University Press for the German History Society of Great Britain, it includes scholarly articles, conference reports, dissertation abstracts, book reviews and announcements of events all dealing with German history.

German Studies Review

This is an interdisciplinary, bilingual journal published three times a year by the German Studies Association. Its issues contain scholarly articles and book reviews in English and German dealing with German history, literature, economics, political science and sociology.

History and Memory: Studies in Representation of the Past

This journal publishes articles on history and memory in European history, with numerous articles on the topic of memory and the Holocaust. It is published twice a year by Tel Aviv University and Indiana University Press.

Journal of Israeli History (formerly *Studies in Zionism*)

Published by Tel Aviv University and Frank Cass Ltd. in London three times per year, this journal publishes articles on the history of the state of Israel, antisemitism, and the Holocaust.

Journal of Modern History

This is a quarterly journal published by the University of Chicago Press in cooperation with the Modern European History section of the American Historical Association. It publishes scholarly articles, review articles, and book reviews on modern European history

Leo Baeck Institute Yearbook

An annual published in English since 1956 by the Leo Baeck Institute of New York, London, and Jerusalem, it is the preeminent scholarly journal for the history of Central European Jewry since the eighteenth century.

Patterns of Prejudice

This journal is published quarterly by the Institute for Jewish Policy Research and the American Jewish Committee. Its articles, reviews and review essays deal with the conditions, causes, and manifestations of racial, religious, and ethnic discrimination and prejudice, particularly against Jews.

Shofar

An interdisciplinary journal of Jewish studies, this quarterly is published by the University of Nebraska Press for the Midwest Jewish Studies Association, the Western Jewish Studies Association, and the Jewish Studies Program of Purdue University. It publishes articles, reviews, and information on Jewish history and culture.

Wiener Library Bulletin

This journal first appeared as a bi-monthly between 1946 and 1965, and then as a quarterly from 1965 to 1981. Published by the Wiener Library, the *Bulletin* contains articles, reviews and news items pertaining to Nazi Germany and the Holocaust, and European Jewish history and the Middle East. It is no longer published.

Yivo Annual

This is an interdisciplinary social science journal devoted to the examination of the history, life, and culture of East European Jews and their descendants throughout the world. Published by the YIVO Institute for Jewish Research in New York, and Northwestern University Press, it contains articles, and translations of Yiddish documents and memoirs.

FILMOGRAPHY

Documentaries

SURVIVOR ACCOUNTS, GHETTOS AND CAMPS
Anne Frank Remembered (117 minutes)

Based on eyewitness testimony, family letters and photographs, and archival film footage, this Academy Award-winning documentary tells the story of Anne Frank's childhood, her years in hiding with her family, and her last days in Bergen-Belsen.

Breaking the Silence: The Generation after the Holocaust (58 minutes)

Survivors and children of survivors examine the ripple effects of the Holocaust on the lives of the post-Holocaust generation. Parents explain why they carried their grief silently, and children explain the difficulties of living with the silence.

Children in the Holocaust (68 minutes)

Survivors tell their stories of life as children in Auschwitz and other extermination camps, combining their stories with film footage and photographs.

Diamonds in the Snow (59 minutes)

Three survivors of a small Jewish community near Auschwitz tell of escape and survival. They talk about a local Christian who protected his Jewish workers and paid for it with his life. There are interviews with Christians from the same town who were children at the time.

The Double Crossing: The Voyage of the St. Louis (29 minutes)

Surviving passengers relive their voyage, with background film footage and photographs. They address past and current issues of racism, refugee quotas, and immigration policies.

Flames in the Ashes (90 minutes)

This video explores the many ways the Jews resisted the Nazis, using film footage and eyewitness testimony of both surviving resistance fighters and Nazi perpetrators. (In Hebrew, Yiddish, French, Italian, and Polish with English subtitles.)

For the Living (60 minutes)

This documentary chronicles the establishment of the United States Holocaust Memorial Museum in Washington, D.C., combining archival film and photographs that focus on the experiences of the victims and survivors.

Forests of Valour (52 minutes)

An Israeli film crew retraces the steps of Jewish partisans from Latvia to the Ukraine. They encounter deserted synagogues, anonymous death pits, and once-thriving Jewish towns that are virtually empty of Jews.

The Holocaust: In Memory of Millions (60 minutes)

This documentary presents an overall history of the Holocaust and introduces viewers to the United States Holocaust Memorial Museum in Washington, D.C.

Image before My Eyes (90 minutes)

This collection of survivor accounts of Jewish life in Poland between the wars examines everyday Jewish life in rural and urban settings, and is illustrated with archival film, home movies, and photographs.

In Our Own Hands (85 minutes)

This documentary traces the history of the Jewish Brigade, the only all-Jewish fighting unit in World War II, from the brigade's early struggles in Palestine to fighting the Germans in northern Italy.

A Journey Back: Remembrances of the Holocaust (60 minutes)

Broadway producer Jack Garfein returns to Auschwitz and finds the spot where as a thirteen-year-old boy he faced Josef Mengele and lied to save his life. He also returns to the small Slovak town where he grew up.

Kitty: Return to Auschwitz (73 minutes)

A survivor returns to Auschwitz thirty-four years after her liberation and recounts her two-year struggle to survive in Auschwitz.

Kovno Ghetto: A Buried History (100 minutes)

Historian Martin Gilbert examines the lives of Lithuanian Jews in the Kovno Ghetto who collected and hid copies of official German orders, minutes of Jewish Council meetings, personal diaries, and photographs of ghetto life.

The Last Days (88 minutes)

Five Hungarian Holocaust survivors describe Nazi Germany's effort to exterminate the Jews of Hungary late in World War II in this Academy Award-winning documentary produced by Steven Spielberg's Shoah Visual History Foundation.

The Last Seven Months of Anne Frank (75 minutes)

Eight women who knew Anne Frank's family tell the story of the plight of the family in transit and in concentration and extermination camps.

Łódź Ghetto (156 minutes)

This documentary combines wartime film footage and photographs of the struggle of the inhabitants of the Łódź ghetto to survive.

The Lost Children of Berlin (50 minutes)

Fifty former students of the last Jewish school in Berlin, closed in 1942, meet in 1996 and recall Jewish life in Berlin in the 1930s and 1940s.

More Than Broken Glass: Memories of Kristallnacht (57 minutes)

This documentary, based on interviews with witnesses, news footage, and photographs, describes the political climate in Germany and the lasting effect of the Crystal Night pogrom on the lives of the survivors.

Nazi Concentration Camps: Witness to Genocide (59 minutes)

This is the official film record of the German camps photographed by Allied forces in 1945. It is intensely graphic, with footage of half-dead survivors, victims of medical experiments, gas chambers, and open mass graves.

Night and Fog (Nuit et Brouillard) (32 minutes)

This award-winning short French documentary combines intensely graphic black-and-white film footage of the horrors of the Nazi camps with color scenes of the same places ten years after World War II. (In French, with English subtitles.)

Not Like Sheep to the Slaughter: The Story of the Białystok Ghetto (150 minutes)

This is the story of Mordechai Tenenbaum and the Jewish resistance fighters in the Białystok ghetto who fought German attempts to liquidate the ghetto in the summer of 1943.

One Survivor Remembers (39 minutes)

In this Academy Award-winning documentary, Gerda Weissmann Klein recounts her survival as a forced laborer in German factories.

Partisans of Vilna (133 minutes)

This film documents the struggle of Abba Kovner and the United Partisans Organization in the Vilna ghetto.

Persecuted and Forgotten (54 minutes)

A group of German Gypsies returns to Auschwitz after World War II and recall their persecution during the Holocaust.

Purple Triangles (25 minutes)

Surviving members of a family of Jehovah's Witnesses describe how they were persecuted as a religious group by the Nazi regime in Germany.

Return to the Warsaw Ghetto (60 minutes)

Three families return to Warsaw on the fiftieth anniversary of the Warsaw ghetto uprising. They come to terms with their past and pass on their experiences to their children.

Shoah (570 minutes)

Claude Lanzmann's epic of the Holocaust is a collection of eyewitness accounts from extermination camp survivors, German officials, and Holocaust scholar Raul Hilberg. (In French, with English subtitles.)

Shtetl: A Journal of the Holocaust (180 minutes)

A Holocaust survivor returns to his native village of Bransk in Poland, where the town's Jewish population disappeared in November 1942. The survivor and a local historian find evidence of Nazi crimes and Polish complicity.

The Story of Chaim Rumkowski and the Jews of the Łódź Ghetto (53 minutes)

The film examines the Jewish Council in the Łódź ghetto, its controversial chairman, Chaim Rumkowski, and the conditions of life in the ghetto.

Survivors of the Holocaust (70 minutes)

This documentary presents a small sample of the eyewitness survivor testimonies collected by Steven Spielberg's "Survivors of the Shoah Visual History Foundation" in Los Angeles.

Theresienstadt: Gateway to Auschwitz (58 minutes)

This documentary on Theresienstadt describes the ghetto as a transit camp for Jewish deportees en route to the extermination camps in Poland, and combines survivor memories, photographs, paintings, and drawings.

Terezin Diary (87 minutes)

Life in the ghetto of Terezin (Theresienstadt) is recounted by survivors who were children and young people during the Holocaust.

Tsvi Nussbaum: A Boy from Warsaw (50 minutes)

This film recounts the life of Tsvi Nussbaum, the boy who was immortalized in the famous photograph taken in the Warsaw ghetto in 1943, including his arrival in the ghetto, the circumstances surrounding the photograph, his survival and life today.

Voices of the Children (80 minutes)

This story of three children imprisoned in Theresienstadt includes interviews with survivors and excerpts from their diaries and drawings from the war years. They attend a performance of the children's opera *Brundibar* and recall its significance during the Holocaust.

The Warsaw Ghetto (51 minutes)

This documentary of the Warsaw ghetto, taken from official films and photographs made by the German army, the SS and the Gestapo, examines the creation of the ghetto, everyday life, and the uprising.

We Were Marked with a Big "A" (Wir hatten ein grosses "A" am Bein) (44 minutes)

Three gay survivors tell of their arrest and incarceration in concentration camps by the Nazi regime. (In German, with English subtitles.)

Witness to the Holocaust (130 minutes)

This two-part program, narrated by Holocaust survivors, deals with the rise of the Nazis, ghetto life, deportations, resistance, the Final Solution, and the liberation of the camps.

ANTISEMITISM

The Cross and the Star (55 minutes)

This documentary examines the relationship of the Christian churches to Nazi persecution and mass murder of the Jews.

Genocide (60 minutes)

This documentary traces the history of Jews in Europe, and Jew-hatred from antiquity to modern antisemitism, and examines the Holocaust through photographs, archival film, and eyewitness accounts.

The Longest Hatred: The History of Anti-Semitism (150 minutes)

Part I of this documentary explores the history of Jew-hatred, from its ancient roots to Nazi Germany. Part II considers anti-Jewish feelings in the Islamic world.

Shadow on the Cross (52 minutes)

After reviewing the early anti-Jewish teachings of the Christian churches, this documentary examines the support of institutional Christianity in Germany for much of the Nazi agenda.

WORLD REACTION, RESCUE

America and the Holocaust: Deceit and Indifference (60 minutes)

America's response to the persecution and mass murder of the Jews from the Crystal Night pogrom to the liberation of the camps reveals indifference and anti-semitism in the Roosevelt administration.

Avenue of the Just (55 minutes)

This documentary contains interviews with "righteous Gentiles" who saved Jewish lives during the Holocaust. Among them are those who hid Anne Frank and her family.

The Courage to Care (30 minutes)

This video profiles several non-Jews who risked their lives to hide Jews.

A Debt to Honor (30 minutes)

Italians remember how they saved more than 30,000 Jews following the German occupation of northern Italy in 1943, hiding Jews in convents, bringing them across the Swiss border, and forging false identity papers.

The Doomed Voyage of the St. Louis (50 minutes)

Almost 1,000 German Jewish refugees aboard the liner *St. Louis*, refused entry into Cuba, the United States, and other countries in 1939, must return to Europe.

Missing Hero: Raoul Wallenberg (52 minutes)

The testimonies of people who knew Raoul Wallenberg in Budapest in 1944 tell of his untiring efforts to save as many Hungarian Jews as he could by issuing them Swedish passports.

My Knees Were Jumping: Remembering the Kindertransports (76 minutes)

This documentary examines the evacuation of almost 10,000 Jewish children from Germany, Austria, Czechoslovakia, and Poland to Great Britain during the nine months preceding the outbreak of World War II.

The Other Side of Faith (27 minutes)

Filmed on location in Poland, this first-person narrative tells the story of a sixteen-year-old Catholic girl who hid thirteen Jews in the attic of her home for two and a half years.

A Place to Save Your Life: The Shanghai Jews (52 minutes)

This film, using interviews with survivors and old photographs, documents the movement of some 17,000 European Jews to Shanghai, a place that did not require immigration visas.

The Power of Conscience: The Danish Resistance and the Rescue of the Jews
(55 minutes)

Based on interviews and archival film, this documentary shows how ordinary Danish citizens committed sabotage against German forces in Denmark, and smuggled almost all of Denmark's 7,200 Jews to Sweden.

Raoul Wallenberg: Between the Lines (85 minutes)

This documentary of Raoul Wallenberg's efforts to save Hungarian Jews in 1944 highlights his diplomatic maneuvers and protests to German authorities in Budapest.

Rescue in Scandinavia (56 minutes)

This documentary describes how Scandinavians improvised an underground railroad to smuggle Jews and others to neutral Sweden.

The Righteous Enemy (84 minutes)

Italian officers and government officials in Italian-occupied areas in Europe resist German efforts to deport Jews to the extermination camps.

Schindler (82 minutes)

This account of Oskar Schindler and his actions that saved his Jewish workers is based on the testimony of both grateful survivors and skeptical witnesses.

They Risked Their Lives: Rescuers of the Holocaust (54 minutes)

Denying that they did anything heroic, more than a hundred Gentiles from twelve countries discuss their efforts to save Jews during the Holocaust

Weapons of the Spirit (90 minutes plus 30-minute interview)

This documentary remembers the residents of the French village of Le Chambon-sur-Lignon, whose efforts during World War II saved some 5,000 Jews. A 38-minute version of this film is available.

Who Shall Live and Who Shall Die? (90 minutes)

Based on interviews and archival and newsreel film footage, this documentary examines the general unwillingness of Americans to rescue European Jews during World War II.

Zegota: A Time to Remember (52 minutes)

This is the story of the little-known Polish resistance organization, Zegota, which provided money, forged documents and other forms of help to Polish Jews during the Holocaust.

HITLER, NAZIS, WAR CRIMES TRIALS

Adolf Eichmann — Hitler's Master of Death: Biography (50 minutes)

This documentary examines Adolf Eichmann's role in the Final Solution against the backdrop of his career as a traveling salesman, Nazi file clerk, and SS officer, followed by his years hiding in South America and his capture and trial in Israel.

East of War (117 minutes)

Former German soldiers who witnessed atrocities in the Soviet Union during World War II exhibit shame, and others fanaticism, as they tell of shootings of Russian prisoners-of-war, the murder of Jews, and the rape and abuse of women.

The Fatal Attraction of Adolf Hitler (90 minutes)

This documentary includes home movies of Hitler's private life and focuses on his charismatic appeal, his rise to power, and the social and economic conditions in Germany that made it possible.

Hitler: The Whole Story (150 minutes)

Based on Joachim Fest's biography, this three-cassette series chronicles Hitler's rise, plans for global conquest, the Final Solution, and Germany's defeat.

Hitler's Henchmen (300 minutes)

Six cassettes profile the lives of six of Hitler's closest collaborators: Hermann Göring, Heinrich Himmler, Joseph Goebbels, Rudolf Hess, Albert Speer, and Karl Dönitz.

Hotel Terminus: The Life and Times of Klaus Barbie (267 minutes)

This award-winning documentary traces the forty-year manhunt for Klaus Barbie, the SS interrogator known as the "Butcher of Lyons."

The Hunt for Adolf Eichmann (100 minutes)

This film examines Adolf Eichmann's career in the Gestapo, his flight to South America after World War II, and his trial in Jerusalem.

In the Shadow of the Reich: Nazi Medicine (40 minutes)

This documentary considers the role of German physicians in Nazi racial and eugenics policies, including the forced sterilization of the handicapped, and medical experiments on Jews, Gypsies, and other victims.

The Legacy of Nuremberg (50 minutes)

This program examines the question of amnesty versus retribution in the Nuremberg trials and relates Nuremberg and the question of war crimes to contemporary issues such as Bosnia and South Africa.

The Life of Adolf Hitler (Das Leben von Adolf Hitler) (111 minutes)

This combination of film and photographs presents a visual history of Hitler's early life, his rise to power, and his dictatorship over Germany from 1933 to 1945.

The Mystery of Josef Mengele (50 minutes)

Josef Mengele successfully eluded justice after World War II with the help of his family and an underground Nazi network. This documentary describes him, his crimes, and his life as a fugitive.

Nazi War Crimes Trials (67 minutes)

This film, made in 1945, uses newsreels and film footage to show the fates of Göring, Hess, Schacht, Streicher, Keitel, and other Nazis brought to trial after World War II.

The Nazis: A Warning from History (300 minutes)

This is a visual history of the Third Reich, combining photographs, archival film footage, testimony by Holocaust survivors and war criminals, and interviews with historians.

Nuremberg (76 minutes)

Produced by the United States War Department, this documentary recounts the history of Hitler's rise to power against the backdrop of the Nuremberg War Crimes Trials. Film footage used by the prosecution is mixed with scenes from the trial.

The Nuremberg Trial: Landmark Cases (50 minutes)

This overview of the Nuremberg Trials uses wartime and trial film footage and commentary to explain the purpose of the trials, review the charges, profile the defendants, examine the tactics of the prosecution and defense, and assess the trials' verdicts and legacy.

Of Pure Blood (100 minutes)

This film examines eugenics, Nazi racism, and the attempt to create a "master race."

The Rise and Fall of Adolf Hitler (150 minutes)

This six-volume video documentary covers Hitler's life from his childhood to his downfall in 1945. It contains interviews with people who served under him, as well as rare film footage.

Witnesses to the Holocaust: The Trial of Adolf Eichmann (90 minutes)

This film looks at the trial of Adolf Eichmann in Jerusalem in 1960, combining his courtroom testimony, witness testimony, and archival film to illustrate his role in the Final Solution.

NAZI PROPAGANDA

The Eye of the Dictator: Propaganda and the Nazis (55 minutes)

This documentary considers the use of film, particularly the weekly newsreel, to inform, disinform, and persuade Germans during the Third Reich, against the backdrop of Goebbels's use of film as propaganda.

The Eternal Jew (Der ewige Jude) (62 minutes)

Directed by Fritz Hippler, this pseudo-scientific Nazi propaganda documentary made in 1940 represents Jewish life and history from the perspective of traditional European antisemitism and Nazi ideology to promote hatred of Jews. (In German, with English subtitles.)

Germany Awake (Deutschland Erwache!) (90 minutes)

This is a collection of clips of motion pictures produced in Nazi Germany to promote Nazi ideology and policies, including antisemitism, euthanasia, hatred of democracy and Marxism, foreign and military policies, and more. (In German, with English subtitles.)

Goebbels: Master of Propaganda (50 minutes)

This documentary focuses on Joseph Goebbels and how he pioneered many of the techniques used by the media today, including the use of political propaganda as mass entertainment.

Good Morning Mr. Hitler (54 minutes)

This color film, shot by an amateur filmmaker in July 1939, captures a three-day Nazi cultural festival that included concerts, dancing, exhibitions, and a huge parade. Elderly Germans watch themselves in the film and remember their lives during the Third Reich.

Triumph of the Will (Triumph des Willens) (80 minutes)

This abridged version of the famous documentary film of the 1934 Nazi Party rally at Nuremberg demonstrates the methods used by Hitler's regime to inspire loyalty. Filmmaker Leni Riefenstahl's innovative techniques raised questions about her role in the Nazi terror. (In German, with English subtitles.)

LIBERATION, DISPLACED PERSONS

Displaced Persons (48 minutes)

This documentary looks at the 250,000 homeless Jews in Europe at the end of World War II and the efforts of some to get to Palestine.

Holocaust: Liberation of Auschwitz (18 minutes)

In this documentary about the Soviet liberation of Auschwitz, the Soviet camera-man shares his impressions of what he saw.

The Last Sea (90 minutes)

This film examines the movement of Jewish Holocaust survivors from Europe to Palestine after 1945.

Liberation (100 minutes)

This documentary examines Germany's two wars, for world power and against the Jews, as well as survival under German occupation and liberation.

Liberation 1945: Testimony (76 minutes)

Jewish survivors and Allied liberators recall how they felt at liberation and describe camp conditions and the problems encountered by the medical relief teams.

The Liberation of KZ Dachau (94 minutes)

This documentary chronicles the American liberation of Dachau, as veterans speak about their reactions to the horrors they discovered.

The Long Way Home (120 minutes)

This Academy Award-winning documentary describes the plight of Jewish Displaced Persons between the end of World War II to the establishment of Israel in 1948.

Opening the Gates of Hell: American Liberators of the Nazi Concentration Camps (45 minutes)

U.S. veterans, including an army doctor, an army psychiatrist, an army chaplain, and several combat soldiers, share their memories of the liberation of the camps at Dachau, Mauthausen, and Nordhausen.

We Were There: Jewish Liberators of the Nazi Concentration Camps (40 minutes)

This documentary deals with American Jewish soldiers and their encounters with the Holocaust as they liberated the camps.

GERMAN RESISTANCE

The Restless Conscience (113 minutes)

This documentary examines the motivations, actions, and fate of those Germans who resisted Nazi tyranny, and focuses on the resisters' belief in an individual's moral responsibility to oppose evil.

Traitors to Hitler (69 minutes)

This documentary focuses on the plot to assassinate Hitler on July 20, 1944. It is based on rare film footage of the infamous show trials of the conspirators against Hitler.

POSTWAR NEO-NAZISM

"The Truth Shall Make Us Free": Inside the Neo-Nazi Network (51 minutes)

This film, the work of a German journalist pretending to be a neo-Nazi who joins the inner circle of the neo-Nazi movement in contemporary Germany, provides disturbing insight into racial and religious hatred among the radical right in Germany today.

Drama, Docudrama

Angry Harvest (Bittere Ernte) (102 minutes)

Set in German-occupied Poland, a Christian farmer saves a young Jewish woman. Their relationship becomes one of interdependence and love, but ultimately ends in tragedy. (In German, with English subtitles.)

The Assisi Underground (115 minutes)

Based on a true story, Catholic priests in Italy help Jews escape via an underground railroad that smuggles them out of German-occupied northern Italy.

The Boat is Full (Das Boot ist voll) (104 minutes)

Switzerland's decision not to admit any more refugees from German-occupied Europe is the backdrop for this drama about a group of Jewish refugees in Switzerland trying to avoid deportation back to Germany. (In German, with English subtitles.)

The Diary of Anne Frank (170 minutes)

This film, based on the Pulitzer-Prize winning play, dramatizes the story of Anne Frank and her family during the Holocaust.

Escape from Sobibór (120 minutes)

This is the 1987 dramatization of the uprising and prisoner escape that took place at the Sobibór extermination camp in 1943.

Europa Europa (100 minutes)

A German Jewish teenager survives World War II and the Holocaust by concealing his identity, living as an Aryan, and spending much of the war in the Hitler Youth. (In Polish and German, with English subtitles.)

Exodus (213 minutes)

This film, based on the novel by Leon Uris, is the story of Holocaust survivors and their determination to enter Palestine shortly after World War II.

The Fifth Horseman Is Fear (Ja, spravedlnost) (100 minutes)

A Jewish doctor in German-occupied Czechoslovakia, forbidden to practice medicine, roams the streets of Prague searching for morphine to treat a wounded resistance fighter he has hidden from German authorities. (In Czech, with English subtitles.)

Fragments of Isabella (80 minutes)

A young Hungarian Jewish woman and her sisters, imprisoned in Auschwitz, struggle to survive, and they escape from a death march.

The Garden of the Finzi-Continis (Il giardino dei Finzi-Contini) (94 minutes)

Set in Italy in the late 1930s, this Academy Award-winning film examines the gradual demise of an aristocratic Jewish family as a result of Mussolini's antisemitic laws of 1938. (In Italian, with English subtitles.)

Goodbye, Children (Au Revoir les Enfants) (104 minutes)

Two schoolboys, one Jewish and one Catholic in German-occupied France, attend a boarding school in which several Jewish children are hiding. (In French, with English subtitles.)

Hanna's War (148 minutes)

This is the true story of Hannah Senesh, a Palestinian Jewish woman, who volunteers for a suicide mission to rescue Jews in German-occupied Hungary. She is captured, tortured, and executed.

Holocaust (450 minutes)

This 1978 Emmy Award-winning television series is a fictional account of two families, one Jewish and one German, and their very different fates in Nazi Germany between 1935 and 1945.

In the Presence of Mine Enemies (96 minutes)

In the Warsaw ghetto in 1942, a rabbi tells the ghetto inhabitants to pray, while young people arm themselves for a revolt.

Jacob the Liar (Jakob der Lügner) (95 minutes)

Jakob Heym, a Jew in a ghetto in Poland, overhears news of a nearby Russian victory on a German radio. He tells his neighbors the good news and feels obligated to continue providing his friends with more "good news" that he invents in order to give them hope. (In German, with English subtitles. An American remake starring Robin Williams was released in 1999.)

Jud Süss (100 minutes)

The notorious Nazi propaganda film depicts a Jew who rises to power in eighteenth-century Württemberg by abusing "Aryans." The physical features and personality traits of the Jews in the film are grossly exaggerated to fit traditional antisemitic and Nazi stereotypes. (In German, with English subtitles.)

Judgement at Nuremberg (187 minutes)

This Academy Award-winning dramatization of the proceedings of the Nuremberg trials addresses the questions of morality, legality, and responsibility.

Korczak (120 minutes)

Dr. Janusz Korczak, Polish physician and author, protects a group of abandoned children in the Warsaw ghetto. Refusing a chance to save his own life in 1942, he accompanies the children to Treblinka. (In Polish, with English subtitles.)

Les Miserables (175 minutes)

An illiterate truck driver helps a Jewish family escape to Switzerland as a member of the family reads Hugo's *Les Miserables* aloud to the driver. Inspired by the character of Jean Valjean, the driver becomes a hero. The film adapts Victor Hugo's themes to German-occupied France. (In French, with English subtitles.)

Life is Beautiful (La Vita è bella) (125 minutes)

This Academy Award-winning film uses humor in the story of a Jewish man, his non-Jewish wife, and their young son who are deported from Italy. The father constructs an elaborate story of their situation in the camp in order to conceal the danger from his son. (In Italian, with English subtitles.)

The Man in the Glass Booth (117 minutes)

An industrialist is brought to trial for Nazi war crimes. Reminiscent of the trial of Adolf Eichmann in Jerusalem in 1960, he is protected in the courtroom by a bulletproof glass booth.

The Man Who Captured Eichmann (96 minutes)

This is the story of the Israeli capture of Adolf Eichmann in Argentina in 1960. Eichmann reveals to his captors his devotion to Hitler, to following orders, and to doing his duty efficiently.

Murderers among Us: The Simon Wiesenthal Story (170 minutes)

This film about survivor and famed Nazi hunter Simon Wiesenthal focuses on his experiences in the camps, and his efforts after the war to gather evidence against Nazi war criminals.

Oppermann (238 minutes)

The Oppermanns are an upper middle-class German-Jewish family in Berlin during the last months of the Weimar Republic and the early months of the Third Reich attempting to survive the growing pressures of Hitler's regime. (In German, with English subtitles.)

The Pawnbroker (116 minutes)

As a result of his experiences, a Holocaust survivor who works in Harlem as a pawnbroker is beyond feeling and caring, and devoid of faith in humanity.

The Quarrel (90 minutes)

Two Holocaust survivors, former Hasidic students and best friends, accidentally meet in a Montreal Park in 1948. One has become a rabbi, the other a skeptical journalist.

Revolt of Job (*Job lazadasa*) (105 minutes)

This is the story of a Jewish couple in Hungary during World War II with an adopted non-Jewish boy. Their relationship as a family develops as the extermination of the Jews closes in around them in 1944. (In Hungarian, with English subtitles.)

The Rose Garden (111 minutes)

A man is on trial for attacking an elderly man whom he recognizes as the former commandant of a concentration camp during World War II. The attacker survived the Holocaust, but his family did not.

Schindler's List (197 minutes)

This is the story of German industrialist and Nazi Oskar Schindler, who saved some 1,100 Jewish workers from certain death.

Ship of Fools (149 minutes)

The passengers on a German ship bound from Mexico to Germany are a microcosm of German society in the early 1930s, as the political conflicts relating to anti-semitism and the Jews are played out.

The Shop on Main Street (*Obchod Na Korze*) (128 minutes)

In German-occupied Slovakia in 1942, an elderly Jewish shop owner and a passive carpenter whom the Germans appoint as her "Aryan controller" become friends.

The Academy Award-winning film reveals the carpenter's confusion and spiritual crisis when the elderly Jewish woman and the rest of the Jews are deported. (In Slovak, with English subtitles.)

Sophie's Choice (150 minutes)

A Polish Catholic woman and mother survives Auschwitz, but her memories and guilt over the deaths of her two children haunt her in her new life in the United States.

Voyage of the Damned (134 minutes)

This film is based on the true story of the ill-fated voyage of the ship *St. Louis* from Germany to Havana with 937 German Jewish refugees in 1939.

The Wannsee Conference (87 minutes)

This is a reenactment of the Wannsee Conference of January 20, 1942, at which leaders of the SS, the Gestapo, the Nazi Party, and the bureaucracy set in motion the Final Solution. (In German, with English subtitles.)

The White Rose (*Die Weisse Rose*) (108 minutes)

Five German students and their professor, who formed the anti-Nazi student resistance group known as the "White Rose," are captured and executed. (In German, with English subtitles.)

ELECTRONIC RESOURCES

H-Net Discussion Networks

H-Net: Humanities and Social Sciences OnLine comprises more than one hundred E-mail lists from different disciplines in the humanities and social sciences. They function as electronic discussion networks linking professors, teachers, students, and others interested in the exchange of information and ideas on research, teaching, book and multimedia reviews, and controversies new and old. The computing center of H-Net resides at Michigan State University, but H-Net officers, editors, and subscribers come from around the world. H-Net discussion networks also provide hyperlinks to a wide variety of Internet sites of related interest.

The following H-Net discussion networks deal with the Holocaust. Readers interested in subscribing to any of these can obtain information and subscription procedures through H-Net's Web site: http://www.h-net.msu.edu/

H-Antisemitism: *Antisemitism* (http://www.h-net.msu.edu/~antis)

H-Antisemitism encourages scholarly discussion of the history of antisemitism and provides diverse bibliographical, research, and teaching aids. It offers subscribers scholarly reviews of books, discussion of topics and issues, occasional papers, and academic announcements. Subscribers are academics and nonacademics.

H-German: *German History* (http://www.h-net.msu.edu/~german)

H-German editors and subscribers are academics in the field of modern German history. Considerable attention is devoted to antisemitism, Nazi Germany, and the Holocaust. It offers exchanges of information and ideas on scholarship and teaching, book and article reviews, academic job postings, a bulletin board for housing in Germany or the United States, and a bulletin board for academic conferences. It maintains an electronic archive of documents in the original German and in English translation.

H-Holocaust: *Holocaust Studies* (http://www.h-net.msu.edu/~holoweb)

H-Holocaust serves academics and nonacademics, making available bibliographical, research, and teaching information and aids. Research issues, teaching methods, historiography, and general discussion constitute most of its business. H-Holocaust also commissions book reviews and posts academic announcements concerning scholarly conferences and grants.

H-Judaic: *Judaica, Jewish History* (http://www.h-net.msu.edu/~judaic)

H-Judaic is a Jewish Studies discussion network for academics and nonacademics. It promotes discussion of research and teaching issues and publishes book reviews and a Jewish Studies Newsletter. Its Jewish Studies Resources Library contains documents, course syllabuses, and a list of scholars by area of specialization.

H-Review: *H-Net Book Reviews* (http://www.h-net.msu.edu/reviews)

H-Net Reviews is an online scholarly review journal. Its book and multimedia reviews enable reviewers, authors, and subscribers to engage in discussions of the books and reviews online. Reviews are posted to individual H-Net discussion networks and subsequently posted to H-Review and placed in an archive on this site.

2G-Legacy: *Children and Grandchildren of Jewish Holocaust Survivors* (http:/www.flash.net/~reyzl/2G-Legacy.html)

This unmoderated network is dedicated to greater awareness among and education of second- and third-generation children of Holocaust survivors, justice for Holocaust victims, and the revival of Jewish-Yiddish culture.

CD-ROMs

REFERENCE

The Encyclopedia Judaica (Windows)

This CD-ROM includes the sixteen-volume edition of the printed Encyclopedia, the Year Books and the Decennials that followed, and a series of selected updates.

Historical Atlas of the Holocaust (Windows)

This is the CD-ROM version of the United States Holocaust Memorial Museum's *Historical Atlas of the Holocaust*. It includes all 221 maps in the book version, and photographs of many sites that are not available in the book. Toolbars enable users to find the maps they seek, and additional toolbars refer users to other options including photographs and explanatory texts.

HISTORY

The Complete Maus: A Survivor's Tale (Mac, Windows)

This CD-ROM contains Art Spiegelman's Pulitzer Prize-winning two-volume comic book that portrays the Jews as mice and the Nazis as cats, with historical commentary by the author linked to the text of *Maus*. It includes audio interviews with Spiegelman's father, color sketches, discussions of the creative process behind the work, and historical documents such as maps, photographs, prisoner drawings, and video clips of Holocaust sites in Germany and Poland.

The Holocaust (Windows)

This is an interactive CD-ROM with a multimedia database, organized primarily around various ghettos and camps. It contains graphic photos, letters of victims, newsreels from the period, reference material, and music.

Images from the Holocaust: A Literary Anthology (Windows)

This is the CD-ROM version of the book edited by Brown, Stephens, and Rubin. It presents a combination of fiction, non-fiction, poetry, and drama that explores the experiences of victims and survivors.

"Into That Dark Night": Nazi Germany and the Jews, 1933–1939 (Windows)

This CD-ROM examines the first six years of Nazi rule, including the coalescence of the regime, social developments and public opinion, antisemitic policies, and Jewish reactions. There is a database with a library, archives, a timeline, a lexicon, and maps.

Lest We Forget: A History of the Holocaust (Mac, Windows)

This CD-ROM contains some 250 pages of text, supplemented by a large collection of archival film and audio clips, some 500 captioned photographs from the Yad Vashem Museum in Jerusalem, detailed biographies of important persons, propaganda posters, interactive maps, charts and timelines.

The Music Survives: "Degenerate" Music Suppressed by the Third Reich (Windows)

This CD contains a sample of works by composers banned by the Nazi regime. There is a forty-minute documentary that examines how and why these composers were labeled "degenerate" by Hitler's regime.

My Brother's Keeper (Mac, Windows)

Through his words and paintings, survivor Israel Birnbaum describes the brutality, injustice, indifference, and heroism he witnessed. The program is organized as a tutorial for students, with quizzes that test students' knowledge. It contains the full text of Birnbaum's book of the same name, the text of *Hitler's War against the Jews* by Lucy Dawidowicz and David Altschuler, and supplementary texts.

Return to Life: The Story of Holocaust Survivors (Windows)

This CD-ROM explores the plight of Jewish survivors immediately after World War II. Combining survivor testimony, archival photographs and film footage, and an analytical narration, the program examines the difficulties faced by survivors.

Stories from the Warsaw Ghetto (Mac, Windows)

This is a collage of stories, images, narrative, and facts examining Jewish life in Warsaw during the first half of the twentieth century. It focuses on the lives of those Jews who played key roles in the Warsaw ghetto resistance, and includes maps, biographies, and a chronology of events.

Survivors: Testimonies of the Holocaust (Mac, Windows)

Produced by Steven Spielberg's Shoah Foundation and narrated by Leonardo DiCaprio and Winona Ryder, this CD-ROM draws upon the stories of four survivors, Bert, Paula, Silvia, and Sol.

The Yellow Star: The Persecution of the Jews in Europe from 1933 to 1945
(Mac, Windows)

Based on the Academy Award-nominated film and introduced by Simon Wiesenthal, this CD-ROM provides access to video clips and a limited amount of text and glossary information. There is an interactive timeline, and video presentations of events.

Holocaust-Related Music

This is a sample of Holocaust-related music, recorded and available on CD. The number of such recordings is growing rapidly. Most of these musicians and some of their music are associated with the ghetto/camp at Terezin (Theresienstadt), a "model camp" established by Nazi Germany in Czechoslovakia during World War II to mislead the world about the persecution and mass murder of the Jews. Many prominent Jewish artists and musicians were sent there, and a vibrant cultural life flourished despite the terrible conditions. Most were eventually deported from Terezin to Auschwitz where they perished.

Much of the Holocaust-related music available today on CD was composed at Terezin. The most prominent of the composers in Terezin were Czech Jews who saw many of their earlier compositions, along with a great deal of other music, placed in the category of music the Nazis called *entartete Musik* ("degenerate music") and banned in Germany. The Germans imprisoned other composers and musicians at other camps, and created orchestras made up of prisoner-musicians who played for camp authorities or for fellow- prisoners as they were marched to gas chambers.

This section is divided into three parts. The first lists the major Terezin composers and the works they composed while prisoners in Terezin or elsewhere. They all perished. The second contains collections of songs sung in ghettos, camps, or among Jewish partisans. The third offers music written or performed after World War II to commemorate the war and the Holocaust.

COMPOSERS

Pavel Haas (1899–1944): Born in Brno in Moravia, Haas was a student of Leos Janacek and wrote a number of instrumental and orchestral works during the 1920s and 1930s, as well as during his internment at Theresienstadt during World War II. His compositions include chamber, piano, and symphonic music. He was deported to Auschwitz in October 1944, where he was killed.
Musica Rediviva: Pavel Haas (Orfeo/186.961) (Stuttgart Wind Quintet)

> This CD includes Haas's "Quintet for Winds, op. 10," "Suite for Piano, op. 13," "The Chosen One, op. 8," and "Suite for Oboe & Piano, op. 17," which was written in response to the German occupation of Czechoslovakia in 1939.

Gideon Klein (1919–1945): Born in Prerov, Czechoslovakia, Klein studied at the Master School in Prague and graduated from there in 1939 as a pianist. His compositions include chamber and choral music, and piano works. He was incarcerated in three camps during World War II. After time at Theresienstadt and Auschwitz, he died at the Fürstengrube camp in January 1945.

Gideon Klein: Piano Sonata, Fantasie & Fugue, String Trio, Choral Works (Koch International/37230-2H1) (Group for New Music; Czech Philharmonic Choir; Allan Sternfeld, piano)

> This CD includes Klein's "Sonata for Piano," "Trio for Violin, Viola, & Cello," "Fantasie & Fugue for String Quartet," and "Madrigals."

Hans Krasa (1899–1944): Born in Prague, Krasa graduated from the German Music Academy in Prague in 1921. He was attracted to the music of Stravinsky and other modern composers. His compositions include chamber and choral music and opera. He was imprisoned in Theresienstadt and deported to Auschwitz in October 1944, where he perished.

Hans Krasa (Koch International/37151-2H1) (Group for New Music; Prague Symphony Youth Chorus)

> This CD includes Krasa's "Brundibar" (A Children's Opera), "Three Songs for Baritone, Clarinet, Viola, & Cello," "Theme with Variations for String Quartet," "Dance for Violin, Viola, & Cello," "Passacaglia & Fugue for String Trio," and "Anna's Song."

Viktor Ullmann (1898–1944): Born in Tesin, Czechoslovakia, Ullmann studied at the Prague Conservatory and with Arnold Schoenberg in Vienna. He composed opera, piano works, songs, and symphonic music. Imprisoned in Theresienstadt in 1942, he was deported to Auschwitz in October 1944, where he perished.

The Emperor of Atlantis (*Der Kaiser von Atlantis*) (Opera) (Arabesque/ARA-6681) (Vermont Symphony Orchestra and Chorus/Robert DeCormier)

Musica Rediviva - Viktor Ullmann Lieder (Orfeo/380952) (Axel Bauni, piano; Christine Schäfer, soprano; Yaron Windmüller, baritone; Liat Himmelhaber, mezzo-soprano)

> This CD includes Ullmann's songs, some composed at Terezin (marked with an asterisk). "Geistliche Lieder, op. 20, nos. 1–6," "Liederbuch des Hafis, op. 30," "Drei Sonette, op. 29, nos. 1–3," "Six Sonnets de Louize Labe, op. 34, nos. 1–6," "Der Mensch und sein Tag, op. 47,*" "Immer inmitten,*" "Vor der Ewigkeit," "Chinesische Lieder, nos. 1–2,*" "Drei Lieder nach C. F. Meyer, nos. 1–3," "Liebeslieder, op. 18, nos. 1–5", "Lieder, op. 17, nos. 1–6," and "Three Hölderlin Lieder.*"

Viktor Ullmann — Sonatas for Piano (Koch International/7109) (Robert Kolben and Edith Kraus, piano; Group for New Music)

This CD contains the last three of Ullmann's *Sonatas for Piano*, composed at Theresienstadt before he was deported to Auschwitz, and a quartet for strings. One sonata, no. 6, is performed by Edith Kraus, who survived Theresienstadt. It includes Ullmann's "Sonata for Piano no. 5, op. 45," "Sonata for Piano no. 6, op. 49," "Sonata for Piano no. 7," and "Quartet for Strings no. 3, op. 46."

Erwin Schulhoff (1894–1942): Born in Prague, Schulhoff studied at the Prague Conservatory, and then in Vienna, Leipzig, and Cologne. He studied composition with Max Reger in Leipzig. As a pianist, he gave recitals with an emphasis on new music, often playing as a jazz pianist. Imprisoned by the Germans in 1941, he eventually died of tuberculosis in the Wülzburg camp in 1942. Schulhoff's compositions include chamber music, piano works, symphonies, operas, and jazz. Virtually all of his compositions were written before his imprisonment. He wrote his Sixth and Seventh symphonies in 1940 and 1941, and was sketching his Eighth Symphony when he died. The following CDs contain a sample of Schulhoff's piano, chamber music, symphonic, and opera compositions.

Schulhoff Concertos alla Jazz (London Classics/444819) (German Chamber Philharmonic Orchestra; Hawthorne String Quartet; Erwin Schulhoff, piano)

This CD contains Schulhoff's "Concerto for Piano and Small Orchestra, op. 43," "Double Concerto for Flute and Piano," "Concertino for String Quartet & Winds," "Jazz Etudes for Piano nos. 2, 3, 4," "Esquisses de Jazz nos. 4, 5," and "Rag Music/Partita for Piano nos. 3, 4, 7, 8."

Flammen (Opera) (London Classics/444630) (German Symphony Orchestra Berlin/John Mauceri, Berlin RIAS Chamber Chorus)

Schulhoff: Piano Works (Supraphon/111870) (Tomas Visek, piano)

This CD includes Schulhoff's "Esquisses de Jazz," "Ostinato for Piano," "Music for Piano, op. 35," "Inventions for Piano," "Themen (10) for Piano, op. 30," and "Jazz Etudes (5) for Piano."

String Quartets; String Quartet — String Sextet (Capriccio/10463 & 10539) (Petersen Quartet)

These two CDs include Schulhoff's "Quartet for Strings nos. 1, 2," "Five Pieces for String Quartet," "Sextet for 2 Violins, 2 Violas, & 2 Cellos," "Duo for Violin & Cello," and "Sonata for Violin Solo."

Schulhoff: Symphonies 4, 6 (Supraphon/112162) (Prague Radio Symphony Orchestra/Vladimir Valek)

ANTHOLOGIES

Al S'fod — Do Not Lament. Hebrew and Jewish Instrumental and Vocal Works
(Koch/7173) (Group for New Music)

This CD contains instrumental and vocal music composed and performed by musicians at Terezin. They include David Grünfeld, Pavel Haas, Gideon Klein, Hugo Löwenthal, Zikmund Schul, Carlo Taube, Viktor Ullmann, and Vilem Zrzavy.

Composers from Theresienstadt: Pavel Haas & Karel Berman (Channel Classics/3191)
(Karel Berman, bass; Alfred Holocek, piano; Premsyl Charvat, piano)

This collection includes two pieces written by Karel Berman when he was imprisoned at Terezin: "Four Songs for Bass & Piano (Poupata)," and "Suite for Piano Solo (Terezin)." It also includes Pavel Haas's "Four Songs to the Text of Chinese Poetry." Berman survived and immigrated to Israel after the war.

Music Written in Terezin (Panton/710524-2) (Czech String Trio, & others)

This collection includes Gideon Klein's "Sonata for Piano" and "Trio for Violin, Viola, & Cello"; Viktor Ullmann's "Sonata for Piano no. 6, op. 49"; Hans Krasa's "Dance for Violin, Viola, & Cello"; and Pavel Haas's "Four Songs for Bass & Piano on Chinese Poetry" and "Suite for Oboe & Piano."

GHETTO, CAMP, RESISTANCE SONGS

Ghetto, camp, and resistance songs often contained new lyrics composed by ghetto and camp inhabitants or partisans, sung in Yiddish to existing popular or traditional melodies. They used such themes as hunger, freedom, revolt, revenge, helplessness, and death.

Hear Our Voices: Songs from the Ghettos and Camps (HaZamir/HZ-909CD) (Zamir Chorale of Boston)

This is a program of music written by young composers who were victims of the Holocaust. There are fourteen choral and solo pieces, sung mostly in Yiddish.

Hidden History: Songs of the Kovno Ghetto (United States Holocaust Memorial Museum/USHMM-03)

This is a collection of topical songs composed in the Kovno ghetto, primarily in Yiddish. They provide a portrait of ghetto life as seen by the inhabitants.

Latcho Drom (Caroline/1776)

This is a collection of Gypsy songs from the soundtrack of the film of the same name. One of the songs is titled *Auschwitz*.

Mordecai Gebirtig — Kraków Ghetto Notebook (Koch/37295-2H1)

This recording contains eighteen songs composed by well-known Yiddish folk poet Mordecai Gebirtig, who perished in the Kraków ghetto.

Partisans of Vilna: The Songs of World War II Jewish Resistance (Flying Fish/ FF-70450)

This is a collection of songs by and about Jewish resistance during World War II. Originally a soundtrack for the documentary film *Partisans of Vilna*, the songs are a mix of Russian-style folk music and Yiddish lyrics. They include the well-known partisan song "Zog Nit Keynmol."

Remember the Children (United States Holocaust Memorial Museum/HMCD-1901)

This is a collection of nineteen songs about children during the Holocaust, sung in Yiddish.

Rise Up and Fight: Songs of Jewish Partisans (United States Holocaust Memorial Museum/USHMM-02)

Eighteen songs sung by Jewish partisans during World War II, sung mainly in Yiddish by Theodore Bikel and others.

Songs from the Depths of Hell (Folkways/37700) (Aleksander Kulisiewicz)

These are Polish and German songs, some written by Kulisiewicz during his incarceration in Sachsenhausen.

We're Riding on Wooden Horses (Koch — unfinished)

This CD will contain songs by Ilse Weber, and cabaret chansons by Karel Svenk, Martin Roman, Otto Skutecky, Evald Weiss, and Adolf Strauss, all prisoners in Terezin.

COMMEMORATIVE MUSIC

Charles Davidson: *I Never Saw Another Butterfly* (Musicmasters/7049-2C) (American Symphony Orchestra and American Boys Choir)

A song cycle composed in the 1960s, set to fifteen poems written between 1941 and 1944 by child inmates of the Theresienstadt ghetto/concentration camp.

Steve Reich: *Different Trains* (Nonesuch/79176) (Kronos Quartet)

This is the composer's response to the Holocaust, written in 1988. It includes string instruments and electronic sounds, with background voices telling parts of stories.

Arnold Schoenberg: A *Survivor from Warsaw*, op. 46, in *Schönberg: Das Chorwerk*(Sony/44571) (BBC Symphony Orchestra/Pierre Boulez)

This short composition is one of the earliest commemorative pieces of music after the Holocaust. The composer wrote it shortly after the World War II, basing it on his conversations in Los Angeles with a survivor.

Dmitri Shostakovich: *Symphony no. 13 "Babi Yar"* (Teldec/90848) (New York Philharmonic Orchestra/Kurt Masur, and New York Choral Artists)

First performed in the Great Hall of the Moscow Conservatory in December 1962, this symphony is based on Yevgeny Yevtushenko's poetry. The first movement, *Babi Yar*, recalls the atrocities committed by the Germans at Babi Yar in 1941.

Franz Waxman: *The Song of Terezin*, and Eric Zeisl: *Requiem Ebraico* (London/LON-460211) (Radio Symphony Orchestra Berlin)

Waxman fled Nazi Germany in the 1930s and became a noted film composer in Hollywood. He composed *The Song of Terezin* in 1964–1965, inspired by a collection of poems, written by Jewish children in Theresienstadt. Zeisl fled his native Vienna in 1938, and also wrote music in Hollywood. His *Requiem Ebraico* is based on the 92nd Psalm.

Web Sites

The following Web sites are not located at organizations, museums, memorial sites, or research and education centers. Those institutions with sites are listed in the next section. The number of Holocaust sites is large and growing rapidly. We have limited this list to sites that are either comprehensive in what they offer or contain information with a particular focus. These sites are not annotated because their contents change routinely. Readers can easily connect to them and learn what each offers. Many have links to other Holocaust sites that readers may find useful.

COMPREHENSIVE WEB SITES

Cybrary of the Holocaust: http://www.remember.org

The History Place — World War II in Europe http://www.historyplace.com/worldwar2

The Holocaust — A Tragic Legacy http://library.advanced.org/12663

Holocaust/Shoah http://www.igc.apc.org/ddickerson/holocaust.html

I*EARN Holocaust Genocide Project: http://www.igc.apc.org/iearn/hgp/

Judaism and Jewish Resources: http://shamash.org/trb/judaism.html

L'Chaim — A Holocaust Web Project: http://www.charm.net/~rbennett/l'chaim.html

The Nizkor Project: http://www.nizkor.org/

The Simon Wiesenthal Center
Multimedia Learning Center Online: http://motlc.wiesenthal.com
A Teacher's Guide to the Holocaust: http://fcit.coedu.usf.edu/holocaust

WEB SITES WITH SPECIFIC FOCUS
Anne Frank
Anne Frank Online: http://www.annefrank.com

Auschwitz
An Auschwitz Alphabet: http://www.spectacle.org/695/ausch.html

Education and Holocaust Courses
March of the Living: http://www.bonder.com/march.html
Modern Jewish and Israel Studies — California State University, Chico
    http://www.csuchico.edu/mjis/
Social Studies School Services: Holocaust Resources:
    http://www.socialstudies.com/holo.html

Music
Terezin Music Memorial Project: http://www.tradoc.com/terezin

Nazi Propaganda
German Propaganda Archive, Calvin College:
    http://www.calvin.edu/academic/cas/gpa/

Neo Nazis/Holocaust Denial
Hate Watch: http://www.hatewatch.org
The Making of a Skinhead: http://www.wiesenthal.com/tj/index.html

Non-Jewish Victims
Holocaust: Non-Jewish Victims of the Shoah: http://www.holocaustforgotten.com
The Patrin Web Journal: Romani Culture and History:
    http://www.geocities.com/Paris/5121/holocaust.htm

Nuremberg War Crimes Trials
The Avalon Project at the Yale Law School:
    http://www.yale.edu/lawweb/avalon/imt/imt.htm
Harvard Law Web Site:
    http://www.law.harvard.edu/library/guides/nuremberg/index.html

Photograph Collections
The Holocaust Album: A Collection of Historical and Contemporary Photographs:
  http://www.rongreene.com/holo.html
Holocaust Pictures Exhibition: http://www.fmv.ulg.ac.be/schmitz/holocaust.html

Rescue
Raoul Wallenberg: http://www.raoul-wallenberg.com
To Save a Life — Stories of Jewish Rescue: http://sorrel.humboldt.edu/~rescuers/

Survivors
The Ernest and Elisabeth Cassutto Memorial Page — Survivors of the Holocaust:
  http://www.fred.net/nhhs/html3/dadmom.htm
Reach and Teach, Worldwide Holocaust Education:
  http://www.flock.mwci.net/~edsdanzig.html
Southern Institute for Education and Research at Tulane University:
  http://www.tulane.edu/~so-inst

Women
Women and the Holocaust: A Cyberspace of Their Own:
  http://www.interlog.com/~mighty

RESOURCE ORGANIZATIONS, MUSEUMS, AND MEMORIALS

This list does not include major public archives, although several of the institutions listed below contain important archival collections for Holocaust and Holocaust-related research as part of their varied functions. Many others are small, local Holocaust memorial and/or information centers. Included too are Jewish history museums and educational or research centers of which the Holocaust constitutes a part of their broader functions and programs. We have not annotated the institutions listed below. Describing the wide variety of resources and programs of many of them would take up considerable space. Readers can access most of them easily on the Internet to determine what each institution offers. Readers should be aware that Web site and E-mail addresses, as well as telephone and fax numbers, frequently change.

United States and Canada

American Friends of the Ghetto Fighters' House
P.O. Box 2153
765 Queen Anne Road
Teaneck, NJ 07666

Tel.: 201-836-1910
Fax: 201-801-0768
Web site: http://www.amfriendsgfh.org

American Gathering of Jewish Holocaust Survivors
122 West 30th Street
New York, NY 10001
Tel.: 212-239-4230
Fax: 212-279-2926
E-mail: mail@americangathering.org

Anne Frank Center, USA
584 Broadway
New York, NY 10012
Tel.: 212-431-7993
Fax: 212-431-8375
E-mail: afc@annefrank.com
Web site: http://www.annefrank.com/

Braun Center for Holocaust Studies
Anti-Defamation League of B'nai Brith
823 United Nations Plaza
New York, NY 10017
Tel.:212-885-7722
Fax: 212-867-0779
E-mail: ptw@pipeline.com
Web site: http://www.adl.org

CANDLES Holocaust Museum
1532 S. Third Street
Terre Haute, IN 47802
Tel.: 812-234-7881
E-mail: Candles@abcs.com
Web site: http://www.candles-museum.com/

Center for Holocaust Studies
University of Vermont
Burlington, VT 05405
Tel.: 802-656-1492
Fax: 802-656-8028
E-mail: kqjohnso@zoo.uvm.edu
Web site: http://www.uvm.edu/~grdept/holocaus.htm

Center for Holocaust and Genocide Studies
University of Minnesota
105 Jones Hall
27 Pleasant Street
Minneapolis, MN 55455-0125
Tel.: 612-624-0256
Fax: 612-624-4894
E-mail: feins001@tc.umn.edu
Web site: http://www.chgs.umn.edu

Dallas Memorial Center for Holocaust Studies
7900 Northaven Road
Dallas, TX 75230
Tel.: 214-750-4654
Fax: 214-750-4672
E-mail: dmchs@mail.swbell.net
Web site: http://www.dvjc.org/education/jec/holocaust.shtml

Facing History and Ourselves National Foundation, Inc.
16 Hurd Road
Brookline, Mass. 02146
Tel.: 617-232-1595
Fax: 617-232-0281
Web site: http://www.facing.org

The Florida Holocaust Museum
55 Fifth Street South
St. Petersburg, FL 33701
Tel.: 727-820-0100
Fax: 727-821-8435
Web site: http://www.flholocaustmuseum.org/

Fortunoff Video Archive for Holocaust Testimonies
P.O. Box 802840
Sterling Memorial Library
Yale University
New Haven, CT 06520-8240
Tel.: 203-432-1879
Fax: 203-432-1879
E-mail: fortunoff.archive@yale.edu
Web site: http://www.library.yale.edu/testimonies

The Holocaust Educational Foundation
3130 Big Tree Lane
Wilmette, IL 60091
Tel.: 847-676-3700
Fax: 847-676-3706
E-mail: HEF3@aol.com
Web site: http://www2.dsu.nodak.edu/users/dmeier/hef/hef.html

Holocaust Education and Memorial Center
4600 Bathurst Street
Toronto, Ontario
Canada M2R 3V2
Tel.: 416-635-2883
Fax: 416-635-0925
E-mail: holmem@ujafed.org
Web site: http://www.feduja.org

Holocaust/Genocide Project
International Education and Resource Network
475 Riverside Drive
Room 540
New York, NY 10115
Tel.: 212-870-2693
Fax: 212-870-2672
E-mail: hgp@copenfund.igc.apc.org
Web site: http://www.iearn.org/hgp/

Holocaust Museum Houston
Education Center and Memorial
5401 Caroline Street
Houston, TX 77004-6804
Tel.: 713-942-8000, ext. 107
Fax: 713-942-7953
E-mail: glendar@hmh.org
Web site: http://www.hmh.org

Holocaust Oral History Project
P.O. Box 1597
Burlingame, CA 94111-1597
Tel.: 650-570-6382

Fax: 650-570-6382
E-mail: hohp@mailexcite.com
Web site: http://members.tripod.com/~HOHP/index-2.html

Leo Baeck Institute
129 East 73rd Street
New York, NY 19921
Tel.: 212-744-6400
Fax: 212-988-1305
E-mail: lbi1@lbi.com
Web site: http://www.lbi.org/

The Montreal Holocaust Memorial Centre
1 Carre Cummings
Montreal, PQ
Canada H3W 1M6
Tel.: 514-345-2605
Fax: 514-344-2651
E-mail: mhmc@total.net

Museum of Jewish Heritage — A Living Memorial to the Holocaust
18 First Place, Battery Park City
1 Battery Park Plaza (mailing address)
New York, NY 10004-1484
Tel.: 212-968-1800
Fax: 212-573-9847
E-mail: webmaster@mjhnyc.org
Web site: http://www.mjhnyc.org

The National Center for Jewish Film
Mailstop 053
Brandeis University
Waltham, MA 02454-9110
Tel.: 781-736-8600
Fax: 781-736-2070
E-mail: ncjf@brandeis.edu
Web site: http://www.brandeis.edu/jewishfilm/index.html

Simon Wiesenthal Center for Holocaust Studies
Yeshiva University
9769 W. Pico Blvd.

Los Angeles, CA 90035-4792
Tel.: 310-553-9036
Fax: 310-277-5558
E-mail: info@wiesenthal.com
Web site: http://www.wiesenthal.com

Spertus Institute of Jewish Studies
Zell Center for Holocaust Studies
618 S. Michigan Ave.
Chicago, IL 60605
Tel.: 312-922-9012
Fax: 312-922-3934
E-mail: musm@spertus.eduE-mail
Web site: http://www.spertus.edu

Survivors of the Shoah Visual History Foundation
P.O. Box 3168
Los Angeles, CA 90078-3168
Tel.: 818-777-4673
Web site: http://www.vhf.org

Terezin Chamber Music Foundation
Astor Station
P.O. Box 206
Boston, MA 02123-0206
Tel.: 617-730-8998
Fax: 617-738-1212
E-mail: info@terezinmusic.org
Web site: http://www.terezinmusic.org

United States Holocaust Memorial Museum
100 Raoul Wallenberg Place, S.W.
Washington, D.C. 20024-2150
Tel.: 202-488-0400
Fax: 202-488-2690
E-mail: education@ushmm.org
Web site: http://www.ushmm.org/

The William E. Wiener Oral History Library
Dorot Jewish Division
New York Public Library

5th Ave. and 42nd Street
Room 84
New York, NY 10018
Tel.: 212-930-0603
Fax: 212-642-0141
E-mail: ngechlik@nypl.org

YIVO Institute for Jewish Research
555 West 57th Street
New York, NY 10019
Tel.: 212-246-6080
Fax: 212-292-1892
Web site: http://www.baruch.cuny.edu/yivo

Germany

Deutsches Historisches Museum Berlin
(German Historical Museum)
Unter den Linden 2
10117 Berlin
Germany
Tel.: 49-30-203040
Fax: 49-30-20304-509; 519
Web site: http://www.dhm.de

Dokumentations- und Kulturzentrum Deutscher Sinti und Roma
(Center for Documentation and Culture of German Sinti and Roma)
Bremeneckgasse 2
69117 Heidelberg
Germany
Tel.: 49-6221-981102
Fax: 49-6221-981190
Web site: http://www.lpb.bwue.de/gedenk/gedenk14.htm

Gedenkstätte Bergen-Belsen (Memorial)
29303 Lohheide
Germany
Tel.: 49-5051-6011
Fax: 49-5051-7396
Web site: http://www.hannovermagazin.de/regional/museum./berbel.html

Gedenkstätte Buchenwald (Memorial)
99427 Weimar
Germany
Tel.: 49-3643-4300
Fax: 49-3643-430100
Web site: http://www.buchenwald.de

Gedenkstätte Dachau (Memorial)
Alte Römerstrasse 75
85221 Dachau
Germany
Tel.: 49-8131-1741
Fax: 49-8131-2235
E-mail: gedenkstaette@infospace.de
Web site: http://www.infospace.de/gedenkstaette/index.html

Gedenkstätte Deutscher Widerstand
(Memorial to the German Resistance)
Stauffenbergstrasse 13-14
10785 Berlin
Germany
Tel.: 49-30-26995000
Fax: 49-30-26995010
E-mail: info@gdw-berlin.de
Web site: http://www.gdw-berlin.de

Gedenkstätte Hadamar (Memorial)
Mönchberg 8
65589 Hadamar
Germany
Tel.: 49-6433-9170
Fax: 49-6433-917175
Web site: http://www.dhm.de/ausstellungen/ns_gedenk/ad_53.htm

Gedenkstätte Haus der Wannsee-Konferenz
(Memorial of the House of the Wannsee Conference)
Am Grossen Wannsee 56-58
14109 Berlin
Germany
Tel.: 49-30-8050010
Fax: 49-30-80500127

E-mail: 100431.1332@compuserve.com

Web site: http://www.brandenburg.de/land/mwfk/kultur/deutsch/gedenkst/bln/
wannseed.html

Gedenkstätte Plötzensee (Memorial)
Hüttigpfad
13627 Berlin
Germany
Tel.: 49-30- 26995000
Fax: 49-30-26995010
E-mail: info@gdw-berlin.de
Web site: http://www.gdw-berlin.de/selbstdarstellung/ploetze1-d.htm

Gedenkstätte und Museum Sachsenhausen (Memorial and Museum)
Strasse der Nationen 22
16515 Oranienburg
Germany
Tel.: 49-3301-803715-17
Fax: 49-3301-803718
Web site: http://www.brandenburg.de/land/mwfk/kultur/deutsch/gedenkst/brb/
sachsenhausen.html

Germania Judaica
Josef-Haubrich-Hof 1
50676 Köln
Germany
Tel.: 49-221-232349
Fax: 49-221-2406963
E-mail: gj@ub.uni-koeln.de
Web site: http://www.stbib-koeln.de/judaica/

Das jüdische Museum Berlin
(The Jewish Museum of Berlin)
Lindenstrasse 9-14
10969 Berlin
Germany
Tel.: 49-30-259933
Fax: 49-30-25993411
Web site: http://www.hagalil.com/brd/berlin/museum.htm

Jüdisches Museum Frankfurt
(Jewish Museum of Frankfurt)
Untermainkai 14-15
60311 Frankfurt am Main
Germany
Tel.: 49-69-21235000
Fax: 49-69-21230705
Web site:
http://www.frankfurt.de/deutsch/2kultur/21museen/juedisches_museum.html

Das jüdische Museum Westfalen in Dorsten
(Jewish Museum of Westphalia)
Julius-Ambrumm-Strasse 1
Postfach 622
46282 Dorsten
Germany
Tel.: 49-2362-45279
Fax: 49-2362-45386
E-mail: juedmuseum_westfalen@t-online.de
Web site: http://www.pomoerium.com/museum.htm

KZ-Gedenkstätte Mittelbau-Dora (Memorial)
Kohnsteinweg 20
99734 Nordhausen
Germany
Tel.: 49-3631-3636
Fax: 49-3631-40181
E-mail: ns000397@frankfurt.netsurf.de
Web site: http://www.nordhausen.de/dora/html/dora_engl.htm

KZ-Gedenkstätte Neuengamme (Memorial)
Jean-Dolidier-Weg 39
21039 Hamburg
Germany
Tel. 49-40-7237403
Fax: 49-40-72374525
Web site: http://www.hamburg.de/Neuengamme

KZ-Gedenkstätte Flossenbürg (Memorial)
Rathaus — Hohenstaufenstrasse 24
92696 Flossenbürg

Germany
Tel.: 49-9603-9206-16
Fax: 49-9603-2895
Web site: http://www.flossenbuerg.de/infozentrum

Mahn- und Gedenkstätte Ravensbrück (Memorial)
Strasse der Nationen
16798 Fürstenberg/Havel
Germany
Tel.: 49-33093-39241; 38370
Fax: 49-33093-38397
Web site: http://www.brandenburg.de/land/mwfk/kultur/deutsch/gedenkst/brb/
    ravensbrueck.html

Das Moses Mendelssohn Zentrum
(Moses Mendelssohn Center)
Am Neuen Markt 8
14467 Potsdam
Germany
Tel.: 49-331-280940
Fax: 49-331-2809450
E-mail: moses@mmz.uni-potsdam.de
Web site: http://www.uni-potsdam.de/u/mmz/m1ueb.htm

Museum Judengasse
Kurt-Schumacher-Strasse 10
60311 Frankfurt am Main
Germany
Tel.: 49-69-2977419
Fax: 49-69-21230705
Web site: http://www.rma.de/eng-rmaweb/kultur/museen/museum-judengasse.htm

Solomon Ludwig Steinheim-Institut
Geibelstrasse 41
47057 Duisburg
Germany
Tel.: 49-203-370071; 72
Fax: 49-203-373380
E-mail: institut@sti1.uni-duisburg.de
Web site: http://sti1.uni-duisburg.de/

Stiftung Neue Synagoge Berlin
(New Synagogue Foundation, Berlin)
Centrum Judaicum
Oranienburger Strasse 28-30
10117 Berlin
Germany
Tel.: 49-30-28401-225; 28401-250
E-mail: cjudaicum@snafu.de
Web site: http://www.snafu.de/~cjudaicum

Stiftung Topographie des Terrors
(Topography of Terror Foundation)
Exhibition and Documentation Center
Stresemannstrasse 110
10963 Berlin
Germany
Tel.: 49-30-254-86703
Fax: 49-30-262-7156
E-mail: topographie@t-online.de
Web site: http://www.dhm.de/ausstellungen/ns_gedenk/ad_11.htm
Library
Budapester Strasse 40 (mailing address)
10787 Berlin
Germany
Tel.: 49-30-254-5090
Fax: 49-30-261-3002
E-mail: topografie@stiftung.b.shuttle.de

Zentralarchiv zur Erforschung der Geschichte der Juden in Deutschland
(Central Archives for Research on the History of the Jews in Germany)
Bienenstrasse 5
69117 Heidelberg
Germany
Tel.: 49-6221-164141
Fax: 49-6221-181049
E-mail: Zentralarchiv@urz.uni-heidelberg.de
Web site: http://www.uni-heidelberg.de/institute/sonst/aj/

Zentrum für Antisemitismusforschung
(Center for Research on Antisemitism)
Technische Universität Berlin

Ernst-Reuter-Platz 7
10587 Berlin
Germany
Tel.: 49-30-314-23154
Fax: 49-30-314-21136
E-mail: zfa10154@mailszrz.zrz.TU-Berlin.de
Web site: http://zfa.kgw.tu-berlin.de/zfa.htm

Poland

Jewish Historical Institute, and
Museum of the History of Polish Jews
ul. Tlomackie 3/5
00-090 Warszawa
Poland
Tel./Fax: 48-22-827-9225
E-mail: reisner@plearn.edu.pl
Web site (for museum): http://www.isjm.org/jhr/no2/museums2.htm#warsaw

Majdanek State Museum
Droga Meczennikow Majdanka 67
20-325 Lublin
Poland
Tel.: 48-81-744-19-55; 744-26-47
Fax: 48-81-744-05-26
Web site: http://www.lublin.pol.pl/majdanek/english.html

Muzeum Stutthof w Sztutowie Museum
82-110 Sztutowie
Poland
Tel.: 48-552-478-353
Fax: 48-552-478-358
Web site: http://www2.3dresearch.com/~june/Vincent/Camps/StutthofEng.html
(this is part of a larger web site on camps and is not located at Stutthof; it contains
information about the camp and its museum)

State Museum of Auschwitz-Birkenau
Ul. Wiezniow Oswiecimia 20
32-603 Oswiecim 5
Poland
Tel.: 48-33-843-2022; 843-2133; 843-2077
Fax: 48-33-843-1934

E-mail: muzeum.auschwitz@um.oswiecim.pl
Web site: http://auschwitz-muzeum.oswiecim.pl

The Research Center on Jewish History and Culture in Poland
ul. Batoreyo 12
31-135 Krakow
Poland
Tel.: 48-12-633-7058
Fax: 48-12-634-4593
Web site: http://www.uj.edu.pl/uj-guide/jewish.html

Europe

The Anne Frank House
Prinsengracht 263
Amsterdam
Netherlands
Tel.: 31-0-20-5567100
Fax: 31-0-20-6207999
Web site: http://www.annefrank.nl

Centre de Documentation Juive Contemporaine
(Jewish Documentation Center)
17, Rue Geoffroy-l'Asnier
75004 Paris
France
Tel.: 33-1-42774472
Fax: 33-1-48871250
E-mail: memcdjc@calva.net
Web site: http://www.calvacom.fr/calvaweb/memorial/cdjc_fr.htm

Gedenkstätte Konzentrationslager Mauthausen (Memorial/Concentration Camp)
Erinnerungsstrasse 1
310 Mauthausen
Austria
Tel.: 43-7238-2269
Fax: 43-7238-3696
Web site: http://www.mauthausen-memorial.gv.at/index.html

The Jewish Museum and Archives of Hungary
Dohany u.2
1077 Budapest

Hungary
Tel.: 36-1-3428-949
Fax: 36-1-3421-790
E-mail: bpjewmus@c3.hu
Web site: http://www.c3.hu/~bpjewmus/

Jewish Museum of Prague
Jachymova 3
11001 Praha 1
Czech Republic
Tel.: 420-2-24810099
Fax: 420-2-2310681
E-mail: zmp@ecn.cz
Web site: http://www.jewishmuseum.cz

Jüdisches Museum Hohenems (Jewish Museum Hohenems)
Villa Heimann-Rosenthal
Schweizer Strasse 5
6845 Hohenems
Austria
Tel.: 43-5576-73989-0
Fax: 43-5576-77793
E-mail: jmh@jmh.vol.at
Web site: http://www2.vol.at/jmh/

Jüdisches Museum Wien (Jewish Museum of Vienna)
Dorotheergasse 11
1010 Wien
Austria
Tel.: 43-1-5350431
Fax: 43-1-5350424
E-mail: info@jmw.at
Web site: http://www.jmw.at/

KZ Mauthausen-Gusen (Concentration Camp)
Postfach 54
4222 Sankt Georgen an der Gusen
Austria
Fax: 43-7229-76920
E-mail: rahd@magnet.at
Web site: http://linz.orf.at/orf/gusen/index.htm

Leo Baeck Institute
4 Devonshire Street
London W1N 2BH
United Kingdom
Tel.: 44-171-580-3493, 4397
Fax: 44-171-436-8634
E-mail: ap@lbilon.demon.co.uk

Mechelen Museum van Deportatie en Verzet
(Mechelen Museum of Deportation and Resistance)
Goswin de Stassartstraat 153
2800 Mechelen
Belgium
Tel.: 32-0-15290660
Fax: 32-0-15290876
E-mail: infos@cicb.be
Web site: http://www.cicb.be/

Terezin Memorial
41155 Terezin
Czech Republic
Fax: 420-416-782245
E-mail: pamatnik@unl.pvtnet.cz
Web site: http://www.siscr.cz/1250/terezin/index.htm

The Wiener Library
4 Devonshire Street
London W1N 2BH
United Kingdom
Tel.: 44-171-636-7247
Fax: 44-171-436-6428
E-mail: lib@wl.u-net.com

Israel

Bet Lohamei Haghettaot Museum
(The Ghetto Fighters' House)
Kibbutz Lohamei-Haghettaot
Galil Ma'aravi 25220
Israel
Tel.: 972-4-9958080
Fax: 972-4-9958007
Web site: http://www.gfh.org.il

Beit Teresienstadt
Kibbutz Givat Chaym Ichud
Emek Hefer 38935
Israel
Tel.: 972-6-369515
Fax: 972-6-369611
E-mail: bterezin@inter.net.il
Web site: http://www.cet.ac.il/terezin/ndx_e.htm

Holocaust Education Center
Givatayyim (Beit Wolyn)
10 Korazin Street
P.O. Box 804
Givatayyim
Israel
Tel.: 972-3-5718197
Fax: 972-3-5717781
Web site: http://www.yadvashem.org.il/education/contacts.html

Massuah Holocaust Studies Institute
Kibbutz Tel-Yitzhak
Tel-Yitzhak 45805
Israel
Tel.: 972-9-899-9997; 9563; 6997
Fax: 972-9-899-7410
E-mail: massuah@netvision.net.il
Web site: http://www.massuah.org/home.htm

Moreshet Archives
Givat Haviva
Menashe 37850
Israel
Tel.: 972-6-6309275
Fax: 972-6-6309305
E-mail: meir_yk@internet.il
Web site: http://www.inter.net.il/~givat_h/givat/moreshet/moreshet.htm

Museum of Hungarian Jewry
P.O. Box 1168

Safed 13111
Israel
Tel. and Fax: 972-6-6923880
E-mail: hungmus@hungjewmus.org.il
Web site: http://www.hungjewmus.org.il

Yad Vashem
The Holocaust Martyrs' and Heroes' Remembrance Authority
P.O. Box 3477
Jerusalem 91034
Israel
Tel.: 972-2-6751612
Fax: 972-2-6433511
E-mail: info@yad-vashem.org.il
Web site: http://www.yad-vashem.org.il/

Tables

Table 1 Jewish Emigration from Germany, 1933–1939

Year	High Estimate*	Low Estimate**
1933	63,400	37,000
1934	45,000	22,000
1935	35,500	20,000
1936	34,000	24,000
1937	23,500	23,000
1938	49,000***	34,000
1939	68,000***	68,000
Totals	318,400	228,000

Note: Estimates of the number of Jews who emigrated from Germany between 1933 and October 1941, when Jewish emigration was stopped in favor of the Final Solution, have ranged from a low of about 270,000 to a high of about 363,000. Lower estimates tended to count only professing Jews, and may reflect an attempt by Jewish organizations to minimize the number of Jewish refugees to dampen fears in destination countries. Higher estimates may include all persons considered Jews under the Nuremberg Laws. The higher figures may also reflect Jewish efforts to show progress to Nazi authorities. The estimates above cover 1933 to 1939. They exclude Austria and the Czech lands of Bohemia and Moravia annexed by Germany in 1938 and 1939. Jewish emigration from Austria between 1938 and 1941 is estimated at 147,000, and from the former Czech lands of Bohemia and Moravia after 1939 at about 30,000. The SS used the higher figures at the Wannsee Conference in January 1942.

* Bundesarchiv Potsdam 75c Re1-31. Reichsvereinigung der Juden in Deutschland, Organisation — Auswanderung 1933–1941, 8 November 1941.

** S. Adler-Rudel, *Jüdische Selbsthilfe unter dem Naziregime* (Tübingen: Mohr, 1974), p. 216; and Herbert Strauss, "Jewish Emigration From Germany — Nazi Policies and Jewish Responses (I)", *Leo Baeck Institute Yearbook* 25 (1980): 326.

*** Includes the Sudetenland.

Table 2 Destinations of German Jewish Emigrants, 1933–1941*

Destinations	Number	% Total
Europe	153,767	40.68
Palestine	53,430	15.17
Asia	16,374	4.65
Africa	14,760	4.19
Australia	4,015	1.14
South America	53,472	15.18
Central America	9,728	2.76
North America	57,189	16.23
Totals	362,735	100.00

Note: The figures for destinations of German Jewish emigrants come from the same source as the higher estimate of Jewish emigration from Germany in Table 1. It is difficult here as well to know with certainty the destination of every German Jew who left Germany between 1933 and 1941. Many receiver countries counted immigrating Jews from Germany as Germans, not as Jews, while others did not keep precise records of incoming Jewish refugees from Germany.

* Bundesarchiv Potsdam 75c Re1. Reichsvereinigung der Juden in Deutschland, Organisation — Auswanderung 1933–1941, 8 November 1941.

Table 3   Estimated Jewish Losses*

	Pre-Holocaust Population	Low Estimate	High Estimate
Austria	191,000	50,000	65,500
Belgium	60,000	25,000	29,000
Bohemia/Moravia	92,000	77,000	78,300
Denmark	8,000	60	116
Estonia	4,600	1,500	2,000
France	260,000	75,000	77,000
Germany	566,000	135,000	142,000
Greece	73,000	59,000	67,000
Hungary**	725,000	502,000	569,000
Italy	48,000	6,500	9,000
Latvia	95,000	70,000	72,000
Lithuania	155,000	130,000	143,000
Luxembourg	3,500	1,000	2,000
Netherlands	112,000	100,000	105,000
Norway	1,700	800	800
Poland	3,250,000	2,700,000	3,000,000
Romania**	441,000	121,000	287,000
Slovakia**	89,000	60,000	71,000
USSR	2,825,000	700,000	1,100,000
Yugoslavia	68,000	56,000	65,000
Totals	9,067,800	4,869,860	5,894,716

Note: Except for Bohemia/Moravia, Slovakia, Hungary, and Romania, the figures given for pre-Holocaust populations are those for 1933. The numbers of those killed, however, include both indigenous Jews and refugees who may have fled from other countries before 1941.

* These estimates are based on statistics in Raul Hilberg, *The Destruction of the European Jews* (New York: Holmes & Meier, 1985), pp. 1201–1220; Israel Gutman and Robert Rozett, "Estimated Jewish Losses in the Holocaust," in Israel Gutman, ed., *Encyclopedia of the Holocaust* (New York: Macmillan, 1990), vol. IV, pp. 1797–1802; and Wolfgang Benz, *Dimension des Völkermords: Die Zahl der jüdischen Opfer des Nationalsozialsmus* (Munich: R. Oldenbourg, 1991).

** The situation in Slovakia, Hungary, and Romania was complicated by the transfer of Eastern Slovakia from Czechoslovakia to Hungary in 1938 and the transfer of Northern Transylvania from Romania to Hungary in 1940. Both areas had large Jewish populations. Hence the figures for pre-Holocaust populations for all three countries are for 1940, and the losses reflect the Jews within the borders of those countries after that date.

Table 4 Estimated Gypsy Losses*

	Pre-Holocaust Population	Low Estimate	High Estimate
Austria	11,200	6,800	8250
Belgium	600	350	500
Bohemia/Moravia	13,000	5,000	6,500
Estonia	1,000	500	1,000
France	40,000	15,150	15,150
Germany	20,000	15,000	15,000
Greece	?	50	50
Hungary	100,000	1,000	28,000
Italy	25,000	1,000	1,000
Latvia	5,000	1,500	2,500
Lithuania	1,000	500	1,000
Luxembourg	200	100	200
Netherlands	500	215	500
Poland	50,000	8,000	35,000
Romania	300,000	19,000	36,000
USSR	200,000	30,000	35,000
Slovakia	80,000	400	10,000
Yugoslavia	100,000	26,000	90,000
Totals	947,500	130,565	285,650

*Statistics on Gypsy losses are especially unreliable and controversial. These figures are based on necessarily rough estimates compiled in Rüdiger Vossen, *Zigeuner: Roma, Sinti, Gitanos, Gypsies zwischen Verfolgung und Romantisierung* (Frankfurt: Ullstein, 1983), pp. 83–86; and Michael Zimmermann, *Rassenutopie und Genozid: Die nationalsozialistische "Lösung der Zigeunerfrage"* (Hamburg: Christians, 1996), pp. 235–292, 381–283.

Table 5 Selected Jewish Displaced Persons (DP) Camps, 1945–1947*

Camp	Country/Zone	Est. Number	Date
Babenhausen	Germany/US	3,350	9/46
Bad Gastein	Austria/GB	1,330	3/46
Bamberg	Germany/US	2,941	8/46
Bergen-Belsen	Germany/GB	10,000	11/45
Biberach	Germany/FR	500	11/45
Deggendorf	Germany/US	1,537	10/47
Ebensee	Austria/US	500	7/45
Feldafing	Germany/US	4,000	10/46
Föhrenwald	Germany/US	6,000	11/45
Fürth	Germany/US	850	12/45
Judenburg	Austria/GB	1,000	10/45
Linz	Austria/US	2,300	11/45
Landsberg	Germany/US	6,000	11/45
Leibnitz	Austria/GB	600	11/45
Leipheim	Germany/US	3,150	10/46
Salzburg	Austria/US	500	11/45
St. Ottilien	Germany/US	1,000	11/45
Zeilsheim	Germany/US	3,563	10/47

Note: This is a sample of Jewish Displaced Persons (DP) camps in Germany and Austria, with estimated populations at given times. Precise figures for Jewish DPs between 1945 and 1949 are difficult to determine, as camp populations fluctuated regularly. At the end of World War II, about 200,000 Jewish survivors gathered in DP camps in Germany and Austria. As many as 150,000 were in the U.S. occupation zone in Germany (including Berlin), about 15,000 were in the British zone, and 2,000–3,000 were in the French zone. In addition, about 30,000 Jewish DPs were in Austria. By early 1947, the number of Jewish DPs reached a peak of almost 230,000. Thousands of Jewish refugees continued to flee from Eastern Europe to the West, arriving as well in camps in Italy, France, Belgium, and Sweden. Some headed for Palestine. By the end of 1948, there were still some 82,000 Jewish DPs in Germany, and about 10,000 in Austria.

* Abraham Peck, ed., *American Jewish Archives, Cincinnati*, in Sybil Milton and Henry Friedlander, eds., *Archives of the Holocaust* (New York: Garland, 1990), Vol. 9, Docs. 18, 22; Sybil Milton and Frederick Bogin, eds., *The American Jewish Joint Distribution Committee*, in Sybil Milton and Henry Friedlander, eds., *Archives of the Holocaust* (New York: Garland, 1995), Vol.10/II, Docs. 244, 248, 249, 253; Angelika Königseder and Julianne Wetzel, *Lebensmut im Wartesaal: Die Jüdische DPs im Nachkriegsdeutschland* (Frankfurt am Main: Fischer, 1994).

APPENDIX II

Maps

German Territorial Losses, Treaty of Versailles, 1919

North Sea

DENMARK

Baltic Sea

NETH.

BEL.

GERMANY

POLAND

Köln

Koblenz
Mainz

CZECHOSLOVAKIA

FRANCE

AUSTRIA

HUNGARY

SWITZ.

ITALY

■	Lost by Germany	▨	Retained by Germany through plebiscite
■	Saar District	⧄	"Anschluss" prevented (Formerly part of Austria-Hungary)
⧄	Occupied territory	····	Demilitarized Zone

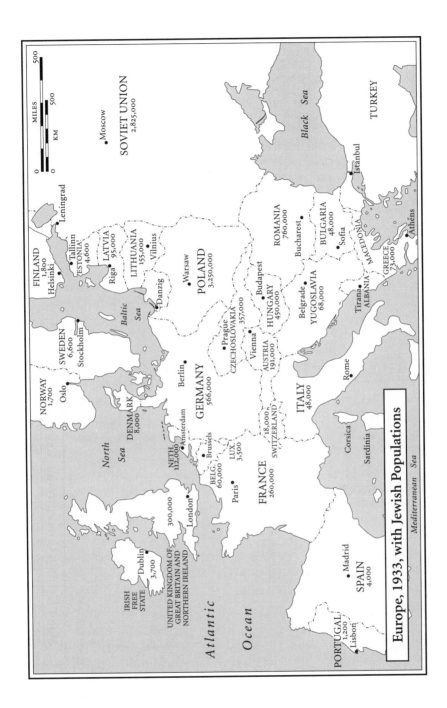

Europe, 1933, with Jewish Populations

SOVIET UNION 2,825,000
Moscow

FINLAND 1,800
Helsinki
Leningrad

ESTONIA 4,600
Tallinn

LATVIA 95,000
Riga

LITHUANIA 155,000
Vilnius

NORWAY 1,700
Oslo

SWEDEN 6,600
Stockholm

DENMARK 8,000

Danzig

Warsaw

POLAND 3,250,000

Berlin

GERMANY 566,000

NETH. 112,000
Amsterdam

BELG. 60,000
Brussels

LUX. 3,500

Prague
CZECHOSLOVAKIA 357,000

Vienna
AUSTRIA 191,000

SWITZERLAND 18,000

Budapest
HUNGARY 450,000

ROMANIA 760,000
Bucharest

Belgrade
YUGOSLAVIA 68,000

BULGARIA 48,000
Sofia

Tirana
ALBANIA

MACEDONIA

GREECE 73,000
Athens

Istanbul

TURKEY

Rome

ITALY 48,000

Corsica

Sardinia

FRANCE 260,000
Paris

London
UNITED KINGDOM OF GREAT BRITAIN AND NORTHERN IRELAND 300,000

IRISH FREE STATE 3,700
Dublin

Madrid
SPAIN 4,000

PORTUGAL 1,200
Lisbon

Atlantic Ocean

North Sea

Baltic Sea

Black Sea

Mediterranean Sea

MILES 500
KM 500

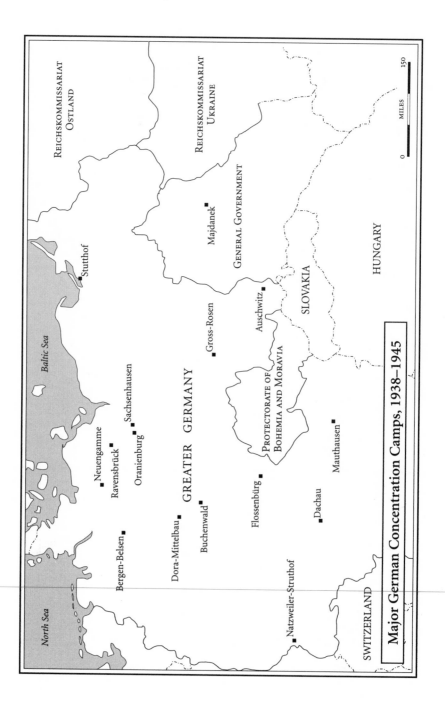

Major German Concentration Camps, 1938–1945

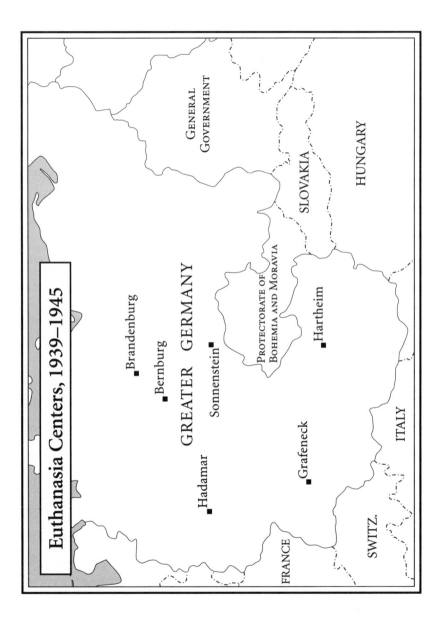

Euthanasia Centers, 1939–1945

GREATER GERMANY

Brandenburg

Bernburg

Sonnenstein

Hadamar

Grafeneck

PROTECTORATE OF
BOHEMIA AND MORAVIA

Hartheim

GENERAL
GOVERNMENT

SLOVAKIA

HUNGARY

FRANCE

SWITZ.

ITALY

German Dominated Europe, 1942

SWEDEN

NORWAY

FINLAND

• Leningrad

North
Sea

DENMARK

Baltic
Sea

GREAT
BRITAIN

U.S.S.R.

Berlin •

• Białystok

GERMANY

Paris •

GENERAL
GOVERNMENT

BOHEMIA
MORAVIA

SLOVAKIA

FRANCE

BESSARABIA

Vichy •

SWITZ.

AUSTRIA

HUNGARY

ITALY

RUMANIA

CROATIA

Black
Sea

SERBIA

SPAIN

BULGARIA

ALBANIA

GREECE

TURKEY

Mediterranean   Sea

Annexed by Germany

Occupied by Germany

Allied with Germany

Occupied by Italy

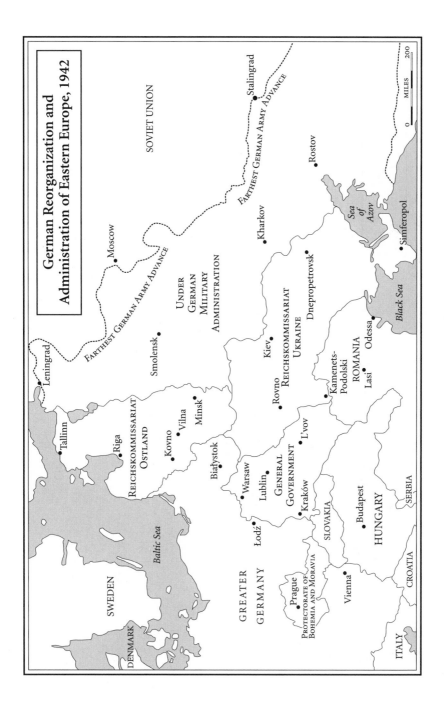

German Reorganization and
Administration of Eastern Europe, 1942

SWEDEN

DENMARK

Baltic Sea

SOVIET UNION

Moscow

Leningrad

FARTHEST GERMAN ARMY ADVANCE

Tallinn

Riga

REICHSKOMMISSARIAT
OSTLAND

Kovno

Vilna

Minsk

Smolensk

UNDER
GERMAN
MILITARY
ADMINISTRATION

Stalingrad

FARTHEST GERMAN ARMY ADVANCE

Kharkov

Rostov

Białystok

Warsaw

Lublin

GENERAL
GOVERNMENT

Kraków

Łódź

Kiev

Rovno

L'vov

REICHSKOMMISSARIAT
UKRAINE

Dnepropetrovsk

Kamenets-
Podolski

ROMANIA

Iasi

Odessa

Sea
of
Azov

Simferopol

Black Sea

GREATER
GERMANY

Prague

PROTECTORATE OF
BOHEMIA AND MORAVIA

Vienna

SLOVAKIA

Budapest

HUNGARY

SERBIA

CROATIA

ITALY

0   MILES   200

Major Ghettos in Occupied
Eastern Europe, 1939–1944

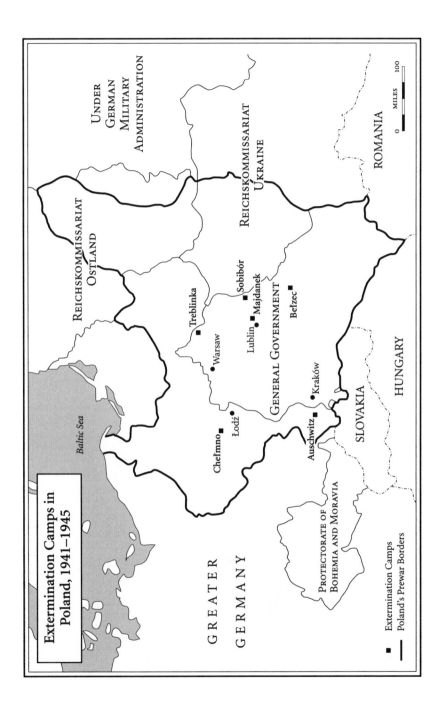

Extermination Camps in Poland, 1941–1945

GREATER GERMANY

Baltic Sea

REICHSKOMMISSARIAT OSTLAND

UNDER GERMAN MILITARY ADMINISTRATION

REICHSKOMMISSARIAT UKRAINE

ROMANIA

Treblinka
Sobibór
Majdanek
Lublin
Bełzec
Warsaw
GENERAL GOVERNMENT
Kraków
Chełmno
Łódź
Auschwitz

HUNGARY

SLOVAKIA

PROTECTORATE OF BOHEMIA AND MORAVIA

■ Extermination Camps
— Poland's Prewar Borders

0   MILES   100

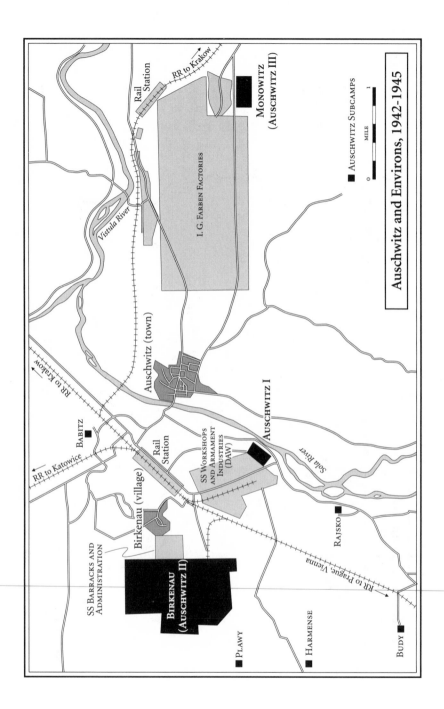

Auschwitz and Environs, 1942-1945

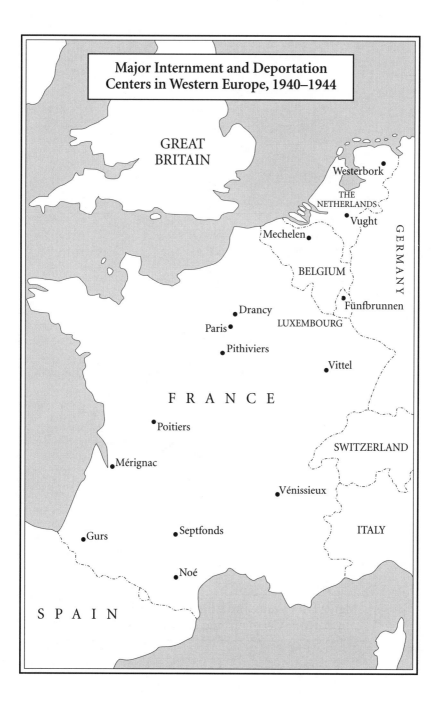

Major Internment and Deportation Centers in Western Europe, 1940–1944

GREAT BRITAIN

Westerbork

THE NETHERLANDS

Vught

Mechelen

BELGIUM

GERMANY

Fünfbrunnen

Drancy

Paris

LUXEMBOURG

Pithiviers

Vittel

FRANCE

Poitiers

SWITZERLAND

Mérignac

Vénissieux

ITALY

Gurs

Septfonds

Noé

SPAIN

POLAND

Bergen-Belsen •

BRITISH ZONE

Berlin •

SOVIET ZONE

G E R M A N Y

Zeilsheim •
Babenhausen •
Bamberg •

FRENCH

Fürth •

U. S. ZONE

CZECHOSLOVAKIA

Deggendorf •

ZONE

Leipheim •

St. Ottilien •

Linz •

Vienna •

Biberach •
Landsberg •

Munich •

Föhrenwald •

U.S.

SOVIET ZONE

Feldafing •

Salzburg •

A U S T R I A

Ebensee •

FRENCH ZONE

ZONE

Judenburg •

SWITZERLAND

BRITISH

Leibnitz •

Bad Gastein

ZONE

YUGOSLAVIA

ITALY

Major DP Camps and Allied Occupation Zones in Postwar Germany and Austria, 1945–1949

0   MILES   100

INDEX

Pages in italics refer to encyclopedia entries

Abella, Irving, 346
Abetz, Otto, 246
Abortions, 147, 222
Academy of German Law, 177
Accommodation, by Jews, 97–99, 103–4
Adelson, Alan, 335
Adenauer, Konrad, 169, 237
Adler, Jacques, 278
Adler, Stanislaw, 335
Ainsztein, Reuben, 100, 322
Aktionen, 206, 208
Albania, 26
Allen, William Sheridan, 294, 69
"All for the Fatherland," *see* Iron Guard
Allies: "blood for trucks" offer and, 122,
    135, 175, 183; Himmler and, 122, 167,
    181; Horthy and, 182; rescue and,
    119–25, 128, 194; sources on, 348, 349,
    351; and suggested bombing of
    Auschwitz, 121, 166, 192; *see also* Tri-
    als of war criminals/International
    Military Tribunal
Altschuler, David, 392
Altschuler, Mordechai, 125
Aly, Götz, 137
American Friends of the Ghetto Fight-
    ers' House, 400–1
American Gathering of Jewish Holo-
    caust Survivors, 401
American Jewish Committee, Oral His-
    tory Library of, 342
American Jewish Congress, 193, 264

American Jewish Joint Distribution
    Committee, 124, 129, 185, 187, *249*,
    264; sources on, 347, 363
American Jewry during the Holocaust,
    124
American Military Tribunal, 167, 187,
    241–42
Améry, Jean, 335
Anglo-German Naval Pact, 147
Angress, Werner, 298
Angry Harvest (Bittere Ernte; film), 385
Anielewicz, Mordechai, 34
Anne Frank House/Museum, The, 176,
    413
Anne Frank Remembered (film), 373
Anschluss (Union), 7, 148, 149, 176, 189,
    214
Anti-Comintern Pact, 148
Antisemitism, *214–15*; Christian, 58, 64–
    65, 67, 133–34, 251–52; continuity ver-
    sus change and, 66–69; Displaced
    Persons and, 221; in Eastern Europe,
    112–15, 173; films on, 378; in France,
    116, 288–89; in Germany, 66, 67–69,
    88–89, 111; history of, 58–59, 60, 61,
    63–69; as motivation of perpetrators,
    88–89, 90; sources on, 278, 287–93,
    353, 370–71, 378, 390; texts on, 293–
    94; *see also* Bonhoeffer, Dietrich;
    Streicher, Julius
Antonescu, Ion, 29, 123, 165, *173*, 197,
    209, 246, 252, 253

Appelfeld, Aharon, 332

Arad, Yitzhak, 100, 104, 272, 283, 319, 335

Arbeitsdienst (Labor Service), 5

Architecture, Speer and, *189*

Arendt, Hannah, 68, 90, 99, 188, 287–88, 307

Armenians, 56; sources on, 350

Armia Krajowa (Home Army), 113, 115, 201

Armia Ludowa (National Army), 201

Army, German, 13, 79, 80, 86, 146, 147, 148, 155, 190, 203, *250*; motivation of, 90, 91; sources on, 307–11; *see also* Einsatzgruppen; Hiwis (Hilfswillige)

Army, Jewish, *see* Partisans, Jewish

Arrow Cross, 27, 87, 115, 166, 182, 192, *250*

Art, sources on, 330–32, 333

Aryanization, 6, 7–8, 83, 179, 216, *216–17*, 224; cultural, 8, 216–17; economic, 7–8, 216, 219–20; privileged mixed marriages and, *236*; Vichy France and, 211

Aryan myth, sources on, 291, 293

Aryans, *215–16*, 229; antisemitism and, 66, 215; Dutch as, 30; German newspapers and, 6; Gypsies as, 47, 215; medical experiments and, 230; *Mischlinge* and, 231

Ascheim, Steven, 295

Asocial elements, concentration camps and, 18, 148, 218

Assisi: film on, 385; sources on, 355, 385

Assisi Underground, The (film), 385

Auschwitz, 20, 21–23, 154, *194–95*, 218, 223, 224, 399; Allies' suggested bombing of, 121, 166, 192; Baeck and, 174; Baum Group and, 238, *251*; crematoria at, 21, 166, 219; evacuation of, 36, 166; films on, 374, 375, 384, 386, 389; Anne Frank and, 176; gas chambers at, 21, 22, 36, 156, 159, 166, 194, 224, 226; gassings of Soviet prisoners in,

14; Gypsies in, 162, 165; Himmler and, 181; Höss and, 22, 154, *182*, 194, 226, 245, 318; Jews deported to, 26, 159, 160, 161, 162, 163, 164, 165, 166, 181, 186, 188, 202, 206, 207, 209; last roll call at, 166; liberation of, 36, 166, 184; medical experiments at, 23, 230; museum on, 412; as secret, 119; selection process at, *240*; Sonderkommando and, 166; sources on, 272, 273, 287, 314, 315, 318, 320–21, 322, 330, 331, 332, 333, 334, 335, 336, 337, 338, 339, 340, 341, 342, 348; survival in, 102–3, 105, 106; tatoos on prisoners of, 18; trials of war criminals and, 169, 241, 242; uprising in, 239; Vichy France and, 211; Wallenberg and, *192*; Weissmandel and, *192*; Westerbork and, 214; *see also* Birkenau; Mengele, Joseph; Monowitz

Auschwitz-Birkenau State Museum, 273

Auschwitz II, *see* Birkenau

Auschwitz III, *see* Monowitz

Auschwitz Trial, 39, 40, 243

Australia, 254

Austria: Anschluss and, 7, 148, 149, 176, 189, *214*; deportation of Jews from, 8, 157; Dollfuss and, 146; Globocnik and, 178; history of antisemitism in, 293; history of Jews in, 60; impact of Holocaust on, 25, 421, 422; independence of, 147; Kaltenbrunner and, 182; responsibility for Holocaust and, 40–41; Seyss-Inquart and, *189*; sources on, 280–81, 291, 292, 304, 369; Stangl and, 190; trials of war criminals in, 39; yellow badges in, *247*; *see also* Central Office for Jewish Emigration

Autobiographies: of German Jews, 301–2; of perpetrators, 318–19

Avenue of the Just (film), 379

Avital, Saf, 321

Avni, Haim, 127, 346–47

Babenhausen, 423

Babi Yar, 13, 80, 157, *195*; sources on, 398

Bad Gastein, 423

Badoglio, Marshal, 163

Baeck, Leo, *173–74*, 320; sources on, 298

Baeck, Leo, Institute, 404, 415

Bak, Samuel, 331

Baker, Leonard, 298

Baldwin, Peter, 359

Balfour Declaration, 192

Baltic states, 100, 113, 234, 260; *see also* Estonia; Latvia; Lithuania

Bamberg, 423

Bankier, David, 111, 353

Barasz, Efraim, 197

Barbarossa, Operation, 13–14, 79, 85, 155, *217*, 250

Barbie, Klaus, 39; film on, 381

Bardossy, Laszlo, 246

Barkai, Avraham, 299

Barkan, Elazar, 288

Barmen Declaration, 257

Baron, Salo W., 68, 300

Barracks seniors, 235

Bartoszewski, Wladyslaw, 335

Bartov, Omer, 90, 276, 307

Bauer, Yehuda, 47, 101, 121, 124, 129, 273–74, 322, 327, 347, 363

Bauman, Zygmunt, 136, 137, 365

Baumel, Judith, 325

Baum, Herbert and Marianne, 250, 251

Baum Group, 97, 238, *250–51*

Bavaria, 142, 180; sources on, 354–55

Bedürftig, Friedemann, 271

Bédzin, 163

Beer Hall Putsch, 73, 141–42, 179, 219, 261

Beinfeld, Solon, 319

Beit Teresienstadt, 416

Belarus, 49, 100, 234, 260

Belgium: deportation of Jews from, 160, 163; impact of Holocaust on, 31, 421, 422; nationalism and, 53; policies on Jews and Gypsies in, 12; Rexists in,

87; trials of war criminals and, 245–46; yellow badge and, 159

Belzec, 14, 20–21, 80, 157, 164, 193, *195–96*, 210, 223–24, 234; gas chambers at, 248–49; Hiwis at, 87; Jews deported to, 159, 160, 161, 203, 210; Karski and, *183*; sources on, 319

Ben-Gurion, David, *174*, 351–52; sources on, 351–52

Benz, Wolfgang, 274

Berenbaum, Michael, 47, 152, 284, 320–21, 327, 369–70

Bergen, Doris, 344–45

Bergen-Belsen, *196*, 199, 218, 423; Anne Frank and, 176; Jews deported to, 201, 214; Jews with foreign passports and, 162; liberation of, 37, 167; memorial to, 406; sources on, 337, 341; trials of war criminals and, 242

Bergmann, Werner, 370

Berkley, George, 320

Berkovits, Eliezer, 133, 365

Berlin, 163, 189; films on, 375; sources on, 296, 301–2

Berman, Aaron, 347

Berman, Karel, 396

Bermuda, 162

Bermuda Conference, *196–97*

Bernadotte, Folke, 167

Bernburg, 223, 233

Bessarabia, 28–29, 113, 156, 157, 173, *197*, 209

Best, Werner, 245

Bet Lohamei Haghettaot Museum (Ghetto Fighters' House), 415–16

Bettelheim, Bruno, 102, 105, 365

Beyerchen, Alan, 314

Bialystok, 155, 156, 162, 163, *197*, 260; film on, 376; Jews deported to, 209; Operation Reinhard and, *234*; sources on, 338; Stutthof and, 208; uprising in, 35, 233; yellow badges in, *247*; *see also* Tenenbaum, Mordechai

Biberach, 423

Bielski, Tuvia, 324
Bielski partisans, sources on, 324
Bierman, John, 127, 347
Biltmore conference, 159
Binion, Rudolph, 72, 304
Biologists, sources on, 314
Birger, Trudi, 105, 106, 336
Birkenau (Auschwitz II), 22–23, 160, 194, 195; Allies' suggested bombing of, 121, 166; crematoria at, 22, 194, 219; family camp at, 23; gas chambers at, 21, 22, 36, 156, 159, 166, 194, 195, 224, 226; Gypsies deported to, 23, 48, 161, 228; sterilization experiments in, 162; uprising in, 35, 104, 239
Birn, Bettina, 359–60
Birnbaum, Israel, 392
Bismarck, Otto von, 56
Black, Peter R., 122, 307
Blacks, sources on, 328
Blatter, Janet, 330
Block, Gay, 353
Block seniors/chiefs, 18, 105, 106, 235; see also Prisoner functionaries
Blok Antyfaszystowski (Anti-Fascist Bloc), 191
"Blood for trucks" offer, 122, 135, 175, 183
Bloomberg, Marty, 270
Boat Is Full, The (Das Boot ist voll; film), 385
Bodemann, Y. Michael, 363
Boder, David, 341
Boehm, Erich, 111, 357
Bohemia and Moravia, see Protectorate of Bohemia and Moravia
Bonhoeffer, Dietrich, 25, 112, 174, 257
"Books of the Dead," 241
Bor, Josef, 331
Borkin, Joseph, 314
Bormann, Martin, 244, 307; sources on, 312
Borowski, Tadeusz, 332
Botwinick, Rita, 274, 284

Bower, Tom, 347
Boycotts, of Jewish businesses, 6, 75, 144, 191, 216
Bracher, Karl Dietrich, 40, 302
Brack, Viktor, 174–75, 223
Braham, Randolph, 115–16, 122, 130, 278–79, 284, 365–66
Braiterman, Zachary, 133, 366
Brand, Joel, 122, 165, 175, 183; sources on, 352
Brandenburg, 223
Braun Center for Holocaust Studies, 401
Breaking the Silence: The Generation After the Holocaust (film), 374
Breitman, Richard, 79, 276, 308, 347, 349
Brenner, Michael, 296, 363
British Military Tribunal, 242–43
British White Paper on Palestine, 151, 159; see also Great Britain
Broszat, Martin, 294, 302–3, 309
Browder, George, 308
Brown, Jean, 332
Browning, Christopher, 80, 92, 93, 276–77, 308, 311
Bruck, Moeller van den, 292
Brundibar (opera), 377
Brustein, William, 295
Buchenwald, 5, 148, 197–98, 218, 338; International Red Cross and, 258; liberation of, 37, 167; medical experiments in, 230; memorial to, 407; sources on, 321, 339, 344; see also Dora-Mittelbau
Buchignani, Walter, 325
Budapest, 166
Buffum, David, 7–8
Bukovina, 28–29, 157
Bulgaria: Allies' pressure on to release Jews, 122, 123; deportations and, 86; government officials in, 87; impact of Holocaust on, 28; nationalism and, 53; sources on, 279; survivors

from, 37; trial of war criminals and, 246

Bullock, Alan, 72, 304

Buna, 22, 161, 164; *see also* Monowitz

Bureaucracy, careerism as motivation of perpetrators and, 92–94

Burleigh, Michael, 46, 137, 303, 327, 366

Burrin, Philippe, 78, 80, 277

Bystanders, 109–17, 123; in Eastern Europe, 112–16; in Germany, 109–112, 353, 354–55, 356, 359; sources on, 275, 346–59, 378–80; in Western Europe, 116–17; *see also* Rescue

Calvinist churches, 257

Camps, *217*, 228; films on, 374–78, 383–84; prisoner self-administration of, 235–36; sources on, 319–22, 396–97; *see also* Concentration camps; Labor camps; Extermination camps; Prisoner functionaries; Transit camps; Euthanasia

Camp seniors, 18, 235; *see also* Prisoner functionaries

Canada: Displaced Persons and, 38, 221; resource organizations, museums, and memorials in, 401, 403, 404; sources on, 346; war criminals in, 254

"Canada," 23

Cancer, sources on, 316

CANDLES Holocaust Museum, 401

Capos, 18, 105, 235; *see also* Prisoner funcationaries

Carbon monoxide gas, 21, 204, 208, 210, 223, 226, 248–49

Careerism, as motivation of perpetrators, 92–94

Cargas, Harry, 270, 366

Carol II, King of Romania, 252

Catholic Center Party, 145

Catholics, 145, *251–52*; euthanasia and, 10, 156; film on, 379, 386; Hitler and,

144, 251; rescue and, 32, 40, 112, 251–52, 358, 379, 386; sources on, 327, 335, 337, 345, 346, 358; Vichy France and, 211; *see also* Vatican

CD-ROMs, on Holocaust, 391–92

Cecil, Robert, 311

Center for Holocaust and Genocide Studies (University of Minnesota), 402

Center for Holocaust Studies (University of Vermont), 401

Central British Fund, sources on, 325

Central European History (journal), 372

Central Europe, history of Jews in, 59–61

Central Jewish Council, 26

Central Office for Jewish Emigration (Zentralstelle für jüdische Auswanderung), 149, 176, 206, 214, 259; *see also* Reich Central Office for Jewish Emigration

Central Office for the Investigation of National Socialist Crimes, 39

Central Office to Combat the Gypsy Menace (Zentralstelle zur Bekämpfung des Zigeunerwesens), 147

Centre de Documentation Juive Contemporaine (Jewish Documentation Center), 413

Chamberlain, Houston Stewart, 66, 293; sources on, 288

Chamberlain, Neville, 149, 154

Chary, Frederick, 279

Chełmno, 14, 20, 80, 157, 158, *198*, 223, 224; gas vans at, 14, 20, 226; Jews deported to, 188, 202, 206; Oneg Shabbat and, *254*

Chetniks, 101

Childers, Thomas, 295

Children: euthanasia of, 94, 10, 151; films on, 375, 377, 379, 387; with Gentile foster parents, 33, 101; Lebensborn program and, 258;

Children (*Continued*)
sources on, 325–27, 338, 339, 340, 341, 342, 343, 344, 397; Zegota and, 265

Children in the Holocaust (film), 374

Children of survivors, 130; electronic resources on, 390; films on, 374, 385, 386; sources on, 365

Christians, 68; antisemitism of, 58, 64–65, 67, 133–34, 251–52; film on, 374, 378, 385; impact of Holocaust on teachings about Judaism, 133–34; rescue and, 374, 385; sources on, 289, 292, 298, 300, 328, 339, 343, 344–46, 353, 366, 367, 368; *see also* Bonhoeffer, Dietrich; Catholics; Gentiles; Lutherans; Protestants

Churchill, Winston, 154, 162, 164, 183; sources on, 348

Civil service: Jews barred from, 6, 144, 147; as perpetrators, 85–86, 94; sources on, 311

Clauberg, Carl, 162, 230

Clerks, 18, 235–36

Codreanu, Corneliu Zelea, 252

Cohen, Arthur, 366

Cohen, Asher, 323

Cohen, Michael, 348

Cohen, Richard, 279

Cohn, Norman, 288

Collaborators, sources on, 317–18

Common criminals, in concentration camps, 5, 18, 199, 218, 236

Communism/communists: Baum Group and, 250; in Germany, 57; Jews and, 61, 66, 73, 112–13, 114; resistance and, 36; in Soviet Union, 13

Concentration camps, 5, 17, 217–18, 224; accommodation in, 104; armed resistance in, 101, 218; common criminals in, 5, 18, 199, 218, 236; Crystal Night and, 219; euthanasia and, 223; evacuation of, 36; evasion in, 33; Himmler and, 21, 36, 84, 154, 160, 167, 180, 195, 198–99, 218, 262; labor camps as, 18, 229; obedience to authority and, 91; Operation 14f13 and, 204, 223, 233; Pohl and, 187; prisoner functionaries in, 18–19, 101, 105, 198, 204, 235–36; prostitutes in, 218; selections (Selektionen) at, 17, 20, 23, 85, 240; sources on, 310, 319–22; SS and, 5, 195, 198, 199, 218, 235; survival in, 102–3, 104–6; *see also* Auschwitz; Bergen-Belsen; Buchenwald; Crematoria; Dachau; Detention camps; Homosexuals; Jews; Medical experiments; Gas chambers; Oranienburg; Dora-Mittelbau; Flossenbürg; Forced labor; Gross-Rosen; Gypsies; Lichtenburg; Majdanek; Mauthausen; Neuengamme; Płaszów; Prisoners of war (Soviet); Ravensbrück; Religious dissenters; Sachsenhausen; Stutthof

Conference of Jewish Material Claims Against Germany, 169

Confessing Church (Bekennende Kirche), 174, 178, 257

Conservative Party (DNVP), 145

Constanza, Mary, 331

"Control Council Law No. 10," 168

Conway, John, 112, 128, 345

Cornwell, John, 345

Council for Aid to the Jews (Rada Pomocy Zydom), *see* Zegota

Council of elders (Altestenrat), *see* Jewish Councils

Courage to Care, The (film), 379

Crematoria, 21, 22, 166, 194, 195, 199, 204, 207, 208, *218–19*, 219, 226, 240–41

Crimea, 260

Criminal Police (Kriminalpolizei or KRIPO), 255, 262; *see also* Police, German

Criminals, *see* Common criminals

Croatia, 25, 27–28, 35, 50, 86, 87, 161, 163, 263–64

Cross and the Star, The (film), 378

Crystal Night (Kristallnacht), 7–8, 75–76, 119, 150, 179, 216, 219–20, 235; concentration camps and, 208, 218; films on, 376, 378; Germans and, 110; Goebbels and, 178–79; Nazi Party and, 110; privileged mixed marriages and, 236; sources on, 298, 300

Culture, 8, 146, 216–17; sources on, 316; see also Art; Literature; Music/musicians

Cyanide, see Zyklon B

Czarnecki, Joseph, 331

Czech, Danuta, 320

Czech lands, impact of Holocaust on, 25

Czechoslovakia, 38, 53, 148, 149, 245, 246

Czerniaków, Adam, 16, 100, 175, 213, 336, 338

Czestochowa, 17

Dachau, 5, 144, 198–99; Eicke and, 218, 199; films on, 384; Himmler and, 198; Höss and, 182; liberation of, 167; Mauthausen and, 204; medical experiments in, 230; memorial to, 407; survival at, 106

Daimler-Benz, sources on, 315

Dallas Memorial Center for Holocaust Studies, 402

Daluege, Kurt, 245, 255

Darre, Walther, 242

Darwin, Charles, 55

Davidson, Charles, 397

Davies, Alan, 367

Dawes Plan, 142

Dawidowicz, Lucy S., 45, 74, 274, 284, 332, 359, 392

Deaf persons, sources on, 218, 328

Death camps, 224; see also Extermination camps

Death marches, 36, 166, 184, 192, 196, 199, 200, 206, 208, 220

Death's Head (Totenkopf) units, 263, 199

Debt to Honor, A (film), 379

De Gaulle, Charles, 187

Deggendorf, 423

Deichmann, Ute, 314

De Jong, Louis, 117

Dekel, Sheila Cohn, 326

Delasem, 32

Delbo, Charlotte, 336

Delzell, Charles, 345

Demjanjuk, John, 132; sources on, 283

Denaturalization Law, 145

Denial, of Final Solution, 34, 98, 124, 34

Denmark, 13; bystander reactions in, 117; film on, 379; government officials in, 88; impact of Holocaust on, 31–32, 421; Jews deported from, 86, 164; sources on, 353, 354; Sweden and, 126; trials of war criminals and, 245; yellow badge and, 247

Dentists, Jewish, 6; sources on, 339

Deportations, 12–13, 25, 78, 79; Eichmann and, 8, 15, 84, 149, 154, 160, 206, 214; German army and, 85; Germans' reaction to, 86, 110; jumping from trains and, 101; SS and, 84; Wannsee Conference and, 15

Deschner, Günther, 308

Des Pres, Terrence, 103, 320

Detweiler, Donald, 286

Deutsches Historisches Museum Berlin (German Historical Museum), 406

Diament, Josef, 206

Diamonds in the Snow (film), 374

Diaries: of German Jews, 301–2; of perpetrators, 318–19; of survivors, 335–44

Diary of Anne Frank, The, 176; see also Frank, Anne

Diary of Anne Frank, The (film), 385

Diaspora, 58, 64

Dietrich, Donald, 345, 367

Dietrich, Otto, 242

Dimensions: A Journal of Holocaust Studies, 371

Diment, Michael, 103, 336

Dippel, John, 299
Disabled, *see* Euthanasia; Handicapped
Disarmament Conference, 146
Displaced Persons (DPs), 37, 38, 129, 184, *220–21*, 249, 423; films on, 383–84
Displaced Persons (film), 383
Dnepropetrovsk, 260
Dobroszycki, Lucjan, 125, 272, 279, 336
Doctors, *see* Physicians
Documentaries, on Holocaust, 373–85
Dokumentations- und Kulturzentrum Deutscher Sinti und Roma (Center for Documentation and Culture of German Sinti and Roma), 406
Dollfuss, Engelbert, 146
Domarus, Max, 304
Donat, Alexander, 106, 336
Dönitz, Karl, 244; film on, 381
Doomed Voyage of the St. Louis, The (film), 379
Dora-Mittelbau, 36, 198, *199*, 218
Double Crossing: The Voyage of the St. Louis, The (film), 374
Dramas/docudramas, on Holocaust, 385–89
Drancy transit camp, 160, *199–200*
Drucker, Malka, 353
Dülffer, Jost, 303
Düsseldorf, 111, 270, 296
Dutch, *see* Netherlands
Dwork, Deborah, 320, 325

Eastern Europe: antisemitism in, 112–13; bystander reactions in, 112–16; evasion by Jews of, 101–2; history of Jews in, 59–60, 61, 66; impact of Holocaust on, 24–29, 129, 421; responsibility for Holocaust and, 41; sources on, 273, 298, 301, 322, 328–29; survivors from, 37–38; *see also* Ghettos
Eastern Galicia, 156, 260
East Germany: reparations and, 40, 237; trials of war criminals and, 39–40, *243*

East of War (film), 381
Ebensee, 423
Economic Administration Main Office, *see* SS Economic and Administrative Main Office
Economy: Aryanization and, 216, 219–20; Jews excluded from, 6, 7–8; Nazis and, 5
Edelheit, Abraham, 270
Edelheit, Hershel, 270
Edelman, Marek, 340
Education, Jews barred from German, 6, 8, 145, 150
Efron, John, 288
Ehrenburg, Ilya, 285
Eichengreen, Lucille, 336–37
Eichmann, Adolf, *175–76*; Brand and, 175; death marches and, 166; deportations and, 8, 15, 84, 149, 154, 160, 206, 214; films on, 380, 381, 382, 387; Hungary and, 26–27; Kasztner and, *183*; motivation of, 90; sources on, 282, 286, 307; trial of, 39, 40, 169; Wallenberg and, *192*
Eicke, Theodor, 199, 218
Einsatzgruppen (action squads), 13, 24–25, 29, 84, 156, 173, *221–22*, 226, 260; gas vans and, 226; German army and, 85, 250; Heydrich and, 180; Himmler and, 181; Hiwis and, 228; Minsk and, 205; Order Police and, 256; Sonderkommando and, 240–41; sources on, 278, 283–84, 310; Soviet Union and, 14, 24, 74, 79, 80, 84, 85, 155, 217, 221, 226, 256, 260; trials of war criminals and, 242; Vilna and, 211
Einsatzkommando, Babi Yar and, 157
Eishyshok, sources on, 300–1
Eitinger, Leo, 130–31, 270, 363
Electronic resources, on Holocaust, 389–92, 398–400
Eliach, Yaffa, 300–1, 337
Emigration, 6, 7, 8–9, 76, 78–79, 157;

ban on, 12, 157; negotiations furthering, 121–22; sources on, 300; SS and,
84; tables on, 419–20; tax on, 7; *see
also* "Blood for trucks" offer; Central
Office for Jewish Emigration; Reich
Central Office for Jewish Emigration

Employment, restrictions on Jewish, 157

Enabling Law (March 24, 1993), 3, 255

Endre, Laszlo, 246

Enforcers, 18

Engel, David, 114, 348

England, history of Jews in, 60; Great
Britain

English Zionist Federation, 192

Enlightenment, sources on antisemitism in, 288–89

Epstein, Eric, 270

Epstein, Helen, 365

Erb, Rainer, 370

Ericksen, Robert, 345

Escape from Sobibór (film), 385

Eschwege, Helmut, 323

Estonia, 24–25, 38, 86–87, 260, 421, 422

Eternal Jew, The (Der ewige Jude; film),
383

Ethnic Germans, *see Volksdeutsche*

Eugenics, 9, 54, 55–56, 66, 222, 223; film
on, 381; sources on, 289, 293, 314

Europa Europa (film), 385

Europe: resource organizations, muse-
ums, and memorials in, 413–15;
sources on Jews in before World War
II, 300–1; *see also* Central Europe;
Eastern Europe; Occupied Europe;
West Europe

Euthanasia, 9–10, 11, 20, 55, 71, 207, 217,
223, 224; beginning of, 151–52; Belzec
and, 196; Brack and, *174–75*, 223;
careerism as motivation of perpetrators of, 93–94; Catholics and, 251;
gassing and, 153, 226; German civil
servants and, 85–86; Goebbels and,
178; Hartheim and, 190, 193, 204, 223,

233; Hitler and, 9–10, 48, 55, 112, 156,
174, 222, 223; Operation 14f13 and,
204, *233*; Operation Reinhard and,
234; physicians and, 89–90, 151–52;
public outcry against, 10, 102, 110,
112, 156; sources on, 315, 327, 366;
Stangl and, 190; T4 program and,
9–10, 11, 48, 74, 76, 85–86, 97, 102,
193, 223, 233; Wirth and, *193*

Evans, Richard, 359

Evasion, as response to persecution,
101–2, 33

Evian Conference, 8, 149, *200*

Exodus (film), 386

Extermination camps, 5, 17, 20–23, 78,
80, 217, 218, 222, 223–24, 225; armed
resistance in, 35, 100, 101, 104, 163,
164, 210, 233, 239; euthanasia and, |10,
223; German physicians and,
85; Himmler and, 181; Operation
Reinhard and, *234*; privileged mixed
marriages and, *236*; selections (Selektionen) at, 17, 20, 23, 85, *240*; Sonderkommando and, 240–41; sources on,
319–22, 340; SS and, 84; survival in,
102–3, 104–6; *see also* Auschwitz;
Belzec; Chełmno; Crematoria; Gas
chambers; Majdanek; Medical experiments; Sobibór; Treblinka

*Eye of the Dictator: Propaganda and the
Nazis, The* (film), 383

Ezergailis, Andrew, 279

Facing History and Ourselves National
Foundation, Inc., 402

Fackenheim, Emil, 133, 367

Falkenhausen, Alexander von, 246

Falkenhorst, Nikolaus von, 243

Farben, I. G., 19, 161, *194–95*, 241, 249;
sources on, 314, 315

Fascism: Arrow Cross and, 27, 87, 115,
166, 182, 192, *250*; Hlinka Guard
and, 27, 87, 150, *252*; Iron Guard
and, 29, 87, 173, *252–53*; Italy and, 32;

Fascism (*Continued*)
sources on, 303, 317, 350; Ustasha and, 27, 87, *263–64; see also* Mussolini, Benito
Fatal Attraction of Adolf Hitler, The (film), 381
Federal Republic of Germany, *see* West Germany
Federation of Swiss Jewish Communities, 185
Fein, Helen, 109, 353
Feinermann, Emmanuel, 300
Feingold, Henry, 120, 348
Feinstein, Stephen, 331
Feldafing, 423
Fenelon, Fania, 105, 337
Fenyo, Mario, 317
Ferderber-Salz, Bertha, 103, 337
Ferencz, Benjamin, 314
Fest, Joachim, 40, 305, 311–12, 356, 381
Feuchtwanger, Edgar, 295
Field, Geoffrey, 288
Fifth Horseman Is Fear, The (*Ja, spravedlnost*; film), 386
Films, on Holocaust, 373–89
Filov, Bogdan, 246
Final Solution (Endlösung), 10, 14–33, 156, 158, 194, 235, 203, *224*, 235; definition of, 46; denial and ignorance of, 34, 98, 124; evasion and resistance to, 33–36, 183, 184; functionalists and, 71, 74–77; Himmler and, 181; immediate origins of, 71–81; intentionalists and, 71, 72–74; *Mischlinge* and, 231; Operation Barbarossa and, *217*; Pohl and, *187*, 241, 263; roots of, 67–69; Sonderkommando and, 240–41; sources on, 274, 275, 276–78, 280, 327, 366; synthesizers and, 71, 77–80; Vichy France and, 211; *see also* Camps; Euthanasia; Forced labor; Genocide; Ghettos; Heydrich, Reinhard; Holocaust; Kaltenbrunner, Ernst; Wannsee Conference

Finger, Seymour, 348
Finkelstein, Norman, 89, 359–60
Finland, 33, 88; sources on, 351
First Supplementary Decree to the Reich Citizenship Law, 231, 233
Fischer, Klaus, 288, 303
Fittko, Lisa, 357–58
Flam, Gila, 331
Flames in the Ashes (film), 374
Fleming, Gerald, 73 68 , 277
Flick, Friedrich, 241
Florida Holocaust Museum, The, 402
Flossenbürg, *200*, 218; memorial to, 409–10; sources on, 343
Fogelman, Eva, 354
Föhrenwald, 423
Forced labor, 15, 17–19, 178, 186, 188, 189, 199, *224–25*, 227, 228; Arrow Cross and, *250*; film on, 376; General Government and, 11, 153, 201, 203, 213, *224–25*; German army and, 85, 250; Jewish Councils and, 253; sources on, 314, 315, 468; SS and, 84; *see also* Labor camps
Foreign Organization of the NSDAP (Auslandsorganisation der NSDAP), 246
Forests of Valour (film), 374
Förster, Jürgen, 49
For the Living (film), 374
Fortunoff Video Archive for Holocaust Testimonies (Yale University), 361, 402
Föster, Jürgen, 308
Four Year Plan, 179, 148
Fragments of Isabella (film), 386
France: antisemitism in, 116, 288–89; armed resistance in, 100–1; bystander reactions in, 116; Catholics in, 251; deportation of Jews from, 159, 160; film on, 380; history of Jews in, 58, 60; impact of Holocaust on, 29–30, 421, 422; International Military Tribunal and, 244; Jewish Army in, 235;

rescue and, 8, 30, 116, 354, 380; sources on, 281, 288–89, 301, 303, 323–24, 354, 362, 369; trials of war criminals and, 39, 246; yellow badge and, 159; *see also* Vichy France

Franco, Francisco, 127, 148; sources on, 349

Frank, Anne, 31, *176*, 337; film on, 373, 375, 379, 385; house/museum of, 176, 413; organization related to, 401; sources on, 358, 399

Frank, Hans, 11, 38, 152, 153, *176–77*, 189, 201, 244, 245

Frank, Otto, 176, 337

Frankfurt Trial, 243

Frankl, Victor, 106, 367

Freeman, Joseph, 337

Freemasons, 255, 262

Frei, Norbert, 303

Freiwald, Aaron, 281

Freudenheim, Tom, 332

Frick, Wilhelm, 143, 244

Friedländer, Albert, 320

Friedlander, Henry, 48, 93–94, 282, 285, 327

Friedländer, Saul, 78, 111, 128, 299, 337, 356, 358, 360, 377

Friedman, Ina, 327–28

Friedman, Saul S., 119

Friedrich, Otto, 320

Fritsche, Hans, 244

Fritzsche, Peter, 354

Fromm, General, 190

Fulda Conference of (Catholic) Bishops, 144, 156

Functionalists, motives for Final Solution and, 71, 74–77

Funk, Walther, 244

Fürstengrube, sources on, 339

Fürth, 423

Galen, Cardinal August Count von, 10, 112, 156

Galicia, Eastern, 156, 260

Gallagher, Hugh, 314–15

Galton, Francis, 55

Garbarz, Moshe, 106, 338

Garden of the Finzi-Continis, The (Il giardino dei Finzi-Contini; film), 386

Garfein, Jack, film on, 375

Gas chambers, 23, 194, 195, 223–24, 219, 225–26; Auschwitz-Birkenau and, 21, 22, 36, 156, 159, 166, 194, 195, 224, 226; carbon monoxide and, 21, 204, 208, 210, 223, 226, 248–49; Dachau and, 199; euthanasia and, 153, 223; Majdanek and, 204, 224, 226; Operation Reinhard camps and, 21, 208, 210, 226; Ravensbrück and, 207; Sachsenhausen and, 208; selection and, *240*; Sondercommandos and, 226, 240–41; sources on, 286; Stutthof and, 208; *see also* Zyklon B

Gas vans, 14, *226–27*; carbon monoxide and, 21, 204, 208, 210, 223, 226, 248–49; Chełmno and, 20, 198, 224; Einsatzgruppen and, 222; Minsk and, 205

Gauleiters (Nazi Party district leaders), 178, 188, 190

Gay, Peter, 301–2

Gebirtig, Mordecai, 397

Gedenkstätte Bergen-Belsen (Memorial), 406

Gedenkstätte Buchenwald (Memorial), 407

Gedenkstätte Dachau (Memorial), 407

Gedenkstätte Deutscher Widerstand (Memorial to the German Resistance), 407

Gedenkstätte Hadamar (Memorial), 407

Gedenkstätte Haus der Wannsee-Konferenz (Memorial of the House of the Wannsee Conference), 407

Gedenkstätte Konzentrationslager Mauthausen (Memorial/Concentration Camp), 413

Gedenkstätte Plötzensee (Memorial), 408

Gedenkstätte und Museum Sachsen-hausen (Memorial and Museum), 408

Geheime Staatspolizei, see Gestapo

Gellately, Robert, 309

Gelman, Charles, 104, 338

General Commissariat for Jewish Affairs (Commissariat General aux Questions Juives), 155

General Government, 152, 156, 189, 200–1, 260; civilians of as target of genocide in, 45, 49–50; Eichmann and, 176; Einsatzgruppen and, 221; forced labor in, 11, 153, 201, 203, 213, 224–25; ghettos in, 11, 152, 157, 227; Gypsies in, 10–11, 24, 76, 152, 153, 154, 422; Nazi racial policies in, 10–12; Order Police and, 256; Radom and, 206; white armband and, 153; yellow badges and, 247; see also Frank, Hans; Ghettos; Kraków; Lublin; Operation Harvest Festival; Operation Reinhard; Poland

Genocide, 132, 222, 225; antisemitism and, 215; Goebbels and, 178; Hitler and, 3–7, 67, 71–81, 156, 181, 215, 216; Holocaust as, 134–36; Operation Barbarossa and, 217; as secret, 15, 97, 110, 119; special treatment and, 15, 240, 241; World War I and, 56; see also Final Solution; Genocide; Heydrich, Reinhard; Holocaust

Genocide (film), 378

Genocide Convention (United Nations), 132, 225

Gens, Jacob, 16, 35, 100, 177, 211

Gentiles: films on, 379, 380; rescue and, 33, 111, 325–26, 343, 353, 355–56, 358–59, 379, 380; sources on, 275, 322, 325–26, 343, 353, 355–356, 358–59; see also Catholics; Christians

Georg, Willy, 273

Gerlach, Christian, 277

German army, see Army, Germany

German Christians, 257; see also Protestants

German Democratic Republic, see East Germany

German Foreign Ministry, 242; deportations and, 86; sources on, 311; see also Madagascar Plan

German Gold and Silver Metallurgical Institute (Deutsche Gold under Silber Scheide-Anstalt or DEGUSSA), 249

German History (journal), 372

Germania Judaica, 408

German Studies Review (journal), 372

German Vermin-Combating Corporation (Deutsche Gesellschaft für Schädlingsbekémpfung mbH or DEGESCH), 249

German Workers' Party (Deutsche Arbeiterpartei or DAP), 141, 232; see also National Socialism (Nazism)

Germany, 421; antisemitism in, 66, 67–69, 88–89, 111; bystander reactions in, 109–112, 353, 354–55, 356, 359; history of Jews in, 58, 60, 66, 67–69; impact of Holocaust on, 25, 421; Jews in, 84, 295–301; nationalism and, 53; resistance in, 111–12, 250, 356–57, 358, 384–85, 407; resource organizations, museums, and memorials in, 406–12; uniqueness/comparability of Holocaust and, 135–36

Germany Awake (Deutschland Erwache! film), 383

Gerstein, Kurt, 25, 111–12, 177–78, 356

Gestapo (Secret State Police), 5, 84, 145, 182,, 190, 255, 256, 262; sources on, 309

Geve, Thomas, 104, 105, 338

Ghetto Fighters' Kibbutz, 194

Ghetto Fighters Museum, 194

Ghettos, 15–17, 227; armed resistance in,

34–35, 100, 113, 162, 201, 212, 213, 233, 239; escape from, 98; evasion in, 33; films on, 374–78; functionalists and, 76; in General Government, 9, 11, 152, 157, 227; German army and, 85; Gypsies in, 9, 202, 206, 213; intentionalists and, 73; Jewish police in, 16, 99, 103–4, 177, 207, 253, 256–57, 341; privileged mixed marriages and, 236; rescue and, 238; sources on, 319–22, 396–97, 341; see also Forced labor; Jewish Councils

Gies, Miep, 358

Gilbert, Martin, 45, 119, 122, 271, 274, 325, 348, 360, 375

Gitelman, Zvi, 115, 360

Glazer, Richard, 105

Globocnik, Odilo, 20, 178, 190, 203, 214, 224, 234

Gobineau, Arthur de, 54, 293–94

Goebbels, Joseph, 143, 144, 178–79; Crystal Night and, 75, 219; culture and, 216; film on, 381, 383; sources on, 312, 313, 316, 318; suicide of, 38–39

Goebbels: Master of Propaganda (film), 383

Goerdeler, Carl, 112

Goetz, Aly, 276

Goldberg, Arthur J., 348

Goldberger, Leo, 354

Goldhagen, Daniel, 88, 111, 277–78, 359–60

Goldmann, Nahum, 169

Goodbye, Children (Au Revoir les Enfants; film), 386

Good Morning Mr. Hitler (film), 383

Gordon, Sarah, 111, 354

Göring, Hermann, 15, 76, 144, 153, 179, 244, 259; Crystal Night and, 219–20; film on, 381, 382; Final Solution and, 74, 75, 79, 80, 156, 180; Goebbels and, 178–79; SA and, 261; sources on, 312–13; trial of, 38

Göth, Amon, 245

Graf, Willi, 264

Grafeneck, 223

Grau, Günter, 51, 328

Great Britain: German navy and, 147; Palestine and, 8, 124–25, 127, 151, 159, 174, 221, 248; rescue and, 8, 120, 162; sources on, 348, 352; trials of war criminals and, 242–43; war criminals in, 254; see also International Military Tribunal

Greater Germany, 157, 158, 247

Great Synagogue (Munich), 149

Greece, 26, 35, 53, 85, 165, 421, 422

Green, Gerald, 331

Greenfeld, Howard, 325–26

Gregor, Neil, 315

Grimm, Hans, 229

Grossman, Chaika, 338

Grossman, Mendel, 272

Grossman, Vasily, 285

Gross-Rosen, 23, 36, 201–2, 218

Grüber, Heinrich, 112

Grünfeld, David, 396

Grynszpan, Herschel, 150, 219

Gunskirchen, 205

Gurock, Jeffrey S., 125, 279

Gurs transit camp, 154

Gusen, 204

Gutman, Yisrael, 47, 100, 113, 270, 283, 320–21, 323, 328

Gutteridge, Richard, 345

Gypsies, 7, 147, 148, 149, 161, 162, 165, 224, 227–28; as Aryans, 47, 215; as asocial, 148; camps for, 9, 23, 97, 148, 161, 162, 165, 227–28; in concentration camps, 18, 162, 165, 197, 198, 199, 205, 207, 209, 210, 218, 227; death marches and, 220; deportations of, 12, 15, 84, 86, 153, 154, 157, 158, 189, 209; Einsatzgruppen and, 13, 24; evasion by, 102; film on, 376; gassing of, 157, 163, 198, 210, 226; in General Government, 10–11, 24, 76, 152, 153, 154, 422;

Gypsies (*Continued*)
   in ghettos, 9, 202, 206, 213; Himmler
   and, 150, 161; history of, 61–62, 69–
   70; impact of Holocaust on, 24, 25,
   26, 27, 28, 29, 30, 31, 32, 33, 47, 422;
   language of, 62, 215; medical experiments on, 230; Nisko and Lublin
   Plan and, 232; Nuremberg Laws and,
   151, 230–31, 233; organizations on,
   406; police surveillance of, 97; and
   registered domiciles, 152; restitution
   to, 40; sources on, 271, 278, 291, 315,
   316, 326, 327, 328, 329, 330, 333; sterilization of, 145; survivors and, 37, 38,
   130, 131; as target of genocide, 9, 45,
   46, 47–48, 51, 71, 84, 85, 87

Haas, Pavel, 393, 396
Haas, Peter, 367
Haavara Transfer Agreement, 145, 76
Habermas, Jürgen, 135
Hackett, David, 321
Hadamar, 223, 407; sources on, 285
Hadamar Trial, 242
Hallie, Philip, 116, 354
Halutz resistance, sources on, 323
Hamann, Brigitte, 305
Hamburg, sources on, 308
Hamerow, Theodore, 112, 356
Hamilton, Richard, 295
Hancock, Ian, 48, 328
Handicapped, 9; children as, 151; eva-
   sion and, 102; history of, 62–63, 69–
   70; Hitler and, 156; sources on, 291,
   314–15, 316, 327, 330; sterilization of,
   9, 70, 145, 222, 223; as target of geno-
   cide, 9, 11, 13, 45, 46, 48, 51, 71; *see
   also* Bonhoeffer, Dietrich; Euthana-
   sia
Hanna's War (film), 386
Harel, Isser, 282
Hartheim, 190, 193, 204, 223, 233
Hartman, Geoffrey, 360
Harzburg front, 143

Hasidic tales, collection of, 337
Häsler, Alfred A., 126, 349
Hass, Aaron, 131, 363, 365
Haushofer, Karl, 229
Hausner, Gideon, 282
Hayes, Peter, 315, 367–68
Headland, Ronald, 278
Health activism, sources on, 316
Hebrew Sheltering and Immigrant Aid
   Society, sources on, 363
Heger, Heinz, 328
Heiber, Helmut, 312
Heim, Susanne, 137, 276
Heinkel, 19
Heller, Celia, 301
Hellman, Peter, 272
Helmreich, Ernst, 346
Helmreich, William B., 130, 363
Heppner, Ernest, 338
Herf, Jeffrey, 360
Hertzberg, Arthur, 288
Herzl, Theodor, 248
Hess, Moses, 248
Hess, Rudolf, 155, 229, 244; film on, 381,
   382
Heydrich, Reinhard, 8, 152, *179–80*, 244,
   255, 259, 307; assassination of, 20,
   159, 160; Final Solution and, 14, 15,
   74, 75, 79, 80, 156; Security Service
   and, 255, 262; sources on, 308;
   Wannsee Conference and, 158, 212;
   see also Operation Reinhard
Hilberg, Raul, 93, 99, 102, 275, 285, 338,
   360–61, 377
Hilfsverein, *see* Relief Organization of
   German Jews
Hilfswillige, *see* Hiwis (Hilfswillige)
Hillesum, Etty, 339
Hillgruber, Andreas, 135
Himmler, Heinrich, 142, 147, 157,
   180–81, 255; concentration camps
   and, 21, 36, 84, 154, 160, 167, 195,
   198–99, 218, 262; film on, 381; Finland and, 33; Frank and, 177; Ger-

man police and, 262; ghetto liquidation and, 163; Globocnik and, 178; Goebbels and, 178–79; Gypsies and, 47–48, 150, 158, 161; Heydrich and, 179–80; Jewish emigration and, 12, 156; Kaltenbrunner and, *182, 183*; negotiations with Allies by, 122, 167, 181; Operation Reinhard and, 160, *234*; sources on, 308, 318; SS and, 84, 262; suicide of, 38–39

Hindenburg, Paul von, 57, 142, 143, 144, 146

Hippler, Fritz, 383

Hirsch, Herbert, 361

Hirschfeld, Gerhard, 317, 328

Historikerstreit (historians' dispute), 135–36

History and Memory: Studies in Representation of the Past (journal), 372

Hitler: The Whole Story (film), 381

Hitler, Adolf, 26–27, 32, *181*, 197, 236; Allies' pressure on to release Jews, 122–23; Anschluss and, *214*; antisemitism in Germany and, 67–69; attempted assassination of, 25, 112, 165, 190, 356, 385; Beer Hall Putsch and,73, 141–42, 179, 219, 261; Catholics and, 144, 251; concentration camps and, 167, 217; Crystal Night and, 219; culture and, 216; euthanasia and, 9–10, 48, 55, 112, 156, 174, 222, 223; films on, 380–82, 385; Frank and, 177; functionalists and, 71, 74–77; genocide and, 3–7, 67, 71–81, 156, 215, 216, 224; German Army and, 148, 250; German citizenship and, 143; Goebbels and, 179; Göring and, 179; Himmler and, 180, 181; *Hitler's Secret Book* and, 305; intentionalists and, 71, 72–74; Iron Guard and, 253; Jewish emigration and, 122; Kasztner and, *183*; *Lebensraum* and, 4, 13, 73, 143, 148, *229*; Madagascar Plan and,

12, *229*; *Mein Kampf* and, 4, 72, 73, 142, 229, 305; Munich Agreement and, 205; Mussolini and, *186*; Nisko and Lublin Plan and, 232; obedience of Germans and, 88–89; Olympics and, 216; Protestants and, 257; rise to power and, 3–4, 5–6, 51–57, 69, 141, 143, 144, 146; Rosenberg and, *188*; SA and, 146, 261; Seyss-Inquart and, *189*; sources on, 294–95, 304–7, 354, 356; Soviet Union and, 13–14, 24, 217; Speer and, *189*; SS and, 84, 262–63; suicide of, 38–39, 167; synthesizers and, 71, 77–80; Tiso and, *191*; Ustasha and, *263*; Waffen SS and, 263; White Rose and, 264; *see also* National Socialism

Hitler's Henchmen (film), 381

Hitler's Secret Book (Hitler), 305

Hitler Youth, 385; sources on, 313

Hiwis (Hilfswillige), 13, 18, 86–87, 94, 132, 183, 196, 210, 222, *228*

Hlinka, Andrej, 252, 317

Hlinka Guard, 27, 87, 150, *252*

H-Net discussion networks, on Holocaust, 389–90

Hochhuth, Rolf, 332–33

Hoffman, Eva, 321

Hoffmann, Peter, 112, 356–57

Höfle, Hermann, 245

Höhne, Heinz, 40, 309

Holland, *see* Netherlands

Holliday, Laurel, 339

Holocaust, 67–69, 132; Allies publicize knowledge of, 123; beginning of genocide and, 9–14; Christian religious thought and, 133–34; definition of, 45–52; disbelief and, 34, 98, 124, 370–71, 399; end of, 36–37; exclusion of "racially inferior" and, 3–9; as genocide, 134–36; historical overview of, 3–41, 53–57, 134–38; history of prejudice and, 63–70; impact of, 13–14, 23–33, 37–41, 129–38, 359–71, 421–23;

Holocaust (*Continued*)
  Jewish religious thought and, 132–33; legal and religious institutions and, 132–34; as modernism, 136–37; perpetrators of, 83–95; philosophical implications of, 365, 366, 367–68, 369–70; public fascination with, 137; religious implications of, 132–34, 365, 366–67, 368–70; roots of, 53–70; sources on, 282, 359–62, 365, 366, 367–68, 369–70, 390, 391–92; uniqueness/comparability of, 134–36; *see also* Final Solution; Genocide; Victims
Holocaust (film), 386
Holocaust (TV docudrama), 40
Holocaust: In Memory of Millions, The (film), 374
Holocaust: Liberation of Auschwitz (film), 384
Holocaust and Genocide Studies (journal), 371
Holocaust Educational Foundation, The, 403
Holocaust Education and Memorial Center, 403
Holocaust Education Center, 416
Holocaust/Genocide Project (International Education and Resource Network), 403
Holocaust Museum Houston Education Center and Memorial, 403
Holocaust Oral History Project, 403–4
Homosexuals: film on, 378; murder of, 5, 9, 18, 45, 50–51, 199, 218; sources on, 327, 328, 329, 330
Horthy, Miklós, 26–27, 87, 115, 122, 124, 165, 166, 181–82, 250
Höss, Rudolf, 22, 39, 154, 182, 194, 226, 245; sources on, 318
Hotel Terminus: The Life and Times of Klaus Barbie (film), 381
Huber, Kurt, 264
Hungary, 122–23; Allies' pressure on to release Jews, 122–23; American Joint Distribution Committee and, 249; Arrow Cross and, 27, 87, 115, 122, 166, 182, 192, 250; "blood for trucks" offer and, 122, 135, 175, 183; bystander reactions in, 115–16; Catholics and, 128; Eichmann and, 176; films on, 375, 388; government officials in, 87; Himmler and, 181; history of Jews in, 61; Horthy and, 26–27, 87, 115, 122, 124, 165, 166, 181–82, 250; impact of Holocaust on, 26–27, 37–38, 421, 422; Jews deported from, 165, 166; Jews in, 87, 165; Kasztner and, 183; Mayer and, 185; nationalism and, 53; rescue and, 238; sources on, 278, 284, 317, 323, 334, 343, 351, 359; Transylvania and, 209–10; trial of war criminals and, 246; War Refugee Board and, 123–24; yellow badges in, 164, 247; *see also* Brand, Joel; Senesh, Hannah; Wallenberg, Raoul
Hunt for Adolf Eichmann, The (film), 381

Ideology, as motivation of perpetrators, 88–90
Ignorance, avoidance of armed resistance and, 34
Image before My Eyes (film), 375
Imperial Germany, 290 236 , 293 272 , 296
IMT, *see* International Military Tribunal
Industrialism, Holocaust and, 54
Industry, 15–16, 22, 36; *see also* Forced labor
In Our Own Hands (film), 375
Intentionalists, motives for Final Solution and, 71, 72–74
Intergovernmental Committee on Refugees, 200
International Military Tribunal (IMT), 38–39, 131, 168, 182–83, 188, 189,

243–45, 244, 256, 263; films on, 381,
382, 387; genocide and, 132, 225;
Gypsies and, 131; medical experi-
ments and, 230; sources on, 278, 282,
283, 285, 286, 287, 399
International Red Cross, *see* Red Cross,
International
In the Presence of Mine Enemies (film),
386
*In the Shadow of the Reich: Nazi Medi-
cine, The* (film), 381
Ioanid, Radu, 317
Ireland, sources on, 351
Iron Guard, 29, 87, 173, *252–53*
Irving, David, 77
Isaac, Jules, 133, 289
Israel: Ben-Gurion and, 174; Displaced
Persons and, 38, 221; establishment
of, 38, 129, 133, 168, 248, 367, 368,
369; Jewish property restitution and,
169; reparations and, 40, 169, *237*; resource organizations, museums, and
memorials in, 415–17; sources on,
363, 367, 368, 369; survivors in, 36,
131; Weizmann and, *192*; *see also*
Palestine; "Righteous Among the
Nations"; Yad Vashem
Italy: Anti-Comintern Pact and, 148; antisemitism in, 150; bystander reactions in, 117; deportations and, 86;
films on, 379, 380, 385, 386, 387;
government officials in, 87; impact
of Holocaust on, 32, 422; Jews in,
149, 164, 421; Mussolini and, 32, 163,
167, *186*, 263, 280; nationalism and,
53; non-Jewish volunteers in, 87;
Pact of Steel and, 151; rescue and, 32,
238, 379, 385; Rome-Berlin Axis and,
148; sources on, 280, 281, 303, 347,
355; *see also* Fascism

Jäckel, Eberhard, 74, 305
Jackson, Robert, 167
Jacobs, Benjamin, 105, 339

Jacob the Liar (Jakob der Lügner) (film),
386–87
Jankowski, Stanislaw, 115, 352
Janówska labor camp, 160, 164, 203
Japan, 148, 352
JDC, *see* American Joint Distribution
Committee
Jeckeln, Friedrich, 245
Jehovah's Witnesses: film on, 376;
sources on, 326, 327, 329; as target of
genocide, 50, 199, 218
Jelinek, Yeshayahu, 317
Jens, Inge, 358
Jewish Agency for Palestine, 153, 159,
192, 261; Auschwitz and, 166; Ben-
Gurion and, 174; Haavara Agree-
ment and, 76; Palestine Office and,
255, 261; reparations and, 168, *237*;
rescue and, 238; *see also* Yishuv
Jewish Army (Armée Juive), 235
Jewish Brigade, film on, 375
Jewish communities, rescue and, 124–25
Jewish Councils (Judenräte), 11, 16–17,
153, 174, 227, *253–54*; Belgium and,
31; of Bialystok, 197; evasion by, 101;
film on, 377; forced labor and, 225;
Jewish police and, 256; of Kraków,
202; of Łódź, 16, 188, 202, 203; of
Lublin, 203; of L'vov, 203; Merin
and, *185–86*; of Minsk, 205; Netherlands and, 30–31; of Radom, 206; resistance and, 16, 34, 35, 99–100, 103,
253; sources on, 322, 338, 340; of
Vilna, 16, 35, 177, 211; of Warsaw, 16,
101, 175, 194, 213
Jewish Documentation Center, Wiesenthal and, 193
Jewish Fighting Organization (Zydowska Organizacja Bojowa or
ZOB), 113, 160, 187, 213, 239
Jewish Historical Institute, and Museum of the History of Polish Jews,
412
Jewish Mischlinge, 233

Jewish Museum and Archives of Hungary, The, 413–14
Jewish Museum of Prague, 414
Jewish Reservation, *see* Nisko and Lublin plan
Jewish resistance, *see* Resistance, Jewish
Jews: history of, 57–61; impact of Holocaust on, 23–33, 129–33, 421; isolation of, 6–8; motives for genocide of, 71–81; reaction of to persecution, 97–107; as target of genocide, 45–46; *see also* Antisemitism; Final Solution; Genocide; Holocaust; Resistance, Jewish; Survivors; Victims
Jews as citizens (Staatsangehörige), 233
Jodl, Alfred, 244
John XXIII, Pope, 133
Jong, Louis de, 354
Journal of Holocaust Education, 371
Journal of Israeli History (formerly *Studies in Zionism*), 372
Journal of Modern History, 372
Journals, on Holocaust, 371–73
Journey Back: Remembrances of the Holocaust, A (film), 375
Judenburg, 423
Judenräte, *see* Jewish Councils
Judgement at Nuremberg (film), 387
Jüdische Museum Berlin, Das (The Jewish Museum of Berlin), 408
Jüdische Museum Westfalen in Dorsten, Das (Jewish Museum of Westphalia), 409
Jüdisches Museum Frankfurt (Jewish Museum of Frankfurt), 409
Jüdisches Museum Hohenems (Jewish Museum Hohenems), 414
Jüdisches Museum Wien (Jewish Museum of Vienna), 414
Jud Süss (film), 387

Kaiser Wilhelm Gesellschaft (later the Max Planck Gesellschaft), sources on, 316

Kaiser Wilhelm Institute for Anthropology, 185
Kalib, Goldie, 339
Kalisch, Shoshana, 332
Kaltenbrunner, Ernst, 180, 38, *182–83*, 214, 244; sources on, 307
Kamenetsky, Ihor, 49–50, 328–29
Kaplan, Chaim, 339
Kaplan, Harold, 361
Kaplan, Marion A., 111, 299
Kapos, *see* Capos
Kappler, Herbert, 246
Karas, Joza, 332
Karski, Jan, 115, *183*, 352
Kasche, Siegfried, 246
Kasztner, Rezsö, *183*
Kater, Michael, 89, 312, 315
Katsh, Abraham, 339
Katz, Jacob, 68, 289
Katz, Steven T., 45, 134, 289
Kauders, Anthony, 296
Keitel, Wilhelm, 244; film on, 382
Keller, Ulrich, 273
Keneally, Thomas, 333
Kenrick, Donald, 47, 131, 329
Kermish/Kermisz, Joseph, 339–40, 338
Kershaw, Ian, 110, 111, 305–6, 354–55
Kersten, Felix, 167, 318
Kesselring, Albert, 243
Khar'kov, 161, 260
Kielce, 37, 161, 235
Kiev, 260
Killing centers, euthanasia and, 10
King, Christine, 329
Kintner, Earl, 285
Kishinev, 156
Kitterman, David, 91
Kitty: Return to Auschwitz (film), 375
Klein, Gerda Weissmann, film on, 376
Klein, Gideon, 393–94, 396
Klemig, Roland, 273
Klemperer, Klemens von, 357
Klemperer, Victor, 302
Koblik, Steven, 126, 349

Koch, Erich, 260
Koehl, Robert, 89, 309
Kogon, Eugen, 321, 285–86
Kolomyia, 161
Korczak (film), 387
Korczak, Janusz, *183–84*, 336, 340; film on, 387
Kosinski, Jerzy, 333
Kovner, Abba, 35, *184*; film on, 376
Kovno, 13, 106, 156, 158, 164, 165, 207, 260; film on, 375; sources on, 336, 343, 396
Kovno Ghetto: A Buried History (film), 375
Kozielewski, *see* Karski, Jan
Kraków, 11, 16, 152, 155, 159, 161, 162, 188, 201, *202*; sources on, 397
Krakówski, Shmuel, 100, 113, 283–84, 323, 328
Krall, Hannah, 340
Krasa, Hans, 394
Krausnik, Helmut, 309
Kraut, Alan, 347
Krell, Robert, 270
Kren, George, 98, 102, 368
KRIPO, *see* Criminal Police
Kristallnacht, *see* Crystal Night
Krosigk, Lutz Schwerin von, 242
Krupp, Alfred, 19, 195, 242
Krystal, Henry, 130, 364
Kühl, Stefan, 289
Kulisiewicz, 397
Kulmhof, *see* Chełmno
Kun, Béla, 66
Kuper, Leo, 132, 282
Kurenets, sources on, 338
Kurthen, Hermann, 370
Kvaternik, Slavko, 246
KZ-Gedenkstätte Mittelbau-Dora (Memorial), 409
KZ-Gedenkstätte Neuengamme (Memorial), 409
KZ-Gedentättte Flossenbürg (Memorial), 409–10

KZ Mauthausen-Gusen (Concentration Camp), 414

Labor camps, 17–18, 217, 224, 225, *228–29*; accommodation in, 104; armed resistance in, 100; concentration camps and, 218; evasion in, 33; functionalists and, 76; Gross-Rosen and, 201; Himmler and, 181; intentionalists and, 73; L'vov and, 203; prisoner functionaries in, 235–36; in Slovakia, 27; Vichy France and, 211; *see also* Forced labor; Janówska; Łódź; Płaszów; Trawniki
LaCapra, Dominick, 361
Lagarde, Paul de, 292
Lages, Willy, 246
Lagnado, Lucette, 326
Lamberti, Marjorie, 296
Landsberg, Henryk, 203, 423
Lang, Berel, 368
Lang, Jochen von, 286, 312
Langbein, Hermann, 106, 340
Langbein, Julius, 292
Langer, Lawrence, 331, 333, 361, 368
Langer, Walter C., 72, 306
Langmuir, Gavin, 289
Lanzmann, Claude, 377
Lapides, Robert, 335
Laqueur, Walter, 98, 124, 349
Last Days, The (film), 375
Last Sea, The (film), 384
Last Seven Months of Anne Frank, The (film), 375
Latour, Annie, 100–1, 323
Latvia, 260; film on, 374; Hiwis from, 86–87; impact of Holocaust on, 24–25, 421, 422; sources on, 279, 326; survivors from, 38; *see also* Riga
Lautmann, Rödiger, 51, 329
Laval, Pierre, 29, 246
Law for the Protection of German Blood and Honor, 147, 232–33
Lazare, Lucien, 323–24

League of Nations, 142, 146, 148
Lebensborn program, 258
Lebensraum, 4, 13, 50, 73, 84, 143, 148,
    181, *229*, 232
Leber, Julius, 25
Le Chambon-sur-Lignon, 30, 116; film
    on, 380; sources on, 354
Lederer, Zdenek, 321
Legacy of Nuremberg, The (film), 381
Legal institutions, impact of Holocaust
    on, 132
Legal system (German): Jews excluded
    from, 6, 144, 149; sources on, 312
Leibnitz, 423
Leipheim, 423
Leitner, Isabella, 105
Lemkin, Raphael, 132, 225, 279
Leo Baeck Institute Yearbook, 373
Lesbians, 50
Less, Avner, 286
Lester, Elenore, 349
Levi, Primo, 104–5, *184*, 333, 340, 368
Levin, Dov, 324
Levin, Nora, 301
Levine, Hillel, 290
Levy, Richard S., 69, 290, 294
Lewin, Abraham, 340
Lewy, Guenter, 47, 128, 329, 346
Ley, Robert, 245
Liberation (film), 384
Liberation, films on, 383–84
Liberation : Testimony (film), 384
Liberation of KZ Dachau, The (film),
    384
Lichtenberg, Bernhard, 40, 112
Lichtenburg (concentration camp), 207
Lidice, Czechoslovakia, 160
Life is Beautiful (*La Vita à bella*; film),
    387
Life of Adolf Hitler, The (*Das Leben von
    Adolf Hitler*; film), 381
Lifton, Robert Jay, 89–90, 315–16
Lindemann, Albert, 290
Linenthal, Edward, 361

Linnea, Sharon, 349
Linz, 190, 423
Lipschitz, C. U., 349
Lipstadt, Deborah, 350, 370–71
Literature: book burning and, 145; on
    Holocaust, 332–35
Lithuania, 260; films on, 375; history
    of Jews in, 59, 61; impact of Holo-
    caust on, 24–25, 421, 422; Jewish par-
    tisans in, 234; resistance in, 100, 324;
    sources on, 279, 300–1, 324, 352; sur-
    vivors from, 38; *see also* Hiwis (Hilf-
    swillige)
Littell, Franklin H., 134, 346, 368
"Little Ghetto," Riga and, 207
Litzmannstadt, 153, 202; *see also* Łódź
Locarno Treaty, 142, 147
Locke, Hubert, 346
Łódź, 11, 16, 153, 154, 157, 158, 165, 166,
    202–3, 227; Chełmno and, 20, 198;
    Einsatzgruppen and, 221; films on,
    375, 377; Gypsy camps and, 228; Jews
    deported from, 153; Jews deported to,
    206, 209; liquidation of, 17; Rum-
    kowski and, 16, 100, 202, *188*, 377;
    Sonderkommandos and, 240–41;
    sources on, 272, 273, 325, 331, 335,
    336, 375, 377,
Łódź Ghetto (film), 375
Łódź Ghetto Chronicles, 202
Löhr, Alexander, 246
Lohse, Heinrich, 259
London Agreement, 168
*Longest Hatred: The History of Anti-
    Semitism, The* (film), 378
Long Way Home, The, film on, 384
Lost Children of Berlin, The (film), 375
Lowenstein, Steven, 296
Löwenthal, Hugo, 396
Lublin, 11, 152, 153, 154, 155, 159, 164,
    165, *203*, 210; euthanasia and, 174–75;
    Globocnik and, 178; Weissmandel
    and, *192*; *see also* Nisko and Lublin
    Plan; Operation Harvest Festival

Luftwaffe, 179

Lukacze, sources on, 336

Lukas, Richard C., 49–50, 114–15, 326, 329

Luther, Martin, 59, 67

Lutherans, 257; sources on, 345; *see also* Protestants

Lutz, Charles, 239

Luxembourg, 12, 33, 421, 422

Luxemburg, Rosa, 66

L'vov, 156, 159, 160, 161, 162, 163, 164, *203–4*, 235, 260; sources on, 321, 343

Maccoby, Hyam, 67

Macedonia, 28

Mach, Alexander, 252

Mackensen, Eberhard von, 243

Macrakis, Kristie, 316

Madagascar, 224

Madagascar Plan, 12, 73, 76, 78, 79, 154, *229*, 232

Mahn- und Gedenkstätte Ravensbrück (Memorial), 410

Maier, Charles S., 135–36, 361

Majdanek, 20, 21, 164, 165, *204*, 218, 223, 224; crematoria at, 22, 194, 219; gas chambers at, 226, 248; Globocnik and, 178; Jews deported to, 197, 209, 213; Lublin and, 203; Operation Harvest Festival and, 234; sources on, 336, 343; survival at, 106, 105; Weissmandel and, *192*

Majdanek State Museum, 412

Man in the Glass Booth, The (film), 387

Manstein, Erich von, 243

Man Who Captured Eichmann, The, 387

Marcus, Paul, 130, 131, 364

Margoliot, Abraham, 283

Marks, Jane, 326

Marr, Wilhelm, 63; sources on, 293

Marriage: Nuremberg Laws and, 6–7, 233; privileged mixed, 7, 149, *236*,

357; sources on, 357; *see also* Mischlinge

Marrus, Michael R., 116, 117, 119, 128, 275, 280, 286, 350, 362

Marshall, Robert, 321

"Martyrs' and Heroes' Remembrance Law," 239

Marxism, 232; *see also* Communism/communists

Marzahn, 227

Maser, Werner, 306

Massing, Paul, 68, 290

Massuah Holocaust Studies Institute, 416

Mauthausen, 5, 23, 149, *204–5*, 218; film on, 384; Gunskirchen and, 205; Gusen and, 204; liberation of, 37; memorial to, 413, 414; sources on, 342; survival in, 105–6

Maybaum, Ignaz, 133, 369

Mayer, Arno J., 80, 275

Mayer, Saly, *184–85*

Mechelen Museum van Deportatie en Verzet (Mechelen Museum of Deportation and Resistance), 415

Medical experiments, 23, 85, 159, 162, 207, *229–30*; *see also* Mengele, Josef

Medical profession, *see* Physicians

Mein Kampf (Hitler), 4, 72, 73, 142, 229, 305

Meister, Barbara, 332

Meltzer, Milton, 355

Memel (Klaipeda), 151

Memoirs: of German Jews, 301–2; of perpetrators, 318–19; of survivors, 335–44

Memorials on Holocaust: in Europe, 413–15; in Germany, 406–12; in Israel, 415–17; in Poland, 412–13; sources on, 362; in United States and Canada, 400–6; *see also* Museums

Mendel, Gregor, 55

Mendelsohn, Ezra, 301

Mendelsohn, John, 286

Mendes-Flohr, Paul, 302
Mengele, Josef, 23, 163, *185*, 230, 341;
film on, 375, 382; sources on, 309–10,
326
Mentally handicapped, *see* Handicapped
Merin, Moshe, *185–86*
Michaelis, Meir, 280
Micheels, Louis J., 105, 340–41
Middle Ages, sources on, 292–93, 300
Milch, Erhard, 241
Milgram, Stanley, 91–92, 309
Miller, Judith, 137, 369
Miller, Richard, 312
Milton, Sybil, 47, 273, 285, 319, 326, 330, 362
Minister for the Occupied Eastern Territories, Rosenberg and, *188*
Minister of Armaments and Munitions, Speer and, *189*
Minister of Public Enlightenment and Propaganda, Goebbels and, 178
Ministry for the Occupied Eastern Territories (Reichsministerium für die Besetzten Ostgebiete), 259, 260
Ministry of Justice, euthanasia and, 86
Ministry of the Interior, euthanasia and, 85–86
Minsk, 13, 156, 157, 158, 159, 160, 164, *205, 206, 209, 260*
Mischlinge (mixed breeds), 6–7, 147, *230–31*, 233; Gypsies as, 47, 151, 231
Miserables, Les (film), 387
Missing Hero: Raoul Wallenberg (film), 379
Mittelbau-Dora, memorial to, 409
Mixed marriage, *see* Privileged mixed marriage
Modernism, Holocaust as, 136–37
Molotov, Viacheslav, 151
Mommsen, Hans, 40, 77, 278, 295
Monowitz (Auschwitz III), 22, 121, 184, 194–95; Buna and, 22, 161, 184; sources on, 340–41

Montreal Holocaust Memorial Centre, The, 404
Moore, Bob, 117, 280
Moravia, *see* Protectorate of Bohemia and Moravia
Moreshet Archives, 416
More Than Broken Glass: Memories of Kristallnacht (film), 376
Morley, John F., 128, 350
Morse, Arthur, 350
Moscow Declaration, 164
Moses Mendelssohn Zentrum, Das (Moses Mendelssohn Center), 410
Mosse, George, 136, 290–91
Mosse, Werner, 296–97
Motivations, of perpetrators, 88–95
Müller, Filip, 104, 341
Müller, Heinrich, 259
Müller, Ingo, 131, 312
Müller-Hill, Benno, 316
Munich Agreement, 149, 205
Municipal police (Schutzpolizei), 255
Murderers Among Us: The Simon Wiesenthal Story (film), 388
Muselmann, 19, 104, *231*
Museum Judengasse, 410
Museum of Hungarian Jewry, 416
Museum of Jewish Heritage — A Living Memorial to the Holocaust, 404
Museums on Holocaust: in Europe, 413–15; in Germany, 406–12; in Israel, 415–17; in Poland, 412–13; sources on, 361; in United States and Canada, 400–6
Music/musicians: electronic resources on, 392; organizations on, 405; sources on, 315, 330–32, 337, 393–98, 399
Mussolini, Benito, 32, 163, 167, *186*, 263; sources on, 280
Myers, Gerald, 369
My Knees Were Jumping: Remembering the Kindertransports (film), 379
Mystery of Josef Mengele, The (film), 382

Names, Jewish, 149
National Center for Jewish Film, The, 404
Nationalism, Holocaust and, 53–54
National Socialism (Nazism), 4, 69, 141, 231–32; Bavaria and, 142; films on, 380–82, 383; German army and, 250; motivation of, 89, 90; obedience to authority and, 91; as only party, 5, 145; propaganda of, 383, 399; as racist, 66; Reichstag and, 142, 143, 144, 146; sources on, 302–4, 290, 298–300, 311–14, 354; *Völkischer Beobachter* and, 187; *see also* Hitler, Adolf; SA; SS
National Socialist German Workers' Party (Nationalsozialistische Deutsche Arbeiterpartei or NSDAP), *see* National Socialism
Nazi Concentration Camps: Witness to Genocide (film), 376
Nazi Party, *see* National Socialism
Nazis: A Warning from History, The (film), 382
Nazi-Soviet Pact, 28, 151, 152
Nazi Storm Troopers, *see* SA
Nazi War Crimes Trials (film), 382
Negotiations: emigration furthered by, 121–22; by Himmler, 122, 167, 181; *see also* "Blood for trucks" offer
Neo-Nazism, film on, 385; sources on, 370–71, 399
Netherlands, 12, 157; bystander reactions in, 117; deportation of Jews from, 160, 164, 166; Gerstein and, 178; government officials in, 88; impact of Holocaust on, 30–31, 421, 422; medical experiments and, 159; non-Jewish volunteers in, 87; rescue and, 31, 117; Seyss-Inquart and, *189*; sources on, 280, 354, 358–59, 369; trial of war criminals and, 246; yellow badges and, 159; *see* Netherlands
Neuengamme, 23, *205*, 218, 230, 409

Neurath, Constantin von, 244
Neutral powers: Allies' pressure on to accept Jews, 122; rescue by, 119–20, 125–28; *see also* Portugal; Spain; Sweden; Switzerland; Turkey; Vatican
Newspapers, Aryans and, 6
Newton, Verne W., 121, 350
New York Public Library, William E. Wiener Oral History Library, 405–6, 415
Nicosia, Francis R., 291, 299–300
Niederland, William G., 130
Nieuwlande, 240
Nieuwsma, Milton, 341
Niewyk, Donald L., 106, 275, 291, 297, 341
Night and Fog (Nuit et Brouillard; (film), 376
Night of the Long Knives, 146, 261–62
Nikolayev, 260
Nisko and Lublin Plan, 11, 73, 76, 78, 79, 153, 203, 224, 232
Noakes, J., 286
Nolte, Ernst, 135, 303
Non-Jewish resistance, *see* Resistance, non-Jewish
Nordhausen, film on, 384
North Africa, 197
Northern Bukovina, 173
Norway: government officials in, 88; impact of Holocaust on, 32–33, 421; Jews deported from, 161; policies on Jews and Gypsies in, 12; registration of Jews in, 161; survivors in, 131, 363; Sweden and, 126
Not Like Sheep to the Slaughter: The Story of the Bialystok Ghetto (film), 376
Novick, Peter, 362
Novitch, Miriam, 332
Nuremberg, sources on, 296
Nuremberg (film), 382
Nuremberg Laws, 6–7, 9, 75, 146, 147, 186, 191, 232–33, 241, 242, 260

Nuremberg Successor Trials, *see* American Miliary Tribunal

Nuremberg Trial: Landmark Cases, The (film), 382

Nuremberg Trials, *see* International Military Tribunal

Nussbaum, Tsvi, films on, 377

Obedience to orders, as motivation of perpetrators, 90–92

Oberg, Karl, 246

Occupied Europe, sources on Holocaust in, 278–81

Odessa, 157, 173

Ofer, Dalia, 103, 125, 326, 350

Office of Special Investigations (OSI), 132, *254*

Of Pure Blood (film), 382

Ohrdruf, 198

Oliner, Samuel and Pearl, 109, 114, 355

Olympic Games (1936), 7, 148, 216, 227

Oneg Shabbat (Sabbath Delight), 17, 113, 187, 213, *254*, 340, 348

One Survivor Remembers (film), 376

Opdyke, Irene, 358

Opening the Gates of Hell: American Liberators of the Nazi Concentration Camps (film), 384

Operation Barbarossa, *see* Barbarossa, Operation

Operation 14f13, 204, 223, *233*

Operation Harvest Festival (Aktion Erntefest), 21, 164, 203, 204, 210, *233–34*, 256

Operation Reinhard (Aktion Reinhard), 20–21, 160, 164, 195, 201, 208, 223, *234*; gas chambers and, 226; Globocnik and, 178; Order Police and, 256; sources on, 319; *see also* Belzec; Sobibór; Treblinka

Operation T4, *see* Euthanasia

Oppermann (film), 388

Oral History Library, of American Jewish Committee, 342

Oranienburg, 208

Order Police (Ordnungspolizei or ORPO), 13, 222, 255, 256, 262

Orders, obedience to as motivation of perpetrators, 90–92

Organisation Todt, 18, 229

Organization for Rehabilitation and Training, sources on, 363

Organizations: rescue and, 238; sources on, 347, 363

Organization Schmelt, 201, 228

Orlow, Dietrich, 303–4

Orphanages, Korczak and, *184*

ORPO, *see* Order Police

OSI, *see* Office of Special Investigations

Other Side of Faith, The (film), 379

Otwock, 103–4; sources on, 341

Overy, Richard, 312

Packard, Jerrold, 350–51

Pact of Steel, 151

Paldiel, Mordecai, 355

Palestine, 151, 159; American Joint Distribution Committee and, 249; Ben-Gurion and, 174; Diaspora and, 58; Displaced Persons and, 221; displacement of Arabs and, 129; film on, 384, 386; Great Britain and, 8, 124–25, 127, 151, 159, 174, 221, 248; Haavara Tranfer Agreement and, 76, 145; immigration to, 8, 38, 76, 119, 120, 248, 249, 254; Jews as fighting unit in, 153; Kovner and, *184*; removal of German Jews to, 112; reparations and, *237*; Russian agricultural settlements in, 248; sources on, 343, 350, 351–52, 364; SS *Struma* and, 127, 159; Weizmann and, *192*; *see also* Jewish Agency for Palestine; Yishuv; Zionism, Palestinian

Palestine Office (Palästinaamt), 255, 261

Papen, Franz von, 244–45

Paris, sources on, 301

Parti Populaire Français, 87

Partisans, Jewish, 98, 100, 104, *234–35*; armed resistance and, 34; Bialystok and, 197; communist, 104; and Croatia, 28; evasion assisted by, 33; German army and, 85, 250; Polish, 113; rescue and, 238, 239; resistance and, 239; Serbia and, 25; SS and, 84; underground formations and, 35

Partisans, non-Jewish, 98, 234

Partisans of Vilna (film), 376

Passelecq, Georges, 346

Passports, Jewish, 150

Patterns of Prejudice (journal), 373

Paucker, Arnold, 300

Pauley, Bruce, 291, 304

Pavelic, Ante, 27, 263

Pawelczynska, Anna, 102–3, 322

Pawnbroker, The (film), 388

Paxton, Robert, 116, 117, 280

Peck, Abraham, 274

Peer pressure, as motivation of perpetrators, 92

Penkower, Monty, 120, 351

Perechodnik, Calel, 103, 341

Perel, Solomon, 341

Perl, Gisella, 105, 341

Perlasea, Giorgio, 239–40

Perpetrators, 83–95; motivations of, 88–95; sources on, 275, 302–19; *see also* Trials of war criminals

Persecuted and Forgotten (film), 376

Pétain, Henri Philippe, 29, *186–87*, 210; sources on, 318

Petliura days, 156

Peukert, Detlev, 355

Philosophical implications of Holocaust, sources on, 365, 366, 367–68, 369–70

Physically handicapped, *see* Handicapped

Physicians, German, 83, 85, 89–90; film on, 381; sources on, 314–16; SS and, 230; *see also* Medical experiments

Physicians, Jewish: films on, 386; restrictions on, 6, 145, 149; sources on, 322, 341

Physicists, sources on, 314

Pinsk, 156, 159, 161

Pinsker, Leo, 248

Piotrków Trybunalski, 152

Pius XI, Pope, 148, 251; sources on, 346

Pius XII, Pope, 127, 128, 151, 187, 251, 333; sources on, 345, 346, 358, 366

Place to Save Your Life: The Shanghai Jews, The (film), 379

Plant, Richard, 51, 330

Płaszów labor camp, 163, 188, 202; sources on, 337, 343

Plenipotentiary-General for Labor Mobilization, Sauckel and, *188*

Plotkin, Diane, 327

Plötzensee, memorial to, 408

Pogroms, 58, 65, 207, 228, *235*; *see also* Crystal Night

Pohl, Oswald, *187*, 241, 263

Pois, Robert, 294

Poland, 151; antisemitism in, 114–15; bystander reactions in, 113–15; Catholics in, 251–52; Displaced Persons and, 221; films on, 375, 377, 379, 385; German invasion of, 151; ghettos in, 9, 152, 227; Globocnik and, 178; impact of Holocaust on, 13–14, 24, 129, 421; Jewish partisans in, 235; Jews in, 24, 59, 61, 74, 76, 78, 79, 152; Karaski and, 183; Kraków and, 202; labor camps and, 228; nationalism and, 53; Nazi racial policies in, 10–12; nonaggression treaty with, 146; Race and Settlement Main Office and, 258; rescue in, 114, 115, 379, 385; reserve police battalion in, 92; resistance in, 98, 239; resource organizations, museums, and memorials in, 412–13; Seyss-Inquart and, *189*; sources on, 272, 284, 290, 301, 308, 319, 321, 323, 326, 328, 329, 335, 338, 339, 340, 343, 344, 348, 349, 352, 356, 358, 360, 362;

Poland (*Continued*)
SS and, 84; survivors from, 37; trials of war criminals in, 39; yellow badges in, *247*; Zuckerman and, *193–94*, 344; Zygelbojm and, *194*; *see also* General Government; Jewish Fighting Organization; Zegota
Poliakov, Leon, 68, 77, 278, 280, 291
Police, German, 13, 15, 84, 94, 147, *255–56*, 262; Gestapo, 5, 84, 145, 182, 190, 255, 256, 262, 264, 309; Heydrich and, 180; Himmler and, 180; Order Police, 13, 222, 255, 256, 262; Security Police, 84, 213, 222, 255, 308; sources on, 307–11; Stroop and, *191*; Wannsee Conference and, 212
Police, Jewish, 16, 99, 103–4, 177, 207, 253, *256–57*; sources on, 341
Polish Bund, Zygelbojm and, *194*
Political prisoners, 190; in concentration camps, 18, 197–98, 199, 204, 224; as prisoner functionaries, 236; sources on, 327, 328, 329; as target of genocide, 45, 50
Poniatowa, Operation Harvest Festival and, 234
Poniatowa labor camp, 164
Poppel, Stephen, 297
Porat, Dina, 124, 351
Portugal, 125, 127; sources on, 351
Posner, Gerald, 309–10
Post-war Jewish communities, sources on, 363–64
Potok, Chaim, 331
Power of Conscience: The Danish Resistance and the Rescue of the Jews, The (film), 379
Prejudice, history of, 63–70; *see also* Antisemitism
Presser, Jacob, 280
Pressler, Mirjam, 337
Pridham, Geoffrey, 286, 295
Prisoner functionaries, 18–19, 101, 105, 198, 204, *235–36*

Prisoners of war (Soviet): sources on, 327, 328, 344; as target of genocide, 13, 21, 45, 46, 48–49, 85, 204, 205, 218, 226, 250
Privileged mixed marriage, 7, 149, *236*, 357
Probst, Christoph, 264
Proctor, Robert, 316
Professions, sources on under National Socialism, 314–17
Professors, sources on, 317
Propaganda, Goebbels and, 144, 178–79
Property, Jewish, 149, 158, 40, 169
Prostitutes, concentration camps and, 218
Protective Detachments, *see* SS
Protectorate of Bohemia and Moravia, 25, 151, 158, 167, 180, 191, *205–6*, 209, 210, 247, 421, 422, 423
Protestants, 252, *257*; Confessing Church and, 174, 178, 257; euthanasia and, 10; impact of Holocaust on teachings about Judaism, 133; reaction of to genocide, 40, 112; sources on, 344–45, 346, 367; *see also* Bonhoeffer, Dietrich
Protocols of the Elders of Zion, sources on, 288
Psychological implications of Holocaust, sources on, 365–66, 367, 364
Public assistance, Jews excluded from, 150
Puhl, Emil Johann, 242
Pulzer, Peter, 68, 291–92, 297
Purple Triangles (film), 376
Puxon, Grattan, 47, 131, 329

Quarrel, The (film), 388
Quigley, John, 129, 369

Race and Settlement Main Office (Rasse- und Siedlungshauptamt or RuSHA), 84, 143, 242, *257–58*, 262

Racial Germans, 9; *see also* Handicapped

"Racially inferior," exclusion of, 3–9

Racism, 229; Holocaust and, 54–55; as motivation of perpetrators, 88–89, 90; scientific, 66; sources on before World War II, 287–93; texts on, 293–94

Radios, ban of Jewish ownership of, 152

Radom, 155, 160, 161, 162, *206*, 210

Raeder, Erich, 245

Rail lines, Allies' bombing of, 121

Ramati, Alexander, 330, 355

Rapaport, Lynn, 364

Rappoport, Leon, 98, 102, 368

Rashke, Richard, 324

Rassenschande, 233

Rath, Ernst vom, 150

Rauter, Hans Albin, 246

Rautkallio, Hannu, 351

Ravensbrück, 5, 23, 151, 159, *206–7*, 218; liberation of, 167; medical experiments in, 230; memorial to, 410; sources on, 336; women released from, 167

Rector, Frank, 51, 330

Red Cross, International, 165, 167, *258–59*; Allies and, 122, 123; Birkenau and, 23; Horthy and, 182; sources on, 351; Theresienstadt and, 17, 167, 209

Reformed churches, 257

Reform Judaism, 59

Reich, Steve, 397

Reich Assocation of Jews in Germany (Reichsvereinigung der Juden in Deutschland), 12, 151, 163, 173, 251, 259, 260–61

Reich Central Office for Jewish Emigration (Reichszentrale für jüdische Auswanderung), 8, 76, 150, 179, 180, *259*; *see also* Heydrich, Reinhard

Reich Chancellery, Speer and, *189*

Reich Citizenship Law, 147, 158, 233

Reich Commissar for the Strengthening of German Nationality, Himmler and, 180–81

Reich Commissariat for the Eastern Territories (Reichskommissariat Ostland), 163, *259–60*

Reich Commissariat for the Ukraine (Reichskommissariat Ukraine), *260*

Reich Commissioner for the Netherlands, Seyss-Inquart and, *189*

Reichmann, Eva G., 68, 292

Reich Press Corps, 242

Reich Representation of German Jews (Reichsvertretung der deutschen Juden), 145–46, 260

Reich Representation of Jews in Germany (Reichsvertretung der Juden in Deutschland), 146, 151, 259, *260–61*

Reichsbank, 242

Reichsdeutsche, 246

Reich Security Main Office (Reichssicherheitshauptamt or RSHA), 15, 152, 176, 180, 182, 212, 234, 255–56; sources on, 307

Reichstag, 3, 142, 143, 144, 146

Reinharz, Jehuda, 302

Reitlinger, Gerald, 278, 310

Relief Organization of German Jews (Hilfsverein der deutschen Juden), *261*

Religious dissenters, 5, 45, 50, 218; *see also* Jehovah's Witnesses

Religious implications of Holocaust, 132–34; sources on, 365, 366–367, 368–70

Rempel, Gerhard, 313

Reparations: East Germany and, 40; West Germany and, 40, 168, 169, *237*, 249

Rescue, 119–28, *237–38*; Allies and, 119–25, 128, 194; Bermuda and, 162; Bermuda Conference and, 196–97; Catholics and, 32, 40, 112, 251–52, 358, 379, 386; Evian Conference and, 200; films on, 374, 378–80, 385;

Rescue (*Continued*)
France and, 8, 116; Gentiles and, 33,
111, 325–26, 343, 353, 355–56, 358–59,
374, 379, 380, 385; Germany and, 111;
Great Britain and, 8, 120, 162; Italy
and, 32, 238, 379, 385; Le Chambon-
sur-Lignon and, 30, 116, 354, 380;
Netherlands and, 31, 117; neutral
powers and, 119–20, 125–28; North
Africa and, 197; Poland and, 114, 115;
social engagement and, 109, 114;
sources on, 274, 275, 339, 342, 343,
344, 346–59, 374, 400; Spain and, 30,
125, 127, 238; Sweden and, 31–32, 33,
126–27, 164, 167, 238; Switzerland
and, 30, 32, 125, 126, 167, 174, 238;
United States and, 8, 120, 124, 162,
164, 200; War Refugee Board and,
123–24, 164, 185, 264; World Jewish
Congress and, 264; *see also* Bonhoeffer, Dietrich; Bystanders; Horthy,
Miklós; Palestine; Partisans, Jewish;
Red Cross, International; Resistance;
"Righteous Among the Nations";
Roosevelt, Franklin D.
Rescue in Scandinavia (film), 380
Research Center on Jewish History and
Culture in Poland, The, 413
Resistance, Jewish, 101, 183, 184, 233,
238–39; armed, 33–36, 97, 99–101,
104, 238; Baum Group and, 97, 238,
250–51; Belgium and, 31; in concentration camps, 101, 218; in extermination camps, 35, 100, 101, 104, 163, 164,
210, 233, 239; films on, 374, 376, 380;
in ghettos, 34–35, 100, 113, 162, 201,
212, 213, 233, 239; Jewish Councils
and, 16, 34, 35, 99–100, 103, 253; Jewish Fighting Organization and, 133,
160, 187, 191, 194, 213, 239; Kovner
and, *184*; obstacles to, 98–99, 100;
sources on, 274, 275, 322–325, 338,
340, 344, 396–397; "spiritual," 33,
101, 238, 239; Zuckerman and,

193–94, 344; *see also* Babi Yar; Res-
cue; Tenenbaum, Mordechai
Resistance, non-Jewish, 25, 30; German,
111–12, 356–57, 358, 384–85, 407;
Stauffenberg and, *190*; *see also* Bon-
hoeffer, Dietrich; White Rose
Resource organizations: in Europe,
413–15; in Germany, 406–12; in Is-
rael, 415–17; in Poland, 412–13; in
United States and Canada, 400–6
Restitution Law, 40
Restless Conscience, The (film), 384
Retail trade, Jews and, 145, 150
Return to the Warsaw Ghetto (film), 376
Reuth, Ralf Georg, 313
Reuther, Rosemary, 133–34
Revisionist-Zionist Jewish Military
Union (Zydowski Zwiazek Wo-
jskowy), 213
Revolt of Job (*Job lazadasa*; film), 388
Rexists, 87
Rhineland, 5, 147
Ribbentrop, Joachim von, 151, 245, 311;
sources on, 311, 313–14,
Richarz, Monika, 302
Riefenstahl, Leni, 383
Riga, 13, 157, 158, 166, 206, *207–8*, 209;
sources on, 279
"Righteous Among the Nations,"
239–40; *see also* Schindler, Oskar;
Wallenberg, Raoul; Zegota
Righteous Enemy, The (film), 380
"Righteous Gentiles," 189, 192, 239, 240;
see also "Righteous Among the Na-
tions"
Ringelblum, Emanuel, 17, 113, *187*, 213,
254, 342, 358
Rise and Fall of Adolf Hitler, The (film),
382
Rittner, Carol, 326
Ritvo, Roger, 327
Röhm, Ernst, 143, 146, 261
Rohrlich, Ruby, 324
Roland, Charles G., 101, 322

Roma, 62; *see also* Gypsies

Romania: Allies' pressure on to release Jews, 122, 123; Antonescu and, 29, 123, 165, *173*, 197, 209, 246, 252, 253; government officials in, 87; impact of Holocaust on, 28–29, 317, 421, 422; Iron Guard and, 29, 87, 173, 252–53; nationalism and, 53; survivors from, 37; Transnistria and, 209; Transylvania and, 209–10; trial of war criminals and, 246; War Refugee Board and, 123–24

Roman, Martin, 397

Rombuli forest, 158

Rome-Berlin Axis, 148

Room seniors, 235

Roosevelt, Franklin D., 120, 121, 124, 162, 167; Evian Conference and, 8, 200; film on, 378; Karski and, *183*; Moscow Declaration and, 164; sources on, 347, 348, 350; War Refugee Board and, 123–24, 164, 264; Wise and, *193*

Rose, Paul Lawrence, 68, 226, 292

Rose Garden, The (film), 388

Rosen, Philip, 270

Rosenbaum, Alan, 130, 131, 282, 364, 369

Rosenbaum, Alan S., 135

Rosenberg, Alfred, 13, 38, *187–188*, 245, 259, 260, 294; sources on, 311

Rosenberg, Maxine, 342

Rosenfeld, Alvin, 333, 369

Rosenstrasse protest, sources on, 357

Rosenzweig, Artur, 202

Rotem, Simha, 342

Roth, John, 326, 369–70

Rothchild, Sylvia, 342

Rousso, Henry, 362

Rovno, 158, 260

RSHA, *see* Reich Security Main Office

Rubenstein, Richard L., 132–33, 136, 137, 370

Rubin, Janet, 332

Rubinstein, William D., 120–21, 122, 123–24, 351

Rückerl, Adalbert, 131, 282, 285–86

Ruether, Rosemary, 133–34, 292

Rumkowski, Mordecai Chaim, 16, 100, *188*, 202; film on, 377

Rundstedt, Karl von, 243

Runners, 18

Rural police (Gendarmerie), 255

RuSHA, *see* Race and Settlement Main Office

Russia, *see* Soviet Union

Ryan, Allan A., 132, 282–83

SA (Storm Troopers or Sturmabteilung), 3–4, 6, 7, 75, 141, 143, 144, 146, 219, *261–62*; motivation of, 89, 91

Saarland, 146

Sabille, Jacques, 280

Sachar, Abram, 364

Sachsenhausen, 23, 182, 205, *208*, 218, 230, 251, 408; *see also* Gross-Rosen

St. James Palace declaration on war crimes, 158

St. Louis (ship), 8; films on, 374, 379, 389; sources on, 334

St. Ottilien, 423

Salonika, 26, 162

Salzburg, 423

Sauckel, Fritz, *188*, 245

Schacht, Hjalmar, 245; film on, 382

Schachter, Raphael, 331

Scharf, Rafael, 273

Schindler (film), 380

Schindler, Oskar, 16, *188–89*, 202, 239, 333; film on, 380, 388

Schindler's List (film), 388

Schirach, Baldur von, 245

Schleunes, Karl, 76, 300

Schloss, Eva, 105, 106, 342

Schmelt, Albrecht, 228

Schmorell, Alexander, 264

Schneider, Gertrude, 280–81

Schoenberg, Arnold, 398

Scholder, Klaus, 346
Scholl, Hans and Sophie, 162, 264; sources on, 358
Scholl, Inge, 357
Schorsch, Ismar, 297
Schul, Zikmund, 396
Schulhoff, Erwin, 395
Schulte, Edward, sources on, 349
Schumann, Horst, 162, 230
Schuschnigg, Kurt, 189
Schutzmannschaften (police) battalions, 86
Schutzstaffel, see SS
Schwammberger, Josef, sources on, 281
Schwartz, Solomon, 281
Schwarz, Jenö, 105–6, 342
Schwarz, Solomon, 125
Science, Holocaust and, 54
Scientific racism, 66
Scientists, sources on, 314, 316
SD, see Security Service
Secret State Police (Geheime Staatspolizei), see Gestapo
Security Police (Sicherheitspolizei or SIPO), 22, 84, 213, 255; sources on, 308
Security Service (Sicherheitsdienst or SD), 179, 180, 222, 255, 256, 259, 262, 308
Segev, Tom, 124, 310, 364
Selections (Selektionen), 17, 20, 23, 85, 240; special treatment and, 15, 241, 250
Self-preservation, as motivation of perpetrators, 94–95
Senesh, Hannah, 342–43; film on, 386
Serbia, 25–26, 35, 53, 85, 157
Sereny, Gita, 105, 310, 313
Sexual relations, Nuremberg Laws and, 6–7, 233
Seyss-Inquart, Arthur, 30, 38, 189, 245
Shadow on the Cross (film), 378
Shanghai: film on, 379; sources on, 338, 352
Sharett, Moshe, 169, 237

Sharon, S., 338
Shaw, Stanford J., 127, 351
Sheftel, Yoram, 132, 283
Ship of Fools (film), 388
Shmuel, Almog, 287
Sho'ah, 45, 240
Shoah (film), 377
Shoah Foundation, 392
Shoah Visual History Foundation, 375, 377
Shofar (journal), 373
Shop on Main Street, The (Obchod Na Korze; film), 388–89
Shostakovich, Dmitri, 195, 398
Shtetl, 240
Shtetl: A Journal of the Holocaust (film), 377
Siberia, 76, 78, 224
Sibyll, Claus, 312
Sicherheitsdienst, see Security Service
Sicily, 32
Siegal, Aranka, 334
Siemens, 195
Sierakowiak, David, 335
Silver, Eric, 355–56
Sima, Horia, 253
Simon Wiesenthal Center, sources on, 399
Simon Wiesenthal Center Annual, 371
Sinti, 62; see also Gypsies
SIPO, see Security Police
Skarzysko-Kamienna, 17
Skutecky, Otto, 397
Slave labor, see Forced labor
Sliwowska, Wiktoria, 343
Slovakia, 150, 151, 159; armed resistance in, 35; Catholics and, 127–28; deportations and, 86; film on, 388–89; government officials in, 87; Hlinka Guard in, 27, 87, 150, 252; impact of Holocaust on, 27, 50, 421, 422; sources on, 317; Tiso and, 27, 191, 246, 252; Weissmandel and, 192
Small town police (Gemeinde polizei), 255

Smelser, Ronald, 313
Smith, Bradley, 283, 287
Snyder, Louis, 271
Sobibór, 20–21, 159, 164, 196, *208*, 210, 211, 223, 234; film on, 385; gas chambers at, 248–49; Hiwis at, 87; sources on, 319, 324; Stangl and, *189–90*, 208, 210, 214, 310; uprising in, 35, 164, 233, 239; Westerbork and, 214
Social Darwinism, 4, 54, 55
Social Democratic Party (SPD), 145
Sofsky, Wolfgang, 310
Sonderkommandos (special commandos), 20, 21, 22, 35, 226, *240–41*
Sonnenschein, 233
Sonnenstein, 223
Sophie's Choice (film), 389
Sorkin, David, 298
Sosnowiec, 159, 163
Sousa Mendes, Aristides de, 239
Soviet Union: antisemitism in, 115; armed resistance in, 35; bystander reactions in, 113, 115; civilians of as target of genocide in, 45, 49–50; Einsatzgruppen and, 9, 14, 24, 74, 79, 80, 84, 85, 155, 217, 221, 226, 256, 260; films on, 381, 384; German army and, 85, 90, 250; Hitler and, 73–74, 78, 79, 80; Hiwis and, 228; impact of Holocaust on, 13–14, 24, 129, 421, 422; Jewish partisans in, 234; Jews in, 61; mass graves at Katyn and, 162; memory of Holocaust in, 369; Nazi-Soviet Pact and, 151, 152; obstacles to resistance in, 98; Operation Barbarossa and, 13–14, 79, *217*, 250; partisans of, 335; Reich Commissariat for Eastern Territories and, 259, 260; Reich Commissariat for the Ukraine and, 260; rescue and, 125, 238; sources on, 279, 280, 283–84, 285, 301, 308, 310, 327, 328, 333, 335, 344, 350, 352, 360, 366, 369; survivors from, 38; trials of war criminals and, 39, 243–44, 245; yellow badges in, *247*; see also International Military Tribunal; Prisoners of war (Soviet)
Spain: civil war, 127, 148; Franco and, 127, 148, 349; rescue and, 30, 125, 127, 238; sources on, 326, 346–47, 349, 350, 351
Spanish Republicans, concentration camps and, 218
Special treatment (Sonderbehandlung), 15, 240, *241*
Spector, Shmuel, 283–84
Speer, Albert, *189*, 245; film on, 381; sources on, 313, 319
Spencer, Herbert, 55
Spertus Institute of Jewish Studies (Zell Center for Holocaust Studies), 405
Spielberg, Steven, 333, 375, 377, 392
Spielvogel, Jackson, 304
"Spiritual resistance," 33, 101, 238, 239
Sporenberg, Jakob, 234
Spraichingen, sources on, 337
SS (Schutzstaffel or Protective Detachment), 84, 141, 144, 147, 155, 250, 262, *262–63*; Anschluss and, *214*; concentration camps and, 5, 195, 198, 199, 218, 235; death marches and, 220; Final Solution and, 212; Frank and, 177; German police and, 255; Gross-Rosen and, 201; Gypsies as *Mischlinge* and, 231; Hiwis and, 228; labor camps and, 235; Madagascar Plan and, *229*; Mayer and, *185*; motivation of, 89, 91; Neuengamme and, 205; Nisko and Lublin Plan and, 232; Operation Reinhard and, 224; physicians and, 230; police and, 84; prisoner solidarity and, 106; Race and Settlement Main Office and, 257–58; SA and, 146, 261–62; Schindler and, *189*; selection and, *240*; Sonderkommando and, 240–41; sources on, 278, 307–11, 318, 321; Waffen SS and, 84; see also Eichmann, Adolf; Einsatzgruppen; Medical experiments; Security Police; Security Service

SS-Aufseherinnen, 207
SS Economic and Administrative Main
    Office (Wirtschaftsverwaltungshaup-
    tamt or WVHA), 187, 224, 241, 263
SS-Verfügungstruppen (Special Purpose
    Troops), 263
Stachura, Peter, 313
Stalin, Joseph, 164, 217
Stangl, Franz, *189–90*, 208, 210, 214, 310
State Museum of Auschwitz-Birkenau,
    287, 412
Statuts des Juifs ("Jewish Laws"), 154,
    155, 211, *241*
Stauffenberg, Claus Schenk Graf von,
    25, 112, *190*
Stauffenberg family, sources on, 356–57
Steinberg, Jonathan, 317
Steinberg, Lucien, 324
Steiner, Jean, 334
Steinert, Marlis, 110, 111, 356
Steinheim, Solomon Ludwig, Institut,
    410
Steinlauf, Michael, 362
Steinweis, Alan, 316
Stephens, Elaine, 332
Sterilization, 145, 230; experiments on,
    162; of Gypsies, 145; of handicapped,
    9, 70, 222, 223; laws on, 70, 147; *Mis-
    chlinge* and, 231; sources on, 315
Stern, Frank, 371
Stern, Fritz, 68, 229, 292
Stern, Kenneth, 371
Stierlin, Helm, 306
Stiftung Neue Synagoge Berlin (New
    Synagogue Foundation, Berlin), 411
Stiftung Topographie des Terrors (Top-
    ography of Terror Foundation), 411
Stoltzfus, Nathan, 357
Storm Troopers, *see* SA
*Story of Chaim Rumkowski and the Jews
    of the Łódź, The* (film), 377
Strauss, Adolf, 397
Strauss, Herbert, 300
Streicher, Julius, 6, *190–91*, 245; film on,
    382; trial of, 38

Streit, Christian, 49, 310
Stresemann, Gustav, 143
Stroop, Jürgen, 34, *191*, 212, 213, 245, 319
Structuralists, *see* Functionalists
Struma (ship), 127, 159
Stuckart, Wilhelm, 242
Sturmabteilung, *see* SA
Stürmer, Michael, 135
Stürmer, Der, 6, 190–91
Stutthof, 23, 106, 206, *208*; sources on,
    336
Styron, William, 334
Suchecky, Bernard, 346
Sudetenland, 5, 149, 150
Sugihara, Sempo, 239
Suhl, Yuri, 324
Survivors, 37–38; in camps, 102–3, 104–
    6; diaries, memoirs, and accounts of,
    335–44; electronic resources on, 392;
    films on, 373–78, 383–84; impact of
    Holocaust on, 129–31; psychological
    aftereffects of, 130–31; reactions of to
    persecution, 103–7; sources on, 322,
    363–64, 365, 400; *see also* Children
    of survivors
Survivors of the Holocaust (film), 377
Survivors of the Shoah Visual History
    Foundation, 405
Survivor syndrome, 130–31
Svenk, Karel, sources on, 397
Sweden: film on, 379, 380; Horthy and,
    182; rescue and, 31–32, 33, 125,
    126–27, 164, 167, 238; sources on,
    349, 351, 353, 354
Sweets, John, 116, 281
Swiebocka, Teresa, 273
Switzerland: American Joint Distribu-
    tion Committee and, 249; film on,
    385, 387; Himmler's transport of Jews
    to, 122; Horthy and, 182; Interna-
    tional Red Cross and, 258; Mayer
    and, *184–85*; rescue and, 30, 32, 125,
    126, 167, 174, 238; sources on, 347,
    349, 351
Sydnor, Charles W., 89, 311

Synthesizers, motives for Final Solution and, 71, 77–81
Szalasi, Ferenc, 250
Szonyi, David, 271

Tal, Uriel, 67, 280, 298
Tarnow, 160, 161, 163
Taube, Carlo, 396
Tauria, 260
Taylor, Telford, 131, 143, 283
Teachers, Jews removed from jobs as, 6
Tec, Nechama, 100, 101, 114, 324, 343, 356
Ten Boom, Corrie, 358–59
Tenenbaum, Mordechai, 35, *191*, 197; film on, 376
Terezin, *see* Theresienstadt
Terezin Chamber Music Foundation, 405
Terezin Diary (film), 377
Terezin Memorial, 415
Ternopol, 163
Tesch & Stabenow Co., 242
Teveth, Shabtai, 351–52
T₄ program, *see* Euthanasia
Thalmann, Rita, 300
Theology, impact of Holocaust on, 132–34
Theresienstadt (Terezin), 17, 23, 163, *209*, 227; film on, 377; International Red Cross and, 165, 167, 258; Jews deported to, 25, 158, 160, 174, 206; memorial to, 415; mixed marriages and, 236; sources on, 320, 321, 331, 344; sources on music in, 332, 393–96, 397, 398, 399, 405; Soviet troops in, 167; Westerbork and, 214
Theresienstadt: Gateway to Auschwitz (film), 377
They Risked Their Lives: Rescuers of the Holocaust (film), 380
Third Reich, 181; sources on, 302–4
Thomas, Gordon, 334
Thorne, Leon, 103, 343
Thrace, impact of Holocaust on, 28

Tiso, Jozef, 27, *191*, 246, 252
Tito, 101
Toll, Nelly, 343
Tong, Diane, 271
Topas, George, 105, 343
Tory, Avraham, 343
Totenkopf division of Waffen-SS, sources on, 311
Trachtenberg, Joshua, 67, 292–93
Traitors to Hitler (film), 385
Transit camps (Durchgangslager), 17; sources on, 339; *see also* Drancy; Westerbork
Transnistria, 29, 157, 173, 197, *209*, 227, 249; sources on, 279
Transvestites, sources on, 330
Transylvania, *209–10*
Trawniki, 20, 86, 164, 187, *210*, 228, 234
Treblinka, 20–21, 160, 164, 184, *210*, 223–24, 234; Czerniaków and, 175; film on, 387; gas chambers at, 248–49; Hiwis and, 87; Jews deported to, 160, 161, 162, 197, 206, 209, 213; Oneg Shabbat and, *254*; sources on, 310, 319, 334, 336, 340; Stangl and, 190, 208, 210; survival in, 105; uprising in, 35, 163, 210, 233, 239
Trevor-Roper, Hugh, 306–7
Trials of war criminals, 38–40, 131–32, 168, *241–46*; American Military Tribunal, 167, *241–42*; British Military Tribunal, *242–43*; "Control Council Law No. 10" and, 168, 169 *241*; Federal Republic of Germany, 39–40, 131, *243*; films on, 380–82, 387; following orders as defense in, 91; genocide and, 132, 225; London Agreement and, 168; Occupied Europe, 39, *245–46*; Office of Special Investigations and, 254; sources on, 281–83, 285, 286, 287; *see also* International Military Tribunal
Tripartite Pact, 154, 155
Triumph of the Will (*Triumph des Willens*; film), 383

Trocme, André, 240
Troller, Norbert, 344
Troper, Harold, 346
Trotsky, Leon, 66
Trunk, Isaiah, 99–100, 101, 322
"Truth Shall Make Us Free, The": Inside the Neo-Nazi Network (film), 385
Tsvi Nussbaum: A Boy from Warsaw (film), 377
Tuchin, 260
Turkey, 56, 125, 127, 238; sources on, 351
Turner, Harald, 26
Tushnet, Leonard, 100, 324–25
Typhus, 196, 199
Tyrnauer, Gabrielle, 271

"U boats," 111
Ukraine: armed resistance in, 100; civilians of as target of genocide in, 49; film on, 374; impact of Holocaust on, 13–14, 129; Jewish partisans in, 234–35; Reich Commissariat for the Ukraine and, 260; sources on, 336; *see also* Hiwis (Hilfswillige)
Ullmann, Viktor, 394–95, 396
Underground, 35–36; sources on, 344
United Nations: Declaration, 158; Genocide Convention, 132, 225; Relief and Rehabilitation Agency (UNRRA), 164, 221; sources on, 282, 353
United Partisans Organization, 184; film on, 376
United States: American Military Tribunal and, 241–42; Displaced Persons and, 38, 221; eugenics and, 222; film on, 378; gas chambers and, 226; immigration to, 38, 420; International Military Tribunal and, 243–44; Jewish communities in, 124; Office of Special Investigations and, 254; rescue and, 8, 120, 124, 162, 164, 200; resource organizations, museums,

and memorials in, 400–6; sources on, 347, 348, 350, 352–53, 362, 363, 369; trials of war criminals and, 167, *241–42*; *see also* International Military Tribunal; Roosevelt, Franklin D.
United States Holocaust Memorial Council, 193
United States Holocaust Memorial Museum (Washington, D.C.), 169, 274, 405; film on, 374; sources on, 361
University of Minnesota, Center for Holocaust and Genocide Studies, 402
University of Vermont, Center for Holocaust Studies, 401
Upper Silesia, 159
Uprisings, Jewish, *see* Resistance, Jewish
Ustasha, 27, 87, *263–64*

Va'da, 175, 183
Vago, Bela, 124, 352
Vagrants, concentration camps and, 218
Van Pelt, Robert Jan, 320
Vatican, 145; Allies' pressure on, 122, 123; early antisemitism of, 65; Eichmann and, 176; Gerstein and, 178; Hitler and, 251; Horthy and, 182; John XXIII and, 133; Pius XI and, 148, 251, 346; Pius XII and, 127, 128, 151, *187*, 251, 333, 345, 346, 358, 366; rescue and, 125, 127–28; Slovakia and, 27; sources on, 332–33, 345, 346, 350, 358, 366; Tiso and, *191*
Versailles, Treaty of, 5, 56, 141, 146, 147
Verschuer, Otmar, 185
Vichy France, *210–11*; bystander reactions in, 116; deportations and, 86; Drancy and, 199–200; Final Solution and, 29–30; General Commissariat for Jewish Affairs and, 155; government officials in, 88; Parti Populaire Français in, 87; Pétain and, 29, *186–87*, 210, 318; policy on Jews in, 12–13; sources on, 278, 279, 280, 318, 354;

Statuts des Juifs and ("Jewish Laws"), 154, 155, 211, *241*

Victims, 45–63, 97–107; accommodation and, 97–99, 103–4; evasion and, 33, 101–2; failure of action by, 123; history of, 57–63; sources on, 275, 319–44, 399; surviving in camps and, 102–3, 104–6; see also Gypsies; Handicapped; Homosexuals; Jews; Political prisoners; Prisoners of war (Soviet); Religious dissenters; Resistance; Survivors

Vienna, 160

Vilna, 16, 156, 164, *211–12*, 260; action (*Aktion*) and, 157; film on, 376; Gens and, 16, 35, 100, *177*, 211; Kovner and, *184*; sources on, 319, 325; uprising in, 35, 100; see also Tenenbaum, Mordechai

Vishniac, Roman, 273

Vital, David, 301

Vitebsk, 157

Voices of the Children (film), 377

Volhynia-Podolia, 260

Völkischer Beobachter, 141, 187

Volkov, Shulamit, 69, 235, 293

Volksdeutsche (ethnic Germans), 11, 178, 208, *246*, 258

Voltaire, 65

Volunteers, non-German, as perpetrators, 86–87

Voyage of the Damned (film), 389

Waffen SS, 84, 87, 175, 178, 180, 185, 222, 263; sources on, 311

Wagner, Richard, sources on, 289

Wahrhaftig, Zorach, 352

Waite, Robert G., 72, 307

Wallant, Edward, 334

Wallenberg, Raoul, 126–27, 166, *191–92*, 239, 359; American Joint Distribution Committee and, 249; films on, 379, 380; sources on, 347, 349, 400

Wannsee Conference, 14, 15, 46, 158, 176, 180, *212*, 231; film on, 389; memorial to, 407–8; sources on, 277

Wannsee Conference, The (film), 389

War-crimes trials, see Trials of war criminals

War criminals, 193; sources on, 334; see also Trials of war criminals

Wardi, Dina, 365

Ware, John, 309–10

War Refugee Board (WRB), 123–24, 164, 185, *264*

Warsaw, 11, 16, 152, 154, 155, 159, 160, 166, 209, *212–13*; Czerniaków and, 175, 213; evasion in, 101; films on, 376, 377, 378, 386, 387; Jewish Fighting Organization and, 160; Karski and, 115, *183*; Korczak and, *184*; Oneg Shabbat and, 17, 113, 187, 213, *254*, 340, 348, 358; Ringelblum and, *187*; sources on, 272, 273, 284, 319, 322, 323, 325, 335, 336, 338, 339, 339–40, 342, 344, 392; Stutthof and, 208; uprising in, 34–35, 100, 113, 162, 201, 212, 213, 233, 239; Zuckerman and, *194*; Zygelbojm and, *194*; see also Stroop, Jürgen; Tenenbaum, Mordechai

Warsaw Ghetto, The (film), 378

Warthegau, 157, 158, 247

Wasserstein, Bernard, 120, 129, 352, 364

Waxman, Franz, 398

Weapons of the Spirit (film), 379, 380

Weber, Ilse, sources on, 397

Web sites, on Holocaust, 398–400

Webster, Paul, 318

Wechsberg, Joseph, sources on, 344

Wegner, Bernd, 311

Wehrmacht, see Army, German

Weimar Republic, 4, 56–57, 69, 88, 141, 142, 143; sources on, 294–95, 296, 297

Weinberg, David, 301

Weinberg, Gerhard, 50, 94, 275

Weinreich, Max, 317

Weisberg, Richard, 281

Weiss, Evald, 397

Weiss, John, 68, 293

Weiss, Peter, 334

Weiss, Sheila, 293

Weissberg, Alex, 122, 352

Weissmandel, Rabbi Michael Dov, *192*

Weitz, John, 313–14

Weitzman, Lenore, 103, 326

Weizmann, Chaim, *192*

Weizsäcker, Ernst von, 242

Werber, Jack, 344

Werner, Harold, 104, 344

Wertheimer, Jack, 298

Westerbork, 164, 166, *213–14*; sources on, 339

Western Europe: bystander reactions in, 116–17; deportation of Jews in, 12–13; history of Jews in, 58–61; impact of Holocaust on, 29–33, 38; responsibility for Holocaust and, 41; yellow badges in, *247*

West Germany: Gypsies and, 131; reparations and, 40, 168, 169, *237*, 249; responsibility for Holocaust and, 40; trials of war criminals and, 39–40, 131, *243*

We Were Marked with a Big "A" (Wir hatten ein grosses "A" am Bein; film), 378

We Were There: Jewish Liberators of the Nazi Concentration Camps (film), 384

White Rose, 25, 162, *264*, 358; film on, 389; sources on, 357

White Rose, The (Die Weisse Rose) (film), 389

White Russia, sources on, 326

Who Shall Live and Who Shall Die? (film), 380

Wiener Library Bulletin (journal), 373

Wiener, William E., Oral History Library, The (New York Public Library), 405–6, 415

Wiesel, Elie, 132, *192–93*, 334–35

Wiesenthal, Simon, *193*, 283, 349, 370; film on, 388; sources on, 344

Wiesenthal, Simon, Center for Holocaust Studies, 404–5

Wilhelmina, Queen, sources on, 354

Wippermann, Wolfgang, 46, 137, 303, 339

Wirth, Christian, *193*

Wise, Rabbi Stephen Samuel, *193*

Wisliceny, Dieter, 245

Witnesses to the Holocaust: The Trial of Adolf Eichmann (film), 378, 382

Wittenberg, Yitzhak, 184

Witts, Max, 334

Wollenberg, Jörg, 359

Women: Gross-Rosen and, 201; labor camps for, 162, 228; lesbians and, 50; sources on, 325–27, 400; Stutthof and, 208; survival of as prisoners, 103; *see also* Ravensbrück

Wood, E. Thomas, 115, 352

World Jewish Congress (WJC), *264*, 193

World reaction: films on, 378–80; sources on, 346–59; *see also* Bystanders

World War I, 56, 66, 88, 141

World War II, 5, 9, 13, 151, 152, 153, 154, 155, 156, 157, 158, 161, 162, 163, 164, 165, 166, 166–67, 168; film on, 375; sources on, 275, 307, 371

World Zionist Organization, *see* Jewish Agency for Palestine

Wurm, Theophil, 112, 257

Wyman, David, 120, 122, 123, 352–53

Wytwycky, Bohdan, 49

Yad Vashem, 416, 169, 39; sources on, 361; *see also* "Righteous Among the Nations"

Yad Vashem Studies (journal), 372

Yahil, Leni, 117, 276, 353

Yale University, Fortunoff Video Archive for Holocaust Testimonies, 361, 402

Yellow badge, 12, 153, 156, 159, 164, 236, 246–47

Yevtushenko, Yevgeni, 195

Yishuv, 124–25, 174, 247–48, 351; sources on, 352; *see also* Palestine

Yivo Annual, 373

YIVO Institute for Jewish Research, 406

Young Plan, 142

Yugoslavia: armed resistance in, 101; Gypsies in, 102; impact of Holocaust on, 25–26, 421, 422; nationalism and, 53; sources on Palestinian Jewish paratroopers in, 343; survivors from, 38; trial of war criminals and, 246; Ustasha and, *263–64*; *see also* Croatia; Serbia

Zamość, Globocnik and, 178

Zegota (Council for Aid to the Jews; Rada Pomocy Zydom), 114, 161, 240, *265*, 335; film on, 380

Zegota: A Time to Remember (film), 380

Zeilsheim, 423

Zentner, Christian, 271

Zentralarchiv zur Erforschung der Geschichte der Juden in Deutschland (Central Archives for Research on the History of the Jews in Germany), 411

Zentrum für Antisemitismusforschung (Center for Research on Antisemitism), 411–12

Zhitomir, 260

Ziegler, Herbert, 311

Zimmermann, Moshe, 293

Zionism, *248*; armed resistance and, 36; Biltmore conference and, 159; Brand and, 165, 175; Displaced Persons and, 221; Eastern European Jews and, 61; Kasztner and, *183*; Palestine and, 120, 159; Palestine Office and, *255*, 261; resistance and, 238; *sho'ah* and, 240; sources on, 291, 297, 299–300, 323, 347, 351, 364; survivors and, 38; Weizmann and, *192*; Wise and, *193*; Yishuv and, 247

Zionist Association for Germany (Zionistische Vereinigung für Deutschland), 254

Zionist Executive, Ben-Gurion and, 174

Zitelmann, Rainer, 313

ZOB, *see* Jewish Fighting Organization

Zrzavy, Vilem, 396

Zuccotti, Susan, 116, 117, 281

Zuckerman, Yitzhak, *193–94*, 344

Zydowska Organizacja Bojowa, *see* Jewish Fighting Organization

Zygelbojm, Samuel Arthur, *194*

Zyklon B, 156, 195, 241, *248–49*; Auschwitz-Birkenau and, 22, 195, 224, 226; Gerstein and, 178; Höss and, *182*, 226; Majdanek and, 21, 204, 224, 226; trials of war criminals and, 241, 242